On the Hill

A HISTORY OF THE AMERICAN CONGRESS

by
Alvin M. Josephy, Jr.

SIMON AND SCHUSTER
NEW YORK

Copyright © 1975, 1979 by American Heritage
Publishing Company, Inc.
All rights reserved
including the right of reproduction
in whole or in part in any form
Published by Simon and Schuster
A Division of Gulf & Western Corporation
Simon & Schuster Building
Rockefeller Center
1230 Avenue of the Americas
New York, New York 10020
Published by arrangement with American Heritage
Publishing Company, Inc.

Manufactured in the United States of America

1 2 3 4 5 6 7 8 9 10

Library of Congress Cataloging in Publication Data

Josephy, Alvin M., date.
On the hill.

Published in 1975 under title: The American Heritage
history of the Congress of the United States.
Bibliography: p.
Includes index.
1. United States. Congress—History. I. Title.
JK1021.J65 1979   328.73′09   79-13018

ISBN 0-671-25048-5

Contents

1. One from Many

At sunset on March 3, 1789, the old guns along the Battery embankment at the foot of Manhattan Island thundered out across the gray waters of New York Harbor. People on the promenade near the crumbling walls of Fort George knew what the din signaled and cheered. The weak and ineffective Articles of Confederation government of the thirteen United States was ended. On the following morning church bells in the city pealed joyously and the cannon boomed again—eleven times now, one for each state that had ratified the Constitution. A new national government (so far without the participation of North Carolina and Rhode Island) was coming into being.

In the expiring Confederation Congress there had been a long argument over the permanent seat of the new government. The question was not settled, but for the time being it would be located in New York, where the old Congress had been meeting. Mayor James Duane and the city government were delighted and had made available City Hall, on Wall Street opposite Broad Street, a short walk north of the Battery. The building was remodeled according to the plans of a thirty-five-year-old Parisian engineer and volunteer officer in the Revolution, Major Pierre Charles L'Enfant, and by the deadline of March, 1789, the eighty-year-old structure had been turned into a handsome and elegantly fitted-out capitol and renamed Federal Hall. Its most striking feature was a second-story porticoed balcony, overlooking the rumbling traffic on Wall Street, where almost two months later the first President would take his oath of office. But as yet there was no President. On this first day of the new republic the city's excitement and hopes were focused solely on the new Congress. Dismayingly, there was a letdown. In habit it seemed unhappily like the legislative body it replaced.

There had been a lackadaisical manner about the late Congress of the Confederation. Its members came and went at will and often there was no quorum. During its last months, attendance dwindled to the point that sometimes no one showed up except its loyal and dedicated secretary, Irish-born Charles

7

Thomson, who had filled the position since the start of the First Continental Congress in 1774. Now, despite great public enthusiasm for the new government, it was clear that Congress was not going to get under way on schedule.

Aside from a small bureaucracy created by the Confederation Congress to deal with the nation's financial, military, foreign, and postal affairs, the bicameral legislative branch given birth by the Constitution was so far all there was to the government of the proud young United States of America. Numerous tasks and problems of enormous gravity awaited the Congress, chief among them the implementation of the constitutional provisions for establishing the rest of the government. Before the executive branch could begin to function, the Congress would have to make arrangements for counting the ballots of the first Electoral College and for inaugurating the President and Vice President. To bring the third branch of the national government into existence, it would have to create a system of federal courts. Yet when the members of the new House of Representatives assembled in their chamber on the ground floor of Federal Hall on that first morning, warming themselves at the fireplaces and then taking seats at desks arranged in two crescent-shaped rows, they numbered only thirteen of the fifty-nine men elected from the eleven states. Upstairs in the smaller Senate chamber, richly hung with crimson damask drapes and with a ceiling painted with the sun and stars, it was no better. Scattered in a semicircle of chairs facing the seat to be occupied by the still-unnamed Vice President were only eight Senators from five states. In accordance with the constitutional directive that "Each House shall keep a Journal of its Proceedings," the first minutes were recorded that day. "The number," read the first entry in the Senate *Legislative Journal,* "not being sufficient to constitute a quorum, they adjourned. . . ."

So it was the next day and on each day thereafter during the entire month of March. Admittedly, travel could be difficult at that season, when winds and ice delayed coastal packets and rain mired the roads. But as the days passed, the legislators, lodged in private homes and boarding houses and meeting each morning at Federal Hall for idle conversation, fretted and grew impatient. Already present were conscientious Senators and Representatives from as far away as New Hampshire and Georgia. If they had been able to meet the scheduled "first Wednesday in March" ordained by the Confederation Congress as the starting date for the new government, so might those who had to travel shorter distances.

The United States of 1789 that they were prepared to represent was a nation of thirteen highly sensitive and self-important states (it was generally taken for granted that North Carolina and Rhode Island would eventually accept the new government), each state jealously protective of its sovereignty and its rights. Collectively, the union comprised a population of almost 4 million, including some 690,000 black slaves but not including Indians, most of whom (perhaps 100,000) lived within the nation's borders beyond the Appalachian frontier. By contrast, France had a population of about 25 million, the British Isles 15 million, and Spain 10 million. The American boundaries, stretching from the Canadian border and the Great Lakes to just short of the Gulf of Mexico and from the Atlantic to the Mississippi River, encompassed about 890,000 square miles, an area as large as France, Italy, Spain, Germany, and the British Isles combined. New York City, with a population of just over 30,000, was the second largest of the centers of population that rimmed the Atlantic coast. Philadelphia was the largest city with 45,000 people. (London was a teeming metropolis of 950,000, and Paris had 600,000.) Inland, in the main, there were only small towns and settlements and isolated farmsteads.

The nation contained many diverse, sometimes perilously clashing interests that the individual members of the new Congress were sure to reflect. Aside from the self-interests of each state—and one problem was that under the new Constitution it was far from clear, and would never be wholly and acceptably clear, what the states' rights were as against those of the national government—there were sectional and regional interests. There were the often opposed interests of the commercial and mercantile groups and of planters and farmers, of creditors and debtors, of western land speculators and western movers, of those of wealth, property, education, and position ("the better sort") and those of "the middling sort" (shopkeepers, artisans, small farmers) and of "the meaner sort" (laborers, servants, the poor). It is inexact to say that there were separate classes in the nation because there was upward and downward mobility, but there were distinctions based on men's callings, qualities, and worth. Since each state had franchise qualifications based on the payment of taxes or the owning of property, only two groups mattered politically, as historian Clinton Rossiter points out in 1787: The Grand Convention—the "rich and well-born," who generally led, and the "body of sober and steady people," who supplied the votes.

There were as yet no organized political parties in which these interests were grouped, but in each state there were individuals and sometimes whole factions whose interests and political feelings had moved them either to support or oppose the ratification of the Constitution. Once ratification had occurred, most of those who had argued against the proposed government swung to its support, or at least endorsed giving it "a good try." Some of them had even run for the new Congress and been elected. But there would continue to be differences between them and the former Constitutionalists, who were now calling themselves Federalists. The opposition, referred to as Antifederalists, would carry on, continuing a concern for the rights of the states and the people, worrying over too much power in the national government, and struggling for more democracy and less elitism.

All these interests had been reflected, at one time or another, by the members of the previous Congresses. But the principal functions of those bodies had been to unite Americans for common goals, such as opposing Great Britain and winning independence; and their powers, after victory when the need for governance became uppermost, were too limited to provide a theater for the settlement, or even the airing, of most of the conflicts that were arising between the interests. Now, with the greatly expanded expressed powers given it by the Constitution, the new Congress—if it ever got going—would become a national arena for contest among all the country's vying interests and points of view.

As the days passed in New York and quorums were still unattainable, impatience grew. Twice the waiting Senators dispatched urgent letters to their missing colleagues: "We apprehend that no arguments are necessary to evince to you the indispensable necessity of putting the Government into immediate operation; and therefore earnestly request, that you will be so obliging as to attend as soon as possible. . . ." Among the signers of these messages were both of Pennsylvania's Senators, one of whom was the celebrated Robert Morris, the "financial genius" of the Revolution and an intriguing figure, with many friends, enemies, and personal business dealings. Morris's Pennsylvania colleague, who was new on the national scene and with whom he had little in common, was Senator William Maclay, a westerner from the Harrisburg area.

The fifty-five-year-old Maclay was a strongly opinionated Antifederalist who had been a frontier soldier in the French and Indian War, a surveyor, lawyer, commissary officer in the Continental Army, judge, Indian commissioner, and member of Pennsylvania's Provincial Assembly and Supreme Executive Council. A strongly built Scotch-Irishman, towering three inches above six feet but lamed by gout in both knees, he was suspicious of the Constitution, believing that its authors had concocted what might turn out to be "the vilest of all traps that was ever set to ensnare the freedom of an unsuspecting people." Sure of his own judgment and integrity, Maclay questioned almost everyone else's, taking particular offense at the least sign of aristocracy. But he had had a classical education and was a learned and inquiring man, vigorously advocating agrarian interests as well as republican plainness. Throughout his term in the Senate, which lasted two years, he kept a frank and revealing diary, providing posterity not only with his own acerbic and rock-ribbed democratic points of view but supplying far more detail on the daily events of the First Congress than is communicated in the spare, dry journals of the two houses.

From day to day the missing legislators at last began to arrive, more of them members of the House than of the Senate. But there were still no quorums. By March 25 the Senate was up to ten members; twelve constituted a quorum. The delay in getting started irritated Representative Fisher Ames from Dedham, Massachusetts, as much as it did Senator Maclay. "This is a very mortifying situation," Ames wrote a Boston friend. ". . . We lose credit, spirit, every thing. The public will forget the government before it is born. The resurrection of the infant will come before its birth."

Ames was thirty-one, a brilliant speaker and a dedicated Federalist who had only recently shot to prominence in his state. He had entered Harvard College when he was only twelve and later taught school while studying law.

In 1788 he participated in the Massachusetts convention called to ratify the Constitution. His oratorical talents there, and in the Massachusetts House of Representatives, to which he was elected the same year, gained him considerable notice and assisted him in defeating the doughty Revolutionary leader Samuel Adams for a seat in the First Congress. Still little known outside his own state in 1789, he would serve with great distinction as one of the leading Federalists in the first four Congresses, returning at last in 1797 to Massachusetts. In 1804, because of ill health, he would have to decline the proffered presidency of his alma mater, Harvard; he died four years later, at the age of fifty. An avid scholar, well versed in history and the classics, Ames wrote numerous and interesting letters during his terms as a Representative. Like Maclay's diary, they provide an illuminating record of many of the details of the daily transactions of Congress that the official journals omit.

Among the missing in both chambers were all the New York members. The state had been torn between Federalists under Alexander Hamilton, centered mainly in New York City, and Antifederalist followers of Governor George Clinton, whose strength was in the countryside and upstate, and the legislature had been forced to adjourn without naming Senators or presidential electors. Not until July, well after Congress had gotten under way, would a Federalist majority finally choose as Senators Philip Schuyler of Albany, a former Revolutionary general and member of the Continental Congress, and Rufus King, who had lately moved to New York from Massachusetts after having played an influential role in the Constitutional Convention. New York's selection of Representatives would also be tardy. Elections were still to be held, and the results would not be known until April. Happily, however, Representative Ames noted that the people of New York City, even though they were not yet represented in the Congress, had not lost their enthusiasm for the new government. Spirits were still high, he reported, and the citizens were busy making plans for fireworks and "a splendid barge" for use when the new President would be inaugurated.

Forced to mark time, Ames and his fellow members of Congress consoled themselves with the fact that New York was a lively and stimulating place. There were almost two hundred taverns and public houses, many of them famed for their food, wine, and conviviality. Wall Street, a hodgepodge of commercial establishments, taverns, shops, churches, boarding houses, and private homes, was a clatter of business and social activity all day long, as was Broadway, which ran for a mile from the Battery to the hills, farms, and swamps beyond The Fields (today's City Hall Park). Along lower Broadway were some of the city's finest homes, the scenes of lavish dinners and receptions to which members of the new government were generally invited. Here lived John Jay, the Confederation's secretary of foreign affairs, and Henry Knox, its secretary of war, as well as the Spanish, French, and Dutch envoys to the United States. There were numerous churches, the most popular of which was St. Paul's, and just off Broadway on John Street was a theater offering the plays of Richard Brinsley Sheridan and Royall

Tyler. For further recreation, Congressmen could take sightseeing tours in coaches or on hired horses, riding northward into the country beyond the Almshouse, Debtors' Jail, and the Gallows at The Fields (where the Liberty Boys had raised their poles of defiance before the Revolution), past picnic areas on Buncker Hill, and on to Greenwich Village, returning via Bloomingdale Road, the Post Road, or Bowery Lane, where Peter Stuyvesant's pear orchard still bore fruit.

For those from rural areas, the daily pace of life in the nation's capital was often adventure enough. One could visit the Battery, the busy wharves, the coffee houses, and the exchanges, where the commercial activity was varied and fascinating. Even a stroll along the board sidewalks could be an experience, especially if one were not on the alert for slops thrown from upstairs windows. The cobblestone streets sloped from the curbs to a central gutter filled with sewage and garbage left to the elements and the thousands of hogs that roamed freely through the city. Carts and coaches clattered over the paving stones, and the air was filled with the racket of draymen and the cries of street vendors.

On Wednesday, April 1, a thirtieth Representative, Thomas Scott from western Pennsylvania, arrived in New York, and a quorum was finally declared in that chamber. The members took their seats and prepared, at last, to deal with the first order of business, the organization of the House. Fisher Ames looked around and observed his fellow legislators, most of whom he had already gotten to know during the long days and evenings of waiting. They were "sober, solid, old-charter folks, as we often say," he wrote. Many of them had served in a state legislature or in one of the previous Congresses and were experienced in government, "and they are not disposed to embarrass business, nor are they, for the most part, men of intrigue." On the whole, they were well educated. There were many college graduates among them (eleven in the first Senate and nineteen in the House —thirteen, in all, from Harvard) and numerous lawyers. As a young novice taking his place among some of the nation's greatest and most famous leaders, Ames felt relieved. "I am rather less awed and terrified at the sight of the members than I expected to be," he wrote. "I assure you I like them very well. There are few shining geniuses; there are many who have experience, the virtues of the heart, and the habits of business."

The star of stars in his opinion, and in the opinion of many others, was the quiet and cultured Representative from Orange County, Virginia, James Madison. Although he was only thirty-eight, Madison's service in the Virginia legislature and the Continental Congress, his principal role in the framing of the Constitution, and his brilliant arguments for that document in *The Federalist* and in the Virginia ratifying convention had made him one of the most respected men in the nation. Very short, frail, and with an almost inaudible voice, he nevertheless commanded attention whenever he rose to speak. A graduate of Princeton College, where he had also studied law, Madison was—thanks partly to the assistance of his friend Thomas

Jefferson, who recommended and sent books to him—perhaps as well read in history, philosophy, and political science as any person in the Congress, if not in the country. But he was also an able politician, skillful at manipulating other men, and his scholarship buttressed and mixed well with his practical talent for public affairs. Ames found him "a man of sense, reading, address, and integrity, as 'tis allowed. Very much Frenchified in his politics. . . . He speaks decently, as to manner, and no more. His language is very pure, perspicuous, and to the point."

The Constitution, very much the product of Madison's keen and logical mind, would be, throughout Congress' history, its constant guidebook for its powers and actions. But it gave few directions to these first members of the House on how they should organize themselves and conduct their business. They "shall chuse their Speaker and other Officers" and, like the Senate, "be the Judge of the Elections, Returns and Qualifications" of their members, said the Constitution. A majority would constitute a quorum, and a smaller number could adjourn from day to day. Each branch of the Congress could "compel the Attendance of absent Members, in such Manner, and under such Penalties" as it might provide. It could "determine the Rules of its Proceedings, punish its Members for disorderly Behaviour, and, with the Concurrence of two thirds, expel a Member." Both houses must keep and publish a journal of their proceedings, "excepting such Parts as may in their Judgment require Secrecy"; the yeas and nays on any question must be recorded in the journal at the request of one fifth of those present; and neither house could adjourn for more than three days nor to any other place without the consent of the other house. That was all.

Following the first directive, the House began its business by electing a Speaker, a presiding officer whose title derived from that of the president of England's House of Commons, who was the spokesman, or speaker, for that body when its members met with the king. In England the speaker was a moderator bound to exercise strict impartiality between the majority and the minority. In colonial days an American speaker in a provincial assembly had generally behaved as a popular leader, often rallying support against the power of the royal governor. Now, in the House of Representatives, he was envisioned simply as one of its members who would be charged with presiding over sessions, preserving decorum, deciding points of order, announcing results of votes, and, as the House soon agreed in its first rules, appointing committees of up to three members. Whenever the House balloted, the Speaker could also vote, but in a day before the founding of parties, no partisanship attached to the position. That would come later and lead ultimately to the Speaker's becoming the unabashed leader of the majority party in the House, invested with enormous prerogatives and powers.

Elias Boudinot, a former president of the Continental Congress and a New Jersey lawyer who could touch heartstrings and move even himself to tears by his oratory, thought he might become Speaker. But the House chose, instead, a Pennsylvanian, Frederick A. C. Muhlenberg, who had had a notable reputation as speaker of his state's house of representatives. A stout, heavy-jowled man who would eventually die of apoplexy, Muhlenberg was a member of what was almost an American dynasty. His father, Henry Melchior Mühlenberg, had emigrated from Germany in 1742 and established the first Lutheran synod in America. Frederick himself had been a Lutheran pastor before becoming a member of the Continental Congress and a political leader in Pennsylvania. His brother, John Peter, also beginning as a Lutheran minister, had served in Virginia's House of Burgesses and then in the Continental Army. Known as Devil Pete, he fought with distinction in many battles, rose to major general, and became a member and vice president of Pennsylvania's Supreme Executive Council. Like Frederick, he was a Pennsylvania Representative in the First Congress. Later there would be more Muhlenbergs in Congress, six in all, including Frederick's great-great-grandson, elected to the Eightieth Congress from Pennsylvania in 1946.

On April 1 the House elected a Virginian, John Beckley, as clerk, and the next day appointed an eleven-member Select Committee on Rules to draw up and report standing rules and orders to guide the House's proceedings. A doorkeeper and assistant doorkeeper were appointed on April 4. (On May 12 a sergeant at arms would also be named. With an assistant, he would become the custodian of the mace, his symbol of authority, setting it to the Speaker's right when the House was in session, lowering it when the members resolved themselves into a Committee of the Whole, and parading it among the members to restore order when sessions became unruly.) On April 7 the report of the Rules Committee was presented by Elias Boudinot, its chairman, read by the clerk, and accepted by the Representatives. The rules covered four subjects, later succinctly summarized by George B. Galloway of the Library of Congress in his *History of the House of Representatives.*

The first rule defined the limited duties of the Speaker. The second, dealing with decorum and debate, stated, in Galloway's words, that "no member could speak more than twice to the same question without leave of the House. No Member could vote on any question in the result of which he was immediately and particularly interested; or in any other case where he was not present when the question was put. Every Member present in the House when a question was put was required to vote for or against it, unless excused. The previous question was to be admitted upon demand of five members and its form was defined. Committees of more than three members were to be chosen by ballot. And any fifteen members could compel the attendance of absentees." The third rule outlined the procedure for a bill. "A committee," noted Galloway, "was to be appointed to prepare every bill which should receive three readings, but no bill could be read twice on the same day without special order of the House. After second reading a bill was to be engrossed or committed either to a select committee or to a Committee of the Whole House. After commitment and report, a bill could be recommitted at any time before its passage. But no bill amended by the Senate could be committed." The fourth rule dealt with Committees of the Whole House, where "bills were to be twice read, debated by clauses, and subjected to amendment."

Committees of the Whole were ingenious legislative devices that permitted the members almost unrestricted freedom of discussion. Like the committee system in general, they had been developed by Parliament, principally during the late Tudor and early Stuart periods, when, under such great leaders as Sir John Eliot, John Hampden, and John Pym, the institution had matured from little more than a debating assembly, passing the king's bills, to a sophisticated legislative body that stood ready to vie with the Crown for supreme power. Since bills in Parliament were ordinarily worked out and drafted in small committees, a Committee of the Whole had been devised to allow and encourage every member to participate in deliberations on important measures. Actually, the Committee of the Whole was the House of Commons itself acting under a different name, with its own special chairman rather than the speaker and with rules that were more informal for free and uninhibited debate.

In America the colonial assemblies had developed their own individual —and often differing—committee systems, some of them probably borrowing more from the business methods of the joint-stock companies that had founded overseas colonies than from Parliament. In several colonies, however, notably Virginia, the Carolinas, Georgia, and New York, important matters had been worked out by the assemblies' full membership sitting as Committees of the Whole, the small select (because only selected members participated) committees being employed principally to draft the wording of the bills. In New England, resort to Committees of the Whole had been rare, but probably as a result of the influence of Virginians the device was frequently employed in the Continental Congress and the Constitutional Convention. Now the House (and later the Senate) adopted the use of such committees.

Their effect, as in Parliament, would be to allow all the members, rather than the small select committees, to join democratically in the framing and amending of important bills. Moreover, the procedures and rules of Committees of the Whole, prohibiting roll calls and such interferences as motions to refer, postpone, or adjourn, would encourage freer, less formal, and often more valuable discussion of the details of a bill than would be possible under the House's regular rules. In practice, the House would merely resolve itself into a Committee of the Whole and the Speaker would give up his place as chairman to another Representative. After discussion and deliberation of a measure ended, the subject would be referred to a small select committee, and the members' intentions would be drafted into a bill. When the select committee had made its report, the House would again become a Committee of the Whole and would consider and amend the bill, once more with the Speaker giving up his seat to the chairman of that Committee of the Whole.

Following approval of the bill, the Speaker would resume his seat and the committee chairman would give the report and the amendments to the members, who would then sit as the regular House. After their agreement and a third reading, the House would pass the bill.

During the first Congresses Committees of the Whole would be frequently employed to allow all members to have their say on important issues. Their use would be encouraged by James Madison and the more democratically minded members. But New Englanders, such as the influential Federalist Theodore Sedgwick, who had served many terms in the Massachusetts legislature, where Committees of the Whole had rarely been used, would prefer the initiation and working out of legislation to be done in small committees in which Representatives unskilled in open debate would not be at a disadvantage. To Fisher Ames and others, moreover, the Committee of the Whole would often seem a tedious and time-consuming mechanism, in which the loquacious and less intelligent could delay important business with inanities and minor details: "We [the Committee of the Whole] . . . correct spelling, or erase *may* and insert *shall*, and quiddle in a manner which provokes me. . . . A great, clumsy machine is applied to the slightest and most delicate operations—the hoof of an elephant to the strokes of mezzotinto. . . . Certainly a bad method of doing business." The device would be retained, however (the freedom of debate would also help Congressmen convince their constituents that they were not neglecting their interests), and through the course of Congress' history it would be developed, under changing rules in both houses, into various Committees of the Whole, each with a particular name, such as the Committee of the Whole on the State of the Union or the Committee of the Whole on Ways and Means, suited to the different types of bills with which the legislators dealt.

On April 13 the House adopted several additional rules concerned with service on committees, members' leaves of absence, and the creation of a Committee of Elections. Seven members were elected by ballot to that committee and were directed to examine and report on the certificates of election of each member. (Later on, the House in this First Congress would change certain of its rules. In January, 1790, the Speaker was permitted to name all the committees, no matter how large, unless otherwise directed, and on January 12, 1791, the rule that no bill could be committed after the Senate had amended it was rescinded.)

On the evening of April 5, meanwhile, one of the best-known political leaders in the nation, Richard Henry Lee of Westmoreland County, Virginia, reached New York and the next day took his seat in the Senate, finally making a quorum in that body. Lee must have awed some of the younger men in Congress who were serving for the first time outside their own states. An incisive and tight-lipped man of dignified, prepossessing appearance, Lee was fifty-seven, the same age as George Washington, and in the minds of many he was linked with Washington as one of the most eminent of Virginia's Revolutionary patriots. He had sat in the House of Burgesses since

1758, becoming one of the first to oppose Great Britain. With Patrick Henry and later Thomas Jefferson, he led Virginia's resistance to British injustices and drew up many of that colony's documents of protest. Patriots everywhere still honored him primarily, however, for the ringing resolution he introduced in the Continental Congress on June 7, 1776. This was his condensed redraft of a resolution passed by a convention in Williamsburg, and it began with the thrilling words: "Resolved: That these United Colonies are, and of right ought to be, free and independent States." John Adams seconded Lee's motion, and it led to the writing and signing of the Declaration of Independence.

Lee had continued to serve Virginia and the new nation, becoming president of the Confederation Congress in 1784. When the completed Constitution was unveiled, he raised opposition to it in Congress. While acknowledging the weaknesses of the Articles of Confederation, he disliked the Constitution's prescription of a strong central government with its danger to the rights of states and individuals, and he condemned the absence of the protections of a Bill of Rights. Allied again with Patrick Henry, who wanted another convention of the states to write a more satisfactory document, Lee presented his case in a series of articles called *Letters of the Federal Farmer*, a sort of Antifederalist's version of *The Federalist* of Madison, Jay, and Hamilton. He lost the anti-ratification fight in his state, but his letters received wide circulation and enhanced his reputation. When the Virginia legislature met to name its two Senators to the First Congress, Henry and his supporters won the day, electing two Antifederalists, Lee and William Grayson. Lee had only a few years to live (he would resign from the Senate in 1792 because of ill health, and die in 1794), but he would play an active role, working closely with his old friend John Adams and becoming eventually, like Patrick Henry, a Federalist himself.

Lee's arrival was the signal for both houses, finally, to get down to the business of the nation. The Senate quickly accepted the credentials of the twelve members who were present and elected a temporary president, Senator John Langdon, a wealthy merchant and trader from Portsmouth, New Hampshire. Langdon's election was necessitated by Article II, Section 1, of the Constitution, which directed that the president of the Senate receive and open the certificates containing the votes of the states' electors for President and Vice President of the United States. The latter, when inaugurated, would be president of the Senate, but as yet there was no one to fill that role, and in a sense Langdon—an ardent patriot and nationalist who had personally paid the expenses of the New Hampshire delegation to the Constitutional Convention—thus became the first, but unofficial, presiding executive of the new nation. Following the balloting for Langdon, Senator Oliver Ellsworth of Connecticut was chosen to go downstairs and inform the House of Representatives that the Senate was organized and ready to carry out the constitutional provision for counting the electors' votes in the presence of the House.

The two bodies began their relationship with strict formality, becoming to the sense of dignity and propriety that, in their minds, the occasion, as well as the new government, required. Ellsworth, a tall, commanding-looking man of forty-four with stern features, had served his state as a legislator, administrator, and judge of the superior court. He was known for his copious use of snuff and his disconcerting habit of talking to himself. But many members of Congress regarded him, also, as having been one of the shrewdest and most useful members of the Continental Congress and the Constitutional Convention, and in 1796 President Washington would acknowledge his political and legal acumen by appointing him Chief Justice of the Supreme Court.

Entering the House chamber, Ellsworth announced stiffly: "Mr. Speaker, I am charged by the Senate to inform this House that a quorum of the Senate is now formed." There must have been a pleased reaction. Ellsworth went on to state that the Senate was ready, in the presence of the House, to count the votes of the electors in the Senate chamber, that it had named a president to open and count the votes, and that it was "submitting it to the wisdom of the House to appoint one or more of their members for the like purpose." The Connecticut Senator then withdrew, and the House, resolving to proceed to the Senate chamber for what was to be Congress' first joint session, named two of its members to oversee the counting of the votes. Continuing to establish formal precedent, Boudinot climbed the stairs to the Senate chamber and informed that body that the House was ready to meet with it. A few moments later the members of the House, led by the imposing Speaker Muhlenberg, filed in and watched while Langdon opened and counted the ballots.

Every step of the procedure was a "first," though the Congress, previously a single body, could look to parliamentary procedure as well as to the bicameral state legislatures for guidance in the working out of the formalities of interhouse relations. In addition, in this instance the members were adhering to the instructions of the framers of the Constitution, who in one of their compromises had worked out the complicated system of electors to choose the President and Vice President. It was no surprise to anyone when Langdon, having completed the tallying, announced to the hushed assemblage that George Washington had received a vote from each of the sixty-nine electors of the reporting states and was therefore the unanimous choice for President. John Adams, with thirty-four votes, was second and would become Vice President.

During the following days the Senate continued with its organization, electing James Mathers of New York as its first doorkeeper (unlike the House, the Senate decided to bar the public and keep its proceedings secret); Cornelius Maxwell as Senate messenger (soon both Houses would communicate with each other by sending their messengers, rather than their own members); and Samuel A. Otis, a former speaker of the Massachusetts House of Representatives and member of the Continental Congress, as secretary. Simultaneously, several committees were appointed. Richard Henry Lee, Oliver Ellsworth, William Maclay, Caleb Strong of Massachusetts, and Richard Bassett of Delaware were named to two committees on April 7, the first to bring in a bill to organize the judiciary of the United States and the second to confer with a committee of the House on the preparation of a system of rules to govern the two houses when they met in conference; it was also ordered to prepare a set of rules for the conduct of business in the Senate. On April 8 the Senators became so annoyed with the noise of the Wall Street traffic that they directed that chains "at each end of the federal building be extended across the street, from the commencement of the Session in the morning, until the adjournment of the Senate, to prevent disturbance by Carriages."

In the House, meanwhile, James Madison, demonstrating the same initiative and leadership he had shown at the Constitutional Convention, had already set the members to considering what he regarded as the nation's most pressing concern—the raising of money to pay the country's bills. The Continental Congress had had no power to tax or lay import duties, and the lack of an adequate revenue was one of the principal reasons for the end of the government of the Articles of Confederation. Now the situation had been rectified; under the Constitution the Congress had power "to lay and collect Taxes, Duties, Imposts and Excises." All bills for the raising of revenue had to originate in the House, but the Senate could propose or concur with amendments. On April 8 Madison started debate in the House on a bill to lay duties on certain imports. On April 11 the matter was referred to a select committee of nine Representatives. The bill they were directed to prepare would become one of the first great controversial issues of the new government.

In a sense, the introduction of the tariff bill symbolized a continuity in the history of the government of the American people that was reflected in the new Congress. Altogether in the first Congress there were eleven Senators and nine Representatives who had helped frame the Constitution. Eighteen of the twenty-six Senators and thirty-six of the sixty-five Representatives had served in the Continental Congress or the Congress of the Confederation. Four members had signed the Declaration of Independence, and one of them, sixty-eight-year-old Representative Roger Sherman of New Haven, Connecticut, had signed every major document of state since 1774, beginning with the Articles of Association of the First Continental Congress. In addition, numerous members of both houses had served as administrators, jurists, or legislators in their own states or had been members of conventions that wrote state constitutions or ratified the federal Constitution; many, also, had been officers in the Continental Army. For them, service in the new Congress would be a continuation of experience in self-government, and conversely, the new government would be influenced and molded to a large degree by what they had learned. At the same time, although the Congress, like the entire government the Constitution's framers had devised, was something the world had never before seen, it was itself an amalgam of numerous ideas and experiences of the recent, as well as the remote, past.

Two principal strands in mankind's history had led to this new American government now waiting to inaugurate its chief executive. The first strand was man's long quest for human rights and freedoms—the men and women of the Revolution had called them the natural rights of man—and for government by the consent of the governed. The Revolutionary generation had fought for these goals and had believed that its victory was the culmination of a struggle whose roots lay far back in antiquity. Their ideas had been formed not alone from their own experiences in opposing Great Britain, but from books and periodicals that gave meaning to their fears and beliefs—from Sir Edward Coke and Sir William Blackstone, the masterful commentators on the common law and the British Constitution, to moralistic sermons hammered at them from church pulpits.

The colonists had been Britons and inheritors of British history, and that history, as the Revolutionary leaders absorbed it from the persuasive writings of eighteenth-century British Whigs (a name derived from the hostile term "Whiggamore" applied in England to certain Scottish insurgents in the seventeenth century), told them of an ancient and happy society of free men and self-governing institutions that the Saxons brought with them from the Continent and planted in pre-Norman England. It was a distorted version of history and has since been discredited. But based largely on the accounts of Tacitus and Sallust and expanded upon by Sir Henry Spelman and a host of other British writers whose books—well read in the colonies—had kept alive the principles of the English struggles against the Stuarts, it related how the Normans brought the tyrannies of feudalism to England, bringing an end to the Saxon heritage of freedom. According to these Whig authors, England's history since then, beginning with Magna Charta in 1215, had been one long struggle to regain those rights. The emergence and development of Parliament (from the Old French *parlement* and Latin *parliamentum*, meaning a place to talk or discuss), the Civil War of 1642, and the Glorious Revolution of 1688–89 had all been forward steps along the way. But to James Otis, John Adams, and scores of other Americans in the colonies steeped in Whig ideology, the rights the English people had won from the king and his ministers, particularly in 1688–89, were being taken away from them in the eighteenth century. Parliament, they could see, had been corrupted by the Georges' ministers and their underlings, and something close to a conspiracy to overthrow the British Constitution was thought to exist, threatening the liberties of every Englishman.

Until the end of the French and Indian War, Britain had pretty much permitted the colonists to rule themselves, and the fiction had grown among them that their own assemblies, generally with power to raise and spend money within their respective colonies, were on a par with Parliament beneath the Crown, representing the people of the colonies as Parliament represented the people of England. To the colonists the power of the purse—the power to raise money from the people and decide how to spend it—was the wellspring of freedom itself. The issue had been at the root of Magna Charta, and it had been among the most basic of all the rights for which the English people and Parliament had struggled through the centuries. But after the French and Indian War the colonists were rudely reminded that their assemblies were not on a par with Parliament and that they did not have power over their own purse. In the eyes of the British government the taxes it levied on the colonies were not unjust. They were needed to pay expenses incurred in America, for the debts of the late war, which ended the French threat to the colonies, and for the continuing defense and administration of the colonies.

The patriots' resistance to this turn of affairs, motivated not a little by a variety of economic self-interests, began with assertions of Parliament's lack of jurisdiction over the colonies, appeals to common-law rights, and republican-style attacks on "taxation without representation," and ended with hostility to the Crown itself and, finally, with the Declaration of Independence. That document, to the American patriots, did more than announce the severing of the bond with the mother country. It represented the climax of years of inspiration from writings on themes of liberty and civil rights, giving notice to the world that the American people had taken up the fight for man's "unalienable" rights—a struggle that the English had begun with Magna Charta and were now losing in their home island.

Victory in the Revolution was a triumph both for independence and for the right of the Americans to control their own purse, and therefore their own state and continental governments and freedoms. This awareness remained strong among many American leaders after independence and would continue as a dominant strain in the First Congress and, indeed, in all succeeding Congresses. Following the Declaration of Independence, it led naturally to another problem, one associated with the second strand in man's history. This related to the type of government that would secure the rights that had been won, and that would not lose them to the tyranny of a despot, the oligarchical rule of an aristocracy, or the anarchy of a mob. Again, historical writings and the experiences of England and other countries, as well as of the colonies themselves, provided abundant examples and precedents from which to learn—and more importantly, on which to bring to bear the reasoning powers of those who would create a new American government.

The history of the colonies had caused men to fear and oppose executive power. In the colonies there had been royal, proprietary, and charter governments, and though their details varied considerably from one colony to another and, indeed, had sometimes changed in individual colonies in response to political forces in England or to altered requirements in America, each colony had experienced the pitting of a people's representative body against the authority of a governor. In most of the colonies, no matter how they were founded, legislative assemblies elected by the colonists under different franchise requirements and often with wide powers of self-government had been encouraged or permitted at an early date. Virginia's democratically elected House of Burgesses had been authorized by the Virginia Company itself and had first met in Jamestown in July, 1619, inaugurating self-government in the colonies. In Maryland, the Carolinas, Pennsylvania, New York, and elsewhere, assemblies of freemen had come into being one by one, each possessing rights of consultation or approval in the making of regulations and laws for their respective colonies. By early in the eighteenth century representative assemblies—usually composed of leading merchants, lawyers, and large property owners who were elected under broadening franchise laws that in time came generally to entitle from fifty to seventy-five percent of the adult male white population to vote—had existed in every colony. Gradually, as the colonies grew, the assemblies increased the number and scope of their interests and powers, basing their authority on the common law and on the liberties won in the Civil War and the Glorious Revolution and modeling their organization and procedures on those of the House of Commons.

Several generations of colonists had acquired practical experience in self-government in these assemblies, but much of it had been frustrating and angering. Ranged against their assertions of authority had always been the executive in the person of royal or proprietary officials, headed by a governor. In the eighteenth-century royal colonies—New Hampshire, Massachusetts, New York, Virginia, and Georgia—the governor was appointed by the Crown. He was bound by instructions from London and held veto power over the assembly. That body was able to appeal a veto to the Board of Trade and the Privy Council in London, but the latter's judgment was final. In the proprietary colonies—Pennsylvania, New Jersey, Maryland, Delaware, and the Carolinas—the governors were appointed by the proprietors but subject to royal inquiry and intervention. The two charter colonies, Connecticut and Rhode Island, were exceptions. They elected their governors and possessed charters that were so satisfactory that they were continued in effect, with the force of basic constitutional law in those states, until well into the nineteenth century.

Aiding the royal governors in the individual colonies had been various types of councils whose members were appointed by the governor, except in Massachusetts, where they were elected by the representative assembly. The typical council was usually composed of the colony's native-born elite, and while its principal function was to advise the governor, it had constituted, in effect, an aristocratic upper house with legislative and occasional judicial powers. Generally, the council had been more responsive and loyal to the governor than the representative assembly, and when the Revolution came it was swept away with the rest of the royal apparatus—though the senates of the new American bicameral legislatures would in a way be its lineal descendants.

During the colonial period the assemblies chipped away at the authority of the governors and their advisers and underlings. The lower houses had some advantages. Funds for the governor and for the salaries and expenses of his administration came from the colonies, and since the assemblies possessed the power to raise taxes and make appropriations, they were often able to wring concessions from governors who needed money. In this way, assemblies were frequently able to influence appointments, decisions, expenditures, and even the acceptance of legislation that the governor might otherwise have vetoed. Furthermore, the colonies had the power— which they sometimes used—to undermine the Crown's support of a governor by creating turmoil against him in the colony or by taking their case against him direct to London, either through their own agents in England or by appeal to the Privy Council. In the main, however, the representative bodies were not able to exert complete control over legislation, nor did they achieve the right of elections free from the governor's interference or a judiciary not dependent on the governor and his followers in the council.

At the same time, the representative assemblies had become the colonists' own political voice and arm. Since assembly members were elected, they constituted the only element of government truly "of, by, and for" the people. They had close contacts with the constituents to whom they were accountable; they usually acted in accordance with the instructions or sentiments of their towns and localities; and, as a rule, it was impossible for the governor to corrupt or unduly influence them. As a result, the people came to regard the members of the lower houses of their legislatures as the guardians of their rights and welfare and the assemblies as the only branch of government on which they could rely. On the eve of the Revolution, when British authority cracked down on the assemblies in reaction to the colonists' resistance to taxation, this perspective became sharper than ever to the patriots. Now fearing and hating executive power, they equated it with tyranny and despotism, and in the first transition governments of their own, they wiped out executives with authority.

On the continental level, revolution was set in motion by extralegal citizens' groups, including Committees of Correspondence formed in the different colonies to communicate information to each other. Following appeals and resolves from different quarters for collective action against Britain's increasing repression, the First Continental Congress—an emergency assembly that possessed no powers but could recommend action to whoever was receptive—met in Carpenters' Hall, Philadelphia, on September 5, 1774. The delegates, fifty-six in number, came from every colony except Georgia. There had been "congresses" of colonial delegates before, notably the Albany Congress in 1754, when a colonial union was discussed, and the angry Stamp Act Congress of 1765 in New York. But the first acts of the new meeting established titles that would endure in American institutions: the assembly was called officially "The Congress," and the man named to be its presiding officer, Peyton Randolph, speaker of Virginia's

House of Burgesses, was termed "The President." He had no powers and little authority, and that was the way it would be until the writing of the Constitution. Like the representative assemblies that had nursed the people's interests through the colonial period, it would be "The Congress" (representing colonies, then states, rather than the people) that, without a separate and independent executive power with which to contend, would shepherd the Americans through the Revolution and into nationhood.

In the beginning the Continental Congress' function—in accordance with the instructions the colonies had given to their delegates—was to devise measures that would obtain redress of American grievances, secure the colonies' rights and liberties, and restore harmony with Great Britain. Each colony had one vote in the Congress, and the delegates' principal concerns were with the colonists' rights under the Crown and with economic countermeasures that the people could take to force an end to Britain's "intolerable" policies. It was inevitable, however, that thoughts would turn to a formal united government. "Government is dissolved. . . . We are in a state of nature, sir," the fiery Patrick Henry exclaimed early in the proceedings. He was answered for all the startled delegates by New York's John Jay. The colonies had given no instructions to create a new government, Jay said. "The measure of arbitrary power is not full, and I think it must run over, before we undertake to frame a new constitution."

With the outbreak of the Revolution in April, 1775, the functions of the Second Continental Congress (which convened on May 10, also in Philadelphia) became more grave. Almost at once, coordination and guidance of the colonies' armed resistance was thrust upon it. Individual colonies appealed to it for powder, help, leadership, and even advice on what to do about establishing new governments. Massachusetts, the principal scene of hostilities, asked Congress to take over the motley rebel army that was ringing Boston. But there had been no substantive changes in the powers or organization of the Congress since it had last met. With John Hancock of Massachusetts sitting as the new president, an office still little more than that of a figurehead, the delegates to this second Congress immediately debated whether to take on the responsibility of running a war or simply to counsel and encourage the actions of the various colonies. Accepting the former course would mean raising and spending money for arms, men, and supplies, which would require that Congress, in effect, assume the role of a central government.

On June 10 the delegates made the first move in that direction, appointing a committee to borrow money for the purchase of powder. Other steps quickly followed. On June 14 it was resolved to raise companies of riflemen in Virginia, Maryland, and Pennsylvania and send them to Boston. On June 15 George Washington (relatively unknown in New England, but recommended to that part of the country by Connecticut delegate Eliphalet Dyer as "clever, and if any thing too modest . . . discreet and virtuous, no harum Starum ranting Swearing fellow but Sober, steady, and Calm") was

24

unanimously appointed to command "all the continental forces, raised or to be raised, for the defense of American liberty." The next day a general plan was accepted for the organization of an army of fifteen thousand men, and on June 22, instead of pursuing the loan, Congress decided to adopt a proposal to issue two million Spanish dollars' worth of paper money, the redemption of which would be pledged by the twelve participating colonies. By these acts Congress, without anyone willing it that way, became something of a central governing body.

In reality, however, Congress continued to be more of an advisory assembly to the colonies than a government. Its members were still delegates to a consultative body that had no expressed powers other than to make recommendations to the colonies and to try to carry out their wishes and meet their needs. Yet, in meeting those needs, it assumed a variety of initiatives. In the following months and years it set up a system for making treaties with Indians to keep them friendly to the Americans. It established a continental postal system and appointed Benjamin Franklin postmaster general. It created a navy and a Marine Committee, the ancestor of the future republic's Navy Department. It set up a standing committee on finance and appointed treasurers; a standing committee called a Board of War and Ordnance and a war office; a committee to import powder and munitions and export produce to pay for the purchases (later called the Committee of Commerce); and a committee to correspond with "friends" overseas and acquire assistance from friendly powers (later called the Committee for Foreign Affairs, the beginning of a Department of State). There was still no executive other than the titular presiding officer. All administrative bodies were made responsible to, and placed under the supervision of, committees of Congress.

Meanwhile, the idea of a stronger and more enduring association of the colonies began to move some leaders to new thinking. From time to time, proposals for a permanent continental government, one of them from the fertile mind of Benjamin Franklin entitled *Articles of Confederation and Perpetual Union,* were presented to Congress, but they received little or no serious consideration. Despite the existence of war, most delegates and the colonies they represented still hoped for a reconciliation with Great Britain, and the establishment of a formal American government was considered contradictory to that goal. But in 1776 public opinion changed rapidly, and with the signing of the Declaration of Independence a government for the "Thirteen United States of America" became essential, not alone to band the states more closely together, but because the new nation desperately required financial and military help from France and other foreign powers. If it were to get that help, there had to be an actual American government with which the European states could deal.

The form of government ultimately worked out and accepted by the Congress and the states was that of the Articles of Confederation. Drawn up in 1776 by a special committee of Congress, it was based largely on

Franklin's original proposal and on a draft by the committee's conservative and legalistic chairman, John Dickinson of Pennsylvania. The delegates argued for many months over the Articles' various sections, but there was never serious debate about the fundamental structure of the new government; it seemed obvious and natural that it would be a confederation of the sovereign states and that, again, it would require only one branch, a single-house Congress to which the states would continue to send their delegates. As before, also, there would be no executive other than a presiding officer, or president, of the Congress, and that body would use committees of its members to appoint and supervise administrative agencies for the nation's business.

The Articles were approved by the delegates on November 15, 1777, and sent to the states for their ratification. Despite the existing Congress' growing problems with finance, inflation, the needs of the army, and the securing of aid from France and Spain, the acceptance of the new government came slowly. Only after the states that owned western lands agreed to cede them to the central government did Maryland, the last holdout, ratify the Articles and make the Confederation a reality on March 1, 1781—seven and a half months before Cornwallis's surrender.

Other than assuming the new title given it by the Articles—"The United States in Congress Assembled"—Congress felt no change. It continued to be the same body, with the same members, the same organization, and basically the same weaknesses. The states retained their sovereignty, independence, and every power not expressly delegated to the Congress. In terms of foreign relations, however, the country became somewhat better off, and John Adams, John Jay, Benjamin Franklin, Thomas Jefferson, and others who had been, or would be, sent abroad were now able to speak for a formally established government. But internally Congress continued powerless in the key area of finance. It was able to vote requisitions of money and supplies from the states, but without the power to make them comply it was forced to beg, wheedle, and cajole them into recognizing their responsibilities. The alternatives for getting necessary funds—loans and the printing of "Continental" paper money—led to huge debts and catastrophic inflation.

After the Revolution the problems of the weak Congress mounted, angering and humiliating those in and out of the government who had fought and labored for independence. On June 21, 1783, even before Congress finally signed the treaty of peace, it almost came to a violent and ignominious end. Rebellious troops, demanding their pay, marched with bayoneted guns from Lancaster, Pennsylvania, to Philadelphia, surrounding the State House, where the Congress was meeting, and sending in a threatening ultimatum with an order for a reply in twenty minutes. Ignoring the "insult," the Congress, after trying in vain to have the Pennsylvania Executive Council send militia to the rescue, sat stoically in a state of siege while the soldiers hurled insults at the members through the windows and "wantonly pointed their Muskets" at them. No violence occurred, however, and at three in the afternoon James Madison and the other delegates adjourned and boldly walked out of the building, pushing their way without harm through the ranks of the taunting soldiers. But the episode had shaken the delegates, and Congress forthwith left Philadelphia for Princeton, deemed a safer location, though its lack of accommodations caused discomfort ("Mr. Jones and my self are in one room scarcely ten feet square and in one bed," Madison wrote unhappily). Thereafter, the Congress moved from one location to another before settling finally in New York on January 11, 1785.

The country's economic problems, meanwhile, became severe. The value of the Continental collapsed, inflation became rampant, divisions sharpened between creditors and debtors, and the Congress' inability to pay its debts undermined confidence in the future of the nation. Added to this were other concerns that demonstrated Congress' helplessness. Since 1781 a national tariff had been seen as an advantageous way in which to raise revenue, and Congress made attempts to acquire authority from the states to regulate foreign commerce and levy duties on certain imports. Almost all the states, recognizing benefits in giving the central government such powers, provided their consent. But the delegation of power required the unanimous action of all the states, and Congress failed to achieve that goal. Instead, the states continued to go their individual ways, some of them even laying on tariffs of their own that caused dissension with other states. Not only was Congress at the mercy of the states, but it became painfully obvious that a single state could block actions deemed necessary by all the others.

In foreign affairs, too, the weakness of the Confederation Congress was felt. Despite the terms of the peace treaty, Great Britain refused to evacuate posts in the Northwest, claiming that the American government, on its part, was not able to make the states comply with treaty provisions to compensate Loyalists for property taken from them. With their continued hold over rich fur country and the Indians who inhabited those regions, the British were able to maintain a threat to frontier settlers and resistance to American fur interests. At the same time Spain, in possession of Louisiana, refused to grant American settlers west of the Appalachians freedom of navigation on the Mississippi and the right to ship their produce through New Orleans, or even to "deposit" their goods in that city while awaiting ships. Even a stronger American government might not have been able to force turnarounds in the British and Spanish policies, but the two situations were bitterly ascribed by many Americans to the weakness of the Congress. These sentiments were more than corroborated by the complaints of American representatives abroad. Both John Adams, who became the first minister to England, and Thomas Jefferson, the minister to France, were angered by the patronizing contempt with which they were treated in those countries, recognizing that it resulted from the Europeans' awareness of the powerless condition of the American government.

To top it off, some of the states themselves, as well as a growing number of delegates, began to act as if they could do without the Congress. Communications to the states went unanswered, and delegates came and went at their pleasure and even vanished. Representation became erratic, affecting the Congress' ability to function. At one point the situation became ludicrous. Congress had recessed and left in its place a special Committee of the States, comprising one member from each state. That group met dutifully for a while and then began to erode. One after another, its members drifted off until there was no quorum and then no government at all. For the next two months, as some of the members tried to reassemble, they were unable to find each other. One delegate from Virginia, searching for the committee in Annapolis and Philadelphia, questioned angrily whether "it is not a prostitution of the name of Government to apply it to such a vagabond, strolling, contemptible Crew as Congress." Another member, Jacob Read of South Carolina, also trying to find whatever was left of Congress, wrote what many others must have been thinking: "I feel more for the Invisible State of the federal government than I can express at this time too when we know the Eyes of Europe are upon us." Fortunately, the recess eventually ended, and Congress reassembled—though with only seven delegates from five states present.

Such a situation, so marked by frustrations and dangerous deficiencies, could not go on forever. In the rising tide of nationalistic pride and enterprise, impatience and irritation with the government's inadequacies increased. Jealous of the international reputation of the country he had led to victory, George Washington castigated the Confederation Congress as "a shadow without substance." Others began to fear that the independence of the country could not endure, or that its liberties would be lost to a despot. From both within and outside Congress came an increasing number of proposals for a new convention to give Congress necessary powers over the states. The appeals aroused the worry of those who feared a tyrannical central government. But even some of them, like Richard Henry Lee, agreed that certain changes had become necessary. On August 7, 1786, a "Grand Committee" of Congress proposed a number of changes, drawn up apparently by Charles Pinckney of South Carolina. In sum, these would have vested Congress with powers to regulate commerce, lay duties on imports and exports, penalize states for noncompliance with requisitions, institute a seven-member federal court of appeals, and enforce attendance by members of Congress. Nothing was done about the proposals, however, and they were soon bypassed by a train of events that had commenced at a convention in Annapolis.

That gathering stemmed from relatively obscure meetings at Alexandria and Mount Vernon in March, 1785, between commissioners of Virginia and Maryland to settle a long-festering dispute over the two states' taxing of each other's commerce on the Potomac River and Chesapeake Bay. As president of a company working to improve navigation on the river, George Washington attended the Alexandria meeting and hosted the one at his home. The conferees worked out an accord and submitted it to the Virginia and Maryland legislatures for endorsement. Recognizing that the interstate nature of the agreement would affect adjacent states, the Maryland legislature called for the participation of Delaware and Pennsylvania. When the subject reached the Virginia legislature, James Madison used the opportunity to propose, instead, a meeting of commissioners from every state to discuss the expanded question of "the power of Congress over trade." Madison's proposal was accepted, and a convention was called to meet in Annapolis on the first Monday in September, 1786.

News of the meeting excited both optimism and fear. Madison hoped it might lead to a revision of the Articles of Confederation, which he had come to believe was necessary "to preserve the Union of the States." In Congress delegates argued over its motives, some suspecting that it was a sly move to defeat the enlargement of Congress' powers, others that it had been called in behalf of the commercial interests of southern planters. Nevertheless, despite the curiosity and mixed expectations, only New York, New Jersey, Pennsylvania, Delaware, and Virginia showed up. The delegates appointed by four states did not bother to attend, and the other states—Maryland included—did not even appoint delegates.

Those who arrived lost no time in agreeing that the central government badly needed strengthening. Madison wanted to amend the Articles; another delegate advocated a national government that would absorb the states; still another proposed an extension of Congress' powers to help the economy. The delegate who won the day, however, was New York's Alexander Hamilton, a sharp and impatient-minded twenty-nine-year-old former aide-de-camp to Washington and an ardent believer in a strong national government. Precocious, handsome, aristocratic in bearing, Hamilton had sat restlessly as a member of Congress, losing faith in the Confederation's ability to solve the nation's problems. On September 14 the convention finished its discussions and passed a resolution. Though this was signed by its chairman, John Dickinson, the author of the first draft of the Articles of Confederation, it was written by Hamilton. It called on all the states to appoint commissioners to meet in Philadelphia on the second Monday in May, 1787, to take necessary steps "to render the constitution of the Federal Government adequate to the exigencies of the Union."

The resolution was laid before Congress for its recommendation to the states. Hesitancies that still existed there had been dispelled by an alarming uprising of debt-ridden farmers under former Revolutionary captain Daniel Shays in western Massachusetts. Attempting to seize the courts to prevent foreclosures, Shays and his angry troops had frightened men of property and standing everywhere, and were put down only by Massachusetts militia paid by private subscription—for the state treasury was empty. Added to that frightening episode had been a disquieting development in Rhode Island that seemed to foreshadow what might happen elsewhere. Under threat of punishment, creditors had been forced by law to accept paper currency in which they had no faith. The Rhode Island Supreme Court finally declared the law unconstitutional (the first decision overriding legislation in the United States), but to many there seemed no doubt that anarchy was in the air and that a more effective central government was essential.

Responding to pressure from several states, Congress finally approved the new convention "for the sole and express purpose of revising the Articles of Confederation," and all the states save Rhode Island named delegates to it. Tiny Rhode Island, under the dominating personalities of truculent states' righters, had been a thorn in the side of the Congress and of those advocating united action since 1781. The two houses of the state legislature were unable to agree on the sending of delegates, and Rhode Island, to the disgust of some of its commercial leaders but to the regret of almost no other state, would not show up at Philadelphia.

Others, too, were not sure what was going to happen. New York, controlled by a faction around its strong governor, George Clinton, could have sent many able and committed nationalists. But Clinton's group had soured because of Congress' lack of support for New York's claim to Vermont, and, feeling that as a sovereign state it could take care of itself if it guarded its powers, it chose one nationalist, Alexander Hamilton, and two Clintonian states' righters with chips on their shoulders, Robert Yates and John Lansing, Jr. Virginia named the most prestigious delegation of all to the convention, headed by Washington and including Governor Edmund Randolph, George Mason, George Wythe, John Blair, James Madison, and Dr. James McClurg of Richmond. Patrick Henry declined an appointment to the delegation, announcing that he "smelled a rat in Philadelphia, tending toward monarchy," and Mason, who in 1776 had written Virginia's Declaration of Rights, the forerunner of the Declaration of Independence, would eventually refuse to sign the Constitution, deploring its lack of a Bill of Rights and believing "it would end in monarchy, or a tyrannical aristocracy."

To avoid just such a destiny, many of the delegates drew once again on history and philosophy. Two of the best-read men in the nation, John Adams and Thomas Jefferson, each the owner of a large personal library, were abroad at their diplomatic posts during the convention. Each maintained a voluminous correspondence with friends at home who had been chosen to go to the convention, sending them observations and ideas of their own, and Jefferson inundated Madison with useful books from Paris, among them works by Diderot, Montesquieu, and Voltaire. Other delegates, meanwhile, were poring through scores of volumes, consulting authorities as varied as Plato, Cicero, Saint Thomas Aquinas, Machiavelli, and Adam Smith, as well as histories of the Greek city-states by Polybius, Sir William Temple's *Observations upon the United Provinces of the Netherlands*, and numerous commentaries on ancient and modern empires, searching for the ingredients of a government that would best permit the American people to promote their welfare as well as protect their hard-won liberties.

On the whole, the men who formed the Constitutional Convention were scholars and jurists, and during the course of debates they took delight in citing and quoting to each other from the classics they had studied. But they also constituted one of the best-grounded and most astute groups of political scientists the world has ever seen, with a maturity acquired not alone from what they had read, but from the long, tumultuous years in which necessity had made them experiment with self-government. Most of this expertise had not been derived from involvement on the national level. While the Confederation Congress was failing, many of the framers of the Constitution had been among hundreds of Americans charting new paths in working out satisfactory governments for their respective states. Their experiences on that level, particularly with checks and balances, the separation of powers, bicameral legislatures, and even a strong executive—all unknown to the government of the Confederation—were to provide the Constitution with many of its saving attributes.

In the thirteen years since 1774, the states had experienced numerous governmental changes of their own. Even before the outbreak of the Revolution, the colonies seethed with quasi-governmental and extralegal patriot groups and committees. In leading the opposition to British oppression, they carried out various executive functions in competition with, and defiance of, the traditional authority of the governors. The need for intercolonial cooperation and the decisions of the First Continental Congress accelerated this development and resulted, also, in the calling of conventions and special meetings of the patriot members of the assemblies to choose delegates and act on measures of resistance. Following the outbreak of hostilities, the provincial assemblies and local Revolutionary bodies assumed power, forcing the flight of the royal governors and their followers and the dissolution of the councils. Until the Declaration of Independence the provincial assemblies, or congresses, exercised the functions of government, many of their members believing that eventually their grievances would be redressed and there would be a reconciliation with Britain. All the colonial governments during this period consisted of unicameral legislatures without executives other than presiding officers and of committees and councils established by the assemblies to carry out policies. These councils' duties were weighty: they raised troops, collected taxes, regulated commerce. But they remained entirely responsible to the legislatures. The judiciary had almost vanished, and judicial powers were exercised largely by local Revolutionary groups from which appeals could be made to the congresses or to one of their committees.

The Whig leaders of the Revolution, mostly men of education and property, had had to secure the fullest support of the people. Consequently, there was a huge upsurge in democracy. More men participated in government, and more people were able to vote and be represented. An egalitarianism, with serious aspects, had appeared. The poorer and less well educated began to challenge authority; others without background or experience gained position and influence; and many men even started evading the payment of taxes and debts. To such Whig leaders as John Adams and George Mason, who believed in the need for legal order and authority to keep men virtuous and counter their natural tendencies to "pride and avarice," it seemed that the overthrow of British institutions had left the colonies open to a dangerous democratic growth that could lead to disorder and the threat of anarchy. Even as they worked for independence, they urged the creation of new constitutionally based governments to check the pendulum that could swing sharply from monarchical tyranny to democratic license; liberty and rights, they felt, could be as easily destroyed by one force as the other.

Even before independence colonies began writing constitutions for formal, legal governments of their own. New Hampshire's provincial congress wrote the first one, legitimizing itself as the center of power but taking a leaf from colonial experience and creating a council, or upper house, whose twelve members it would select. There was no executive. After independence the roll of constitutional conventions and new governments swelled rapidly, and so too the number of innovations and new ideas. Despite long-standing fears of an executive, experiences with the domination of strong or unscrupulous men and their cliques within some legislatures gave rise, also, to anxiety about legislative tyranny. More quickly than most Americans would have guessed a year or two earlier, sentiment grew for some sort of executive, not only to check legislative license but to administer efficiently the mounting details of government. In the first rush of state constitutional government-making, contests arose between those who would strengthen democracy, extending suffrage and creating popularly based institutions close to the people, and those who would limit suffrage with qualifications based on wealth and create interlocking governmental institutions with checks upon each other's powers. To the latter group, the notion of a strong executive had become appealing, but the first steps to create one were tentative and cautious and took a different form in almost every state.

Throughout the Revolution and in the years of peace that followed, many of the states periodically held new conventions, rewriting their constitutions and revising their governments to conform to new thinking, new needs, and new relations of society within their states. The basic contest over democracy continued and shaped many of the institutional changes in the different governments. The Whigs, who distrusted too much popular power, pushed steadily for a stronger executive, a meaningful upper house, or senate, that would represent the propertied interests and check the lower house, the independence of executive officials, indirect elections, and limited suffrage. Their opponents worked for widened suffrage, direct elections, a weak executive with a short term of office, and either only one house with control over the executive or a bicameral system whose upper house would be as accountable to the people as the lower one.

By 1783 the social democratization created among the men who had fought the war had its counterpart in a wider political democratization in the states. Under many of the state constitutions, new democratic procedures were adopted. There was a broader franchise with fewer and lower property qualifications, and there was ballot voting. Reapportionment and the distribution of seats both by districts and population resulted in more seats to be filled and therefore in a wider participation in government. It also tended to shift power toward the West and to agrarian groups in the countryside that had previously counted for little in political life. Annual elections, open sessions of legislatures, roll-call votes, and the publication of bills and journals all became an established part of government.

As far as governmental systems were concerned, the tugging and hauling between Whigs and democrats in the states produced many desirable innovations but no single model upon which a satisfactory national government could be based. Though many people were now ready for a stronger executive, most of these remained weak and more or less dependent on the legislature. In eight states the executive (called president in three of them) was still chosen by the legislature, and in ten states his term of office was limited to one year. Ten states, also, had bicameral legislatures, and the senates had generally become stronger, with many powers equal to those of the lower house. No longer, however, did they resemble the councils of colonial days; recognition of the value of separation of powers had worked to strip them of executive and judicial functions.

The contests over powers, relative strengths, and working relations among the components of government brought into prominence the principle of the separation of powers, with accompanying checks and balances. It was not a new idea. In the seventeenth century some English Whigs had popularized the concept in a slightly different context when referring to the king, the aristocracy, and the Commons as separate sources of power. In actual fact, England had developed a government that mixed and balanced, rather than separated, the powers of government. But Locke and Montesquieu, both widely read in the colonies, had focused attention on the importance to the British Constitution of what they saw as a separation of powers, and they favorably influenced many Americans on the subject. "When the legislative and executive powers are united in the same person, or in the same body of magistrates, there can be no liberty," Montesquieu had written in *The Spirit of the Laws* in 1748. When the First Continental Congress composed its Declaration of Rights in 1774, one of its points recognized the principle of the separation of powers as a necessity of good government, and many of the state constitutions, in various ways, accepted and developed the doctrine. Its greatest impact on the framers of the Constitution, however, came on the eve of the Philadelphia convention, with the publication of the first volume of the powerful *Defence of the Constitutions of Government of the United States of America,* written in Paris by John Adams in answer to an attack on the American states' bicameral legislatures and division of powers by the French philosopher A. R. J. Turgot. Adams, who had made the principle the hallmark of a constitution he wrote for Massachusetts in 1779, demolished Turgot's thesis that in a "perfect common-wealth, a single assembly is to be possessed of all authority, legislative, executive, and judicial," and in arguing for the system the states had been developing, he provided the framers of the Constitution with an overwhelming brief for a triadic structure of separated powers in the new national government.

Beginning on May 14, 1787, the delegates to the Constitutional Convention hammered out that government, concluding their work in under seventeen weeks. Vague in many of its clauses, full of compromises that made its acceptance possible, the Constitution they wrote nevertheless rectified almost every weakness and deficiency that had hobbled the government of the Confederation. It created a single strong executive, a bicameral legislature, and an independent judiciary, each with separate powers but all inter-related in a delicate system of checks and balances. It devised an equally delicate structure of shared sovereignty between the nation and the states, giving the federal government certain powers over the states, but otherwise leaving the states as they had been. And it made the government one whose authority stemmed from the people rather than from the states.

Eighteen specific powers, many of them identified with the national needs with which the Confederation had not been able to cope, were given to Congress. They included the power to lay and collect taxes, duties, imposts, and excises with which to pay the debts "and provide for the common Defence and general Welfare of the United States"; to borrow money; to regulate foreign commerce and commerce among the states and with Indian tribes; to make rules and laws on naturalization and bankruptcies that would be uniform among all the states; to coin money, regulate its value as well as that of foreign currency, and fix standards of weights and measures; to punish counterfeiters; to establish post offices and post roads; to issue patents and copyrights; to establish federal courts beneath the Supreme Court; to punish piracy; to declare war, grant "Letters of Marque and Reprisal," and make rules concerning captives in war; to raise and support armies, though no appropriation for that use could be for a term longer than two years; to establish a navy and make rules for the administration of the nation's land and naval forces; to provide for calling out, equipping, arming, and training the militia when necessary and for employing it in the service of the nation; to establish and make laws for a federal seat of government not exceeding ten miles square; to make rules and regulations for territories or other property of the United States and to admit new states; to follow several methods for amending the Constitution; and to make all laws necessary and proper for carrying out Congress' expressed powers and all other powers vested by the Constitution in the federal government. As part of the convention's "great compromise" that settled the manner of the states' representation in Congress, the House was given the power to originate all money bills—already the custom in ten of the states—but it was then added that the Senate could propose, or concur with, amendments to those bills.

The struggle between large and small states over representation was resolved by giving the states equal representation in the Senate and apportioning seats in the House of Representatives among them according to their population, which would be determined by counting all free persons and three fifths "of all other persons" (principally slaves), but excluding "Indians not taxed." A census would be taken within three years of the first meeting of Congress and every ten years thereafter, providing Congress with a basis for a decennial reapportionment of Representatives. The number of Representatives could not exceed one for every thirty thousand inhabitants, and the Constitution apportioned sixty-five seats for the first House among the thirteen states.

Senators (two from each state) would serve for six years (provision was made for dividing the first Senators into classes, with one class serving two years, the second four years, and the third six years, so that one third of the Senate would be elected every two years), and Representatives would serve for two years. A Senator would have to be thirty years old and a citizen for at least nine years, a Representative twenty-five years old and a citizen for seven years. Both had to be inhabitants of the states they represented. Unlike many of the states that had subjected their legislators to property and religious qualifications, the Constitution placed no other qualification on them and, in fact, expressly stated that "no religious Test shall ever be required as a Qualification to any Office or public Trust under the United States." The time and place of elections of members of the House was left to each state to decide, but the qualifications for voting for Representatives had to be the same as those of the electors of the most numerous branch of a state's legislature. Senators were to be named by the state legislatures.

The Vice President, with no vote except to break a tie, would be president of the Senate, and the House would choose its Speaker. Each house would be the judge of the elections, returns, and qualifications of its own members and could make its own rules. The old threat of being prorogued or dissolved, a practice of former kings against Parliament and of governors against colonial assemblies, was also precluded by clauses giving the two houses control of their own sessions and by provisions prohibiting adjournment for more than three days, or removal of place of sitting, by one house without the consent of the other. Stemming also from parliamentary custom, members of both houses were given privileges of freedom from arrest while in Congress or going to or from it (save in cases of treason, felony, or breach of the peace) and freedom from questioning of anything said in a speech or during debate in Congress (a freedom, for instance, against legal action for such an alleged offense as libel or slander).

After long argument in the Constitutional Convention, it was decided that members of both houses would be paid by the federal government and not by their respective states, with compensation "to be ascertained by Law." Conflict also developed over whether a member of Congress would be eligible to hold a national or state office. Many delegates had resented the

Confederation Congress' appointments of its own members to diplomatic and other positions and had raised the fear of a President's making corrupt bargains with Congressmen whom he appointed. The matter was settled by deciding that no member of Congress could be appointed to any civil office that had been created—or had its emoluments increased—during his term in Congress. Although George Washington would strictly observe this provision during his administration—even recalling the nomination of a Senator for associate justice of the Supreme Court—other Presidents would repeatedly fuzz its observance with constitutionally questionable appointments of members of either house to diplomatic posts and conferences, Cabinet positions, and even the Supreme Court.

Additional constitutional provisions spelled out House and Senate roles in the system of checks and balances. Two thirds of both houses could override a presidential veto of an act passed by Congress. Presidential appointments of ambassadors, Supreme Court judges, and all other high officials of the government would require the advice and consent of the Senate; treaties would require the advice and consent of two thirds of the members of that body. The President from time to time was to give Congress information on the state of the union and recommend "such Measures as he shall judge necessary and expedient." The House was given the sole power of impeachment of the President, Vice President, and all civil officers of the United States for "Treason, Bribery, or other high Crimes and Misdemeanors" (a phraseology derived from parliamentary precedents), and the Senate received the sole power to try all impeachments, a conviction requiring the concurrence of two thirds of the members present. In the election of the President, the House was awarded another power: if no person received a majority of the votes in the Electoral College, the House, with one vote for each state, would decide the election (it was to happen twice, in 1801 and 1825).

The framers of the Constitution, finally, proclaimed that document as the "supreme Law of the Land . . . any Thing in the Constitution or Laws of any State to the Contrary notwithstanding." The people and the states received certain protections, ranging from things that Congress could not do (it could not pass bills of attainder or ex post facto laws or levy taxes on exports or—against the opposition of many—prohibit the importation of slaves until 1808) to things that it must do (honor the people's right to know by keeping journals, guarantee a republican form of government to each state, and protect the states against invasion and, on application of a state legislature or governor, against domestic violence). To many Americans, including some delegates to the convention, these protections, however, seemed far from adequate. When the framers' work, drafted in final form probably by Gouverneur Morris, was made public, it appeared to support the worst fears of those who had earlier worried about the calling of the convention. Instead of following Congress' instructions solely and expressly to revise the Articles of Confederation, the delegates had created a brand-new central government, powerful enough, the critics said, to crush the rights of the states and the people.

The Constitution was signed by thirty-nine delegates on September 17, 1787, and sent to the Confederation Congress, which was still sitting in New York—though in penniless and near-moribund state. Opposition arose almost immediately, but Madison and other delegates who were also members of Congress came to New York and argued for it. The opponents finally agreed to let the fight be carried on in the states—nine of which were needed for ratification—and on September 28 the Congress transmitted the Constitution to the legislatures of the states to be submitted to conventions, as called for by Article VII of the document.

The ratification process was an uphill struggle, marked by great debates in most of the conventions, by thunderous denunciations of almost every clause in the document, and by the brilliant defense of the proposed new government by Hamilton, Jay, and Madison in *The Federalist*. In every state even supporters of the Constitution wondered at the failure to include a Bill of Rights. Others attacked the powerful executive, the seemingly aristocratic Senate, and the small House of Representatives. The House, according to many persons, *was* the people. Like the people and the states, the House, it was charged, was not adequately protected against the executive. The framers had believed from the experience of the recent past that a legislature would tend to become stronger than an executive, and that the states would tend to become stronger than a central government. In the quest for balance, they therefore favored the executive and the central government. They were wrong, argued opponents such as Patrick Henry: the executive and the central government would prove to be the stronger. In the seesaw trends of American history, both questions would surface again and again.

One by one, often by close votes, the state conventions ratified the document. In Pennsylvania a mob had to drag two Antifederalists to the state legislature to constitute a quorum that could call a ratifying convention, which then voted for ratification. In North Carolina all kinds of fears were raised. One delegate suggested that the treaty-making power, confined to the President and two thirds of the Senate, might result in a treaty "with foreign powers to adopt the Roman Catholic religion in the United States." Others complained that national taxes could be so heavy that the people would not have enough left to pay taxes to support the states, and that such rights as trial by jury had been left unsecured. In the end, North Carolina withheld its approval of the Constitution and did not ratify it until November 21, 1789, long after the First Congress had begun its work. Rhode Island, absent from the convention, ignored ratification and did not change its mind until 1790. In Massachusetts there was much questioning and long and lively debates, particularly over the absence of a Bill of Rights. Finally John Hancock, president of the convention, paved the way for ratification by proposing that the new government be requested to add necessary amendments to the Constitution. Friends of the new government in New York City thereupon celebrated ratification by sacking the offices of a hostile newspaper, the *Patriotic Register*.

New York was split between followers of Governor Clinton, who strenuously objected to the powers given to the Congress ("Our lives, our property, and our consciences are left wholly at the mercy of the legislature," one delegate declaimed), and Alexander Hamilton and his friends. The latter finally staged a huge pro-Constitution parade in New York City, where Federalist sentiment was strong. A replica of a frigate, dubbed *Hamilton* and manned by marines and seamen, was drawn up Broadway to a farm near Grand Street, where five thousand people were treated to an outdoor meal and speechmaking. Two and a half weeks later the state convention at Poughkeepsie, having heard threats that New York City would secede from the state and join the union, voted ratification, but with a rider asserting that New York would expect a new general convention of the states to revise the Constitution.

A month before New York's action, New Hampshire, on June 21, 1788, became the ninth state to ratify, thus assuring the start of the Constitution's government. Shortly afterward Virginia, too, ratified, but only after a dramatic and protracted debate between the Federalists and Antifederalists, each of whose ranks in that state's convention included some of the nation's leading partisans for and against the Constitution. For almost four weeks Patrick Henry, aided by George Mason, James Monroe, and others, stormed and questioned and were answered by Madison, George Wythe, Henry Lee, Edmund Randolph, and a future Chief Justice of the Supreme Court, thirty-two-year-old John Marshall. Washington, who was a firm supporter of the Constitution and was undoubtedly aware that he would become the first President, exerted a strong influence for ratification. Another Virginian, Thomas Jefferson, still in Paris as minister, was critical of the Constitution but remained neutral. He wrote to John Adams in London that he was displeased by the failure of the Constitution to limit the length of time a President might serve (a point with which Adams totally disagreed, finding as his main criticism Congress' powers over the President). Jefferson also made it clear that he missed a Bill of Rights. In addition, there is an apocryphal story, told later, that when Jefferson finally returned from France, he asked Washington at breakfast why he had agreed to a two-house Congress. "Why did you pour your tea into that saucer?" Washington replied. "To cool it," Jefferson said. "Just so," Washington answered; "we pour House legislation into the senatorial saucer to cool it." It was an answer guaranteed to displease democrats who were worried about the power of the Senate—which the people did not elect—over the small body of people's representatives. During Virginia's convention, however, Jefferson remained aloof from the debate and was not distressed by his state's decision.

Following New Hampshire's ratification, the Confederation Congress spent several months, amid the competing rivalries of members, trying to determine where to locate the new government. Then, deciding temporarily on New York, it wrote its own warrant of extinction on September 13, 1788, resolving that the states should appoint electors on the first Wednesday in January, 1789, that the electors should vote for President on the first Wednesday in February, and that the new Congress should meet on the first Wednesday in March (a date that happened to be March 4 and thus became fixed as Inauguration Day until passage of the Twentieth Amendment in 1933). The Confederation Congress then gradually evaporated.

Meanwhile, in the states, voting had taken place. In some states the electors were chosen by popular vote, in others by the legislatures. For the election of Representatives some states were divided into districts, each of which elected one man. Other states elected Representatives at large for the whole state, or used a combination of the two systems. The state legislatures chose the Senators. The total vote for Representatives in the first election has been estimated by historian Charles O. Paullin at from 75,000 to 125,000, or from three to three and a half percent of the free citizens of the nation. Infrequent polling places, scattered and remote populations, poor communications and traveling conditions, a variety of voting qualifications, and lack of democratization all accounted for the low vote, which was probably exercised in the main by a minority of property owners. The elections were won overwhelmingly by supporters of the Constitution, but in general these were moderates, even veering toward middle-of-the-road views.

As they came into New York to take their seats in the First Congress, the winners provided a foretaste of what most future members of Congress would be like. They did not constitute a monolithic body, able to stand like a granite block against an executive. They were so many individuals, representing not states alone, as before, but many differing constituencies. Moreover, the voters, limited in number as they were, had demonstrated already what would become familiar in American political life—a tendency to shy away from extremes and select centrists, even at the risk of picking mediocrities. Many of the most fiery defenders and opponents of the Constitution, men famed as patriots, Revolutionary leaders, and founding fathers, were missing from the First Congress. "Candidates of the type of Hamilton and Henry did not run well," observed Paullin. "Already, availability, inoffensive partisanship, and a fairly neutral record were elements of successful candidacy."

Finally, if there were statesmen who shone with the virtue that John Adams and others had equated with the desire to serve one's country even at a pecuniary hardship, there were also statesmen who worried and schemed over personal affairs, who connived for advantages, who traded and bargained and compromised and made deals, who detested and fought one another, and who played politics to the hilt. It was not long—as the new Senators and Representatives waited for the arrival of the first President and Vice President—before they began to reveal their human frailties. In time Senator William Maclay would be questioning the integrity of Senator Richard Henry Lee; accusing Pennsylvania Congressman Thomas Fitzsimons, who was also a merchant, of holding up a tariff bill until his imports could be landed and escape the new duties; and persuading himself generally that he was serving with "a set of vipers" in the Congress. And in time the distinguished Senator from Connecticut, William Samuel Johnson, delegate to the Stamp Act Congress, judge of the Connecticut Supreme Court, member of the Continental Congress and of the Constitutional Convention, would be whispered about by his colleagues for having charged the government for travel to and from Connecticut when he maintained his residence in New York City, where he was also president of Columbia College—the first example of the padding of a congressional expense account.

2. The First Congress

In the third week of April, 1789, Vice President-elect John Adams came down from Massachusetts to New York. At the northern end of Manhattan Island at Spuyten Duyvil Creek—where the Boston and Albany post roads crossed by a rude pontoon bridge that replaced the old King's Bridge British troops had destroyed—he was met by a grand welcoming committee that included his friend and Harvard classmate Senator Tristram Dalton of Massachusetts, Oliver Ellsworth, the stately Senator from Connecticut, and three members of the House of Representatives. The ceremonial party, accompanied by a troop of horse, made its way south through the countryside to the vicinity of present-day MacDougal and Charlton streets in what was then the northern outskirts of the city, where with further pomp and greetings Adams took up formal residence in a home already famous, a hilltop estate of oaks and pines known as Richmond Hill, which thirteen years before, during the Revolution, George Washington had used as his New York headquarters.

The President-elect had not yet arrived from Virginia, but on April 21 Adams was conducted downtown to the Senate chamber in Federal Hall for his inauguration as Vice President. To most Americans who were flocking into New York for the celebrations, the serious and self-confident little man from Braintree was a familiar—though scarcely known—symbol of the young nation, a senior statesman who was linked in people's minds not alone with the great events of the struggle for independence but with the peace treaty and the notable successes abroad that had gained the United States international recognition and assistance. Adams, however, had been out of the country almost the entire time since 1778, and few people had any idea what he was really like. Benjamin Franklin, who served with him on the peace commission, observed in 1783 that he was "always an honest Man, often a wise one, but sometimes and in some things, absolutely out of his senses." All that was true, as some of the Senators over whom he would preside would soon discover to their chagrin or amusement. But there was more to him than that.

Adams was fifty-three years old, a stout, dumpy-looking man who wore a tight, side-curling wig on his balding head. His arms and legs looked too small for his body, his head seemed to come right out of his shoulders as if he had no neck, and his heavy-lidded eyes and small, prim mouth were flanked by large jowls. Characteristically (for he felt his own importance and like many short men craved respect), he was immensely bothered by his physical appearance. But his personality also gave him problems. He was socially awkward, tactless, and often smug and haughty. He was uncomfortable with, and even distrustful of, most other people and once wrote his wife, Abigail, "There are very few people in this world, with whom I can bear to converse." At the same time he was fussy, sensitive to criticism, jealous, and highly irritable. When he was aroused he would throw his arms about and speak impulsively without restraint or caution, reaping criticism and mockery from his listeners.

But Adams was also a man of great principle, morality, and integrity, whose courage and erudition (sometimes worn on his sleeve) were admitted even by his detractors. James Otis, the fiery Boston attacker of the notorious British search warrants known as writs of assistance, had first inspired him to patriotic political activity in 1761, when he was twenty-six years old and just getting started as a lawyer. Four years later, as a member of the Sons of Liberty, he argued with Otis against the Stamp Act, but in 1770 he confounded Massachusetts patriots by defending the British troops accused of the Boston Massacre. That required a defiant boldness on his part, but it reflected a dominant strain in his make-up—a fervent regard for the upholding of law and justice and an almost fanatical dread of democratic license and mob action. In 1774 he was named to the Continental Congress, where he served until 1778, making a reputation as an outstanding intellect and leading spokesman for independence. The Congress sent him abroad that year as a joint commissioner with Franklin and Arthur Lee to the court of France. Later, appointed minister to Holland, he was hailed for his diplomatic achievements in obtaining from that country recognition of American independence, a treaty of friendship and commerce, and a much-needed loan of about $2 million. After joining Franklin, John Jay, and Henry Laurens in negotiating the peace treaty with Great Britain in Paris, he was named first minister to England and filled that post until April, 1788, when he finally returned home.

Save for a brief sojourn in 1779, when he drafted a constitution for Massachusetts, Adams had been away for ten years. In the interim both he and the country had changed, and in some respects grown out of step with each other. The spread of democratization, characterized in the extreme by Shays's Rebellion in his own state, disturbed him greatly. But with equal dismay he observed a decline in what he regarded as American virtue and morals: the rise of commerce and industry was corrupting even the best people; speculation in government securities and public lands was rife; patriotism and selfless desire to serve the country had given way to ambition and intrigue. As a meticulous, searching scholar who had pondered and written for many years on the governmental structure best suited to cope with what he believed was a natural conflict between men's reason and passions, he now saw more need than ever before for a strong, authoritative government that would check and control men's weaknesses.

To some extent, Adams's antidemocratic feelings had been heightened by his experiences at the courts of Europe, where he had noticed the effects of titles, symbols, and ceremonial pomp in encouraging respect for law and authority. He even came to reverse some of his opinions on European aristocracy, persuading himself that it played an important role in controlling both monarchy and the mob. As a Whig, he had always been on guard against too much democracy. He could remember an episode near his home in Braintree in 1775 after the Revolution had broken out when "a common Horse Jockey" accosted him excitedly, exclaiming, "Oh! Mr. Adams, what great Things have you and your Colleagues done for Us! We can never be grateful enough to you. There are no Courts of Justice now in this Province, and I hope there never will be another!" Adams had reacted with abhorrence at the time, noting that "We must guard against this Spirit and these Principles, or We shall repent of all our Conduct."

In those days his Whiggish distrust of democracy had been more or less in the mainstream of American ideas of government. In the late 1790's, during his presidential administration, after he had carried his thinking to an approving consideration of an American government patterned somewhat after that of Great Britain, with a hereditary executive and Senate, he would be so far out of the mainstream that it would bring him crashing down. But even now, in 1789, he was advancing in that direction and would soon reveal how far the distance had widened between himself and many of his countrymen. Despite his protests that he was being misunderstood, his ideas would have him charged with being "monarchical" and antirepublican —or, as Benjamin Franklin had said, "absolutely out of his senses."

When he first received the news of his election to the vice presidency, Adams must have done considerable thinking about what he could accomplish in that office. In addition to forcing him to live in the giant shadow of George Washington, of whom he had always been jealous, the job would provide him with no duty save that of presiding over the Senate. Even that minor task had been assigned to the Vice President by the Constitutional Convention because, according to Connecticut's Roger Sherman, "If the Vice President were not to be President of the Senate he would be without employment, and some other member by being made president [of the Senate] must be deprived of his vote, unless when an equal division of votes might happen in the Senate, which would be seldom." Normally, moreover, the presiding officer would not be expected to participate in Senate debates. Even his presence and power to break tie votes were violations of a strict separation of powers (though they were part of the delicate system of checks), since the Vice President was a member of the executive branch. As he went to his inaugural on April 21, however, Adams had long since concluded not to be bothered by any such obstacles.

In the Senate chamber that morning he was greeted by Senator Langdon, the president *pro tempore*, and conducted to the broad chair of his office, placed beneath a canopy on a raised platform. It was clear that all but a handful of the members were in general agreement with him on the special responsibility, prerogatives, and role of the Senate. They had been elected by their state legislatures and were removed from the transient clamors and passions of the people. In their deliberations, which they conducted behind closed doors, they could reinforce their aloofness from the public and dedicate themselves to exercising a steadying influence on the government. Even the name of their body—derived from Rome—lent weight to their importance. In time, members of the House of Representatives would scoff at them, calling them a "divan" of aristocrats who looked down on "the common herd," but that, from Adams's point of view, would be the natural reaction of those whose power the Senate checked.

It was toward the end of his inaugural address that Adams provided the Senators with a hint of the kind of relations that he, in his role as Vice President, had decided to have with them. Those who had visited him told him that they valued the great gifts of knowledge and experience that he would bring to the Senate. This had pleased him, but he had not needed their encouragement. He knew himself better than they, and he now reminded them: "Not wholly without experience in public assemblies, I have been more accustomed to take a share in their debates, than to preside in their deliberations." In short, John Adams was not going to be a silent ceremonial fixture. He made good on his warning almost immediately, and especially during his first two years as Vice President, he frequently intruded into Senate debates, lecturing the Senators and making known his opinions and learning.

He took the lead at once in raising an issue designed to meet what he considered one of the most pressing needs of the national government. It was a first step in his mission to endow the central government with respect and authority greater than those of the states and to strengthen it with a dignity that would command awe and enduring support from the general populace. For almost a month it resulted in his plunging the Senate into pompous debates that bordered on the inane. In Europe, Adams said, he had noticed that nothing aroused the affections of people for their governments as much as the distinctions of titles; and there was "no people in the world so much in favor of titles as the people of America." Some Senators must have raised their eyebrows (that arch-democrat, Senator Maclay, could scarcely believe what he heard). But Adams was persuasive, and from April 23 to May 14 the Senate, thanks largely to the Vice President, wasted much of its time on a profitless debate over titles for the President and other high officials of the government.

Led by the prestigious Richard Henry Lee, the Senate first tried to involve the House of Representatives in the matter. The Representatives, it turned out, had no use for titles and voted their satisfaction in addressing the chief executive simply as "George Washington, President of the United States." This set Adams off: the word *president* had no dignity, he told the Senate, because it was so commonly used. There were even presidents of fire companies and cricket clubs. What, he asked, would be the reaction of "the common people of foreign countries [to] 'George Washington, President of the United States'? They will despise him *to all eternity*."

The Senate appointed a committee to wrestle with the problem, and it came back the next day with the suggestion "His Highness, the President of the United States of America and Protector of the Rights of the Same." When South Carolina's Ralph Izard and others tried to postpone further discussion, hoping the subject would go away, Adams rose from his chair and, according to Maclay, who was fast working up a hearty dislike for the Vice President, "for forty minutes did he now harangue us from the chair." As the debate went on periodically from day to day, the Representatives found humor in what was going on in the upper chamber (so called because it was on the second floor of Federal Hall). They began bestowing titles of their own, naming a Representative from Pennsylvania "His Highness of the Lower House" and dubbing Maclay "Your Highness of the Senate." This induced Maclay to ridicule the subject in a long speech to the Senate on the meaning of *highness* ("the excess of stature" that one man possessed over others), concluding that the title rightfully belonged "to some huge Patagonian." In the end, nothing was accomplished save Izard's bestowing on Adams the title "His Rotundity."

In the meantime, more important matters were occurring. On April 23, amid great excitement in the city, George Washington arrived, rowed across New York Harbor from Elizabethtown Point, New Jersey, in a splendid barge manned by thirteen masters of the New York Marine Society. More than a week before, a joint committee of the House and Senate had drawn up plans for his reception and living quarters in the city. The two houses approved the report and then appointed another committee of three Senators and five Representatives to greet the President-elect.

All the way from Mount Vernon, Washington's trip had been a triumphal procession. Dignified, austere, the very model of a nation's greatest hero, he was the center of frenzied celebrations in town after town. It had always been obvious that no one else could have been the first President, but at the time few recognized how fortunate this would be. Even as he made his way to New York, Washington's association with the government set up by the Constitution was bringing it prestige and added support, even from doubters and Antifederalists. The "epitome of propriety," he would become in time the symbol of the presidency, establishing by his character and conduct the accepted image of that office. But now he was being equated with the whole government; under his leadership the national government was worth trusting—if only because he had tied his own fate to it.

New York outdid all the other celebrations. From every part of the harbor vessels of all sizes fell in behind Washington's barge, accompanying it across the choppy waters to Manhattan, whose shoreline was thronged by thousands of people. The din was so enormous as the barge neared Murray's Wharf at the foot of Wall Street that the noise of the pealing bells and the booming guns at the Battery could scarcely be heard. On the wharf, which was decorated with crimson velvet, Washington was greeted by Governor Clinton, Mayor Duane, and other New York officials and then taken by coach through the pressing crowds to the Franklin House at 3 Cherry Street, just east of present-day City Hall, which Congress had rented for him, furnished, from its owner, Samuel Osgood, for £900 a year. The next day members of the House and the Senate called on the President-elect to pay their respects, and a joint committee briefly discussed with him the arrangements for his taking the oath of office as prescribed by the Constitution. It was decided to have the chancellor of the state of New York (there was still no federal judicial officer) administer the oath in the House chamber (later changed to the balcony outside the Senate chamber, so that the people could witness it) on the following Thursday, April 30, the intervening days being needed to prepare Federal Hall.

The impending ceremony gave John Adams something else to worry about. What would be his official status when the President of the United States entered the Senate chamber, he asked the bewildered Senators. "Gentlemen," he appealed to them, "I feel great difficulty how to act. I am possessed of two separate powers; the one in *esse* and the other in *posse*. I am Vice-President. In this I am nothing, but I may be everything. But I am president also of the Senate. When the President comes into the Senate, what shall I be? I can not be [president] then. No, gentlemen, I can not, I can not. I wish gentlemen to think what I shall be."

According to Maclay, who could scarcely keep from laughing, a "solemn silence ensued. . . . Ellsworth thumbed over the sheet Constitution and turned it for some time. At length he rose and addressed the Chair with the utmost gravity: 'Mr. President, I have looked over the Constitution (pause), and I find, sir, it is evident and clear, sir, that wherever the Senate are to be, there, sir, you must be at the head of them. But further, sir (here he looked aghast, as if some tremendous gulf had yawned before him), I shall not pretend to say.'"

That ended it—but only temporarily. On the great day, April 30, the Senate assembled at eleven-thirty to await the members of the House and the President-elect. Outside Federal Hall a great crowd was already gathering in Wall and Broad streets. But Adams was still concerned. "Gentlemen," he addressed the waiting Senators, "I wish for the direction of the Senate. The President will, I suppose, address the Congress. How shall I behave? How shall we receive it? Shall it be standing or sitting?"

"Here," Maclay reported, "followed a considerable deal of talk from him which I could make nothing of." To some of the other Senators, however, the

Vice President was again raising legitimate questions. Not only were there no American precedents for guidance, but there was the matter of the dignity of the Senate, no small concern to men who took seriously the need to maintain the high prestige of that body, especially when it would be on public view. A discussion got under way on how protocol was observed in Parliament during the delivery of the king's speech. "Mr. Lee," said Maclay, "began with the House of Commons (as is usual with him), then the House of Lords, then the King, and then back again. The result of his information was, that the Lords sat and the Commons stood on the delivery of the King's speech. Mr. Izard got up and . . . made, however, this sagacious discovery, that the Commons stood because they had no seats to sit on, being arrived at the bar of the House of Lords. . . . Mr. Adams got up again and said he had been very often indeed at the Parliament on those occasions, but there always was such a crowd, and *ladies along*, that for his part he could not say how it was. . . ."

The discussion was suddenly thrown in a new direction when the clerk of the House appeared at the Senate door with a communication. Now, Adams wanted to know, what was the proper way for him to receive the clerk? Even that matter needed settling. The debate moved to this new question, while the clerk waited, until it was announced that the Speaker and the whole House of Representatives were now at the door waiting to come in for the joint inaugural session. "Confusion ensued," said Maclay, but the next instant the door opened and the magisterial Speaker Muhlenberg entered, bowing affably, followed by the Representatives. Added chairs had been placed for the Representatives on the left of the center aisle, and there was so much formality and conversation as the newcomers streamed in and took their seats that for a time the three-member Senate committee charged with meeting three Representatives at Washington's residence to escort him in the parade to Federal Hall forgot to depart on their mission. This oversight caused a delay in the schedule, and the members of the two houses waited for an hour and ten minutes before the roar of the crowd and the noise of drums, bagpipes, and clattering horses coming up Broad Street announced the arrival of the inaugural procession.

The joint congressional committee, headed by Senator Izard, led Washington and a crush of dignitaries that included New York's redheaded Chancellor Robert R. Livingston, who would administer the oath, Governor Clinton, Generals Henry Knox and Arthur St. Clair, and the Prussian inspector general of Washington's Continental Army, Baron von Steuben, through the vestibule of Federal Hall and up the stairs. Maclay's diary reported the historic scene as they entered the Senate chamber:

"The President advanced between the Senate and Representatives, bowing to each. He was placed in the chair by the Vice-President; the Senate with their president on the right, the Speaker and the Representatives on his left. The Vice-President rose and addressed a short sentence to him. The import of it was that he should now take the oath of office as President. He seemed to have forgot half what he was to say, for he made a dead pause and stood for some time, to appearance, in a vacant mood. He finished with a formal bow, and the President was conducted out of the middle window into the gallery, and the oath was administered by the Chancellor. Notice that the business [was] done was communicated to the crowd by proclamation, etc., who gave three cheers, and repeated it on the President's bowing to them.

"As the company returned into the Senate chamber, the President took the chair and the Senators and Representatives their seats. He rose, and all arose also, and addressed them. . . . This great man was agitated and embarrassed more than ever he was by the leveled cannon or pointed musket. He trembled, and several times could scarce make out to read, though it must be supposed he had often read it before. . . . I sincerely, for my part, wished all set ceremony in the hands of the dancing-masters, and that this first of men had read off his address in the plainest manner . . . for I felt hurt that he was not first in everything."

At the conclusion of the address the members of Congress joined the new President and others in a solemn and dignified procession to St. Paul's Chapel on Broadway, where Bishop Samuel Provoost conducted a special prayer service. The Senators returned to their chamber after the service to establish precedent in another matter—how to respond to a presidential address. Adams, as might have been expected, made it difficult.

"There are three ways . . . by which the President may communicate with us . . .," he told the Senate. "If he comes here, we must have a seat for him. In England it is called a *throne*. . . . The second is by a minister of state. The third is by his chamberlain. . . ." It was finally decided that the Senators would call on the President, taking carriages to his residence, and a committee was appointed to prepare the Senate's reply (which took more than two weeks). On May 18 the Senators called on Washington at the Franklin House on Cherry Street to deliver their response, and again Maclay—who was opposed to the whole business—recorded the scene, noting in a tart preamble that "having no part to act but that of a mute, I had nothing to embarrass me."

"We were received in an antechamber," Maclay wrote. "Had some little difficulty about seats, as there were several wanting, from whence may be inferred that the President's major-domo is not the most provident, as our numbers were well enough known. We had not been seated more than three minutes when it was signified to us to wait on the President in his levee-room. . . . We made our bows as we entered, and the Vice-President, having made a bow, began to read an address. He was much confused. The paper trembled in his hand, though he had the aid of both by resting it on his hat, which he held in his left hand. He read very badly all that was on the front pages. The turning of the page seemed to restore him, and he read the rest with more propriety. . . .

"The President took his reply out of his coat-pocket. He had his spectacles in his jacket-pocket, having his hat in his left hand and the paper in his right. He had too many objects for his hands. He shifted his hat between his forearm and the left side of his breast. But taking his spectacles from the case embarrassed him. He got rid of this small distress by laying the spectacle-case on the chimney-piece. . . . Having adjusted his spectacles, which was not very easy, considering the engagements on his hands, he read the reply with tolerable exactness and without much emotion. I thought he should have received us with his spectacles on, which would have saved the making of some uncouth motions. . . .

"After having read his reply, he delivered the paper to the Vice-President with an easy inclination, bowed around to the company, and desired them to be seated. This politeness seems founded on reason, for men, after standing quite still some time, want to sit. . . . The Vice-President did not comply, nor did he refuse, but stood so long that the President repeated the request. He declined it by making a low bow, and retired. We made our bows, came out to the door, and waited till our carriages took us up."

The House of Representatives had managed the same question with far more dispatch. On the day after the inauguration, the Speaker laid a copy of the President's address before the House, which discussed it in Committee of the Whole and directed a five-member committee, headed by Madison, to prepare a reply. The President's speech had been a purely ceremonial one, with no call for legislative action by the Congress. Madison's committee prepared a polite reply, conveying congratulations and complimentary sentiments to the President, which the whole House approved. Since the President's office (as well as all the offices of the government) was located in the same building as the Congress, it was a simple matter to ask Washington for a meeting. On May 8 the President met with the Representatives in a room next to the House chamber, Speaker Muhlenberg read their reply to the President, and the matter was finished.

The custom of a President addressing the Congress in person, and each house acknowledging the address with a ceremonial response of its own, continued through the administrations of both Washington and Adams. Historian Forrest McDonald, in his *The Presidency of George Washington*, noted that "beneath all this nonsensical ostentation and formality . . . lay some deadly serious jockeying for power. . . . The exaggerated deference toward the president was designed, at least in part, to ensure that if court politics developed, the senators would have first rank as courtiers. The exaggerated insistence on formality, on the other hand, was part of a design by the senators to protect their prerogatives against executive encroachment." Be that as it may, the custom of replying to the President smacked of regal ritual, and Jefferson was prompt to put an end to it in his first administration.

During the first months of the new Congress, meanwhile, both houses began to take up a host of more serious matters. High in priority, still, were questions of organization and procedure, many of which resulted in heated discussions and sometimes in jealous disagreements between the two bodies. The Senate established a set of twenty rules for its own conduct and debate (among them: "No member shall speak to another, or otherwise interrupt the business of the Senate, or read any printed paper while the Journals or public papers are reading, or when any member is speaking in any debate"; members should rise, stand in their place, and address the chair when speaking, then sit down; and all committees would be appointed by ballot vote of the Senators). The two houses agreed, without difficulty, to the appointment of two chaplains of different denominations who would interchange weekly between the two bodies. There was, also, no quarrel over the rules for holding conferences between the two houses to reach consensus on legislation. By April 17 both bodies had agreed that "in every case of an amendment to a bill agreed to in one House and dissented to in the other, if either House shall request a conference, and appoint a Committee for that purpose, and the other House shall also appoint a committee to confer, such Committees shall, at a convenient time to be agreed on by their Chairman, meet in the conference Chamber and state to each other, verbally or in writing, as either shall choose, the reasons of their respective Houses, for and against the amendment, and confer freely thereon." (The briefly stated method—refined and altered by practice and law during Congress' history until it fills numerous pages in the Senate *Manual*—had been worked out in bicameral state legislatures. But what no member of Congress knew, perhaps, was that essentially the same method had been observed by colonial leaders in the formal practices of the League of the Iroquois in New York, whose decision-making sachems had also been divided into two bodies that reached consensus through small meetings of spokesmen.)

More difficult was the reaching of agreement over the method of communication between the two bodies. Here again the Senate's sense of its superior prestige and prerogatives caused friction that upset the House and moved its members to resist. The Senate decided that when sending a bill or other message to the House, it should be carried by the secretary of the Senate, who should make proper "obeisances" to the Speaker and the House on entering and departing; but that a bill from the House should be brought up by two of its members, who would make bows to the president of the Senate and the Senators on entering and leaving. The House would have none of this ("We hear the House laughed at it," Maclay reported with mirth) and replied, in conference, that it would decide for itself how it sent bills and messages to the Senate. In the end, it was agreed merely that messages between the two houses should be carried "by such persons as a sense of propriety in each House may determine to be proper." The clerk of the House and the secretary of the Senate gradually assumed the role of interhouse messengers, and the Senate swallowed its pride. Other joint rules concerning the enrollment, examination, and signature of bills and other details of procedure were also established.

In the House of Representatives Madison, if not always in the lead, was at least usually at the center of all the discussions, resolutions, and agreements that were establishing rules for the future. "In every step the difficulties arising from novelty are severely experienced . . .," he wrote. "Scarcely a day passes without some striking evidence of the delays and perplexities springing merely from the want of precedents." Working generally in Committee of the Whole, the Representatives referred question after question to special committees set up for each purpose. Most of them were concerned with legislation, but committees considered such varied matters as supplies needed for the current year, the state of the western lands, and the provision of seats "within the bar" of the House for visits from the President or for joint sessions with the Senate. Other committees joined those of the Senate to settle such questions as the furnishing of newspapers to members of both houses at public expense and the selection of a person to print the proceedings and acts of Congress. In later days the rights, prerogatives, and powers of the House committees—and especially of their chairmen—would grow until they became national problems. But in the beginning they had no autonomy. "In those early years, before the rise of the standing committee system," wrote George B. Galloway in his *History of the House of Representatives*, "the committees were regarded as agents of the House which kept control over them by giving them specific instructions as to their authority and duties." The same applied to the Senate.

The first legislation passed by both houses was a bill to carry out the provision of the Constitution's Article VI, requiring the taking of oaths to support the Constitution by Senators, Representatives, members of state legislatures, and all executive and judicial officers of the federal and state governments. Discussion of the act—designed to regulate the time and manner of administering the oaths—centered, first, on whether Congress could legislate on that subject for state officers (it decided that it could) and then on the proper phraseology of a bill's enacting clause. Again, there was no precedent to follow. On May 4, principally at the insistence of South Carolina's Senator Izard that it lent more dignity and pre-eminence to the Senate, the clause "Be it enacted by the Senate and Representatives of the United States of America in Congress assembled" was substituted for the bill's original version, "Be it enacted by the Congress of the United States," and the style for all future acts of Congress was set. The bill in its final form passed the Senate on May 7 and the House on May 18. By May 22 it had been signed by Speaker Muhlenberg and Vice President Adams; on June 1 the House notified the Senate that on that day the President had affixed his signature to it, and the bill had become law. Three days later Senator Langdon administered the oath designated in the bill to Vice President Adams; Adams, in turn, administered it to the members of the Senate; and a similar procedure was followed in the House. In the states members of the legislatures and executive and judicial officers soon followed suit, binding themselves for the first time by oath to support the Constitution.

There were more procedural and housekeeping matters to settle. On

May 15 ballots were drawn in the Senate to determine, according to the Constitution, which members of the first Senate would serve for two-, four-, and six-year terms. "I fell in the first [two-year] class," said Maclay with no further comment. On June 4 and 5 the Senate and House respectively resolved to furnish the executive of each state with two copies of every act of Congress so that the states could be kept informed of national legislation. Compensation for members of the executive branch, from President Washington on down through clerks in the different departments, as well as for members of both houses of Congress and their various officials and employees, was settled in a series of bills passed by both houses in September. In his inaugural address Washington had suggested that, as during the Revolution, he not be paid an annual salary but receive only reimbursement for "such actual expenditures as the public good may be thought to require." Recalling that those bills had run high during the war and might in the future run even higher (Washington's liquor expenses alone in 1789 were to amount to almost $2,000), the Congress thought otherwise and voted the chief executive $25,000 a year, which would have to include his expenses. After much wrangling in the Senate over whether the dignity and prestige of its members required them to receive higher pay than the Representatives (Maclay, who was for no discrimination, found himself the target of "the rage and insult of the bulk" of the Senators), Congress settled for a salary of $6 a day while in session and up to the same (at $6 per twenty miles) for daily travel expenses to and from Congress for members of both houses. Most of the Senators were incensed at being placed on the same financial level as the Representatives. South Carolina's Izard, according to Maclay, said that delegates from his state had previously been paid £600 a year and "could live like gentlemen," not in "holes and corners," associating with "improper company . . . so as to lower their dignity and character"; Pierce Butler from the same state huffed that "a member of the Senate should not only have a handsome income, but should spend it all"; and Pennsylvanian Robert Morris, proud of his expensive manner of living and his "disregard of money," announced curtly that he did not care for "the common opinions" of people or what they thought of him. But the Representatives would not stand for any discrimination, and the Senators finally had to accept equal pay.

There were also numerous petitions, personal appeals, and applications for contracts and jobs to divert the two houses. Beginning with Washington, every President was besieged by office seekers. But they also applied by message or in person to members of Congress for influence in their behalf. One of the first instances of congressional interest in the filling of a position seems to have occurred in August, 1789, when Connecticut Congressman Jeremiah Wadsworth offered support for a Treasury job to young Oliver Wolcott, Jr., the son of a Connecticut signer of the Declaration of Independence and a prominent officer in the Revolution, and sent Wolcott's application to Washington. Wolcott was appointed auditor, and later became controller and then secretary of the treasury, succeeding Alexander Hamilton. By 1790 Washington and members of his Cabinet were regularly receiving recommendations for appointments from Congressmen, as well as pleas against the firing or displacing of postmasters or other jobholders in whom they had an interest. At the same time, it became common for the President or one of his top executives to consult with members of Congress over prospective appointments of men in their respective states.

Another matter that concerned the Senate's relations with the executive branch was the method of providing what the Constitution phrased as its "advice and consent" in the appointing of ambassadors and other officials and, by a two-thirds vote, in the making of treaties. On June 17 the question arose for the first time when John Jay, still filling the role of secretary of foreign affairs, appeared in the Senate to announce that Thomas Jefferson, the minister to France, was coming home on leave, and that President Washington desired the advice and consent of the Senate to appoint William Short to replace Jefferson in his absence. The question appeared to require only a simple vote of approval or disapproval by the Senators, but immediately a controversy broke out over whether this should be a voice vote or a secret ballot. Once again Maclay was at the center of the conflict. If a Senator voted against the President's wishes, and his vote were known, what might be the consequences to him, he asked. Conversely, might not a Senator vote against his better judgment simply to win "the warmth" of the President's favor? These and other arguments moved a majority to support Maclay's motion for a secret ballot, and the Senators then went on to declare their advice and consent to Short's appointment.

Two months later, however, word was received that the President was coming to the Senate with "some propositions" regarding an Indian treaty and that he desired the Senate's advice and consent, as called for by the Constitution. The question of the method of voting was abruptly reopened, and this time, despite Maclay's protest that the matter had been settled, the Senators resolved that they would record their advice and consent positions to the President by a voice vote. On Saturday, August 22, Washington entered the Senate chamber accompanied by General Henry Knox, who carried a number of papers involving negotiations with the Cherokee, Chickasaw, Choctaw, and Creek nations of the South. What the President wished was the Senate's advice and consent to proposals for treaties with those tribes. The meeting soon proved an awkward one. Knox handed a paper to Adams, who read it aloud to the Senators. "Carriages were driving past," said Maclay, "and such a noise, I could tell it was something about 'Indians,' but was not master of one sentence of it. Signs were made to the doorkeeper to shut down the sashes. Seven [articles], as we have since learned, were stated at the end of the paper which the Senate were to give their advice and consent to."

The Vice President read the first article, asking whether the Senators gave their advice and consent to it. He was interrupted by Robert Morris, who said that there had been so much noise from outside that he had not heard the body of the material "and prayed that it might be read again." This was done, and when Adams again began asking for advice and consent to the first article, "there was," said Maclay, "a dead pause." The Senators had not been able to digest and form an opinion on the matter that quickly, but all of them were in awe of Washington, hesitating to ask him questions. Finally, after whispered goading from Morris, Maclay boldly asked for a reading of the treaties and other documents to which Knox's paper had referred. "I cast an eye at the President of the United States," said Maclay. "I saw he wore an aspect of stern displeasure."

The proposed treaties, however, were produced and read. But when Adams again asked for advice and consent, the Senators, growing more bold, moved and voted that decision on each article be postponed. Morris, in turn, moved that the papers be referred to a committee for a report to the Senate on the following Monday. Seeing "no chance of a fair investigation of subjects while the President of the United States sat there, with his Secretary of War, to support his opinions and overawe the timid and neutral part of the Senate," Maclay seconded Morris's motion, adding a few words of his own in justification. "As I sat down," he reported, "the President of the United States started up in a violent fret. '*This defeats every purpose of my coming here,*' were the first words that he said. He then went on that he had brought his Secretary of War with him to give every necessary information; that the Secretary knew all about the business, and yet he was delayed and could not go on with the matter."

Washington finally "cooled" and agreed to return to the Senate on the following Monday. The papers went to a committee, and when he reappeared at the Monday session, the President "wore a different aspect . . . was placid and serene, and manifested a spirit of accommodation." The Senators were now ready to debate the articles. They did so in front of Washington, adding some amendments and changes, but at last giving their approval to all his treaty proposals.

The embarrassing confrontation had considerable significance. Washington and many others may have held vague ideas that the Senate was to play a role in relation to the presidency somewhat similar to that of the colonial executive councils, legislative bodies that also advised the governors. The episode ended that idea forever, for the Senate had vigorously asserted its independence of the executive. There was an apocryphal story that Washington was so offended by his treatment that he swore "he would be damned if he ever went there again." Indeed, he never did revisit the Senate, but established the precedent of communicating with it entirely by written messages. Moreover, taking foreign affairs entirely into his own hands, he soon set the custom—frequently, though not always, observed by future Presidents—of having the executive branch conduct treaty making without the Senate's participation, leaving to that body merely the right of accepting or rejecting a treaty after it had been negotiated.

During the long period of precedent setting, a stream of legislation, initiated principally in the House of Representatives under the eager and competent leadership of Madison, had been moving through the committee processes. The first need was to raise operating revenue for the new government, and the proposal to lay duties on imports that Madison introduced in Committee of the Whole of the House on April 8, only two days after the Senate announced a quorum, had originally been designed simply to meet that single goal. As debate got under way, however, the aim of the measure took on an additional cast.

Spring was the importing season, and Madison hoped that the Congress would pass an act in time to collect revenues at the ports that year. He submitted a proposed schedule of specific duties of so much a gallon or pound on certain articles such as rum, molasses, tea, pepper, and sugar, and an *ad valorem* tax (a fixed percentage of value) on all other imports. In deference to a public opinion that might still not be ready to accept such a law from a national government for an unlimited period of time, he suggested making the act a temporary one. The next day a number of Representatives were on their feet, urging that a tariff not be temporary or limited in its aim of raising revenue, but that it also be planned "to encourage the productions of our country and to protect our infant manufactures." Congressman Thomas Fitzsimons of Pennsylvania, a wealthy and prominent Philadelphia merchant who had been one of the least productive delegates to the Constitutional Convention, opened the floodgates with an amendment to that effect, and almost immediately Representatives were proposing a host of high duties that would keep out foreign imports of goods produced in their home areas.

In a short time the debate became enmeshed in sectional interests and rivalries. George Clymer, another Pennsylvania merchant, urged placing duties on imported steel, noting that a furnace in Philadelphia "made three hundred tons in two years" and deserved protection. He was opposed by Thomas Tudor Tucker of South Carolina. Southern agriculturists needed steel for tools, Tucker exclaimed; he would fight any tax on that product. At the same time, his South Carolina colleague Aedanus Burke, joined by Andrew Moore of Virginia, asked for protection for the planters of the South, proposing a duty on hemp, which Burke said had a good future in such states as South Carolina and Georgia, and on cotton, which was "in contemplation" (Eli Whitney's cotton gin had not yet revolutionized the production of that crop). New Englanders wanted a high protective duty on rum, which they produced, but no duty on the molasses they imported to make the rum. Benjamin Goodhue of Massachusetts got anchors, tinware, and other products manufactured in his state added to the list of imports to be taxed; Roger Sherman of Connecticut obtained a duty on manufactured tobacco high enough for him to term it a "prohibition" on imports; Theodoric Bland and Josiah Parker of Virginia, claiming that their state's coal mines could supply the nation, got foreign coal added to the list; and Daniel Carroll of

Maryland and Clymer of Pennsylvania got protection for their respective states' glassmaking and papermaking industries.

Madison did not oppose the protective aspect of the duties, but he fretted over the delays caused. "The prospect of our harvest from the spring importations is daily vanishing," he pleaded. The proposals went to a select committee of the House and were held there for days by John Laurance of New York, Elbridge Gerry of Massachusetts, and Fitzsimons of Pennsylvania. At length gossip arose that the committee members had business interests of their own that induced them to delay the bill deliberately until their spring imports arrived. The charges were undoubtedly true. Gerry was a shrewd, dapper little merchant-politician who was both a patriot (he had made many contributions to the Continental Congress since 1776) and a protector of his considerable financial interests. He was a thin, sharp-looking man (Maclay called him cadaverous), but he considered himself a favorite with the ladies. Fitzsimons was involved in banking and the China trade, and like his fellow Pennsylvanian Senator Robert Morris, he had fingers in many business ventures. Even Fisher Ames, who was usually generous in his observations of most of his colleagues, did not think too well of Fitzsimons. He "is artful, has a glaring eye, a down look, speaks low. . . . He is one of those people, whose face, manner, and sentiments concur to produce caution, if not apprehension and disgust," Ames said. Meanwhile, merchants in different cities began to raise their prices by the amount they understood the duties would be, according to the House's published debates, and reaped windfall profits at the expense of the public.

Under pressure, the committee finally returned with a bill, and on May 16 the House passed it and sent it to the Senate. As an adjunct to the tariff, Madison had also proposed a tonnage duty—a tax on the carrying capacity of all ships arriving from foreign ports. In consultation with Washington (well before Congress had met and before Washington had even been notified formally of his election), Madison had shaped a schedule of tonnage duties to make them something of an instrument of foreign policy. The smallest duties were to be laid on American ships, somewhat higher ones (thirty cents per ton) on the ships of France and other European powers with whom the United States had treaties of friendship and commerce, and the highest duties (sixty cents per ton) on vessels of the recent enemy, Great Britain, which since the Revolution had not only refused to discuss a commercial treaty with the United States but had angered most Americans by her failure to observe points in the peace treaty. The Congress supported wholeheartedly the principle of the lowest rates for American ships, but the discrimination against Great Britain—in effect, an attempt to shift American commerce from England and her colonies to France—seemed like an undeclared economic war on Britain and drew opposition from many sources, both in and out of Congress. In New York Alexander Hamilton, who was practicing law as a private citizen, voiced the concern of many by predicting that such discrimination would reduce British imports without increasing French ones, and that the resulting drop in import and tonnage duties would cut American revenues and strangle the new government. Hamilton's arguments were echoed in Congress during debates over the tonnage duties, and the principle of discrimination against British ships and imports was finally killed in the Senate.

After being subjected to numerous amendments that changed the duties on most items, the tariff bill passed the Senate on June 11. During the next week the House rejected almost all the amendments and sent the bill back to the Senate. A conference was arranged between committees of the two houses, and on July 1 the Senate and House agreed to final terms on tariff and tonnage duties. The bill was enacted on July 4 and was generally a compromise between those who had viewed the tariff as strictly a revenue-producing measure and those who had fought for high protective duties. The act placed equal tonnage duties on all foreign ships (fifty cents per ton, versus six cents per ton on American-owned ships) and levied specific taxes of up to fifty percent on some thirty items and a straight five percent *ad valorem* tax on all other imports. Duties were not as high as all the protectionists had wished them to be, but, in general, the manufacturing and shipping interests of the North were favored at the expense of the agricultural South, which imported much of what it used. South Carolina's intemperate Pierce Butler set the tone for what might be viewed as the beginning of strain between the two sections of the nation. Not only would the South have to pay more for its imports, he railed, but the tonnage duties would tax its exports of agricultural products to the North. At the same time, the law foreshadowed the combining of revenue and protection as twin aims of future American tariffs. As a postscript, the Congress also passed a bill to provide for the collection of duties at the ports. The law had missed taxing the spring imports, but federal collectors were quickly installed and revenue was soon coming in to the government.

On May 4 Madison had interrupted a discussion of the import duties in the House to mention another matter. At the end of the month, he announced, he would introduce the subject of amending the Constitution to include in it a Bill of Rights. Madison was probably under pressure from home, for the next day his Virginia Antifederalist colleague Theodoric Bland, a doctor and planter who was a follower of Patrick Henry's, presented an application from the Virginia legislature, bearing Henry's touch, reminding the Congress that Virginia had ratified the Constitution only on "a full expectation of its imperfections being speedily amended." Time had gone by, nothing had been done, and Virginia now wanted another convention of the states to revise the Constitution. The danger seemed great to Madison, for New York, Massachusetts, and other states had ratified the Constitution with similar reservations and at any time might join Virginia's plea. A new convention was intolerable for Madison to contemplate, because much of what had been accomplished could be undone by opponents of a strong central government, who might take the nation back to something like its helplessness under the Articles of Confederation.

Bland wished Virginia's application to be considered at once in Committee of the Whole, but a majority of the members thought the question should wait until Madison introduced his amendments. Two hundred ten amendments, specifically restricting the federal government's powers, had come in to Congress in formal proposals from the constitutional ratifying conventions in five states and in informal proposals from two others. They covered a broad range of concerns, although every state had recommended restrictions on the federal government's power to tax, as well as an amendment to make it clear that all powers not delegated to the national government were reserved to the states. Madison eliminated duplicates and combined the rest into eighty subjects, which—when reduced to their final number—he thought might be woven into the body of the Constitution. Eventually, however, Roger Sherman convinced him that Congress had no right to alter the wording or meaning of what the states had already ratified, and Madison agreed to the adding of separate amendments at the end of the Constitution.

Madison labored carefully, trying to frame the desired rights without imperiling or weakening any of the powers already given to the national government by the Constitutional Convention. To a large extent he was guided by the Virginia Declaration of Rights, which George Mason had written in 1776 and which had been incorporated in the Virginia Constitution. From that document he drew inspiration for what were to become the first eight amendments of the federal Bill of Rights—though, by using such commanding language as "shall not" instead of Mason's "ought not," he made his prohibitions on governmental power much stronger than those in the Virginia document. Dropping the least popular subjects and those considered unsuited to the Constitution and combining and rewriting others, he reduced the proposed amendments to nineteen and on June 8 was finally able to introduce them in the House.

Madison hoped that prompt endorsement of the amendments would end the threat of another convention by satisfying the sincere Antifederalists and winning them away from those who, like Patrick Henry, used their objection to the absence of a Bill of Rights to obscure their real desire to rewrite the Constitution and return power to the states. The House debate, however, produced a jumble of conflicting points of view. Such amendments regarding the rights of the people and the states had been debated by the Constitutional Convention and deemed unnecessary, Roger Sherman reminded the House. Whatever powers the national government possessed had been expressly mentioned, and it had been considered irrelevant and foolish to go on and enumerate the powers that the government did not have. Sherman was supported by Fisher Ames, Elias Boudinot, and other Federalists, who added—as they had been stating during the preceding weeks—that there were more urgent matters than a Bill of Rights for the Congress to settle. Decision on the tariff and tonnage duties was up in the air; the executive branch was not yet organized; and there was still no federal judiciary, which would have to enforce the revenue act and all other federal laws and establish the power of the federal government over that of the states. They were soon joined in their arguments by the waspish and unpredictable Elbridge Gerry, who had refused to sign the Constitution partly because it contained no Bill of Rights, and by James Jackson of Georgia and two Representatives from South Carolina, all of whom had loudly proclaimed their desire for such amendments. Now they seemed slyly united in wanting to prevent the endorsement of amendments so that—as Henry hoped and Madison feared—there would be another convention.

In the face of such a mixture of objections, Madison delivered a speech—considered by some to be one of the major state papers in American history—finally persuading a majority of the House that the government must take up the amendments. "There is a great number of our constituents who are dissatisfied with [the Constitution]," he said, "among whom are many respectable for their talents and patriotism, and respectable for the jealousy they have for their liberty." There were also two states that had not yet ratified the Constitution because of the absence of a Bill of Rights. "We ought not to disregard their inclination, but, on principles of amity and moderation, conform to their wishes, and expressly declare the great rights of mankind secured under this constitution." Provide the amendments, he counseled, and he had no doubt but that those who were sincere and still opposed to the Constitution would at last give it their support.

Madison spoke in a low voice, so low that most members had to strain to hear what he was saying. But his manner was pleasing, "sweet," and kind, according to some of them, and what he said was thoughtful and convincing. The Federalists knew that he, too, had originally seen no need for a Bill of Rights, but there was logic now in his appeal to broaden the support for the national government and undermine the threat of those who would weaken it in a new convention. Moreover, they were aware that Washington agreed with Madison; the President, too, wished to remove this obstacle to the uniting of his fellow countrymen. On July 21 a select committee of eleven members—one from each state, with Madison at its head—was named to work on the amendments. The committee reported back, and on August 13 the Committee of the Whole took up the subject.

In the intermittent debates that ensued, additional amendments were suggested. One of them, supported principally by Elbridge Gerry of Massachusetts and John Page of Virginia and opposed by Madison, Sherman, and many others, proposed permitting constituents to instruct their Congressmen how to vote. This was a hazy and ill-conceived idea, but it struck at a legitimate question about representative government and produced a vigorous debate. It was unclear whether instructions from voters were to be considered binding, but the Representatives—arguing at length over the right to exercise their own wisdom and judgment and also over the practicability of acquiring the majority viewpoint of the voters in a district—finally rejected the proposal with the consensus that Representatives had an obligation to act in the best interests of the whole nation as well as of their particular constituencies. It was a tentative conclusion to a question that would not, and could not, ever be satisfactorily settled.

On August 24 the House approved seventeen of Madison's amendments and sent them to the Senate. During the next month that body worked them over and suggested a number of changes, including the combining and elimination of some of them. Late in September conferees of the two chambers agreed on the final form of twelve amendments to be submitted to the states. One of Madison's proposals that was dropped was a prohibition on the violation *by states* of the rights of freedom of speech, press, and conscience, and trial by jury. Its elimination (in deference to states' righters) was to cause considerable trouble through much of America's history, for while persons were secured against federal violations of their rights, they were legally defenseless against similar infringements by the states unless they were protected by their state constitutions. Even after post-Civil War constitutional amendments were designed to end the double standard, court decisions proved slow in giving satisfaction.

The twelve amendments were passed by both houses and submitted to the states on September 25, 1789. All but the first two (concerning the number of Representatives and the timing of changes in the compensation of members of both houses) were ratified by the states and became part of the Constitution on December 15, 1791—the day of ratification by Virginia, satisfying the constitutional requirement of assent by three quarters of the states. By that time the amendments had had the effect hoped for by Madison. North Carolina ratified the Constitution and joined the other states on November 21, 1789, two months after Congress endorsed the Bill of Rights. The following year, on May 29, 1790, Rhode Island also ratified the Constitution, spurred to action (in a breathtakingly close 34–32 vote) perhaps not so much by the Bill of Rights as by a vote of the exasperated citizens of Providence to secede from the state. In Virginia Patrick Henry had been outmaneuvered by Madison, for although the Ninth and Tenth amendments guaranteed to the people and the states all rights and powers not given to the federal government, the amendments did not return to the states any of the powers that the Constitution had taken from them. Throughout the country, new support was gained for the government. So great was the general satisfaction and the increased respect for the Constitution, in fact, that Massachusetts, Connecticut, and Georgia even forgot to ratify the amendments until 1939, when, during the celebration of the sesquicentennial of the Bill of Rights, they discovered their oversight and moved briskly to correct it.

The Senate's own notable contribution to the first session of the First Congress, meanwhile, had been the writing of the Judiciary Act of 1789, which created the nation's third branch of government and was, in effect, almost an appendage of the Constitution. The legislation was principally the work of one man, Oliver Ellsworth, though the tall, trim Connecticut Senator received valuable assistance from legally minded William Paterson of New Jersey and Caleb Strong of Massachusetts. A select Senate committee, headed by Ellsworth, had been set up to write the act on April 7, the day after the Senate achieved its first quorum. The Constitution said that the judicial power of the United States would be vested in a Supreme Court "and in such inferior Courts as the Congress may from time to time ordain and establish." The questions faced by the Senate committee, however, were much more complex than the Constitution's directive made them seem.

By coincidence, Ellsworth, Paterson, and Strong were all forty-four years old. Ellsworth, a serious, hard-working man who used common sense and logic with good effect to overcome gaps in his learning and experience, had gone to Yale, then transferred to the College of New Jersey (Princeton). He tried both preaching and teaching before turning to the law, but he had a difficult time getting started in that profession, even having to chop wood for an income. Finally he made a good marriage, moved from Windsor, Connecticut, to the state capital at Hartford, and through perseverance and the force of his personality began to make a reputation. In time he rose politically, becoming state attorney, going to the Continental Congress, serving on the Governor's Council (which constituted a supreme court of errors), and being appointed a judge of the Connecticut Superior Court. He also had many business and investment interests, and by the time he went to the Constitutional Convention in 1787, he was one of the most influential men in Connecticut.

His Senate colleagues, Paterson and Strong, had also gained reputations in law and politics in their respective states. Paterson, born in Ireland, was raised in Princeton and had gotten both his B.A. and M.A. at the College of New Jersey (graduating from the college three years earlier than Ellsworth). He kept a store with his brother before building up a law practice and then served in the legislature and became state attorney general. A very short man, able and tough-minded, he was a leader in the fight of the small states at the Constitutional Convention. In 1790 he would be elected governor of New Jersey and would resign from the Senate, and in 1793 Washington would name him an associate justice of the Supreme Court. Strong, from Northampton, was a Harvard graduate and an experienced lawyer and Massachusetts political leader with a number of investment interests on the side. Suffering from seriously impaired eyesight, the result of a bout with smallpox, he was sober, industrious, and extremely devout. He, too, would go on to become governor of his state.

Antifederalists and states' righters greatly feared a system of federal courts. If there was one part of the new government that might swallow up state sovereignty and ride unchecked over the people's rights, they believed, it would be a new, all-powerful national judiciary that would wipe away the bulwarks provided by state courts and sanction and enforce the actions of the central government. Although Ellsworth, Paterson, and Strong were all Federalists who believed in the need for a powerful federal judiciary to unite the nation and win the respect of the people, they were acutely aware of the states' fears—articulated vigorously in the Senate by Richard Henry Lee and William Grayson of Virginia, Pierce Butler of South Carolina, John Langdon and Paine Wingate of New Hampshire, and the irrepressible Maclay of Pennsylvania. With remarkable ability and ingenuity they beat a middle path, devising a federal judicial structure and an intricate system of jurisdictional interrelationships between federal and state courts that paralleled, in a sense, the shared sovereignty between the central government and the states achieved by the Constitutional Convention.

Largely reflecting Ellsworth's innovations, common-sense thinking, and reliance on his experiences in Connecticut, the Judiciary Act established a Supreme Court of one Chief Justice and five associate justices; thirteen federal district courts (one in each state) whose judges would have to be residents of the states in which they served; and three traveling circuit courts of appeals presided over by two touring members of the Supreme Court and the district-court judge of the state in which the court was sitting. The state judiciaries would be untouched save in the necessity to observe national laws, and they were further protected and empowered by a new, highly complex mixture of jurisdictions that, instead of swallowing up the state courts, fitted them into a state-and-national framework of concurrent jurisdictions and systems of appeals. In this way state courts could continue their functions within their respective states and also share in protecting the rights and carrying out the obligations of the federal government. In matters not under federal jurisdiction, the decisions of the highest courts in the states were final and without appeal to federal courts. In most matters concerned with federal laws and treaties or arising under the Constitution, cases might also be adjudicated in state courts, but they could be appealed to the Supreme Court in order to protect the national government's rights. The act thus established the principle of federal judicial review over state legislation, though it was not mentioned in the Constitution.

At the same time, Section 13 of the act somewhat innocuously gave the Supreme Court original jurisdiction in cases involving federal public officials. This section broadened and conflicted with the Constitution's own Article III, Section 2, which spelled out the cases that could start at the Supreme Court level, though no one in either house seemed to be concerned about it. The Senate passed the bill, 14 to 6, on July 17, and after debate in the House it became law on September 24, 1789. Two days later John Jay, the distinguished New Yorker who had been filling the role of secretary of foreign affairs, was confirmed by Congress as the first Chief Justice of the Supreme Court.

The federal courts were instituted and the regulatory provisions of the

Judiciary Act were put into effect, and in 1803 a new Chief Justice, John Marshall, at last caught the defect in Section 13. In the celebrated case of *Marbury* v. *Madison* he called it an unconstitutional extension of the Supreme Court's original jurisdiction by Congress and with that decision established the principle of judicial review of federal legislation. Marshall had caught the one flaw in an otherwise brilliant and largely enduring contribution by Oliver Ellsworth and his Senate colleagues to the basic structure of the American form of government.

Simultaneously, both houses were grappling with the organization of the various departments of the executive branch. It was agreed that there should be three major departments of the new government, Foreign Affairs, War, and Finance, though lesser offices of an attorney general (to advise the President on legal and constitutional matters) and a postmaster general, both responsible to the chief executive and later raised to Cabinet level, would also be created. An additional proposal by Representative John Vining of Delaware for a Home Department, concerned with western territories, patents, surveys, the census, and other internal matters, was turned down with the argument that those functions could be divided among the three great departments. (In later years, however, Congress would create various domestic departments to handle most of these activities, as well as many others.)

During the House debate over the secretary of foreign affairs, a controversy arose that, according to Fisher Ames, "kindled some sparks." Under the Constitution it was clear that the President could make certain appointments only with the advice and consent of the Senate. But did the President need the Senate's concurrence to *remove* such appointees? The Constitution was silent on the point. Some Representatives, such as Bland and Alexander White of Virginia, who feared executive power, argued that while they trusted Washington a future President might abuse the right of removal unless the Senate had the power to check him. The Constitution, they believed, gave the Senate the right to approve a removal because "the party who appoint ought to judge of the removal." Most members of the House disagreed with this argument, though they divided over whether the Constitution implied that the President could remove appointees without Senate approval, or whether Congress should explicitly confer such a power on the President by law. The first argument got the House into the difficult situation of trying to interpret the Constitution, and the second raised the specter of Congress' passing a law to permit something that was already conferred by the Constitution. Nevertheless, the argument raged, with members suggesting that unless the President had the power of removal it might prove impossible ever to dismiss a secretary save by the lengthy and involved process of impeachment, trial, and conviction—a possibility that distressed Elias Boudinot, who asserted that impeachment was "intended as a punishment for a crime, and not as the ordinary means of rearranging the Departments."

Once more Madison's logic and eloquence were brought into play and proved persuasive. The Senate had *expressly* been given the right to advise and consent on appointments, he argued, but it had *not* been given the right on removals. Therefore, not having been taken away from the President, the power of removal was part of the general grant of power to the executive under Article II of the Constitution, which Congress could not lessen or change. Moreover, the President, by that article, had been made responsible for the administration and conduct of the executive branch. If he could not remove the head of a department without Senate approval, the President, said Madison, "is no longer answerable."

Both houses of Congress eventually went along with Madison's thinking. The debate, however, was to have strange fruit. In 1867 the Congress, at odds with President Andrew Johnson, passed the Tenure of Office Act, by which the President was prohibited from removing officials appointed by and with the advice and consent of the Senate without senatorial approval. When Johnson was impeached and charged with violating this act, the arguments of the 1789 losers—those who had wanted to curb the President's powers—were used against him. In 1926 the Supreme Court finally ruled against the Senate's power to concur on such removals, in effect upholding the congressional verdict of 1789.

Despite resentment by some Senators over the way the House had clipped their power on removals, the bill organizing a new Department of Foreign Affairs became law on July 27. On September 15 its name was changed to the Department of State, and eleven days later Thomas Jefferson, who was on his way back to Virginia on leave from his post in France, was named by Washington as the first secretary of state. In the spring of 1790 Jefferson finally traveled from Virginia to New York, and on March 22 of that year he took his oath of office as head of a staff that included a messenger, an office keeper, and four clerks. A War Department bill was passed on August 7, 1789, after considerable debate between a few men such as Maclay and Lee, who opposed a standing army or even a War Department in time of peace, and others such as Senator Pierce Butler of South Carolina, who in Maclay's words "blazed away.... Declared over and over that Georgia would seek protection elsewhere if troops were not sent to support her [against danger from Indians]." General Henry Knox, convivial, efficient, and a favorite of Washington's (and weighing three hundred pounds, so that he and his wife—also gargantuan—were known as the biggest couple in New York), was continued in the job of secretary of war, which he had filled under the Confederation government.

The organization of the Treasury gave Congress the most trouble. Elbridge Gerry (really an independent who moved back and forth between Federalist and Antifederalist points of view and quite often could find third positions for himself) was among those who were adamant in wanting to have the nation's financial affairs continued in the hands of a three-man board rather than a single person. Gerry and his supporters did not wish to concentrate financial power in the hands of one man, and although their resistance was overcome in a close vote, many other Representatives also feared the possibility of Congress' losing control of the power of the purse to a strong secretary, and under Madison's guidance unique rules were written regarding the Treasury and its head.

Unlike the provisions for the secretaries of other departments, the bill concerning the Treasury—while recognizing the President's right to appoint and remove its head—required the secretary to work directly with Congress rather than with the President. He would have to make his reports to Congress, and Congress could examine his financial documents and ask him for information without going through the President. The intent was to circumscribe the President's power in this field and ensure Congress' control. Viewing the secretary as something of a liaison officer with the responsibility to plan fiscal measures, Madison wished to authorize him to "digest and report" his financial proposals to Congress. But this was opposed by a majority in the House, who feared that it would transfer the initiative from Congress to the secretary, paving the way for him to become a powerful British-type minister able to turn Congress into a rubber stamp for his measures. Instead the House, jealous of its constitutional prerogative to originate all money bills, directed that the secretary must "make report and give information . . . respecting all matters referred to him by the Senate or House of Representatives," not on his own initiative.

By going as far as they did in tying the secretary of the treasury to the Congress, Madison and his colleagues unwittingly established the ground not only for the intrusion of a strong secretary into the affairs of the Congress, a significant melding of the executive and legislative branches, but —just what they had hoped to avoid—for the emergence of an American version of Britain's chancellor of the exchequer who could ram his own measures through Congress with the support of a loyal majority. At the moment, all this was unforeseen. The Treasury bill was enacted on September 2; earlier, on July 24, the House had set up a Committee of Ways and Means to advise it on financial matters. But on September 11 Alexander Hamilton, who enjoyed the confidence of the Federalist majority in Congress, was appointed secretary of the treasury, and six days later the House discharged the committee, indicating that it would rely on Hamilton instead. (Not until 1795 would the House establish a permanent standing Committee on Ways and Means.)

Hamilton was thirty-four years old, a small, lean, handsome man far beyond his years in experience and abilities. Born on Nevis in the West Indies, the illegitimate son of a Scottish merchant, he had pretty much shifted for himself from the age of eleven, when his mother died and his father went bankrupt. Raised for a time by relatives, he displayed an unusual intelligence and aptitude for business and in 1773 was helped by friends to get to New York to attend King's College. In the growing Revolutionary ferment he joined the city's patriots, gaining celebrity among them by his flaming speeches and brilliant writings. He entered the army, rose to colonel at twenty-two, became an aide-de-camp and trusted friend of Washington's, and distinguished himself for outstanding bravery at Yorktown. Returning to New York after the war, he married the daughter of the rich and influential Philip Schuyler, and as an ambitious but graciously charming and self-assured lawyer and leader in business, civic, and political affairs, he added to his luster and stature. His interest in finance had convinced him early of the inadequacy of the government of the Articles of Confederation, and hand in hand with his developing ideas of how to cope with the nation's economic ills there had grown in him an almost fanatical belief in the necessity of a strong central government. This conviction had placed him in opposition to Governor Clinton and the Antifederalists and had given him the reputation of being antidemocratic and a monarchist.

To a large extent, both charges were true. Hamilton thought that a limited monarchy was the best guarantee of the people's liberty, and he feared the excesses that could stem from too much democracy. But though he was aristocratic—even autocratic—in bearing, temperament, and instinct, he wanted no oligarchy running the American government. "Give all power to the many," he said, "and they will oppress the few. Give all power to the few, they will oppress the many." At the same time, his ideas of what was necessary to cure America's economic problems and promote the growth of a strong nation would have the initial effect of favoring the wealthy. In his view this was both necessary and desirable. Measures had to be taken, he insisted, to reduce the power and independent-mindedness of the states and draw that power to the federal government. To do so, the allegiance of all classes and ranks must be lured from the states to the central government. Since people, he believed, were moved by their ambitions, interests, and even greed, he would use economic means that would make it worthwhile and, indeed, necessary for them to deal with the federal, rather than a state, government in their financial and business affairs. In time, those measures would help everyone. But their first beneficial impact would be on the creditors of the government—the wealthy, whose attachment the national government most needed. He would not shrink, moreover, from charges that his measures would tend to corrupt men. He admired—and got many of his ideas from—the workings of Great Britain's economic system, and he sometimes shocked others in private conversation by saying that England's system worked so successfully only because it rested on corruption. He did not see anything wrong in the encouragement of a financial aristocracy, for it would give strength to the much-needed growth of the American economy. Nor did he see anything wrong in appealing deliberately to men's baser instincts if it served the end of strengthening the national government.

In September, 1789, these ideas of Hamilton's were only hazily known to Congress. Most Federalists had a high regard for his administrative abilities and understanding of finance. In 1780–81, some of them recalled, he had drawn up several plans to rescue the Continental dollar. Moreover, Madison, who had collaborated closely with Hamilton in the past, not only was still his friend and admirer but had had him in mind as the first secretary of the treasury when he proposed giving ample powers to the secretary during the writing of the Treasury Department bill, and had then been in the forefront of those who persuaded Washington to appoint him to the position. But to states' righters and democrats such as Maclay, Hamilton was disturbing. In the Constitutional Convention the New Yorker had proposed a plan that would have made the states mere administrative districts of the national government. Even Madison, essentially a nationalist, was too loyal a Virginian to share Hamilton's views on the submergence of states, and he differed with him on some of the provisions of the Constitution and on how to meet the financial needs of the government. But despite these differences, Madison looked forward to a harmonious working relationship between Congress and the new secretary of the treasury, and Hamilton, in turn, felt he could count on the Virginian's support in Congress.

Earlier, Congress had received a memorial from some citizens in Pennsylvania requesting payment of the interest on the Continental securities that they held, and it was referred to the new secretary of the treasury. At the same time the House, making use at once of its hold on the secretary, directed him to provide it with a survey of the public debts of the different states—how they were being serviced, and how much of the Continental debts the states owned—and also to prepare a plan "for the support of the public Credit." A huge and complicated problem that had hung precariously over the new government since its first day was thus finally brought to the fore, but the House, in asking for the submission of a plan, was going beyond a request for information and was opening the door wide for what it had opposed—the initiation of legislation by the secretary. Hamilton was asked to have his reports ready for presentation when Congress convened again, and on September 29 the two houses ended their first session, having organized the federal government and gotten it off to a good start.

The problem of the nation's credit, on which Hamilton labored during Congress' recess, was an enormous one. Some $11,710,000 in principal and interest (as Hamilton would report) was owed to France, Spain, and private Dutch bankers, and another $44 million was due American citizens for outstanding Continental securities and the accrued interest on them and for unliquidated claims and currency. Interest payments to France were $1.5 million in arrears, and the Dutch had received their interest only by lending more money to the United States. Not only could this not go on, but if the country were to become stabilized and grow it would require further loans—and they would not be forthcoming while such a large debt was outstanding and unserviced. Everyone, including Hamilton and the members of Congress, knew that America's credit would have to be restored. To complicate the matter, there had been widespread speculation in the securities held in the United States. Originally these had been issued during and after the Revolution to pay soldiers, farmers, and others for services or goods, but their value had depreciated greatly and many of the poorer people had been forced to sell their securities at from ten to fifty cents on the dollar. Now a relatively small number of the wealthy held them in large amounts, hoping for the day when the government would redeem them at their face value or something close to it. However, there were some who did not want their value to rise, for they had contracted with the federal or state governments to buy public lands in the West, paying over a period of time in government securities at par value. As long as they could buy the securities in the market at less than par, they stood to make money—and sometimes fortunes. Finally, many of the Continental securities were held by the states, which in turn owed an estimated $25 million in debts of their own.

On January 6, 1790, the members of both houses, having returned to New York from their recess, achieved quorums for their second session, and two days later Washington, in person, delivered a State of the Union message in a joint session in the Senate chamber. This time the President proposed subjects for legislation. He wished Congress to authorize the raising of troops; establish a uniform system of weights and measures; appropriate funds for diplomats and his own diplomatic expenses (his salary was pinching); establish post roads; fix the terms for the naturalization of new citizens; take steps to further public education by helping schools already established or by creating a national university; and, receiving the suggestions prepared by the secretary of the treasury, enact laws for the national credit.

On the day after Washington's address, Speaker Muhlenberg delivered to the House a message from Hamilton, announcing his readiness to deliver the report on the public credit to which the President had alluded. Elbridge Gerry, alert to the need for the House to keep an upper hand over the secretary, moved that the report be submitted in writing rather than in person. The motion carried, and on January 14 the House received Hamilton's *First Report on the Public Credit*. The forerunner of several papers on economic matters that the secretary would submit to Congress, it was explosive.

After presenting the factual information on the debts that Congress had requested, the report recommended that the government fund the nation's entire foreign and domestic debt, including approximately $13 million of interest in arrears, by issuing new stock with which to pay off the debt and by pledging to pay the interest and principal on the new loan with a certain portion of the government's annual revenues. Subscribers could pay for the new stock with the old securities, and the purchasers would have a choice of receiving their new holdings in a variety of attractive forms, including different types of securities as well as options to acquire western lands at bargain prices. In addition, Hamilton proposed that the government also assume the unpaid debts of the states, redeeming them in the same way.

There was virtually no opposition in Congress to paying off the foreign obligations; both national honor and practicality demanded that the country establish its credit among the powers of the world. But bitter controversy arose immediately over the plan to fund the domestic debt. Hamilton proposed to redeem the old securities at their face value, a recommendation heartily supported by speculators and others who held the certificates but angrily opposed by debtors, farmers, and others who had had to sell their holdings at a fraction of the original value. Moreover, the scheme lent itself to new speculation by those able to afford to do so, and charges began to arise of "stock jobbing" and corruption by persons, both in and out of Congress, who sought to make a quick fortune. Three fast ships had sailed suddenly from New York to buy up as many securities as possible from "uninformed though honest citizens of North Carolina, South Carolina, and Georgia," thundered Georgia Congressman James Jackson. It was whispered that among the owners of the ships, dispatched to arrive in the South before news of the high redemption prices could reach the back-country people, were two Representatives, the aristocratic young William Smith of South Carolina and Jeremiah Wadsworth of Connecticut, a former seaman and commissary general in the Revolutionary Army. "My soul rises indignant at the avaricious and moral turpitude displayed!" roared Jackson.

A New York newspaper stated baldly that Wadsworth would make $9 million from the funding plan and that Senator Robert Morris (who was absent from the Senate attending to his private land and security speculations almost as much as he was present) would profit by twice as much. Maclay, of course, needed no urging to believe the worst. "I really fear the members of Congress are deeper in this business than any others," he confided to his diary. Some members of the House, noting the sudden rise in the market value of the old securities, hoped to nick the profit making by proposing that the payment of accrued interest be repudiated. Others, including Jackson, Thomas Scott of western Pennsylvania, and Samuel Livermore of New Hampshire, insisted angrily that only the market value of the certificates be paid. But they were opposed as vehemently by Federalists such as Thomas Fitzsimons of Pennsylvania, Roger Sherman of Connecticut, and Fisher Ames and Theodore Sedgwick of Massachusetts. "Shall it be said of this government, evidently established for the purpose of securing property, that in its first act it divested its citizens of Seventy Millions of money which is justly due the individuals who have contracted with Government?" asked Ames.

For about a month during the debate, Madison, the acknowledged leader of the House, sat silently. As a Virginian he could not go along with Hamilton's plan, since more than four fifths of the national securities and most of the state debts were held in the North. But Madison knew less about finance than Hamilton, and he was unprepared. The secretary had seized the initiative in the legislative process, and the Virginian was on the defensive. On February 11 Madison finally rose to advance his own plan—a weak compromise proposal to give the present holders of securities bonds equal in value to the highest market price of the old securities, and to the original holders, who had sold their securities at less than face value, a bond equal to the difference between the highest market price and the original face value. This, he felt, would provide justice to both groups. The proposal angered Hamilton, who was bent on establishing absolute faith in the nation's willingness to live up to its financial obligations. Taking over the leadership of the fight himself, he gathered together those in the House who supported him, directing their strategy and tactics, providing them with arguments, and having them undermine Madison with the untrue assertion that his plan was impractical because it would not be possible to distinguish in the Treasury's records between the original and present holders of certificates.

On February 22 the Virginian's proposal came to a vote, and Madison suffered his first defeat, 36 to 13. Many Federalists and friends of Madison's, some of them speculators guarding their own interests, others anxious to establish the nation's credit in view of future borrowing needs, deserted him to give Hamilton the victory. Boudinot, who said he thought that Madison's plan was an admirable attempt to provide justice to those who had sacrificed during the Revolution but that he had to vote against it because of its impracticability, gently chided the Virginian for having been "led away by the dictates of his heart." Much later, however, it was revealed that Boudinot stood to profit personally by passage of Hamilton's funding plan. So did almost forty of its most vocal supporters in both houses, including Representatives Fisher Ames, Theodore Sedgwick, Elbridge Gerry, Thomas Fitzsimons, George Clymer, William Smith, and Jeremiah Wadsworth, and Senators Robert Morris, Caleb Strong, John Langdon, Oliver Ellsworth, Pierce Butler, Rufus King, and Philip Schuyler, Hamilton's own father-in-law.

The fight over the assumption of state debts was a different story. In return for the federal government's paying what the states owed, the plan required that the states surrender their own right to tax and agree to vest taxing powers in the federal government. Hamilton viewed assumption as an essential part of his overall funding plan, for it would not only wed state creditors to the federal government, but also provide him a field for levying the taxes necessary to finance the funding. Some states, principally in New England, had large unpaid debts and supported assumption; New York, New Jersey, and South Carolina also stood to benefit. But others, including Maryland, Delaware, North Carolina, and Georgia, had either paid off their debts or were satisfactorily on their way to doing so, and they opposed federal taxation of their own citizens to pay for the debts of others. Pennsylvania, with a modest debt, was divided over the plan, while Massachusetts and Virginia, both with large debts incurred in certain state military operations during the Revolution, threatened to block assumption unless these debts too were assumed. In addition numerous Congressmen, including Gerry, Theodoric Bland, and William Smith, possessed large holdings of state securities and would gain personally by passage of the proposal. But as the debate continued, waged contentiously and with high emotion off and on for almost six months, Hamilton failed to marshal a clear majority. He won Massachusetts to his side by agreeing quietly to meet all its debts, but he made no headway with Virginia.

Chief among his opponents was Madison, who not only opposed assumption because of the "injustice" it would do his state, but was greatly disturbed by Hamilton's overt direction of his supporters in the Congress—an interference in the legislature that was also resented by others (Maclay called the secretary's followers "the crew of the Hamilton galley" and Hamilton's "gladiators"). Hamilton's best efforts got nowhere, however, as Madison and his forces (which the Virginian was beginning to term the "republican interest") introduced amendment after amendment. They would have negated Hamilton's overall plan, and the secretary's supporters managed to beat them back, but the votes were close and filled with tension. On one occasion Representatives Bland and Huger, one of them lame and the other sick, had to be carried into the House chamber by Hamilton's supporters in order to vote, while Clymer's leave to go home to Pennsylvania was delayed until he had cast his vote. On another occasion Maclay found a dispirited and somewhat frightened Pennsylvania Representative, Henry Wynkoop, sneaking off with his wife to return home so as to avoid the pressure coming at him from both sides. "He certainly is wanting in political fortitude," said Maclay. "Benson, Laurance [both New York Representatives], the Secretary, and others have paid attention to him, and he has not firmness of mind to refuse them his vote. But he has done what equally offends them and subjects himself to ridicule; he has abandoned the whole business and deserted the cause of his country at a time when an honest vote is inestimable."

By April the supporters of Madison and Hamilton were virtually deadlocked, and some of the secretary's followers were proposing compromises. Hamilton would not accept them, however, and on April 12 assumption was finally put to a climactic vote in a Committee of the Whole House. This time Madison won, 31 to 29. Maclay visited the House to watch the vote, and he recorded with unconcealed glee the reactions of Hamilton's defeated adherents, who also faced the prospect of personal financial losses: "Sedgwick, from Boston, pronounced a funeral oration over it. He was called to order . . . he took his hat and went out. When he returned, his visage, to me, bore the visible marks of weeping. Fitzsimons reddened like scarlet; his eyes were brimful. Clymer's color, always pale, now verged to a deadly white; his lips quivered, and his nether jaw shook with convulsive motions; his head, neck, and breast contracted with gesticulations resembling those of a turkey or goose nearly strangled in the act of deglutition. . . . Ames's aspect was truly hippocratic . . . he sat torpid, as if his faculties had been benumbed. Gerry exhibited the advantages of a cadaverous appearance, at all times placid and far from pleasing; he ran no risk of deterioration. . . . Wadsworth hid his grief under the rim of a round hat. Boudinot's wrinkles rose in ridges and the angles of his mouth were depressed. . . ."

For almost two months Hamilton's forces tried to reverse the vote, but despite threats by some of the New England Representatives that their states would secede from the union, Madison's majority stood firm. On June 2 the House adopted the funding bill without assumption and sent it to the Senate. In that body Robert Morris, Ellsworth, and a number of members who held both state and Continental securities argued for the restoration of assumption, without which, they knew, the funding part of the bill would be crippled. On June 14 a Senate committee recommended amending the funding bill to restore assumption, and the stage was set for an impasse between the two houses. At that point Hamilton turned desperately to a complex political deal that he tried to work out with the help of Thomas Jefferson. The tall, lanky, reddish-haired, sandy-complected Virginian, forty-seven years old, graceful and easygoing on the outside but a torrent of conflicting ideas and emotions within, had arrived in New York to serve as secretary of state. Washington had recently changed his residence from Cherry Street to a larger and more comfortable house on Broadway just south of the recently rebuilt Trinity Church, and one day late in June Jefferson was about to enter the President's house when Hamilton came up to him.

The treasury secretary, Jefferson later recalled, "was sombre, haggard, and dejected beyond description." For half an hour the two Cabinet members walked back and forth in front of the building while Hamilton pointed out the danger to the new government and to the country's finances if assumption was not adopted by Congress. Hamilton "was determined to resign" if the measure failed, he told Jefferson, but he appealed to the Virginian for help, for "the administration and its success was a common concern" and the two Cabinet officers should "make common cause in supporting one another." Though Jefferson professed little knowledge of, or interest in, the economic measures, he agreed to try to help, and the following evening brought Madison and Hamilton together at a private supper party.

During the meeting, according to Jefferson, a deal was consummated designed to settle not only the assumption fight but also a long-drawn-out competition among rival interests, dating back to the days of the Continental Congress, over a permanent location for the national government. That argument had been waged in open debates and in private conversations on the streets and in the boarding houses throughout both sessions of Congress, with the most devious intrigues and attempts to deal for votes. Maclay had come close to winning support for a location on the Susquehanna River near his home in Pennsylvania; it passed the House and was agreed to by the Senate. But his Pennsylvania colleague Robert Morris, wanting the capital closer to an area of business activity, had first plumped for a location at the Falls of the Delaware River and had then got the Senate to substitute Germantown for Maclay's Susquehanna River. This made the feelings between the two Pennsylvania Senators no better and ended with the Senate dropping both Germantown and the Susquehanna. In June debate reached a climax, and tensions became almost as high as over the assumption bill.

Many members of Congress were now agreed to moving at least temporarily to Philadelphia, with Baltimore, Wilmington, and the Potomac River, where Lee, the Virginia delegation, and most southerners wanted the new capital, all being considered for the permanent site. When votes were taken no place ever received agreement, despite energetic means by various partisans to round up support for their favorites.

The agreement worked out at Jefferson's home, according to the secretary of state's recollection, bound Hamilton to seek Pennsylvania's votes "through the agency of Robert Morris" to locate the capital at Philadelphia for ten years, then move it permanently to a site on the Potomac River, as desired by the Virginians. In return, while Madison personally would not have to support the Senate's assumption amendment when it returned to the House, he would give his "acquiescence" to the inducement of two Virginia Representatives from Potomac River districts, Richard Bland Lee and Alexander White, to switch their votes in behalf of assumption. Jefferson believed that this agreement was carried out, and that the bargain made at his home was responsible for the ultimate passage of both measures.

Recent scholarship, however, principally that of historian Jacob E. Cooke, suggests convincingly that while the agreement was probably made, it actually played little or no role in the working out of both bills. Even before Jefferson's supper party, Cooke noted, Virginia and Pennsylvania had begun collaborating on moving the capital temporarily to Philadelphia and then permanently to the Potomac, although the Pennsylvanians hoped that Congress would become so satisfied with Philadelphia that it would stay there permanently. Hamilton's principal role may have been in quietly undermining northern opposition to the Virginia-Pennsylvania coalition. According to Cooke there is no evidence that he secured even one vote for the Philadelphia-Potomac decision; instead, agreement on the location of the capital was finally achieved after a series of votes in the Senate, accompanied by maneuvers totally unassociated with assumption. The measure, passed by the Senate on June 30, approved by the House, and enacted into law on July 16, 1790, located the permanent national capital in a district ten miles square on the Potomac (its precise site along a 105-mile stretch of the river was left to the selection of President Washington and commissioners whom he would appoint) after a temporary move to Philadelphia for ten years beginning the following December.

The course of assumption was more complicated and, again, was so marked by political maneuvers, shifting positions, and changing votes as to seem unrelated to the agreement described by Jefferson. Even though the Senate voted to put assumption back in the funding bill, the full measure was returned to the House modified by compromises that made it more palatable to some of the assumption opponents. These included not only a compromise on interest rates to be paid on the funded debt, but modifications that held out to those states with little or no debts promises of what amounted to large outright grants to remunerate them for the debts they had already paid. Nevertheless, on July 24 followers of Madison in the House again tried to eliminate assumption from the bill. The proposer of the motion, Congressman Jackson of Georgia, wrote Fisher Ames to a friend in Massachusetts, "made a speech, which I will not say was loud enough for you to hear. It disturbed the Senate, however; and to keep out the din, they put down their windows." Despite Jackson's stentorian oratory, his motion was beaten. Two days later the assumption plan passed the House, and on August 4 the entire funding bill became law. True enough, the two Virginians, White and Lee, had switched their positions to support assumption, but to ascribe assumption's passage to their votes is too simplistic; other votes, also, had changed on both sides of the issue.

History soon revealed Hamilton's wisdom and vision. Though Madison continued to the end to vote against both assumption and funding, the measures brought a new climate of economic stability and confidence to the country, strengthened the national government, established its credit, encouraged business optimism and growth, and drew foreign capital to America to assist in the nation's development. At the same time it increased political and ideological divisiveness. The act enriched a handful of the wealthy and convinced large numbers of people, principally southerners and the defenders of agrarians, that Hamilton wished to create a class of wealthy northern masters, that he was an enemy of agriculture, and that he was scheming to impose a monarchical system on the country. The bill's effects in giving power to the national government at the expense of the states led Jefferson to have second thoughts about Hamilton and his own naiveté in trying to help arrange the assumption deal. In Virginia it was generally accepted that Hamilton had sacrificed the states to the central government, the South to the North, and the interests of agriculture to those of manufacturing and commerce. Despite the ameliorating compromises in the final version of the bill, the Virginia legislature on December 16, 1790, sent Congress a steaming "Protest and Remonstrance," framed by the untiring Patrick Henry, declaring that assumption and the funding system were "repugnant to the Constitution of the United States" and "dangerous to the rights and subversive of the interests of the people."

On August 12, 1790, Congress adjourned again and said good-by to New York. Its second session had been stormy but also productive. Among other accomplishments, in addition to adopting Hamilton's funding and assumption schemes and settling the permanent location of the capital, it had authorized the first United States Census; defined various crimes against the federal government and their punishment; set up a government for the western territory south of the Ohio River; enacted the first patent law and established a patent office, which opened on July 31, 1790 (it was said that a dozen inventors from Connecticut were waiting at the door); passed the first Copyright Act, which protected books, maps, and plays for fourteen years, with the right of renewal for another fourteen; and bought land at West Point from an owner who had hit hard times and needed cash.

On December 6 Congress reassembled in Philadelphia, a larger but quieter and cleaner city than New York. Its most famous citizen, Benjamin Franklin, had died and been buried in the yard of Christ Church the previous April, but the warmth and wisdom of his spirit still hung over the red-brick State House and its companion buildings on State House Square, where so many great events had already taken place. In 1789 the county of Philadelphia had completed a county courthouse just west of the State House, and it was now made available to Congress. The House met in a large hall on the first floor (with a seating capacity on the main floor and in a gallery for almost five hundred spectators), and the Senate, again the "upper chamber," convened in a room on the second floor. In addition, a wing of the State House was used by the House of Representatives as offices for its clerk and committees, the rest of the building housing the government of Pennsylvania and for a few days the United States Supreme Court.

Washington, who had frightened everyone by almost dying of pneumonia during an influenza outbreak in New York in May, took residence in Philadelphia in a handsome four-story brick mansion on High Street belonging to Robert Morris. Once more the President opened Congress with an address to a joint session, and once more both houses responded with formal acknowledgments. Washington spoke of a military expedition dispatched to the Northwest Territory under General Josiah Harmar to punish Indians who were resisting trespass on their lands by settlers and hinted that Harmar might have had a disaster. (Later, when confirmation came that Harmar had been routed with the loss of two hundred dead, Washington said, "I expected little from the moment I heard he was a drunkard.") The announcement of the expedition upset a number of members in both houses, who considered it the waging of hostilities without a declaration of war by Congress.

But the matter was soon overshadowed by preoccupation with two new economic reports submitted by Hamilton. The first, received by the Senate on December 23, recommended the chartering of a national bank to serve several functions stemming from the funding and assumption bills. Hamilton wished the bank to store government funds, serve as an agency for the collection and expenditure of tax revenues, and issue bank notes, which were needed as a medium of exchange in the expanding economy. The institution, to be called the Bank of the United States, would issue $10 million in stock, one fifth of which would be bought by the government and the rest sold to private investors. Control of the bank, moreover, would rest in private hands, for the government would appoint only five of its twenty-five directors. The second report dealt again with the nation's credit, setting forth the need to levy taxes for revenues with which to carry out the provisions of the funding and assumption measures and recommending an excise tax on the producers of "spiritous liquors."

The bills were immediately taken up by Congress, and once again Hamilton, to the chagrin and resentment of Jefferson, Madison, and republican-minded members of both houses, actively directed his supporters in the House and Senate, calling them together before sessions to plan strategy in private caucuses (an Algonquian Indian word for "counselor," first picked up by the settlers at Jamestown from Powhatan Indians). The development, which in effect violated the Constitution's separation of powers—indeed creating something of a ministerial form of government—also had the coloration of the start of a faction or party, which was not lost on Hamilton's opponents. "There had been a call of the Secretary's party last night," Speaker Muhlenberg said to Maclay at one point, using the word *party* as if it denoted something that already existed.

Despite recognition that the bank bill would again benefit northern commercial groups and the wealthy (investors would receive dividends earned on public funds), the measure, thanks to Hamilton's expert management, sailed easily through the Senate without even a roll-call vote. In the House Madison opposed it, aided by a vociferous and able twenty-eight-year-old newcomer, William B. Giles, a fellow Princetonian and Petersburg, Virginia, lawyer. Admitting the bank's usefulness, Madison branded it unconstitutional. The Constitutional Convention, he recalled, had overruled his own proposal to give Congress the power to create national corporations. What the convention had denied, he insisted, Hamilton could not now go ahead and do. Giles backed him up, giving sharp voice to Virginia's Antifederalist anger and condemning the bank bill as another Federalist grab for power. Nevertheless, Hamilton had the votes, and the House passed the measure.

Madison's argument, however, had worried Washington, and when the bill went to him for signing he asked Attorney General Randolph, Jefferson, and Hamilton for written opinions on its constitutionality. Both Randolph and Jefferson supported Madison, employing many arguments but citing in particular one of the Bill of Rights amendments that Congress had passed and the states were then in the process of ratifying—"the powers not delegated to the United States by the Constitution, nor prohibited by it to the States, are reserved to the States respectively, or to the people." The two papers were so persuasive that Washington asked Madison to draft a veto message for him. On February 23, however, Hamilton submitted his paper, titled *Defense of the Constitutionality of the Bank*. It was a brilliant work, setting forth for the first time a "loose constructionist" interpretation of the Constitution based on Congress' power, under Article I, Section 8, "to make all Laws which shall be necessary and proper for carrying into Execution the foregoing Powers"; since the bank was necessary and proper to carry out the funding and assumption laws, Congress had the implied power to create it. This argument, which Chief Justice John Marshall would later expand upon in his 1819 decision in *McCulloch* v. *Maryland*, convinced Washington, and on February 25, to the dismay of Jefferson and Madison, he signed the bank bill.

The proposal for an excise tax also went through both houses, emerging from Congress on March 3 as the nation's first internal revenue law. It levied a tax of twenty to thirty cents a gallon on distilled spirits and set up fourteen revenue districts in the nation, with officials to collect the taxes. Once more federal power was enhanced, and the legislatures of Virginia, North Carolina, and Maryland registered their disapproval—in time even more serious trouble would come from western Pennsylvania. But the law stood, and on the evening of March 3, 1791, amid the hurry and bustle of the rushing through of last-minute bills and overlooked appropriations, the First Congress came to an end by candlelight. During its three sessions, totaling 519 days of work, it had received 268 bills and enacted 118 of them —more than 60 being major statutes.

During Congress' last months, new elections had taken place in the states. Most incumbents in both houses were re-elected—but not all. In Georgia General Anthony Wayne, a new resident of the state, beat the noisy James Jackson, though his victory was achieved with the use of fraudulent votes, which would ultimately cause Congress to declare the seat vacant. In New York Senator Philip Schuyler was retired by the legislature in favor of an ambitious and charismatic lawyer and political leader, Aaron Burr. And in Pennsylvania—as he had expected would happen—William Maclay, who had made enemies on all sides by his blunt honesty and independence, was dropped by his state legislature. Few would miss the acidulous Maclay, but in his place eventually would come Albert Gallatin, far more dangerous to the Federalists than the man from the Susquehanna had ever been. This republican, also from western Pennsylvania, would give enormous strength to Jefferson—who up to that time had been in the shadow of Madison, supporting the leader of the House—and to Madison, who was becoming a Jeffersonian, and all that that would mean.

3. Years of Tumult

By the opening of the first session of the Second Congress in Philadelphia on October 24, 1791, Americans were on their way toward a division into two political groups that would become increasingly—and dangerously—combative. Support of or opposition to the Constitution was disappearing as an issue. In its place came a rising angry distrust between those who feared a trend toward monarchy and aristocracy, perhaps modeled on the British system, and those who feared too much republicanism and democracy. The two sides were personified by their most highly placed and therefore most influential and powerful partisans, Jefferson and Hamilton, both Cabinet members and both vying for the support of Washington. While the President deplored the split in his executive family, trying to remain neutral but more often than not leaning to Hamilton, the fissure spread, dividing the Cabinet, the Congress, and the people.

Jefferson's ideal of an agrarian republic, based on sturdy yeomen "tied to their country, and wedded to its liberty and interests, by the most lasting bonds," put him in natural opposition to most of Hamilton's policies; to Jefferson they appeared designed to lead to the growth of an affluent, favored commercial class and to urban ills and corruption at the expense of agriculturists, particularly those in the South and the expanding West. In addition, Jefferson's vision aroused him against extensions of federal power and especially against anything that hinted of monarchy. In the previous year he had been perturbed by a series of essays by John Adams entitled *Discourses on Davila*, which seemed to be a plea for a limited monarchy in the United States, and in a letter to Washington he raised objection to the Vice President's "apostasy to hereditary monarchy & nobility." For a time Jefferson thought of Adams as the "bellwether" leading the Federalists into "political heresies," but he soon saw the aggressive Hamilton as the more committed "monocrat" and the more dangerous of the two men. Hamilton, of course, returned the compliment. The secretary of state, in his view, was too radical to be trusted, and his closeness to Washington made him more threatening than any other man to Hamilton's own policies and goals.

This Cabinet-level contest, exacerbated by Hamilton's uninhibited Anglophile leanings and Jefferson's pro-French feelings, dramatized and intensified the growing division within the nation. The debates over almost every major piece of legislation in the First Congress, pitting the republican-minded like Maclay against the Federalists, provided evidence that the roots of the conflict were already present. Washington's decision on the United States Bank had stung Jefferson, Madison, and their followers and turned Jefferson fully against Hamilton, who he felt was gaining control of the administration and would, if unchecked, turn it into a British-style ministry.

With much to concern him, Jefferson in May and June had accompanied Madison on a "botanical" vacation excursion through New York and New England. While conclusive evidence is lacking, they probably met briefly with various northern Antifederalist political leaders, including New York's Governor Clinton, Chancellor Robert R. Livingston, and newly elected Senator Aaron Burr, to discover how strong the secretary of the treasury was in the North and to exchange sentiments regarding a possible anti-Hamilton coalition. Nothing was formalized, however, and by October neither side had coalesced into anything resembling an organized party. But common ideas and concerns were fast binding men together, and when Congress met, many individuals in both houses became more or less firmly aligned into two voting groups—Federalists on one side and the republican-minded on the other. Above them were the two Cabinet officers, locked in an ideological conflict that inspired their followers in and out of Congress.

In the Congress few matters were unaffected by the growing division. Twenty-eight of the sixty-five members of the old House had been replaced by newcomers, but supporters of the administration were still firmly in control. The Federalists, with their principal leadership and support in the New England delegations, could count on about fifteen fairly consistent votes, while the republicans, led by Madison and based principally among southern delegations, had a core of about seventeen votes. The Middle Atlantic delegations usually divided on roll calls, with the majority going to the Federalists. But divisions on issues were rarely consistent. As a rule, they reflected alignments of individuals who had different economic or sectional reasons for standing together on particular pieces of legislation.

In the Senate John Adams still sat in the Vice President's chair, though he had learned to be somewhat more silent. Despite his complaint that "my country has in its wisdom contrived for me the most insignificant office that ever the invention of man contrived or his imagination conceived," Adams was able to cast twenty-nine tie-breaking votes during his eight years in the office, more than any Vice President since. Richard Henry Lee of Virginia, now turned Federalist, was elected president *pro tempore* of the Senate, succeeding John Langdon of New Hampshire. His term was of short duration, however. On October 8, 1792, failing health forced him to resign from the Senate, and he died less than two years later. Langdon again became president *pro tempore* of the Senate, and Lee's seat was taken by tall, courtly John Taylor of Caroline County, Virginia, a thirty-eight-year-old redheaded planter and scholar of economics who championed the farmer and agricultural interests. As an enemy of "the moneyed aristocracy of the North," Taylor would later write exposé-type books against the Hamiltonians. He was a close friend of his fellow Virginian in the Senate, James Monroe. Monroe—large, muscular, four years younger than Taylor—was fast becoming the leader of the republican-minded faction in the upper house, consulting closely with Madison and Jefferson. On the House side, the Federalist majority ousted Speaker Muhlenberg, whom the Hamiltonians did not consider helpful to their policies, and elected Connecticut's Jonathan Trumbull, a loyal Federalist.

On October 25 Washington addressed a joint session of the two houses and immediately raised the temper of a number of Antifederalists. Again he reminded Congress of the war being waged against the Indians of the Ohio country, and he asked for legislation designed to secure the frontier so that the country could utilize the potential abundance of its western lands. No one would deny aid to protect the lives of innocent settlers, but to some members of both houses that was not the issue. Two of the most notable achievements of the old Confederation Congress had been the enactment of the Land Ordinance of 1785, which established the method of surveying and selling western lands, and the Northwest Ordinance of 1787, which created a government for the Northwest Territory and provided for its eventual division into states. Together they had set a pattern for the orderly westward expansion of American society and its institutions—but the pattern was not yet operating. The Land Ordinance, calling for the sale of township subdivisions of 640-acre sections—too large for most families to afford—had encouraged widespread land speculation by the wealthy. Speculators and settlers alike simply took up land, some of it ceded by Indians in formal treaties but most in areas unceded and unsurveyed. When whites moved onto the lands the tribes still claimed, the Indians tried to drive them away. The ensuing border warfare, compounded by frontiersmen's outrages against the Indians, kept the West in turmoil.

During the First Congress legislation had been passed, at Washington's urging, to try to deal with the problem. Federal licenses were required for all traders with the Indians; settlers were prohibited from moving onto lands not formally ceded to the government by the tribes; and punishment was provided for whites who committed crimes against Indians. But some Antifederalists had raised serious objections to this extension of federal power, and Congress turned down other proposals by Washington and limited the act it did pass to a duration of two years.

The act had proved largely unenforceable, and as conflict continued, Washington sent troops to try to pacify the Ohio country. When the expedition under General Josiah Harmar met disastrous defeat, in March of 1791

Washington ordered out another army under white-haired Arthur St. Clair, who had been serving as the first governor of the Northwest Territory. Most Federalist members of Congress were determined to support Washington's new requests, which would extend the provisions of the earlier act and add various trade and other measures designed to bring the Indians into peaceful relations with the national government. Opposition to these measures, however, now broadened. A second large army was engaged in a war that some members of Congress felt was constitutionally and morally questionable. The army was invading Indian territory to protect people who had no right being there and to open new lands for "land jobbers." Moreover, it was expensive, which meant increased taxes (five sixths of the government's general expenses were used in the Indian war). There was opposition even to the existence of a federal army. Why have one, opponents asked, for any purpose save the defense of the country against a foreign enemy?

The recommendations in the President's message were referred to a select committee in the House, which eventually reported a bill. But before it could be debated, the stunning news reached Philadelphia on December 9 that St. Clair had met with a defeat worse than Harmar's. On November 4, near the present Ohio-Indiana border, his army had been almost destroyed by Miamis, Shawnees, and Delawares under Little Turtle, Blue Jacket, and Buckhongahelas; of fifteen hundred regulars and militia, St. Clair lost six hundred dead and three hundred wounded, the greatest victory ever won by Indians over American troops. The blow scandalized the nation, providing ammunition for the Antifederalists in Congress. But the Federalists, too, wanted to know what had happened, confident that when the facts came out, opposition to the government's pacification policy would melt. "The war will be pursued against the Indians . . . ," wrote Federalist Fisher Ames; "the public will be made to see that the charges of violence and oppression on the part of the United States, the disturbance of the Indian possession of their lands, and a hundred others, are Canterbury tales."

On February 2, 1792, Representative John Steele, a North Carolina Federalist, moved that Congress direct the President to conduct an inquiry, hoping that it would still "the clamor against the war." The motion was stoutly opposed on the grounds that under the doctrine of separation of powers, Congress had no right to instruct the President in a matter affecting the conduct of the executive branch. A second motion by Representative Hugh Williamson, another North Carolina Federalist, proposed, instead, that the House appoint a select committee of its own to conduct the inquiry. Backed by Madison, who carefully put the investigation on a solid constitutional base by adding that the committee's purpose would be "to inquire relative to . . . the expenditures of public money," the motion for an investigating committee with power "to call for such persons, papers and records as may be necessary to assist in their inquiries" was approved by the House on March 27. There was ample precedent in parliamentary and colonial legislative history for such a committee, and it was the first of a long series of investigations by both houses of Congress. Moreover, like many of those that would follow, its principal motive lay beneath the surface.

Federalists and their opponents publicly agreed that its function should be to inform Congress what had happened, and why, so that it would not happen again. But the Federalists also recognized that the Antifederalists, prodded principally by Madison's fellow Virginian William B. Giles, who detested Hamilton, were on what would later be called a fishing expedition. Giles hoped to uncover evidence that would fix the blame on the secretary of the treasury, who had been responsible for the army's supply contracts, and from the beginning that unspoken aim put the Federalists on guard.

When the committee wrote to Secretary of War Henry Knox for all relevant papers, Knox realized what was happening and, vulnerable himself to criticism that could harm the Federalists, presented the matter to Washington. The President called a Cabinet meeting at once, "to consult," reported Jefferson, "merely because it was the first example, and he wished that so far as it should become a precedent, it should be rightly conducted. He neither acknowledged nor denied, nor even doubted the propriety of what the House was doing, [but] he could readily conceive there might be papers of so secret a nature, as that they ought not to be given up." The Cabinet could not come to agreement about what to do, and asking for time "to think and enquire," it met again on April 2 after having studied parliamentary precedents. Now "of one mind," said Jefferson, it agreed that "the House was an inquest" and that "the Executive ought to communicate such papers as the public good would permit, and ought to refuse those, the disclosure of which would endanger the public. Consequently, [the executive] were to exercise a discretion."

On the question of "the power of the House to call on Heads of Departments," however, Jefferson noted that Hamilton had bridled. Slyly, he commented that Hamilton was concerned about a congressional inquiry into financial speculation by government officials, the most notorious of whom was William Duer, Hamilton's former assistant secretary of the treasury. Duer had resigned under a cloud in April, 1790, but he continued large-scale financial manipulations—largely on the basis of "inside" information from the Treasury—that had recently brought about his collapse as well as a financial panic that ruined many others. Nevertheless, the Cabinet agreed that "neither the committee nor House had a right to call on the Head of a department, who and whose papers were under the President alone, but that the committee should instruct their chairman to move the House to address the President." This was done, and on April 4 Washington, with a recommendation from the Cabinet that "there was not a paper which might not properly be produced," directed Knox to furnish the House committee with all the records it requested.

Though the seven-member select committee had a Federalist majority, its republican members worked hard to develop their contention that St. Clair's defeat had resulted from corruption by Hamilton's Treasury agents.

In large measure they succeeded. After reviewing all the records and examining St. Clair and others, the committee made its report to the House, unanimously exonerating St. Clair and laying the blame on the War Department and on the "gross and various mismanagements and neglects" of the quartermaster and the contractors. Treasury corruption was not specifically mentioned, but Hamilton nevertheless felt that he had been implicated. By November, when the next session of the House took up the committee's report, Hamilton had raised angry opposition to it among his followers, and some of them demanded that both Hamilton and Knox be invited to answer the charges. Madison objected to a precedent of permitting the attendance of Cabinet members in the House—one that could lead to British-style Cabinet government—and the House supported him. However, the Federalists succeeded in recommitting the report for further consideration by the committee. On February 15, 1793, after receiving voluminous critiques from Knox and rebuttals from St. Clair, the committee again reported, sustaining its earlier conclusions and pointing an indicting finger at the discredited Duer, who had gone bankrupt and been jailed. Federalists again leaped to the defense of Knox and Hamilton, and on February 26 the report was laid aside and never acted on. With the expiration of the Second Congress the matter died. Since the committee's report had not been made public, St. Clair's exoneration was not known, and he suffered unjustly under a cloud for the rest of his life—a victim, in effect, of the politics of the growing Federalist-republican conflict.

Meanwhile, as Fisher Ames had foretold, the administration relentlessly pursued the war against the Ohio Indians, supported in Congress by Federalist measures designed to pacify and develop the West. Early in 1793, a third army under General Anthony Wayne (who, on March 16, 1792, had been ordered by a House vote of 58 to 0 to give up his seat in that body because of overwhelming evidence that he had won his election in Georgia by fraud) arrived in the Ohio country, and on August 20, 1794, at the Battle of Fallen Timbers in northwestern Ohio, decisively defeated Little Turtle's forces. But although Indian military defense of their lands in that region of the Northwest Territory collapsed, the Federalists were still unable to realize their goal of devising a peaceful and orderly method for westward expansion. Again and again Washington sought stronger legislation to permit the federal government to protect the Indians, regulate commerce with them, and acquire their lands through peaceful negotiations. In 1796 Congress finally passed an act formalizing permanent federal authority over "intercourse" with the tribes and setting up a system of government trading houses. Although these measures were continued in force until 1822, they failed to stop border strife, ending up finally in what was to become a large waste heap of doomed and discarded Indian policies.

In other respects, too, westward expansion was a continuing source of division and frustration. While the Federalists wished to pacify the western lands, many eastern Hamiltonians opposed their being settled too rapidly, fearing the depopulation of the coastal states, the luring away of their labor force just when manufacturing was on the rise, and the loss of their own political power to the interior areas. After the victory at Fallen Timbers and the Indians' enforced cession of land by the Treaty of Greenville in 1795, interest in acquiring western property surged among speculators. The rush for land on every border bred scandals, and even Congress was tainted. Amid considerable embarrassment, South Carolina Federalist William L. Smith, chairman of the Land Office Committee in the House, revealed that he had been sounded out concerning his receptivity to a bribe in connection with the granting of some twenty million acres in the Northwest Territory. It then turned out that other Representatives, including Madison and Giles, had also been approached. The distress quickened the members' desire to legislate for the orderly sale of newly ceded western lands and led to the passage of the Land Act of 1796. The bill represented a victory, however, for the fearful eastern Federalists. Despite vigorous attempts by republicans and westerners to tailor the act for the average small settler with limited funds, the legislation required the purchase of a minimum of 640 acres at $2 an acre (four times the price of equivalent state-owned lands), with credit terms too exacting for the average small settler to meet.

In the context of the growth of the national conflict between the Hamiltonians and their opponents, western questions were of secondary importance. More vitally at stake were the country's basic political and economic structures. On December 5, 1791, Hamilton submitted to the Second Congress what many historians consider his ablest and most visionary state paper, the *Report on Manufactures*. In it he proposed a comprehensive plan for converting the United States from an essentially agricultural country into an industrialized one, with an integrated, self-sufficient economy. Hamilton's scheme, which involved a system of protective tariffs, government subsidies to industry, exemptions from duties on essential imports, and rewards for inventions and improvements in product quality, would primarily benefit the northern business and commercial groups—though Hamilton believed that by integrating agriculture into the plan as supplier for the industrialization, he would tie the nation together and minimize sectional rivalries. Every part of the country, he argued, would eventually profit from industrial growth.

The report was greeted with scorn and anger by Jefferson, Madison, and their congressional supporters, who felt that Hamilton had gone too far. Southern agriculturists complained that the treasury secretary wanted to reduce them to the status of exploited producers of raw materials for northern manufacturers. Any plan that would turn the country into a nation of factories and wage workers was abhorrent to Jefferson. But it was Madison who effectively quashed the report in Congress with a constitutional objection. The general-welfare clause of the Constitution's Preamble, Hamilton maintained, would sanction all the bounties, subsidies, and aids that he wished government to give to business, for the general welfare covered all aspects of American activity. Though Hamilton qualified his explanation to say that he meant that Congress could appropriate, but not necessarily legislate, for anything considered to be for the general welfare, Madison saw no distinction between the two. By appropriating, Congress was making itself the judge of what constituted the general welfare, he said, and could thus take every aspect of American life under its control. "If not only the means, but the objects are unlimited," he argued, "the parchment [the Constitution] had better be thrown into the fire at once."

Some northern Representatives who feared that high tariffs would hurt foreign trade supported Madison and the anti-Hamiltonians, and no action was ever taken in Congress on the report—though many of its recommendations were included in a new tariff act that Congress passed in May, 1792. From a historical viewpoint, the future would again prove Hamilton more visionary than the republicans. As put by one of Jefferson's biographers, Nathan Schachner, "the inexorable forces of the industrial revolution eventually brought Hamilton's plan to fruition and left the Jeffersonian philosophy in this particular respect an outworn memory. For good or ill, it was Hamilton rather than Jefferson who had anticipated the future."

Much of the Second Congress' first session was spent in debate on governmental measures, one of which resulted in the first presidential veto. The measure in question dealt with reapportioning the membership of the House after the first census. A compromise bill enacted after seven months of deadlock and acrimonious debate was regarded as unconstitutional by Washington, and when Jefferson, Madison, and Attorney General Edmund Randolph agreed with him, he had the trio draw up "the instrument" for him "to negative the bill." When the veto message reached the House "a few of the hottest friends of the bill expressed passion," reported Jefferson, "but the majority were satisfied, & both in and out of doors it gave pleasure to have at length an instance of the negative being exercised." The House tried but failed to override the veto.

Congress adjourned on May 8, 1792, and reassembled in Philadelphia for the second session on November 5. During the summer the first signs of a coming storm over Hamilton's excise tax on whiskey, which Congress had enacted in 1791, appeared in the back country of North Carolina and in western Pennsylvania. The frontier farmers had much to complain about—the high rate of the tax (twenty-five percent of the net price of a gallon), the invasion of privacy by hated tax collectors, the hauling of evaders away from their farms to the nearest federal court, sometimes three hundred miles distant. In the interior the distilling of grain was the most feasible way of getting it across the mountains to a market. In addition, in an area where bank notes and hard money were scarce, whiskey served as a medium of exchange. During the original congressional debate over the tax, Hamilton had shown impatience with frontier farmers' resentment. If they did not like the tax, he said, let them stop drinking; Americans, in his view, drank too much for their own good anyway. When the College of Physicians in Philadelphia supported Hamilton, Representative James Jackson of Georgia leaped to the defense of his constituents, asserting angrily that "they have been long in the habit of getting drunk . . . in defiance of a dozen colleges or all the excise duties which Congress might be weak or wicked enough to impose."

The most serious resistance was now rising in Pennsylvania, where farmers, as historian John C. Miller said, "reckoned their fluid wealth in Monongahela rye." On August 21, 1792, representatives from four western Pennsylvania counties met at an inn in Pittsburgh to denounce the tax and recommend measures to obstruct its collection. Among the leaders at the meeting was Albert Gallatin, a thirty-one-year-old state representative and republican, who had been born and educated in Geneva, Switzerland. A sparrowlike man with a French accent and manners, Gallatin had an aristocratic background. He had come to Massachusetts in 1780 to sell tea, served in the Revolution, taught French at Harvard, and in 1785—influenced by Rousseau's writings on the freedom of natural man in the wilderness—used his inheritance to buy land in western Pennsylvania. There his learning, ardent republicanism, and brilliant political talents won him a following. He served in the state constitutional convention and in 1790 was elected to the Pennsylvania House of Representatives. Ironically, though he failed as a speculator and even as a farmer, his reputation as a republican expert in the field of finance—one who might eventually challenge even Hamilton—was already spreading beyond the borders of his state.

News of the meeting disturbed Hamilton, who was quick to equate the tax protests with treason against the national government. Washington, who agreed with Hamilton on the need to nip another Shays's Rebellion before it got started, issued a proclamation on September 25 warning "malcontents" to "desist from all unlawful combinations" and declaring that the collection of the excise taxes would be enforced. A short time later former Federalist Representative George Clymer, now Hamilton's supervisor of the excise for Pennsylvania, sent the secretary a disquieting report from Pittsburgh implying that the entire West was disaffected. It was a harbinger of dramatic developments to come.

The summer and fall of 1792 also saw the public feud between Hamilton and Jefferson grow more vicious. Jefferson had had thoughts of retiring, but he recognized that Hamilton was trying to force him out and reconsidered. It was also the last year of Washington's term in office, and the President, too, was hoping to retire the following March and return to Mount Vernon. Indeed, he even asked Madison to help him prepare a farewell address. But the financial panic that occurred after Duer's collapse, together with a growing uneasiness about foreign and domestic tensions that were emerging from the French Revolution, unsettled him. In addition, the dangerous schism between his two Cabinet officers and their followers appeared to dictate that he stay at the helm of the country. Many men of all factions, including Hamilton and Jefferson themselves, appealed to him to accept a second term and hold the government together, and eventually he agreed to do so. Under Hamilton's leadership, a caucus of Federalists from different states decided to work together, on a national basis, to assure the re-election of both Washington and Adams.

Jefferson, Madison, and their supporters, now designating themselves Republicans or Democratic-Republicans, in contrast to their image of the Federalists as aristocrats, supported Washington but decided to try to unseat Adams and secure the election of as many Republican-oriented Congressmen as possible. Their campaign to select a strong vice-presidential candidate and unite the different Antifederalist factions behind him went far, in the fall and winter of 1792, to set the country on the road to party politics, though the formation of durable, formally structured parties still lay in the future.

Serving Jefferson and Madison as something of a combination campaign manager and communications center was their fellow Virginian John Beckley, clerk of the House of Representatives. Beckley, a self-important but adroit politician, was a fountainhead of gossip and a master of trouble-shooting and dirty tricks for the Republican cause. The previous summer he had visited Boston to sound out opinion on Adams, and he reported back to Madison that the Vice President was highly unpopular even in his home domain. Now the clerk took on the job of finding a Republican to succeed him. In September, 1792, Beckley journeyed to New York. It was hoped that that key state could be yanked completely away from Hamilton and brought into an influential position of national leadership, along with Virginia, on the Republican side. The Virginia Republicans had pretty well decided on supporting New York's governor George Clinton for the vice presidency. But the New York situation was confused, with Senator Aaron Burr at the heart of the confusion.

Burr, whose political orientation was still a matter of question (which made him both acceptable to, and suspect by, almost everyone), had had a meteoric rise in politics. A short, slight man with luminous, piercing eyes and a gracious, lively manner that made him a charmer of women, he had been born thirty-six years before in Newark, New Jersey, the grandson of the fiery colonial theologian Jonathan Edwards and the son of one of the founders and the first president of the College of New Jersey at Princeton. Left an orphan at two, he was tutored for a time by his brother-in-law, Tapping Reeve (who later founded the first American law school at Litchfield, Connecticut), and was graduated from Princeton at the age of sixteen. He began the study of theology and then became Reeve's first law student. His legal training was interrupted by the Revolution, in which he served with distinction until illness forced his resignation from the army. After working in several New Jersey law offices, Burr was admitted to the Albany bar and began practice there in 1782. His charm, legal abilities, and hustling political skill made him many friends and followers, and he rose quickly, moving to a home on Wall Street in New York and being elected to the state legislature in 1784. Five years later he was one of New York's most powerful politicians, with an intensely loyal statewide following.

His methods, however, had often appalled men of sensibilities. After one of his victories, a friend wrote that Burr's "twistings, combinations, and maneuvers to accomplish this object are incredible. . . ." Sometimes he worked with the Federalists and sometimes with the Republicans of Governor Clinton. Hamilton had come to despise him, at one time writing, "As a public man, he is one of the worst sort—a friend to nothing but as it suits his interest and ambition. . . . 'Tis evident that he aims at putting himself at the head of what he calls the 'popular party,' as affording the best tools for an ambitious man to work with. . . . if we have an embryo Caesar in the United States, 'tis Burr."

By the fall of 1792, when Beckley reached New York, Burr, though disliked and distrusted by many, was considered one of the ablest politicians in the nation. Moreover it was well known that he had ideas of running for Vice President himself and had been making efforts for more than a year to win friends and supporters. Beckley now sized him up, advising him that he would have some backing in Pennsylvania. The clerk of the House returned to Philadelphia with the impression that Burr would be willing to be substituted for Clinton, a fact that satisfied some of the Republicans but caused others, including James Monroe, to have doubts about Burr's integrity. On the evening of October 16 Beckley called a private meeting of some of the Republican leaders in Philadelphia "to conclude *finally* & *definitely* as to the choice of a V.P." Present, with Jefferson and Beckley, were a number of Pennsylvanians, Melancton Smith, a New York supporter of Burr, Senator Pierce Butler of South Carolina, and several others. In this first version of a nominating convention (or of a "smoke-filled room"), the participants agreed to unite in supporting Clinton, who they felt was older and more experienced than Burr and would be better known and more acceptable to the nation. A few days later a joint letter arrived from Madison and Monroe in Virginia, advising also against switching from Clinton.

Burr seemed not dissatisfied. Later he said that he had received hints of support from the South for the next election in 1796. The word was soon out that Adams had a rival. Though Hamilton had a personal distaste for the Vice President, he tried to take charge of Adams's campaign, fearing that Clinton's candidacy was a plot to split the New England and Middle Atlantic votes between Adams and Clinton and allow the South to elect Jefferson over both of them. Like Washington, Adams made no effort in his own behalf, preferring to affect indifference. This drove the anxious Hamilton to distraction, and other Federalists were also worried. "The poor Vice will be hard run . . . ," wrote Fisher Ames. "Is it not strange that a man, unblemished in life, sincere in his politics, firm in giving and maintaining his opinions, and devoted to the Constitution, should be attacked, to place Mr. Clinton in the chair . . .?"

Adams was saved by the electoral system. In nine of the fifteen states the electors who voted for the President and Vice President were selected by the state legislatures, and in another one, Massachusetts, the legislature named eleven of the state's sixteen electors. This complicated the task of those Republicans who had originally united behind Clinton. When the ballots were tallied, it was discovered that Washington had received 132 out of a possible 136 electoral votes, and that Adams had gotten 77, Clinton 50, Jefferson 4, and Burr 1. The votes for the new Congress that would meet in December, 1793, were a different matter. In the Senate the Federalist majority would be seventeen to thirteen. But Hamilton had lost control of the House. There were now some fifty-seven members who on key issues would vote rather consistently with the Republicans, and forty-eight who would generally side with the administration. There would still be no such thing as party loyalty, and individuals and interest blocs would shift on various issues. But the stage was set for an even more intense partisanship in the House.

The anti-Hamilton offensive got under way almost immediately. With Jefferson giving direction from behind the scenes, the Republicans in the House set about trying to drive the New Yorker from the Cabinet, just as he had earlier tried to force Jefferson to retire. In November, 1792, Hamilton asked the House for authorization to borrow $2 million from Dutch bankers at five percent interest in order to pay off in full the government's debt to the Bank of the United States, on which it was paying six percent. The proposal to save the government $20,000 a year in interest made sense, until Madison and other Republicans began to raise questions about the Treasury's handling of earlier loans and the operations of the bank itself. Hamilton then revealed that he had taken it upon himself to intermix the funds from two different loans and that he had used some of the funds for unauthorized— though legal—purposes. In addition, after the overthrow of Louis XVI, he had halted payments to France because, as he explained, there was no competent government in that country. Charges of Treasury mismanagement and corruption were made, and Hamilton's personal honesty was questioned. Objecting to the plan of paying off the bank loan while ignoring the country's debt to the French people, Madison on December 26 put through a motion to limit the bank repayment. Republican tempers were hot, and Virginia's short, rotund William Giles continued the attack.

On January 24, 1793, with shrewd and quiet assistance from Jefferson, Giles introduced five resolutions in the House, directing Hamilton to submit clear and specific accountings of all the foreign loans, the operations of the sinking fund, the relations between the government and the bank, and the state of federal finances. Tensions began to mount as the resolutions were approved in the House and similar ones were passed by the Senate. Fisher Ames noticed that the ranks of his opponents were holding together and becoming expectant of victory over the treasury secretary. "Virginia moves in a solid column," he wrote, "and the discipline of the party is as severe as the Prussian."

But in the end, however, it all seemed to come to nothing. Hamilton was found blameless of everything save asserting executive discretion over the administration of congressional actions, intermixing the funds of the two loans (which he explained had been done for bookkeeping purposes), and not keeping Congress well enough informed. But Giles, still questioning Hamilton's integrity, could not let the matter drop. Drawing largely on extravagant charges the Republican *National Gazette* had already publicly leveled at Hamilton, Jefferson framed a series of resolutions to censure the secretary of the treasury, and Giles introduced them. On March 1, with the House galleries packed with partisans of both sides, motions were introduced "to disagree" with Giles's resolutions. Hamilton's stalwarts took on the Republicans, and as the angry debates continued by candlelight into the evening, the Federalists managed to strike down the censuring motions one by one. Only Madison and four others voted in favor of all of them.

It was an awkward and overwhelming defeat for Jefferson's forces. Nevertheless, the debates had raised what was to become a perennial issue between the executive and Congress—how much discretion the executive could assert in administering appropriations. Giles and the Republicans had sought to censure Hamilton for not strictly carrying out the laws that had made specific appropriations, but the Federalists had managed, for the time being at least, to win approval for broad administrative discretion.

On another subject, before the Second Congress ended on March 2, the Republicans won a victory. Largely at their insistence, Congress passed the Fugitive Slave Act, requiring state officials to enforce the return of any slave who fled into a free state. There was almost no argument over that measure. It passed unanimously in the Senate, and with a lopsided 48–7 vote in the House.

On March 4 the Congress met for one day in special session, Washington and Adams were inaugurated, and then the Representatives and Senators left for home. But the Republican-Federalist conflict went on, freshly fueled by events in Europe. Most Americans had sympathized with the outbreak of the French Revolution in 1789, but its increasing coloration as an apparently atheistic and anarchistic uprising bent on world revolution gradually divided American opinion, widening the cleavage between Republicans who deplored the execution of Louis XVI and the excesses of the Terror but still supported the French people, and Federalists who feared the spread of French lawlessness and radicalism to America. With France's declaration of war on Great Britain, Spain, and Holland on February 1, 1793, the partisanship intensified. Hamilton's whole system rested on good relations with England, for America and Great Britain were each other's best customers. Jefferson and the Republicans, however, saw America benefiting from a policy of friendship with France and an open, free, honorable commerce with all the world. Moreover, they were on guard against England, believing that the anti-French coalition of monarchies was also the enemy of republicanism in the United States.

The French declaration of war induced Washington, who feared involvement in the conflict, to return to Philadelphia from his vacation and summon the Cabinet to meet with him. Hamilton, whose intrusion into the area of foreign affairs had steadily grown bolder—conducting private discussions with British officials and giving them secret advice and commitments—had drawn up materials for a proposed proclamation of neutrality for Washington to issue. Jefferson raised objections to it. He argued that such a declaration would be a statement that the United States would not go to war, which was constitutionally for the Congress rather than the executive to decide, and that breaking or suspending the treaty of alliance which had bound the American and French people together since 1778 would be a breach of a solemn agreement. Washington decided at length on a middle course, agreeing not to suspend the treaty but to issue a proclamation that, though not employing the word *neutrality*, would declare the nation's friendship and impartiality toward both Great Britain and France and prohibit Americans from unneutral activity against any of the warring powers. None of the Cabinet members thought that Congress had to be called into session to approve the proclamation, and it was issued on April 22, setting a precedent for executive initiative in foreign relations—an initiative that Washington would increasingly assert during his remaining years in office.

France, meanwhile, assumed that she had the support of the American people, and on April 8 Edmond Charles Genêt, minister of the French Republic, landed at Charleston, South Carolina. Republicans gave him an enthusiastic welcome, which greatly disturbed the Hamiltonians and troubled Washington. But Genêt's arrogance and impolitic activities, culminating in rudeness to Washington and highhanded attempts to persuade Americans to defy the neutrality proclamation, eventually embarrassed Jefferson and Madison. They acquiesced in the Federalists' demand that Genêt be recalled, though that proved unnecessary. The Revolution took a new turn in France, and the Jacobins ordered Genêt to return to face trial and the guillotine for his "crimes." Washington generously refused to extradite him, and he married Governor George Clinton's daughter and settled down as a farmer on Long Island.

But the Genêt episode was only the start of an increasingly emotional polarization over foreign affairs in the United States. Beginning in June, harsh policies instituted by Great Britain partly in response to America's neutrality proclamation played into the hands of the Republicans. France was blockaded, and neutral ships carrying food and other contraband to her ports were ordered seized. The British Navy was directed to stop neutral vessels on the high seas and search them for deserters. An influx of French refugees from Haiti horrified Americans in the South with tales of Britain's support of burnings and killings on that island by rebellious black slaves under Toussaint L'Ouverture. England was accused of stirring up the Indians in the Northwest against frontier settlements, and she was denounced for actions in the Mediterranean imperiling American commerce with southern French ports. Finally, on November 6, a secret order in council authorized British warships to seize neutral vessels engaged in commerce with French possessions in the West Indies, and beginning the next month the order was implemented by the capture of some 250 American merchant ships in Caribbean waters.

As these developments became known in the United States they aroused a storm of anti-British feeling, putting the Federalists on the defensive (they considered the British actions blunders) and swelling the ranks of the Republicans. Republican societies, inspired by the Jacobin clubs of France, were formed; newspapers poured out anti-British invective; and mass meetings against Federalists and Great Britain were accompanied by mob violence. The societies and the turmoil gradually politicized new elements of the population—artisans, mechanics, ethnic minorities, the urban working class—that had not previously voted in elections, and their involvement, in turn, created a base for the broadening and increased democratization of the electorate and for the development of a Democratic-Republican national party. The components of the new Republican following were diverse, ranging from cultural and intellectual inheritors of the radicalism of the Revolutionary Sons of Liberty to members of such local groups as New York City's Tammany Society (named after a Delaware Indian chief), which had been mainly a nativist fraternal organization. Like the other groups now turning with patriotic fervor to politics, Tammany synchronized its local interests with the national policies of the Republicans.

By December 2, 1793, when the Third Congress assembled in Philadelphia, it appeared that the Republicans might at last have the upper hand in the legislature. In the House the burly, rigid forty-seven-year-old Hamiltonian Theodore Sedgwick of Massachusetts was put up for Speaker by the Federalists and was beaten by the Republican-backed candidate, former Speaker Frederick Muhlenberg, by ten votes. In the Senate, however, Monroe's Republican forces were reminded that they were still not in control of that body when newly elected Albert Gallatin became its first member to be denied his seat.

In February, 1793, the Pennsylvania legislature had elected Gallatin to the Senate. From his able performance in the Pennsylvania legislature, Federalists were already aware of his shrewd fiscal skills and his extreme Republican sentiments, and they did not welcome his arrival. Within minutes after Gallatin took his oath of office, Vice President Adams read a petition from nineteen residents of York, Pennsylvania, protesting his election on the ground that he had not been a citizen for the required nine years. It was a highly technical and complex charge, based on a constitutional interpretation that could have disqualified all the members of the first Senate in 1789. National citizenship had existed only since 1781; prior to that time, Americans were citizens of their states. Gallatin had come to Massachusetts from Switzerland in 1780 and ended his constitutional status as an alien only in 1785 by taking his oath as a citizen of Virginia (the possessor, at the time, of the area in western Pennsylvania to which he had moved). Perhaps recognizing that it was purely a partisan stab at Gallatin, Adams tabled the York petition, and later in the day Senator Robert Morris told his fellow Pennsylvanian that, even though he himself was a Federalist, he had refused to introduce the document and would remain "perfectly neutral." Nine days later, however, Adams referred the petition to a committee of five Federalists, headed by John Rutherfurd of New Jersey. On December 31 the committee reported to the Senate what Gallatin and the Republicans expected to hear, that the Pennsylvanian had not satisfied the nine-year requirement of the Constitution.

The Federalists were not sure of their majority in the Senate, however, and decided to postpone further action until they felt confident of victory. In the meantime, Gallatin kept his seat. He immediately launched an attack on Hamilton's fiscal policies, taking up where Giles and Madison had left off in the House in the previous session. This time Hamilton faced a rapierlike financial inquisitor. Gallatin had a long nose and a receding chin, and he looked innocent and boyish. But his eyes were accusatorial, and when he leaned forward, delivering his remarks in a sharp, demanding voice with a French accent, he seemed like a prosecutor. The Republicans were delighted with him; the Federalists considered him the incarnation of the French Revolution in their midst. On January 8, 1794, after questioning the Treasury's affairs, he asked that Hamilton provide the Senate with details of the domestic and foreign debts and all the government's receipts and expenditures for each year since 1789. With the help of some votes from the Middle Atlantic states, his resolution was carried. Infuriated by the new requests, Hamilton twice complained to the Senate about the annoyance, cost, and waste of time involved in once again compiling such information.

The Federalists now determined to try to get Gallatin out of his seat. After several days of partisan debate on the Rutherfurd report, the matter was referred to a new committee of four Federalists and three Republicans. On February 20 the majority of that committee also reported against Gallatin, and the subject again came before the full Senate. Since February, 1791, Monroe had been introducing bills, at the request of the Virginia legislature (which felt it should know what its Senators were doing), to open the upper chamber's proceedings to the public. Each time Monroe had lost, beaten by those who maintained that secrecy insured freedom of discussion. But now he won, and the Senate doors were opened for the first time for the debate on Gallatin's fate. (They were finally permanently opened to the public in December, 1795, after adequate gallery space had been constructed.) For a good part of seven days the public crowded into the one small gallery in the Senate chamber as Federalist Rufus King of New York, aided by William Lewis, a dour Philadelphia Quaker lawyer serving as counsel, conducted the legalistic and technical case against Gallatin, and Aaron Burr, Monroe, and John Taylor of Virginia spoke lengthily for the defense. Everyone knew that the Federalists were fighting to gain a much-needed vote in the Senate and also to remove this new enemy of Hamilton. At times the Hamiltonians appealed to nativistic prejudices, striking low blows at the Swiss-born Republican. "One of the ancient Republics made it death for an alien to intermeddle in their politics," the Quaker Lewis snapped at Gallatin at one point.

As the debate reached its climax, Senator Benjamin Hawkins of North Carolina, who had often voted Republican and on whom Gallatin depended, left Philadelphia to avoid having to vote. Realizing that the decision now rested on his vote, Robert Morris broke his promise to remain neutral and joined the Federalists against Gallatin, and on February 28 the Pennsylvania Republican was unseated, 14 to 12. His departure from the body brought relief to Hamilton. The Senate put aside Gallatin's resolutions and never required the secretary of the treasury to submit the information that Gallatin had requested.

The nation's most prominent Republican had meanwhile left the Cabinet. Tired by the political infighting and by Washington's tendency to favor Hamilton's judgment over his own, Jefferson had tendered his resignation to the President on July 31, 1793, to take effect the end of September. Washington asked him to stay until the end of the year, however, and Jefferson had done so, partly because of the turmoil over the Genêt episode and partly because of governmental confusion resulting from a terrible yellow fever epidemic that struck Philadelphia in August. As carts piled high with corpses were trundled through the streets and the city filled with the putrid smell of death, the government, somewhat in chaos, transferred its activities to crowded rooms in Germantown. Jefferson, who stayed in Philadelphia after many others left, had been untouched, but the fever downed Hamilton and for a time it was feared that he was dying. By December 2, the scheduled date for the start of the Third Congress, Hamilton had recovered ("saved by Doctor Stevens's cold bath, and bark," said Fisher Ames), the epidemic had run its course after killing four thousand people, one tenth of the city's inhabitants, and the government had returned to the mourning capital. Jefferson, however, was now determined to retire, and on January 4, 1794, he did so, returning to Monticello. He was succeeded as secretary of state by his fellow Virginian Attorney General Edmund Randolph, who in Jefferson's opinion was a weak, vacillating man and too flabby against Hamilton.

Before he left Philadelphia, Jefferson completed and submitted to Congress a report on American commerce that he had been asked to prepare for the legislature almost three years before. It was a long argument, buttressed with statistical material, for protective and restrictive trade measures against Britain (which, he said, sought to maintain an "unnatural" monopoly over American commerce); for favoritism toward France because she was friendly to the United States; and, ultimately, for free trade among all countries. The document's proposals were exactly opposite the policies of Hamilton, who complained that Jefferson "threw this FIREBRAND of discord into the midst of the representatives of the states . . . and instantly *decamped* to Monticello."

The anti-British and pro-French thrust of Jefferson's ideas received enthusiastic support from Republican members of Congress. But implementing the proposals was another matter. In his opening address to Congress, Washington, with the same aims of ensuring the country's safety and securing its markets for trade, pointed the legislators in a more evenhanded direction, which appealed to the Federalists. Recalling the tenor of the Proclamation of Neutrality, he announced friendship for all countries, but urged Congress to strengthen the nation's military establishment so that America would be prepared for any eventuality in the warring world.

Supporters of the two options presented by Jefferson and Washington filled the House and Senate chambers with patriotic oratory, but many of them were confused and hesitant about the implications of individual measures introduced in their behalf. As men began to react more from the perspective of their local interests, it became clear that there was no solid Republican majority in the House of Representatives. Once again voting reflected the polarization of two extremes, with a smaller middle bloc of shifting factions holding the balance of power. Oddly, this time the middle group used its power to negate, rather than support, the measures of one side or the other. Despite abundant zeal, maneuvering, and speechmaking, the result was an abdication in the field of foreign affairs by that session of the House and the delivery of the initiative to the executive and the Senate.

On January 3 Madison directed the House to Jefferson's report on commerce, introducing a series of resolutions for discriminatory tonnage duties and tariffs against nontreaty nations (Great Britain), higher tariffs on certain manufactured goods that came from Britain, indemnification for seized American ships, and various retaliatory measures, all designed to carry out Jefferson's suggestions. The resolutions were immediately opposed by Fisher Ames and other Federalists, who asked for ten days to prepare a reply. Hamilton supplied the response, which was delivered in an all-day speech by William L. Smith, the wealthy young South Carolina Federalist. Another all-day address by Madison the next day was followed by weeks of debate, which an independent Representative, Abraham Clark of Essex County, New Jersey, characterized as "a waste of time" by members who merely wished "to see their speeches published in the newspapers" and "felt so big with their speeches that they would burst."

The House chamber rang with nationalism, but it was obvious to Clark and the Republicans that too many of the Representatives both feared the impact of the tariffs and other proposed anti-British measures on their local and sectional economies and shared the Federalists' concern about bringing on a war with Great Britain. On February 5 Madison and his supporters postponed further consideration of the resolutions for a month, hoping that time and new antagonistic measures by Britain would work in their favor. They reckoned correctly. Later in the month a report of a speech by the governor general of Canada announcing to Indians that a British rupture with the United States was imminent was followed by the receipt of official word of the British seizure of American ships trading in the West Indies. A wave of patriotism swept the country, moving even pro-British Federalists to demand retaliation. Republicans united with Federalists in both Houses to authorize a general one-month embargo, hoping that it would force a change in British policies. On military matters the Republicans were put in a delicate position. They could not oppose measures for the nation's defense, but they still balked at authorizing the creation of a costly military establishment that would be controlled by the monarchical-oriented Federalists. The army, they understood, would even be under the command of Hamilton himself. When the Federalists presented a bill authorizing the President to raise fifteen thousand troops if he felt the country was threatened by an invasion from Canada, the Republicans solved their dilemma by adroitly turning the bill into one that empowered the President, instead, to summon eighty thousand state militia if necessary. Measures were also passed authorizing the construction of six frigates for the beginning of a navy. (The ships, including the *Constellation* and the *Constitution*—"*Old Ironsides*"— were eventually built, becoming the most powerful ships of their class afloat, and the Navy became a separate department in 1798.)

The tension with Britain, lessened by the arrival of news in March that England had repealed the obnoxious order in council to seize ships in the West Indies, had deeply disturbed the Federalists. As Republicans in the House moved to convert the embargo into one aimed specifically at trade with England, a group of four Federalist Senators conferred with Hamilton, and then with Washington, to urge that an effort be made to reach a settlement with Great Britain by diplomacy. The Senate had no standing committee that dealt with foreign affairs, but on previous occasions the four rock-ribbed Federalists who called on Washington—Senators Oliver Ellsworth of Connecticut, Rufus King of New York, and Caleb Strong and George Cabot of Massachusetts—had constituted themselves as something of an unofficial Senate advisory body on foreign affairs for the President. The Senators proposed that Hamilton be sent to England as "envoy extraordinary" with powers to negotiate a treaty between the two countries. When Monroe and other Republicans caught scent of what was in the air, they objected vigorously to the suggestion, particularly to the United States being represented by so pro-British a partisan as Hamilton. Recognizing that the secretary of the treasury's controversial status might imperil the nation's acceptance of whatever he accomplished, Washington was advised, instead, to select Chief Justice John Jay of the Supreme Court for the mission. This did little to mollify the Republicans, who distrusted the Federalist Jay almost as much as Hamilton.

When Jay's nomination reached the Senate, Monroe and John Taylor led an angry but unsuccessful attack against it. The Federalist Senators were able to defeat a series of resolutions by Monroe and Taylor by large majorities, and Jay was finally confirmed by a 17–8 vote. Soon afterward Jay left for England, armed with detailed, Federalist-oriented instructions written by Hamilton, who was having no difficulty elbowing Randolph aside in the handling of foreign policy. Though the Republicans would now expect the worst from Jay's mission and would look forward to trying to tear to pieces whatever he brought back, they were dejected over the seizure of the initiative by their pro-British opponents.

A few months later both Monroe and Taylor left the congressional scene of combat. When France requested the recall of Gouverneur Morris, the hostile Federalist minister to that country, Washington was urged to nominate the pro-French Monroe in his place. The Republicans in Congress advised Monroe to accept the appointment, which he did, resigning from the Senate on May 27, 1794. This followed by two weeks the resignation of his friend and fellow Virginian Senator John Taylor, who had become disgusted with the political developments. It was months before Virginia could fill both its vacant seats, but the loss of the two antiadministration leaders was greater to the embattled Republican forces in Congress than to Virginia.

During the remainder of the session Congress coped with ways to increase revenues to meet the rising costs of debt service and military expenses. Excise taxes were finally levied on a number of new items, including carriages and snuff, but only after bitter debates in which members of Congress reflected the economic impact that the taxes would have on their districts. The new taxes on snuff and other tobacco products would hit southern growing areas, and such men as Madison and Giles led an unsuccessful fight against them. The tax on carriages—a Hamiltonian schedule of annual levies ranging from $2 for a two-wheeled vehicle to $10 for a coach —also disturbed the less-urbanized South, whose wealthy planters, widely separated from one another, relied heavily upon the use of coaches for transportation. The tax was enacted after John Taylor left the Senate, but three years later he called upon the Supreme Court to declare it unconstitutional; in his opinion, it was a direct tax and had not been apportioned among the states "in proportion to the census or enumeration, of the inhabitants of the United States," as directed by the Constitution. Acting as counsel for David Hylton, a Virginian sued for evasion of the tax, Taylor challenged Hamilton's assumption that the tax was an excise, not a direct tax. The Supreme Court upheld Hamilton's argument and refused to rule the act unconstitutional—leaving that sort of landmark precedent for John Marshall to establish in the *Marbury* v. *Madison* case in 1803. The impact of the excise taxes of 1794, however—generally supported by such New Englanders as Fisher Ames, who argued that they were necessary to support the public credit—added to the growing sectional antagonism between the North and South. Northern manufacturers, who at first opposed taxes on their products, soon learned that they could pass on the added cost to consumers, and the Supreme Court decision on the carriage tax finally helped to establish a tax policy for the nation that laid increasing dependence on excise levies.

During the 1794 summer recess the storm long building over the whiskey tax finally broke in western Pennsylvania. Hamilton ordered his agents to serve processes, returnable in the federal district court in Philadelphia, on more than sixty persons in western Pennsylvania who had failed to register their stills. The move set wild rumors racing across the mountains and resulted in confused and demagogic appeals among the westerners to resist the process servers. Republicans throughout the nation accused Hamilton of deliberately trying to provoke a violent crisis so that he could demonstrate the need for a standing army to enforce the law and exert federal authority over the West. Events seemed to bear out the Republicans' charges. Large meetings of armed farmers in western Pennsylvania resulted in threats of rebellion, acts of violence against the Treasury officials, and enough turmoil to give Hamilton an excuse to move with severity. On August 7 he had Washington issue a proclamation that he had written calling the resistance an insurrection. Immediately thereafter Washington, sharing Hamilton's view that resistance to the national government was intolerable, asked the governors of Virginia, Maryland, New Jersey, and Pennsylvania to supply thirteen thousand militiamen for a march to the West.

Albert Gallatin, meanwhile, together with Congressmen William Findley and John Smilie, both Antifederalist Pennsylvanians, did his best to try to calm the more hotheaded westerners. They had partially succeeded when the trooops, with Washington at their head, commenced their march over the mountains. Washington soon left the army and returned to Philadelphia, giving the nominal command to Virginia's governor, Henry Lee, but the actual charge of suppressing the rebellion to Hamilton. There was little rebellion to suppress. On the approach of the army the ringleaders fled to the Ohio wilderness, where they were never heard from again; the farmers returned to their homes without offering opposition; and Hamilton rounded up some twenty suspects and then went on an unsuccessful search for Gallatin, who he thought must have been a leader of the resistance. Though friends informed Gallatin that Federalists had gone "so far as to offer large Rewards for your Head" for having kept "so severe an Eye" on the secretary of the treasury, Hamilton had to accept the fact that the Pennsylvanian was not only innocent but had tried to moderate the tempers of the westerners.

In the spring of 1795 the affair ended with the conviction for treason of two of the men whom Hamilton had rounded up and marched back to Philadelphia. Washington pardoned both of them, one because he was "insane" and the other because he was a "simpleton." In the meantime, Hamilton achieved his goal: a body of federal troops was stationed in Pittsburgh to maintain national authority over the West; resistance to the central government had crumbled beyond the mountains; and the right of the federal government to put down rebellion, within limits that it would draw itself, had been asserted. The Republicans were outraged but helpless. "An insurrection was announced and proclaimed and armed against, but could never be found," said Jefferson. As for Gallatin, his stock again rose. In October, while Hamilton was still seeking him for treason, the western Pennsylvanians elected him simultaneously to the Pennsylvania State Assembly and to Congress. Since no charges could be placed against him, he served in the state legislature until December 7, 1795, then entered Congress as a Republican Representative, more dangerous than ever before to the Federalists.

The rebellion in Pennsylvania, unorganized and ineffective as it had been, had angered Washington as much as Hamilton. Certain that it was "the first formidable fruit of the Democratic Societies," which he viewed as dangerous agencies of division and dissension, he startled the country with a stern attack on such "self-created societies" in his State of the Union message to Congress soon after it had reassembled on November 3. The Whiskey Rebellion, which he felt was treasonable, had been fomented by these societies, he charged, and if they were not suppressed "or did not fall into detestation . . . they would shake the government to its foundation." In its formal reply to his speech the Senate gave polite support to his remarks. But the Republicans in the House were more critical of the President, some of them noting that resistance to the whiskey tax had appeared long before the start of the political societies and that members of many of them had been in militia bodies that marched west to put down the insurrection. More significantly, Madison, who at first wanted the House to ignore Washington's remarks, pointed out the constitutional restrictions on the government's right to censure the clubs for their political ideas. "The censorial power is in the people over the Government, and not in the Government over the people," he warned.

After a series of close votes, the House's reply to the President was framed so as barely to acknowledge his condemnation of the political clubs. Nevertheless, the Federalists' maneuvers, together with the President's testy attack and the Senate's support of it, reflected a growing impatience with opposition and an inclination on the part of the Federalists to assert, in effect, the right of the federal government to be its own judge of what measures it had to take to establish and maintain its security. In a sense, the debate also tended to confirm that defenders of the central government— having now established that government—were no longer revolutionists who would in practice acknowledge the "Right of the People to alter or to abolish" it if they deemed it oppressive. That principle, boldly proclaimed in the Declaration of Independence, had served the men and women of the American Revolution and the framers of the Constitution; now, in the Federalists' view, the government had what amounted to an unrestricted right to meet any challenge to its continued existence.

It was no coincidence that this issue, raising questions about the limit and control of federal power that would continue to tear the country apart, became important when it did. John Jay was still in England. There had been no word on the progress of his negotiations. But information would have to come soon, and the country was becoming tense about it. Characterizing the tenseness was a growing intolerance in which Washington himself had indulged. The President had hurt his carefully nurtured public image, for the first time descending from his lofty role as a neutral above the partisan battle. He had bared himself, instead, as a Federalist and Hamiltonian, and now he was open to personal political attack and vilification.

On January 31, 1795, Hamilton resigned from the Cabinet, tired at last of the abuse and political fighting and dismayed by Gallatin's election to the House of Representatives. Succeeded in the Treasury by his assistant, Oliver Wolcott, he returned to private law practice in New York but continued to wield great influence over Washington and members of his Cabinet as well as Federalists in Congress. In 1794 the high-living secretary of war, Henry Knox, had also resigned, unable to make ends meet on his government salary. No longer wishing anyone in his Cabinet who did not agree with his policies, Washington appointed as Knox's successor Timothy Pickering, a stern and uncompromising Federalist.

Late in January news arrived in Philadelphia that Jay had signed a treaty with the British on November 17 and that copies of it were on their way from England. On March 7, four days after the Third Congress came to an end, the first copy of the treaty finally reached Philadelphia. Waiting long enough for some friendly Senators from the new Congress to arrange to take their seats, Washington called the Senate into special session on June 8 and submitted the treaty for ratification by two thirds of the Senators.

Though there was much in the document that in the long run would benefit the United States, there was much to anger the Republicans and even disappoint the Federalists. The British had driven a hard bargain, agreeing only to evacuate their posts in the West by June, 1796; to pay reparations for ships they had seized; to permit American ships to conduct a restricted commerce with India; and to open the British West Indies to American vessels of seventy tons or less, provided that the products taken on would be consumed in the United States and not re-exported to any other country. In return, Jay, in effect, had to renounce America's demand that its right as a neutral be respected on the high seas, agreeing to British terms concerning what American ships could carry to enemy ports and submitting to Britain's "Rule of 1756," which prohibited trade by a neutral in wartime with ports normally closed to it in time of peace. Britain, furthermore, was given a "most favored nation" status, precluding the United States from using the weapon of discriminatory duties on British goods. Various disputes, including the settlement of the northwest boundary between the United States and Canada, were referred to arbitration by joint commissions. Nothing was said about several issues important to the United States, notably the impressment of American seamen by the Royal Navy and compensation to American citizens for slaves carried away by the British Army in the South after the Revolution.

Though the Senate decided at once to keep its debates, and the treaty itself, secret until the exchange of ratifications by the two nations, South Carolina's Pierce Butler and several other Senators evinced a trait that was to become common among members of Congress throughout history; within weeks, they were leaking copies of the treaty to friends. In the debate on the treaty, the Federalist majority had little difficulty. Hamilton, now a private citizen, was still guiding Rufus King and other Federalist leaders, and on June 17, on his advice, they proposed that the Senate approve all of the treaty save the article relating to trade with the West Indies (there was objection to an ambiguity of wording). That article, the Federalists recommended, should be renegotiated with the British.

In a long, impressive speech, Aaron Burr for the Republicans attacked the treaty's shortcomings, but his motion to postpone ratification and reopen full negotiations with Great Britain was defeated 20 to 10, and on June 24 the Senate ratified the document, with the exception of the article on the West Indies. Every New England Senator save two voted in favor of the treaty; both of Virginia's Senators voted against it. Five days later one of the Virginians, Senator Stevens T. Mason, a thirty-five-year-old lawyer who had finally filled the seat vacated by James Monroe, caused a national explosion. Mason gave a copy of the still-secret treaty to Pierre Adét, the French minister to the United States. Hoping that the American people would force the Senate to undo the ratification, Adét gave it to Benjamin Bache, publisher of the Philadelphia *Aurora*. Bache promptly printed it.

The fury that was raised against the treaty was, said Washington, "like that against a mad dog." The Republican societies, attacked earlier by the President, had been effectively preparing for this day, and throughout the country public opinion was methodically whipped up against "the humiliation" to which Jay had subjected the nation. Protest meetings, petitions, and riots rocked the North. In New York Hamilton was pelted with stones when he tried to address a crowd of five thousand. Frenzied mobs in Philadelphia so frightened John Adams that he thought they would bring down the government. It was the same in the South. In Kentucky the legislature denounced Senator Humphrey Marshall, who had voted for the treaty, and urged an amendment to the Constitution that would enable state legislatures to recall Senators. When Marshall returned home he was manhandled by a mob and only by fast talking saved from being thrown into a muddy pond. In Charleston the distinguished John Rutledge, a framer of the Constitution and Federalist senior statesman whom Washington had just nominated to succeed Jay as Chief Justice of the Supreme Court, went totally berserk, raving and ranting in the streets against the injustices in the treaty. (His demented behavior shocked his friends and cost him senatorial confirmation of his nomination to head the high court.) Jay himself had just been elected governor of New York, replacing George Clinton, but he was the nation's most unpopular man; he could walk from one end of the country to the other in the middle of the night, it was said, and find his way by the light of fires burning him in effigy.

The intensity of the uproar threw the Federalists on the defensive, but only temporarily. Soon Hamilton and others were writing persuasive defenses of the treaty, while local Federalist groups organized meetings and circulated petitions to counteract those of the Republicans. By October emotions had been calmed and the Republican attack had lost its momentum. Meanwhile, Washington had signed the treaty. At first the public clamor against it had caused him to waver, and then Great Britain angered him by beginning again to seize American ships. Finally, however, he had been outraged by evidence implying that the French had bribed Edmund Randolph, his secretary of state. Though modern scholarship tends to exonerate Randolph, his explanation to the President did not satisfy Washington, and the secretary resigned in disgrace. Angry, shaken, and growing increasingly weary of the intrigues and trials of his office, Washington made Timothy Pickering the new secretary of state and then, almost in a fit of pique over France's arrogance, signed the treaty.

But Washington's tribulations were only beginning. His support of the treaty now subjected him to the same public abuse and vilification that Jefferson and Hamilton had experienced. Moreover, the need for congressional appropriations to fund the arbitration that had been agreed to in the treaty would expose the document to another abrasive controversy, this time in the House of Representatives.

The Fourth Congress convened on December 7, 1795, with the doors of the Senate permanently opened to the public. In the new House Fisher Ames counted "fifty-six *antis*, forty-nine feds," though he admitted that many were not firm and might "shrink from the edge of the pit, to which their leaders would push them." The events of the last year, however, had accelerated the trend to party organization and discipline. In many of the states, particularly New York and Pennsylvania, formal party machinery was beginning to appear, and in numerous localities committees worked to nominate and elect candidates. Though ties between the committees and organizations in the various states were not yet as developed as they would be in the presidential elections the next year, unity among like-minded men in the House was strong enough to make possible in this session the first party caucus ever held in Congress.

The new Speaker of the House was Jonathan Dayton, a thirty-five-year-old highly ambitious politician from Elizabeth, New Jersey. It was typical of him that though he had entered Congress as a Federalist, he had voted enough times with the Republicans to have received their support. Dayton was a large, heavy-set man with narrow, searching eyes. A tireless intriguer, he would later be associated with dreams of personal power and enrichment in the West (Dayton, Ohio, would be named for him), and he would end his public career in 1807 by being arrested for having conspired treasonably with his Republican friend Aaron Burr.

While the Representatives waited for Washington to notify them that Britain had ratified the treaty and made it operative, Albert Gallatin, now safely in his congressional seat, again took on the Treasury Department, asking once more for an examination of the public debt and the nation's revenues and expenditures. With Hamilton gone from the Treasury, many members saw need to rely more on the House's own initiative and authority over finance, and on December 21, responding to Gallatin's suggestion, they voted to create a permanent standing Committee on Ways and Means in the House. Thereafter, as the Republicans grew stronger, the policy-making influence of the Treasury rapidly disappeared and the threat of that department's assuming a permanent ministerial-type power over the national purse vanished. Gallatin himself was placed on the Ways and Means Committee, and in the ensuing years he played an influential role in making congressional appropriations more specific than they had been, at the same time narrowing the limits of executive discretion in the spending of the appropriations.

On March 1, 1796, Washington at last notified Dayton that Great Britain had ratified Jay's Treaty and that the House could proceed to vote the necessary funds (about $90,000) for its implementation. The Speaker informed the House of the receipt of the ratified treaty, and the next day a first-term Republican Representative, Edward Livingston of New York, moved that Washington provide the House with copies of all papers, documents, and instructions relating to Jay's Treaty. A wealthy and rather aristocratic young man of thirty-one, Livingston was a brother of Robert R. Livingston, who had administered the oath of office to Washington in 1789. Originally Federalists, he and his family had broken with Hamilton and now constituted the leadership of a strong Republican-oriented bloc in New York.

Though Madison and other Republicans thought the wording of Livingston's motion too brusque and peremptory, they agreed with the tactic and closed ranks behind the New Yorker. Uriah Tracy, a Connecticut Federalist, asked with sarcasm whether Livingston wanted the papers for the impeachment of Washington or Jay. When Livingston replied that that would depend on what the papers revealed, William Smith of South Carolina and other Federalists raised the issue of constitutionality, arguing that the treaty was now the law and that the House had no right to do anything about it save vote the funds that it required. The Federalist challenge was taken up principally by Gallatin and three Virginians, Madison, Giles, and John Nicholas, against whom the Federalists were a poor match in debate. Though the Constitution limited treaty making to the President and the Senate, Gallatin argued, the Constitution also gave the House the right to originate all money bills, and if a treaty depended on an appropriation, then the House had a veto power over the treaty. It was a loose construction of the Constitution, resting on the acceptance of implied powers, but Hamilton had used such reasoning in his defense of the United States Bank, and the Republicans now employed it against the Federalists. Madison added support to Gallatin's thesis. On March 24, after he amended Livingston's resolution with the qualification "excepting such of said papers as any existing negotiation may render improper to be disclosed," the House passed it 62 to 37. It was the strongest antiadministration vote yet recorded, and it reflected the desire of many members to shore up the House's sagging prestige in the face of the growing influence of the executive and the Senate.

On the advice of Hamilton, Washington refused to turn over the requested papers, with the curt implication that they were none of the House's business. Apparently on Madison's initiative, opponents of the treaty met in the first party caucus in Congress and agreed to stand firmly against the treaty but to "avoid as much as possible" a direct confrontation with Washington. To the Federalists' claim that the treaty was now the "supreme law of the land" and that the House was bound by it, as were all other branches of the government, Madison replied with a resolve that "when a Treaty must depend for its execution . . . on a law or laws to be passed by Congress . . . it is the Constitutional right and duty of the House of Representatives . . . to deliberate on the expediency or inexpediency of carrying such Treaty into effect." Although the House supported Madison's resolution— established since that time as traditional doctrine—the Virginian had won only a skirmish. In the end he lost the battle. Hamilton and the Federalists put enormous pressure on the Representatives, using businessmen, public rallies, petitions, and even a threat by Federalists in the Senate to postpone the ratification of two treaties with Spain and Algiers, which most of the country, Republicans included, supported. Gradually, the Republican strength in the House was undermined, and as the President stood firm, even Madison, it seemed, lost the will for an all-out fight against him. The climax came on April 28, when Fisher Ames, sick and believing that he was dying, delivered an emotionally charged speech in the House. After pointing out the benefits that would come to the United States because of the treaty, he conjured up what would be forfeited if it were rejected, concluding with a dramatic appeal for the safety of the western settlers who, he claimed, would again be exposed to the cruelties of Indians if the House brushed aside the British offer to transfer the posts in the West to the Americans. By turning down those posts, he warned, "we light the savage fires, we bind the victims. . . . You are a father—the blood of your sons shall fatten your cornfield: you are a mother—the war whoop shall wake the sleep of the cradle."

Ames was one of the most gifted orators the House of Representatives ever knew, and this was his supreme effort. Dr. Joseph Priestley, who was in the galleries and who had heard Pitt, Burke, and Fox in England, observed that it was "the most bewitching piece of parliamentary oratory" he had ever listened to. John Adams, who was also present, said that there was hardly a dry eye in the House, "except some of the jackasses who had occasioned the necessity of the oratory." Ames lived for twelve more years, long enough to see his speech become a classic, memorized by schoolboys and recited on patriotic occasions.

On the day after Ames's address, the vote to support the treaty came before a Committee of the Whole, chaired by Frederick Muhlenberg. The result was a tie, which Muhlenberg, though a Republican, broke in favor of the treaty. His action caused an uproar: a few days later he was stabbed by his brother-in-law, an infuriated Republican, and in the next election his Pennsylvania constituents failed to re-elect him because of his "base desertion." But the damage had been done. On April 30 Speaker Dayton, also voting with the Federalists, twice broke ties to defeat Republican resolutions that condemned the treaty, after which resistance to it collapsed and the House voted 51 to 48 to carry it into effect. Washington, also, had won his fight against having to submit the Jay's Treaty papers to the House, and ever afterward chief executives would lean on the precedent he set—though the question of the latitude of "executive privilege" would never be settled between the executive branch and Congress.

Washington had now had enough. He had been vilified "in such exaggerated and indecent terms as could scarcely be applied to a Nero, a notorious defaulter, or even a common pickpocket," and he let it be known that he would not be a candidate for re-election. During the summer recess of Congress he had Hamilton and Jay help him prepare a farewell address to the nation (it included some of the material that Madison had written for him for a similar purpose when he had considered retirement in 1792), and in September it appeared in newspapers around the country. Though Washington never delivered it orally, it was a valedictory to his fellow countrymen, summing up the achievements of his administration, advising maintenance of the public credit, and warning against permanent foreign alliances and internal divisiveness. The nation had moved far along the last path, however, and reversal would be impossible.

The choice of presidential candidates and the 1796 election did little to ease the country's schism. The conflict over Jay's Treaty had at last resulted in the coalescence of the various Antifederalist factions and vote-getting organizations in a nationwide Democratic-Republican party, and by November its leaders had agreed to support Jefferson for President and Aaron Burr (now converting New York's Tammany Society into a powerful Democratic-Republican political organization) for Vice President. A caucus of Federalist members of Congress had meanwhile settled on a ticket of John Adams for President and Thomas Pinckney of South Carolina for Vice President. In 1795, during the tension over Jay's negotiations, Pinckney—a polished and popular statesman who had been minister to Great Britain—became a national hero by wrangling concessions from Spain, in the Treaty of San Lorenzo, that all Americans could hail. The agreement established the borders between the United States and Spain in Florida and Louisiana, opened the Mississippi River to free navigation by Americans, and won them the right of deposit for the transshipment of their goods at the river's mouth. Pinckney was Hamilton's choice for President—the former secretary of the treasury disliked Adams's headstrong independence, which had made him an unreliable supporter of Hamiltonian policies and tactics—and he secretly tried to cut the electors' votes for Adams so that Pinckney would run higher and win the top position. But it was too difficult to control the electors. Of the total of 138, 59 were still chosen by state legislatures. The rest were elected by the voters either in districts or at large within a state. The campaign was a vituperative one, with partisan newspapers and orators engaging in an orgy of scurrility. When the votes were counted it was seen that the electors had marched off independently in all directions. New Englanders, getting wind of Hamilton's plot to defeat Adams, had deliberately cut Pinckney's vote so that he would not run first. On the Republican side Virginia had given only one of its second round of votes to Burr, casting its other fifteen for elderly Samuel Adams of Massachusetts. John Adams barely squeaked through to victory for the presidency, winning with a total of 71 votes; Jefferson, the Federalists' most feared enemy, ran second, with 68 votes, and would be Vice President; Pinckney, with 59 votes, and Burr, with 30, headed the list of also-rans.

The election of 1796 left scars. Burr would not forget how Virginia's Republicans had turned their backs on him, and Adams resented deeply the treachery of Alexander Hamilton. But more significantly, the new state of affairs boded ill for the future of the Federalists. To Hamilton and the Federalist members of Congress, Jefferson's election as Vice President was a catastrophe and a dangerous development for the safety of the nation. But Hamilton, in addition, knew that no one—and most importantly he himself —could control Adams, who had never ceased to irritate him with his unflattering and oft-repeated views of corrupt speculators, stock jobbers, and banks and bankers who profited through the taxation of the public. Adams's holdover Cabinet members, Pickering (State), Wolcott (Treasury), and James McHenry (War), however, were all Hamilton's henchmen, and from the start of Adams's administration they formed a cabal behind the new President's back. They stayed in secret communication with Hamilton in New York, reporting to him on Cabinet meetings and on Adams's proposals and plans and doing nothing of major importance, including supplying an opinion to Adams, without first seeking Hamilton's advice. Through them, as well as through Federalist leaders in Congress, Hamilton was still able to bring his influence to bear on the course of the nation. Inevitably, it would lead to a contest between him and the President and to a ruinous split among the Federalists.

Jefferson, meanwhile, was kept totally on the outside. The day before his inauguration, Adams visited the Virginian to consult with him, but the friendly gesture so upset the Hamiltonian Cabinet members and other Federalists that Adams, according to Jefferson, never again sought his opinion or help. For the next four years Jefferson confined himself to his single constitutional duty of presiding over the Senate while giving advice and leadership to the Republicans.

During Washington's last months in office a new crisis in foreign affairs had begun to build, this time with France. The passage of Jay's Treaty, with its unfavorable implications for France, had angered that country, which announced that it would take retaliatory measures against American shipping. Swept by his own intense anti-French feeling, the arch-Federalist secretary of state, Timothy Pickering, persuaded Washington to recall James Monroe, the Republican and pro-French minister to France, for ineffectively representing the administration's policies. Monroe's abrupt and angry departure from France made matters worse. When Charles Cotesworth Pinckney, a pro-British Federalist, was sent to Paris as Monroe's replacement, he was refused official recognition by the French Directory. In the United States, at the same time, the French minister openly interfered in the American elections, trying to help the pro-French Jefferson. When Adams won, the Directory, swollen with haughtiness as a result of the growth of French power on the Continent, took his victory as an affront from a puny nation that had forgotten its Revolutionary debt to France. By the time Adams was inaugurated, it was clear that the French had broken off diplomatic relations with the United States. Soon afterward it became clear also that the Directory was dismissing America's rights as a neutral, seizing United States ships on the high seas and confiscating their cargoes.

Patriotic fervor again filled the country, this time aimed at France, whose arrogance and contempt for the United States seemed worse than Britain's had ever been. Amid a rising clamor for action, Adams called Congress into a special session on May 15, 1797, to announce his intention to try to avoid hostilities by sending a three-man commission to Paris to attempt to negotiate with the Directory. At the same time, he asked Congress to pass measures for the defense of the country, if that were to become necessary.

The Fifth Congress was again almost evenly divided between Federalists and Democratic-Republicans, though on most important issues the former could command a slim majority in the House and a broader one in the Senate. Many veterans were gone from the two chambers. Madison and Ames had both retired from the House to give their attention to private affairs—Ames to try to regain his health, Madison to enjoy life with his bride, the young widow Dolley Payne Todd, whom he had married in September, 1794. Aaron Burr was out of the Senate; the New York legislature, again controlled by Federalists, had replaced him with Philip Schuyler. It would be a temporary setback for Burr. He maintained his political control over New York City's strong Republican organization and through contacts and correspondence kept himself in the forefront of the national Republican leadership. Such staunch old Federalists as Caleb Strong of Massachusetts and Oliver Ellsworth of Connecticut were also gone from the Senate (Ellsworth had succeeded John Jay as Chief Justice of the Supreme Court in 1796). Theodore Sedgwick, Ames's friend and a strong Hamiltonian, was now a Massachusetts Senator and would give Federalist leadership to the upper house.

In the lower chamber, where New Jersey's slick Jonathan Dayton was again the Speaker, Federalist leaders now included Roger Griswold of Connecticut, Harrison Gray Otis of Massachusetts, and William L. Smith and Robert Goodloe Harper of South Carolina. Madison's mantle in the lower house had fallen on Albert Gallatin, but Edward Livingston of New York and William B. Giles and John Nicholas of Virginia were still strong Republican voices.

In addition, a new strain of frontier-tinged democracy, plainly at odds with the scholarly and well-born sophistication that had dominated previous Congresses, was present in both chambers. In the House it was typified by Matthew Lyon of Vermont, a free-swinging democrat who had come to America as a redemptioner from Ireland in 1765, been in on the capture of Fort Ticonderoga with Ethan Allen, and become a printer, editor, and extreme Antifederalist, popular in rural Vermont and belligerent and radical in his politics. In the Senate, the new strain was personified by a tall, slim frontiersman with long hair and a cue down his back tied in an eelskin, thirty-year-old Andrew Jackson from Nashville, Tennessee. As a boy Jackson had been thrown into a stockade in South Carolina by the British during the Revolution; he had then been a saddler, a teacher, and a lawyer and in 1788 was appointed solicitor in western North Carolina. When that region became the state of Tennessee in June, 1796, Jackson was elected to Congress as a Democratic-Republican. In March, 1797, the Tennessee legislature elevated him to the Senate, where, Jefferson later recalled, ". . . he could never speak on account of the rashness of his feelings. I have seen him attempt it and as often choke with rage."

Because of the French provocations, the Republicans were on the defensive. Debate in the House over a reply to Adams's speech was bitter and personal. The Republicans, led by Gallatin and Livingston, accused the Federalists of wanting war with France. The Federalists denied this, but Robert Goodloe Harper—who, when he was fifteen years old, had fought as a cavalryman under Nathanael Greene against the British in North Carolina and was still ready to fight any enemy of American liberty—cried so savagely against France's oppression that Speaker Dayton had to admonish him against "arraigning the French government like a criminal at the bar of the House." Neither Adams nor Hamilton wished war with France, however, and their followers in Congress were ultimately content to endorse a moderate line of seeking only those measures necessary to convince France of the determination of the United States to stand up for its rights while at the same time building up America's defenses.

On May 31 Adams appointed his commission to France, consisting of Charles Cotesworth Pinckney, Virginia's eminent lawyer John Marshall, and Francis Dana, the chief justice of the Massachusetts Supreme Court.

All were Federalists, and their nominations were quickly confirmed by the Senate. Soon afterward, however, Dana declined the appointment because of poor health, and without consulting his Cabinet or Federalists in Congress Adams replaced him with Elbridge Gerry. The action shocked the Hamiltonians, not alone because they distrusted Gerry—whom they considered a Republican, though he was still more of an independent—but because Adams had ignored them in making the appointment. Pickering and others fussed and fumed, but there was nothing they could do. Adams defended Gerry as "an honest and firm man," and the Senate confirmed the nomination, though six Federalists voted against him.

On June 2, meanwhile, the House agreed 62 to 36 on its reply to Adams's message, approving the President's policy of negotiation, after which both houses turned to the defense measures. By July 10, when the special session ended, Congress had appropriated $115,000 for port and harbor fortifications, the construction of three of the frigates authorized in 1794 but still unbuilt, and an increase of eighty thousand in the militia. In addition, it authorized the government to borrow $800,000. A number of other proposals, including the strengthening of the regular army, were defeated. Even the amount voted to build up defenses was deemed vastly inadequate for the job, but it reflected a consensus among the Republicans and some of the Federalists to hold back expensive, warlike commitments until the President's commission had had a chance to end France's belligerency.

When the Fifth Congress reassembled for its second session on November 13, 1797, the French situation had grown no worse, but it had not improved. No news had come from the three-man commission in France, and French depredations on American shipping had continued. In his opening address on November 23 the President repeated essentially his requests of the previous May, asking for an increase in the standing army, a naval force to protect American commerce, legislation for a provisional army, and new taxes for additional revenue. In the months since adjournment, France's continued truculence had broadened Adams's support in both houses, and among many legislators the earlier attitude of "wait and see" had given way to feelings that France was not going to change and that the country had best prepare for the worst. The shift in opinion was accompanied by a growth of intolerance toward opponents of the administration, and many Republicans had become more defensive, fearful not only of hasty measures that would plunge the country into a war against France, but of congressional approval of a standing army and other legislation that might be used against the liberties of the American people.

As Congress began again to debate measures to implement Adams's program, stalling in the hope that news would soon arrive from France, the growing tension among the members was reflected in a lively "breach of decorum" that threw the House of Representatives into an uproar lasting through most of January and February, 1798. Following a sharp exchange of personal insults, on January 1 the fiery Matthew Lyon spit a stream of tobacco juice into the face of aristocratic Roger Griswold of Lyme, Connecticut. A motion was made immediately to expel the Vermont Republican for "gross indecency," but the issue was prolonged through weeks of arguing along party lines until February 12, when the motion was finally put to a vote and failed to gather the necessary two-thirds support of the members. Three days later the Connecticut Federalist, smarting over his failure to gain legal redress, came up behind the seated Lyon and began beating him over the head with a hickory cane. Lyon staggered to the fireplace on the House floor, seized the fire tongs, and flailed back at his assailant. As the two men closed and wrestled each other to the floor, the other members cheered them on with partisan delight. Finally Griswold pinned Lyon on his back and was pulled off by some of his supporters. A new motion to expel both members was then debated, but was defeated 73 to 21. The two men kept their seats, but the Vermonter was pilloried as "the Spitting Lyon" and "Ragged Mat, the Democrat."

Early in March the first dispatches finally reached Secretary of State Pickering from the commissioners in France. When they were deciphered they told a sordid story. After delaying an official meeting with the three Americans, Talleyrand, the French foreign minister, had sent three agents to call on them and suggest a United States loan of $12 million to France, a bribe of $250,000 for Talleyrand, and an apology by President Adams for anti-French remarks he had made in his message to Congress in May, 1797. The Americans refused the proposal, and after recognizing the hopelessness of their mission, they asked for their passports.

The dispatches inflamed Adams, who prepared to tell Congress about them. Pickering proposed an immediate American declaration of war, but Hamilton, who was informed of the results of the mission, counseled that Adams ask Congress only for preparations for a defensive war. Agreeing that Congress and the people would probably not support a war declaration, Adams on March 19 informed Congress that he had received dispatches from the mission reporting a failure in the negotiations. Since the United States now faced a state of limited hostilities with France, he called on Congress to enact speedily necessary defense measures to protect American ports and shipping, to build up the land and sea forces and increase the manufacture of arms, and to raise revenue for these purposes. Not having seen the documents, the Republicans responded angrily to Adams's militancy. To some Republicans the President's message seemed a declaration of war without Congress' consent. In the course of the ensuing debate a demand arose that the President submit the documents of the mission to Congress. Some Federalists had been told what was in them, and aware of how damaging they were to France, they gleefully lent their support, looking forward to the Republicans' embarrassment. Though Gallatin and Giles suspected a trap ("You are doing wrong to call for those dispatches. They will injure us," Giles told his Republican colleagues), the House, on April 2, voted 65 to 27 to demand the complete dispatches of the mission.

On April 3 Adams sent all the papers to the House after substituting X, Y, and Z for the names of the three agents of Talleyrand who had demanded the bribe from the commissioners. The documents shocked the Republicans, who recognized at once that their publication would arouse the American people to support a war declaration. Despite Republican objections, however, the House on April 6 voted to print twelve hundred copies of the documents, and the Senate, which had also examined the papers, passed a similar resolution three days later. As expected, the disclosures shocked the nation, creating a frenzy of anti-French feeling that amazed even Adams and Hamilton. "Millions for defense but not one cent for Tribute" (reported falsely in one newspaper as Pinckney's reply to the would-be bribers; Pinckney had actually said, "It is no, no, not a sixpence") became a national slogan. Turned into a hero overnight, Adams relished his new popularity, denouncing France and the Republicans and encouraging demands for war. As the hysteria mounted, he received hundreds of addresses and resolutions praising his patriotism. He greeted delegations dressed in full military uniform, with a sword at his side, and was pleased when a black cockade that his wife had presented to one visiting group caught the public fancy and was quickly adopted by thousands as an anti-French symbol.

In mid-April rumors that the French were planning to invade the United States increased the excitement. Liberty poles were erected, mobs roamed the streets, and Republicans and pro-French editors were physically attacked. The violence of the public's reaction panicked some of the Republicans in Congress. Giles departed from Philadelphia in terror, resigning his seat in October, and several others also left hastily for home. On April 9 Samuel Sewall, a Massachusetts Federalist, had introduced the defense measures sought by the administration. From then until mid-July, despite the brave opposition of Gallatin, Livingston, and the outnumbered Republicans, the Federalists put through some twenty bills in behalf of the nation's defense. (In the Senate, Vice President Jefferson wrote resignedly to Madison that the Federalists "will carry what they please" and went home before the session ended.) The enacted laws included the establishment, on May 3, of an independent Navy Department, followed by the appointment of Benjamin Stoddert, a prominent Federalist merchant of Georgetown, Maryland, as the first secretary of the navy; vast increases in naval power and the authorization of the President to use the navy and commissioned private ships to seize armed French vessels anywhere in the world; an embargo, to take effect on July 1, against all commerce with France; the creation of an "additional army" of ten thousand men to serve during the dispute with France and a "provisional army" of fifty thousand men to be raised in case war broke out or if the national security demanded it; authorization for the President to call out eighty thousand militia; the re-establishment of a Marine Corps, whose existence had lapsed after the Revolution; authorization for the administration to issue six percent bonds to private citizens who contributed to the building of ships; a direct tax on property, houses, and

111

slaves to raise $2 million (originally proposed in 1796 by Gallatin, this tax, now supported by the Federalists as a necessary revenue measure, proved unpopular and in February, 1799, led to a brief uprising in three Pennsylvania counties that ended when its leader, John Fries, was convicted of treason, sentenced to death, but pardoned by Adams); the suspension of the 1778 treaties of commerce and alliance with France; and finally, four bills that became known collectively as the Alien and Sedition Acts.

These last measures stemmed from a paranoid fear that the pro-French Republicans had become a threat to the nation's survival and also from a determination by some Federalists to muzzle opposition and criticism within the country until the crisis had passed. They were initiated by Federalist members of Congress, particularly Robert Goodloe Harper and Senator James Lloyd of Maryland, and despite their oppressive nature and violation of constitutional liberties, they were accepted approvingly by both Adams and Hamilton. They included the Naturalization Act, raising from five to fourteen years the length of residence required for citizenship; the Alien Act, authorizing the President to deport any alien considered dangerous to the public safety or suspected of "treasonable or secret" inclinations; the Alien Enemies Act, authorizing the President, in time of a declared war, to arrest, imprison, or deport aliens who were subject to an enemy power; and the Sedition Act, levying a fine of up to $2,000 and imprisonment for as long as two years on anyone convicted of writing, publishing, or speaking anything "false, scandalous, and malicious" against the United States government, the President, or either house of Congress, of entering into unlawful combinations to oppose the execution of national laws, or aiding or attempting "any insurrection, riot, unlawful assembly, or combination."

The acts were the most intolerant ever passed by Congress and reflected the extent of division and suspicion within the country. The Naturalization Act, which was repealed in 1802 in favor of a return to the milder law of 1795, was based on the belief that most immigrants, and particularly the large numbers coming from Ireland, gave their support to the Republicans and to radical, pro-French ideas and movements. "If some means are not adopted to prevent the indiscriminate admission of wild Irishmen & others to the right of suffrage, there will soon be an end to liberty and property," Federalist Harrison Gray Otis of Massachusetts (a nephew of the pre-Revolutionary lawyer James Otis) had declared. Gallatin and Matthew Lyon, both immigrants, had good reason to suspect that the act's sponsors had had them in mind. Though the two Alien Acts were never enforced and were allowed to expire in June, 1800, they caused the voluntary exodus of a number of Frenchmen who had been living in the country, as well as the taking out of naturalization papers by many aliens. The greatest storm was set loose by the Sedition Act, whose avid enforcement, particularly by Pickering and Supreme Court Justice Samuel Chase, a ruthless anti-Republican from Maryland, visited on the country what the Republicans termed "an American reign of terror" against liberties supposedly protected by the

Constitution and its Bill of Rights. Twenty-five persons, including the editors of leading Republican newspapers, were arrested under the act, and ten were convicted and sent to jail. Among the notables caught in the Federalist net was Matthew Lyon, who was convicted of alleged slanderous attacks on Adams, fined $1,000, and imprisoned for four months. While he was still in jail, his outraged Vermont constituents made him into a martyr for liberty and re-elected him to Congress.

The enforcement of the Sedition Act represented a high-water mark of Federalist power in the United States. Gradually, its excesses brought about a reaction, symbolized by the Virginia and Kentucky Resolutions composed by Jefferson and Madison and asserting the supremacy of the power of states over that of the federal government. The Kentucky Resolutions, written by Jefferson in answer to the Alien and Sedition Acts and presented to the Kentucky legislature on November 16, 1798, held that a state could declare unconstitutional—null and void—any federal law that it considered a violation of its constitutional rights. Madison's Virginia Resolutions declared that the states had the right and duty "to interpose for arresting the progress of the evil." Seven northern states protested against the resolutions, insisting that it was up to the Supreme Court, not the states, to determine the constitutionality of a federal law—a contention rebuffed by Jefferson, who noted that all the Supreme Court justices were Federalists. Nothing came immediately of the resolutions, though ironically they would become in time paving blocks on the road leading to secession and civil war.

In the meantime, newly built American frigates and smaller warships, as well as hundreds of commissioned privateers, had taken to the high seas, and an undeclared naval war that was to last for two years had commenced with France. All through the spring and early summer of 1789, following the disclosure of the XYZ papers, Adams and some of the more extreme Federalists had plumped for a declared war, and most of the American people lived in tension, expecting such a declaration by Congress from week to week. But too many moderate Federalists in the House shied away from taking that last drastic step, still afraid of the Republican opposition, worried about facing France without British help (Napoleon was threatening to invade Britain), and persuaded that the American people would take every measure for defense but would not support an offensive war. Despite the worst Republican fears, therefore, the momentous second session of the Fifth Congress ended on July 16, 1798, with the country still not formally at war, thanks largely to the fears and inhibitions of some of Adams's own supporters.

That summer and fall Adams himself changed. He was informed that Tallyrand and the Directory desired peace and new negotiations with the United States. A division in the Federalist party—first evident in the last session of Congress—between the war-hawk followers of Pickering and the moderates who had resisted a war declaration was now clearly apparent to the President, and he gave increasing credence to the possibility of avoiding war through another attempt at negotiation. A second factor in his thinking was his growing suspicion of the loyalty of the Cabinet. The doughty little President, his ego built by his new popularity among the people, began to eye more coldly the hold that the insufferable Hamilton had over the officers of his administration, and this distaste, according to some historians, influenced the shift he was making from saber rattling to advocating peace. An explosive split in the Federalist party was brewing.

On February 18, 1799, the blow fell on the Federalists. Without consulting his Cabinet or any Federalist leader in Congress, Adams, now the voice of peace, submitted to the Senate the nomination of William Vans Murray to be minister to France. The extreme Federalists, who still wanted a declaration of war, were horrified, as were Hamilton and Pickering, Wolcott, and McHenry of the Cabinet. Overnight the party split apart on the issue of negotiating with France. When a delegation of Federalist Senators called on the President to tell him that they would not vote for the nomination, Adams threatened to resign and turn over his office to Vice President Jefferson. That was worse. Thinking that the headstrong Adams had gone mad, the Senators compromised, finally agreeing with Adams on the appointment, instead, of a commission of three Federalists. The President thereupon named Murray, Chief Justice Oliver Ellsworth, and Patrick Henry (who declined and was replaced by William R. Davie, the Federalist governor of North Carolina). The commissioners were ultimately successful, on September 30, 1800, signing a treaty with the government of Napoleon, now first consul, that waived American claims for depredations against United States shipping but won release from all treaties with France, ended the undeclared war, and re-established friendly relations between the two countries that paved the way for the Louisiana Purchase three years later.

Adams's independent handling of the crisis turned many members of his party irrevocably against him. Nevertheless, the elections of 1799 reflected a popular support for the President and his policies, and when the Sixth Congress convened on December 2, 1799, the Federalists were firmly in control of both houses. Theodore Sedgwick, the Massachusetts Federalist who had served three years in the Senate, was re-elected to the House and was chosen Speaker over Nathaniel Macon, a North Carolina Republican. With the abatement of tension over France, the nation had become more tranquil. Yet deep fears and animosities still divided Republicans and Federalists and rent the latter between Hamiltonians who resented Adams's willful independence and those who, like Fisher Ames, now a lawyer in Massachusetts, still patronizingly supported the honest but often "imprudent" old man.

In May, 1800, as Adams began to face the prospect of another election, he at last lost patience with his treacherous Cabinet members. On May 6 he demanded McHenry's resignation, replacing him with Senator Samuel Dexter of Massachusetts, and four days later he asked Pickering to resign. When that arch-Hamiltonian resisted, Adams fired him, leveling a blast also at Hamilton. In Pickering's place Adams appointed John Marshall of Virginia. These actions enraged Hamilton, who became determined to prevent Adams's re-election. During the summer he prepared a "Letter from Alexander Hamilton Concerning the Public Conduct and Character of John Adams," attacking the President's "disgusting egotism," "jealousy," "indiscretion," and "vanity without bounds" and characterizing him as a man of passion, spite, envy, and malice. When the letter was published, Adams retorted coldly that Hamilton was "a bastard." The unseemly quarrel horrified many Federalists, determining some of them, including Sedgwick, Robert Goodloe Harper, and Harrison Gray Otis, to get out of national politics, and further split and weakened the party.

In June, after Congress had recessed, the executive departments of the government were moved to the new Federal City still being built near Georgetown on the Potomac River. The site was one of mud, mosquitoes, huts, claptrap boarding houses, and half-finished government buildings, but the law of 1790 had directed that the seat of government be transferred there from Philadelphia by the first Monday in December, 1800. Early in November, when members of Congress began to appear, they were appalled by the mire, the unfinished Capitol, and the lack of amenities. Adams and his family had already moved into the President's House, whose interior was far from complete. As the Senators and Congressmen searched out lodgings in the frontierlike settlement, Gouverneur Morris, now a Senator from New York, observed that the new seat of the American government needed only "houses, cellars, kitchens, well informed men, amiable women, and other little trifles of this kind to make our city perfect."

The second session of the Sixth Congress commenced on November 17, 1800, with the House and Senate crowded into the Capitol's north wing (which they shared with the Supreme Court), the only part of the "Congress House" that was completed. (A year later the House would assemble amid great discomfort in an oval brick structure that stood temporarily where the south wing was to be erected and that the members dismally called the Oven.) Since October the sixteen states had been voting for their presidential electors, and the session was dominated by interest in the progress of the elections. In May a caucus of Federalist Senators and Representatives had agreed on Adams and Charles Cotesworth Pinckney as their standard-bearers. A Republican caucus of members of Congress, as well as state leaders, had chosen Jefferson and Burr. Both groups now represented true, nationwide parties, with roots firmly planted among local and state vote-getting organizations. The electors, however, were still chosen by a variety of means, some by popular vote and some by state legislatures.

From the beginning the Federalists had trouble. In the key state of New York, where the legislature named the electors, Burr's Republicans—augmented by many small merchants and businessmen who felt the Federalists had grown too conservative and represented only those who were wealthy and powerful—swept the state elections and guaranteed a slate of

Republican electors. The Federalists also gave up hope for Pennsylvania, where a newly elected Republican governor, Thomas McKean, introduced the spoils system into American politics by throwing out Federalist incumbents and creating a machine of Republican replacements. Even in South Carolina, the home state of the Federalists' vice-presidential candidate, another Charles Pinckney, this one a Republican, won the state legislature for Jefferson and Burr by promising ample patronage to the legislators. Hamilton himself was of no help to the Federalists. Once again he connived busily to try to rig the electors' vote so that Pinckney would run higher than Adams. His antagonism to the President only intensified the party split.

The national parties and grassroots organizations also worked for congressional candidates, and in most districts the campaign was bitter and emotional. Adams's writings were used against him to prove that he was a monarchist, a believer in an aristocracy and a hereditary Senate, and was hell-bent on delivering the United States into the hands of Great Britain. Jefferson was attacked as a blood-drenched Jacobin and atheist. The loss of pivotal states made the Federalists fight harder elsewhere. In New Jersey, where the people chose the electors, the Federalists discovered a law dating back to colonial days that did not bar women from voting; making use of it, the women members of scores of Federalist families went to the polls and helped elect a New Jersey slate for Adams and Pinckney.

In the end opposition to the Alien and Sedition Acts and the Federalists' land tax, as well as resentment over a loss of trade with France and a new growth of anti-British sentiment caused by that nation's stepped-up policy of impressing American seamen, resulted in a landslide victory of Republican Congressmen (the Federalists lost about forty seats) and a triumph for the Jefferson-Burr ticket. Jefferson and Burr each received 73 votes, Adams got 65, Pinckney 64, and Jay 1. The balloting reflected a high degree of party discipline, for the electors had voted almost unanimously for their parties' two choices. (One Rhode Island elector, however, had thrown his vote to Jay, so that Adams would be sure to run higher than Pinckney.)

But the tie between Jefferson and Burr meant that the House of Representatives would have to choose which man would be President, with each state having one vote in the balloting. It was a ticklish question, for the Federalists controlled six states in the House and split the control with the Republicans in two others. The Republicans controlled only eight states, and the winner needed nine to be elected. Hamilton detested Burr more than he feared Jefferson, and he counseled the Federalists to give their votes to the Virginian. They refused to do so, however, and for thirty-five ballots, from February 11 to 17, denied Jefferson the victory by voting for Burr. Finally, through an intermediary, word was circulated among the Federalists that Jefferson had given assurances that he would preserve the public credit, retain subordinate Federalist officials, and continue Adams's foreign policy. The situation by then had grown tense. Rumors were afloat that the Federalists intended to end the impasse by giving the presidency to the Federalist president *pro tempore* of the Senate, and that to counter such a usurpation Republicans in the Middle Atlantic states were preparing to march on Washington.

The report of Jefferson's "assurances" brought relief to some Federalists, who were growing worried over the rumors of an uprising. When Federalist James A. Bayard, the lone Representative from Delaware, announced he would switch his vote to Jefferson, however, it precipitated a crisis among the Federalists. Foreseeing the end of the world with Jefferson's election, extremists among the leadership fought to hold the Federalists in line for Burr. Their efforts not only failed but turned some Federalists irrevocably away from the leadership—and, in time, turned them into Republicans. Meanwhile, they agreed that no Federalist vote need be cast *for* a Republican President and approved an arrangement by which the Federalists in Vermont and Maryland would cast blank ballots, permitting the Republican members to vote their states for Jefferson. On the thirty-sixth and final ballot, with Republican Matthew Lyon exultingly announcing Vermont's switch to Jefferson, the Virginian was elected, ten states to four for Burr. Delaware and South Carolina refrained from voting. No one wanted to repeat the experience, however, and in 1803 Congress passed the Twelfth Amendment to provide for separate balloting by the electors for President and Vice President. It was ratified by the states a year later.

The election was a bitter blow to Adams. During the few remaining weeks of his term he nursed his wounds in the President's House, feeling resentment against both Hamilton and Jefferson. Fearing that great calamities would occur to the nation under a Republican administration, he began sending to the Senate a stream of nominations of reliable Federalists to fill national offices as bulwarks against Jefferson after March 4. On January 20 he appointed John Marshall Chief Justice of the Supreme Court to succeed Oliver Ellsworth, who had retired in 1799 to join the mission to France. Now, on February 27, in one of its last actions, the Federalist-controlled Sixth Congress passed a new Judiciary Act, reducing the number of Supreme Court justices to five but creating sixteen circuit courts, each with its own judge, and providing for a large number of new marshals, lawyers, and clerical personnel. It opened more jobs for Adams to fill, and he worked right up till 9 P.M. on March 3, his last night in office, sending nominations to the Senate, whose Federalist majority obligingly voted confirmations. The Republicans were infuriated. Jefferson protested that Adams's appropriation of offices which the new Republican administration should have the right to fill was an "outrage on decency." Gallatin was less charitable; Adams's conduct, he thought, was "almost insanity."

The little man from Braintree, who had done his best for his country, who had taken the slings and arrows from his own party as well as from the Republicans, but who had saved the peace, was hurt, but he knew what he was doing. If the reign of antichrist was coming, the continuation of orderly government and the protection of liberty and property would be in the hands of the Federalists whom he would leave behind him in office, like guardians of a fortress. Before dawn on March 4, with mixed feelings of wounded pride, bitterness, and satisfaction that history would treat him better than his contemporaries, he left, unobserved, on the long road that led to home.

In the Federal City on the Potomac, his successor, in the company of Adams's secretaries of the treasury and the navy, some Republican members of Congress, a ragtag group of citizenry, and a unit of Maryland artillerymen pulling a cannon, walked a few hundred yards from his boarding house to the Capitol. At noon he entered the Senate chamber and sat down in the Vice President's chair, with Aaron Burr, militarily erect and dignified, on his right and Chief Justice John Marshall on his left. After several moments of silence, he rose and in a low, almost inaudible voice began to read his inaugural address to the members of the Republican-dominated Seventh Congress seated before him. The time had come for national reunification. The tumultuous years of division were past. "We are all Republicans," said Jefferson. "We are all Federalists."

4. Out of the Wilderness

When the Senate finally opened its galleries to the public in 1795, visitors found its proceedings staid and dull in comparison with the livelier give and take of the House. The thirty Senators, according to one observer in the closing years of the century, conducted debate with "the most delightful silence, the most beautiful order, gravity, and personal dignity of manner. They all appeared every morning full-powdered and dressed, as age or fancy might suggest, in the richest material. The very atmosphere of the place seemed to inspire wisdom, mildness, and condescension." The "courtesy" of the upper chamber, a number of whose members were sometimes hard pressed to regard themselves as legislators rather than as counselors to the national government, was in "striking contrast to the independent loquacity of the Representatives below stairs, some few of whom persisted in wearing, while in their seats and during the debate, their ample cocked hats, placed 'fore and aft' upon their heads."

Within ten years the republicanism and antimonarchical plain ways of the party of Thomas Jefferson made an impact on the rising little city of Washington (population approaching sixteen thousand, including five thousand slaves and twenty-five hundred free blacks) and on the Congress. The President, tall, thin, freckled, and graying, received visitors in the Executive Mansion in old, soiled clothes and slippers with holes in their toes, and he kept the doors of the gleaming stone edifice overlooking muddy, rutted Pennsylvania Avenue open to everyone (more and more, people were calling it the White House, rather than the President's House). The Senate still had an air of pomposity and dullness, but stiff, old-line Federalists such as New York's Gouverneur Morris, Connecticut's Uriah Tracy, and Massachusetts's Timothy Pickering were in the minority. Democratic newcomers from the West and South munched on apples and cakes in the Senate chamber and strode around the floor, often walking unconcernedly between members engaged in debate with each other. The House was cruder, dominated by Republican members whose brashness, slovenly dress and manners (they often sat in sessions with their hats on their heads and their feet on desks), addictive use of chewing tobacco, and loquacious belligerency dismayed foreign diplomats in the rustic American capital. "This undoubtedly is a miserable place," wrote the secretary of the British legation to his mother, the duchess of Devonshire, in 1805, "but the elect of all the states are assembled in it, and really such a gang to have the affairs of an empire wanting little of the size of Russia entrusted to them, makes one shudder." The British minister, Anthony Merry, was even less flattering. "To judge from their Congress," he commented, "one should suppose the nation to be the most blackguard society that was ever brought together." The "excess of the democratic ferment in this people is conspicuously evinced by the dregs having got up to the top," his office reported to London.

In theory, Jefferson and many of the Republican congressional leaders believed in the separation of powers between the executive and the legislature, and Jefferson assumed office expecting Congress to take the initiative and responsibility for legislation. "The Executive is the branch of our government which . . . is already too strong," he said. In neither his inaugural address nor his first annual message to Congress in December, 1801, did he do more than proclaim his seemingly modest republican aims: to reduce government spending and the national debt, cut the army and navy, repeal excise taxes, support the states "in all their rights," and end such abuses to liberty as the Alien and Sedition laws. (He dramatized his republican principles by having his secretary deliver by hand his first annual message, in writing, to each house, partly because he opposed the monarchical-style personal address followed by formal congressional processionals to convey the legislators' "replies to the throne," and partly because he was such a poor and mumbling reader. The custom he set of sending written messages to Congress—and expecting no formal acknowledgments from the legislators—was continued thereafter by all Presidents up to Woodrow Wilson.) Several factors, however, soon had Jefferson taking the lead in proposing specific legislation, directing his majorities in Congress, and becoming one of the strongest of Presidents.

Although there were many Republican luminaries in Congress who had made reputations on their own, the party, by and large, owed its nationwide electoral success to Jefferson. In a sense the President *was* the Republican party and the principal fountainhead of its philosophy, policies, and programs, and numerous Senators and Representatives naturally looked to him for guidance. But in some respects, also, Jefferson's coming to power represented a fundamental political revolution—in the view of the Jeffersonians, the securing, at last, of what the American Revolution had been about. The Republicans had taken office in an unprecedented peaceful transference of power from the adherents of one philosophy of government to those of another. The task they set for themselves was to make this new direction for the American people an enduring one, ending forever the dangers of the monarchical or oligarchical trend the Federalists had appeared to represent. In this mission Jefferson could not play a secondary role. He was the architect of the Republican structure, and in a remarkably short time, with Albert Gallatin, his able and forceful secretary of the treasury (and, to a much lesser extent, James Madison, his scholarly secretary of state), he began to exert as strong an influence over Congress and the legislative process as Alexander Hamilton had ever wielded, and, in addition, to create a new mechanism for binding Republican Congressmen to his policies and programs.

In the beginning the Speaker of the House had been viewed as an unbiased presiding officer. But rather quickly the majorities that elected him came to require that he be one of their own—and the more helpful to the majority, the better. During Adams's last two years, Theodore Sedgwick of Massachusetts, the Federalist Speaker of the Sixth Congress, was so biased in favor of the Federalists and against their enemies that the Republicans refused to join in the customary resolution of thanks to the Speaker at the conclusion of that Congress. Neither Washington nor Adams, however, ever utilized the Speaker, or any other member of either house, as a personal representative of the President—though Hamilton, to be sure, had frequently guided and directed Federalist members in both chambers to assist administration legislation. Now, on Jefferson's accession to power, the House elected as Speaker Nathaniel Macon of North Carolina, a genial and popular but obviously partisan Republican planter who, though fair-minded, would be expected to help the administration. While many were to fuss at his lack of leadership ("No man in history has left a better name than Macon," John Quincy Adams later wrote, "but the name was all he left"), he assumed his office in 1801 as a loyal Jeffersonian, willing to follow the President's guidance. More importantly, he appointed his twenty-eight-year-old close friend, the blazing and erratic second-term Congressman John Randolph of Virginia, to be chairman of the House Ways and Means Committee as well as something of an assistant to him. The nervous, quick-witted Randolph (who claimed to be a descendant of Pocahontas and added "of Roanoke" to his name in order to avoid confusion with a cousin, "Possum" John Randolph) was a spectacle. Known to be sexually impotent ("You pride yourself upon an animal faculty, in . . . which the negro is your equal and the jackass infinitely your superior!" he once lashed out at a colleague), he swaggered around the House floor like a strange, tormented autocrat, booted and spurred, swinging a riding crop imperiously, often with one or two foxhounds at his heels. Described by a contemporary as "lean and sallow," with a small head, a face lined with "premature and unhealthy wrinkles," a short body, and long "protracted" legs, he was soprano-voiced and shrill. But no one was sharper or more devastating in debate. Despite his youth, he demolished opponents with invective, obscenity, and satire. Working closely with both Macon and Randolph, Jefferson soon began to use the aggressive young Virginian as his own personal representative, or floor leader, to guide his legislation through the House.

This development of a formal, working tie between the executive and Congress was further expanded and strengthened during Jefferson's eight years in the White House. When the tempestuous Randolph eventually turned against the President, drawing Macon part way along with him in rebellion, Jefferson dropped them both. The Republicans elected another Speaker, and Jefferson chose a new personal agent in the House. Joseph H. Nicholson of Maryland, Caesar A. Rodney of Delaware, and Barnabas Bidwell of Massachusetts were among those who served for periods as presidential lieutenants, looking after party interests in the House and taking orders from Jefferson. At the same time, the increased membership and workloads during the eight years (the House went to 142 members after the census of 1800) led to the creation of a number of standing committees in both houses. In addition to the Ways and Means Committee, which became permanent in 1802, with the responsibility for all taxing and spending, the House by 1809 had created nine standing committees whose interests ranged from interstate and foreign commerce to public lands and the post office and post roads. In the Senate four standing committees were created, all concerned chiefly with the administrative affairs of that body. Party men generally chaired the committees, and particularly in the House, they could be counted upon to assist the President. Jefferson also had loyal agents in the Senate, though none was as important as the floor leader in the House, which was still the principal legislative arena. In the upper chamber John Breckinridge of Kentucky, who had introduced Jefferson's anti-Sedition Law resolutions in the legislature of that state in 1798; James Jackson, now returned as a Senator from Georgia; and De Witt Clinton of New York, the young nephew of George Clinton and an ambitious, anti-Burr politician, were among those on whom Jefferson could usually rely. The final element in Jefferson's control of the Congress was the party caucus, in which his leaders, often under Gallatin's direction, guided the Republican membership to desired legislative decisions.

The House, complained Federalist Representative Josiah Quincy of Boston toward the end of Jefferson's administration, "acts, and reasons, and votes, and performs all the operations of an animated being, and yet, judging from my own perceptions, I cannot refrain from concluding that all great political questions are settled somewhere else than on this floor." Like other Federalists, he had by that time become a victim of Jefferson's party machine, one of the most effective, in welding together the national executive and legislature, that the country would ever see. It was, however, dominated and directed by the executive, and that would soon change. But its various elements—the key roles of floor leaders and committee chairmen in the legislative process, a system of standing committees, and caucuses that bound party members to decisions—would continue as institutions and sources of power within the Congress.

During Jefferson's first term Burr sat as president of the Senate, but

Jefferson rarely saw or spoke to him. Like many Republicans, he had come to resent Burr's conduct during the House balloting for President in 1801, when the New Yorker, who the nation knew had professed to run for the vice presidency, had permitted the Federalists to try for thirty-six ballots to give him, rather than Jefferson, the presidency. Burr was now treated scornfully as a man without a party. The suave little New Yorker continued, however, to baffle men of both parties, behaving as if nothing bothered him, posing as a Republican and then almost deliberately affronting Jefferson with outrageous infidelities covered by an air of innocence. One series of episodes that occurred early in 1802 finished Burr with the national Republican leadership.

The year before, on the eve of his inauguration, Jefferson had been angered by the Federalists' last-minute action in ramming through the new Judiciary Act, which permitted Adams's "midnight" appointments of a host of stolid Federalists to judicial jobs. The maneuver, coupled with Adams's naming of the Virginia Federalist John Marshall as Chief Justice of the Supreme Court, had accomplished Adams's aim: the federal judiciary, filled from top to bottom with men hostile to Jefferson and the Republicans, loomed as an enormous threat to the new administration. To Jefferson, the specter of an enemy judiciary, whose judges he could not fire or replace, was intolerable. Coping with the problem was one of his highest priorities. As an initial step, he was determined to force the congressional repeal of the offensive Judiciary Act of 1801, thus nullifying all Adams's eleventh-hour appointments by the simple expedient of ending their jobs. A resolution to repeal the act was introduced in the Senate on January 6, 1802, by Jefferson's Kentucky ally John Breckinridge. The Republicans' edge in the Senate was much more tenuous than in the House, and the bill seemed in danger of defeat. For the moment, however, it was saved by Burr; the vote was 15 to 15, and the Vice President's deciding ballot carried it over the hurdle. But the next day Burr created a storm. His friend the New Jersey Federalist Jonathan Dayton moved suddenly to send the bill back to committee for further consideration, slyly urging a revision of the *entire* federal judiciary. Once more the vote was 15 to 15, but this time Burr sided with Dayton and the Federalists and voted to recommit. Jefferson and the Republicans were furious. On February 2 Breckinridge was able to call up the bill again, and the next day it successfully passed the Senate. The Republicans had no trouble with it in the House, where John Randolph managed it on the floor and Jefferson's caucus ran like clockwork. ("The Jacobins," wrote Matthew Lyon's old adversary, the testy Federalist Roger Griswold of Connecticut, ". . . have adopted the plan of meeting in divan and agreeing on measures to be pursued and passed in the House and then they vote in mass without admitting any alteration in the plan proposed. The wickedness of such a course has never been equalled but by the Jacobin club in Paris; the spirit is intolerant and must lead to ruin.") Jefferson signed the repeal on March 8,

1802, and the Republicans followed through by legislating a new Judiciary Act. Jefferson had won his first round, but there was no forgiveness for Burr's treacherous support of the Federalist Dayton.

Yet the full drama of the relationship between Burr and Jefferson was far from ended. As Burr became aware that the Republicans would not support him again in the next presidential election, he turned his attention to the rough-and-tumble theater of his New York political base. There, early in 1804, he decided to run for governor. Even in his home state, however, there was much against him. In November, 1803, De Witt Clinton had resigned from the Senate to become mayor of New York City. Burr now had to fight the Clintonians, headed by the tough, ambitious mayor, as well as his old enemy Alexander Hamilton, still a leader among what was left of the New York Federalists. Like most of Burr's involvements, the gubernatorial campaign had numerous crosscurrents of intrigue. So intemperately did Hamilton participate in the opposition to Burr that when the latter was defeated for governor, he turned on Hamilton and demanded satisfaction on the field of honor for questionable remarks the one-time treasury secretary had circulated against him. The quarrel ended in a horrendous climax when Burr, still the Vice President of the United States, mortally wounded the famous Federalist on the dueling grounds at Weehawken, New Jersey, before daybreak on July 11, 1804.

The shocking affair made Hamilton a martyr. Burr was indicted in New Jersey for murder and in New York City for having sent the challenge to the duel. In most parts of the country, however, dueling was still considered a legal and acceptable method for gentlemen to settle affronts to their personal honor, and the clamor against Burr gradually subsided. After a brief flight to the South, the Vice President returned to Washington and on November 5, 1804, the opening day of the second session of the Eighth Congress, nonchalantly occupied his seat again as president of the Senate as if nothing had happened. "What a humiliating circumstance that a man Who for months has fled from justice—& who by the legal authorities is now accused of murder, should preside over the first branch of the National Legislature!" fumed New Hampshire's Senator William Plumer. But, he added, "The democrats, at least many of them, appear attentive to him—& he is very familiar with them."

Jefferson's lieutenants and followers, as a matter of fact, were more than attentive to Burr; Virginia's William B. Giles, now a Senator, even petitioned the governor of New Jersey to quash the murder charge against the Vice President and end the Senate's embarrassment at having its presiding officer pictured to the world as a "common murderer." But the Jeffersonians' new desire to wean Burr's loyalty had a selfish and more subtle motive. During the previous months Jefferson had resumed his campaign against Federalists in the judiciary. The President's real target was Chief Justice John Marshall, but he first went after lesser prey, intending as a necessary preliminary step to undermine and destroy the Federalists' claim of the "sanctity" of the courts against the government's other two branches.

On February 24, 1803, John Marshall added fuel to Jefferson's crusade against the judiciary by a stunning decision in the case of *Marbury* v. *Madison*. A Federalist from Maryland, William Marbury had been one of Adams's "midnight" appointments, but before going out of power the Federalists overlooked handing him his official commission as a justice of the peace for the District of Columbia. When Jefferson directed his secretary of state, Madison, to withhold delivery of the commission, thereby annulling the appointment, Marbury—under Section 13 of the Judiciary Act of 1789— appealed directly to the Supreme Court for a mandamus (an order to Madison to give him the commission). Marshall's decision went off in a different and totally unexpected direction: he ruled that Section 13 of the 1789 act was unconstitutional because it enlarged the Supreme Court's original jurisdiction, which could be done only by a constitutional amendment. Thus, while averring that the high court did not have original jurisdiction under the Constitution to issue Marbury a mandamus, Marshall asserted the doctrine of judicial review of legislation and made it clear that the courts, too, could pass judgment on the constitutionality of executive actions. Marbury had not received his mandamus, but Marshall had affirmed new power and independence for the third branch of the government, a challenge that did nothing to lessen Jefferson's determination to proceed full tilt against the Federalist-dominated judiciary.

In March, 1804, Federalist District Judge John Pickering of New Hampshire, impeached by the House for intoxication, bullying, and other breaches of good behavior on the bench, was tried by the Senate, found guilty, and removed from office. Jefferson now moved on to a larger target: Samuel Chase of Maryland, the ablest and most distinguished justice of the Supreme Court after Marshall himself. To the Republicans, Chase had long been a marked man, a Federalist of violent antidemocratic feelings who had presided tyrannically over some of the most notorious of the Sedition Act trials. In May, 1803, Chase had delivered a political tirade to a Baltimore grand jury, denouncing Congress' repeal of the Judiciary Act of 1801 and attacking Jefferson's administration as a "mobocracy" whose doctrine "that all men . . . are entitled to enjoy equal liberty and equal rights" would destroy "peace and order, freedom and property." Jefferson had been incensed by the "seditious" attack, and at his request the House voted articles of impeachment against the judge. The case, much more important to the Republicans than the Pickering removal, was also more politically charged and would be more difficult for the Jeffersonians to win. Chase, a tall, powerful man who had been a signer of the Declaration of Independence and who was called by some the Demosthenes of Maryland, was a dangerous adversary in his own right; in addition, to his defense had hastened some of the outstanding Federalist lawyers in the country, who were convinced that his conviction would imperil Marshall and the entire federal judiciary. Jefferson was also determined to win. It was to this tense atmosphere, on the eve of Chase's trial by the Senate, that Burr returned after his duel with Hamilton and found himself wooed by the Jeffersonians. As Vice President he was in a key position, for he would preside over the court and would have the power to assist or make more difficult the administration's prosecution of the associate justice.

As it turned out, Jefferson's case was lost disastrously by John Randolph, who headed the prosecution for the House of Representatives. The unstable Virginian handled his presentation in a weird and inept manner and was outclassed by Chase and his distinguished battery of lawyers. From the outset Randolph was nervous and unprepared, and at times he screamed in his high voice, was forgetful and irrational, and groaned as if he were ill. At the end he broke down and sobbed, telling the Senators that this was "the last day of my sufferings and yours." On March 1, 1805, Chase was acquitted on all eight articles of impeachment. Marshall had been saved, and Jefferson thereafter had to live with a judiciary of which he did not approve.

Burr had conducted the trial proceedings with such skill and impartiality that both sides were moved to acknowledge new respect and admiration for him. Even Senator Plumer had kind words for the man who had killed Hamilton. "Mr. Burr has certainly, on the whole, done himself, the Senate & the nation honor by the dignified manner in which he has presided over this high & numerous Court," he wrote. Burr, however, was now almost through as Vice President. On March 4, 1805, he was to be succeeded by the aging George Clinton, who had been elected to serve during Jefferson's second term. On March 2, the day after Chase's acquittal, Burr appeared in the upper chamber for the last time. Although he had a sore throat, he rose to deliver a farewell address. It proved to be one of the most stirring speeches ever made in the Senate. The assault on the judiciary by his enemy, Thomas Jefferson, and the conscientious role of the Senate in turning back that assault, were fresh in his mind. His words were emotional, and tears welled in the eyes of some of his listeners. In closing he referred to the national legislative body that he was leaving, and there was a stillness among both friend and foe. "This House," he said, "is a sanctuary; a citadel of law, of order, and of liberty; and it is here, in this exalted refuge, here, if anywhere, will resistance be made to the storms of political phrensy and the silent arts of corruption; and, if the Constitution be destined ever to perish by the sacrilegious hands of the demagogue or the usurper, which God avert, its expiring agonies will be witnessed on this floor."

When Burr had finished, according to one member, the whole Senate was in tears and so transported that it could not come to order for half an hour. The scene was "one of the most affecting of my life," said Senator Samuel Mitchill of New York. As soon as the Vice President bowed and took his departure from the chamber, his colleagues expressed their appreciation and voted "entire approbation of his conduct." Burr thought it best not to return to New York, but headed west where he would soon get into the greatest difficulty of his life, being charged with a conspiracy against the nation. His farewell words to the Senate were eventually forgotten by most people (though a later Speaker of the House, John White of Kentucky, used them in an eloquent speech, pretending they were his own, and when exposed was so ridiculed and humiliated that he committed suicide in 1845). What Burr had said, nevertheless, was destined to come true in the Senate on more than one occasion in the future.

Despite the anticlimactic end of his designs on the judiciary, Jefferson during his first term had had little trouble winning his way with the legislation that passed through Congress. Among the principal achievements of his administration on the domestic front was the implementation of a new financial policy that Secretary of the Treasury Gallatin fashioned to carry out the Republicans' economic principles. In March and April, 1802, under Jefferson's direction, Republican-led majorities in both houses repealed Hamilton's hated excise taxes. The loss of revenue was more than offset by actions of Jefferson and Gallatin that effected large economies: useless jobs and offices were eliminated, the army and navy were drastically cut, the Treasury was reorganized to make collection of income more efficient, Congress was asked to make specific appropriations for specific purposes, and the discretionary spending power of administrative officials was severely limited. The resulting drop in annual expenses permitted an accelerated liquidation of the national debt; by 1809, when he left office, Jefferson had reduced that figure from $83 million to $57 million. The economic accomplishments, moreover, quickened the disintegration of the Federalist party in Congress and in the country at large. Far from turning out to be devils, the Republicans had retained the essentials of Hamilton's financial system and had proven economically conservative and good for the country. The impact was conclusively apparent in the election of 1804, when large numbers of Federalists left their party to vote for Republican electors. Jefferson and George Clinton carried every state but Connecticut and Delaware. Congressional elections went heavily Republican. In the next session of the legislature, in 1805, the Federalists were outnumbered in the House eighty-one to twenty-five, and in the Senate twenty-seven to seven.

The main concerns of the United States, however, had continued to be in the area of foreign affairs, and there, too, Jefferson's actions, supported by his followers in Congress, won converts among the electorate. In his first inaugural Jefferson, no longer partisan to France (Napoleon ended the last of the republican idealism of that country's revolution), had proclaimed a policy of "peace, commerce, and honest friendship with all nations, entangling alliances with none." Maintaining that policy of neutrality toward the big powers—whose wars with each other threatened increasingly to crush the United States between them—proved less difficult in Jefferson's first administration than in his second. At the same time, it did not keep America out of a shooting conflict with the small, piratical nations of the Barbary Coast of North Africa.

That situation broke upon Jefferson soon after he took office. The Western powers for years had been paying tribute to Algiers, Morocco, Tunis, and Tripoli to keep those countries from seizing their merchant ships in the Mediterranean and holding their seamen for ransom. After a brief opposition in the 1790's, the United States had agreed to pay the annual blackmail to protect its commerce. Suddenly, early in 1801, the pasha of Tripoli raised his demand. His men cut down the flag at the American consulate in Tripoli, symbolizing the end of the treaty, and the other Barbary nations joined him in resuming raids against American ships. Congress was not in session, but on May 14, 1801, Jefferson decided to resist paying the increased tribute. Backed by his Cabinet, he dispatched three frigates and a sloop of war to the Mediterranean to protect American ships, with orders to take no offensive action since Congress had not declared a state of war. In time the undeclared war turned hot, and the American warships had to meet attacks by the pirates. As the conflict dragged on, Jefferson each year asked for a low level of appropriations, Congress voted them, and the Mediterranean squadron was modestly enlarged. But no war was declared.

Finally, in 1805, the combination of a blockade of the Tripoli coast and the dramatic capture of Derna in Tripoli by a motley force of Turks, Greeks, and eight American Marines forced the truculent pasha of Tripoli to sue for peace. Hostilities ended, and the United States paid a final ransom of $60,000 to the pasha for prisoners he still held. The other Barbary powers also demanded settlements, and in November, 1805, Sidi Suleiman Mellimelli, the personal emissary of the bey of Tunis, arrived in Washington on an American frigate. Dressed in scarlet and gold, wearing a white muslin turban, and smoking a pipe more than four feet long, he set up headquarters in Stelle's Hotel near the Capitol and created a sensation. He was taken to visit the House of Representatives and the Senate, being offered a chair of honor in each chamber. In the House the Tunisian envoy watched a debate, and in the Senate he conversed in Italian with Senator Buckner Thruston of Kentucky. He was curious about the House, he told Thruston; if each member were allowed to talk on an issue, would it not take a year for that body to come to a decision? Later he got down to business in Washington with Secretary of State Madison. To the disgust of many Americans—but to the satisfaction of others, who thought that the appropriation of tribute would be less burdensome than the cost and problems of continued warfare—periodic payments to all the Barbary states other than Tripoli were finally agreed upon and were continued until 1816, when the marauding power of the North Africans was at last broken.

In 1802 another threat to American interests suddenly arose. Early that year an alarmed Jefferson received confirmation of rumors that, by the Treaty of San Ildefonso in 1800, Spain had agreed to turn over Louisiana

A New York City parade for the new Constitution in 1788

Washington's inauguration outside the Senate chamber in New York's Federal Hall, April 30, 1789

The first home of the House of Representatives in Federal Hall

An impression of the first Senate, with members seated
around Vice President John Adams

The highly partisan Alexander Hamilton

Senator Robert Morris of Pennsylvania

The first Speaker, Pennsylvania's Frederick Muhlenberg, a former Lutheran pastor

*Senator William Maclay,
the diarist*

*Veteran statesman Richard
Henry Lee*

The Federalist leader Fisher Ames

John Adams of Massachusetts

A 1798 view of the Lyon-Griswold brawl in the House

A Federalist caricature of Albert Gallatin

Vice President Aaron Burr

Georgia's Senator William H. Crawford

The Capitol after the British burned it in 1814

James Monroe

The erratic John Randolph of Roanoke

John Quincy Adams, President and then Congressman

John Quincy Adams, "Old Man Eloquent," fatally stricken at his desk in the House in 1848

Daniel Webster and Andrew Jackson at a White House ball, 1824

COLONEL CROCKETT DELIVERING HIS CELEBRATED SPEECH TO CONGRESS.

A contemporary version of a Davy Crockett speech

An 1832 campaign attack on Jackson

BORN TO COMMAND.

OF VETO MEMORY.

HAD I BEEN CONSULTED.

KING ANDREW THE FIRST.

Champion of states' rights:
John C. Calhoun of
South Carolina

The great Speaker Henry Clay   *The imposing Daniel Webster*

The Senate, with packed galleries, in the 1840's

SCENE IN UNCLE SAM'S SENATE.
17TH APRIL 1850.

"Hangman" Foote threatens "Old Bullion" Benton in 1850

Clay's memorable appeal for the Compromise of 1850

Stephen A. Douglas, who precipitated the Kansas-Nebraska crisis

Scenes in the Senate and House at the start of the session in 1853

Senator Sumner caned by Representative Brooks in 1856

Pre–Civil War mayhem in the House over the Kansas issue

Congress in turmoil on the eve of disunion in 1859

New York Zouaves quartered in the House chamber, 1861

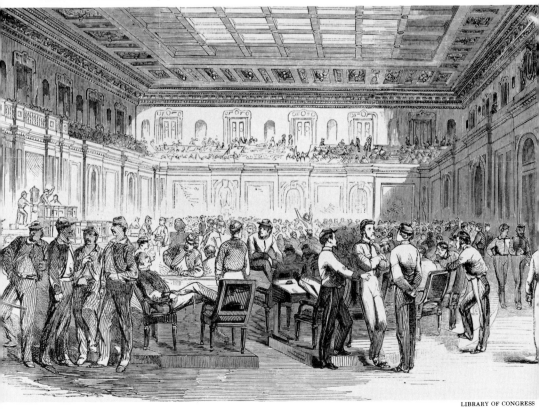

Troops baking bread in the basement of the Capitol

HARPER'S WEEKLY, MAY 25, 1861

Carrying the mace into the House of Representatives

to Napoleon. In October came worse news: although the transfer had not yet been made, the Spanish intendant at New Orleans had closed that port to Americans. The news aroused the westerners, who set up a clamor for war against Spain. They were soon joined by enthusiastic Federalists, who saw a chance to embarrass Jefferson—who was opposed to a war—as well as an opportunity to win converts for themselves in the West. With mounting concern, the President pondered the situation and gradually came to a decision.

There was nothing in his annual message of 1802 about the western developments, but delicate plans, worked out with his congressional lieutenants, were already afoot. Two days after Congress received the presidential message, John Randolph rose in the House and moved that the government submit to Congress all documents relating to the closure of New Orleans. On December 22, 1802, Jefferson submitted the documents, and the House went into closed session. When it opened its doors on January 7, 1803, it announced what Jefferson wanted to hear. By a vote of 50 to 25 the Representatives resolved to give the chief executive authority to take "such measures" as were necessary "for asserting the rights and vindicating the injuries of the United States." Four days later in the House, once again behind closed doors, Samuel Smith of Maryland moved for an appropriation of $2 million "to defray any expenses which may be incurred in relation to the intercourse between the United States and foreign nations . . . to be applied under the direction of the President of the United States . . . an account whereof, as soon as may be, shall be laid before Congress." The resolution was referred to a committee headed by Maryland's Joseph H. Nicholson, another loyal Jeffersonian, who moved its adoption. When it returned to the House it was passed. To the Senate, at the same time, Jefferson sent the nomination of James Monroe as envoy extraordinary to France to join the resident minister, Robert R. Livingston. The nomination was quickly approved, and Monroe set sail for France on March 8, 1803. Jefferson's plans were now fairly well known: without recourse to war, he would secure access to the sea for Americans in the interior West and South by buying from France New Orleans and the two Floridas (which he erroneously thought were included in Spain's cession to Napoleon).

To some extent, Jefferson was moved by his own dreams of empire. The unknown wilderness of the West had always intrigued him, and he envisioned its settlement and exploitation by an American people who would grow prosperous by looking westward rather than toward Europe. His vision included extinguishing the Indians' title to their lands, by fair means if possible, by foul if necessary, and their removal west of the Mississippi, where they could be isolated from hostile whites until they became civilized husbandmen.

At the time Monroe left for France, Jefferson had no idea of buying from Napoleon the vast Louisiana country. But he had long wished to know about it—and indeed about the entire trans-Mississippi West—and the

129

new developments reawakened his interest. He now thought that it might be explored with the aims of opening it to the American fur trade and finding an overland route to the Pacific. Just a week after asking the House for $2 million to treat with "foreign nations" over the New Orleans closing and sending Monroe's nomination to the Senate, he delivered a confidential message to Congress requesting an appropriation of $2,500 for an exploratory expedition across the country "for the purpose of extending the external commerce of the United States." To allay the suspicions of France and Spain, the undertaking would be announced as "a literary pursuit," implying a purely scientific aim. Both houses of Congress agreed, and within a year the Lewis and Clark Expedition was under way. By the time those explorers set off, however, all of Louisiana, as far west as the Rocky Mountains, had become American through a surprise development in France.

In Paris Monroe and Livingston found that, because of a changing military situation, Napoleon wished to sell the United States not only New Orleans but the entire province of Louisiana. Exceeding their instructions, the American envoys consummated the deal for some $15 million. The agreement, which more than doubled the geographic size of the United States, reached the United States at the end of June. It created a sensation and raised a number of serious questions, among them whether the government had the constitutional right to buy a foreign country. At first Jefferson considered submitting to Congress a constitutional amendment to permit the transaction. But word came from the envoys in Paris that Napoleon might change his mind if the purchase agreement was not ratified by the agreed-upon date, and aware of the need for speed, Jefferson summoned Congress into early session, opening on October 17, 1803. Apprising his stalwarts in both houses of the necessity for "as little debate as possible, & particularly so far as respects the constitutional difficulty," he asked the Senate to ratify the purchase and the House to authorize the issuance of bonds to make up the difference between the $2 million already appropriated and the full purchase price.

The agreement contained several guarantees that concerned members of both houses, particularly the Federalists. The inhabitants of the new territory were eventually to become American citizens, and the area itself was to be divided in the future into new states rather than governed as a province or colony. To the Federalists this spelled doom. Despite their earlier support of a war to secure New Orleans, they now recognized more realistically that the new western states would more likely be permanently Republican than Federalist and would shift economic and political power away from the Northeast. At the same time, many legislators were disturbed by the prospect of what amounted to a huge foreign land suddenly being made a part of the United States, with its inhabitants soon to become equal to all other Americans and its lands enabled to enter the Union as states with the same rights and powers enjoyed by the other states. Raising a cry that the new territory would "absorb" the rest of the country and cause the dissolution of the Union, the Federalists in both houses abruptly took the old position of the Republicans and argued that the issue involved an unconstitutional extension of federal power that usurped the rights of the states. In words reminiscent of Jefferson's and Madison's Kentucky and Virginia Resolutions, they demanded that the question of ratification be decided by the states. The Republicans, in turn, argued like Federalists, declaring that the federal government could make the purchase under the "implied powers" construction of the Constitution.

In the end, the sheer size of the Republican majorities in both houses gave Jefferson the votes he requested. On October 20, 1803, the Senate overwhelmingly ratified the purchase, 24 to 7. The House moved more slowly, but by November 10 it too approved the purchase, appropriated the necessary funds, and vested the President with the necessary powers to take over Louisiana. On December 30, 1803, the American flag was raised above New Orleans, signifying the transfer of the territory.

The problems of the Southwest were now increasingly to attract the attention of the President and Congress and lead to several dramatic developments, including a split between Jefferson and Randolph. The latter had already shown signs of independence from the President, chafing at Jefferson's occasional use of other members of the House to give leadership on certain administration measures and on a number of issues going his own way in opposition to Jefferson's wishes. The fiasco of the Chase impeachment did not help relations between Randolph and the President, and with the opening of the first session of the Ninth Congress on December 2, 1805, matters came to a head. Macon was re-elected Speaker, but only on the fourth ballot after a contest with Joseph B. Varnum, a distinguished Massachusetts jurist and Republican who had first entered Congress in 1795. The challenge to Macon reflected not only an antagonism to Randolph and his friends on the part of the growing number of northern Republicans in the House, but the beginnings of a sectional rivalry characterized by the northerners' opposition to the hardening of the states'-rights feelings of southerners in their own party. The unwavering loyalty of the states' righters to their old principles had been evident during the debates on the Louisiana Purchase, when a number of them deserted Jefferson to oppose the extension of federal power and join the Federalists in urging that the acquisition be voted upon by the states. But Randolph posed still another threat. It was part of Jefferson's greatness that he could change with changing situations and adopt tactics and points of view representing total reversals from earlier positions. Randolph, despite his eccentricities, had great integrity and hated sham and fraud, and he considered Jefferson's maneuverings devious and dishonest. Under the circumstances, it was disastrous when Macon, upon winning re-election to the speakership, again named Randolph to head the House Ways and Means Committee.

At stake was a growing controversy with Spain over the status of West Florida, which controlled the access to a number of important rivers flowing through the South to Gulf ports such as Mobile. Though the wording of the Louisiana Purchase agreement was ambiguous on the subject, Congress had been sure that West Florida was included in the acquisition. On November 30, 1803, Randolph had introduced a bill formally annexing that district and authorizing the President to organize the Mobile area and all the waters entering the Gulf of Mexico east of Mobile for the collection of customs. Congress passed the bill and Jefferson signed it. But Spain soon objected that she had never ceded the region to France and still owned it. Though France confirmed this to the United States, the matter remained in controversy, and serious clashes occurred in the area between Spaniards and Americans. As a new war fever mounted against Spain, Jefferson vacillated. Finally, he learned that, for a payment, France would intercede and see that Spain peaceably turned over West Florida to the United States. Jefferson decided to pursue that course, but he recognized that he could not reveal publicly that the settlement would rest on a bribe to France.

On December 3, 1805, in his annual message to the new Congress, he rattled the sword against Spain, recounting American grievances against that country and implying readiness to use force to seize West Florida. Three days later, however, he bewildered Congress by sending it a confidential message hinting that war against Spain might not be necessary. When the message was turned over to Randolph's committee, that Congressman, in some puzzlement, went to see Jefferson to learn what he had meant. The President was now on guard against Randolph, but he told him that he wished Congress to appropriate, in the same secrecy with which it had handled the Louisiana negotiations, $2 million for him to purchase West Florida. Randolph blew up; he wanted no more secrecy, and he was opposed to paying for West Florida, which he felt the United States already owned. His committee met on December 7 and he denounced Spain for extortion and Jefferson for dishonorable tactics in not having submitted his request for the appropriation openly in his official message. But the worst was still to come. From Madison, Randolph learned that the money would be paid to France as a bribe. This information was the final straw. Randolph said he was disgusted and wanted nothing more to do with men capable of such double-dealing. Breaking with the administration, he ultimately formed a new coalition of about a dozen like-minded Republicans, including for a while Macon and Joseph Nicholson. In time this independent group, in effect America's first third party, became known as the Tertium Quids and gave Jefferson much trouble.

Meanwhile, despite considerable opposition to the President's method of acquiring West Florida, a bill for the $2 million finally went through the House—managed by a new Jeffersonian lieutenant, freshman Congressman Barnabas Bidwell of Massachusetts—and passed the Senate, though four Republicans voted against it and three others absented themselves. John Quincy Adams, who had entered the Senate in 1803 nominally as a Federalist but as independent and ruggedly honest as his father and eventually to become a Republican, wrote following the vote: "The measure has been very reluctantly adopted by the President's friends, on his private wishes. . . . His whole system of administration seems founded upon this principle of carrying through the legislative measures by his personal or official influence. There is a certain portion of the members in both Houses who on every occasion . . . have no other inquiry but what is the President's wish." Randolph was, as usual, more acid. Bitterly he denounced those who had supported Jefferson as "pages of the presidential water closet." The President signed the bill on February 7, 1806, but in the end it was all for nothing. Napoleon, turning aside Jefferson's emissary, now decided that West Florida should remain in Spanish hands, and there it stayed for the time being.

The West had one more dramatic event in store for Jefferson. Like a magnet, the Louisiana Purchase had drawn all manner of American adventurers and fortune hunters, as well as settlers, into the country beyond the Appalachians. Far from the reach, as well as the aid, of the American government and placed on their own resources, they lived in a raw world of self-reliance and independence, filled with talk of intrigue, plots against, and with, Spain, and even separatism from the United States and the erection of new western empires. Into that country, after his term as Vice President ended, had gone Aaron Burr, traveling down the Ohio and Mississippi rivers to New Orleans and on his way visiting every notable along the route. Burr had become interested in a number of projects, but he told those he visited of one particular scheme that he had in mind—the leading of an assault against Spain in the Southwest that would liberate Mexico and perhaps even South America—and they had all given him patronizing (and patriotic) encouragement.

By December, 1805, however, rumors began reaching Washington from the West that Burr was really organizing a military expedition to separate the western states from the rest of the United States. Evidence of a large-scale conspiracy began to accumulate, and in August, 1806, it was confirmed that Burr had recruited a private armed force and started down the Ohio River with it. Meanwhile, one of Burr's fellow plotters, General James Wilkinson, had panicked and sent Jefferson a cipher letter he had received from Burr, seemingly corroborating the worst suspicions about the former Vice President's plans and stating that Burr had British support for his venture. Though all was still mystery, the affair now appeared menacing to the safety of a large part of the United States. In alarm, Jefferson ordered the arrest of all participants in the plot and informed Congress fully.

On February 19, 1807, Burr was arrested in the Southwest, and though by that time it was well established that reports of his force and his plans had been grossly exaggerated, he was sent back to Richmond, Virginia, to be tried for treason. Unwilling to believe anything but the worst about his former Vice President, Jefferson practically directed the prosecution himself and became infuriated when he realized that most of his enemies, including Federalists and dissident Republicans, were lining up behind Burr.

In addition, all Jefferson's hatred for the independent, Federalist-dominated judiciary was reawakened by the fact that Chief Justice John Marshall presided over the trial. And, as a final horror, he learned that none other than John Randolph was foreman of the jury.

Though the weakness of the case against Burr was apparent almost at once, Jefferson tenaciously tried to develop evidence against him. He not only failed, but had the tables turned against him when Marshall, at the request of the defense, issued a subpoena for the President's appearance at the trial with all the letters and papers on which he had based the information about the alleged conspiracy that he gave to Congress. Jefferson exploded in fury, but though he did not go to Richmond, he sent the requested papers, and Marshall dropped the issue of his personal appearance, preferring not to press a constitutional confrontation over that question. Soon afterward the trial ended abruptly. The defense moved for a dismissal on the grounds that no evidence of an overt act by Burr had been produced, and the jury rendered a decision of acquittal. Burr thereafter went into hiding and eventually ended up in Europe. During the War of 1812 he returned to the United States and lived the rest of his life quietly.

Jefferson, meanwhile, fulminated against the decision and tried to launch a new attack on the federal judiciary, hoping to bring it under control this time by a constitutional amendment. In November, 1807, bills were introduced in the Senate by Edward Tiffin of Ohio and in the House by George Washington Campbell of Tennessee for an amendment that would limit federal judges to a term of years and provide for their removal by the President on the request of two thirds of the members of both houses. The amendment would have destroyed the independence of the judiciary, making it subservient to the other two branches of government, but it was sent to committees in both houses and never reported out. At the same time, responding to Jefferson's urging of legislation that would prevent a repetition of what he considered a miscarriage of justice in the Burr case, William Giles introduced in the Senate a tyrannical bill advocating the death sentence for all persons assembling to resist a law as well as for anyone, even if not present, who assisted the purpose of the assembly. The measure, which outdid anything conceived by the Federalists in the days of the Alien and Sedition Acts, passed the Senate but was killed by the House. The hysteria, mostly politically produced and motivated, gradually subsided, leaving to history continued puzzlement over what "Burr's conspiracy" had actually been about and equal wonderment at the savage fanaticism of Jefferson's reaction to it.

To some extent, the President's handling of the Burr trial and his followers' overreaction during its aftermath reflected a serious "ungluing" of the Republican party, and of Jefferson's hold over it, that set in during his second administration. Randolph's defection was only a part of the problem, as was the loss of political influence of a "lame-duck" President. The real source of difficulty was the foreign situation, which month after month—as

Britain fought for her life against Napoleon—frustrated the President, the Congress, and the nation. In the process, tempers ran exceedingly short.

The situation first became grave early in 1805, when Britain stepped up her harassment of American ships and impressment of American seamen. Ports such as New York were literally blockaded by British warships that stopped every ship passing in or out. Dead set against rebuilding the navy, Jefferson, in March, 1805, asked for and received authority to construct up to twenty-five small gunboats and to take various legal steps to halt the British activities at American ports. Nothing proved effective, however, and as the nation's humiliation and the financial losses of shippers mounted, he delivered a sober State of the Union message to the first session of the Ninth Congress in December, 1805, asking for new measures, short of war, to cope with Britain. Various nonimportation resolutions, designed to bring England to terms by halting imports from her or from her colonies until she relented in her hostile acts against the United States, were immediately introduced by a number of members of both houses. In the view of Randolph, nonimportation was a dastardly policy that was merely cover for the protection of American merchants and shippers who made profits as neutrals by carrying the products of a belligerent, and that would lead inevitably to war. When debate got under way in the House on one of the first resolutions, Randolph screamed his opposition to the "incipient war measures." "If this great agricultural nation," he declaimed, "is to be governed by Salem and Boston, New York and Philadelphia, and Baltimore, and Norfolk and Charleston, let gentlemen come out and say so. . . . I, for one, will not mortgage my property and my liberty, to carry on this trade. . . ."

When this resolution was turned down in Committee of the Whole, another one, introduced by Maryland's Joseph Nicholson and approved by Jefferson, was taken up. Once again Randolph led the attack, delivering long tirades against the President and Madison and heaping abuse on everyone who disagreed with him. His harangues were so violent and dramatic that Senators left their own chamber to watch him, as if he were a performer. At length Jefferson let it be known that Randolph had to be beaten, and on March 26, 1806, Nicholson's nonimportation bill won, 93 to 32. In the Senate, meanwhile, a resolution was passed urging Jefferson to send negotiators to England to try to settle the conflict by a new treaty with that country. Suspending the implementation of the newly passed Nonimportation Act so that it would not interfere with the treaty negotiations, Jefferson dispatched James Monroe and William Pinkney of Maryland to London, but the document they signed on December 1, 1806, and sent back to Washington was more disastrous than Jay's Treaty had been. It said nothing about America's principal complaint, the impressment of her seamen, and was otherwise so meaningless that Jefferson rejected it and did not even send it to the Senate.

The second session of the Ninth Congress, meanwhile, assembled in Washington in December, 1806. Among northern Republicans, who had had enough of Randolph, there was a spirit of revolt. Congressman James Sloan of New Jersey listed a score of complaints against the chairman of the Ways and Means Committee, among them his imperiousness with other members and his highhandedness—tying up committee business, keeping appropriation estimates for the army and navy "in his pocket, or locked up in his desk," and holding up important bills till the end of the session "when many members are gone home." Sloan moved that all standing committees be elected by ballot and "choose their own chairmen." The motion was defeated, but Speaker Macon recognized the majority sentiment and the inadvisability of continuing to place leadership in the hands of Jefferson's bitterest enemy; and though it upset him greatly to have to do so, he appointed a northerner, Joseph Clay, a Pennsylvania banker, as chairman of the Ways and Means Committee.

Except for one piece of legislation, it was a short and relatively uneventful session. In his annual message Jefferson reminded the lawmakers that under the Constitution Congress now could—and should—bring an end to the slave trade after January 1, 1808. Resolutions were introduced, and despite much wrangling between the two houses (and many more violent speeches by Randolph) over southern amendments regarding the right to transport slaves between states, a bill was finally passed on March 2, 1807, and the importation of slaves into the United States was at last prohibited by law as of the end of that year.

The Ninth Congress ended on March 3, and in June, with no Congress in session, a new crisis with England suddenly arose. A few miles off the Virginia coast the British frigate *Leopard* halted the American warship *Chesapeake*, carrying Commodore James Barron to take command of the Mediterranean squadron. When Barron refused to permit the British to come aboard and look for British deserters in his crew, the British opened fire and killed three men and wounded eighteen others. The British seized four crewmen as deserters (only one was an Englishman), and the *Chesapeake* limped back to port. The news of the unprovoked attack on an American naval vessel raised a patriotic storm. Jefferson issued a proclamation ordering British warships to leave American waters, demanded reparation and apologies, and called the Tenth Congress into session in October—more than a month early, but long enough away to allow tempers to cool.

Save for Randolph and about twenty Quids, the new Congress began as a solid Jeffersonian one, replacing Macon as Speaker with Joseph B. Varnum of Massachusetts and appointing another Jefferson ally, Scottish-born, Princeton-educated George Campbell of Tennessee, chairman of the House Ways and Means Committee. In addition to the *Chesapeake-Leopard* affair, British orders in council and French decrees, setting up blockades and counterblockades, were bringing America close to war with one or both of the belligerents. Jefferson asked Congress for appropriations to organize and arm the militia, continue the fortifying of harbors, and build more small gunboats for coastal defense, and they were voted (though

Randolph flailed away at the requests, ridiculing the navy as "the Gunboat Department" and denouncing a policy that built gunboats to protect the coast and forts to protect the gunboats). But with the failure of Monroe's mission, the ineffectiveness of the Nonimportation Act, and the measures by both Britain and France to enforce their orders against American shipping, the President now recommended a new economic step designed to bring the belligerents to terms without going to war. On December 18, 1807, he asked Congress to pass an embargo on all foreign commerce. It was a drastic step that would halt all of America's foreign trade, but Jefferson hoped that this would be so sorely missed by Britain or France, or both, that America's rights as a neutral would again be recognized. Dispensing with all rules, the Senate rushed the proposal into a committee. Helped by John Quincy Adams, who had become an enthusiastic administration supporter, it was reported back almost immediately as a bill ("The President has recommended the measure on his high responsibility. I would not consider, I would not deliberate; I would act!" Adams told the Senate) and was passed, 22 to 6, on the same day that Jefferson asked for it. In the House, Randolph and the Quids, along with angry Federalists, held it up temporarily, attacking it as unconstitutional (Congress could regulate commerce, not destroy it); but Campbell, Jefferson's floor leader, insisted on a loose construction of the Constitution, and on December 22 it passed, 82 to 44.

Meanwhile, Jefferson, who would retire in 1809, was considering his successor. He had selected Madison, but a number of Virginians, aided by Randolph, pushed Monroe, whom they considered more loyal to Republican principles. To pull things together, Jefferson again relied on the political maneuverings of John Beckley, who, in addition to his duties as clerk of the House, was serving as the first librarian of Congress. (The Library of Congress, housed, together with the Senate, in the north wing of the Capitol, had been established by a congressional act in 1800, with a $5,000 appropriation for books deemed helpful to the Senators and Representatives. Along with his duties as clerk, Beckley kept watch over the books.) The librarian-politician personally preferred Monroe, thinking Madison "too timid and indecisive as a statesman, and too liable to a conduct of forebearance to the federal party which may endanger our harmony and political safety." But he did Jefferson's bidding, and at a caucus in the early spring of 1808 in Washington, some eighty-nine Republican Senators and Congressmen nominated Madison. George Clinton was once more chosen for Vice President. To run against Madison and Clinton the Federalists again chose their 1804 slate, Charles Cotesworth Pinckney and Rufus King, and again they were beaten.

The embargo, in the meantime, was having little effect on England and France but was proving a disaster for the United States. By the fall of 1808 merchants and shippers, particularly in New England, New York, and Pennsylvania, were approaching a state of rebellion. The Federalist party, almost defunct, came aggressively back to life. In New England old Federalists of the "Essex Junto"—a small group of extremists who for many years had tried to guide Federalist opposition to Jefferson—secretly negotiated with British officials for an alliance with England and openly called for nullification of the Embargo Act and even secession from the Union. In Connecticut former Federalist Senator Jonathan Trumbull, now governor, refused to enforce the embargo, and in northern Vermont, where smugglers used fleets of rafts on Lake Champlain to move goods to Canada, Jefferson declared a state of insurrection and called on civil and military powers to enforce the law. Elsewhere in the country the situation was no better. People relying on imports suffered, and exporters in the South— including Jefferson himself—were losing fortunes as crops lay in warehouses and rotted.

The mounting chaos around the country was reflected in Washington. As the economy stagnated and local riots and mob action increased, Gallatin turned against the embargo, but he could not persuade Jefferson to drop it. Soon every member of the Cabinet but Madison was opposed to the policy. In the 1808 elections the Federalists for the first time in years cut heavily into the Republican vote, sweeping New England and much of New York. By that time the Republicans themselves were divided. When Congress reassembled in November, 1808, for the last session under Jefferson, party lieutenants and stalwarts faced demands on every hand for the repeal of Jefferson's catastrophic "experiment." In the Senate Giles, carrying the struggle for Jefferson and Madison, fought off a Federalist resolution to repeal the embargo, and his committee reported out two administration bills, one for a stricter enforcement of the Embargo Act and the other for the use of the navy against violators. The Federalists were wild with fury, but the enforcement bill was passed and sent to the House. In that body a repeal resolution was also beaten, and measures for stronger enforcement were introduced. Macon, who had deserted Randolph's Quids and was back with the administration forces, threw his help behind Jefferson's floor leader, George Washington Campbell. Though citizens' petitions for repeal flooded the House, Campbell held his forces in line for the President. Speeches were long and inflammatory, and personal fights broke out.

On January 6, 1809, the House passed the Senate's enforcement act, with some amendments, and the stern measure became law three days later. It was greeted by anguished outcries and new resistance, particularly in New England. Obviously it could not last long, for, as many pointed out, even the enforcement act could not be enforced. With insurrection spreading and the battered and wearied Jefferson looking forward anxiously to his retirement, the Republicans in Congress (in "panic," said Jefferson) finally forced an administration about-face. On February 28, with such loyal Jeffersonians as Giles leading the way, Congress repealed the Embargo Act, substituting the Nonintercourse Act, which permitted American trade with every country except England and France. "Never did a prisoner, released from his chains, feel such relief as I shall on shaking off the shackles of power," Jefferson wrote to a friend on March 2. The next day, divided, shaken, and leaderless, the Tenth Congress came to an end, and on March 4 Madison was inaugurated.

A week later Jefferson left for Monticello, never to return to Washington. In retirement he struck up a friendly communication again with his old Revolutionary colleague—and political opponent—John Adams. By an odd stroke of fate, the two ex-Presidents were to die on the same day, July 4, 1826, the fiftieth anniversary of the Declaration of Independence, which owed as much to them as to any other two men. Like many Presidents, neither left office under happy conditions. But the perspective of time, by 1826, had confirmed them both as among the foremost of America's illustrious founders. The phenomenon of their death on the fiftieth birthday of the nation awed all Americans and reawakened a patriotic regard for their accomplishments. The "like has never happened in the world, nor can it ever happen again," wrote the New York *National Advocate* of the news of their death. The "beauteous moral must forever stand alone on the page of history."

Madison, though conscientious, was not the right man for the crisis in which Jefferson had left the country. Now chief executive of the government he had played so large a role in launching, he proved to be weak and indecisive as President. It was almost as if the drubbings he had taken in Congress from the Hamiltonians during Washington's administration had disheartened the earlier, confident Madison. He had retired from politics in 1797, and when he came back to become Jefferson's secretary of state he was another man—older, wearier, less innovative and inspiring, less willing to get into a fight and be bruised. When Washington Irving saw the President and his wife, Dolley, in 1811, he observed, "Mrs. Madison is a fine, portly, buxom dame, who has a smile and pleasant word for everybody . . . but as to Jemmy Madison—ah poor Jemmy!—he is but a withered little apple-john." Even before the inauguration, three Republican members of Congress— Giles, Senator Michael Leib of Pennsylvania, and Representative Wilson Cary Nicholas of Virginia—dictated to him the selection of his secretary of state, persuading him that the Senate would block his own choice, Albert Gallatin, and making him take Nicholas's inept, guileful brother-in-law, Robert Smith, Jefferson's do-nothing secretary of the navy. Smith was an intriguer and caused division in the Cabinet. He was a brother, moreover, of Senator Samuel Smith of Maryland, who was a corrupt, conspiratorial ringmaster of a small antiadministration faction in the upper chamber, and the combination of the two Smiths often undermined the President. Madison, passive and vacillating, was willing to let Congress lead, and the primacy of power in the national government passed quickly and without contest from the executive to the legislative branch. And yet, to a nation that was divided, frustrated, and in serious economic difficulties, the Congress, too, was of little help. It had grown used to looking to the administration for leadership. Now it was rent by factions, filled with mediocre men, and without strong leadership of its own. For two years the United States would flounder.

Madison tried to carry on Jefferson's policy of economic coercion against England and France, but the Nonintercourse Act, in which he had little confidence, was as unworkable as the Embargo Act. He made no significant recommendation for new action, preferring to leave decision to "the wisdom of the national Legislature." The Congress, however, was more divided and rudderless than before. Gallatin, who had been persuaded to remain as secretary of the treasury, warned of an impending Treasury deficit due to the decline of customs receipts. In an effort to break the impasse and permit an increase in imports and duties, he, Madison, and Macon drew up a tortuous bill that retained most prohibitions on trade, but planned to allow the entry of British and French goods if they were carried in American vessels. The measure, introduced by Macon, was passed by the House, amended into uselessness by Senator Smith, and finally killed. This was followed by protracted wrangling over a series of resolutions introduced by Randolph to reduce the armed forces. By April, 1810, all Randolph's resolutions had been killed. Another measure—known as Macon's Bill No. 2, though Macon voted against it himself—was finally enacted. It was a strange measure, reflecting a growing desperation. It ended the Nonintercourse Act, removing all restrictions on trade with both Britain and France, but authorized the President to revive nonintercourse against either power if the other one should "cease to violate the neutral commerce of the United States." In other words, it offered something of a bribe to both powers: end your violations against us, it said to each country, and we will apply nonintercourse against your opponent. The act became law on May 1, 1810.

Trade with Britain immediately rose, but it was only temporary. Learning of Macon's Bill No. 2, Napoleon in August communicated word to the United States that France would repeal her decrees that had interfered with American commerce provided that Britain did the same and, if not, that the United States reinstituted nonintercourse against that nation. Madison received information that the French decrees had actually been canceled, accepted Napoleon's word, and on November 2 proclaimed the reopening of commerce with France and a halt, once again, to trade with Britain unless she repealed her offensive orders in council by February 2, 1811. Although Great Britain claimed that France was deceiving Madison and had not canceled her decrees (a suspicion entertained, as well, by many members of Congress), Madison clung to his decision either because he was being duped or because he hoped to force Britain into favorable action toward the United States. On March 2, 1811, also relying on France's assurance, a new session of Congress supported Madison and sanctioned his action against Britain. The American course impelled angry and vigorous British retaliatory moves, including a renewal of the blockade of New York and a redoubling of the impressment of American seamen. Great Britain had been correct about the French: Napoleon had deliberately deceived

Madison. Madison was now helpless, unwilling to admit to the nation that Napoleon had tricked him and unable to reverse American policy again.

In the meantime, Congress had to deal with other matters. The most important was the renewal of the charter of the United States Bank, established by the Hamiltonians in 1791 for a twenty-year period. On December 10, 1810, a petition from the bank directors for renewal, strongly supported by Gallatin, had been received by the Senate and referred to a five-man committee headed by Senator William H. Crawford of Georgia. Crawford, a huge, handsome man of thirty-nine, six feet three inches in height and weighing over two hundred pounds, exemplified a new breed of forthright southerners and westerners who, self-assured, intensely patriotic, and raised amid the rawness, violence, and cocky "half a horse, half an alligator, I can lick anything on earth" atmosphere of the frontier, were beginning to enter Congress. During his rise to the Senate, which he reached in 1807, only eight years after having begun the practice of law in Georgia, Crawford had fought two duels and killed one of his opponents. Still somewhat unpolished, he had a blunt, good-humored intelligence and would eventually become one of America's leading statesmen and—until paralyzed by a series of strokes in 1823—the front runner for the presidency in 1824. On February 5, 1811, he reported a bill from his committee to extend the bank's life for another twenty years. The measure ran into trouble at once from many old-line Republicans, who revived the issue of the bank's constitutionality. But there were additional opponents also, notably the brothers Smith and others (known as the Invisibles), who waged a furtive and devious opposition because of their dislike for Gallatin. The most vocal opponent, however, was Senator Henry Clay of Kentucky, who reflected the opposition of his state to a national bank and attacked the holdings of British investors in the bank as dangerous to the United States.

Clay was a magnetic personality, thirty-four years old, tall and slender, usually dressed in a flowered waistcoat. He had been born and raised in Virginia and trained in law and the classics in Richmond by the noted George Wythe, a signer of the Declaration of Independence and the first American professor of law (Jefferson, Monroe, and Marshall were among his students). After moving to Kentucky, Clay had begun the practice of law in Lexington in 1797 and then entered that state's house of representatives. He had first come to the Senate to fill a vacancy in 1806, when he was under thirty—a violation of the Constitution—but he served only a few months. Returning to Kentucky's House of Representatives, he became its speaker, gaining a reputation also as the most successful criminal lawyer in the state. In January, 1810, he was again elected to the Senate to fill a vacancy, and he startled that body by a challenging speech in favor of war against Britain and the conquest of Canada. America, he proclaimed, needed "a new race of heroes" to achieve "deeds of glory and renown" like those of "the illustrious founders of our freedom." The conquest of Canada, he boasted to the Senators, "is in your power. I trust I shall not be deemed presumptuous when I state that I verily believe that the militia of Kentucky are alone competent to place Montreal and Upper Canada at your feet."

Bold and dramatic as an orator, Clay was also extremely personable, charming, and tactful. In time he would become, in the words of Clement Eaton, one of his biographers, "the epitome of the American politician," fighting to preserve the Union with a mastery of political arts and skills seldom equaled in Congress. Like Crawford, he was of the new breed. The West flowed in his veins and poured forth in his oratory. As spokesman for western interests, he gained many nicknames—"Gallant Harry of the West," "the Cock of Kentucky," and "the Western Star," among them. Randolph came to hate him and reviled him with what John F. Kennedy in *Profiles in Courage* characterized as "perhaps the most memorable and malignant sentence in the history of personal abuse"—"this being, so brilliant yet so corrupt, which, like a rotten mackerel by moonlight, shines and stinks." Most men, however, loved him. "I don't like Henry Clay," John C. Calhoun said. "He is a bad man, an imposter, a creator of wicked schemes. I wouldn't speak to him, but, by God, I love him." He was a radiant, whiskey-drinking, card-playing, horse-loving, one-hundred-percent American, and he would be one of the greatest Speakers the House of Representatives ever had, elected to that office six times and never seriously contested. "Decide, decide promptly, and never give your reasons for the decision," he once advised another Speaker. "The House will sustain your decisions, but there will always be men to cavil and quarrel about your reasons." In a few months, he would begin to give his brand of self-confident leadership to the House.

Crawford did his best to push the bank renewal bill through the Senate, but the combined opposition of the anti-Gallatin forces, the strict constitutionalists, and Henry Clay was too strong. Though Madison had now come to favor the bank, he refrained from interference, and the measure finally lost by a 17–17 tie vote and a deciding vote in the negative cast by Vice President Clinton. Gallatin was so resentful that he submitted his resignation, but Madison refused to accept it and, instead, fired Secretary of State Smith, with whose intrigues he had finally lost patience. In April, 1811, he appointed his old rival, James Monroe, to succeed Smith. At the same time Henry Clay, who would later regret his stand against the bank—which now went out of business and would be sorely missed to help with loans and other financing during the War of 1812—decided to leave "the solemn stillness" of the Senate and run, instead, for the more active House of Representatives. He was elected and that November—along with a whole group of young nationalists, most of them newcomers, whose election reflected the voters' impatience with the continued insults to American honor and pride and the frustrations, timidity, and confusion of the administration's policies —arrived in Washington for the opening of the fateful Twelfth Congress.

On November 4, 1811, the first day of the new Congress and Clay's first day in the House of Representatives, he ran for Speaker, and, as a testament to his winning personality, style, and reputation, he was elected on the first ballot. Thereafter the young nationalists, who were charged with energy and purpose and at whom Randolph would soon hurl the angry catchall epithet "War Hawks," grouped around Clay as if they were members of a team. Clay roomed with some of them in a boarding house on New Jersey Avenue, where around the dinner table they shared ideas and plans for legislative strategy and tactics (the building became known in the capital as the "war mess"). Among Clay's fellow lodgers was Felix Grundy of Tennessee, who had once been chief justice of the supreme court of Kentucky, though even now he was only thirty-four years old. Three others were from South Carolina: Langdon Cheves, born thirty-five years before in a frontier stockade to which settlers had retreated during a war with the Cherokee Indians and who had become a lawyer and attorney general of his state; William Lowndes, a planter, captain of militia, and the twenty-nine-year-old younger brother of a former Federalist member of Congress; and John Caldwell Calhoun, a somber, humorless man, also twenty-nine, with a pronounced brow, a heavy shock of long hair, and deep, smoldering eyes. A graduate of Yale and of Tapping Reeve's law school in Litchfield, Connecticut, Calhoun was intelligent, bookish, and among the keenest logicians who would ever come to Congress. Formidable and distant in his relations with others, he was a brilliant and awesome debater. Like Clay, at this stage of his life he was a nationalist; later he would become the greatest spokesman for the South. Unlike Clay, he did not smoke or play cards and he limited his drinking to a polite glass or two of wine.

This group had like-minded allies from other states: Peter B. Porter, a stout, pontifical thirty-eight-year-old trader and lawyer (also educated at Yale and Tapping Reeve's school) from the Niagara frontier of New York State, who was itching to have his country seize Upper Canada; William W. Bibb, a Georgia physician who had entered politics and gazed expansively south and west into Spanish Florida and Creek Indian country and would become the first governor of those lands after they were organized as the Territory of Alabama; John A. Harper of New Hampshire, a graduate of Phillips Exeter Academy, a lawyer, state militia officer, and merchant who had been financially hurt by the Embargo and Nonintercourse acts; Richard Mentor Johnson of Kentucky, thirty-year-old frontiersman, soldier, lawyer, and ambitious politician who would become a colonel in the Kentucky Volunteers during the War of 1812, fight in the West under William Henry Harrison, and then base a long political career on his participation in the killing of the great Shawnee Indian leader, Tecumseh, at the Battle of the Thames in 1813; and the quiet sixty-six-year-old veteran backwoodsman John Sevier of Tennessee, Revolutionary hero of the Battle of King's Mountain, democrat in the First Congress from North Carolina, and the first governor of Tennessee.

Madison's annual message, delivered to the two houses on November 5, reviewed the familiar trade grievances against Great Britain. The situation was as bad as ever, Britain showed no signs of relenting, and, somewhat weakly, Madison called on Congress to "put the United States into an armor and attitude demanded by the crisis." Clay and the westerners were ready for the challenge. News had just arrived of the fierce Battle of Tippecanoe in Indiana between William Henry Harrison and Indian followers of Tecumseh, who many believed were urged on by the British in Canada, and it ignited new demands to take Canada, end the Indian menace, and open new lands for American expansion. The newly elected Speaker at once appointed three select committees in the House—on foreign relations, the military, and the navy—to consider the President's recommendation. To head each committee he named one of the firebreathing nationalists, and the teamwork began to operate.

On November 29 the Committee on Foreign Relations, headed by rotund, wispy-haired Peter B. Porter, reported to the House, intruding enthusiastically into military affairs by urging an increase of ten thousand men for the regular army, fifty thousand volunteers, the repairing and fitting out of all American warships, and permission for merchant ships to arm in their own defense. Randolph took issue with the report, pointing out that the committee had exceeded its responsibility and arguing spiritedly and long against the trend to war. But for the first time, he met his match. Clay called him to order and even had the doorkeeper remove his dog from the floor of the House. When Randolph spoke, there were such men as Calhoun, with greater oratorical talents and more agility in the use of parliamentary tactics, to subdue him. A war fever was now in the air, generated by the passion of the War Hawks and caught up by others, including even the President and Monroe, who were approaching the limit of their frustrations and were beginning to breathe war themselves. "Mr. Monroe has given the strongest assurances that the President will cooperate zealously with Congress in declaring war, if our complaints are not redressed by May next," Representative Lowndes wrote his wife in December, 1811.

A bill to raise an army of twenty-five thousand regulars passed both houses in January, 1812, and an authorization for the President to accept fifty thousand militia followed in February. On January 17 Langdon Cheves, chairman of the Committee on Naval Affairs, reported a bill calling for the construction of ten 38-gun frigates. Clay was aware of the Republicans' traditional opposition to a navy and decided to get into the debate himself. In another significant departure from the traditional role of the Speaker, he arranged with his friends to have all matters on which he wanted to speak referred to a Committee of the Whole so that he could appoint a chairman of that committee, give up the chair, step down on the floor to be recognized, and then add his oratorical talents to the subject under discussion. Despite his arguments for Cheves's navy bill, however, old-time fears and prejudices were still too strong, and Clay's forces and the measure were beaten on January 27—though Porter's proposals for repairing the old ships and allowing merchant ships to arm were passed. At the same time, to Gallatin's consternation, little realism was given to the question of financing the preparedness acts. The United States Bank could no longer render help, and Congress had no stomach for voting new taxes. The Treasury, instead, was authorized to borrow money.

Events moved quickly. On March 15, 1812, Clay asked Monroe to consider having the President "recommend an embargo to last, say, thirty days, by a confidential message; That a termination of the embargo be followed by war. . . ." The embargo, this time, was to give American ships time to return to home ports before a war declaration. Two weeks later, Monroe met with the members of Porter's Foreign Relations Committee. After Calhoun, who was on the committee, assured the secretary of state that the administration could count on Congress' raising money to fight a war, Monroe agreed to have Madison recommend the embargo. Fearful that the country was still too unprepared for a war, and hoping that if he delayed Britain might yet repeal its orders in council and remove the reason for a war declaration, Madison sent the secret message to the House the next day, April 1, 1812, but asked for a sixty-day rather than a thirty-day embargo. The Senate changed the embargo to ninety days, and the measure was passed in secret sessions of both houses.

While the administration tried hurriedly—and with little success—to increase the army to its new, authorized strength, prepare to arm and equip it, and negotiate the borrowing of $11 million to pay for it all, tension against the war moves grew in the Northeast. Although Randolph provided the most vocal opposition to the War Hawks in Congress, a small but outraged band of Federalists led by Josiah Quincy, mostly from New England, opposed Clay and the administration at every turn. Their anger reflected a fury that was building in their home states, especially among the merchant and shipping groups, over the course the country was taking. Trying to hold Massachusetts for the Republicans against a Federalist onslaught in the spring state elections, the Republican legislature in that state, together with the governor, Elbridge Gerry, rearranged the state senatorial districts to favor Republican candidates. One of the districts assumed an absurd geographic shape that looked like a salamander, and a Boston newspaper published it as a cartoon, calling it a Gerry-Mander. The word entered the political lexicon, and the resulting ridicule, together with the growing antiwar feeling in Massachusetts, defeated Gerry's own bid for re-election. In Washington, however, a caucus of 83 of the 133 Republicans in Congress renominated Madison for President on May 18, 1812, and named Gerry for Vice President. In the electoral vote that winter, Madison carried the South and the West, defeating Federalist De Witt Clinton 128 to 89. The New Yorker, reflecting the North's deep dissatisfaction with the war, won every state north of the Potomac except Vermont and Pennsylvania. Gerry was also elected, but in the congressional elections the Federalists swept the Northeast, doubling their strength in the house.

145

The nation, meanwhile, had marched to war. On May 22 word from Europe dashed Madison's last hope for peace: the British, apparently, had no intention of ending the orders in council. On June 1 the President finally asked Congress to declare war against Great Britain. The receipt of his message brought to a climax the vigorous struggle that the Federalists and the antiwar Republicans had waged against the War Hawks in both chambers. Though the right of debate was essentially unlimited and was cherished in both houses, various Representatives from time to time had flirted with means to cut off long, obstructionist speeches that held up important business in the House. A year earlier, before Clay became Speaker, a majority in that body had used the device of the previous question (a motion, not debatable, by any member for an immediate vote on the motion under discussion) to bring to a halt a rambling, long-winded speech by Representative Barent Gardenier of New York that, until two o'clock in the morning, had held up a vote on a critical bill. Though the action indicated that thereafter a majority could employ a call for the previous question to cut off debate, it was generally regarded unpopularly as a "gag" that could be turned against anyone and was not frequently invoked. When Clay became Speaker he relied more on parliamentary tactics and the gavel to outwit and overawe those who, like Randolph, tried the patience of the House. In the emotional days preceding Madison's war message, however, this had become an almost impossible task, and Calhoun and other War Hawks often assisted Clay in asserting control over debate. The process—a ruling by Clay, supported by a majority vote of the members—had the effect of establishing a number of new rules of procedure. As Clay gained mastery over the lower chamber during his six terms, becoming its undisputed leader, his rules for the order and procedure of that body's business and debates swelled—and from then on the House's rules continued to grow, change, and be honed and refined under later Speakers.

Now, despite the efforts of the War Hawks to ram through approval of the declaration of war, their opponents nevertheless were able to block a vote for three days. As recounted by Neil MacNeil in *Forge of Democracy,* the outnumbered Federalists and other antiwar members had been conducting a filibuster against the war in the lower chamber for weeks, using "every parliamentary trick they knew." According to Henry Wise, a later Virginia Representative whose story MacNeil reported, the "Federalist leaders had organized a phalanx of debaters" to follow each other in speaking and not lose control of the floor. Finally, with Madison's message before them, the exasperated War Hawks burst into the chamber one night while a Federalist speaker was droning on and his companions were drowsing, and seizing spittoons from the House floor, they set up a clamor by beating them and throwing them around. In the chaos, the Federalist who had been speaking was so taken aback and frightened that he sat down, whereupon a prowar member moved the previous question. With Clay in the chair, the majority accepted it, thus halting the filibuster. Clay then put the main question—the declaration of war, and the House passed it, 79 to 49. That was June 4. The Senate followed on June 18 by a vote of 19 to 13, and the nation was at war. Ironically, five days later, Britain suspended the orders in council, but it was too late.

Through most of its course, the war was a humiliation to the nation and to the War Hawks in Congress. Though rousing naval victories were won at sea and on Lake Erie, military debacles occurred in the West and along the Canadian border. The nation was unprepared, divided, and—in New England and New York—even in rebellion against the war. There American contractors openly supplied beef, flour, and other necessities to British vessels and the enemy armies in Canada, and in December, 1813, Congress had to pass another embargo act to try to stop this trade. Predictably, it worked its greatest hardship on the South and West, which not only could not export their agricultural products but had to pay war-inflated prices for northeastern-manufactured goods. Specie drained rapidly out of those areas into New England banks, eventually causing the collapse of every state bank outside New England and forcing the repeal of the embargo in April, 1814. The army was untrained, understrength, ill-equipped, incompetently led, and without centralized command. Offensives into Canada were launched, cut to pieces, or abandoned because the militia refused to leave American territory and assist the regulars. The Northeast, the financial center of the country, was of almost no help in funding the war. When Gallatin pressed Congress for money, it refused again, at first, to vote new taxes, and washed its hands of the problem by authorizing the desperate Treasury head to seek an additional loan—when he had already been unable to raise the first one. In 1813 Congress finally had to vote taxes on a long list of items, recommended by Gallatin, including whiskey, salt, stamps, carriages, and sugar—the same Hamiltonian taxes against which Jefferson and Gallatin had once railed, and which the Republicans had repealed when they first came to power.

The Twelfth Congress, which had begun the war, came to a close on March 3, 1813, but because of the gravity of the situation Madison called the Thirteenth Congress into its first session on May 24, months ahead of the December date when it would normally have convened. John Randolph was out, beaten in the previous election because of his antiwar stand, but there was a host of new Federalists from the Northeast ready to do battle with the administration. Rufus King had returned to the Senate from New York after a seventeen-year absence, and there was a formidable new Federalist Senator from New Hampshire, Jeremiah Mason, who had been attorney general of his state. To the House New Hampshire had sent an ardent opponent of embargoes and the war, Daniel Webster, a dark, brooding man with a large head, an expansive forehead, deep-set eyes that Thomas Carlyle would later liken to anthracite furnaces, and an imposing appearance of firmness and strength. Thirty-one years old, Webster had been educated at Phillips Exeter Academy and Dartmouth College, shifted from teaching to the law, and had already gained a reputation in New Hampshire as an outstanding lawyer and a spellbinding speaker. He had a powerful voice, an immense command of the vocabulary, and a skill in oratorical delivery that would soon focus attention on him in the capital. He liked good living and was improvident, sought the respect of "the best people" (and would often champion their interests), and frequently changed positions to go with prevailing opinion—but in time he would loom in Congress as a pillar of moral strength and, with Calhoun and Clay, would be one of the giants of the national legislature.

Almost at once Webster went on the attack, complaining about Clay's tight control of the Republican caucus to "arrange" everything before bills reached the House floor (the majority members were "moved by wires" like puppets, he said) and introducing resolutions designed to embarrass Madison. But the President suffered a more telling rebuff from Rufus King and the new Senate. The previous September the czar of Russia, faced by Napoleon's invasion and worried by the new diversion of his British ally, had offered to mediate the conflict between America and England. His proposal reached Madison in March, 1813, and the President dispatched Gallatin and the Delaware Federalist James A. Bayard to St. Petersburg as peace commissioners to join John Quincy Adams, the American minister to Russia. Led by King, with the support of Gallatin's old enemies, Giles, Leib, and Smith, the Senate rejected Gallatin's appointment and severely chastized Madison for having used a Cabinet member as an envoy. The matter soon came to nothing when Britain announced that she was not interested in the czar's mediation, but in November Lord Castlereagh, the British foreign secretary, suddenly informed Monroe that he would welcome direct negotiations with the United States. Madison leaped at the opportunity and nominated John Quincy Adams, Bayard, Henry Clay, and Jonathan Russell, American minister to Norway and Sweden, as peace commissioners to meet with the British in the Flemish city of Ghent. The Senate confirmed these nominations, and a few days later Madison announced the resignation of Gallatin as secretary of the treasury and added him to the group. This time the Senate approved Gallatin's nomination. Clay resigned from the House and the commissioners left for Europe.

During the summer of 1814 British military pressure on America increased. Maine was invaded, upper New York State was threatened (and saved by Thomas Macdonough's victory on Lake Champlain), the coast was blockaded, and Washington and Baltimore were attacked. Congress was not in session on August 24 and 25, when British forces, having scattered American defenders at Bladensburg in Maryland, marched unopposed into the capital city and set fire to every government building except a decrepit structure that housed the post office and patent office (the superintendent of patents pleaded that the destruction of the patent models would be a crime against civilization, like the Saracens' burning of the Alexandria library). Madison, Monroe, and the rest of the Cabinet had been with the troops at

Bladensburg and had fled, along with all other government officials, to Virginia, where the President joined his wife, Dolley, who had saved the original copy of the Declaration of Independence and Gilbert Stuart's portrait of George Washington. After the British withdrew from the capital, having taken souvenirs and defaced the interior walls of buildings, the government returned to the fire-blackened city, which had been saved from total conflagration by a violent thunderstorm.

A few weeks later the Senators and Representatives began to arrive. The Capitol building was a smoke-stained ruin, its central section destroyed, the roof of the House wing collapsed in rubble on desks and chairs, the Senate wing in ashes, the library burned, the mace of the House of Representatives taken, and all the windows gone. On September 19 the dazed and angry Congress convened in the undamaged patent office building, the members of the House crowded into a room so small and uncomfortable that "every spot up to the fireplaces and windows" was taken. When a motion was made, however, that the government relocate in Philadelphia or Lancaster, Pennsylvania, it was patriotically voted down by both houses, and an offer of a $500,000 loan from Washington bankers to help with the rebuilding was accepted. Congress continued to meet in the patent office building, with the House using a wooden replica of the mace, until the end of 1815, when it moved temporarily into a newly constructed brick building. Jefferson donated his own library to replace Congress' destroyed books—it became the basis of the present-day great collections of the Library of Congress—and in December, 1819, after Benjamin Latrobe and Charles Bulfinch had redesigned and renovated the Capitol, the national legislature finally moved back into its own building. The resplendent columned Hall of Representatives (the Capitol's present-day Statuary Hall) was hung with tasseled crimson curtains to muffle a terrible problem with echoes and adorned with a theatrical crimson canopy above the Speaker's desk and brass cuspidors by the seat of every legislator.

Despite the almost bankrupt state of the government, the Congress that convened in September, 1814, proved ineffective and helpless. When a new secretary of the treasury, Alexander J. Dallas, recommended the re-establishment of a national bank that could lend funds to the Treasury, the House and Senate emasculated the proposal so badly that, after a bill was finally passed, Madison vetoed it and Dallas had to settle for an authorization to increase taxes and try to borrow another $25 million. A conscription bill for a draft of men for the army was similarly buffeted around between the two houses and ended up being shelved, despite the urgent need for more troops. To cap the dismal state of affairs, a convention of antiwar Federalist delegates from the legislatures of Massachusetts, Connecticut, and Rhode Island, together with Federalists from New Hampshire and Vermont, assembled behind closed doors in the Hartford State House and adopted resolutions calling for constitutional amendments and various measures that smacked of a breakup of the Union. Three of the delegates were sent to Washington to negotiate with the national government. They arrived in February, 1815, just after fortunes had turned abruptly and dramatically. News reached the capital, almost simultaneously, of Andrew Jackson's stirring victory at New Orleans and of the signing of a treaty of peace with Great Britain in Ghent. Overnight, ecstatic pride and patriotic fervor supplanted gloom. The delegates from New England turned back amid ridicule and scorn, their secret actions in Hartford equated with treason and their Federalist party now nationally discredited and beyond recovery.

When the new Fourteenth Congress met in December, 1815, it was as if all the nation's problems had blown away with the war. The humiliations and setbacks of the conflict had been a sobering trial, but, in Madison's words, the final outcome asserted "the rights and independence of the Nation." Britain had agreed to end most of America's reasons for going to war, and in the coming years she would negotiate a settlement of the other complaints. In Congress the members reflected a new spirit of nationalistic pride, and most of them evinced a desire to drop old antagonisms and seek harmony. Clay had been re-elected to the House from Kentucky, and the Republican caucus again named him Speaker. John Randolph, too, was back, older but still unchastened. Madison's State of the Union message, delivered on December 5, 1815, was a ringing call to rectify the weaknesses revealed by the war and to consolidate the country. He recommended a national bank and a uniform currency, a strong national defense, the protection and nurturing of domestic manufactures, and a system of roads and canals. It was a nationalistic speech, foreshadowing a new era in American politics. Madison himself had come full circle; he was again the advocate of a strong central government, back where he had been during the Constitutional Convention before changing to fight Hamilton and the Federalists. But his views, far from mirroring the narrow, sectional, pro-British stance of the Federalists, coincided with those of the new nationalistic Republicans in Congress. A majority in both houses now responded to his recommendations with enthusiasm.

Bills were passed authorizing a regular army of ten thousand men and appropriating $1 million for the navy. In the House Calhoun introduced a new bill to charter a second United States Bank and received support from Clay, who had helped kill the first bank in 1811. Now, as a result of the financial difficulties during the war, Clay had changed his mind, and he stepped down from the Speaker's chair to declare that Congress had the constitutional right to authorize the bank. Though he and Calhoun were vigorously opposed by Webster, the bank—which eventually provided a reliable, convenient national currency—was approved and established on April 10, 1816, for twenty years. At the same time the three men, who more and more would come to dominate legislative arguments on major issues, led a debate on whether to continue the high wartime duties as a protective system for American manufactures. Calhoun, again supported by Clay and opposed by Webster (who represented the New England shipping interests' opposition to high duties and was joined in his arguments by Randolph), finally steered through the House the nation's first peacetime protective tariff act, which the Senate endorsed and the President signed.

As usual, Clay had employed the Republican caucus to win passage of the bills, carefully canvassing the members before the measures came to the House floor and then seeing that the party decisions were faithfully carried out. But Clay and his close associates had larger designs, determining to control not only party members, but the Congress, the government, and the national budget as well. The House majority, under Clay's direction, established six standing committees on expenditures, each one to keep an account of the finances of a different executive department—State, War, Navy, Treasury, the Post Office, and one on public buildings. Calhoun was as insistent as Clay on overseeing the administration. "Not a cent of money ought to be applied but by our direction and under our control," he said. The Senate, too, set up new standing committees. To its four existing standing committees it added eleven new ones—Foreign Relations, Finance, Commerce and Manufactures, Military Affairs, the Militia, Naval Affairs, Public Lands, Claims, the Judiciary, the Post Office and Post Roads, and Pensions—most of them composed of five Senators. Their subjects reflected the expanding interests and needs of the maturing nation. Congress' own needs were reflected in a measure that raised the per diem pay from $6 to $8 for members of both houses.

By December, 1816, a caucus of 119 of the 141 Republicans in the Senate and House had picked James Monroe over William H. Crawford to succeed Madison as President. Madison's second Vice President, Elbridge Gerry, had died suddenly in 1814, and Daniel D. Tompkins, the Republican governor of New York, was chosen to run with Monroe. What was left of the Federalists put up Rufus King for President. He made a poor showing, carrying only Massachusetts, Connecticut, and Delaware and admitting after his defeat that from then on the Federalists would have to be content with supporting "the least wicked section of the Republicans." He was the last Federalist to run for President.

The final session of the Fourteenth Congress began on December 2, 1816. Responding to one of Madison's recommendations to the previous session, Calhoun, backed enthusiastically by Clay, introduced a measure to finance a federally subsidized network of roads and canals to assist the internal development of the country. "Let us then bind the Republic together with a perfect system of roads and canals," Calhoun declared in presenting the bill. "Let us conquer space." Though Madison and various members of Congress believed that a constitutional amendment would be required to permit the government to build roads and canals within states, Calhoun employed the old Hamiltonian doctrine of implied powers and argued that Congress had a right to authorize such projects under the general-welfare clause of the Constitution and through its power to build post roads. When the bill passed both the House and Senate, however, Madison vetoed it on strict constitutional grounds. The veto, which ran counter to the rest of Madison's nationalist thinking, dumfounded Clay, who as a representative of the West and a spokesman for western expansion knew the need for arteries of transportation and communication in the country's undeveloped interior. "Not even an earthquake," he said of the veto, "could have excited more surprise than when it was first communicated to this House." Though the Speaker tried hard to dragoon members into overriding the veto, and even cast the first vote himself, he failed to muster the necessary two-thirds majority.

The President's show of independence angered Clay, who became more determined than ever to assert the authority of Congress over the executive. When Monroe came to the presidency—the fourth Virginian to hold the office—the confrontation over the subject was instantly renewed. In his first annual message to Congress, Monroe announced that he agreed with Madison on the unconstitutionality of federally financed internal improvements. Congress had not yet introduced a new bill on the matter, and Clay, who now had presidential ambitions, blew up at the President's commenting on a bill that the Congress had not yet even introduced, "telling us what we may or may not do." The issue, said Clay, "is now a question between the Executive on the one side, and the Representatives of the people on the other." He delivered a stirring speech in behalf of government support of western expansion and called for a resolution stating baldly that Congress had the power to make appropriations for that purpose. "We will assert, uphold and maintain, the authority of Congress," he announced, adding that the members must vote quickly lest the President's view be accepted. Act, "or the power is gone—gone forever," he warned. Despite his appeal, the matter bogged down for several weeks in debate, but in the end the House passed the resolution, settling nothing but demonstrating a majority's willingness to stand with Clay in his battle for congressional mastery over the executive.

Monroe's attention was primarily focused on foreign affairs, but his running fight with Clay continued, first over Latin American countries that had revolted against Spain, and then over Florida. With Secretary of State John Quincy Adams working carefully to negotiate a peaceful cession of Florida from Spain, Monroe tried to remain neutral over Spain's troubles with her South American colonies. But with a genuine humanitarianism, Clay demanded recognition of the Latin countries that were in revolt and tried to win congressional approval for an appropriation to send an American minister to Buenos Aires as recognition of the independence of those who were fighting "to burst their chains and be free." He was defeated in this effort, but in November, 1818, he was again on the attack, though this time denouncing an offense committed by the United States against Spain. In March of that year Andrew Jackson, now a celebrated hero for his victory at New Orleans, had, with only the vaguest orders, led American troops into Spanish Florida. That province had become a haven for runaway slaves from Georgia and a hotbed of intrigue by British agents, who whipped up the escaped blacks and local Creek and Seminole Indians against marauding Americans who came looking for their slaves. In a whirlwind expedition, Jackson obliterated some Indian towns, captured the Spanish cities of St. Marks and Pensacola, and executed two British subjects.

Monroe's chagrined report to Congress on what had happened shocked both the House and Senate and led to a three-day speech by Clay, during which the galleries were packed by Washingtonians, who had learned to look forward with excitement to the Speaker's orations. There was confusion over whether Monroe had actually authorized Jackson's expedition. If he had done so, said Clay, "the Constitutional provision is a dead letter which confides to Congress the power of declaring war"; if he had not, then Jackson had usurped Congress' power. "Remember that Greece had her Alexander, Rome her Caesar, England her Cromwell, France her Bonaparte," he exclaimed. The galleries loved it, for it was high theater (during Clay's pauses, gentlemen on the floor of the House of Representatives added to the gala atmosphere by handing up oranges wrapped in handkerchiefs on long poles as refreshment for the ladies in the galleries). Though a move to censure Jackson failed, the general resented Clay's speech as a personal attack and thereafter viewed Clay with hostility. The Florida problem was finally solved in February, 1819, by a treaty in which Spain ceded Florida and defined the western boundary of the Louisiana Purchase. The year before, the government had also signed a pact with Great Britain agreeing to establish the forty-ninth parallel as the boundary between the United States and Canada from the Lake of the Woods to the Rocky Mountains and sanctioning the joint occupation of the Oregon country. With the two treaties, the United States now had a continental gaze.

The settling of far-distant boundaries matched an expansionism that had accelerated after the end of the War of 1812. Indiana became a state in 1816, Mississippi in 1817, Illinois in 1818, and Alabama in 1819. The country east of the Mississippi was beginning to fill up, the forests disappearing to settlers' clearings and towns in the North and cotton fields spreading across the flatlands of the South. People were even beginning to move across the Mississippi; Daniel Boone had emigrated to Spanish-owned Missouri in 1798 to get away from civilization in Kentucky, and now Americans, mostly from the South, were overspreading that area. In December, 1818, Missouri asked to be admitted to the Union, and the House prepared an enabling act. It was the start of a grave new division in Congress.

On February 13, 1819, while the act was under discussion, Representative James Tallmadge, Jr., from Poughkeepsie, New York, offered amendments to bar the importation of slaves into Missouri and to emancipate, at the age of twenty-five, all slave children born thereafter in that state. The amendments made sense to antislavery northerners. The Northwest Ordinance had banned slavery in any states created north of the Ohio River, and while nothing had been said about slavery in the area of the Louisiana Purchase, most of Missouri lay north of a line extended west from the Ohio River. Nevertheless, Clay and others attacked Tallmadge's amendments as unconstitutional (Congress had no right to place such restrictions on the citizens of a state as a condition of admittance, they maintained) and as a violation of the Louisiana treaty (states created from the purchased territory were to enter on an equal basis with the original thirteen states). Northerners had the votes, however, and they passed the enabling act with the amendments. The Senate, in turn, knocked them out—the Senators were keenly aware of another problem: the Union now consisted of eleven free states and eleven slave states; another slave state would swing the balance in the Senate against the North—and sent the original bill back to the House, which promptly restored the Tallmadge amendments and returned them to the Senate. Once more the Senate killed them and sent back the original bill. The House refused to concur, and the matter died with the adjournment of that session of Congress.

When Congress convened again in December, 1819, Maine, too, applied for admission. That provided an opportunity to maintain the balance between free and slave states, but once more an amendment was introduced to bar slavery in Missouri. In the Senate the debate raged with increasing excitement for three weeks. Overflow crowds of spectators, including many women, were permitted on the Senate floor and escorted to sofas and seats reserved for visiting Representatives, while southerners such as the elegant William Pinkney of Maryland, in gloves and ruffled sleeves, battled against any federal interference with slavery, and northerners, led by the veteran Federalist Rufus King, now sixty-five years old, fought for the amendment. The antislavery forces finally lost, but Senator Jesse B. Thomas of the new state of Illinois followed up with a new amendment, permitting slavery in Missouri but barring it thereafter from all states created out of the Louisiana Territory north of 36 degrees, 30 minutes, north latitude, approximately the line of the Ohio River. This amendment passed the Senate, and the proposed compromise was sent to the House, which was also being wracked by the issue.

There, too, the galleries were packed, the presence of large numbers of Washington ladies nettling John Randolph, who pointed angrily at them and demanded, "Mr. Speaker, what, pray, are all these women doing here, so out of place in this arena? Sir, they had much better be at home attending to their knitting." For four days straight Randolph stormed against any prohibition of slavery. Even the Thomas compromise did not satisfy some of the extremists on both sides, and the debate went on, endangering the passage of other important measures. The House was accustomed to take up matters in the order in which they were entered on the docket, or calendar. Now it was moved and accepted to rearrange schedules and the order of business to meet urgent problems. The decision seemed unimportant at the time, but it established a procedure in the House that would later give its leaders the enormous power to decide when, and if, specific matters would be considered. During the debate, also, a new American expression came into the language. Gaining the floor, Representative Felix Walker of North Carolina, whose district included Buncombe County in that state, announced to his colleagues that there was no need for them to listen to what he had to say, because he would just be speaking for the voters in Buncombe. "Speaking for Buncombe" became a laughing expression in the House and soon ended up as the word *bunk*.

The debate dragged on, and finally, after one Congressman fainted on the floor of the House and even Henry Clay became exhausted from the day and night sessions, a joint conference committee of the two houses worked out a two-part compromise that included the Thomas amendment and admitted Missouri as a slave state and Maine as a free state, and the measure passed. But it was not the end. Monroe signed the Missouri Compromise on March 3, 1820, but the whole issue erupted again in the next session of Congress, when Missouri presented its newly enacted constitution for acceptance. That document outraged northerners by provisions that forbade the Missouri legislature to interfere with slavery and prohibited free Negroes from entering the state. A southern motion to accept Missouri's constitution was defeated, 93 to 73, and another wild and angry debate ensued in the House for six weeks, even throwing into pandemonium the formal counting of the electors' ballots for Monroe's re-election when northerners and southerners contested whether Missouri was yet a state and had a right to cast a vote. (Actually, it did not matter; Monroe received the vote of every elector in the nation except that of former Senator William Plumer of New Hampshire, who thought that Washington should be the only President accorded the honor of a unanimous election and voted for John Quincy Adams.) With Missouri's admittance still unsettled and the adjournment of Congress only two weeks away, Clay (who had resigned the speakership before the session began so that he could devote more time to his personal affairs) put together a special joint Senate-House committee of twenty-three members whom he chose himself and induced them to recommend a compromise, admitting Missouri if she would agree to "respect the rights and privileges of all citizens of the United States." Although no one expected that this would guarantee the right of free blacks to enter the state, Clay's compromise was accepted by the tired legislators. Missouri was admitted with its offensive constitution on August 10, 1821, and the first great national contest over slavery was ended. But to the aged Thomas Jefferson at Monticello, the conflict had been "like a fire bell in the night." The Missouri settlement had been "a reprieve only" for the nation.

In the fall of 1821 Clay resigned from Congress to return to law in Kentucky and make some money; he had lost heavily in gambling and had been left in debt by the failure of a friend whose note he had endorsed. When he had given up the speakership in October, 1820, he had been succeeded by

John W. Taylor of New York, but Taylor had been opposed by Lowndes of South Carolina, and the contest, reflecting the North-South rivalry of the Missouri Compromise conflict, had taken two days and twenty-two ballots to settle. In 1821 the fight for the speakership went twelve ballots, with Philip P. Barbour of Virginia finally being elected. Clay was out of Congress for only one term; he missed politics, and in December, 1823, he was back in the House for the first session of the Eighteenth Congress. Immediately, he was re-elected Speaker over Barbour, 139 to 42. It would be Clay's last term in the House and his last in the national legislature until he entered the Senate in 1831.

The opening of the Eighteenth Congress was a memorable one. On its second day, December 2, 1823, the President delivered his annual message, enunciating in it the principles of the Monroe Doctrine, which was aimed specifically at Russian expansionist designs in the Pacific Northwest and at threats by the Holy Alliance to restore Spain in Latin America. But it proclaimed to all the world that "the American continents, by the free and independent condition which they have assumed and maintain, are henceforth not to be considered as subjects for future colonization by any European powers" and that European intervention in the Western Hemisphere would be viewed as a "manifestation of an unfriendly disposition toward the United States." Listening to the reading of the sober pronouncement were men in both houses who would, in time, become major national figures.

Daniel Webster, for one, was back in the House after an absence of seven years. In 1816 he had moved from New Hampshire to Boston and been defeated for re-election. In the interim he became a national figure as a result of his roles in the *McCulloch* v. *Maryland* and the *Dartmouth College* cases before the Supreme Court. Now Massachusetts returned him to Congress. Also in the House was a future President, James Buchanan, an earnest, industrious, thirty-two-year-old lawyer from Lancaster, Pennsylvania. Andrew Jackson, a long, lean man, usually fierce and unsmiling, was in the Senate, and the hero of Tennessee was already being touted for President. Near Jackson sat a man who was personally offensive to him, huge, burly Thomas Hart Benton, who had come to the Senate two years before from the new state of Missouri. Benton was a master of high-flown language, but he was also a vain, blusterous, and pugnacious fighter who had served with Jackson on the rough southwestern frontier in the War of 1812. Both men were used to donnybrooks and duels, and in 1813, in a wild melee in Nashville that had climaxed a quarrel between them, Jackson had attacked Benton with a horsewhip and had, in turn, been shot in the shoulder. In the Senate the two men for a time did not speak to each other. Finally, while serving on the same committee, they shook hands, and eventually Benton became one of Jackson's most loyal supporters. Also in the Senate was still another future President, New Yorker Martin Van Buren. An enemy of De Witt Clinton's, Van Buren was clever and cunning and had organized a strong machine of his own, employing the spoils system to maintain the loyalty of his followers. His busy maneuvering and ability to avoid taking stands on issues gave him the nicknames "the Red Fox of Kinderhook" (his home town in New York) and "the Little Magician." On the House side was another man linked to Jackson, tall, restless Sam Houston, who had moved from Virginia to Tennessee, where he had served with both Jackson and Benton during the War of 1812. Washington Irving would call Houston fascinating, but that was an understatement. In 1829 Houston would abruptly resign the governorship of Tennessee to disappear from the white man's world and live among the Cherokees in present-day Oklahoma. Seven years after that he would be in the forefront of the white man's affairs again in the Southwest, leading Texas to independence and becoming its president.

There were other notable figures in the same Congress: Monroe's old Virginia ally, John Taylor of Caroline, was back in the Senate, still an ardent states'-rights Republican; Edward Livingston, who as a brash newcomer to Congress had precipitated a confrontation with Washington over the Jay's Treaty papers in 1796, was now a Representative from Louisiana; and from South Carolina had come a new Senator, Robert Y. Hayne, a strict believer in states' rights and a tariff "for revenue only." He was also a magnificent debater. Hayne arrived in Congress in time for a debate over a new tariff law, but this was a year that belonged to Henry Clay. The bill, which would increase certain tariffs, had originated in the House and provided Clay with an opportunity to proclaim a grand dream of an "American system" of protective tariffs and internal improvements to expand domestic markets and make the United States more self-sufficient. Again stepping down from the chair so that he could speak in Committee of the Whole, Clay delivered one of the most memorable orations of his career on March 30 and 31, 1824, pleading for the development of home manufactures by protecting industry with a tariff. Envisioning a majestic continental future when "the wave of population, cultivation, and intelligence shall have washed the Rocky Mountains and have mingled with the Pacific" and appealing to the patriotism of all sections of the country, he tried to convince the agricultural South and West that they, too, would benefit by an increased demand for their products within the United States. In a way, it was an echo of the planned national economy of Alexander Hamilton's visionary *Report on Manufactures*, and, like Hamilton, Clay failed to convince the South. Nevertheless, the higher tariffs passed the House, 107 to 102, with almost every southerner voting against them. When the bill also moved through the Senate, the new tariffs were enacted. (There was a "footnote" to the close vote in the House. Clay had counted on the support of both Samuel Foote of Connecticut and Charles Foote of New York. Both, however, voted against the bill. "We made a good stand," quipped Clay after the tally, "considering we lost both of our Feete.")

With the approach of the presidential election of 1824, a new factionalism began to devil the Congress. The collapse of the Federalist party and Monroe's unopposed victory in 1820 had given birth to an optimistic belief that the nation had entered what a Boston newspaper termed an "Era of Good Feelings," but it did not last long. By 1821 the Republicans were splitting into busily conniving factions that supported as many as seventeen potential successors to Monroe. In time the number was reduced to five serious candidates. Clay and Andrew Jackson were both being boosted, and so were three Cabinet members, Secretary of State John Quincy Adams, Secretary of War John C. Calhoun, and Secretary of the Treasury William H. Crawford. In the summer of 1823 Crawford suffered a serious stroke that impaired his mental faculties, almost blinded him, and left him partly paralyzed. Nevertheless, Monroe continued him in office (Crawford had a seal made with his signature, which his daughter helped him press down on papers), and he remained in the presidential race. Meanwhile, the accelerated democratization of the nation that was accompanying its rapid economic growth and expansion to the west was greatly extending the franchise, and large segments of the population, together with various state legislatures, were demanding an end to the caucus method of selecting presidential nominees, urging instead that the state legislatures or the people themselves be permitted to instruct the electors. To act before this pressure became too strong, some 66 of the 261 Senators and Representatives called a caucus on February 14, 1824, and nominated Crawford and Gallatin. The vote was meaningless, since a majority of the members of Congress obviously supported other candidates—the caucus caused such an outcry, in fact, that it was the last one ever held to nominate a presidential candidate—and gradually Crawford's physical condition became worse and his chances of victory faded. Prior to the voting, also, Calhoun withdrew, accepting the vice-presidential position from both Adams and Jackson.

The voting took place at various times during the fall in the twenty-four states. In eighteen of them the voters, rather than the legislatures, instructed the electors for whom to vote among the four nominees. The final result gave no one a majority. Andrew Jackson, garnering the largest popular vote, ran first with 99 electoral votes; Adams had 84; the ailing Crawford 41; and Clay 37. Instead of withdrawing for Jackson, Adams decided to stay in the contest, and the vote went to the House of Representatives as in 1801. Clay was suddenly in the position of being able to help name the next President by throwing his influence to either Jackson or Adams. Intrigue, bargaining, and political maneuvering reached a height of intensity in Congress before Clay finally announced that he would vote for Adams. Soon afterward a communication from an anonymous member of Congress appeared in a newspaper, accusing Clay of having made an "unholy" bargain with Adams, who, the writer alleged, had agreed to name him secretary of state. Both Adams and Clay denied the accusation, and the anonymous writer was exposed as a slightly odd Pennsylvania Representative, "Honest George" Kremer, who was noted for his overcoat made of leopard skins. Clay demanded an investigation by the House, and when Kremer refused to appear the Speaker was sure that James Buchanan, one of Jackson's Pennsylvania supporters, had actually composed the letter.

Adams finally was elected—though only by the vote of Alexander Hamilton's brother-in-law, New York Representative Stephen Van Rensselaer, a wealthy old man whom Clay and Webster frightened by suggesting that a Jackson victory might endanger the safety of his property. Rensselaer, the last of the great Hudson River patroons, closed his eyes and prayed for divine guidance on how to vote. When he opened his eyes he saw a ballot lying by his seat with Adams's name on it. Interpreting it as God's will, he cast his vote for the secretary of state, breaking a tie in the New York delegation and giving Adams just the number of states he needed—thirteen —for victory. When Adams soon afterward named Clay his secretary of state, the Jacksonians turned their wrath on the Speaker, Jackson himself terming him the "*Judas* of the West." The charge of a "corrupt bargain," though repeatedly denied by both Adams and Clay, hurt Adams all through his administration and haunted Clay all his life, crippling his many attempts to win the presidency for himself.

In his relations with Congress, Adams, dour, introspective, and as impeccably honest and moralistic as his father, was doomed from the start. Clay helped him with the House, where the friendly New Yorker John W. Taylor was elected Speaker. But in the Senate the new President's problems were immense. For the first time that body was beginning to challenge the House as the principal legislative forum of the nation. While the large increase in the number of Representatives had forced the adoption of rules that inhibited the role of and opportunities for debate in the House, the growth of the Senate to a membership of almost fifty had worked to the contrary, making it a more lively and rewarding forum for those who wanted to lead and be heard. Moreover, the equality of state representation in the Senate, and the growing concern over divisions between the free and slave states that had been underscored by the Missouri controversy, heightened the Senate's importance as the arena in which southerners could block the action of an antagonistic House majority. The Senate was a body "of equals, of men of individual honor and personal character, and of absolute independence," Daniel Webster would soon say. Prior to 1823 Senate committees had been named by ballot, but in that year the chamber conferred the authority on its presiding officer, and the president *pro tempore* had been making the appointments. Now Vice President Calhoun— growing increasingly disenchanted with the nationalistic policies of Adams and Clay, which he himself had espoused—assumed the right to name committees and their chairmen and put Jackson men into the most influential positions. It was not long before all Washington was aware that supporters of Jackson, Calhoun, and Crawford were combining to ensure that Adams would serve only four years and that Jackson would become President in 1828.

The reaction to Adams's first annual message to Congress in December, 1825, hinted at the extent of the new President's troubles. Reversing the position of Madison and Monroe—who had insisted on an authorizing constitutional amendment—he called for a vast program of federally financed internal improvements. What Clay had earlier proposed now drew fireworks from old states' righters such as Randolph and Macon and from others who were moving to join them, fearful, as Randolph warned them, that if Congress had the right to authorize such projects under a loose-constructionist doctrine of implied powers, "they may not only enact a Sedition law . . . but they may emancipate every slave in the United States." Adams was bitterly attacked as a "usurper of power" and a would-be tyrant, and Congress ignored his recommendations. It passed instead various isolated, planless bills for land grants, stock subscriptions, and other aids for individual roads and canals that primarily benefited specific constituents, districts, or states—the beginning of what came to be called bringing home the bacon, or pork barrel, legislation.

The behavior of John Randolph in the Senate (which he entered in 1825, filling a vacancy) was obviously that of an ill, unbalanced man, and now it went from bad to worse. He would gain the floor for hours, making long, rambling, often incoherent speeches, calling out every ten or fifteen minutes to the assistant doorkeeper for another tumbler of whiskey or porter, and then shrieking out epithets at whomever he chose to attack. Many appeals were made to Calhoun to call Randolph to order, but the Vice President, masking his enjoyment at the Virginian's attacks on the administration and its supporters, gravely insisted that, since he was not a member of the Senate but merely its presiding officer, he had no wish to usurp power and interfere with debate. Most Senators, afraid to ask for a rule that might limit the freedom of debate of all Senators, chose instead to leave the chamber whenever Randolph got up to speak. (In later years, rules were adopted by the Senate that governed the propriety of the members' remarks so that the Vice President could call to order any member casting aspersions against another Senator, the House of Representatives, one of its members, or a state, but the right to criticize the executive was carefully retained.)

One consequence of Randolph's invective was a dueling challenge from one of his favorite targets, Henry Clay. Neither man made the ideal image of a duelist nor was considered expert in the handling of arms, but nonetheless they met in the late evening of April 8, 1826, in a clearing on the Virginia side of the Potomac (if he were to die, Randolph wanted to do so on the soil of his native state). The Virginian arrived wearing a dramatic white flannel wrapper. Both men missed with their first shots; on the second shot, Randolph fired in the air and Clay put his bullet through Randolph's garment, though without hurting him. The two then shook hands and departed. Watching in awe was Senator Thomas Hart Benton, the dueling *aficionado*, who later recalled that it was "about the last high-toned duel" he ever saw.

In the elections of 1826 supporters of the administration in the Virginia legislature managed to replace Randolph, but the winds of change were blowing hard, much of the South was rapidly shifting to the hard anti-national position that Randolph had championed for so long, and his own district returned him again to the lower house. Increasingly, the issue of states' rights was coming to the fore—once more, as in the first years of constitutional government, in a predominantly southern context. Extreme southerners, demanding a strict observance of the Constitution, were against the United States Bank, internal improvements, and a high tariff, but linked to their objections was a pervading fear of the national government's interference with slavery. The slave economy was extending westward quickly, encouraged by its supporters to expand and give birth to new states that would maintain balance and strength against the free states in the Congress. The hardening of sectional interests began to pose a dilemma to such men as Calhoun, who had to represent and defend their sections and yet hoped to seek national office that would require support from all sections of the country.

The problem confronted Calhoun early in 1827, when the House passed a woolens bill, which would have raised the tariffs on imported manufactured wool. In the past Calhoun had been an advocate of protectionist tariffs, going along with Clay and other nationalists because of the plausible argument that South Carolina and other southern states, with adequate water power with which to manufacture textiles, might become industrialized. But few plants had been built in the South, and now tariffs (as well as internal improvements, most of which linked the North and West, encouraging the growth of those sections rather than the South) worked to the disadvantage of the southern states. Conversely, northerners such as Daniel Webster (who in December, 1827, entered the Senate) began to support protective duties, reflecting the rising importance of manufacturing interests above those of shippers and traders in the North. When the woolens bill reached the Senate in February, 1827, it was held up by a tie vote in that body. Faced with having to break the tie, Calhoun finally made his decision, voted no, and killed the tariff.

The defeat of the bill roused a northern demand for a new measure that would protect many different products, and in the Twentieth Congress, which convened on December 3, 1827, the House Committee on Manufactures prepared such a bill. This new Congress was filled with Jackson supporters, many of them swept into office in the elections of 1826. Andrew Stevenson of Virginia, a Jackson man, was elected Speaker, and nearly all the committee chairmen in the House were Jackson partisans. In the Senate, where Jackson support was stronger than ever, Martin Van Buren, Thomas Hart Benton, John H. Eaton of Tennessee, and others watched over Jackson's interests, waging a subtle campaign that was intended to advance Jackson's candidacy and embarrass and discredit Adams in every possible way.

When the new tariff bill of 1828 was prepared in the House Committee on Manufactures, Jacksonians played a devious game, joining the Adams protectionists and loading the bill with so many outrageously high duties that they were sure Congress would kill it, and they could then blame the Adams forces for its defeat. Instead, to their surprise, the bill passed both houses and became law on May 19, 1828. The act, which became known as the Tariff of Abominations (it levied duties as high as forty-five percent on woolen goods and many other manufactured articles), was denounced by the legislatures of South Carolina, Georgia, Mississippi, and Virginia. It also moved Calhoun, now fully identifying himself with southern interests, to write an anonymous and widely circulated essay expounding the doctrine of the right of a state to nullify what it considered an unconstitutional law, such as the tariff, making it null and void in that state until a constitutional amendment gave the disputed power to Congress—at which time the state, if it still opposed the law, could secede from the Union.

Jackson, meanwhile, had been nominated for the presidency by the Tennessee legislature and resigned from the Senate to pursue his campaign. The "feel" of a Jackson victory was in the air, and when it came in the winter of 1828, it was a substantial one, 178 electoral votes to 83 for Adams. It was a great triumph for "the common man," particularly in the West and South, where Jackson was lionized. Under the vastly liberalized franchise laws, large numbers of Americans voted who had never done so before. The popular vote jumped from 400,000 in 1824 to more than 1.1 million in 1828. In only two of the twenty-four states, Delaware and South Carolina, did the legislatures still choose the electors; in the rest the people now had that power. Calhoun was re-elected Vice President.

Adams regarded his defeat as a sectional victory for the planters of the South, who with Martin Van Buren's help had forged a coalition with "plain Republicans of the North." Southerners also read the returns as a triumph for their interests, particularly slavery. They were both wrong. During the campaign the Jacksonians had begun to be called Democrats. On March 4, 1829, all Washington saw the real meaning of that word as masses of farming, frontier, and working-class families swarmed into the capital to hail "Old Hickory," the symbol not of slavery or of sectionalism but of a new democracy that had brought the common people of America, at last, to political power. "It was a proud day for the people," Amos Kendall, a Kentucky newspaperman, wrote his paper. "General Jackson is *their own* president."

5. Struggle for the Union

Although Andrew Jackson's support had come from all sections of the country and from all elements of the voters, the tall, aging military hero owed his victory in large measure to the rapidly increasing and more democratic electorate that was emerging from the nation's growth and expansion. On the whole, the new voters opposed aristocratic influences and special privilege and felt that all men were of equal importance and had an equal right to participate in government and receive equal representation by the government. Already this anti-elitist trend was having an effect on state politics, and it would also be felt by Congress.

For one thing, the increase in voters—accelerated by a proliferation of new laws and state constitutional provisions that extended white male suffrage—required bigger and better-organized political machines to present candidates, direct campaigns, attract and hold voters, and get out the vote. Such organizations, in turn, needed rewards to enlist and retain the loyalty of party workers. In many states, particularly New York, where Martin Van Buren and William L. Marcy had created a powerful Democratic machine called by its enemies the Albany Regency, party strength had been built by patronage. The dispensing of jobs to the faithful was not new on the national level; John Adams's "midnight appointments" had infuriated Jefferson, and Jefferson had rewarded many of his own supporters. But patronage as a device to strengthen a national party now came to Washington with a vengeance. With his "Kitchen Cabinet"— a group of intimate friends and advisers including Van Buren, who had succeeded Henry Clay as secretary of state—Jackson replaced scores of long-time federal officeholders in Washington and in the states with deserving Democrats who had worked for and supported him. Van Buren had motives of his own—he would do everything possible to destroy the followings of Vice President Calhoun and Clay (who was out of office and had gone back to Kentucky), his principal rivals as successor to Jackson. But in justification, Jackson himself cited the benefit of rotation

—replacing entrenched bureaucrats who had grown old and inefficient in their jobs—and the right to rid his administration of enemies who would be disloyal to him and oppose his policies. Altogether, during his eight years in office, Jackson dismissed fewer than twenty percent of the approximately ten thousand government jobholders, but the first spate of nominations he sent to the Senate—a majority of whose members were on guard against signs of executive usurpation or tyranny by the headstrong general in the White House—roused opposition in that body. Many of the nominations were fought over, rejected by the anti-Jackson Senators, and submitted again by the President. "Recess appointments" and other political maneuvers were used by Jackson, angering Senators who declaimed against the demeaning of the "honor and dignity" of the contested positions and warned that a precedent was being set for mass scrambles for public office after every future presidential election. In reply William Marcy, who entered the Senate from New York in 1831 as a Jackson loyalist, roared, "to the victors belong the spoils of the enemy!" and the Senate gradually gave way, permitting the development of a spoils system in which the Senators themselves would acquire enormous new power and influence through their constitutional right to approve the nominations.

Meanwhile, the new electorate was changing the complexion of Congress. In the states the bestowing of patronage—franchises, contracts, and other favors, as well as jobs—often made the fortunes of a party more important than the advancement of issues, and the winning of elections sometimes became an end in itself. To win elections, the parties needed men who wanted to win and could win. The old idea that gentlemen should not seek public office but that the office should seek them out began to disappear in most places, and the country became filled with candidates for positions on all levels, including Congress, who were eager to prove that they would make ideal servants and representatives of the people because they were "of the people." Since successful candidates generally did reflect the majorities that elected them, the extension of manhood suffrage soon lowered the quality of men sent to Congress. During the period between the accession of Jackson and the outbreak of the Civil War, some of the ablest and most statesmanlike legislators in the nation's history occupied seats in both houses, but they were greatly outnumbered by mediocrities, nonentities, and even oddities, who were no better or worse than the average "common man" majorities that elected them, and who, indeed, often pandered deliberately to the ignorance and prejudices of the lowest, but most numerous, element of their constituencies.

Davy Crockett of Tennessee was perhaps the most extreme example of this new breed of the people's representatives. A backwoodsman, bear hunter, and veteran of the Creek Indian wars, he served two terms in the Tennessee legislature and first came to Congress in 1827, when he was forty-one years old. Though he was a genuine frontiersman with a rough border constituency, he played a slick role, pretending that he was more

164

ignorant than he was and modeling himself after a popular character of the contemporary American stage, the boastful Colonel Nimrod Wildfire, a "ring-tailed roarer" who could leap the Mississippi River and whip his weight in wildcats. With the help of a ghost writer Crockett published his autobiography, which spread his fame, relating how he electioneered in his district with a bottle of liquor and a twist of tobacco (before taking a drink, a voter usually spit out his quid of tobacco, which Crockett would then replace for him, thus leaving the man no "worse off than when I found him") and popularizing such Crockett expressions as "Root hog or die" and "Be sure you are right, then go ahead." Crockett became a legend in his own time as an "unlarned" rustic braggart and wit, but he was unimportant in the House. He turned against Jackson and was defeated in his district in 1831. In 1833 he was re-elected, but in the next campaign he was beaten again. At that time he is supposed to have announced to his unimpressed Tennessee constituents, "I am going to Texas, and you can go to Hell." The next year, on March 6, 1836, he died with the defenders of the Alamo.

Many other members of both houses, though failing to win Davy Crockett's glory, were of a type that was similarly caricatured and laughed about as "colorful." Their antics and eccentricities, usually emphasizing their "common man" backgrounds, often delighted their constituents and were good for votes, though in time they gave rise to unflattering and contemptuous stereotype thinking about all Congressmen by the American people. Among a host of such "characters" were William "Sausage" Sawyer, a former blacksmith from Ohio who got his name from his crude habit of standing by the Speaker's chair munching sausages; and Felix Grundy McConnell, a bull-voiced, fun-loving Representative from Alabama who wore a blue swallow-tailed coat and a scarlet waistcoat and once broke up a violin concert in a Washington hall by shouting at the artist, "None of your high-falutin, but give us *Hail, Columbia*, and bear hard on the treble!" On another occasion he appeared at a dignified Washington gathering with two French shop girls on his arms. As he reached President Polk in the receiving line, he tried to present them: "Mr. Polk, allow me the honor of introducing to you my beautiful young friend, Mamselle—Mamselle—Mamselle . . . whose name I have forgotten." Not a few Congressmen, far from the moral restraints of home, looked for easy entertainment in Washington and were not disappointed. Saloons, gambling rooms, and bawdyhouses proliferated, and such picturesque individuals as "Beau" Hickman, who made a living piloting statesmen to such resorts, became familiar fixtures in Washington hotels and the lobbies of the Capitol.

The Senators, who were still chosen by their state legislatures (they were "the elect of the elect," said Senator Benton), were generally a broad cut above the Representatives in erudition, ability, and manners, and most of the more capable and respected legislators, reversing the sentiment of earlier years, tried to graduate from the House to the Senate at the first opportunity. In 1831, when Alexis de Tocqueville, the French politician and writer, visited Washington, he praised the Senate as a body "of eloquent advocates, distinguished generals, wise magistrates, and statesmen of note, whose language would at all times do honor to the most remarkable parliamentary debates of Europe." The House of Representatives, on the other hand, dismayed him with its "vulgar demeanor," presenting an image totally different from that of the eminent and learned body in which Madison had sat during the first days of the republic. "The eye," Tocqueville wrote, "frequently does not discover a man of celebrity within its walls. Its members are almost all obscure individuals, whose names present no associations to the mind; they are mostly village lawyers, men in trade, or even persons belonging to the lower classes of society. In a country in which education is very general, it is said that the representatives of the people do not always know how to write correctly." Most other visitors to the Capitol during the three decades before the Civil War would have agreed with him.

Both houses were using young boys, generally orphans or sons of acquaintances of members, as runners. The clerk of the House first noted their employment in his annual report in 1827. By 1839 they were being called pages. The first one in the Senate was nine years old and was appointed at the behest of both Webster and Clay. They ran errands for the Senators and Representatives, carried messages on horseback from the Capitol to the scattered executive offices in the Federal District, worked in the Capitol's cloakrooms preparing speeches and documents for mailing, and received $1.50 per day, extra pay for overtime, and an additional payment of $250 at the end of a session.

Even before Jackson's inauguration, the Senate had been rising in esteem as a body of great debates, "a lofty pulpit with a mighty sounding-board" from which to address the nation, as Senator Charles Sumner of Massachusetts would later characterize it. The small, semicircular Senate chamber, with plain walls and a domed roof, had excellent acoustics and was ideal for the ringing voices of eloquent men. The Senators sat at desks of mahogany, placed on semicircular platforms, each row higher than the one ahead of it. Like the members of the House, the Senators—unless they were chairmen of standing committees—had no clerks, no assistants, and no offices of their own in which to work in private. (They would not begin to have clerks of their own until 1884, and they would not acquire personal offices until the first Senate Office Building was constructed in 1909.) Save for the work they did in other rooms in the Capitol, such as that in which the Congressional Library was housed, the Senators carried out all their business at their desks in the intimacy of the Senate chamber, studying documents, preparing speeches, and answering correspondence. All such labors ceased when the galleries and the floor became packed with spectators who came crowding in to hear the debates on national issues. Thronged along the walls and standing even among the Senators' desks, they heightened the excitement and drama in the little chamber.

The Webster-Hayne debate, one of the most memorable in the Senate's history, occurred soon after the opening of the Twenty-first Congress, the first one to meet after Jackson assumed office, and it began quite by accident. On December 29, 1829, Senator Samuel A. Foote, an anti-Jackson man from Connecticut, introduced a resolution to have the Committee on Public Lands inquire into the expediency of limiting the sale of western public lands and abolishing the office of surveyor general. The proposal was angrily attacked by Senator Benton, a loud and persistent champion of western expansion. He denounced the Foote resolution as a diabolical plan of the Northeast to safeguard its cheap labor by closing opportunities for poor people "to go to the West and get land," and at the same time to halt land revenues so as to make high tariffs necessary. It was, he summarized, "a most complex scheme of injustice which taxes the South to injure the West, to pauperize the poor of the North!"

His appeal drew approving nods from Vice President Calhoun, who must have felt frustrated that he could not get into the debate. By that time Nathaniel Macon had finally retired from the Senate, worn with old age, and John Randolph was gone too, sent by Jackson as minister to Russia. (Randolph soon fled its climate for England, returned to the United States, was elected to the lower house again in 1833 but, fighting off insanity, died in May of that year—saying, first, that he wished the House to take no note of his passing, and then almost having his wish dramatically fulfilled when a Virginia colleague who rose to announce his death dropped dead himself at his seat just as he finished imparting the news about Randolph.) But there was now another determined advocate of the states'-rights cause in the Senate, South Carolina's Robert Y. Hayne, thirty-eight years old, slim and handsome, aristocratic, socially popular, and an able and compelling debater. On January 19, 1830, he rose to pick up and expand upon Benton's theme that the South and West should unite against the Northeast. As Hayne began to speak, charging the Northeast with a host of sins against the South and West, attacking the "American system" of a high protective tariff and western land restrictions as a deliberate policy to create a dependent class of low-wage workers in the Northeast, denouncing the use of western lands simply to raise revenue and increase the federal government's power, and asserting that "there is no evil more to be deprecated than the consolidation of this government," Daniel Webster, wearing his customary blue coat with bright brass buttons, buff waistcoat, and high white cravat, entered the Senate, having come from the chamber of the Supreme Court in the basement, where he had been conducting some private law business. Webster listened to Hayne with rapt attention and the next day rose to answer the southerner's charges against the East and to question him severely on his views of the powers of the national government. Remarking that he deplored the tendency of some southerners habitually to "speak of the Union in terms of indifference, or even of disparagement," he called attention to the support being given in South Carolina to Calhoun's doctrine of nullification and challenged Hayne to oppose or defend the right of a state to pass on the constitutionality of, and resist, federal legislation such as a tariff.

On January 21 and 25, with Calhoun registering obvious approval, Hayne gave his reply, satirically reminding the Senate of the anti-Union activities of Massachusetts's Federalists at the Hartford Convention during the War of 1812 and going on to deliver a brilliant defense of the doctrine of state sovereignty and nullification. The Senate chamber was crowded with spectators, and most of them considered the southerner's arguments unanswerable. But the debate had now become a battle of giants over the nation's most perplexing—and possibly insoluble—issue, the powers of the Union and the state governments. On January 27 Webster rose again, and with the packed chamber hanging on every word, he delivered the most powerful and eloquent plea for the American Union that any man has ever made. Demolishing Hayne's arguments one by one, he assailed nullification as impractical, ruinous, and unconstitutional. His deep, majestic voice sounded like an organ and his words filled his hearers with emotion. "The Constitution is not the creature of the State government," he told them. "It is, sir, the people's Constitution, the people's government, made for the people, made by the people, and answerable to the people. . . . The very chief end, the main design, for which the whole Constitution was framed and adopted was to establish a government that should not . . . depend on State opinion and State discretion." Whatever was left of the Benton-Hayne theme of an alliance between the South and the West disappeared as the ultranationalist western legislators in the chamber thrilled to the patriotic fervor of Webster's final words, which many American schoolboys would thereafter have to memorize: "When my eyes shall be turned to behold for the last time the sun in heaven, may I not see him shining on the broken and dishonored fragments of a once glorious Union; on states dissevered, discordant, belligerent; on a land rent with civil feuds, or drenched . . . in fraternal blood! Let their last . . . glance rather behold the gorgeous ensign of the republic . . . not a stripe erased or polluted, nor a single star obscured, bearing for its motto, no such miserable interrogatory as 'What is all this worth?' nor those other words of delusion and folly, 'Liberty first and Union afterwards'; but everywhere, spread all over in characters of living light, blazing on all its ample folds, as they float over the sea and over the land, and in every wind under the whole heavens, that other sentiment, dear to every true American heart—Liberty *and* Union, now and forever, one and inseparable!"

In the ensuing tumult, the tenuous southern hope for an alliance with the West vanished, and Foote's original resolution, almost overlooked, was eventually defeated. But another question buzzed through the Capitol. Where did the new President, a southerner and a westerner, stand? As with most issues, he had never committed himself on the question of the rights of states. As Jackson's silence continued, Calhoun and his South Carolina colleagues, aware of the spread of nullification sentiment in their state that might lead to a confrontation with the administration, became concerned. Finally they forced the issue, inviting Jackson to a dinner at Brown's Indian Queen Hotel honoring Jefferson's birthday on April 13, 1830. The President was surrounded by states' righters, and twenty-four prepared toasts were given supporting South Carolina's position. When Jackson was introduced, everyone stood and cheered. He fixed his eyes on Calhoun. "Our Union—it must be preserved," he said. Then he raised his glass. Calhoun's hand shook as he lifted his own tumbler. Hayne rushed up to the President, trying to save something. Could the text be changed for the newspapers to read, "Our Federal Union"? he asked. The President agreed. A moment later Calhoun was called on. Regaining his composure, he faced his friends. "The Union," he said, "next to our liberty, most dear."

From then on, the already strained relations between Jackson and the Vice President went from bad to worse. Soon after the Jefferson birthday affair, Jackson discovered that Calhoun, as secretary of war in Monroe's Cabinet, had wanted to punish him for his unauthorized invasion of Florida in 1818. The revelation led to a complete breach between the two men and set the stage for a bitter confrontation over nullification, which Calhoun's supporters in South Carolina continued to push. To try to conciliate the South, Jackson asked Congress to revise the harsh 1828 Tariff of Abominations, and on July 14, 1832, a slightly milder tariff—though retaining the protection principle, which Jackson considered constitutional—was enacted. The new law created a crisis: dissatisfied nullifiers in South Carolina swept the state elections and called a convention in November, 1832, which adopted an ordinance nullifying the federal tariff acts, prohibiting the collection of duties within the state beginning on February 1, 1833, and declaring that the use of federal force would be cause for the state's secession. At the same time, the South Carolina legislature authorized the use of the militia to resist the national government. Calhoun continued to publish papers reaffirming the constitutionality of nullification. As the crisis deepened, his position as Vice President, as well as his personal safety, became precarious. On December 10 Jackson issued a proclamation to the people of South Carolina, asserting the supremacy of the federal government, declaring that no state could refuse to obey its laws or leave the Union, and announcing that "disunion by armed force is treason."

Two days later, recognizing that Jackson might already consider him a traitor, Calhoun was chosen by the South Carolina legislature to fill the Senate seat of Hayne, who had been elected governor. On December 28 Calhoun resigned as Vice President and returned boldly to Washington—now alive with rumors that Jackson had sworn to hang him—to plead his state's case on the Senate floor. He arrived just in time to lead a fight against the so-called Force Bill, which had been introduced in Congress to authorize Jackson's use of the army and navy to enforce the revenue laws in South Carolina. The struggle was marked by another notable debate, this time between Webster and Calhoun, over the question of the constitutionality of nullification and secession. Meanwhile, to try to end the crisis, administration supporters had introduced a measure for the immediate lowering of the tariff. Henry Clay was now back in the Senate, and neither he nor Calhoun wished to see the bill pass, for it would permit Jackson and Van Buren to take credit for settling—and winning—the issue. Instead, Clay formulated his own compromise tariff bill, which would lower the rates over a ten-year period, and Calhoun gave it his support. The new measure was introduced on February 12, 1833, and by March 1 it had passed both houses. The Force Bill kept pace with it, passing the Senate on February 20 (with Calhoun, Clay, Benton, and many others abstaining from voting) and the House on March 1. Both bills were signed by Jackson on March 2. On learning of the introduction of the administration's original bill to lower the tariff, South Carolina—given no support by any other southern state and losing heart in the face of Jackson's determined moves to proceed against her—had suspended the nullification ordinance. In March, after the Clay-Calhoun compromise bill was passed, a state convention formally rescinded the ordinance, and the crisis ended. Both sides claimed victory, but Calhoun, sullen, bitter, a lonely, leonine figure in the Senate, had learned a lesson. No state standing by itself could successfully carry out the doctrine of nullification. The South would have to become united, each state guarding its own rights but joining with the others for their common sectional interests.

Despite his strong stand for the supremacy of the Union, Jackson had given ample evidence on other issues that he would support the exercise of national authority only in limited areas and that, in many matters, he would back the states'-rights forces. Though he endorsed internal improvements, he thought, like Madison and Monroe, that federal financing would require a constitutional amendment. In the meantime, he proposed distributing surplus federal revenues among the states to be used at their discretion. Congress did not respond to this recommendation for what amounted to an early form of revenue sharing, but instead continued passing pork-barrel legislation that provided federal aid to individual projects, developing within both houses the practice of "logrolling" ("I'll vote for your bill if you vote for mine"). The trading of votes and cooperation, either for the passage or defeat of bills, would in time become a basic and complicated part of congressional procedure in the movement of legislation through committees and on the floors of both houses, but in 1830 the states' righters saw it being used as a tool by the supporters of Henry Clay and his "American system" to frustrate their opposition to the federal financing of internal improvements.

Hoping to strike at the system, and particularly at the Clay party that would oppose him as Jackson's successor, Martin Van Buren finally induced the President on May 27, 1830, to exercise his first veto, negating a bill to authorize the government to subscribe to $150,000 worth of stock for the building of a sixty-mile turnpike from Maysville to Lexington in Clay's state of Kentucky. Pointing out that the road lay within a single state,

Jackson pleased the states' righters by justifying his action on constitutional grounds, but he reaffirmed his support of internal improvements and again suggested a constitutional amendment. Clay's supporters were unable to override the veto, but in Kentucky Clay made much of the issue. Meanwhile, Jackson (who during his administration vetoed twelve measures—three more than his predecessors combined—and was the first President to use the "pocket veto," killing a measure at the end of a congressional session by letting it die without his signature or a formal veto) continued to veto logrolling bills for canals and roads, though he signed measures for river and harbor improvements (justified for defense, but generally supported also by southern and western exporters).

The day after the Maysville Road veto the states' righters, again with Jackson's assistance, won another victory by the passage of the Indian Removal Bill, which appropriated $500,000 for the forced removal of all Indians still living east of the Mississippi River to lands farther west. The measure fulfilled the policy of dispossessing the eastern Indians that Jefferson had first proposed, and it also climaxed a long fight between Georgia and such northern nationalists as John Quincy Adams and Daniel Webster. When Georgia had ceded its western land claims to the federal government in 1802, Jefferson's administration had promised Georgia to extinguish all Indian land titles within that state's borders as quickly as possible. Through the years, however, the powerful Cherokee nation had refused to cede its lands and move west, as Jefferson had hoped it would, and gradually it came to constitute an Indian political entity within Georgia's boundaries—most of its people as "civilized" as the neighboring whites, but occupying lands that the whites wanted. Finally Georgia lost patience and began a program of terrorization against the Indian people. An attempt to drive the Cherokees and Creeks out of Georgia and Alabama was temporarily thwarted during John Quincy Adams's administration by the President and various northern Congressmen, but pressure against the Indians was increased when gold was discovered on Cherokee lands in 1829. A Georgia law assumed state authority over the Cherokee territory, but white missionaries living with the Indians contested it in the courts, and in March, 1830, Chief Justice John Marshall ruled that the federal government had exclusive jurisdiction in the Cherokee lands and called the Georgia law unconstitutional.

His decision brought matters to a head. Jackson, a strong supporter of the policy of forcing all Indians out of the East, was in the White House, and when Georgia defied the court decision, he supported the state. "John Marshall has made his decision, now let him enforce it," he is reported to have said. Despite his contrary, and almost simultaneous, stand against South Carolina on the nullification issue, he ignored the angry protests of northern Senators and Congressmen, who wanted him to send troops to enforce the Court's decision and protect the Indians, and, instead, gave his backing to the Removal Bill. After impassioned debate, it passed.

From then on most members of Congress lost interest in the Indians, considering them a people destined to disappear; the victory of the states' righters, supported by Jackson and his successor Van Buren, forced tribe after tribe from their ancestral lands and sent streams of Indians trekking on "trails of tears," often under the bayonets of escorting troops, to present-day Oklahoma and the eastern plains of Kansas and Nebraska. Some tribes, including Black Hawk's Sauk and Fox in Illinois and the Seminoles in Florida, resisted removal (an eight-year undeclared war against the Seminoles, launched by Jackson in 1835 and causing another brief but ineffective congressional flare-up against the administration's Indian policy, took several thousand lives on both sides and cost the government almost $60 million), and segments of some of the tribes managed to evade the removal agents and hang on, in hiding in the east, until the nation lost interest in the small, isolated, and seemingly useless pockets of land they still inhabited. On June 30, 1834, Congress set apart the western section of the Arkansas country (today's Oklahoma) as Indian Territory—in time, it would be a dumping ground and end of the road for defeated tribes from every part of the nation—and in 1836 a Bureau of Indian Affairs was established to assert governmental authority over the tribes and take from them whatever sovereignty they still possessed. Placed at first in the War Department, the bureau was transferred in 1849 to the newly created Department of the Interior.

An issue of far greater contention between Jackson and his opponents in Congress had meanwhile arisen over the Second Bank of the United States, whose twenty-year charter was due to end in 1836. In his first message to Congress in December, 1829, Jackson revealed his basic antagonism to the bank, suggesting an investigation of the institution. With a number of his supporters in Congress, most notably Senator Benton, Jackson viewed the bank as something of a national monster, established unconstitutionally and run privately and in dictatorial fashion by its president, Nicholas Biddle of Philadelphia, for the benefit of the privileged financial and commercial interests of the Northeast to the detriment of the government and the agrarian interests of the South and West. To many, including numerous newspapers and members of Congress, however, the memory of the country's difficult fiscal experience during the War of 1812 after the death of the first bank had not faded. The bank still seemed to them the source of the nation's economic stability, and Congress paid little attention to Jackson's proposal for an investigation. But the President meant business. In his next annual message to Congress, in December, 1830, he served notice on the bank that it faced a contest by recommending that it be replaced by a new government bank established as a branch of the Treasury. Behind the scenes, and unbeknownst to Jackson, Biddle began quiet negotiations with Secretary of the Treasury Louis McLane for a recharter, but in the Senate Benton took up the President's cause.

Believing in a solid gold and silver "currency of the Constitution,"

Benton considered that the bank's great influence over state banks and over the supply of credit and currency in all parts of the country gave it life-and-death powers over every section of the economy, permitting it to determine the prosperity or depression of one group or region at the expense of another. The bank, he charged, moreover, was run by "a company of private individuals, many of them foreigners [British investors], and the mass of them residing in a remote and narrow corner of the Union, unconnected by any sympathy with the fertile regions of the Great Valley [the Mississippi West] . . . and none of these elected by the people, or responsible to them." On February 2, 1831, he tried to introduce a resolution against the recharter of the bank. The bank's friends, led by Clay's supporters, still held a slim majority in the Senate, however, and despite a fiery speech that lasted for several hours, Benton was denied permission to present his resolution. His speech, nevertheless, was widely circulated, and with the help of various newspaper editors who supported Jackson, anti-bank arguments began to make an impact on the electorate. Meanwhile, congressional elections were held, and Henry Clay, fighting mad over the Maysville Road veto, returned to the Senate to add strength to the antiadministration forces.

Confident of a majority in the current Congress and wary of increased Jackson strength in the next Congress, supporters of the bank applied at once—four years ahead of time—for a renewal of the charter. The move led to frantic maneuvering in both houses that increased still further the public's interest in the contest. In the House a freshman Representative and pro-Jackson man, Augustin S. Clayton of Georgia, recited a list of fifteen charges against the bank—written out for him by Senator Benton on a small piece of paper that Clayton wrapped around his finger to refresh his memory while he spoke—and called for a committee to investigate the charges. A fight then developed over whether the investigation should be conducted by the Ways and Means Committee, headed by Representative George McDuffie of South Carolina, a supporter of the bank, or by a special committee appointed by Speaker Andrew Stevenson of Virginia, an anti-bank man (customarily, resolutions were not referred to committees hostile to their purpose). The vote on what to do ended in a tie, and Stevenson appointed a committee with an anti-bank majority. Despite its investigation and majority report against the bank, the committee failed to win over the House, and on July 3, 1832, that body voted, 107 to 86, to recharter the bank. Three weeks earlier, the Senate had done the same, 28 to 20. The House committee's report, however, provided Jackson with all the ammunition against the bank that he needed, and on July 10 he vetoed the bill with a message apparently drafted for him by Attorney General Roger B. Taney, charging the bank with being a monopoly, having foreign influence, and conferring special privilege; challenging the Supreme Court's decision that it was constitutional; and making the question the primary 1832 campaign issue.

His opponents accepted the challenge and were badly defeated in the first campaign utilizing national nominating conventions of party leaders from the different states—an idea first proposed in 1822 by Thomas Ritchie of the Richmond, Virginia, *Enquirer* and given increasing support as the electorate expanded and dissatisfaction with the congressional caucuses spread. On December 12, 1831, a convention of National Republican delegates met in Baltimore and nominated Clay for President and John Sergeant, a former Federalist and then Republican Congressman from Philadelphia, for Vice President. Jackson's supporters, now calling themselves the Democratic party, met on May 21–22, 1832, also in Baltimore, and unanimously chose Jackson and Van Buren. The campaign, revolving largely around the vetoes and other strong-willed acts of the President, whom his opponents labeled "King Andrew" and attacked as a would-be tyrant over Congress and the nation, witnessed the first use by the parties of such popular vote-getting devices as torchlight processions for the candidates. On election day Jackson overwhelmed Clay, 219 electoral votes to 49, carrying sixteen of the twenty-four states, and Van Buren did almost as well.

The election chastened Jackson's enemies in Congress but did not halt their opposition to his attacks on the bank. When in December, 1832, he launched a new assault, proposing the withdrawal of government funds from the institution (he was angered by charges that the bank had used its resources to help finance the campaign against him), Clay and Calhoun supporters in the House united in adopting a resolution against such an action. Jackson, however, viewed the election as a mandate to proceed against the bank, and on September 26, 1833, it was announced that the government would begin removing its deposits from the United States Bank and place them in selected state banks (labeled "pet banks" by opponents). Biddle had meanwhile begun a campaign of restricting loans and tightening credit to create financial distress and arouse protests that would force Jackson to change his policy. Like many members of Congress who continued to practice private law or pursue personal business interests while they served in the national legislature (few could live on their $8 per diem congressional remuneration, and most—though not all—members fastidiously guarded themselves against charges of conflict of interest), Daniel Webster represented outside clients, among them the bank. "My retainer has not been renewed or refreshed as usual," he wrote Biddle near the end of 1833. "If it be wished that my relation to the Bank should be continued, it may be well to send me the usual retainers." Biddle hastened to meet the Massachusetts Senator's complaint, and when the new Congress convened in December, 1833, Webster—indifferent to the ethics of his behavior—helped the bank's campaign to pressure the legislature against the President's policy. As manufacturers and commercial groups were squeezed for lack of credit (Biddle told them that the government's removal of deposits left the bank with insufficient money to lend), they inundated Congress, as well as the administration, with petitions to replace the deposits. Day after day, with Webster often in the lead, Senators held up other business to read the "distress memorials." In time delegations began to show up from the states to lobby their Representatives and Senators. So-called lobby-agents were not new to Congress. Since the first days of Washington's administration, special pleaders and their representatives had frequented the rooms outside the House and Senate chambers, as well as the taverns, boarding houses, and other haunts of the members of Congress, seeking attention for their personal concerns and interests. In the 1820's, when debates raged over the tariffs, the rotunda and corridors of the Capitol had often been filled with spokesmen for the various manufacturing and commercial interests in the different parts of the country, some of them having no means of income other than the fees they received from the special groups they represented. But never before had so many persons descended on Congress simultaneously with their complaints. Webster and the other opponents of the administration welcomed them, and once Webster ushered a group of thirty of them onto the floor of the Senate, placing them in various spots around the chamber while he read aloud their petition.

In the end it did no good. Jackson supporters also began to arrive with their petitions, and—more to the point—Jackson closed his ears to the opposition's protests and continued to transfer government deposits from the national bank to different state banks. On December 11, 1833, the Senate, on Clay's motion, asked Jackson for a paper he had earlier read to his Cabinet in which he defined that group as a personal organ of the President's and directed its members to support removal. When Jackson refused to submit the paper, stating, "I have yet to learn under what constitutional authority that branch of the Legislature has a right to require of me an account of any communications, either verbally or in writing, made to the heads of Departments acting as a cabinet council," Clay decided angrily that the time had come for the Congress to halt the President. On December 26 he introduced a Senate resolution censuring Jackson for assuming "a power not granted to him by the Constitution and laws, and dangerous to the liberties of the people," and a joint resolution, requiring House concurrence, criticizing the Treasury for the removals. Once again the Senate galleries were packed as Clay and Benton locked horns in an emotional debate over the censure resolutions. The nation, declared Clay in a three-day speech, was "in the midst of a revolution . . . rapidly tending toward a total change of the pure republican character of the Government, and to the concentration of all power in the hands of one man. . . . If Congress do not apply an instantaneous . . . remedy . . . we shall die—ignobly die—base, mean, and abject slaves; the scorn and contempt of mankind; unpitied, unwept, unmourned!" The cheers that followed his speech were so loud and sustained that Vice President Van Buren had to order the galleries cleared. Benton answered Clay with a bellowing four-day oration, charging that Clay's censure resolution was, in fact, "a direct impeachment of the President of the United States," and Calhoun replied to Benton. On March 28, after the wording of the censure of the President had been slightly changed, charging him with assuming "authority and power not conferred by the Constitution

175

and laws, but in derogation of both," the Senate passed the resolutions.

The House, now up to 242 members, at which level it stayed for the next forty years, and numbering among its members three future Presidents— Millard Fillmore, an anti-Jackson man from New York; Franklin Pierce, a Democrat from New Hampshire; and James K. Polk, a Tennessee Democrat who was chairman of the Ways and Means Committee—could not act on the Senate resolution that censured the President. Its pro-Jackson majority, however, promptly tabled the concurrent resolution criticizing the Treasury and instead passed a series of resolutions of its own, produced by Polk's committee, endorsing the removal of deposits and declaring that the bank should not be rechartered. In the Senate the confrontation with the President continued. On April 15, 1834, Jackson protested angrily to the Senate that he had been charged with what amounted to an impeachable offense without the opportunity to defend himself. A week later he sent the Senate a milder message of protest. On May 7, by a vote of 27 to 16, the Senate defiantly asserted that the President had no authority to question its action and refused to receive his messages of protest or place them on the record. In the following weeks it rejected a series of the President's nominations. On June 30, 1834, just before that turbulent first session of the Twenty-third Congress adjourned, Senator Benton, adding to the drama of the break between the President and the Senate, warned his colleagues that he would propose a resolution to expunge the censure of Jackson from the official record of the Senate at every session of Congress until it was passed.

During that year many of the anti-Jackson groups coalesced into the beginning of a new national party that—because it was fighting the executive tyranny of "King Andrew"—called itself Whig, after the English party that had fought the usurpations of the British kings. Based essentially on a union of the Clay National Republicans and the southern states'-rights supporters of Calhoun, who together had secured the passage of the censuring resolutions in the Senate, the party also included eastern supporters of Webster and the bank and westerners who opposed Jackson's stand against the federal funding of internal improvements. It was a loose coalition, and by the time of the 1836 elections it was still not well enough organized to choose a single candidate. Instead, its various elements put up a number of individuals with strong followings, hoping that the election would have to be decided by the House. A Massachusetts legislative caucus named Daniel Webster, and other anti-Jackson men were nominated by similar caucuses in Ohio and Tennessee. In addition, a third party, the Anti-Masonic, meeting in Harrisburg, Pennsylvania, nominated General William Henry Harrison of Ohio. None of them had a chance. The Democrats met in convention in Baltimore and unanimously chose Van Buren to be Jackson's successor, and in the election the New Yorker, promising to "tread generally in the footsteps of President Jackson," swept the field.

Meanwhile, the Senate had been completely frustrated on the bank issue and Jackson's popularity with the general public had soared. Friends of the bank accepted the fact that it would not be rechartered, and Biddle made plans to turn it into the Bank of the United States of Pennsylvania, with a state charter, after the expiration of its national charter on March 1, 1836. The passions aroused by the bank conflict, however, did not die. On January 30, 1835, an unemployed house painter, who claimed he was the rightful heir to the British throne and blamed Jackson's opposition to the bank for his difficulty in finding work, ran out of a crowd and tried to shoot the President with two pistols as he emerged from the Capitol rotunda after attending the funeral of Representative Warren R. Davis of South Carolina. Both pistols misfired, and Jackson sprang at his assailant with his cane. The man was captured, judged insane, and put in a lunatic asylum. Though an examination of him failed to link him to a conspiracy, Jackson was convinced that he was the agent of his political opponents.

On June 23, 1836, after Biddle's bank had finally become a state bank, Congress passed the Deposit Act, requiring the secretary of the treasury to select at least one bank in each state and territory that would receive deposits of federal funds and carry out the services previously provided by the United States Bank. The stability of the country's economy, however, had been gravely shaken by the disappearance of the old national bank, and a serious financial crisis was developing. With government money going into a variety of state banks, an uncontrolled inflation had begun. The banks issued huge amounts of paper money against the new funds in their vaults; the bank notes were used to buy and sell public land; and prices rose to unprecedented levels. On July 11, 1836, after Congress had adjourned, Jackson issued the Specie Circular, drafted for him by Senator Benton, the hard-money advocate soon to be known as "Old Bullion," announcing that after August 15 the government, to curb the "ruinous extension" of paper money and credit and to combat monopolistic speculation, would, with minor exceptions, accept only specie—gold and silver—in payment for public lands. The circular burst the inflationary bubble, but it started the nation toward a financial panic. The state banks did not have enough specie to cover all the paper money in circulation, loans could not be covered, and land prices plummeted. In December, 1836, with Congress back in session, a Whig resolution in the Senate called for repeal of the circular. In the House a bill providing for the government's acceptance of notes from specie-paying banks and for the discontinuance of the issuing of paper money of less than $10 denominations was amended to rescind the circular. By March 1, 1837, it had passed both houses, but Jackson, who was going out of office on March 4, pocket-vetoed it on the ground that the bill was "liable to diversity of interpretation." The veto—a final example not only of his pioneering use of the pocket veto but of his killing of bills for other than constitutional reasons, something not done before—climaxed one of Jackson's most significant impacts on the relations between the executive and Congress. Though his opponents viewed his thwarting of Congress' will as tyrannical, he had established, within his constitutional rights, the power of a President to influence legislation through the use of the veto threat.

In the meantime, Jackson—with Benton's help—achieved a final, satisfying triumph. True to his word, the Missouri Senator had introduced a resolution in each session of Congress since 1834 to expunge the censure of Jackson from the Senate *Journal*. At the same time, the President and his supporters had put pressure on some of the Senators through the state legislatures that elected them. As a result, a few anti-Jackson Senators had been replaced and others had been induced by their home-state legislatures to support Benton's resolution. By 1837 Jacksonian Democrats were in control of the Senate, and on January 16 of that year Benton's expunging resolution finally passed, 24 to 19. In accordance with the directions of the resolution, the secretary of the Senate brought the manuscript copy of the *Journal* of 1834 into the Senate and in a dramatic ceremony drew black lines around the censure resolve, writing across its face, "Expunged by order of the Senate this sixteenth day of January in the year of our Lord 1837." The supporters of Benton's resolution repaired to the room of the Committee on Finance, where refreshments awaited them to help celebrate their victory and where, according to Ben Perley Poore, a contemporary journalist and author of a volume of reminiscences of Washington life, "several Senators showed by their actions that they were not members of the then newly organized Congressional Temperance Society, before which Mr. Webster [who was noted for fortifying himself with a drink or two before making a speech] had delivered a brief address."

As Van Buren came into office in March, the so-called Panic of 1837 burst with full fury. Specie drained out of the East, banks failed, interest mounted to four percent a month, bankruptcies multiplied, unemployment increased, farm prices fell, and there were rent, food, and fuel riots among the poor and hungry in the cities. The short, affable New Yorker, bald, florid-faced, with bushy side whiskers, spent his entire four years in office trying to cope with the fiscal chaos and economic depression that Jackson had bequeathed to him. Calling an extra session of Congress in September, 1837, he proposed that the government manage its funds in an Independent Treasury instead of placing them in private banks, but, other than that, he urged the lawmakers to allow the depression to run its course. "The less government interferes with private pursuits the better for the general prosperity," he told them. His laissez-faire approach, in the face of the widespread suffering, drew sharp attacks from the Whigs, including Daniel Webster, who accused the new President of "leaving the people to shift for themselves." Congress' record was no better, however. An administration bill to set up an Independent Treasury was introduced, and despite opposition from Clay and Webster, who still wanted to reinstitute a national bank, it was passed by the Senate in a close vote. But under pressure from many of the nation's bankers it was tabled in the House, and Congress adjourned without taking any other steps to meet the depression. Reintroduced and fought over each year (the offensive Specie Circular, at least, was repealed in 1838), the Independent Treasury Act was finally passed by Congress on July 4, 1840, repealed the next year by a legislature dominated by Whigs, and reinstated by the Democrats in 1846. The scheme it finally instituted that year—regional subtreasuries with their own vaults, collecting all federal receipts, disbursing all payments in silver and gold, and serving the financial needs of the different sections of the country—was retained, essentially unchanged, as the organizational basis of the nation's fiscal system until the passage of the Federal Reserve Act in 1913.

In 1835, while Jackson was still in office, the slavery issue, never far beneath the surface in Congress, had re-emerged. In a message to the legislature on December 2 of that year, Jackson had noted that abolitionist publications tending to incite slave insurrections were flooding into the South through the mails and that pressure had been exerted on postmasters to intercept such material. In response to Jackson's recommendation of a law to prohibit the use of the mails for antislavery material, a special Senate committee, headed by Calhoun, had produced a bill giving postmasters so broad a censorship power that the Senate refused to pass it. The rise of northern abolitionist groups, and the new attention paid to the slave question in Congress, however, had marked the start of a sectional struggle that would divide both houses for twenty-five years.

Soon after the defeat of Calhoun's bill, Pennsylvania's James Buchanan, now a Senator and a loyal Jacksonian, presented a memorial from Quakers calling for the abolition of slavery in the District of Columbia. A heavyset bachelor with a large head and pudgy features, Buchanan was the object of cruel jokes in Washington resulting from his conspicuous intimacy with his "better half," the fastidious Senator King of Alabama, also a bachelor and once called by Jackson Miss Nancy. Defensive and cautious (he wore a high-collared coat to conceal a neck scar, and an eye defect caused him to tilt his head slightly forward and to one side so that he seemed attentively polite), Buchanan was quick to dissociate himself from the intent of the petition. Calhoun, however, protested that Congress had no right even to consider such a memorial and plunged the Senate into a heated two-month debate over whether it should receive the Quakers' petition. Calhoun lost again (though the request contained in the petition was rejected), but the intensity of the debate stirred fears and animosities on both sides and widened the gap between supporters and opponents of slavery. Believing that northerners were now dedicated to ending slavery, Calhoun set about on a deliberate campaign to unite southerners behind his principles of nullification and secession by waging an aggressive counteroffensive in behalf of "the peculiar domestic institution of the Southern States" and making the rights of the slaveholding interests into a national issue. When a resolution to recognize the independence of Texas came before the Senate in June, 1836 (Texas, under Sam Houston, the friend of both Jackson and Benton, had declared its independence of Mexico after the Battle of San Jacinto on April 21), Calhoun enraged the abolitionists and frightened many northerners by calling for the immediate annexation of Texas to extend slavery. Though Benton opposed him and Calhoun's proposal lost, a new dimension was added to the simmering slavery issue.

The abolitionists' petitions had, meanwhile, also flooded into the House and in that body had led to the passage of a "gag resolution" against the petitions and to the start of a courageous crusade for the right of petition and against slavery by sixty-nine-year-old John Quincy Adams, who two years after his term as President had ended in 1829 had come back to Washington as the Representative of his Massachusetts district. The ambitious Henry Clay had feared that Adams meant to run again for the presidency, and he welcomed his potential rival back to the capital in 1831 rather warily, asking him, "How do you feel upon turning boy again to go into the House of Representatives?" Adams was not averse to moving to higher positions that might lead him back to the White House, but he was now something of an anachronistic figure in the new American politics—scholarly, highly moralistic, disdainful of party regularity, still of the old gentlemanly school of the founding fathers, who believed that public service, based on integrity in ideals, was its own reward. By-passed by party leaders and the electorate when the stakes were higher than his Representative's seat, he missed out on presidential, gubernatorial, and senatorial opportunities during the early 1830's and was content to stay in the House, where he became one of its most valuable—and independent-minded—members, respected as a senior statesman of learning, experience, and honesty. As chairman of the Committee on Manufactures he played a leading role in fashioning the compromise tariff that ended the nullification crisis in 1832 and supporting the bank against Jackson (he was horrified when his alma mater, Harvard, conferred an honorary degree of Doctor of Laws on Jackson in 1833, and, though a member of the Board of Overseers, he stayed away from the ceremony, not wanting to see "my darling Harvard disgrace herself by conferring a Doctor's degree upon a barbarian and savage who could scarcely spell his own name"). Two years later, however, he took Jackson's side against Webster in a conflict over Jackson's threat of reprisals against France in a claims dispute dating from the Napoleonic Wars, and he delivered such a powerful defense of the President and the Democrats that Jackson's enthusiastic supporters fondly dubbed Adams "Old Man Eloquent," a term taken from one of John Milton's sonnets.

Adams was not an abolitionist, but he viewed slavery with abhorrence and felt that Congress possessed the constitutional right to end slavery through its war powers—if it ever chose to do so. A humorless stickler for proper procedure (he fathered a significant rule, requiring the House to vote to authorize a proposal—thus knowing exactly what it was supporting—before appropriating money for it), he was appalled by the attacks that broke out in Congress in 1836 over the people's constitutionally guaranteed right of petition. Though the House since 1792 had refused to consider petitions and memorials on the subject of slavery (the argument having been made that Congress constitutionally could do nothing about it), the right to address Congress with appeals on any subject had been held sacred, and every Monday morning the clerk of the House called the roll by states for the Representatives to present summations of the petitions they had received and to refer the memorials, if they wished, through the Speaker to an appropriate committee. Now, however, a move was under way in the House, much like Calhoun's attempted action in the Senate, to halt the antislavery petitions coming into the lower chamber. On May 18, 1836, three resolutions on the subject of slavery were introduced, including one providing that "all petitions, memorials, resolutions, propositions, or papers, relating in any way, or to any extent whatever, to the subject of slavery, or the abolition of slavery, shall, without being either printed or referred, be laid upon the table, and that no further action whatever shall be had thereon." Adams was on his feet immediately, trying to object, but was called out of order by Speaker James K. Polk. When the roll was called, and Adams's name was read first, he stood up and shouted, "I hold the resolution to be a direct violation of the Constitution of the United States, of the rules of this House, and of the rights of my constituents." Largely because of a desire to eliminate from the House the emotional rancor and division that discussion of slavery caused—a motive that partly accounts for the gag resolution's long reign in the lower chamber—the southerners were joined by many northerners and the ban on slavery petitions was passed, 117 to 68. But Adams had sounded a call to battle that he would wage on principle—single-handedly at first—for the next eight years within the House for one of the American people's basic rights.

His determined struggle was marked by one dramatic highlight after another. Despite the gag, he used every possible parliamentary device to read the abolitionist petitions that now came pouring in to him. In 1837 he threw the House into an uproar by asking Speaker Polk whether he could read a petition signed by twenty-two slaves. Amid angry shouts from the southerners to expel him, Adams disclosed that the petition opposed, rather than supported, abolition. That only fed the fire, and Representative Waddy Thompson of South Carolina introduced a resolution, amended by Virginia's furious, alcoholic George C. Dromgoole, to censure the aged ex-President for "contempt of this House" and for having "given color to the idea that slaves have the right to petition. . . ." After a long debate, filled with abuse and threats against Adams, the motion was beaten, and Adams's fight went on. The gag resolution was renewed each year, backed by northern Democrats trying to hold the party together and ensure southern support for Van Buren; in each session, day after day, Adams defied the ban, reading petitions and welcoming a support that was slowly growing for him among restless northerners and westerners.

In February, 1838, the feelings of northerners in Congress against southerners were intensified by a tragic duel. In the course of heated remarks, Jonathan Cilley, a freshman Representative from Maine, made comments that led to his being challenged to a duel by another first-termer, William J. Graves of Kentucky. Graves's second was Representative Henry A. Wise of Virginia, a fiery defender of slavery who later, as governor of his state, would sign the order to hang John Brown. A bitter opponent of Adams and of all those who took his side in the reading of petitions, Wise was more furious than Graves at the young Maine Congressman and seemed eager for his death. The two contestants chose rifles at a hundred-yard range and on February 24 met on the old dueling grounds at Bladensburg near the capital. Both took the customary two shots and missed. Wise, however, insisted that the duel continue, and on the third shot Graves killed Cilley. The affair shocked Congress as well as the public, and Wise's murderous role was investigated by a House committee, whose report was tabled by a majority vote contending that there had been no breach of Cilley's privilege as a member of the House and that therefore no action required. In the Senate, however, a bill was passed banning the giving, delivering, or accepting of a challenge to a duel thereafter in the District of Columbia. Adams led the fight for the bill in the House, and it became a law on February 20, 1839. The act later drew bitter comments from the unchastened Wise, who complained that members of Congress would now call each other cowards and liars on the floor, "And, Sir, there the matter will drop. *There will be no fight."*

Friction had, meanwhile, increased over the growth of abolitionist activity and the question of annexing Texas, now an independent republic with a constitution permitting slavery. Fearful that Texas could be carved into several new slave states and that annexation would also bring on a war with Mexico, northerners, including the legislatures of a number of states, bombarded Congress with memorials against the admission of Texas. In the House attempts by southerners to table the petitions under the gag rule incensed Adams, who felt that they should be considered by the House Committee on Foreign Affairs. The tyranny of the gag rule was daily becoming more evident, and for three weeks Adams was able to conduct something of a filibuster against annexation and the slave interests. (At almost the same time Clay, who wanted the presidential nomination in 1840 and feared that his Whig party was becoming too closely identified with northern antislavery leaders, delivered a scathing attack on the abolitionists in the Senate. When Senator William C. Preston of South Carolina suggested that he might have repelled a lot of northern Whigs, Clay replied somewhat hollowly, "I had rather be right than be President".)

Though respect for Adams had increased, even among his enemies, the gag rule remained, and Adams continued reading petitions, even from persons who questioned his patriotism and sanity and threatened him with harm. In 1841, in another great display of courage and conviction—and despite the opposition and fear of his own family—he defended the Africans of the *Amistad* case, who had mutinied on a Spanish slave ship and landed on Long Island, where American officials seized them and put their fate to the courts. Adams introduced resolutions in their behalf in the House and finally helped free them by an eloquent plea before the Supreme Court. The next year he caused another tumult in the House by reading a petition from forty-six citizens of Massachusetts who asked that Congress dissolve the Union. When he moved that the petition be given to a select committee to report to the House why the appeal should not be granted, all the old attacks were renewed against him. The southerners met in caucus and the next day introduced another resolution to censure him. Adams, now seventy-five years old, white-haired and slightly bent, his hands shaking with palsy and his eyes red and watery, stood at his seat, fighting back against his attackers. When Henry Wise charged him, as well as his father, with having been in alliance with Great Britain against the South, Adams's shrill voice rose. "Four or five years ago," he cried, alluding to Wise's role in the killing of Cilley, "there came to this House a man with his hands and face dripping with the blood of murder, the blotches of which are yet hanging upon him, and when it was proposed that he should be tried by this House for that crime, I opposed it."

Adams got through the ordeal without being censured. The next month, however, a new ally, Joshua Giddings of Ohio, was censured for attacking a southern demand for the return of escaped slaves. Giddings resigned but was immediately re-elected by his constituents and re-entered the House, a vigorous and dangerous opponent of the defenders of slavery. His return reflected changes taking place in the North, where voters in increasing numbers were supporting antislavery candidates. By the end of 1843 the Democrats were beginning to split in political and factional disputes over the approaching 1844 presidential nomination, and in January, 1844, in the first session of the Twenty-eighth Congress, many of the northern Democrats, no longer feeling bound to support the southerners, for the first time backed Adams's resolution to abolish the gag. Adams lost by one vote, but after eight years of trial and defeat, victory was near. It came on December 3, 1844, the second day of the second session. Once more Adams introduced his resolution to rescind the gag, and this time enough northern Democrats, angry at southerners in their party for having overthrown Van Buren and nominated Polk at their convention, joined the northern Whigs and passed Adams's motion, 105 to 80. "Blessed, ever blessed be the name of God," Adams wrote in his diary that night. "The great battle for the freedom of petition and of debate in Congress was over . . . ,"observed historian Samuel Flagg Bemis in *John Quincy Adams and the Union*. "It was a turning-point in American history, from slavery toward freedom."

Adams had three more years of life. Hailed by his supporters as "the Representative of the Whole Nation," he opposed the annexation of Texas and the Mexican War, oversaw the passage of legislation in 1846 establishing the Smithsonian Institution (funded by a gift of $501,169 from James

Smithson, an amateur British scientist, in 1835 to the United States government "to found at Washington . . . an Establishment for the increase and diffusion of knowledge among men"), suffered a cerebral hemorrhage in November, 1846, recovered, continued to serve in Congress, and while seated at his desk in the House on February 21, 1848, suddenly slumped over during the clerk's reading of some resolutions on which the members were about to vote. The old man was lifted to the area in front of the Speaker's table, then placed on a sofa and carried into the rotunda of the Capitol. A short time later he was moved to the Speaker's room, which was warmer. Reviving enough to call for Henry Clay, who came in and, with tears in his eyes, took Adams's hand, the dying ex-President said weakly, "This is the end of earth, but I am composed." He fell into a coma, lingered for two days, and died in the Speaker's room on the evening of February 23. He was eighty years old and had been in Congress for seventeen years. In the Senate Benton delivered a eulogy. "Where could death have found him but at the post of duty?" he asked.

Meanwhile, other affairs in Congress had been entwined with political events. In 1840 the nation had had enough of Van Buren and the depression that had followed Jackson's administration. Certain that the coming presidential election would at last go to the Whigs, and that he, rather than Webster, would be their candidate, Clay arranged a deal to attract southern votes and carry Virginia by securing the vice-presidential nomination for his friend John Tyler of that state, who although a states' righter was stubbornly independent and often supported Clay. Much to his anger, however, Clay was by-passed by the Whig convention at Harrisburg. Wanting desperately to win, and fearing that both Clay and Webster were too controversial, the Whigs aped the Democrats, who had swept the nation with Jackson, a military hero, and nominated Ohio's General William Henry Harrison of Tippecanoe and War of 1812 fame. "I am the most unfortunate man in the history of parties: always run . . . when sure to be defeated, and now betrayed for a nomination when I, or any one, would be sure of an election," Clay mourned. The campaign was the most ludicrous in American history. Again mimicking the Democrats of 1828, the Whigs presented no platform and carefully hid from the nation any views that Harrison might have had on issues. Instead, they whipped up an emotional circus, promoting the myth that Harrison, a man of means and the son of a wealthy signer of the Declaration of Independence from Virginia, had been born in a frontier log cabin and raised on hard cider and was truly "a man of the people." With newspapers such as *The Log Cabin*, edited in New York by young Horace Greeley (it was a forerunner of his powerful national paper, the *Tribune*), and hundreds of rallies and parades, whose participants sang such campaign songs as "Tippecanoe and Tyler Too," Harrison overwhelmed Van Buren. Exactly a month after his inauguration, however, on April 4, 1841, the new President died of pneumonia, and Tyler, a thin, blue-eyed man of fifty-one with a long nose and a face that looked as though it had been pinched and drawn downward, entered the White House.

Clay intended to lead a Congress that would assert its authority over the executive. When the Twenty-seventh Congress met, Whigs were in control of both houses. Clay quickly introduced a set of resolutions in the Senate, embodying a legislative program that the Whig Senators had worked out in caucus, and implied somewhat arrogantly that he expected the President to support the measures. At first there was no difficulty. To clear the way for the re-establishment of a national bank—the Whigs' principal project—Whig majorities in Congress passed and Tyler signed a measure repealing Van Buren's Independent Treasury Act. A week later the Federal Bankruptcy Act, providing relief to some victims of the depression, also became law. But then Tyler, smarting over Clay's highhandedness, suddenly asserted his independence and shocked Clay and the Whigs by twice vetoing their bills for the re-establishment of the bank, terming them unconstitutional because they provided for the creation of branch banks within states without giving the states the right to approve them—a stipulation that Tyler insisted upon and Clay refused to accept.

The southern states' righters and Democrats, who had tried unsuccessfully to kill the bank by a two-week filibuster in the Senate, were overjoyed, and some of them called on the President, whose cordial meeting with them—marked by champagne toasts unflattering to the party that had elected him—infuriated Clay and the Whigs. They now saw that by accident they had a stubborn states' righter back in the White House—they began calling Tyler His Accidency—and a break between them and the President came quickly. On September 11, 1841, every Cabinet member but Secretary of State Webster (who was engaged in delicate negotiations with Great Britain) resigned; the Whig Senators and Representatives, unable to override Tyler's vetoes of the bank bills, met in caucus and voted to dissociate themselves from the administration; and Tyler drew around himself a coterie of advisers, most of whom were southern states' righters. Clay, in turn, had the President read out of the Whig party and dismissed the small number of men around Tyler as less numerous than "a Corporal's Guard" (which was what they were then called). Tyler, however, was unbowed. Hoping to build a new party for himself, he turned over the dispensing of federal patronage to his new advisers, which led to an unashamedly mercenary rush for lucrative jobs by double-dealing politicians, few of whom displayed any long-lasting loyalty to the President. At the same time the Senate rejected many of Tyler's nominations, including four of his new Cabinet appointments.

While the Whig Senators were having their difficulties with Tyler, the House was torn by long squabbling, exacerbated by sectional conflict, over other measures in the Whig program, including land and tariff bills. Having abandoned the hope of direct federal subsidies for internal improvements, the Whigs now pushed for their funding by a distribution to the individual states of federal money received from the sale of public lands, proposing, in addition, that the distributed funds be made up by receipts from a higher tariff. The intermixing of the measures—which fitted together neatly in Clay's scheme of things—so tied the Representatives in knots that they were unable to muster the two-thirds vote necessary to end debate in Committee of the Whole and had to change the rule to permit a majority vote to discharge the Committee. After another rule was passed limiting a member to one hour in debate, a distribution bill was passed, amended by southerners to provide that distribution to the states would halt if the tariff were raised above the level of twenty percent.

In the next session of the Twenty-seventh Congress, which began on December 6, 1841, hostility between Tyler and the Whig majorities in both houses brought the legislative process almost to a standstill. Recommendations by the President were brushed aside or subjected to weeks of purposeless wrangling that aroused public anger and inspired irreverent newspaper reporters to call the House of Representatives the House of Rips and the National Bear Garden. Finally the Whigs pushed through both houses a bill that raised the tariff above the twenty-percent level without repealing the Distribution Act. Since it was a violation of the southerners' amendment of the previous session, Tyler vetoed it. Unable to override the veto, the two houses passed practically the same measure again, and once more Tyler vetoed it. The Distribution Act finally had to be repealed so that a tariff act that Tyler would sign could be passed, but not before a select House committee, chaired by John Quincy Adams, to consider what to do about presidential vetoes, reported a resolution to censure Tyler ("The power of the present Congress to enact laws essential to the welfare of the people has been struck with apoplexy by the Executive hand," the report said) and recommended a constitutional amendment allowing a majority rather than a two-thirds vote to override a veto. The House adopted the report but did nothing about the proposed amendment. In the meantime Henry Clay, once more deciding to run for the presidency, resigned from the Senate on March 31, 1842, in order to organize the Whigs for the 1844 elections. His emotional valedictory speech, delivered in his familiar style—stepping gracefully forward, backward, and from side to side, and flourishing a silk handkerchief as he spoke—provided the Senate with another of its great dramatic moments, causing Benton to burst into tears and the usually cold, frowning Calhoun to walk over and embrace the Kentuckian as he left the chamber.

Clay was unfortunate again. The congressional elections of 1842, bringing the Democrats back in control of the House, were a foretaste of what would happen in 1844. The annexation of Texas was now a major national issue, and while many Americans, including Clay, Calhoun, and other political leaders, viewed it primarily as a sectional conflict over the spread of slavery, the bulk of voters were motivated more by a new sense of national expansionism, expressed as America's "manifest destiny" and reflected by an increasing interest in extending the nation's boundary to the Pacific and enfolding not only Texas but California and Oregon. Senators Benton and Lewis F. Linn, both of Missouri, were the principal advocates of the settling of the question of Oregon, which since 1818 the United States had shared in joint occupation with Great Britain. Early in the 1840's American settlers had begun taking the Oregon Trail to that territory, and in 1843, in the third session of the Twenty-seventh Congress, Benton and Linn had engaged in "spread-eagle" oratory advocating that the pioneer travelers be given military protection and grants of land in Oregon. Calhoun and his supporters recognized that Oregon would become another antislave, or "free-soil," state and for the time being effectively quashed further consideration of the subject. But Texas, sure to become at least one, and possibly as many as five, slave states, was another matter, and one that had the support of Tyler. The serious connotation for Clay began when Webster, out of step with the administration's Texas policy, resigned as secretary of state and was eventually succeeded by Calhoun. Since the nullification conflict, Calhoun and his supporters had been following an independent course, but the appointment brought them back to the Democratic party, whose policies increasingly showed their influence.

The northerners' fears about Calhoun's appointment were confirmed on April 22, 1844, when Tyler submitted to the Senate a treaty for the annexation of Texas, the negotiations for which Calhoun had secretly completed and which Tyler had signed, also secretly. Though some southerners threatened the dissolution of the Union if the treaty were not ratified by the Senate, the combination of abolitionist fury, Whig opposition, and warnings by Benton and others that the treaty would bring on an unnecessary war with Mexico (the treaty defined Texas as extending to the left bank of the Rio Grande, incorporating territory that Mexico claimed was not part of Texas) resulted in the failure of the treaty to win a two-thirds vote in the Senate. In an unprecedented action, Tyler then sent the treaty to the House, proposing that Texas be annexed by a joint resolution of Congress, which required only a majority vote of each house. Before a vote could be taken, however, Congress adjourned, and Texas and Oregon both became issues in the presidential campaign.

At Baltimore, on May 1, 1844, the Whigs had nominated Henry Clay and former Senator Theodore Frelinghuysen of New Jersey. The Democrats, far from united, met in the same city on May 27. Van Buren, favored to win the nomination, had incensed the southern Democrats and alienated Jackson by declaring that annexation would probably lead to war with Mexico, and he finally lost the nomination to a "dark horse," former Speaker of the House James K. Polk of Tennessee, whose name was placed before the convention only on the eighth ballot.

Now, at last, the annexation question overtook Clay. Polk ran a strong campaign based on the sole occupation of all of Oregon, which at the time extended northward to the parallel of 54 degrees, 40 minutes, across the center of present-day British Columbia, and on the "reannexation" of Texas (the Democrats maintained that Texas had been part of the Louisiana Purchase but had been foolishly given back to Spain by the treaty of 1819). Despite an attempt to derogate Polk by using the campaign slogan "Who is James K. Polk?" Clay, in the end, did himself in. Hoping to gain southern support, he suddenly modified his annexation stand, announcing that "far from having any personal objection to the annexation of Texas, I should be glad to see it, without dishonor, without war, with the common consent of the Union, and upon just and fair terms." Angry northerners deserted him in droves, switching to the Liberty party, which had nominated James G. Birney of New York, a former Kentucky slaveowner turned abolitionist, who ran on an antislavery platform. As a result of Birney's personal vote in New York, as well as Clay's flirtation with the anti-Catholic American Republican party (a forerunner of the Native American and Know-Nothing parties), which turned New York Irish voters against him, Clay lost that state to Polk and with it the election.

Viewing the result as support for annexation, Tyler reintroduced the subject to the last session of the Twenty-eighth Congress when it convened in December, 1844. A number of bills were produced and excitement ran high in both houses. To the issues of the extension of slavery and possible war with Mexico was added what a newspaper editor in Washington termed "the organ of *acquisitiveness* [that] is very strongly developed in our people." Texas bondholders showed up at the Capitol, lobbying for the United States to take over Texas's unpaid debt. "Texas scrip and Texas bonds and Texas lands are said to be distributed freely among members," wrote Ohio's anti-slavery Representative Joshua Giddings in disgust. After many maneuverings and efforts by Benton and others to effect compromises, a joint resolution providing for the admission of Texas as a state (with her right to approve the forming of up to four additional states from her territory) had passed both houses by March 1. The votes reflected a variety of motives, though none as questionable as that advanced by a future President of the United States, thirty-seven-year-old Andrew Johnson, who had entered the House as a Democrat two years before. Reared in poverty and without a day of formal education, Johnson had risen from an apprentice tailor to the leadership of a Tennessee workingman's organization and membership in the Tennessee state senate. A sincere champion of the poor, though sometimes so defensive as to be demagogic and dissembling, he announced that he had voted for annexation because Texas (where slavery was legal) would "prove to be the gateway out of which the sable sons of Africa are to pass from bondage to freedom." No one apparently asked the still-obscure Johnson what he was talking about.

On March 28, claiming that the area between the Nueces River and the Rio Grande belonged to her and not to Texas and that the United States was therefore seizing some of her territory, Mexico broke off diplomatic relations. Troops under Zachary Taylor were dispatched to defend Texas, and on

December 29, 1845, that state entered the Union. By then Tyler's term had ended, his final day in office, March 3, 1845, being marked by the Senate and House finally overriding one of his vetoes. It was the first time that Congress had ever passed a bill over a presidential veto, and it reflected the low regard in which the legislature held the outgoing President.

Polk, slightly built and in his fiftieth year, was a dour, taciturn man, but a far more astute and able politician than Tyler. Moreover, he was strong-willed and determined and used every weapon and tactic, including the giving and denying of patronage, the trading of votes and support, the press, and the whipping up of home-state constituencies and political organizations against recalcitrant Representatives and Senators, to get Congress to do what he wished. Facing not only Whig opposition but considerable infighting among factions and powerful individuals within his own Democratic party, he established precedents of personal leadership and initiative over legislation that strong chief executives in future years would emulate to an even greater degree to gain dominance over the legislative branch.

In domestic affairs Polk managed to get the first session of Congress to pass almost all the measures he requested, including a reduced tariff and the reinstitution of the Independent Treasury. He was spared the opposition of Clay, who had returned to private life after the 1844 campaign, but Webster was back in the Senate, subsidized by an annuity endowment of $100,000 subscribed by a group of rich Bostonians ("All Webster's political systems are interwoven with the exploration of a gold-mine for himself," observed John Quincy Adams caustically). Joined by Senators from Pennsylvania and other protectionist states, Webster fought Polk's tariff to a tie vote in the upper chamber, then lost when Vice President George M. Dallas cast a deciding vote for the bill.

With a combination of boldness and bluff, Polk, meanwhile, conducted the settling of the Oregon question with Britain. In his inaugural address he announced an American claim to all of Oregon, setting off a wave of militant patriotism and the cry of "Fifty-four forty or fight!" by expansionists. Armed with this support, he then privately informed Richard Pakenham, the British minister in Washington, that he would settle the boundary at the forty-ninth parallel. When Pakenham rejected the offer without even submitting it to London, Polk renewed his public demand for the whole area, and on December 2, 1845, he asked Congress for authority to give Great Britain the necessary one-year notice of intention to end the 1818 treaty of joint occupation. British officials in London now reversed Pakenham's earlier attitude, suggesting negotiation or arbitration, but Polk turned them down. At the same time the introduction in both houses of the resolution that Polk requested precipitated a stormy debate between bellicose expansionists and those who feared an unnecessary and ruinous war with Britain and argued for a peaceful settlement. Among the noisiest expansionists were Michigan's Senator Lewis Cass, a massive and pompous man of sixty-three who had been secretary of war under Jackson, and Representative Stephen A. Douglas, who was serving his second term in the House from Illinois. Though Cass was a national figure with a varied background (including service as governor of Michigan Territory), which had made him a serious Democratic presidential contender against Polk in 1844, his detractors maintained that he was knowledgeable about many things but profound about nothing, and that he avoided or straddled most controversial issues. Douglas, on the other hand, though only thirty-two, was already a commanding figure in the House. He had a powerful upper body, short limbs, and a huge head with deep-set eyes and hair that hung to his shoulders. A gregarious politician and lawyer who also made money in real estate, he was a florid, arm-flailing orator who could speak for hours. Against the expansionists was arrayed a peace group, led in the Senate by Benton, who wanted a settlement at the forty-ninth parallel, and by Calhoun, who—having retired from office after his stint as Tyler's secretary of state—had become alarmed at the prospect of a war with Great Britain and had gotten Daniel Huger of South Carolina to resign his Senate seat so that he could return to that body in December, 1845, and participate in the Oregon debate.

Despite personal attempts by Benton, Calhoun, and others to prevail on Polk and James Buchanan, the new secretary of state, to negotiate with Great Britain, the President was immovable, and in April both houses passed the resolution that Polk requested, though expressing the hope that the President could effect a peaceful settlement. On May 21, 1846, risking war with Great Britain (the United States was then at war with Mexico), Polk notified the British that he intended to abrogate the 1818 treaty. As the crisis mounted, a change of circumstances in England led suddenly to that country's proffering a draft treaty to settle the boundary at the forty-ninth parallel. Polk submitted the treaty to the Senate, and though he was attacked by the expansionists for treachery and deception in abandoning the fight for all of Oregon, he accepted the decision of the majority of the Senate, which ratified the treaty, 41 to 14, on June 15, 1846, and brought the Oregon issue to a peaceful close.

In addition to his domestic program and the desire to settle the Oregon question, Polk had come to the White House with one other major goal—the acquisition of California. This required a shooting war, which the President methodically manipulated after Mexico refused to negotiate with an emissary he had sent to Mexico City. Encouraging the drumming up of anti-Mexican feeling, Polk, in January, 1846, ordered General Zachary Taylor to move his troops across the contested Texas territory from the Nueces to the Rio Grande. On May 9 word reached Washington that Mexicans had crossed the Rio Grande and killed some of Taylor's men. Polk was ready for the news. Two days later, in a highly distorted and self-serving version of the clash, he told an excited Congress that war "exists by the act of Mexico herself" and asked the legislature to "recognize the existence of war." At the same time his lieutenants in the House introduced a measure, worked out the day before between the President and Democratic leaders of the House Military Affairs Committee, appropriating $10 million and authorizing Polk to call for fifty thousand volunteers. Everything had been carefully planned. The House was permitted only two hours for debate. When angry antiwar Representatives pointed out that Congress had not yet voted to declare war, the Polk men attached a preamble to the money-and-troop bill stating, "Whereas, by the act of the Republic of Mexico, a state of war exists" and announced that this would serve in lieu of a war declaration. Opponents, willing to vote support for Taylor's exposed men on the Rio Grande but not for a war of aggression, struggled in vain to separate the preamble from the bill, Whig Representative Garrett Davis of Kentucky crying out, "It is our own President who began this war!"

Amid jingoistic oratory that raised the fear of disloyalty among those opposed to the war, the measure finally passed the House, 174 to 14, and that same afternoon it was taken up in the Senate, where Calhoun and Benton were able to separate its two parts, sending the preamble to the Foreign Relations Committee and the rest of it to Benton's Military Affairs Committee. Their momentary victory disintegrated that night when Polk put pressure on Benton, sending a battery of intermediaries to threaten his political future. The big Missourian, who had once proclaimed that "Benton and the people, Benton and Democracy are one and the same, Sir," finally surrendered early the next morning, telling one caller, "I see *you are right.*" That afternoon administration supporters, including Cass and Sam Houston—newly elected to the Senate from Texas, wearing a sombrero and a waistcoat of panther hide with its hair still on and normally sitting silently in the Senate chamber whittling away at small pine sticks—took up the fight. All resistance finally collapsed, and the measure passed, 40 to 2.

Begun as an expansionist act, the war quickly took on a new cast, feared by older men in both houses who had struggled for so long to quiet the issue of slavery in order to hold the Union together. Since a military victory would give the United States new territories, it now became inevitable that Congress would have to decide whether they would be free or slave. The issue arose abruptly in the same first session of the Twenty-ninth Congress. On August 8, 1846, two days before the scheduled adjournment of the long session, Polk asked the House for an appropriation of $2 million to use in negotiations for land cessions from Mexico at the end of the war. The House quickly voted the funds but attached a proviso, introduced by Representative David Wilmot, a northern Democrat from Pennsylvania, prohibiting slavery in any new territory. The next day was Sunday, but on Monday morning the measure went to the Senate. Before Polk's supporters could vote down the proviso, John Davis of Massachusetts, one of the two Senators who had voted against the war, secured the floor and filibustered till noon, when the session ended, thus killing the whole bill. The same request for an appropriation, though raised to $3 million, was introduced by the administration in the second session, which began on December 7, 1846, and again the House passed it with an amendment embodying the principle of the

Wilmot Proviso against the spread of slavery. The Senate drew up its own bill, however, without the rider, and after a heated debate over the constitutionality of the war, during which Polk charged opponents with giving "aid and comfort to the enemy," both houses passed the money bill, omitting from it any mention of slavery in the territories. At the same time the House attached the Wilmot Proviso to a bill to organize the Territory of Oregon. When that measure reached the Senate, Calhoun launched into a vigorous defense of slavery and southern rights and a harsh attack on the North, which he said was trying to destroy the balance between the two sections. If that happened, he warned, it would lead to "political revolution, anarchy, civil war, and widespread disaster." The Oregon bill was tabled by the Senate, but slavery was at last surfacing as the nation's largest issue, and Calhoun was beginning to achieve his goal of uniting the South.

In the North, meanwhile, the Free-Soil movement, demanding that "not another inch" of the United States be opened to slavery, was growing. During 1847 and early 1848, as American forces conquered northern Mexico, the Southwest, and California and gradually brought the war to a close by General Winfield Scott's triumphant campaign in central Mexico, the legislatures in ten of the fourteen northern states sent resolutions to Congress calling for the prohibition of slavery in any new territory. When the first session of the Thirtieth Congress assembled on December 6, 1847, Democrats still controlled the Senate but Whigs held a slim majority in the House and were able to elect Robert C. Winthrop, a Massachusetts Whig, as Speaker. Among the newcomers, sitting in the middle of the back row on the Whig side of the House, was long-legged Abraham Lincoln from Illinois, thirty-eight years old and still something of a country-bumpkin lawyer. Risen from obscurity and frontier poverty, Lincoln had served four terms in the Illinois legislature and had come to the House after working out with two Whig rivals in his district a "rotation" deal by which each of them would serve only one term in the national legislature, a not uncommon practice in many congressional districts in the nineteenth century to spread the honor of service in Washington among party rivals and to assure the voters that no one Representative would become "too big for his breeches." Though Lincoln roomed with a number of abolitionist Whigs, including Ohio's Joshua Giddings, at Mrs. Sprigg's boarding house on the site of the present-day Library of Congress (where his easy manner and store of jokes made him a favorite), he was not an abolitionist himself and in the beginning had even supported the war. But he idolized Henry Clay, and after being elected he had been moved by speeches of Clay and other Whigs to view the war as an unjust act of aggression against Mexico. It was a time when many men were changing their minds, and the two major parties were beginning to come apart. Near Lincoln sat two southern Whigs, very much against Polk's war but almost ready to join Calhoun's southern Democrats in defense of slavery—Georgia's Alexander H. Stephens, a pale-faced, sickly-looking little man who would one day be vice president of the

Confederacy, and Robert Toombs, also from Georgia, who would be a secretary of state in Jefferson Davis's cabinet. Davis himself, a thirty-nine-year-old Mississippi Democrat, was in the Senate. A wealthy cotton planter, he had graduated from West Point, served in the Black Hawk War, married Zachary Taylor's daughter, and done a stint in Congress before he resigned to assume a command in the Mexican War. After distinguishing himself in battle in northern Mexico, he had been appointed by Mississippi to the Senate in August, 1847.

Because of his commitment to his rivals, Lincoln—who served on two committees, the Post Office and Post Roads and War Department Expenditures—retired after only one term in the House. But after Polk opened the session with a message asserting that the war was a just one, Lincoln joined the debate on an administration resolution concerning the indemnity to be asked of Mexico by introducing a series of his own resolutions designed to force the President to admit that Mexico, not the United States, owned the exact spot between the Nueces River and the Rio Grande where Americans had first been killed. He followed it up with a scathing attack on Polk for having started an unnecessary and unconstitutional war and forcing Congress to accept it. "Allow the President to invade a neighboring nation . . . *whenever he may choose to say* he deems it necessary . . .," he told his colleagues, "and you allow him to make war at pleasure." The House passed a resolution condemning Polk, but on March 10, 1848, the war ended with the Senate's ratification of the peace treaty by which Mexico ceded California and New Mexico to the United States, and both houses turned their attention to the issue of slavery in the territories.

The House had again passed an Oregon territorial bill that included the Wilmot Proviso. Despite the fact that Oregon's geographical location and climate offered no future for slavery, southerners in the Senate opposed a restriction on slavery in any new territory, and Calhoun, Jefferson Davis, and others got the proviso killed. As tension increased, the Senate, after twenty-one hours of continuous debate, adopted a complicated compromise for territorial governments in Oregon, California, and New Mexico, with a decision on slavery in each territory to be left to the Supreme Court. The work of a committee headed by Whig Senator John M. Clayton of Delaware, the compromise was promptly tabled by the House, which repassed its original bill. The Senate, in turn, amended it to extend the old Missouri Compromise line of 36 degrees, 30 minutes to the Pacific. This proved unacceptable to the House (Oregon would have been free soil, but much of California and the Southwest would have been slave), and after another exciting session that lasted twenty-four hours and was marked by applause for Webster, Houston, and other speakers from the partisan crowds in the galleries and lobbies, the Senate approved the House bill on Oregon alone, with the Wilmot Proviso included, early in the morning of August 13, 1848, by a vote of 29 to 25. Calhoun failed to persuade Polk to veto the bill

Despite the growing division in the nation over slavery, the campaign of

1848 was a dull one. Neither Cass, whom the Democrats nominated after Polk refused to run again, nor Mexican War hero "Old Rough-and-Ready" Zachary Taylor, whom the Whigs united behind in a cynical attempt to emulate their success with another general, William Henry Harrison, in 1840, spoke out on the territory question (or any other issue), and Taylor defeated both Cass and Van Buren of the new Free-Soil party, carrying seven free states and eight slave states, thus showing that sectional feelings had not been aroused. In Congress it was a different matter. The attitude of an individual member on almost all questions was beginning to be affected by his position on slavery. As a result, the rules, procedures, and sectional leanings and loyalties of the chairmen and members of committees in both houses became more important than ever before. In December, 1846, at the start of the second session of the Twenty-ninth Congress, the Senate had instituted a significant change in the manner of selecting the chairmen and members of committees. Prior to that time—with temporary exceptions— they had been chosen by secret ballot, a method that had permitted the Senators a maximum of independence from the discipline and control of their party. Now it was agreed that representatives of caucuses or confer- ences of both major parties, the Democrats and Whigs, would make up lists of committee choices and the Senate would routinely accept them. The new procedure gave the parties a tighter control over their members, binding them to substantive issues, and it also worked to introduce a seniority system to committees, for the ranking of members began to be based on their experience and length of service on the committees. By 1859 the result was solidly favoring the South; selection by party, rather than by secret ballot, and ranking by seniority, complained one Senator, "operated to give to Senators from slaveholding states the chairmanship of every single com- mittee that controls the public business of this Government. There is not one exception."

In the House, where for many more years the Speaker would retain the power to appoint committees and their chairmen (delaying the development of seniority in the lower chamber's committees), sectional rivalry led to bitter battles over the election of a Speaker. Facing an intensely partisan contest in settling the problem of slavery in the territories acquired from Mexico, the first session of the Thirty-first Congress, assembling on Decem- ber 3, 1849, found the Senate in Democratic hands and the House evenly divided between Democrats and Whigs, with thirteen Free-Soilers holding the balance of power. A year before, in December, 1848, Calhoun, fearful of the effects of the Whig presidential victory on the Congress, had called a secret caucus of all southern members in both houses and in three meetings had tried to unite them in behalf of southern rights. Although most southern Whigs had refused to sign the "Address of the Southern Delegates," which Calhoun wrote, Georgia's Robert Toombs and Alexander Stephens now led other southern Whigs in the House in opposition to the re-election of Robert Winthrop, the Massachusetts Whig, as Speaker in the new Congress. Other issues had also arisen, including northern pressure to end slavery in the District of Columbia as well as a southern demand for a stricter fugitive slave law, and at stake was the proslavery or antislavery complexion of the chairmen and majorities of the committees, which the bias of the Speaker would determine. The contest for Speaker, which began with eleven candidates, including Howell Cobb, a Georgia Democrat, took three weeks and sixty-three ballots to settle, filling the Representatives' Hall with inflammatory speeches that threatened disunion and civil war, stirring men to the edge of violence (the sergeant at arms had to rush the mace to the side of a New York Representative to protect him from physical assault and restore order), widening the split between northern and southern Whigs, and seeming at times insolvable. Finally the House, for the first time in its history, abandoned majority rule, and on December 22, 1849, agreeing to accept a Speaker by a plurality vote, gave the victory to Cobb. It was an important triumph for the South at the start of a tempestuous session.

On December 24 Taylor sent his first and only message to Congress, amusing some because of a slip ("We are at peace with all the nations of the world and the rest of mankind," he said) and outraging most southerners by urging the admission of California and suggesting that the territories be allowed to decide for themselves whether they wished to accept slavery. Immediately Congress was in a new crisis: since California had adopted a constitution that forbade slavery, her admission would tip the balance, sixteen to fifteen, against the slave states in the Senate. In both houses southerners stormed against the proposal, denouncing it as the beginning of the end for slavery in their own part of the country and proclaiming that the South's only recourse was secession. Henry Clay, now seventy-three years old, aged, gray-haired, but as tall and magnetic as ever, had returned to the Senate. He had been excused from serving on any standing committees, but as the tumult rose and talk of the dissolution of the Union increased, the Kentuckian, already known as the Great Pacificator, began to work quietly with Stephen Douglas, now a Senator and chairman of the Committee on Territories, seeking a compromise formula to solve all the problems that were driving the North and South apart. On the stormy night of January 21, 1850, he called on Daniel Webster, won his support, and on January 29 introduced before the Senate a grand program to save the Union. In a series of resolutions, he proposed the admission of California as a free state; the organization, without mention of slavery, of territorial governments for New Mexico and Utah; the assumption of Texas's pre-annexation debt; the prohibition of the slave trade in the District of Columbia, but noninterference with slavery in the District as long as it existed in Maryland; a more effective fugitive slave law; and a declaration denying congressional authority over the interstate slave trade. The resolutions, embodying every concession to the South that Clay believed necessary as her price for California's admission, aroused new excitement in Washington and led to another great debate, involving for the last time the triumvirate of legislative giants, Clay, Calhoun, and Webster, as well as almost every other major figure in the Senate.

With the galleries and Senate floor once more packed with visitors who crowded into the Capitol to see the drama, Clay—greeted by a tremendous ovation as he rose to speak—commenced the debate on February 5 and 6, 1850. Wearing a black suit and a high white collar that reached to his ears, he argued against secession and, despite a bad cough and shortness of breath, pleaded lengthily and eloquently for tolerance and concessions by both sides. When he finished he was surrounded by admirers who congratulated and embraced him. Calhoun had been stricken by tuberculosis and was not present, but on March 4 the gravely ill southerner, wrapped in flannels and a great cloak, his face pallid and drawn and his eyes burning like coals, was helped into the chamber. Slumped in his seat, he listened in defiant silence while his speech was read for him by his friend Senator James M. Mason of Virginia. It was Calhoun's last blow for southern unity against the rest of the country, which he believed was growing stronger and more menacing to the South. Somewhat fanatically, he demanded that the North suppress the abolitionists and halt even the discussion of slavery. Clay's compromise measures were brushed aside; the North must yield on everything to the South. If not, Calhoun ended, "let the States . . . agree to separate and depart in peace. If you are unwilling we should depart in peace, tell us so, and we shall know what to do. . . ." Calhoun was helped from the chamber and four weeks later was dead at the age of sixty-eight, leaving as a legacy to the nation his doctrines of state interposition, nullification, and secession, based on states' rights. The last two were quashed by a civil war; the first one was still being asserted by states more than a hundred years after his death.

On March 7 the "Godlike Daniel" Webster, also sixty-eight, arose, dark, solemn, and booming. "I wish to speak today," he began, "not as a Massachusetts man, nor as a Northern man, but as an American. . . . I speak today for the preservation of the Union. 'Hear me for my cause.'" The chamber was hushed as Webster supported Clay's compromise, item by item, hurting himself among antislavery groups in Massachusetts and the North by his backing of the concessions to southern slaveowners, particularly of a more stringently enforced fugitive slave law. He was followed by two opponents of the compromise, one an antislavery northerner, the former governor of New York and newly elected Senator William H. Seward, and the other Jefferson Davis. Seward, a pragmatic politician who had acquired great influence over President Taylor, was usually motivated more by practical than moralistic aspects of a question. But now he inspired the North with an idealistic attack on Clay's concessions to the South as "essentially vicious" and appealed to a "higher law" of justice than that of the Constitution. Davis, a cold, calculating disciple of Calhoun's, denounced the resolutions as offering nothing to the South and demanded that, as a minimum, the line of the Missouri Compromise be extended to the Pacific. After them came Salmon P. Chase of Ohio, who would settle only for the Wilmot Proviso, and then Thomas Hart Benton, who opposed the compromise and with furious belligerency defended the preservation of the Union against talk of secession.

Clay had intended having the Senate vote, one by one, on the resolutions, but when southerners expressed the fear that after admitting California the northerners might turn down the concessions to the South, he agreed to combine all the measures into a single omnibus bill and supported a resolution introduced by Senator Henry S. Foote of Mississippi to appoint a select committee for that purpose. On April 17 Foote's resolution was passed and a Committee of Thirteen, headed by Clay, was elected by ballot. On the same day, Foote threw the Senate into pandemonium. A violent and homely little man of forty-six, he was a veteran of four duels (he had been shot down in three of them), had grappled in the Senate aisles with the much bigger Senator Simon Cameron of Pennsylvania, and had gained for himself the name "Hangman Foote" for having threatened to hang Senator John P. Hale of New Hampshire from the tallest tree should he ever visit Mississippi. Although he was a Unionist, Foote regarded Benton as a traitor to the South and had been baiting him unmercifully. Benton and his friends joked about the belligerent little man (how could an adversary in a duel "look into such a funny face and fire?" they asked), but Benton also took him seriously and warned the Senate, "Mr. President, sir . . . I never quarrel, sir. But sometimes I fight, sir; and whenever I fight, sir, a funeral follows, sir." On April 17, as Benton spoke on the select committee resolution, Foote rose with an aggressive retort and stopped suddenly as he saw the Missourian advancing on him. Drawing a pistol, Foote aimed it at Benton, who kept on coming. As other Senators finally held him, the Missourian shouted, "Let him fire! Stand out of the way! Let the assassin fire!" Panic broke loose as members scattered. Foote was finally overcome and relieved of his pistol and Benton led back to his seat. In the tensions over slavery the dignity and decorum of both houses were fast deteriorating, and numerous Senators and Representatives, frequently close to the boiling point in the angry debates, were coming to sessions carrying concealed bowie knives, derringers, and other weapons. In his defense Foote registered surprise; he had assumed, he said, that Benton was also armed.

On May 8 Clay reported his committee's omnibus bill, and for weeks in the hot weather he led the debate in favor of it. Eventually he had to give up, overwhelmed by the opposition of individual members on both sides who attacked different elements of the package as well as by the President, who, under the influence of Seward, insisted adamantly on his own plan to bring California into the Union and threatened to veto all the other proposals. On July 9 Taylor died suddenly and was succeeded by Vice President Millard Fillmore, an uninspired and ineffectual New York politician who was an enemy of Seward's and a friend of Clay's. When the omnibus bill was defeated in the Senate on July 31, Senator Stephen Douglas devised a new strategy, supported by Fillmore and aided considerably by the lavish use of lobbying funds from Washington banker W. W. Corcoran and other holders of Texas bonds. The individual resolutions were again broken into separate bills, and with Douglas in charge, they were this time maneuvered successfully through both houses. By September 20 all of them had been passed and signed by Fillmore. Known collectively as the Compromise of 1850, they were hailed by all but extremists on both sides as a final solution to the problems that had been dividing the nation. In Congress most members of the two houses, worn out by the exertions of the struggle, felt that the slavery issue had been settled; few wanted to hear or say anything more about it. "I have determined never to make another speech on the slavery question," said Douglas to his colleagues. "Let us ... drop the subject."

For several years it seemed, indeed, that they might be right. In the South followers of Calhoun took beatings from unionists in state elections in 1851 in South Carolina, Alabama, and Mississippi (where Jefferson Davis tried unsuccessfully to win the governorship as a secession candidate). Congress turned to other matters. On July 4, 1851, a cornerstone was laid for a new extension of the Capitol, the beginning of a massive redesign of the building that added the present-day quarters of the Senate and House as well as the huge handsome dome. The Representatives moved into their new hall in 1857. Two years later, on January 4, 1859, the Senators moved, complaining almost immediately of the poor acoustics and ventilation of their new chamber. The stale air and torturous heat and humidity in summer afflicted their health and humor until the installation of air conditioning almost a century later. And the vastly increased size of the chamber, together with its bad acoustics, inhibited the kind of oratory that had flourished in the smaller room (which the Supreme Court now moved into), and gradually most Senators ceased trying to pit their lungs against the architectural obstacles. Shouting matches continued, but anything else became too much of an effort.

Meanwhile, on June 29, 1852, Henry Clay died in the National Hotel in Washington. Webster, who had left the Senate in July, 1850, to become Fillmore's secretary of state and had then suffered a great disappointment when southern Whigs and northern extremists had both deserted him— after being deadlocked for five days and fifty-two ballots at the Whig convention in Baltimore—to nominate a noncontroversial political innocent, General Winfield Scott, for President in 1852, died four months after Clay, on October 24, at his home in Marshfield, Massachusetts. Another of the great voices, that of Thomas Hart Benton, disappeared from the Senate in 1851 when the Missourian, after thirty consecutive years in the upper chamber—a record at the time—was defeated by a Whig. Benton was elected to the House of Representatives for one term in 1853, fought on with a thundering voice for the preservation of the Union from the sidelines in Washington, and died of intestinal cancer in the capital in 1858 at the age of seventy-six. Less celebrated than Webster, Clay, or Calhoun, he exemplified the stratum of the national legislature's greatest figures, who combined political acumen, integrity, courage, and scholarship to contribute, in John F. Kennedy's words, a "sense of liberty to the affairs of his State and Nation."

By the time of his death, the peace established by the Compromise of 1850 had long since been shattered, despite valiant attempts by members of both houses to muffle sectional divisiveness. In 1851 a fire in the Capitol's west wing had destroyed most of the volumes of the Library of Congress, which was housed in that area of the building, and when the Joint Congressional Committee on the Library had begun the task of rebuilding the collection, its chairman had even gone to the extent of directing that no books be purchased that might exacerbate the sectional feelings of the members of Congress. But Clay's compromise, it became increasingly clear, had only temporarily saved the Union. Northerners, defying the Fugitive Slave Act, were encouraging antislavery agitation and helping runaway slaves to freedom, and southerners, deserting the Whig party for the Democrats, were again talking secession. The election of 1852, in which the Democratic candidate, Franklin K. Pierce—sympathetic to the south though he came from New Hampshire—defeated General Scott, marked the beginning of the disintegration of the Whig party. It also brought to the House of Representatives a thirty-year-old New York Democrat, William M. Tweed, who had come up through Tammany Hall as the foreman of a volunteer fire company and a city alderman. The future archetype of political bosses served only one term, but he managed to leave his distinctive mark, even in Congress, by securing passage of a bill that gave one of his relatives a contract to supply the House with some chairs, which turned out to be shoddily built and were soon replaced. During the same period, in January, 1854, Stephen A. Douglas, in the Senate, lit the fuse of the bomb that would begin the blowing apart of the nation.

6. The Senate Supreme

When Stephen A. Douglas first entered the House of Representatives in 1843, John Quincy Adams was shocked at the wild gesticulations and ravings that marked the speeches of the powerfully built little Democrat from Illinois. "In the midst of his roaring," Adams wrote, "to save himself from choking, he stripped off and cast away his cravat, and unbuttoned his waistcoat, and had the air and aspect of a half-naked pugilist." In the West Douglas, scarcely five feet tall but supercharged with energy, enterprise, and ambition, was known as "a steam engine in breeches." Born in 1813 in Vermont, he went to Illinois in 1833 and plunged into law and politics as an ardent Jacksonian Democrat. Appointed to the Illinois Supreme Court—he used the title "Judge" till the end of his life—he made a fortune in real estate and in the 1850's had landholdings worth close to a million dollars. As he grew older, entering the Senate and becoming one of the Democratic leaders and a principal contender for the presidency, he became more dignified, though he still had characteristics that, while serving him well in the guerrilla warfare of Congress, were defects in a man who would give courageous and moralistic leadership to a nation in crisis. Among them were a cynical expediency and a tendency to play with the truth when it suited his purpose.

On January 4, 1854, a month after the opening of the first session of the Thirty-third Congress, Douglas, as chairman of the Senate Committee on Territories, reported out a seemingly innocuous bill for the organization of the Territory of Nebraska. Written with great care to try to obscure its explosive implications, it shunted aside a congressional role in whether the territory would be free or slave by incorporating the principle of popular sovereignty—leaving the question to the decision of the inhabitants of the territory and in contested cases to the local courts with appeal to the Supreme Court. In addition, it carried a specious explanation to Congress that the bill continued the successful and peaceful policy for creating new territories laid down by the Compromise of 1850. The measure fooled no one. The Compromise of 1850 had applied to territories south of the 1820

Missouri Compromise line. Nebraska Territory, the last huge, unorganized section of the old Louisiana Purchase, stretching westward to the Rockies from Missouri, Iowa, and Minnesota Territory, lay north of that line, where slavery supposedly had been barred forever. Northern Democrat Douglas was, in effect, arbitrarily repealing the Missouri Compromise and opening the Northwest to the potential formation of a whole new group of slave states. Overnight an antislavery storm, more emotional than any the country had yet experienced, swept the North and projected Congress into the most turbulent years of its history.

Douglas's bill stemmed from many motives. As an expansionist he, with numerous others, had been urging the building of a transcontinental railroad, and in 1850 he devised a method of getting federal subsidies for railroads without risking vetoes on constitutional grounds. Interested at the time in a north-south railroad from Chicago to the Gulf of Mexico that would bind the West and South (and, incidentally, increase the value of his landholdings along the projected Illinois Central route in his state), he managed to push through both houses a land-grant bill that transferred federal land to the states through which the railroad would run; the states, rather than the federal government, could then use the land by sale or grant to fund the railroads, quieting the states' righters' arguments against the national government's financing of internal improvements. By 1853 attention had shifted to a railroad to the Pacific, and Jefferson Davis, now secretary of war in Pierce's Cabinet, dispatched expeditions of topographical engineers to seek the best route. Davis was bound to champion a southern route that would favor the South's commerce, but Douglas (again with landholdings and business relationships that would benefit) supported a central route from Chicago and St. Louis that would cross the proposed Nebraska Territory. There was one fly in the ointment. Missouri's influential Senator David R. Atchison, a hard-drinking, vehement advocate of slavery and president *pro tempore* of the Senate, had pledged Missouri voters to secure the repeal of the Missouri Compromise so that Nebraska could be a slave territory.

In December, 1853, Senator Augustus C. Dodge of Iowa had introduced a Nebraska bill in the Senate, with no mention of slavery. It was referred to Douglas's committee. Immediately, Douglas was under strong pressure from Atchison, who threatened to resign as president *pro tempore* and displace Douglas as chairman of the Committee on Territories if he did not produce a bill that repealed the Missouri Compromise. Douglas, who hoped to run for President in 1856 and was eager for southern support, needed little urging. A sincere believer in the principle of popular sovereignty, he was convinced that slavery would not take hold in the new territory, and thus the people's vote would produce the same result as the Missouri Compromise. While the North, furiously, saw at once what was being proposed, Atchison and other proslavery Senators also found fault with the measure, objecting to Douglas's ambiguous wording and demanding that the bill proclaim explicitly the repeal of the 1820 compromise. To put additional pressure on Douglas, Senator Archibald Dixon of Kentucky announced that he intended to offer such an amendment to the bill. Consideration of the measure was put over until January 23, 1854, and in the interim Atchison and a delegation of his supporters in both houses, accompanied by Douglas, conferred with the Cabinet and the President, readily acquiring administration backing for repeal. Shrewdly, Douglas had Pierce, who was pro-South in sympathy, write out the repeal clause in his own hand. At the same time, provision was made to split the area and organize two territories, Kansas and Nebraska.

On January 23 Douglas introduced the rewritten measure—the Kansas-Nebraska Bill—declaring flatly that the Missouri Compromise was "inoperative" (a word that reflected an attempt to deceive but again fooled no one) and commencing a furious debate in which shocked and angry northern Senators, led by Salmon Chase and the acid-tongued Charles Sumner of Massachusetts, denounced the bill as a "gross violation of a sacred pledge," a "criminal betrayal of precious rights," and "part and parcel of an atrocious plot." Sumner, a tall, handsome, humorless man of forty-three, was unsparing in his hatred of slavery and those who defended it. Long before he first came to Congress as a Senator in 1851, he was notorious among southerners as a leading abolitionist and a founder of the Free-Soil party. Regarding him as a loathsome fanatic, "outside of any healthy political organization," they tried to ostracize him in the Senate, denying him an assignment to any committee. Their opposition had not deterred him. At every opportunity he stung them with his rebukes, often employing provocative language that made his friends worry for his safety. Typical of his vituperation was his likening of Douglas to a "noisome, squat, and nameless animal" that filled the Senate chamber with an offensive smell.

Though the violent attacks by the Kansas-Nebraska Bill's opponents helped fan new flames of antislavery sentiment across the North, Democrats controlled both houses, and the southerners, backed by the administration, needed the votes of only a few pliant northerners to create majorities. On March 3 the Senate passed the bill, and on May 22 it passed the lower chamber and became law on May 30, 1854, ending the truce of the Compromise of 1850 and creating a crisis for the nation that would lead to the Civil War. The measure, announced Sumner with cold fury, "annuls all past compromises with slavery and makes any future compromise impossible."

There were southern Unionists in both houses—old-time Whigs, Jacksonians such as the "magnificent barbarian" Sam Houston ("I know neither North nor South; I know only the Union"), and conservative Democrats—all of whom feared the divisive course the country was taking. But events were now in the hands of such spiritual followers of Calhoun as Lucius Quintus Cincinnatus Lamar, a fire-breathing gentleman and scholar from Mississippi, Robert Barnwell Rhett (he had changed his last name from

Smith) of South Carolina, David Atchison, who left the Senate and hurried West to help win Kansas for slavery, former Congressman William L. Yancey of Alabama, and others, all bent on forcing the nation to accept slavery on their terms or breaking up the Union. Unlike Andrew Jackson, who had forced the would-be secessionists to back down, Pierce, who was greatly under the influence of Jefferson Davis—a man "ambitious as Lucifer and cold as a lizard," said Houston—followed a weak, permissive course, favoring and strengthening the southern extremists. Kansas became the fulcrum of their confrontation with the rest of the country, and within a year that hapless territory was wracked by a bloody struggle between militant proslavery and antislavery forces that made a mockery of Douglas's hopes for a peaceful decision by popular sovereignty.

In the North the passage of the Kansas-Nebraska Act led to a rapid realignment of political forces. On February 28, 1854, northern Whigs, Free-Soilers, and antislavery Democrats, meeting at Ripon, Wisconsin, recommended the organization of a new antislavery party to be called Republican. Another gathering at Jackson, Michigan, on July 6 formally adopted that name and called for the repeal of the Kansas-Nebraska Act and the Fugitive Slave Act and the abolition of slavery in the District of Columbia. The movement spread quickly across the northern states, enrolling numerous antislavery leaders, including Sumner and Chase. At the same time the breakup of the old parties gave added strength to another movement that had appeared a few years earlier, the anti-Catholic, anti-immigrant American party, popularly called the Know-Nothing party because its members, bound by oaths of secrecy, used as their password "I don't know." In reaction to the Kansas-Nebraska Act, both these parties scored dramatic triumphs in the congressional elections in the North in the fall of 1854. The Know-Nothings, who appealed more to a nativistic patriotism than to antislavery feelings, elected more than forty members to the House of Representatives, and the anti-Nebraska Act forces won more than a hundred seats. In all, only seven of the forty-two northern Democrats who had voted for the Kansas-Nebraska Act were re-elected.

When the first session of the Thirty-fourth Congress met in December, 1855, the Democrats still controlled the Senate, which named a proslavery northerner, Jesse D. Bright of Indiana, as president *pro tempore*. The House, however, was in chaos, almost evenly divided between southern Democrats and northern anti-Nebraska men, with the Know-Nothings holding the balance of power. The two latter groups could not unite on a candidate for Speaker, and once again the House went through a tumultuous battle, filled with personal threats and near fights. This one lasted for nine weeks, until on the 133rd ballot Nathaniel P. Banks, a mild-mannered Free-Soiler from Massachusetts who had joined the Know-Nothings, was elected. As in 1849, the House had had to reach a decision by a plurality rather than a majority vote to end the two-month contest.

In the meantime, amid violence and illegalities, both the proslavery and antislavery forces in Kansas set up governments, each clamoring for recognition. On January 24, with the House still unorganized and balloting for a Speaker, Pierce sent an undisguisedly biased message to Congress, in effect recognizing the proslavery Kansas government (which a temporary invasion of some five thousand Missouri residents had helped to vote into existence) and condemning the organization of the free-state government (by more legitimate settlers) as an act of rebellion. The message, generally believed to bear Jefferson Davis's touch, drew scorn from the anti-Nebraska men in Congress but was supported in the Senate by Douglas, who on March 17 introduced an act to enable Kansas to become a state. The antislavery majority in the House would have none of it and two days later, with Banks, one of their own, safely in the Speaker's chair, authorized the appointment of a three-member committee to investigate the true state of affairs in Kansas. Banks appointed one proslavery Representative from Missouri and two northern anti-Nebraska men, including a first-term Republican from Ohio, thirty-two-year-old John Sherman, who was just beginning a long and distinguished governmental career and whose brother, William Tecumseh Sherman, would become one of the great Union generals in the Civil War. While the committee was in the West, proslavery forces sacked the free staters' settlement at Lawrence, Kansas, and civil war began in earnest in the territory.

Meanwhile, Congress itself had been rocked by violence. On May 19 and 20, with tempers running high in both houses, Sumner delivered a long, intemperate tirade titled "The Crime Against Kansas," which he had already had printed for mailing around the country. His speech denounced the "slave oligarchy" and contained offensive personal attacks on other members of the Senate, particularly sixty-year-old Andrew Pickens Butler of South Carolina, who was not present. Sumner's stinging insults inflamed the southerners and embarrassed even some of his supporters, who considered them ill advised. On May 22, just after the Senate had adjourned and while Sumner was writing at his desk, two South Carolina Representatives, Laurence M. Keitt and Preston S. Brooks, the latter a tall young veteran of the Mexican War who was Butler's nephew, entered the Senate chamber carrying stout gutta-percha canes. Going up behind Sumner, Brooks began flailing away at his head while Keitt faced the other Senators to keep them from interfering. Sumner's long legs were stretched under his desk, so that when he struggled to rise, with blood pouring from his head, he was pinioned until he wrenched the desk loose from the floor and fell unconscious over it. None of the Senators present, including Douglas, made a move to stop the murderous assault. As Brooks finally backed away, some of them congratulated him. Others carried Sumner out of the chamber to a sofa in an anteroom. Brooks had seriously injured him, and for two years Sumner was out of the Senate under medical care. During that time, the Republicans honored him as a martyr, and Massachusetts kept his chair in the Senate empty as a symbolic reminder that the state supported him and that he would be back. On the day after the attack the Senate, at the request of William H. Seward and Sumner's colleague from Massachusetts, Henry Wilson, appointed a committee of investigation; but the Democratic majority allowed no Republican to be appointed to the committee, which eventually reported that though the incident was regrettable the Senate could take no action. In the House, whose antislavery members were seething, a motion to expel Brooks and Keitt was introduced but failed to receive the necessary two-thirds vote, though, in addition to the beating of Sumner, both men had been guilty of a gross breach of the rules against members of one house interfering in the affairs of the other. After a less-stern motion of censure was voted against Keitt, the two Representatives resigned, but within a month both were re-elected by their constituencies and reoccupied their seats as heroes among their southern colleagues.

Peace had not returned, however. In each house threats and abusive remarks punctuated the tense debates over Kansas, and men openly announced that they were carrying guns for their personal safety. At one point a pistol fell out of a Representative's pocket, clattering on the House floor and almost causing a riot. Congressman Philemon Herbert, who had been born in Pine Apple, Alabama, and was a proslavery Representative from California, where he had gone during the gold rush, contributed to the violent atmosphere by shooting a waiter in a restaurant. Despite the law against them, a number of duels were almost held. The hot-tempered Keitt, a South Carolina aristocrat who considered no northerner a match for a southerner, got into another scrape, challenging Sumner's friend Senator Wilson to a duel. Wilson declined with contempt, but Representative Anson Burlingame of Massachusetts accepted the challenge for Wilson, only to have Keitt back down when Burlingame insisted that the duel take place on the Canadian side of Niagara Falls, which would necessitate Keitt's traveling through the hostile North. Against this angry background the House received the report from its Kansas investigating committee, and in July, 1856, it voted to admit Kansas as a free state. When the Senate rejected the bill, passing instead the enabling act Douglas had introduced in March, the antislavery majority in the House, in turn, ignored the Douglas measure and continued its opposition to the administration and its deadlock with the Democratic-controlled Senate. When Congress adjourned, the question of a government for Kansas was left unsettled.

In the presidential election that fall, the fate of "Bleeding Kansas" was the principal issue. On June 2 the Democratic convention at Cincinnati, sensitive to the unpopularity of Pierce and Douglas in the North, had "dumped" both men in favor of the inoffensive James Buchanan, who as minister to Great Britain had been out of the country and was unsullied by the Kansas controversy. Buchanan campaigned on a platform supporting popular sovereignty in Kansas but promised to bring peace by stopping the violence and holding fair elections. The Republicans, still more of a movement than a strongly organized nationwide party, bypassed Seward and

Chase as too controversial and nominated the inexperienced John C. Frémont, who was something of a popular hero for his western explorations and his well-publicized role in the conquest of California and who supported the admission of Kansas as a free state. Despite Frémont's small political stature and the Republicans' spotty organization, Buchanan's electoral-vote majority was only a slim 52.

When the Thirty-fourth Congress met for its last session after the election, in December, 1856, both houses turned temporarily away from the Kansas issue to await the new administration. With attention now focused on tariff and economic matters, the Washington correspondent of the New York *Times* suddenly charged that "a corrupt organization of Congressmen and certain lobby-agents" existed in the capital, and an embarrassing bribery scandal shook the House. To most members of Congress (who in this session finally raised their salaries from $8 per day, which they had received since 1818, to $3,000 per year), it was no news that bribery, in one form or another, was part of the congressional scene and had existed since William Maclay complained about it during the First Congress. Though not flaunted openly, the corrupt activities of some lobbyists were taken as a matter of course. The best known of them, Edward Pendleton, enjoyed a popular reputation as the owner of an elegant gambling house on Pennsylvania Avenue called the "Palace of Fortune" or, as certain Congressmen dubbed it, the "Hall of the Bleeding Heart," where the affable host paid his bribes in the form of "fixed" winnings at the card tables or "loans" in return for the support of measures in which his clients were interested. The *Times*'s charges, nevertheless, nettled the House, which ordered an investigation behind closed doors. Despite the fact that the *Times*'s correspondent refused to testify and reveal his sources, the committee had no trouble finding evidence of bribery by lobbyists for railroads and manufacturers, as well as attempts by certain northern Representatives to buy the votes of others for particular bills. A motion was passed to expel guilty Representatives and punish those who would not testify. No one was expelled or punished, however, and when three New York Representatives at whom evidence pointed resigned their seats, the matter was dropped.

Pierce's southern sympathies and support of the slavery interests had gravely wounded the nation, but Buchanan's irresolution and fear of southern extremists were disastrous. On March 4, 1857, the new President delivered his inaugural address. Concealing the fact that he had already learned, improperly, the Supreme Court's decision in the Dred Scott case, he nevertheless aroused suspicion among northerners by stating that the Court would soon settle the Kansas controversy. Two days later Chief Justice Roger B. Taney issued the decision, shocking the North by declaring the Missouri Compromise unconstitutional, denying Congress the power to legislate against slavery, and implying that Congress must act to protect slavery in a territory. Buchanan, who wished to avoid involvement in the controversy, was pleased by the decision, for it seemed to support his solution: when the Kansans wrote their constitution, they could decide for themselves whether they wished to be free or slave. The history of the conflict in Kansas was proof enough of how fatuous this thinking was, and now the slavery interests redoubled their efforts, using force and a host of illegal devices. Though it was evident that an overwhelming majority of the settlers in Kansas were for a free state, a small, rigged proslavery convention at Lecompton drew up a constitution that protected slavery. With amazing effrontery, the proslavery leaders decided that the people would not vote on the constitution itself but on a hoodwinking and meaningless proposition "for the constitution with slavery" or "for the constitution with no slavery" but protecting the "property" of slaveowners. Either way the state would be slave. This, at last, was too much for Douglas, who recognized the travesty being made of the principle of popular sovereignty. Another crisis began to build. The Kansas free staters boycotted the fraudulent election, and the proslavery forces, announcing a victory for "the constitution with slavery," sent the constitution to Washington with a request for the admission of Kansas as a slave state. Douglas appealed to the President to turn down the request, but Buchanan was under great pressure from the southern members of his Cabinet, some of whom played on his fears of spreading violence and secession. The President had become "panic-stricken," wrote former Senator Henry Foote, the man who had once threatened Benton with a gun and who, though a Mississippian, was now a Unionist and an enemy of Jefferson Davis. "The howlings of the bulldog of secession" were frightening Buchanan "out of his wits," Foote warned.

When the Thirty-fifth Congress assembled in December, 1857, Douglas, who almost four years before had begun the whole Kansas controversy, led the opposition to the Lecompton constitution, telling the Senate that it was "a trick, a fraud upon the rights of the people." On January 4, 1858, the free-state legislature in Kansas conducted a new and more honest vote, in which the constitution was overwhelmingly rejected. Despite this evidence, Douglas's entreaties, and growing defections among northern Democrats, Buchanan took the fateful step of submitting the Lecompton constitution to Congress, giving it his endorsement. The brazen victory of the southern extremists who had worked on Buchanan's cowardice outraged Douglas, who immediately split with the President. "By God, sir!" he bellowed, "I made James Buchanan, and by God, sir, I will unmake him!" There followed three months of debate in both houses, angrier and more violent than ever before. Jefferson Davis was now back in the Senate, and under his imperious leadership the administration forces gradually overcame Douglas, Seward, Benjamin Wade of Ohio, and other furious opponents who tried to block the President's bill. On March 23 the Senate voted to admit Kansas as a slave state. Douglas's eyes were now opened. "In making the fight . . . ," he said, "I was enabled to stand off and view the men with whom I had been acting. I was ashamed I had ever been caught in such a company. They are a set of unprincipled demagogues, bent on perpetuating slavery, and by the exercise of that unequal and unfair power, to control the government or break up the Union. . . ."

In the House, once again ruled by Democrats thanks to Buchanan's victory and presided over by James L. Orr of South Carolina as Speaker, the bill's fate was uncertain. Sessions ran late and in one of them, at half past one in the morning, a wild-swinging, free-for-all fight erupted on the House floor when Laurence Keitt of South Carolina, again in a belligerent mood, called Representative Galusha Grow of Pennsylvania "a black Republican puppy" and Grow shouted back at him, "No Negro-driver shall crack his whip over me!" As the two men rushed at each other, Representatives came from all sides of the chamber to help, and in a moment more than thirty members of all ages were wrestling and punching each other. As Speaker Orr shouted and banged his gavel for order, the sergeant at arms strode into the middle of the melee with the mace. Still the fight went on, and ended only when one member, intending to seize another one by the hair, pulled off his wig, starting laughter that became contagious and halted the fighting. Members were soon making up and shaking hands.

When the bill reached the House floor it was beaten, 120 to 112, by a coalition of Republicans and Democratic followers of Douglas who deserted the administration. After passing its own bill calling for a new vote in Kansas on the Lecompton constitution, the House sent conferees to meet with members of the Senate, and in conference a new bill was worked out incorporating a complicated compromise providing for another vote on the contested constitution, and it finally passed both the House and the Senate. On August 2, however, Kansas voters rejected the Lecompton constitution. For the time being Kansas remained a territory, with slavery legal under the Dred Scott decision, and Congress was unable to solve the question. In time, as the population of free staters increased, Kansans wrote themselves a new constitution, and in 1861, after southerners had departed the Congress, the northerners admitted Kansas as a free state.

The issue had propelled the country closer to civil war, further polarizing the extremists on both sides, strengthening the Republicans, splitting the Democrats both sectionally and within the North, and weakening Buchanan. The damage to the Democrats became apparent in the fall elections of 1858, when the Republicans won every northern state except Illinois and Indiana. In Illinois Douglas was challenged for his Senate seat by Abraham Lincoln, who was still largely unknown outside the Northwest. In his acceptance speech to the state Republican convention, Lincoln attacked the Kansas-Nebraska Act for having increased slavery agitation, which, he said, would not cease until the nation had reached and passed a crisis. "'A house divided against itself cannot stand,'" he reminded his audience. "I believe this government cannot endure permanently half slave and half free." During the campaign Lincoln and Douglas engaged in a series of debates, which, because of Douglas's stature and association with the crisis, were followed by the whole nation. At Freeport, Illinois, Lincoln maneuvered Douglas into a difficult position, forcing him to explain how he could reconcile his doctrine of popular sovereignty with the ruling in the Dred Scott case. "It matters not what way the Supreme Court may hereafter decide . . . ," answered Douglas. "The people have the lawful means to introduce or exclude it as they please, for the reason that slavery cannot exist . . . unless it is supported by local police regulations." This assertion that despite the Dred Scott decision the people of a territory could legally exclude slavery before they wrote a state constitution was designed to satisfy the Illinois voters, but it further damaged Douglas's standing among southern Democrats and continued the split in the party. On the other hand, the debates enhanced Lincoln's reputation, and he won the popular vote in Illinois, though the Democrats carried the state legislature, which returned the embattled "Little Giant" to the Senate.

The last session of the Thirty-fifth Congress, assembling after the elections, accomplished little. Sectional tensions were as strong as ever, and both sides stood guard against any legislation that might benefit their opponents. Presidential recommendations to purchase Cuba from Spain and establish a protectorate over northern Mexico were contemptuously ignored by the northerners, who viewed them as new schemes for the expansion of slavery. At the same time the southerners blocked bills for a higher tariff, river and harbor improvements, and a transcontinental railroad. A homestead bill, giving the head of every family the right to buy 160 acres of western land for $1.25 an acre, also went down to defeat. For almost ten years Pennsylvania's Galusha Grow had been urging the adoption of such a bill, but land speculators, as well as southerners who feared that the measure would fill the western territories with antislavery settlers, successfully opposed it. Another bill, sponsored by Representative Justin S. Morrill, a Vermont Whig farmer who had gone into banking and trade, got further. It would grant public land to states and territories to be used for the establishment of public colleges. Like Grow's crusade for a homestead law for needy settlers, Morrill's dream of land-grant colleges, specializing in agriculture and mechanics and open to those with meager funds, would eventually be realized. This year the bill passed both houses but was vetoed by Buchanan on the old states'-rights ground that the federal financing of such activities was unconstitutional.

Far more newsworthy were John Brown's raid and hanging, which occurred after Congress had adjourned. Three days after the abolitionist's execution on December 2, 1859, the Thirty-sixth Congress convened, with sectional feeling more intense than ever. The Democrats still controlled the Senate, and on the first day the upper chamber approved the appointment of a committee to investigate Brown's financial backers. They failed in this purpose, but their wrath reflected the alarm and anger sweeping their home states and fast bringing the country to disunion. Republican Senator Seward, at Rochester, New York, had warned of an "irrepressible conflict" that would make the United States "sooner or later . . . either entirely a slaveholding nation or entirely a free-labor nation." To southern extremists, who were gaining the upper hand in their states, such threats, suggesting that John Brown's "invasion" was only a prelude to federal intervention and to slave insurrections in the South, were grounds for taking the offensive in behalf of slavery, confident that if the North denied the southern states their rights they would secede.

The House, meanwhile, had difficulty even getting organized. Despite the fact that Republicans outnumbered administration Democrats in the lower chamber, the fight for Speaker again lasted two months and took forty-four ballots to settle. During the struggle the galleries were crowded with emotional partisans of the candidates who applauded and hissed, and on the floor the excited members, some of them flourishing pistols and knives, shouted insults at each other and threw the chamber into one uproar after another. At the end of January, 1860, the Republicans' candidate, John Sherman, deeply resentful of personal attacks the southerners had made against him, finally withdrew from the contest, and on February 1 the Republicans managed to elect a sixty-three-year-old Representative from Newark, New Jersey, William Pennington, who had once been governor of his state but was serving his first term in Congress and was completely unknown to most members. Pennington, who aside from Henry Clay was the only Representative ever elected Speaker in his first term, recognized that he had been chosen because he was not controversial, and "as an act of patriotic duty" he accepted the honor, which was short-lived because this turned out to be his only term in Congress.

The presidential election of 1860 carried the nation inexorably closer to civil war. At the Democratic convention in Charleston, South Carolina, on April 23, the delegates of eight southern states walked out when Douglas's supporters put over a platform that refused to endorse federal protection of slavery in the territories. Douglas was then unable to secure the necessary two-thirds vote for his nomination, and all the delegates reconvened in another convention at Baltimore on June 18. Again they split, and the two wings of the party met separately, the northern Democrats nominating Douglas and the southerners Buchanan's Vice President, John C. Breckinridge of Kentucky. On May 9 a coalition of old-time Whigs and Know-Nothings formed the Constitutional Union party, with a platitudinous platform for the preservation of the Union and the enforcement of laws, and nominated former Senator John Bell of Tennessee, who had first entered Congress in 1827 and had been William Henry Harrison's secretary of war in 1841. On May 16 the Republicans met at Chicago and after rejecting Seward, whose antislavery record was considered too extreme for victory, nominated Lincoln and Senator Hannibal Hamlin of Maine.

With the Democratic party divided and four candidates in the field, the oligarchical leadership of the South, which had been able to dominate the nation's policy-making apparatus for so long, grew fearful at the prospect of a Republican victory that for the first time would put antislavery forces in control of the huge power and patronage of the presidency. As secession threats spread, Douglas went south to try to persuade the southern states to stay in the Union, but he accomplished little. The idea of remaining in the nation without power to protect slavery was becoming intolerable to contemplate. On November 6 Lincoln was elected, receiving a million fewer votes than the combined tally of his opponents but winning 180 electoral votes against 72 for Breckinridge, 39 for Bell, and 12 for Douglas. Within a week South Carolina's two Senators resigned their seats, and on December 20 that state seceded from the Union. In the crisis the last session of the Thirty-sixth Congress assembled on December 3, looking to Buchanan for leadership. Instead the President was torn and frightened, pulled between Jefferson Davis, who pressured him to support the constitutional right of a state to secede, and the northern members of his Cabinet, who urged him to follow the examples of Jackson and Webster and declare firmly that a state had no right to secede and that he would take all steps necessary to preserve the Union. Wishing that Lincoln were already in the presidency, Buchanan finally sent a message to Congress that tried to satisfy both sides by announcing that while no state had a right to secede, the federal government lacked the power to keep it in the Union. The timid message, treated with contempt in both the North and the South, gave a further go-ahead to the secessionists.

Turning away from the President, Congress sought desperately to cope with the emergency by itself. The House created a committee of thirty-three members to see what could be done, and the Senate set up a committee of thirteen with a similar aim. On December 14 Jefferson Davis and a group of Senators and Representatives from nine southern states signed an address entitled "To Our Constituents" stating that "we are satisfied the honor, safety, and independence of the Southern people require the organization of a Southern Confederacy—a result to be obtained only by separate state secession." Nevertheless, now that the crisis had come, Davis was reluctant to leave the Union and hoped that some compromise could still be worked out. Nervously, but still frigid and self-righteous, he joined the select Senate committee of thirteen, which was now chaired by a venerable seventy-three-year-old Kentucky Whig, John J. Crittenden, whose intermittent service in the Congress went back to the years immediately after the War of 1812. Crittenden assumed the peace-making mantle of Henry Clay, and during the last tense weeks of December he guided the committee to a compromise that was acceptable to both northern and southern members. But Lincoln sent word to Seward, who was on the committee, that he would not accept one of the provisions, which would have extended the Missouri Compromise line to the Pacific, making all the land south of it, including California, permanently slave, and the compromise fell apart. As the new year commenced, the confrontation over Fort Sumter began in South Carolina, and the rest of the lower tier of southern states, one by one, seceded. Mississippi left the Union on January 9, 1861, and on January 21, with crowds of hushed spectators filling the Senate galleries, the corridors, and all the adjoining rooms in the Capitol, five southern Senators—beginning with David Levy Yulee, the nation's first Jewish Senator, whom Florida had originally sent to the upper chamber in 1845 when it was admitted as a state, and ending with Jefferson Davis himself, gaunt, pale, suffering from neuralgia brought on by the emotional strain—rose to announce the separation of their states from the United States. Speaking passionately of the common heritage of the two sections of the nation, Davis pleaded for peace between them. "I am sure I feel no hostility toward you, Senators from the North," he said. "I am sure there is not one of you, whatever sharp discussion there may have been between us, to whom I cannot now say, in the presence of my God, I wish you well. . . ." The eyes of many of his hearers were wet with tears as the Mississippian concluded, "Mr. President and Senators, having made the announcement which the occasion seemed to me to require, it only remains for me to bid you a final adieu."

Calhoun's successors had finally achieved his goal, and in the following days other Senators and Representatives from seceded states formally resigned, withdrew, or simply packed up and silently left Washington. After the Civil War commenced and passions became inflamed, both houses took official note of those who had left, voting that they had been "expelled as traitors." At the moment, however, no one could gauge how serious the secessionists were or whether their departure would be permanent. With northerners now in control of the two houses—their memberships reduced by one third—business moved ahead speedily. Vacancies on committees were filled and acts were passed admitting Kansas as a free state and raising tariffs on manufactured goods. The tariff bill, bearing the name of its author, Vermont's Representative Morrill, who had tried unsuccessfully to put it through in the previous session, began a policy of subordinating the aim of raising revenue to that of protecting American products that would persist amid controversy for the next half century.

On February 4, 1861, a so-called Peace Convention, proposed by the legislature of Virginia, which had not yet seceded, and attended by delegates from twenty-one northern and border states, met in Washington and, under the chairmanship of ex-President Tyler, tried to seek a way to peace between the North and the South. The group continued to meet during most of the month but accomplished nothing. Meanwhile, in Montgomery, Alabama, the Confederate States of America came into existence, with Jefferson Davis as provisional president, Alexander Stephens as vice president, and many former southern Senators and Congressmen filling high administrative posts. On February 23 Lincoln arrived in Washington. The Thirty-sixth Congress ended on March 3, and the new President was inaugurated the next day. At 4:30 A.M. on April 12 Confederate shore batteries opened fire on Fort Sumter in Charleston Harbor. Three days later Lincoln called for seventy-five thousand three-month volunteers and summoned the Thirty-seventh Congress to meet on July 4.

As war fever swept both sides, Virginia, followed by Arkansas, Tennessee, and North Carolina, seceded, and the Confederacy established its capital at Richmond. In both the North and the South men who had been in the national Congress helped their state governors organize militia units, and some of them donned uniforms to command companies and regiments. On the south side of the Potomac a growing force of Confederate soldiers began to appear, menacingly close to Washington. Northern units, some of them attacked as they came through Baltimore, hurried to the defense of the national capital, and the first of them were temporarily quartered in the empty halls and corridors of the Capitol. Four companies of Pennsylvanians, most without arms or uniforms, were the first to reach Washington and were wildly cheered as they marched from the railroad station, up the steps of the Capitol, and through the corridors to the large, newly built Hall of the House of Representatives. A bearded black member of one of the companies, Nick Biddle, had been struck on the head with a rock in Baltimore and wore his cap over a blood-soaked handkerchief. In the rotunda he took off his cap and the wound began to bleed. As he marched to the Representatives' Hall, he left a trail of blood spots behind him on the floor, and Biddle was hailed as the first man to spill blood for the Union in the war. The next day the Massachusetts Sixth Regiment arrived and was quartered in the Senate chamber, its colonel occupying the Vice President's chair and its men cooking bacon and making coffee at the furnaces in the Capitol's basement and sleeping on the floor and in the galleries of the Senate chamber. A week later they were joined by New York's Seventh, a unit of wealthy and socially elect young men, who moved into the Hall of the Representatives but marched to restaurants downtown for their meals, and by the Massachusetts Eighth, commanded by Benjamin Franklin Butler, a stout, cross-eyed, dictatorial Democratic politician and military amateur, who would have a flamboyant career during the war and in Congress as a Radical Republican after the war. Butler's men bivouacked in the rotunda and helped to establish bakeries in the committee rooms in the basement for all the troops in the Capitol. After a while the units were moved out of the building to new camps guarding Washington, and on July 4 the new Congress assembled.

With the city and the offices of the government still filled with southerners, and Confederate troops encamped across the Potomac, Lincoln and members of his Cabinet, particularly Secretary of State Seward, took numerous extralegal steps to safeguard the national government and combat the Confederacy. Although Congress had not declared war, Lincoln ordered a blockade of the South, directed an increase in the regular army and navy, called on the governors for more volunteers, and authorized the army to suspend the writ of habeas corpus when necessary to cope with sedition. When Congress met, its angry and impatient Republican majority was quick to endorse every emergency action that Lincoln had taken and to clamor for more of the same. Throughout the war, freedoms were violated by arbitrary arrests and infringements of rights—including, from time to time, the widespread interception of mail and the tapping of telegraph wires —by the federal government. The House set up an inquisitorial Select Committee on the Loyalty of Clerks, under the chairmanship of pugnacious John F. Potter of Wisconsin, who two years earlier had offered to duel Virginia's hotheaded Representative Roger A. Pryor with bowie knives. Potter's committee, a watchdog over the loyalty of government personnel, used spying and tale-bearing to ferret out and discharge, or arrest, anyone suspected of southern sympathies in the various Washington bureaus.

Lincoln's determination and abilities were matched by similar qualities among the Republican leaders of the new Thirty-seventh Congress, and for a while they worked together harmoniously, with the Congress supporting the President and his Cabinet, helping the administration frame necessary legislation, and then quickly passing it. In the Senate the militant Charles Sumner, preachy and pedantic but overwhelming in his moral fervor, forged into leadership, becoming chairman of the Committee on Foreign Relations and being supported by his Massachusetts colleague, Henry Wilson, who headed the Committee on Military Affairs. William Pitt Fessenden, a popular Republican from Maine, presided over the important Committee on Finance, cooperating closely with Salmon P. Chase, whom Lincoln had made secretary of the treasury, and with the House Committee on Ways and Means, led by Thaddeus Stevens of Pennsylvania. Stevens, a ferocious, angular sixty-nine-year-old man with dark brows, a black wig, and a club foot, could terrorize younger men by his sharp voice and cynical, despotic manner. For years, on the local, state, and national levels, he had fought for the extension of suffrage, public schools, free soil, the opening of the public domain, and the encouragement of industry and trade; believing that freedom was a prerequisite of American progress and prosperity, he venomously hated the feudalism of the southern aristocracy. The owner of a small Pennsylvania iron foundry (which Lee's army destroyed during the war), Stevens was a bachelor, had a black housekeeper who some gossiped was his mistress, and did not care a hoot what anybody thought. In the House, by force of intellect, personality, and autocratic will, he became more of a power than the Speaker, his fellow Pennsylvanian Galusha Grow. John Sherman, at the same time, had gone to the Senate to replace Chase and was of great help to Fessenden on the Finance Committee. Andrew Johnson, hating the wealthy and aristocratic slavery leaders of the South, had broken angrily with those in his state who took Tennessee into the Confederacy, and he remained a dedicated Union Democrat in the Senate. The ablest Democrat of all, however, Stephen Douglas, was gone. For three months he had tried to help Lincoln, but then, on June 3, 1861, he died at Chicago. Had he lived, the history of Reconstruction and of the postwar Democratic party might have been entirely different.

Under the Republican leadership that, through skillful use of party caucuses, steering committees, parliamentary procedure, patronage, and subcommittee action, quickly built a close-knit, efficient machine in the two houses, the first session of the Thirty-seventh Congress passed a stream of war legislation, and on August 6, one month after it had assembled, adjourned. During the brief, hectic session it authorized an army of five hundred thousand men, appropriated money for a vast increase in the navy, voted a $250 million bond issue, raised the tariff, enacted the first income tax in American history (3 percent on incomes over $800 and 1.5 percent on income from government securities, both to start on January 1, 1862) and a tax on land, and passed the Confiscation Act, directing the seizure, with adjudicated compensation, of all property, including slaves, used by enemies against the United States. Some of the emergency legislation supported Lincoln's actions, some was unprecedented, and much of it was open to constitutional question. The income tax, which was later increased, expired in 1872, though some years later the Supreme Court, in deciding a case that had arisen under it, declared that it had been constitutional. There were frequent debates and arguments over the bills, but the Republican leaders employed informal "whippers-in" (a term derived from the House of Commons and later in the century shortened to "whips," used to refer to specific party leaders on the floor) to round up votes and with threats or promises hold them obediently in line for the fast-moving measures.

After adjournment a strain developed between the more radical antislavery Republicans and conservatives and moderates such as Lincoln who felt that the immediate task was to restore the Union. Those who came to be called Radical Republicans, remembering the trials they had endured in the prewar Congresses, were determined to smash the southern slave-owning oligarchy forever, stripping it of its property, including slaves, and guaranteeing Republican control of the national government and Congress for years to come. They included such Senators as Sumner and Wilson of Massachusetts, Lyman Trumbull of Illinois, Zachariah Chandler, a millionaire Michigan Republican who had been mayor of Detroit, and square-jawed, vengeful "Bluff" Benjamin Wade of Ohio; and in the House, Thaddeus Stevens, Schuyler Colfax and George W. Julian of Indiana, and many others. Lincoln and the moderates were more cautious about the slavery question, hoping not to antagonize the loyal border states and the northern Democrats, who supported a war to preserve the Union but not one to force an end to slavery.

The first significant conflict between the two groups arose in the fall of 1861 when General John C. Frémont, on his own authority, decreed the emancipation of the slaves of all persons in Missouri who had taken up arms against the government. Northern antislavery forces hailed his edict but others protested, and Lincoln ordered Frémont to make his proclamation conform to Congress' Confiscation Act, which directed compensation through the judicial process. When Frémont resisted, Lincoln dismissed him, raising the wrath of abolitionists. Congress had given Lincoln the powers of a dictator, said Sumner; "how vain to have the power of a God and not to use it godlike." The Radicals also fretted increasingly over the lack of military activity against the secessionists. In July, 1861, Lincoln himself had pressured General Winfield Scott to start the march on Richmond by dislodging the Confederate forces in northern Virginia. Scott thought that his troops were still unready, but he gave in and launched the offensive. On Sunday, July 21, many members of Congress joined the Washington throngs that followed in the rear of the army to watch the fighting. At Bull Run the battle turned into a northern disaster, and everyone, troops and Congressmen included, fled back to Washington. After that, for months, the Union troops along the Potomac, now under General George B. McClellan, drilled and did nothing else, and then, on October 21, came another northern defeat near Washington, at Ball's Bluff, where the popular Oregon Senator Edward D. Baker was killed leading Union soldiers. Four days later the Radical antislavery Senators Wade, Chandler, and Trumbull came to Washington from the midwest to scold Lincoln for McClellan's procrastination in not marching against Richmond and ending the rebellion.

Though Lincoln agreed with them and could do nothing himself to hasten McClellan, the Senators held him responsible as the Commander in Chief, and when the second session of the Thirty-seventh Congress convened on December 2, 1861, the Radicals launched fierce attacks against the "do-nothing" administration, pressing not only for military action but for the emancipation of the slaves. The Radicals' resentment at the North's frustrations, despite the great war powers that Congress had given Lincoln, led them to appoint a seven-member joint House-Senate Committee on the Conduct of the War, designed, insofar as possible, to compete with the President in the direction of the war. Composed of such determined men as Chandler, Wade, and Andrew Johnson, and guided and pushed by Sumner and Stevens, the committee exercised great influence over the conduct of the war, probing conspiracy, incompetence, and waste, supporting or condemning military leaders as well as members of the executive branch, and bringing the impact of the antislavery point of view to bear on political and military policies. The committee could not force Lincoln to fire McClellan, but when its investigations revealed widespread inefficiency and corruption in the War Department, Lincoln removed his secretary of war, Simon Cameron, the Republican leader of Pennsylvania, and promoted Cameron's chief legal officer, Edwin M. Stanton, in his place. Stanton, a fierce, dynamic man with a long straggly graying beard, was a tyrannical but efficient administrator, and he soon whipped the department into shape. One part of the committee's work involved the security of the government. Washington was filled with Confederate spies and agents, and at one time even Mrs. Lincoln, who had relatives on the southern side, was the target of rumors. To dispel them the President voluntarily appeared at a closed committee session and satisfied the legislators concerning his wife's loyalty. The North's frustrations, however, continued to increase congressional impatience. In February, 1862, Jesse D. Bright, the Indiana Democrat who three times before the war had been elected president *pro tempore* of the Senate, was expelled from that body for alleged sympathy for the Confederacy.

Meanwhile, Lincoln could not continue to resist the growing antislavery pressure. On March 6, 1862, he recommended that Congress pass a joint resolution offering to provide funds to any state that would undertake the gradual, compensated freeing of its slaves. Congress passed the resolution as a statement of policy on March 10, but none of the members from such loyal border states as Delaware and Kentucky, at which the resolution was aimed, voted in favor of it. Lincoln continued to bring pressure on the border-state Senators and Representatives throughout the session, but without success. The antislavery men, in turn, continued to pressure the President for more drastic action on his part, and in two measures of their own took the nation farther along the road toward emancipation. On April 16 the two houses abolished slavery in the District of Columbia, the bill providing for the compensation of those who freed their slaves. On June 19, ignoring the Dred Scott decision, Congress also abolished slavery in the territories, but without compensation. The latter action might have been held unconstitutional or, as John Quincy Adams had once maintained, Congress, under its war powers, might now have been upheld. It was never tested. At the same time Congress passed other bills that the Republicans had long advocated and that southerners had blocked. The President signed a Homestead Act on May 20, 1862 (which within a generation established 350,000 families on farms of 160 acres each), and Justin Morrill's "land-grant college" measure for the donation of 30,000 acres of public land for each member of Congress to finance a public agricultural and mechanical college (with obligatory military training) in every state and territory.

Among the busiest committees were those dealing with the financing of the war. On February 25 a Currency Act authorized the issuance of government paper "greenbacks" as legal tender. It was the first national paper currency, and by the end of the war some $450 million worth was in circulation. New loans were also voted; an internal revenue system, with a commissioner of internal revenue, was established on July 1 to collect taxes; a second Confiscation Act was passed, enlarging upon the first one and authorizing the President, in certain cases, to issue pardons or grant amnesty; tariffs were again raised; and without the presence of southerners to protest, a bill to incorporate the Union Pacific Railroad to build a transcontinental road that would follow a central route across the West was finally adopted. In conjunction with another measure enacted two years later, the bill subsidized the railroad builders by giving them rights of way through the public domain, huge grants of twenty sections of public land for every mile of track laid, all the materials needed for construction, and virtually unsecured credit of up to $48,000 per mile.

By the time Congress adjourned on July 17, 1862, Lincoln was far more disposed than ever before to issue an emancipation proclamation. On July

22 he read to his Cabinet a draft of such a document, freeing all slaves in the seceded states. For psychological reasons, Seward and the others urged him to wait for a military victory. It finally came at Antietam on September 17, and five days later Lincoln issued a preliminary proclamation, warning that on January 1, 1863, he would declare the emancipation of slaves in whatever states were still in rebellion. The antislavery forces hailed his announcement, but it set off widespread criticism among northern Democrats, who as a result made large gains in the fall congressional elections. Many people, it appeared, still only supported a war fought for the Union, not for the blacks.

On January 1, 1863, Lincoln issued his Emancipation Proclamation, which freed only slaves in the Confederate states and did not apply to those in the loyal border states or in Union-occupied areas of Louisiana, Virginia, and Tennessee (where Andrew Johnson, much admired in Congress because of his aggressive loyalty to the Union, had been named military governor). The proclamation and a decision to recruit freed slaves into the Union army were denounced in the South and also by many northern Democrats, who now claimed that Lincoln had deceived the nation regarding the true purpose of the war. As northern war losses mounted and victories eluded the Union side, a peace movement of "Copperheads" grew in the North, named not only for the snake but for its supporters' custom of cutting the head of Liberty out of a copper penny and wearing it like a badge. Mostly Democrats—their chief spokesman being Ohio Democratic Representative Clement L. Vallandigham—they resented continuing the war for the purpose of ending slavery and, believing that the South could not be beaten, urged a compromise settlement. The nation's first conscription bill (though the Confederacy had already enacted one) was being debated in Congress, and Vallandigham, a fiery and eloquent debater, outraged many antislavery Representatives by the seemingly treasonable remarks with which he opposed the measure.

The conscription bill went through Congress on March 3, making all men from twenty to thirty-five (all bachelors from twenty to forty-five) subject to the draft and containing highly controversial provisions permitting those whose numbers were called to avoid the draft by paying a commutation fee of $300 or hiring a substitute to enlist for three years. The measure, which favored the rich and marked the end of the long-cherished American freedom from enforced military service, resulted in tumultuous draft riots in some northern cities, particularly New York, and provided the peace advocates with additional ammunition for their attacks on the continuation of the war. After Congress adjourned, Vallandigham, who had not been re-elected to the next Congress, was arrested by General Ambrose Burnside in Ohio for treasonable utterances, but was ordered banished to Confederate territory by Lincoln. Meanwhile, to cope with the growing opposition, Thaddeus Stevens introduced a bill giving Lincoln the right to suspend habeas corpus at his discretion for the duration of the war.

It passed both houses, endowing the executive branch with more power over the lives of the people than it had ever had before and permitting in the last years of the war numerous military arrests, suppressions of constitutional rights, and violations of personal freedom.

The Thirty-eighth Congress assembled in December, 1863. Aided by the lobbying of influential friends, including the favor-seeking railroad tycoon Commodore Cornelius Vanderbilt, Schuyler Colfax—described by detractors as a "miserable popinjay, charlatan, and small potatoe demagogue"—was elected Speaker. Among the newly elected Republican members of the House who would soon rise to leadership were James G. Blaine, a thirty-three-year-old teacher, editor, and recent speaker of the Maine House of Representatives, and thirty-one-year-old General James A. Garfield of Ohio, who despite his youth had already had a full career as a college professor and president and possessed, as well, a distinguished record in the army, from which he had just resigned. Once again Stevens's Ways and Means Committee and the Senate Committee on Finance—the latter benefited by Ohio's able and dedicated John Sherman—poured forth legislation to meet the rising war costs and keep the nation's economy sound and productive. Bills were passed raising tariff rates to an average of forty-seven percent, more than double that of the immediate prewar years; increasing the income tax in a graduated scale from five percent on incomes of $600 to ten percent on incomes over $5,000; levying excise taxes—the first ones since Jefferson had ended them—on stamps and a long list of products; and expanding on the National Banking Act, which had first been passed the previous session and which established a system of national banks that were required to invest one third of their capital in United States securities —against ninety percent of which they could then issue currency notes under the direction of a newly created controller of the treasury.

These economic measures, generally reflecting the Republicans' Hamiltonian and Whig legacy of the use of strong federal powers to assist the national economy, again, in a Hamiltonian fashion, favored the country's wealthiest interests. This time they were the emerging industrial capitalists who were growing fat on the war as well as northern financiers, bankers, and smaller manufacturers. The process of shaping such legislation brought these interests together with the professional politicians of the Republican party on both the state and national levels; and gradually the alliance, buttressed by a growing apparatus of lobbyists and bribes, turned the party into an instrument that, at one and the same time, pursued and financed the idealistic war aims of the Radicals, supported the growth of a northern industrial revolution, and encouraged an atmosphere in which war profiteering, corruption, and the exploitation of public resources flourished.

During the session the Radicals in the Senate also pushed through the Thirteenth Amendment, to abolish slavery throughout the nation, but the House failed to give it the necessary two-thirds vote. At the same time a new confrontation arose between Lincoln and the congressional Radicals, this one over authority for the reconstruction of the South. In December, 1863, Lincoln issued a proclamation of amnesty for southerners who took an oath of loyalty to the Union and also announced that he would extend recognition to governments of southern states which agreed to emancipation and in which ten percent of the 1860 electorate took the oath of loyalty. Lincoln had already set up reconstructed governments in the conquered states of Louisiana and Arkansas, and they now fulfilled the required steps. But both houses of Congress, with the constitutional right to accept or reject the credentials of their members, refused to seat the men sent to Congress by the new governments of the two states, raising the issues of whether the reconstructed states were, indeed, actually back in the Union and whether the President or the Congress had the authority to make that decision. Lincoln felt that people, rather than states, had left the Union (since he believed that the states had no legal right to secede), that the states therefore were still in the Union—though in a temporarily improper relationship with the rest of the nation—and that because of the President's position as Commander in Chief and his powers to grant pardons and a general amnesty, he had the authority to direct Reconstruction. The Radicals, on the other hand, were persuaded that, by secession, the southern states had left the Union, and that Congress, representing the sovereign power of the people with a constitutional duty to guarantee all states a republican form of government, had authority to direct their return to the Union. "Until . . . Congress recognize a state government organized under its auspices, there is no government in the rebel states except the authority of Congress," declared Representative Henry Winter Davis of Maryland.

With the help of Wade in the Senate and Stevens in the House, Davis—challenging Lincoln as being far too lenient with the South—drew up a much harsher Reconstruction measure, whose provisions included the abolishment of slavery, a requirement that a majority, rather than ten percent, of the electorate in each seceded state swear to past and present loyalty, and prohibitions against the voting for delegates to state constitutional conventions or the serving as delegates by anyone who had held state or Confederate offices or had voluntarily carried arms against the United States. Known as the Wade-Davis Bill, it passed both Houses by July 4, 1864, the final day of the session. Lincoln pocket-vetoed it, however, announcing in a proclamation that he would not commit himself inflexibly "to any single plan of restoration" but that he also would not set aside the free-state governments organized in Louisiana and Arkansas and did not accept Congress' power to abolish slavery in the states. The Radicals fumed at him, and on August 5 they published the Wade-Davis Manifesto to "Supporters of the Government," declaring that "the authority of Congress is paramount and must be respected" and that if the President "wishes our support he must confine himself to his executive duties—to obey and to execute, not to make the laws—to suppress by arms armed rebellion, and leave political reorganization to Congress." Lincoln ignored the manifesto, and the issue was left unsettled.

In the meantime, the Republicans held their presidential convention at Baltimore on June 7. After a brief flurry of support for Chase from the anti-slavery forces, Lincoln was renominated. To appeal to Democrats, Andrew Johnson was named for the vice presidency, and the two men ran on a Republican-Union ticket. In July the continued heavy casualties of the war forced Lincoln to issue a draft call for 500,000 more men, and opposition to him grew. Nevertheless, when the Democrats nominated the former Union commander, George B. McClellan, at Chicago on August 29 and confronted him with a platform containing a peace plank written by Vallandigham, it was so anti-Union and defeatist that McClellan refused to endorse it. Soon afterward the cheering news of the fall of Atlanta swung support back to Lincoln, and in November he defeated McClellan by 400,000 votes.

When the second session of the Thirty-eighth Congress met in December, 1864, the end of the war was in sight and Lincoln now pleased the Radicals by asking the House to join the Senate in passing the Thirteenth Amendment, abolishing slavery. The House did so, and the amendment, finally ending slavery in every part of the United States, became part of the Constitution on December 18, 1865. The Wade-Davis Bill, reintroduced, was decisively defeated, suggesting that Congress might ultimately accept Lincoln's charitable Reconstruction policy, and the Freedmen's Bureau Bill was passed, setting up a comprehensive agency to assist the freed blacks in meeting the economic, medical, educational, and other problems they faced as they emerged from slavery. On March 3, 1865, after authorizing a new loan of $600 million and a ten percent tax on state bank notes to drive them out of circulation, the Thirty-eighth Congress ended. The next day, Lincoln was inaugurated for his second term, preparing the ground for a lenient Reconstruction policy by his appeal, "With malice toward none; with charity for all. . . ." There was one jarring note that day: Andrew Johnson, nervous and feeling unwell, overimbibed in brandy, and when he appeared in the Senate chamber to deliver his own inaugural address he was reeling drunk. His unfortunate performance disgusted his audience, and many of the assembled Senators would never forgive or forget the embarrassing episode.

On April 9 Lee surrendered, and on the evening of April 11 Lincoln spoke to a joyous crowd gathered outside the White House, urging in serious vein the practicality of his premise that the seceded states, in law, had never left the Union. His remarks upset Stanton and the Radicals, but Congress was not in session and the resolution of the conflict over a Reconstruction policy would have to wait for the start of the Thirty-ninth Congress in December. How Lincoln's plans would have developed would never be known. On April 14, at Ford's Theater, he was assassinated, and the next day, amid the wild shock and grief of the nation, Johnson took the oath of office. As Lincoln's body lay in state, first in the East Room of the White

House and then in the rotunda of the Capitol, a spirit of revenge swept the North. Seward, who had also been attacked and seriously wounded by the plotters, calmed Johnson, who hysterically blamed Jefferson Davis for the crime; and gradually, after Lincoln's funeral and the execution of the conspirators, tranquillity returned to the capital.

Though the Radical Republicans were the spiritual inheritors of Henry Clay's belief in legislative dominance over the executive, Lincoln, a consummate politician, had more than held his own against them. Johnson, however, was marked for trouble with Congress. He was tactless, insulting, and headstrong. A southern poor white, he was full of envy and insecurity, which he often covered with an offensive imperiousness. Being a Democrat among victorious Republicans (like Tyler, he was another "His Accidency") did not help him; he hesitated to make up his mind, but when he did so he became inflexible and uncompromising, even violently so. Nevertheless, when after Lincoln's death congressional Radicals hastily met with Johnson to size up his views on Reconstruction, they felt that they would have no conflict with him. Far from being a second Lincoln whom they would have difficulty steering, Johnson echoed their own sentiments. "Treason must be made odious, and traitors must be punished and impoverished," he kept repeating. This pleased such Senators as Michigan's vengeful Zach Chandler. Johnson "is as radical as I am and as fully up to the mark," he said. Expecting that the new President would take no important steps without calling them back into session for their approval, the members of Congress went home. "Johnson," exclaimed Senator Ben Wade patronizingly as he said farewell, "we have faith in you. By the gods, there will be no trouble now in running the government."

Within weeks, however, the new occupant of the White House began to confound the Radicals, putting into effect, on his own and without calling back the Congress, a mild, simple, and quick Reconstruction program that hewed closely to the conciliatory policy advocated by Lincoln. In two proclamations on May 29, Johnson provided for the establishment of loyal governments in the seceded states (provisionally appointed governors would call state conventions to name the new governments, which would have to nullify their secession ordinances, repudiate Confederate debts, and ratify the Thirteenth Amendment) and for the granting of amnesty and pardons and the return of all property except slaves. Amnesty would be granted to everyone who took the oath of allegiance, except those in fourteen special classes—including Confederate civil and military leaders and persons owning more than $20,000 worth of property—but they could apply directly to Johnson for individual pardons. Only those receiving amnesty or pardons would be eligible to participate in the conventions or the new state governments. The states lost no time in carrying out the provisions. Amnesty was granted wholesale; thousands of southerners or their agents flocked to Washington and, in personal meetings that puffed up Johnson's ego, were issued pardons; and in state conventions and elections the President's few requirements for "restoration" to the Union were quickly met.

All this satisfied Johnson, whose aims, it was becoming apparent, were not those of the Republicans. Politically, indeed, there was a wide gap between the new President and the party that had chosen and elected him. Johnson was a Jacksonian Unionist who had wanted to preserve the Union and smash the rebellion; but he was also a Jacksonian small *d* democrat whose roots and sympathies lay with the workingman and the small farmer and against the northern capitalists as well as the landed aristocracy in the South. Furthermore, he was a Jacksonian states'-rights Democrat who would return powers to the states as quickly as possible, and, though he supported the Thirteenth Amendment, he was bigoted and cynical about blacks and felt that after they were freed their fate should be left entirely to the states. As the southern states during the summer went through the motions of meeting the requirements of his policy, he had an uncomplicated goal in mind: the establishment of loyal, orderly governments whose power would rest not on the planter oligarchies, as before the war, but on the more democratic masses of less-affluent white southern farmers. It was a hopeless dream, for Johnson's own policy of pardons and the return of property to big landowners put the same old southern aristocracy back in power and leadership. In the elections for the men who would go to Washington in December to represent the southern states in the first postwar Congress, the new "loyal" governments named six of Jefferson Davis's Cabinet members, fifty-eight members of the Confederate Congress, nine Confederate Army officers, and Confederate Vice President Alexander Stephens. At the same time, through the passage of notorious "Black Codes" and vicious "vagrancy" and "apprentice" measures, the new southern governments established a pattern for turning the freed slaves into a class of controlled, propertyless rural laborers, without rights and often bound without pay to white masters as securely as if they were still slaves. The oppressive new measures not only negated the intent of the Thirteenth Amendment, but in the absence of any protection for southern blacks in Johnson's Reconstruction program, threatened to condemn them permanently to a serflike status.

Johnson's go-it-alone actions and the resulting developments in the South infuriated the Radical Republicans, who were loud in their denunciations of the President. "The whole fabric of southern society *must* be changed . . . ," lectured Stevens angrily. "How can republican institutions, free schools, free churches, free social intercourse exist in a mingled community of nabobs and serfs? . . . If the south is ever to be made a safe republic let her lands be cultivated by the toil of the owners, or the free labor of intelligent citizens. This must be done even though it drive her nobility into exile!" Just before the opening of the Thirty-ninth Congress on December 4, 1865, the Republicans met in secret caucus in Washington under Stevens's leadership. The Radicals were determined to force Congress into a Radical mold and make it dominant over the President, but they were in the minority. The moderate majority, however, shared an important concern with them. The Republican party had become a powerful institution, through which they themselves enjoyed power. None of them wished to see the return of unreconstructed southerners who, with northern Democrats, might well turn the Republicans again into a minority party. The elemental desire to stay in power helped to unite the Republicans, and the caucus decided to sidetrack Johnson and his program by supporting the establishment of a joint committee of fifteen members of the House and Senate to investigate conditions in the South and report to Congress whether any of the southern states should be seated.

When Congress convened, Colfax, a Radical, was again named House Speaker. In the previous session Stevens's overworked Ways and Means Committee had been divided into three standing committees—Ways and Means, Banking and Currency, and Appropriations. Colfax named Justin Morrill to head Ways and Means, and Stevens took the chairmanship of the more strategic Appropriations Committee, with House authority over all government spending. Then Stevens moved for approval of the fifteen-member Joint Committee on Reconstruction. It was accepted in both houses, and six Senators and nine Representatives were named to it. Chaired by Senator Fessenden of Maine, it included more moderates than Radicals. Two days later Johnson sent his first annual message to Congress, announcing bluntly that the Union had been restored and that representatives from the southern states were waiting to be seated. Though it debated the message, Congress made no decision until February, 1866, when, in a rebuff to the President, it announced that no Senator or Representative from a southern state would be seated until both houses had "declared such state entitled to such representation."

In the meantime, the Joint Committee met almost every day, receiving testimony from scores of witnesses who had traveled in the South. Later in the spring it issued its report—another rebuke to the President. Since the majority of southerners were still hostile to the United States, since civil rights were not secured in the South, and since public offices were filled by leaders of the rebellion, it announced, the states were not entitled to representation in Congress. In addition, it sternly asserted Congress' authority over the Reconstruction process. By then Congress had had a series of clashes with the President, which strengthened the hand of the Radicals. Recognizing from its investigations that the freed slaves were in great need of protection from vindictive southerners, Congress, in February, extended indefinitely the life of the Freedmen's Bureau, which had been providing medical, educational, and a host of social and economic services to southern blacks, and gave it judicial powers to protect their rights in special courts. Johnson, however, vetoed the bill as a violation of states' rights, drawing new fire from the Radicals, particularly from Stevens and Sumner. Satisfied that he was constitutionally correct, Johnson replied with intemperate speeches, calling both Stevens and Sumner traitors. In response the House overrode his veto of the Freedmen's Bill. In the Senate, however, the vote to

JAMES F. WILSON, Iowa.   GEORGE S. BOUTWELL, Mass.   JOHN A. LOGAN, Ill.

BENJAMIN F. BUTLER, Mass.   THADDEUS STEVENS, Penna.   THOMAS WILLIAMS, Penna.   JOHN A. BINGHAM, Ohio.

Managers of the House of Representatives of the Impeachment of Andrew Johnson.

The losers in the fight to remove President Andrew Johnson

A cartoon depicts the first black Senator, Hiram Revels of Mississippi, filling Jefferson Davis's former seat.

"TIME WORKS WONDERS."

IAGO. (JEFF DAVIS.) "FOR THAT I DO SUSPECT THE LUSTY MOOR HATH LEAP'D INTO MY SEAT: THE THOUGHT WHEREOF DOTH LIKE A POISONOUS MINERAL GNAW MY INWARDS." — OTHELLO.

Settling the Hayes-Tilden election dispute in 1877

FARMER GARFIELD
Cutting a Swath to the White House.

An 1880 Currier & Ives boost for Garfield

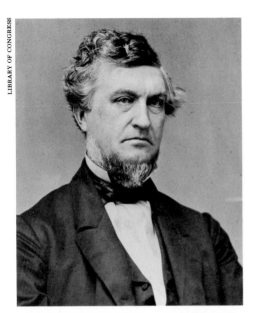

Michigan Senator Zachariah Chandler *Boss Roscoe Conkling of New York*

*Blustering Ben Butler
of Massachusetts*

An 1884 Puck *cartoon hit at James G. Blaine's hidden deals.*

Vice President Schuyler Colfax

Blaine, Speaker from 1869 to 1875

*A cartoon gibe at the
Populists in the 1890's*

THE WAY WE BECOME SENATOR NOWADAYS.

PUCK, JANUARY 22, 1890

*A Puck satire on the Senate
as a "millionaires' club"*

THE DEMOCRATIC ANDROMEDA AND HER PERSEUS.

Another 1890's cartoon attacks free silver.

Republican Speaker, "Czar" Thomas B. Reed of Maine

The cluttered Library of Congress when it was housed in the Capitol

Dictatorial Speaker "Uncle Joe" Cannon of Illinois

A gallery of Senators drawn in 1910

Setting back the clock in the House to allow the finish of business

The first woman Senator, Rebecca Felton of Georgia, 1922

Insurgents go at Coolidge in the 1924 campaign

Congress receives bonus petitions from World War I veterans in 1922

*New Deal enemy, Senator
Huey P. Long of Louisiana*

Secretary of War Stimson at a Senate hearing during World War II

Republican Senate leader Everett McKinley Dirksen of Illinois

*Sam Rayburn, the last
of the strong Speakers*

One of the Senate's ablest Majority Leaders, Lyndon B. Johnson

override failed and led to a concerted effort by the Radicals to unseat Senator John P. Stockton of New Jersey, a Democratic supporter of Johnson's, whose election had been contested. The Radicals were successful, ousting also a Johnson man from the House, and on July 16 a second Freedmen's Bureau Bill, similar to the first one, was passed over another presidential veto.

Johnson, meanwhile, had compounded his difficulties, also vetoing a Civil Rights Bill, which, like the Freedmen's Bureau Bill, had been introduced by Senator Lyman Trumbull of Illinois with a warning from the moderate Republicans to the President that a veto would lose his administration their support. The measure was intended to undo the ruling of the Dred Scott decision by conferring citizenship on blacks and granting them the same civil rights possessed by all persons born in the United States, except untaxed Indians. When Johnson ignored the warning and vetoed the bill, again as an invasion of states' rights, Congress overrode the veto. Nevertheless, doubt about the bill's constitutionality (the Supreme Court did call it unconstitutional in 1883) induced the Joint Committee of Fifteen to introduce the Fourteenth Amendment, which passed Congress on June 13, 1866, and was sent to the states for ratification three days later. The heart of the amendment, its first section, mostly drafted by Representative John A. Bingham, an Ohio corporation lawyer, defined American citizenship to include the freed slaves and then went on to prohibit states from enacting laws abridging "the privileges or immunities of citizens"; depriving "any person of life, liberty, or property, without due process of law"; or denying "to any person within its jurisdiction the equal protection of the laws." The section occasioned much controversy in later years. Although the Supreme Court for almost a century interpreted it as inapplicable for the protection of blacks against individuals' violations of the Bill of Rights, thus making it useless as a safeguard of their civil rights, it did make the "due-process clause" a valuable weapon of corporations against federal and state taxation and regulatory laws.

Johnson could not veto the amendment, whose ratification was made another condition of a state's restoration to the Union, but he did denounce it severely, with the result that every southern state save Tennessee, believing that the 1866 fall elections would oust the Radicals and repudiate their Reconstruction policies, rejected it. On July 19 Tennessee ratified the amendment, its Radical governor notifying the Senate in a telegram that ended, "Give my respects to the dead dog in the White House." Five days later Congress readmitted that border state to the Union—though only a few days after that, whites went on a rampage against blacks in Memphis (the violence was eclipsed by even worse anti-black rioting a short time afterward in New Orleans). Johnson, meanwhile, was far from being a "dead dog." In late August, after the adjournment of Congress—which on its final day increased the annual pay of members of both houses from $3,000 to $5,000—the President set off on a speaking "swing around the circle," campaigning in various cities for his Reconstruction policy and lambasting his Radical opponents. The vulgarity of his speeches and his undignified brawling with hecklers, however, drew widespread criticism, and the tour backfired against him disastrously. In addition, by then he had lost large numbers of moderate Republicans on aspects of the Reconstruction issue that were beginning to hit home in the North.

In congressional debates, and in the northern press, it had often been pointed out that the abolition of slavery would mean that, for representation in the House, a southern black would now have to count as a full person rather than as three-fifths of one (the original constitutional agreement), thus greatly increasing the number of Representatives to which the South would be entitled. This would be all right if blacks received the franchise and voted Republican; but if blacks were denied suffrage, the increased white southern representation, combining with the Copperhead Democrats of the North, would again control the House. Such a development, northerners could now see, posed threats to Republican policies that were deemed essential to their prosperity, such as high protective tariffs, subsidies to railroads, homestead laws, and grants of western natural resources for timber and mineral exploitation. Even worse, the southerners, by repudiating the federal war debt, could hurt the holders of government securities and gain complete revenge by ruining the entire economy of the North. (The fear was so great that the Fourteenth Amendment, which the southern states were refusing to ratify, contained a prohibition against questioning the validity of the public debt.) Johnson charged that the Republicans were more interested in punishing the South than protecting the rights of the blacks. To a large extent, he was correct. Aside from the idealists and abolitionists among the Radicals, there was little pro-black crusading spirit among the moderate Republicans and, conversely, considerable anti-black sentiment. But Johnson misgauged the Republicans' *need* for the blacks' votes in the South. Even Sumner appealed to the moderates to support the Radicals for this reason. "Only through him [the black] can you redress the balance of our political system and assure the safety of patriot citizens," he warned them. "Only through him can you save the national debt from the inevitable repudiation which awaits it when recent rebels in conjunction with Northern allies once more bear sway. He is our best guarantee. Use him." By the fall of 1866 large numbers of northerners felt this self-interest keenly. The Republican party hammered home the specter of a government again in the hands of the leaders of the rebellion, and, amid rising support for suffrage for the southern blacks, the Republicans swept the elections, gaining a two-thirds' control of both houses of Congress.

When the second session of the Thirty-ninth Congress convened in December, the Radicals quickly seized the initiative. Stevens, now a wrathful, hard-driving commander flushed with a sense of triumph over the executive, took control of patronage and demanded "iron party discipline" in the House. He got it. The run-of-the-mill members of Congress, said Gideon

Welles, who had been secretary of the navy since 1861, were "small party men, creatures of corner groceries, without any knowledge of the science of government or of our Constitution. With them all the great, overpowering purpose and aim are office and patronage." Such men knew that defiance of Stevens and the party caucus could mean their political life, and they did not test it. Like unquestioning soldiers, they went along with the leaders. Bills were introduced and passed giving blacks the right to vote in the District of Columbia and in all territories. On December 19 Stevens, as powerful now as any member of Congress had ever been, charged that since the South refused to ratify the Fourteenth Amendment, new legislation was needed to protect the blacks. On January 3, 1867, he introduced a measure that, when reported by the Reconstruction Committee in February, became known as the Military Reconstruction Bill. As Congress' Reconstruction policy, it was at last the legislature's stern and determined answer to the President's bankrupt program and to the South's failure to accept the Fourteenth Amendment. "It is now our turn to act," said Ohio's Representative James A. Garfield. "They [the southern states] would not co-operate with us in rebuilding what they destroyed. We must remove the rubbish, and build from the bottom." The measure divided the South into five military districts, whose commanders were given broad powers, under martial law, to protect blacks, preserve order, and carry out political reconstruction, enrolling qualified voters, including blacks, and holding elections for new constitutional conventions which would establish state governments that guaranteed black suffrage and ratified the Fourteenth Amendment. Ex-Confederates disqualified by the Fourteenth Amendment would be denied the right to vote, and Congress itself would decide when to end military rule and seat the state representatives. As expected, Johnson vetoed the bill, but on March 2 Congress overrode the veto, and the harsh measure went into effect.

Johnson and his attorney general, as well as whites in the southern states, looked for loopholes by which to subvert its intention, and on three later occasions Congress had to pass supplementary acts, each time over Johnson's veto, tightening various of its provisions and safeguards. By 1868 six of the southern states had been readmitted to the Union, and the ratification of the Fourteenth Amendment was announced on July 28 of that year. The other states delayed meeting all the requirements for readmission, but by 1870 they too were again represented in Congress. On February 25, 1870, the first black Senator, Hiram R. Revels of Mississippi, who had organized and served as a chaplain with black troops on the Union side during the war, entered the upper chamber, occupying the seat once filled by Jefferson Davis. Two Senators, from Kentucky and Delaware, tried to disbar him, but their motion was defeated, 40 to 8. Later that year South Carolina sent the first black man, Joseph H. Rainey, to the House of Representatives. Despite the blacks' entry into government, Congress' attempt to reconstruct the South had—as Stevens recognized—one large oversight.

The Radicals had urged the confiscation and division of the large landholdings of former slaveowners and the distribution of forty acres and a mule to every freedman who wanted to farm on his own. This was never done, and the southern blacks were left without an economic base on which to build.

The passage of the Reconstruction Act was accompanied by a series of legislative attacks on the President himself, designed to limit his powers and bring him tightly under Congress' control. "Though the President is Commander-in-Chief," declared Stevens, "Congress is his commander; and, God willing, he shall obey. He and his minions shall learn that this is not a Government of kings and satraps, but a Government of the people, and that Congress is the people." The polarization of the executive and legislature had led some friends of Johnson's to suggest that he brand Congress an illegal body because of its refusal to seat the southern states and even use the army to dissolve Congress. Despite the fact that there was little fear of the President's taking such action, the Radicals were distrustful of what he might do between Congress' sessions, and on January 22, 1867, the legislators, in an unprecedented move, voted that the Fortieth and all succeeding Congresses would meet immediately on the adjournment of the preceding ones. The vote, applying also to special sessions, would have the effect of keeping Congress in almost continuous session; but, in addition, it bestowed on Congress the right to call itself into special session—a power previously exercised exclusively by the President. On March 2 the Republicans followed up by attaching a rider to the Army Appropriation Act, circumscribing the President's power as commander in chief by directing him to issue all military orders through the General of the Army, Ulysses S. Grant, and forbidding the President either to remove Grant or to send him elsewhere without the Senate's consent. On the same day, determined to cripple Johnson's power of patronage as well as to protect Secretary of War Stanton, the only Radical member of the Cabinet, Congress passed the Tenure of Office Act, making it a "high misdemeanor" for the President to remove federal officials without the Senate's approval, though he could make temporary suspensions when Congress was not in session.

All these actions were of serious constitutional significance, for they reflected a deliberate attempt to alter the balance of power between the legislative and executive branches, bringing the latter dangerously under the domination of the former. But some of the Radicals, convinced that Johnson had become a menace to the country and would yet sabotage Congress' Reconstruction program, went further and began to seek his impeachment. On January 7, 1867, Representative James M. Ashley of Ohio had introduced a resolution instructing the House Judiciary Committee to "inquire into the conduct of Andrew Johnson." The House had adopted the resolution, but after a long investigation of a mass of charges against the President, the Judiciary Committee voted, 5 to 4, on June 3 not to recommend impeachment. In the following months, however, new actions by Johnson, some of them attempts to undermine the Reconstruction program in the South, angered Congress. On July 20, after holding two special sessions, Congress adjourned. Some two weeks later, Johnson asked Stanton for his resignation. When Stanton refused to give it, Johnson suspended him and prevailed on General Grant to take Stanton's place *"ad interim."* The development excited the Republicans, and in a third extra session, beginning on November 21, 1867, the Judiciary Committee reversed itself and recommended, 5 to 4, the impeachment of the President. Two minority reports, however, insisted so strongly that no evidence yet existed that Johnson had committed a crime or a misdemeanor for which he could be impeached that the full House on December 7 voted down the recommendation for impeachment, 108 to 57.

On December 12 Johnson, following the legalistic requirements of the Tenure of Office Act, sent a message to Congress enumerating the reasons why he had suspended Stanton. The next day the Senate, by a vote of 36 to 6, refused to concur in the suspension. At the same time the Radicals persuaded Grant to turn over the secretary of war's office again to Stanton. Grant did so, infuriating Johnson, who lost his temper, accused Grant of treachery, and drove him completely over to the side of the Radicals. On February 21, 1868, Johnson, now defiantly violating the Tenure of Office Act with the expectation of testing its constitutionality, fired Stanton and appointed Adjutant General Lorenzo Thomas in his place, again *ad interim.* Barricading himself in his office, Stanton sent word of the President's action to the Capitol. The news caused wild excitement in both houses. After seven hours of debate in executive session, the Senate resolved that "under the Constitution and laws of the United States, the President has no power, to remove the Secretary of War and to designate any other officer to perform the duties of that office *ad interim."* In the House a resolution offered by Representative John Covode of Pennsylvania that "Andrew Johnson, President of the United States, be impeached for high crimes and misdemeanors in office" was referred to Stevens's Committee on Reconstruction, which recommended it to the House the next day. By a vote of 126 to 47, the Representatives two days later approved impeachment and then appointed a committee of seven members, including Stevens, Bingham of Ohio, George W. Julian of Indiana, and John A. Logan of Illinois, to prepare articles of impeachment—something that, but for the frenzy of the moment, they might have been expected to do before the voting of impeachment.

Stevens and Bingham formally notified the Senate of the impeachment, and on March 2 and 3 the House adopted eleven articles—eight of them concerned with the attempted removal of Stanton, the ninth charging a violation of the rider on the Army Appropriation Act of March 2, 1867, the tenth accusing Johnson of undignified conduct as President, and the last repeating the first ten and adding an accusation that Johnson had brought the legality of Congress' acts into question by referring to the Thirty-ninth Congress as "a Congress of only a part of the United States." On March 5, with Benjamin Wade, the president *pro tempore* of the Senate and next in line in succession, confident that he would soon be President, and with Salmon P. Chase, now Chief Justice of the Supreme Court, presiding, the trial began in the Senate, climaxing the two years of anger against the President that had existed in Congress and the North. Seven members of the House, led by Stevens, George S. Boutwell of Massachusetts, and the redoubtable Benjamin F. Butler, the Civil War general and now a noisy Representative from Massachusetts, presented the case. The President was defended by his attorney general, Henry Stanbery, who resigned to represent him, and four able lawyers, including Benjamin R. Curtis of the Supreme Court and William M. Evarts, one of the leading members of the American bar, who would later become President Hayes's secretary of state.

The House managers pursued two lines of attack, first the legal one that Johnson was guilty as charged of having violated the Tenure of Office Act and of having defamed Congress, and second a contradictory argument that impeachment was a political and not a judicial process and therefore the Senate did not have to decide whether the President had committed an indictable offense but only whether he was fit to continue in office. Insisting that impeachment was a judicial and not a political procedure, Johnson's lawyers were able to demonstrate flaws in the legal charges, and the case against Johnson gradually weakened. It was shown that there was nothing wrong in his having removed Stanton in order to test the constitutionality of the Tenure of Office Act—a measure that contravened the First Congress' decision on the President's right of removal (and whose doctrine the Supreme Court would finally call unconstitutional in 1926). Moreover, the act itself provided that the Cabinet officers were to "hold their offices . . . for and during the term of the President by whom they may have been appointed . . . ," and since Lincoln, and not Johnson, had appointed Stanton, the act, on that technicality, was held not to protect Stanton against removal.

Despite arguments over such points, a secret Republican caucus alarmed the Radicals with the revelation that six Republican Senators, viewing impeachment as a legal process in which guilt beyond question would have to be established, intended to join the twelve Democrats in voting for acquittal. If the Republicans were to convict Johnson by a two-thirds vote, they could not afford to lose a single additional Senator, and yet one other Republican, Senator Edmund G. Ross of Kansas, a Radical of impeccable credentials who had fought slavery in Kansas before the Civil War, had not made up his mind on how he was going to vote. Enormous pressure was put on Ross, but on May 16, when the first vote was taken (on the comprehensive eleventh article), he courageously voted for acquittal, saving Johnson. The vote, 35 for conviction to 19 against, was just one vote short of the two-thirds necessary for conviction. Once more great pressure was put on all seven Republicans to change their votes on the next two articles to be decided, but despite attacks on their patriotism and threats to their political future, they refused to waver and the results were the same. After that

Stevens—whose health had faded suddenly during the proceedings—and the other House managers gave up, and the Senate adjourned without taking any further votes. In Washington as well as in their own states, the Republican dissenters, who included the eminent Senators Fessenden of Maine and Trumbull of Illinois, were looked upon as traitors, and not one of them served another term in the Senate. Gradually, however, others accepted their point of view that impeachment, used as a political weapon, would imperil the constitutional system of checks and balances and destroy the independence of the executive branch. "Once set the example of impeaching a President for what, when the excitement of the hour shall have subsided, will be regarded as insufficient cause," said Senator Trumbull, "and no future President will be safe who happens to differ with a majority of the House and two-thirds of the Senate on any measure deemed by them important."

While the final votes were being taken, the Republican convention meeting in Chicago on May 20 and 21, 1868, nominated General Grant and the popular Radical Speaker, Schuyler Colfax, for the presidency and vice presidency. Grant, who earlier in his life had been a Democrat, accepted the nomination with the terse admonition to the nation, "Let us have peace." On July 4 the Democrats in New York named a ticket of Horatio Seymour, the former governor of that state who had often been accused of being a Copperhead, and Francis P. Blair of Missouri, who had once been a Free-Soil and Republican member of Congress. On August 11 Thaddeus Stevens, still honored in the North as a great "commoner," died in Washington at the age of seventy-six, his body lying in state for a day in the rotunda of the Capitol before being taken to Pennsylvania for burial. In November Grant and Colfax were elected, and in the last session of the Fortieth Congress the House was presided over by a Speaker who was also the Vice President-elect. Johnson, nursing bruised feelings and grudges, finished out his term quietly. On February 26, 1869, Congress passed the Fifteenth Amendment, forbidding any state to deny a citizen the right to vote because of race, color, or previous condition of servitude. Most members of Congress were satisfied that it would finally settle the question of black suffrage, but some, such as Senator Oliver H. P. T. Morton, who had been the wartime governor of Indiana and was determined to create a solid Republican South, were more realistic. "Sir," Morton warned angrily, "if the power should pass into the hands of the conservative or Democratic population of those [southern] states, if they could not debar the colored people of the right of suffrage in any other way, they would do it by an educational or property qualification."

On March 4, 1869, Grant entered the White House, and the Republican party entrenched its command over the government and the political life of the country. Andrew Johnson returned to Tennessee and in 1874 was elected again to the Senate. On March 22, 1875, he made his last speech in that body, attacking the Radicals' Reconstruction and ending, "God save the Constitution." To men like him there seemed reason for such a cry, for the

Supreme Court had not yet received cases that would permit it to rule on the constitutionality of most of the questionable legislation passed during the war and postwar periods. But by 1875, too, the leaders of the Republican party, corrupted by power, had run roughshod not only over a reconstructed South of obedient Republican state governments kept in office by the military, but over the whole nation as well. Soon after Johnson's last speech a stroke paralyzed him and he died on July 31, 1875, his populist championing of the little man and his loyalty to the Union at the time of its crisis all but forgotten as a result of the losing fight he had waged with the Radicals. A copy of the Constitution was buried with him.

The commencement of the Grant administration marked the beginning of more than a generation of almost uninterrupted Republican hegemony, stained by widespread political and economic corruption. The nation had weak Presidents, and after its experience with Johnson, the Congress by and large kept them weak. "The executive department of a republic like ours should be subordinate to the legislative department," Senator John Sherman pronounced icily, as if it were gospel. "The President should obey and enforce the laws, leaving to the people the duty of correcting any errors committed by their representatives in Congress." Within the Congress the Senate—with its longer terms and lengthier continuity of membership, its opportunities for fuller expression, its clublike committee system based generally on seniority, its prestigious members, and above all its hold over patronage, appointments, and removals, and the awarding of subsidies, charters, grants of natural resources, and various legislative favors—became the fount of political power. In many states strong political machines came into being, or grew stronger than they already were, financed by dues and assessments of jobholders, contributions by businessmen, industrialists, and bankers, and by graft and plunder unequaled before or since in the history of the country. In most cases the bosses of the machines were Senators—men such as Oliver Morton of Indiana, Roscoe Conkling of New York, Simon Cameron of Pennsylvania, Zach Chandler of Michigan, and after 1871 General John A. "Black Jack" Logan of Illinois, who had built the machines or come up through their ranks and who sustained them with a stream of federal jobs and opportunities for graft and in turn were sustained by them. The Senate and House, both, became filled with professional politicians, creatures of the machines, but the Senators generally were the men of power. The United States, wrote Henry Adams in his novel *Democracy* in 1880, had a "government of the people, by the people, for the benefit of Senators."

In later years such nonprofessionals as Leland Stanford, the California railroad mogul; Nelson Aldrich, the Rhode Island wholesale grocer and banker; Philetus Sawyer, the Wisconsin lumber tycoon; Henry M. Teller, the Colorado lawyer and promoter; and George Hearst, Horace A. W. Tabor, and James G. "Bonanza" Fair, the western mining kings, who made their wealth outside politics, would enter the Senate and give it the flavor of a "millionaire's club." But in the beginning, with a few exceptions, wealth came through politics to shrewd, able men, who—as was said of the influential Speaker of the House, Maine's dynamic James G. Blaine—had no visible means of support other than their government salaries yet lived and entertained like nabobs in expensive Washington homes. To such men opportunities came via two channels—from boodle siphoned off by the ranks of machine henchmen from industry and state and national government salaries and appropriations, and from bribes and various forms of financial favors from private industry. To an extent, in the postwar period of explosive expansion of capitalist industry and finance, there was an unspoken alliance between the professional politicians and the industrial barons. The competing businessmen, striving to build monopolies, reaching hungrily for natural resources in the public domain, and outwitting or bending the law when it dared to assert the public interest, needed the influence and help of the party machines and their bosses. The big men of money and enterprise were the "chief stockholders" of the Republican party, said Seward. In return for their contributions to the machines and favors to the leaders, the railroad builders, oil and steel men, pork packers, mining and timber interests, and scores of other corporate groups got public lands, rights of way, charters, subsidies, franchises, and other legislative advantages. Sometimes the capitalists dealt directly with the lawmakers: Collis Huntington of the Central Pacific Railroad, who came to Washington with some $200,000 in cash in a trunk, Jay Cooke and his brother, Henry, Commodore Vanderbilt, and many others were confidants of individual Senators. Other favor-seeking interests dealt through intermediaries, including a new breed of lobbyists such as Sam Ward, the self-styled "King of the Lobby," John L. Hayes of the National Association of Wool Manufacturers, and others who maintained expensive offices and staffs, entertained lavishly, and helped plan the content and thrust of legislation. Whatever expenses were required, the rewards were usually worth the cost. The promoters of four western railroads, for instance, received as donations from the government as much land as the states of Ohio, Indiana, Illinois, Wisconsin, and Michigan combined, the Northern Pacific alone making off with forty-seven million acres.

The corruption of the period, stemming both from the relaxed morals of the postwar social atmosphere and the frantic pace of the industrial revolution, enmeshed the executive branch as well as Congress, Democrats as well as Republicans, and cities and states as well as the national government, and flourished in all parts of the country. The champion political plunderer of all was the Democrat William M. "Boss" Tweed in New York City. Republican "carpetbag" and "scalawag" governments in the South plundered almost at will, but they were outdone by many of the southern Democratic governments that followed them. In the Congress, however, where the Republicans for years had almost no opposition from the executive branch or from a strong Democratic party, corruption, feeding on power, affected the governing of the country. The problems of staying in power, of maintaining the machines, of pursuing politics night and day for its political rewards, became all-important. Men wasted their talents in petty political infighting and gave short shrift to the pressing needs of the changing country. Few issues were seriously debated; indeed, few of the urgent problems—those of the farmers, the workers, and the burgeoning urban centers—were even accurately perceived. One of the largest issues—the future of the South and its blacks—was treated purely as a political matter of guaranteeing the votes of the southern states for the Republicans. Denied land, credits, or the benefits of the Homestead Act, the blacks were viewed merely as voters and were then abandoned, without ability to fend for themselves, when they were no longer useful to the northern machines.

At the same time, while party caucuses and strong men with followers gave leadership on organizational matters in both houses, there was little or no leadership on issues or substantive concerns. In the House of Representatives, where no one arose to take the place of the iron-willed Thaddeus Stevens, the most respected man was Blaine, thirty-nine years old in 1869, warm-hearted and friendly, an astute politician (he never forgot a name), and magnetic as an orator. He served as Speaker from 1869 to 1875, presiding with good humor over a House that had deteriorated into what historian John A. Garraty described as "one of the most disorderly and inefficient legislative bodies in the world." Members visited with each other, walked around aimlessly, read newspapers, puffed on cigars, slammed their desk lids, shouted for pages, cleared their throats noisily and spat at pink and gold china spittoons, and called out to each other while one or two Representatives tried to carry on debate above the din and confusion. These were the smaller fry of the machines; facing re-election every two years, they preoccupied themselves much of the time with paying attention to the folks back home, making the fullest use of their franking privileges and sending their constituents copies of their occasional remarks as well as packets of free garden seeds that the Department of Agriculture made available to them. Few of the Representatives had any personal stature. When one of them—such as Ohio's James A. Garfield—stood out above the rest because of his intellect and breadth of national vision, he was usually slated for a rise in political station. But in an arena of mediocrities, a Garfield's true worth was only relative. An obliging party man, he seemed strong and able as part of a team on the floor and as a committee member. When he had to act alone, he was vacillating and indecisive and begged almost everyone else for advice and opinions.

The Senate, on the other hand, was filled with a large number of potential leaders, but they worked in unity only on organizational matters—doling out committee assignments through the powerful Committee on Committees—and then went their own ways, largely nullifying their talents in political rivalries and in essentially trivial concerns and showing few signs of true statesmanship. If there was a national Republican party—and there was one—it was more like an organized confederacy of many individual Senator-bosses, with no central direction over all of them. In the Capitol the Senators acted like so many autonomous headmen. "No one is *the* Senator," observed Woodrow Wilson in his study *Congressional Government* in 1885. "No one may speak for his party as well as for himself; no one exercises the special trust of acknowledged leadership. The Senate is merely a body of individual critics." For many years after Johnson's trial, however, two things held the Republicans together—a determination to keep the Republican party in power and a belief that the Congress was dominant over the executive, and the Senate was dominant over the House.

Grant had scarcely entered the White House in March, 1869, when the Senate put him in his place. Despite his great personal prestige, the new President was a political innocent who, without consulting the Senators—hungry for the thousands of jobs, high and low, that would result from the ousting of Johnson's appointees—began filling Cabinet posts with his cronies and nonpolitical wealthy friends. The Senators were shocked, and they blocked the appointment of Grant's choice for secretary of the treasury, Alexander T. Stewart, a New York dry-goods merchant, forcing the President to take instead the Radical Republican Representative George S. Boutwell of Massachusetts, who had led in the impeachment proceedings against Johnson. Immediately thereafter Grant asked the Senate to repeal the Tenure of Office Act. Again he was rebuffed. "Is the race of bad Presidents extinct?" asked Senator George F. Edmunds of Vermont. The Senators changed the wording of the act slightly but kept the measure in force until 1887. The double blow, underscored by a visit to the "baby politician" in the White House by a Senate committee that threatened him with continued congressional opposition, was all the lesson Grant needed. The national hero agreed to "harmony," and by his capitulation confirmed, in his first month in office, control by the Senate Republicans over patronage and the government.

For a short time Charles Sumner, chairman of the Foreign Relations Committee, was the most prestigious member of the upper chamber. But the scholarly Massachusetts Senator, more interested in issues than spoils, was soon out of place in the new order, and intrigue and cynicism, centering on Grant's insidious personal secretary, Colonel Orville E. Babcock, finally brought him down. Babcock, a thirty-four-year-old West Pointer who had been Grant's wartime military aide, was perhaps the most evil of all Grant's betrayers, a slick, double-dealing conniver who set himself up as the guardian of the President's office; he decided who would see Grant and who would not, in the process becoming the President's closest counselor, feeding him rumors, lies, and false advice when it suited his purpose. Five months after Grant assumed office Babcock, in league with some shady promoters, went with the President's blessings to Santo Domingo in the Caribbean, then in the throes of a revolution, and returned with a treaty he had secretly negotiated with the beleaguered president of that country for the United States to annex Santo Domingo. Secretary of State Hamilton Fish was appalled, but at Grant's urging he agreed to send the treaty to the Senate for ratification. The document, the way it had been negotiated, and administration promises to give certain members of Congress concessions on the island outraged Sumner, who, after a long fight, in which he attacked America's becoming involved in a rebellion in a foreign country, managed to scuttle the scheme. But the conflict upset those Republicans who thought they could prosper from the annexation and created such animosity between Sumner and the President and the secretary of state that on March 9, 1871, the Republican caucus in the Senate, on the ground that it would not do to have a chairman of its Foreign Relations Committee who could not communicate with Grant or Fish, replaced Sumner with the next Republican committee member in seniority, Simon Cameron. It was a blow to Sumner's prestige, but he continued to fight the Grant administration on other issues, allying himself eventually with the Liberal Republican reformers. A man of great drama, he died on March 11, 1874, and to the surprise of many members of Congress was eulogized in an emotional speech in the House of Representatives by Mississippi Representative Lucius Quintus Cincinnatus Lamar, the archenemy of abolitionists before the Civil War who had been pardoned and re-elected to Congress in 1872 and was now anxious for reconciliation between the North and South. "My countrymen!" Lamar exclaimed after praising his former adversary, Sumner, as an "earnest pleader for the exercise of human tenderness and charity"—"know one another, and you will love one another!"

By that time both the executive and legislative branches of the government were deep in corruption. In September, 1869, a conspiracy by Jay Gould and Jim Fisk, the Wall Street railroad buccaneers, to run up the price of gold, aided by the influence of Grant's brother-in-law and Treasury insiders who were to keep the government from selling any of its gold, resulted in the catastrophic "Black Friday" financial panic when Grant wrecked the plot by ordering government gold reserves to be sold. It was the beginning of a long series of debacles that shook Grant's two-term administration, filling the newspapers with lurid accounts of massive graft in a huge postwar construction program of new government buildings in Washington; a giant Whiskey Ring of thievery and fraud in the Treasury Department; and embezzlement, plundering, bribery, fraud, and theft in the Indian Service, the Interior Department, the War Department, the Post Office, the Navy Department, the Attorney General's office, and the Freedmen's Bureau that resulted in indictments and convictions, or resignations, of scores of federal officials, including one Cabinet member after another as well as such intimates of the President's as Colonel Babcock, who escaped the penitentiary only by a deposition in behalf of his character from Grant.

Again and again public pressure, as well as certain conscientious legislators, forced Congress into conducting investigations, sometimes many of them concurrently, by different select and standing committees, which looked into the "horrors" of the executive branch and often skirted close to embarrassing revelations that would have implicated members of both houses. The great senatorial bosses of the state machines and the Republican leaders in the House protected themselves and each other and kept the focus of attention on the administration. Though they managed to come through the scandals relatively unscathed, they were no more virtuous, in the public's mind, than many of those who went to jail. Chief among them were the "Stalwarts," who worked closest with Grant and the leaders of his administration and who consequently profited the most. The greatest in influence at first was the highhanded Senator Oliver Morton of Indiana, who, even though his legs became paralyzed so that he had to walk with two canes or be wheeled around in a chair and sometimes deliver his speeches from his seat, swaying from side to side as he spoke in a grating voice, nevertheless held a commanding dominance over relations with the administration. Morton was a swarthy man with long black hair and a black mustache and chin whiskers; his province was the southern states, whose reconstruction governments he packed with loyal northern job seekers and despoilers. His principal rival, who eventually rose above him in influence, was the theatrical and vain Roscoe Conkling of New York, six feet, three inches tall, forty years old in 1869, and athletically trim and handsome. Conkling, with auburn hair and a golden beard, was a favorite of the ladies and cultivated his looks; he wore fawn-colored vests and pants, combed his hair so that it came down in a single dramatic curl in the center of his broad forehead, and usually looked and smelled as if he had just come out of a hot bath and had groomed himself with an expensive cologne water. When he walked it was with a swagger—Blaine gained his eternal enmity by once mocking him cruelly for his turkeylike strut—and when he orated, as he did magnificently, it was with a slow, deliberate accentuation of almost every consonant. He was arrogant, sarcastic, and politically brilliant, and in New York he ruled an army of ward heelers and hacks whose principal power base was the more than one thousand jobs and enormous booty of the New York Custom House, presided over by several top henchmen, including Chester A. Arthur, an amiable and foppish man who owned one hundred pairs of pants and who one day, to his own surprise, would become President of the United States.

Vying with Morton and Conkling in the Senate, and often outstripping them in greed, were Zach Chandler, gaunt and horse-faced, one of the few independently wealthy spoilsmen, who controlled hordes of collectors, postmasters, and other state and federal jobholders in Michigan while he lived above it all, entertaining like a potentate in his Washington mansion; John Logan, whose Illinois machine sold every form of political job and favor and who organized northern war veterans into the powerful Grand Army of the Republic as a political support for the Republican party; Matthew H. Carpenter, an able and debonair lawyer from Wisconsin, who had his hand in more than one of the administration's scandals; Timothy Howe of the same state, and after 1873 John P. Jones, a mine owner from

Nevada, both of them allies of Conkling's; and also after 1873 Aaron Sargent, friend and tool of the California railroad promoters. Much like them in the House was the crass, scheming demagogue Ben Butler, whose pillaging organization in Massachusetts matched Conkling's New York machine.

The brigands in Congress did not get off scot-free. As early as 1871 a reform movement of Liberal Republicans, initiated by ex-Senator B. Gratz Brown and Senator Carl Schurz, both of Missouri, rebelled against corruption and the excesses of the carpetbag governments in the South and swept into power in their state on a platform that called for universal suffrage, total amnesty in the South, and a Civil Service to end the corruption of patronage and the spoils system in the federal government. Schurz, described by a contemporary as looking like Mephistopheles with eyeglasses, was a shrewd and formidable publicist and operator. Born in Germany in 1829, he had come to the United States in 1852 and eight years later was a delegate from Wisconsin to the Republican convention that nominated Lincoln. He had gained celebrity as a Union general during the war and as a Missouri newspaperman and general political busybody after the war. The movement that he and Brown began in Missouri quickly gained adherents elsewhere, including Sumner and Lyman Trumbull in the Senate as well as various industrialists who were becoming tired of the increasing brazenness of the machines. Despite the bosses' contempt for the reformers, the latter, in March, 1871, put through a mild Civil Service Reform Act, which authorized Grant to set up a commission to investigate establishing a federal civil service of persons who took examinations for their jobs. Congress passed the act only because the bosses intended it to be a sham. A commission head was appointed, but no money was ever appropriated for him. When, even so, he made recommendations, they were ignored, and finally, in 1875, he resigned in frustration and the act died.

Meanwhile, the movement of the Liberal Republicans gathered force, and on May 1, 1872, its supporters, in convention at Cincinnati, nominated the New York publisher Horace Greeley for President and B. Gratz Brown for Vice President against Grant. Their candidacy was aimed against the bosses, who, they charged, were seeking to control the Republican party and the Senate. Though their platform embraced a return to specie payments (rather than the continued use of greenbacks) and a law to end the speculators' abuse of the Homestead Act, civil-service reform was their principal goal, and when the Democrats, at their convention in Baltimore, also endorsed them, the Republican machines finally took them seriously, sparing no effort to trounce them in the campaign. With Grant and Senator Henry Wilson of Massachusetts as their candidates, the regular Republicans shamelessly "waved the bloody shirt" (a term originated when a Massachusetts Congressman displayed in the House, for its emotional effect, the bloodstained shirt of an Ohio carpetbagger who had been beaten in Mississippi), whipping up again Civil War patriotism and linking the Liberal Republicans with the Copperheads of the North and the unreconstructed rebels of the South. In response Greeley ran a floundering, amateurish campaign and was thoroughly beaten. He died within a month after the election, and the Liberal Republican movement gradually disintegrated.

Its threat to the bosses had hardly disappeared, however, when a more ominous development engulfed them. During the campaign Charles A. Dana of the Democratic New York *Sun* had published charges that members of the Cabinet, numerous Senators and Representatives, Vice President Schuyler Colfax, and vice-presidential nominee Henry Wilson had all received bribes in 1867 totaling $9 million worth of stock in the Crédit Mobilier, a construction company that the promoters of the Union Pacific Railroad organized to divert to themselves the excess profits—made at the government's expense—in building the line. In return for the stock, it was alleged, the beneficiaries helped defeat a bill that would have regulated the railroad's rates. Public sentiment demanded an investigation, and on December 2, 1872, to the horror of many members in both houses, Speaker Blaine—who, though one of those accused, knew that he was innocent—left the chair to take the floor and move for the appointment of an investigating committee. Three committees were finally created, two in the House and one in the Senate, but the principal evidence was uncovered by one of the House committees, headed by Representative Luke P. Poland of Vermont. One by one those who had been accused testified, many of them such as Colfax and Garfield becoming panicked and lying or telling contradictory stories; others—with a blind sense of morality and an aggrieved feeling that they had done nothing wrong—admitting to complicated arrangements by which they had purchased varying amounts of Crédit Mobilier shares (at prices well under the market value), either giving them back or paying for them out of the high dividends they later received; and still others, such as Blaine, Conkling, and Treasury Secretary Boutwell proving, with a good deal of outraged dignity, that they had been mistakenly accused. Anxious to sweep the mess out of sight as quickly as possible, the committee accepted the confused and contradictory testimony, whitewashed many who were patently guilty, and fastened all blame on two scapegoats, Representative James Brooks of New York, the Democratic leader in the House, who had received more stock than anyone else and whom the Republicans were happy to condemn, and Representative Oakes Ames of Massachusetts, a director of the Crédit Mobilier and the man who had distributed the shares to the others. "I shall put them where they will do most good to us. I am here on the spot and can better judge where they should go," Ames had written to another stockholder in the Crédit Mobilier in an 1867 letter that the committee revealed. Though the committee recommended the expulsion of the two Representatives, the Judiciary Committee, headed by Ben Butler, decided against it, and the full House finally voted on February 27, 1873, that they be "absolutely" condemned for their conduct. After the vote members came over apologetically, assuring both men that they had been forced to vote for the resolution because of public opinion. Brooks and Ames were broken by the verdict, however, and within a few weeks both of them died. The Senate, for its part, took no steps to punish those of its members who had been implicated. Colfax, who left everyone puzzled by his contradictory explanations, was a special case. As Vice President he could only be impeached. His term of office ended in a few days, however, and the House took no action against him, letting him retire under a cloud that lasted the rest of his life.

With the end of the investigation, a feeling of relief and even of exhilaration swept Congress. Six days after the censure vote the two houses, with an utter disregard for the public's sensibilities, passed an act, introduced by Butler, doubling the President's salary (to $50,000 a year), increasing certain other salaries, including those of the Supreme Court justices and the Speaker of the House, and raising the compensation of Senators and Representatives from $5,000 to $7,500 a year. The last increase, in addition, was made retroactive over the two preceding years so that the members of Congress, in effect, would receive a bonus of $5,000 each. The uproar that followed was unforeseen. The session ended and the Senators and Representatives went home to find themselves scourged and lashed by a public infuriated by what the newspapers called the "Salary Grab" Act. In the next session the chastened legislators repealed the section of the act referring to their own increase, but, on top of all the scandals, they had done themselves irreparable harm, confirming the general public's low opinion of members of Congress and giving further credence to the stereotype image of the national legislature projected half in jest by Mark Twain: "It could probably be shown by facts and figures that there is no distinctly American criminal class except Congress."

Amid the politics and corruption, sporadic attention had been paid to the nation's problems. In the South the Ku Klux Klan had arisen, terrorizing blacks and undermining the reconstruction governments. Investigations were held, first by the Senate, then by a joint Senate-House committee, and three different acts were passed in 1870 and 1871 to enforce the Fourteenth and Fifteenth Amendments in the turbulent southern states. Though the Klan soon died out on its own, Grant, supported by the Republicans in Congress, took stern measures to restore the authority of the Reconstruction governments, invoking martial law, moving troops from one trouble spot to another, and visiting stern justice on lawbreakers. At the same time there were those in the North who recognized that the harsh measures, while guaranteeing southern support for the northern Republican politicians, were also creating an atmosphere of enormous resentment and hatred among the whites in the South. Under pressure from Schurz's Liberal Republicans, Congress, after several attempts, passed the Amnesty Act on May 22, 1872, restoring all the rights of citizenship to every white person in the South, save about five hundred of the "great criminals" of the war. Sumner, growing old and ill and without the influence he had previously enjoyed, tried to amend the act by a provision outlawing discrimination against blacks on juries or in public places or on public means of transportation in the South. Though he failed, his crusade for equal rights for blacks was carried on by others after his death, and on March 1, 1875, despite an attempted filibuster in the House, Congress passed another Civil Rights Act, giving the blacks the rights for which Sumner had fought in 1872. In 1883, however, the Supreme Court ruled the act unconstitutional, opening the way for the long reign of the Jim Crow "separate but equal" doctrine of racial segregation in the South that was legally ended only in the 1950's and 1960's.

Meanwhile, an economic conflict—over the heads and beyond the interest of many legislators—had been waged in the financial committees of both houses. In the campaign of 1868 the Democrats had supported the "Ohio Idea" of former Congressman and 1864 vice-presidential candidate George H. Pendleton, now the Democratic candidate for governor of Ohio, proposing the payment of the national debt in greenbacks. The Republicans, however, opposed further inflation, and, supporting the use of "hard" money and the withdrawal of the wartime greenbacks from circulation, they passed the Public Credit Act on March 18, 1869, providing for the payment of the government's debt in gold. At the same time it was left unsettled whether to redeem the remaining $356 million in greenbacks still in circulation. Four years later, on February 2, 1873, Congress passed the Coinage Act, seemingly an innocent measure at the time, dropping the use of silver in coins (for years no silver had been presented to the mint) and making gold the sole metal used in coinage. That fall the failure of Jay Cooke's banking firm (brought on partly by the Crédit Mobilier scandal, which had made it difficult for him to market his Northern Pacific Railroad bonds to European banking houses, which were now leery of western American railroads) resulted in the Panic of 1873 and a deep economic depression. Attempts to cure it were marked by debates between those who favored and those who opposed inflation, the former urging an increased supply of money in the form of greenbacks, as well as gold and silver coins. Though silver was now pouring from Nevada mines it could no longer be coined, and the Coinage Act was assailed by the bimetallists as the "Crime of '73." On April 14, 1874, however, Congress, under the guidance of John Sherman, chairman of the Senate Finance Committee, passed a moderate and cautious inflation bill, permitting the issuance of legal tender notes up to a total of $400 million in circulation. Business interests, regarding it as a repudiation of the promise to redeem government securities with specie, besieged Grant in protest, and he vetoed the measure. Midwestern Republican Senators such as Morton and Logan, reflecting the needs of their hard-pressed farmer constituents, registered their dismay, but eastern Republicans saw the veto as a commitment of their party to stand by the conservative business and financial interests, and Congress was unable to override the veto.

A new national issue that would go on for the rest of the century was now taking shape. Against the eastern Republican interests would be arrayed Grangers, Greenbackers, Populists, advocates of the free and unlimited coinage of silver, and others representing the inflationist agricultural interests of the Mississippi Valley and the South and the far western miners, all seeking a larger supply of money to combat hard times. Eastern-minded Republicans, however, were still in control. On June 20, 1874, following the failure to override Grant's veto, Congress put a ceiling of $382 million on greenbacks in circulation. That fall the Republicans received a warning. The depression, the scandals, the defection of Liberal Republicans, all combined to give the Democrats a victory in the congressional elections. The following March, for the first time since the Civil War, they would control the House. But on January 14, 1875, before the old session ended, the Republicans climaxed their anti-Greenback campaign, passing the Specie Resumption Act, which—hailed by the financial interests—provided for the reduction of greenbacks to $300 million and the resuming of payments of the government's debt in specie by January 1, 1879.

When the Forty-fourth Congress met in 1875, the Democrats elected Representative Michael C. Kerr of Indiana as Speaker of the House, and Blaine became the leader of the opposition. Flushed with their new power, the Democrats pressed investigations of every aspect of Grant's battered administration, and many of the worst scandals were now exposed. Even Blaine, who was emerging as one of the leading contenders for the Republican presidential nomination in 1876, was suddenly thrown on the defensive when he was charged with having used his position as Speaker to put up some nearly worthless railroad bonds as collateral against a payment to him of $64,000 from the Union Pacific. On May 31, 1876, a subcommittee of the House Judiciary Committee, set up to investigate the matter, received testimony from a man named James Mulligan, who claimed he possessed letters that would incriminate Blaine. By a ruse, Blaine got hold of the letters and refused to turn them over to the committee, claiming that they were his property and were not "relevant." As rumors filled the capital, harming Blaine's reputation and undermining his presidential candidacy, the former Speaker suddenly announced that he would rise to a question of privilege in the House on June 5. That day the Hall of the Representatives was filled with tense spectators, most of them hoping that the dazzling Blaine would pull a coup. He did not disappoint them. Waving the packet of letters, he announced first that he had vindicated his right to protect his private property. Then, in dramatic fashion, he said that he would read the letters to prove that they contained nothing derogatory to him. He proceeded to do so, obviously picking and choosing various parts that sounded innocent but covering his tactics with such flourishes and theatrical tones of voice that every sentence seemed to prove his case. To make any sense of what he read was impossible, but it sounded magnificent, and cheers greeted his explanations and running comments, which seemed to make everything clear. As he concluded, he stood by the seat of J. Proctor Knott of Kentucky, the Democratic chairman of the House Judiciary Committee, his chief tormentor, and delivered a final, telling blow. He knew that Knott had received a telegram that a friend had sent for Blaine to try to exonerate him. Whether the facts in the telegram were accurate or not was irrelevant; Knott, deciding on his own that the information in the telegram was spurious, had made a blunder by not letting anyone know that he had received it. Blaine now made Knott admit to the House that he had concealed the telegram, which Blaine asserted was proof of his innocence, and he flustered Knott so badly that the Kentuckian was unable to establish that the information in the telegram might, after all, be untrue.

The House, in which James Madison and John Quincy Adams had once fought for constitutional principles, exploded in applause for Blaine's performance, and a few weeks later Robert G. Ingersoll, a master of extravagant oratory, placed Blaine's name in nomination for the presidency at the Republican convention in Cincinnati, describing him as "a plumed knight" who "marched down the halls of the American Congress and threw his shining lance full and fair against the brazen forehead of the defamers of his country and maligners of his honor. . . ." Blaine was now up against cynics in his own party, however, chief among them Morton and Conkling, who were both competing against him for the nomination. Conkling had never forgiven Blaine for mocking his "strut," and Senator Morton had no love either for the "smart" Representative from Maine. In the end, they knocked each other out, and the Republicans nominated Governor Rutherford B. Hayes of Ohio, "a third-rate nonentity, whose only recommendation," wrote Henry Adams, "is that he is obnoxious to no one." Ten days later the Democrats named the popular New York reformer Samuel Tilden as their candidate. With good reason, the Republicans "ran scared," waving the bloody shirt frantically and hoping that the Democratic congressional victory of 1874 had been an aberration. On Election Day their worst fears were realized. Tilden won the popular vote by a margin of about 250,000 and carried enough states, including New Jersey, New York, Connecticut, Indiana, and all the southern states—where power was again back in the hands of the southern white population—to give him a close electoral-vote victory. But Hayes's lieutenants claimed South Carolina, Florida, and Louisiana—whose votes would give the election to Hayes by one electoral vote, 185 to 184—and on their orders, telegraphed to carpetbag officials in those states, tens of thousands of Democratic votes were thrown out and the tallies were doctored so that eventually two sets of returns, one Republican and one Democratic, each showing victory, were sent to Washington from those three states. Congress was in a quandary. The Constitution said that "the President of the Senate shall, in the presence of the Senate and House of Representatives, open all the Certificates, and the Votes shall then be counted." But counted by whom? The House was Democratic, the Senate Republican. Each would claim the three states—which would determine the election—for its own candidate.

On January 29, 1877, after days of confusion, Congress created an

Electoral Commission of five Senators, five Representatives, and five justices of the Supreme Court to decide the contest. The Senate named three Republicans and two Democrats to the commission, the House three Democrats and two Republicans, and the Supreme Court two Republicans, two Democrats, and one independent jurist, David Davis of Illinois, whose political leaning was not known. Before the group could meet, the Illinois legislature created another crisis by naming Davis to the Senate. He resigned from the Electoral Commission, and the Supreme Court filled the vacancy with another Republican judge. Voting on strictly partly lines, the commission gave the victory to Hayes. For a time matters grew tense. Angry Democrats threatened a march on Washington to force the acceptance of Tilden. In Congress some members talked of a filibuster that would prevent an electoral count. Finally, with the assent of Lamar and other Democrats on the commission, who did not want to see more sectional violence, a compromise was worked out. The Democrats accepted Hayes, with promises from the Republican leaders to withdraw all federal troops from the southern states, to appoint at least one southerner to the Cabinet, and to appropriate large sums of money for internal improvements that would help rebuild the South.

Since March 4, 1877, was a Sunday, Hayes was sworn in privately at the White House on the evening of March 3 by Chief Justice Morrison R. Waite, taking the oath again on Monday at a large public ceremony at the Capitol. In April the last federal troops were withdrawn from the southern states. The blacks were abandoned (few northern business or political leaders any longer felt threatened by a return to power of a vengeful South), and Reconstruction was over. The besmirched Grant took off on a long trip around the world, and the Senate, filled with political bosses—whom one of them pointed out on the Senate floor to a freshman in the chamber as "the jackal—the vulture—the sheep-killing dog—the buzzard—a damned, hungry, skulking, cowardly wolf"—still dominated the presidency. The upper house was no longer a forum of great debates over the foundations of the nation. If the improvident Webster had still been alive, said a newspaperman of the day, he would have been "neither in debt nor in the Senate."

7. Politicians and Millionaires

"God reigns and the government at Washington still lives," said Congressman James A. Garfield. To many Americans in 1877, after all the turmoil the nation had been through—years of division over slavery, the Civil War, the shock of Lincoln's assassination, Reconstruction, the impeachment of Johnson, the Grant administration's endless scandals, the election crisis of 1877—it might have seemed a miracle. Now a long period of relative peace and stability—even dullness—characterized at the start by the drab, respectable figure of the new President, Rutherford B. Hayes, settled over the political life of the nation. In place of the fierce ideological conflicts that had strained and tested the foundations of the American government came new commotions in the halls of Congress, many stemming from the tensions and problems created by the gigantic surge of industrialization and economic growth rapidly building the United States into a world power, others reflecting little more than Tweedledum-Tweedledee party rivalries over essentially trivial issues, but none of them menacing in any way to basic American institutions.

The compelling facts of life during the era, which Mark Twain termed the Gilded Age, were the explosive expansion of the economy, the aggressive force of the highly competitive captains of finance and industry who directed it, and the influences for change that both exerted on all aspects of American society. The response of Congress, which by and large still lorded it over the executive branch, was to keep hands off of—or to help—the development, but certainly not to get in its way. Industrial barons such as Andrew Carnegie, John D. Rockefeller, and scores like them believed in Social Darwinism, which proclaimed the doctrine of the survival of the fittest in economic life, and they believed that the best government was the least government—unless they could mold it as a weapon and tool to help the strongest have their way over the weak. On the one hand, all branches of government, imbued with that philosophy, worked to ensure a maximum of laissez faire and a minimum of interference in the country's business life. On the other hand, business succeeded in making the Congress, the executive, the courts, and the Constitution its handmaidens in assuring support for money-making and protection against opponents.

The link between businessmen and Congress was gradually strengthened, but subtle changes marked the relationship. As industry grew more powerful, better organized, and more varied in its interests and needs, a reaction set in among its leaders against the more brazen piracy of political bosses and their machines. More than ever before, business needed the men in politics, but it required not plunderers but efficient, centralized political organizations that, like synchronized arms of business itself, could effectively and economically guarantee favorable representation in the nation's legislative bodies. Continuing their financial support of campaigns, corporations increased their influence over the organizations of both parties, in some states taking control of them. Businessmen put their own men in positions of power and even entered politics themselves and assumed leadership of the machines. As the politically ambitious moved upward through the organizations—to the state legislatures, the House of Representatives, then the Senate—they shared an identity of interests, no longer with boodle-collecting bosses but with the business interests that influenced, or controlled, their state parties.

At the same time, on both the state and national levels, there were numerous contradictions and exceptions to this political development. Industry itself was fragmented, composed of many different and often competing interests, so that even within individual states there were those, for instance, who wanted high tariffs and those who wanted low tariffs. The leadership often strove mightily to effect compromises, and when it was unable to do so, the stronger elements won and there were temporary splits or permanent defections. At other times the national parties divided, the business-oriented state organizations in the East and West separating, for example, over currency issues. In some states the organizations were oriented more to agricultural than industrial interests, or to mining rather than manufacturing concerns. Even in states where tightly disciplined machines ruled, voters had a frequent habit of electing independents, mavericks, reformers, and populists, who provided a noisy—but largely ineffective —opposition to the conservative pro-business majorities of both parties.

In the South, which after Reconstruction became solidly Democratic, state organizations were often built around popular individuals. At first the old oligarchy seemed to come back to life, and aristocratic, gentlemanly, well-educated men such as Lucius Q. C. Lamar and Wade Hampton of South Carolina represented their states in Congress. Now that they knew the southern cause was lost they espoused union and racial harmony (though not necessarily equality), and their principal concern was the rebuilding of the South. But the days of most of them were numbered. Eventually, as democratization spread across the South, they were toppled by new groupings of poorly educated white merchants and small farmers who hated the blacks and the old aristocrats alike and who sent to Congress

246

lower-grade, locally oriented politicians hungering for power and plunder. Sometimes they could be lined up with the business interests, but more often they allied themselves with the agriculturists and populists. Among their ranks were occasional extreme racist demagogues such as South Carolina's "Pitchfork Ben" Tillman (who threatened to stick his pitchfork into President Grover Cleveland's ribs). Such ranters usually followed erratic, tub-thumping courses of their own.

Business's many different and conflicting interests, as well as the large number of uncontrolled members in both houses, made lobbying more essential than it had ever been; and it, too, became institutionalized into a more businesslike and effective mechanism. In the early postwar years the uninhibited rascality of the most active economic groups, such as the railroads, spelled trouble for legislators and industry alike. Lawmakers were bribed by "loans," gifts of railroad passes and other favors, jobs for relatives, and opportunities to buy stock at low prices. Collis Huntington of the Central Pacific Railroad, who in 1876–77 employed some two hundred agents to push his interests on Capitol Hill, characterized all Senators and Representatives as "clean" (so sympathetic that they did not have to be bought), "commercial" (open to being bought), and "communists" (who could not be bought). Yet Huntington's methods were expensive and unreliable, and other industrialists increasingly shied away from the most blatant dealings, which, if exposed, could involve them in another Crédit Mobilier scandal and lay them open to ruin by competitors and the public.

Gradually, as tariff and currency measures drew increasing numbers of lobbyists to Washington, their activities became respectable, aboveboard, and even a necessary adjunct to the work of Congress. Though the use of personal influence and various forms of bribery did not disappear, and lobbying in general continued to conjure up a sinister image in the mind of the average citizen, the practitioners (sometimes retired or defeated Senators and Representatives) were often honorable, hard-working experts in their fields who exerted influence not by offering bribes but by providing the legislators with research and technical advice on bills and with speeches and documentary materials in behalf of their clients' interests. In time, however, the most effective lobbying was done in the caucuses, the committee rooms, and the cloakrooms by the legislators themselves. Sometimes bills came up that affected a business in which particular lawmakers had a personal interest. Only rarely, in such cases, was their partisanship inhibited by a sense of ethics or by recognition of a conflict of interest. More significantly, many of the most powerful and influential members of both houses came to be advocates of class interests, first of the industrialists and then of the monopolists and finance capitalists, with whom they identified their own interests. Men like Blaine charted the path for them, championing freedom from government interference for their business friends and benefactors. Later on, individuals who entered Congress with interests of their own in capitalist enterprise strove to make the government their own possession, attuned to the needs of the nation's ruling economic stratum. "The members of the Senate," pointed out Senator George Hearst of California, one of the richest mining titans in America, "are the survivors of the fittest," and the Senate would reflect their economic, social, and political credo. It was not a day for the weak, the unorganized, or the powerless; little, if any, lobbying was done for labor, minorities, consumers, or the crowded poor in the cities.

The attack on the power and excesses of the professional political spoilsmen who had dominated Congress since the Civil War began haltingly under Hayes. During the 1876 campaign both he and Tilden, responding to the public reaction against the Grant administration scandals, promised civil-service reform. Hayes, devoid of glamour and popular appeal, was nevertheless honest and meant what he said. He appointed a strong Cabinet, including William M. Evarts, the distinguished leader of the bar who had helped defend Andrew Johnson during his impeachment trial, as secretary of state, Senator John Sherman as secretary of the treasury, and—shocking to Zach Chandler and other bosses in the Senate—Carl Schurz, the Liberal Republican agitator for a civil service, as secretary of the interior.

These were only Hayes's preliminary moves. With the support of Evarts and Sherman, who had many ties to businessmen tired of paying tribute to the New York Custom House, he launched an investigation of that base of Senator Roscoe Conkling's machine. A report submitted to him on May 24, 1877, laid bare an overwhelming record of graft and corruption presided over by Conkling's lieutenants, Chester A. Arthur and Alonzo Cornell. Hayes wrote to Sherman, whose Treasury Department administered the Custom House, expressing his opinion that "the collection of the revenues should be free from partisan control, and organized on a strictly business basis" and added, "the party leaders should have no more influence in appointments than other equally respectable citizens." He followed with an executive order, issued on June 22, prohibiting government officials from taking part "in the management of political organizations, caucuses, conventions, or electoral campaigns" and barring the assessing of government jobholders for political purposes. Arthur and Cornell were charged with "laxity" rather than with any criminal activity of their own, but they were informed that their resignations were requested.

The Conkling machine rose at once to the challenge of a President who did not seem to know his place. The two men refused to resign, and Conkling, deriding talk of a "snivel service," delivered a withering attack on reformers and the President. When a special session of the Forty-fifth Congress convened in October, 1877, Hayes sent the Senate nominations of two businessmen to replace Arthur and Cornell. Conkling appealed to "senatorial courtesy" (no Senator should approve an appointment in the state of a colleague who was opposed to it), and in a caucus of Republican Senators he let it be known that if Hayes could dictate to New York the President could similarly assume mastery over every other Senator and each state organization. Asserting the "dignity of the Senate," the upper chamber rejected Hayes's nominations, 35 to 21, and Conkling temporarily won the battle.

"I am right, and shall not give up the contest," Hayes confided to his diary; but he remained silent and did nothing at once about the New York Custom House, and his efforts for reform in other areas of the government were carried out with little direction. Finally, in July, 1878, he suspended Arthur and Cornell, and when Congress met again on December 2 of that year he submitted two new nominations as replacements. Sherman now went to work to help him get votes from Republican Senators who were tiring of Conkling's constant diatribes against the President. After much wrangling the Republicans split, and on February 3, 1879, enough of them joined the Democrats to approve the nominations and defeat Conkling. It was a serious blow to the oligarchical bosses, but who had really won was a question. Hayes had lost stature with half the party, and the party—torn among administration adherents, Conkling's "Stalwarts," and "Half-Breeds," who stood between them and looked to the more urbane and respectable Blaine for leadership—had lost stature in the nation. In the elections of 1878, though other factors contributed to the results, the Democrats won control of both houses for the first time since the Civil War.

Conkling made a swift recovery from his defeat, achieving a measure of revenge in 1879 by putting up Cornell for governor of New York and Arthur for Senator and electing them both, and by 1880, despite his loss of the Custom House spoils, he was virtual dictator of politics in New York. Scheming to regain control of the Republican party and the presidency, he led a movement of Stalwart followers to nominate Grant for a third term. By the time the Republicans met in convention at Chicago in June, 1880, the former President had again assumed the role of Civil War hero and was the front runner, opposed principally by Blaine and by John Sherman, whose campaign was managed by the Republican House leader, James A. Garfield. Grant's opponents, fearful that the Democrats would revive memories of all the scandals of his administration, united to keep him from being nominated: Conkling held 306 votes solidly for Grant for thirty-six ballots, but they were not enough to win, and on the thirty-fourth ballot Garfield, who had been fighting hard for Sherman, suddenly began to receive votes. On the thirty-sixth ballot a stampede of switches from Blaine and Sherman gave the surprised Ohio legislator the nomination. As a sop to try to hold the Stalwarts' loyalty in the election, the convention nominated Conkling's somewhat-stained henchman, Chester A. Arthur, for Vice President.

The Democrats nominated the Civil War Union general Winfield S. Hancock, but it was the struggle for future power, patronage, and spoils between the Stalwart and Half-Breed Republican factions of Conkling and Blaine that made the campaign a nightmare for the weak and insecure Garfield. He rushed back and forth in confusion, attending secret meetings that bewildered the public and left the bosses with whom he met confused as to what he promised them. In the wings Carl Schurz and his reformers, constituting a third group whose support Garfield needed, watched in alarm. Gradually all elements of the party got behind Garfield, but more significant for the future was the support given him by private capitalists, who during the campaign began converting the national Republican organization into the party of American business. Blaine, who numbered Andrew Carnegie among his close friends, was one of the principal catalysts for this development, encouraging the counsel and participation, as well as the financial help, of prominent businessmen. Numerous industrialists, promoters, and financiers, including the Rockefellers, Jay Gould, and the Vanderbilts' lawyer and agent Chauncey M. Depew, played active roles behind the scenes in the campaign. In New York Conkling's wealthy "angel," Levi P. Morton, raised funds for Garfield in Wall Street, and in Ohio Marcus Alonzo Hanna, an energetic forty-three-year-old millionaire with interests in coal, iron, banking, and shipping, organized businessmen into fund-raising political clubs to work for the Republican ticket.

Hancock, a notably clean and honorable candidate, carried the Solid South, but Garfield won the election, 214 electoral votes to 155. It was the first time that the presidential electors had been chosen by popular vote in every state. Garfield's headaches now began in earnest as the competing politicians buffeted him for payoffs on his promises. The few advances toward reform that Hayes had made went down the drain, and an unseemly contest for spoils was waged, much to the disgust of the public and the horror of the reformers. Blaine, about to become secretary of state, soon wielded a commanding influence over Garfield, steering patronage to Half-Breed leaders. The final blow to Conkling was the shooting of Garfield at Union Station in Washington on July 2 by a frustrated office seeker, who cried out, "I am a Stalwart and Arthur is President now." It was an enormous shock to the nation and the bosses, overnight dooming Conkling and the entire Stalwart wing of the Republican party. All elements of the population turned against the spoils system and its defenders, and an angry demand, joined by the business community, for civil-service reform swept the country. Garfield clung to life during the summer, but he died on September 19. The shooting had other consequences. Blaine now suddenly lost his power. The chief lieutenant of his worst enemy had become President, and soon after Arthur was sworn in he resigned from the Cabinet. On the other hand Arthur, the political hack, a "nobby dresser" with a gray mustache and Dundreary-style side whiskers, straightened out with a start. Severing his ties to the Stalwarts, he responded to public opinion by giving his full support to civil-service reform. As he pressed genuinely for good government the worst fears about him disappeared, and he proved a better President than his early career would have suggested.

In his message to the Forty-seventh Congress in December, 1881, Arthur strongly endorsed passage of a civil-service reform act. The previous year Democrat George H. Pendleton, whom Ohio sent to the Senate in 1879, had introduced a bill prepared by the Civil Service Reform Association, and on January 16, 1883, Congress finally passed it. It set up a three-man bipartisan Civil Service Commission to hold examinations and make appointments on a merit basis; provided a list—which the President could extend—of positions to be filled by examination; and forbade the levying of political contributions on federal officeholders. The act was only a beginning. During Arthur's term some 14,000 of 110,000 government civil-service positions were filled by examination. Future Presidents would make advances and retreats under the law. In his first term Grover Cleveland, the first Democratic President since Buchanan, dismayed the supporters of the act by adopting Andrew Jackson's philosophy—that bureaucrats needed a shaking up and should be rotated out of office every so often—thus justifying the replacement of some two thirds of all government workers by deserving Democrats. But Cleveland gave greater support to the law in his second administration, and other Presidents gradually extended the list of positions that required examinations. Broadened from time to time, civil service brought an end to the spoils system in the federal government.

In other areas of national interest, the passage of important legislation during the years of the Gilded Age was a relatively rare phenomenon. Partly responsible—along with the ruling laissez-faire philosopy—was the frequently divided political control of branches of the government that began with the Democrats' return to power in the House of Representatives in 1875. The first Democratic Speaker, Michael C. Kerr of Indiana, died in 1876, and the Democrats replaced him with Samuel Jackson Randall, a forty-nine-year-old forceful and able parliamentarian from Philadelphia. When he was Speaker, Blaine had made committee assignments deliberately calculated to aid legislation in which he was interested. This was the beginning of a trend, continued by Randall, that gave the office of the Speaker considerably more power than it had ever had before. Randall, who served till 1881, not only influenced legislation by his appointments to committees, but in 1880 headed a five-man committee that thoroughly revised the House rules, making the Committee on Rules a five-member standing committee chaired by the Speaker. Designed to "secure accuracy in business, economy of time, order, uniformity, and impartiality," the revised rules, employed by the committee that the Speaker controlled, strengthened his power over numerous procedures of the House, including committee access to the House floor, the amount of time for debate on major bills, suspension of the rules, privileges of reporting, the offering of amendments, and the distribution of certain bills to committees. The new rules, however, did not cope with some growing practices that were being criticized and called disreputable. Among them were the old maneuver, revived by the Democrats from pre-Civil War days, of attaching nonrelevant "riders" to urgent appropriation bills (which the President had to accept, or veto, *in toto*); "disappearing quorums" (the frustration of business by basing quorums on the number of those who voted rather than on those who were actually present); and repeated roll calls and other dilatory tactics that permitted a minority to block action by the majority. Both parties supported these practices as devices to have their way or to oppose and delay measures when they were in the minority, and the 1880 rules reform ignored them.

In the Senate a foundation was laid for future party control of legislation: the Republican caucus, still more concerned with procedural than substantive matters and often diverted by political intrigues, appointed an *ad hoc* committee to work out an order of legislative interests. Eventually this would lead to the institutionalizing of a businesslike Republican Steering Committee with great powers over party members and legislation in the Senate. The Democrats in time copied the Republicans.

The primary issues taken up by Congress pertained, in the main, to economic matters. Though Hayes and his secretary of the treasury, John Sherman, were determined to maintain the gold standard to assist business, the continuing effects of the depression that began in 1873 increased agitation among farmers, workers, and debtors for an inflated currency of silver as well as greenbacks. In 1875 the uniting of agricultural interests with the silver-mining advocates of the West had helped to give the Democrats control of the House, and in December, 1876, the House passed a bill introduced by Representative Richard "Silver Dick" Bland, a Missouri Democrat, for the free and unlimited coinage of silver and the end of the Coinage Act of 1873, which had made gold the sole metal used in coins. The Republican Senate took no action on the measure, but the next year, when the House again passed Bland's bill, popular support for the coinage of silver was so strong that it seemed probable that both houses would muster enough votes to pass the measure over a presidential veto.

Warned by August Belmont and other New York bankers that enactment of Bland's bill would imperil the government's credit, Sherman enrolled William B. Allison of Iowa, the astute and influential Republican chairman of the Senate Finance Committee, to amend the measure into a compromise that would appease both sides. Allison, a quiet "politician's politician," would in time become one of the most powerful men in Congress. Forty-eight years old, a short, stocky man with a spade beard, he had entered the House in 1862 and ten years later began what would be thirty-five years of service in the Senate. Although a westerner with a largely agricultural constituency, he was a friend of the railroads and of banking interests and basically supported the gold standard, protective tariffs, and other conservative positions. But he was also a conciliator and compromiser who believed in reasonableness and worked constantly behind the scenes to smooth quarrels and bring opponents together. His air of caution led some to maintain that he never ventured an opinion of his own. "He was so pussy-footed," said one of his Senate colleagues, "he could walk from New York to San Francisco on the keys of a piano and never strike a note." Allison thoroughly amended Bland's bill, eliminating the features most opposed by the eastern moneyed interests—especially the *unlimited* coinage of silver, which posed the most dangerous threat of inflation—but authorizing a controlled silver coinage of between $2 million and $4 million a month. The compromise, which satisfied the bankers more than the inflationists, finally passed with majorities of both parties. As the Bland-Allison Act it then passed the House, was repassed over Hayes's veto by both houses, and became law on February 28, 1878.

To inflationists, still appealing for a vastly increased volume of circulating currency as the best means of raising farm prices and industrial wages, the act spelled deception by both major parties. On February 22, 1878, the Greenback Labor party, advocating the redemption of government bonds with greenbacks—"the same money for the plow-holder and the bondholder"—free silver coinage, and a graduated income tax, was formed at Toledo, Ohio, and that fall elected fourteen members to the House of Representatives. The resurgent Democrats gained majorities in both houses, but their margin of control in each chamber was slender, and the Forty-sixth Congress, which met during the last two years of Hayes's term, was unproductive, marked by party wrangling and impasses with the President.

The new Democratic Congress was called into an extra session by President Hayes on March 18, 1879, to pass appropriation bills that the previous Congress had failed to enact. The Democrats at once seized the opportunity to try to repeal the various Force Acts of the Reconstruction period that still authorized the President to use federal troops in southern states during elections. In the South the old aristocrats and the new politicians were speeding the process of disenfranchising black voters. The last black Senator, Blanche K. Bruce of Mississippi, a handsome, able, and personally popular thirty-eight-year-old former slave, still sat in the upper chamber and would do so for two more years. But unfair and discriminatory voting laws, as well as intimidation, were making a mockery of the Fifteenth Amendment in the South—an ironic development that distressed many Republicans. The Fourteenth Amendment, with a provision to reduce proportionately the congressional representation of states that denied suffrage to blacks, had been passed with an eye to preventing the South from using a nonvoting black population as a basis for increasing its representation in Congress. Some now thought that the Fifteenth Amendment should never have been passed, for its practical effect, they believed, was to nullify the intention of the representation provision in the Fourteenth: the South was acquiring increased representation and power in Congress (after the census of 1880 the House would go from 293 to 332 members, and the South would benefit), and, as the Radical Republicans had feared, the black population that conferred the increase was being denied political power. To the Republicans it seemed essential that every means be retained to enforce the Fifteenth Amendment.

Nevertheless, throughout the extra session of 1879 the Democrats in the House attached riders to the administration's appropriation bills forbidding the federal government to use money, troops, or marshals to police the southern polls. Despite Republican dilatory tactics in the House and angry filibusters in the Senate, the appropriation bills with the riders passed Congress but were vetoed by Hayes, who stood up to the Democrats, attacking the notion that the House of Representatives had the right "to withhold appropriations upon which the existence of the Government may depend unless the Senate and the President shall give their assent to any legislation which the House may see fit to attach to appropriation bills." If not abandoned, he said, the principle would "result in a consolidation of unchecked and despotic power in the House." Despite Speaker Randall's leadership, the Democrats were unable to override the vetoes, and Congress finally passed the supply bills without the riders. In the next session the Democrats made another try, attaching riders once more to appropriation bills to prohibit the use of money and marshals at southern polls. Again Hayes's vetoes could not be overridden, and in 1881 the Republicans regained control of the House, temporarily stifling the issue.

Toward the end of Hayes's administration prosperity returned to the nation. Agrarian agitation subsided and manufacturing and industrial profits and wages increased; the currency issue faded and the Greenbackers dwindled in numbers. At the same time the taxation policies inaugurated during the Civil War and based largely on high protective tariffs were bringing into the Treasury embarrassing surpluses, which Congress was hard put to spend on a steadily mounting pension largesse for Civil War veterans (whose votes gratefully supported the Republican machines that took credit for the payments) and on pork-barrel legislation. Gradually a new demand arose for an end to the protective tariffs that subsidized huge profits for monopolists and kept prices high for farmers and other consumers. By the time Chester Arthur succeeded Garfield in 1881, even many industrialists, while demanding the retention of protection, were willing to support a moderate revision of the tariff structure.

When Arthur submitted a tariff-reform report, together with suggested schedules, to Congress, however, Republican members of the House Ways and Means Committee, led by a sixty-eight-year-old veteran Pennsylvania protectionist, William D. "Pig Iron" Kelley, ignored it and proceeded to devise a bill of their own. At the same time the Senate Finance Committee set about independently to draw up still another version of a new tariff. Lobbyists flocked to assist both committees. Taking leading roles, also, were a group of younger legislators who, reflecting the changes occurring in politics, spoke for steel, coal, sugar, textiles, and other powerful and respected segments of private industry. Among them were Senator Nelson W. Aldrich of Rhode Island and Representatives William McKinley of Ohio and Thomas Brackett Reed of Maine. Aldrich, a distinguished-looking forty-one-year-old wholesale grocer and banker, had entered Republican politics in his state to help rid it of its spoilsman leadership and make it more responsive to the needs of businessmen. He had served one term in the House and in 1881 was elected to the Senate, where, as a rich, knowledgeable, and hard-working expert on fiscal and economic affairs, he became a pillar of the Finance Committee. Cold and aloof, a firm believer in a protective tariff, sound currency, and private enterprise free from government interference, he worked mostly behind the scenes, saying little on the Senate floor but increasing his influence among his colleagues by his strong, businesslike leadership in committees. Headed for great power in Congress, he would also become very wealthy through his private investments, and his daughter would marry John D. Rockefeller, Jr., the son of America's richest man.

McKinley, handsome, affable, the grandson and son of iron manufacturers, was thirty-nine years old. He was a lawyer and had been elected to the House in 1876. As a member of the Ways and Means Committee, he specialized in the tariff, becoming known as a "one-idea man," and worked earnestly for the protection of the iron and steel interests in his eastern Ohio district. Reed was forty-three, an elephantine man, six feet, three inches tall, weighing almost three hundred pounds, with a large, round baby face and thinning hair. An able lawyer with a delightfully sarcastic wit, integrity, the erudition of a scholar, and a formidable reputation as a debater and parliamentarian, he had been elected to Blaine's seat in the House when the latter moved to the Senate in 1876. His influence rose rapidly until, as a member of the powerful Rules Committee, he became the acknowledged strong man of the Republicans in the House, asserting even more authority than the new Republican Speaker, J. Warren Keifer of Ohio, who turned out to be weak and inept, so fearful of violence in the House that he carried a pistol in his pocket for protection. Cool and impassive, though a nimble tactician, Reed too was a protectionist and an accommodating—but thoroughly honest—partisan of New England textile and manufacturing interests.

As the two committees worked over their bills, defeating the intention of the tariff reformers by yielding to the demands of the hordes of lobbyists, an emergency arose for the protectionists. In the fall elections of 1882 the Democrats, capitalizing on the sordid Republican patronage fights, won by a landslide, and the next House, under their control, would be anti-protectionist. The new tariff, Reed and other Republicans recognized, would have to be passed by the present Congress, yet only a few weeks remained till the end of the session. The House version went to the floor, where even though it was supported by former Democratic Speaker Sam Randall, it was subjected to opposition and attempted filibusters. Faced with the problem of eventually having to reconcile the House bill with the Senate version, Reed suddenly pulled a series of parliamentary coups, ending House debate four days before the end of the session and sending the bill directly to a conference committee of the two houses, which the protectionists dominated. In twenty-four hours the joint committee wrote an entirely new bill, combining many increases and minimal reductions, which on the whole kept the protectionist principle inviolate and lowered the schedules by an average of less than five percent. On March 3, 1883, the last day of the session, the "mongrel" bill, as its opponents called it, passed both houses and was signed into law by Arthur.

When the Forty-eighth Congress assembled the following December, Randall's protectionist stand cost him the speakership, and the Democrats elected John G. Carlisle of Kentucky, who had led the fight against the House protectionists. Carlisle, another strong Speaker, further increased the power and stature of the office, even going beyond his predecessors in asserting his own legislative policies and using every means at his command to achieve them. More than a mere representative of his party, he imposed his personal will on the House through his committee appointments and his power of recognition. Asking, "For what purpose does the gentleman rise?" he was often dictatorial in withholding recognition from members with whom he disagreed. Nevertheless, he was popular with Representatives of both parties and was considered able and generally fair, and he served throughout a six-year Democratic reign in the House, until 1889.

Randall, meanwhile, gained power in another area, becoming chairman of the Appropriations Committee but continuing as a controversial figure within his party. His insistence on economies in appropriations caused him trouble, antagonizing many of his colleagues and playing into the hands of power-seeking heads of other committees. With their support, in 1885 members of both parties joined to transfer authority over appropriations for the army, navy, military academy, consular and diplomatic affairs, post office and post roads, and Indian affairs from his committee to the respective standing committees that handled their legislation. Earlier, his committee had also lost jurisdiction over appropriations for rivers and harbors and agriculture, and the new dispersal, as Woodrow Wilson pointed out in *Congressional Government* that same year of 1885, increased the scattering of the House's power among the committee chairmen, all of whom, rising by seniority, were becoming omnipotent barons in their individual bailiwicks. Wilson concluded that there was a lack of party control in Congress, since legislation shaped in standing committees seemed to him to reflect compromises between majority and minority members of the committees. In the Senate there was indeed as yet little party control over legislation. But in the House party authority was becoming increasingly strong in the person of the Speaker. "He who appoints those committees is an autocrat of the first magnitude," said Wilson of the Speaker. Two years later, in 1887, Carlisle tightened party authority, making the chairmen of the Ways and Means and Appropriations committees members of the five-man Rules Committee, which the Speaker chaired. The powerful trio, forming a majority, now constituted a party steering committee with enormous influence over all legislation in the lower chamber.

In March, 1885, the Democrats under Grover Cleveland took over the executive branch. As a reform mayor of Buffalo and governor of New York, Cleveland had gained a reputation for honesty as well as conservatism, and many Republicans, ranging from leading industrialists to Carl Schurz's reformers (now termed Mugwumps—fence-sitters, with their mugs on one side, their wumps on the other), supported him against the ambitious Blaine, whose shoddy ethics they could no longer stomach. Determined originally to observe the spirit of the hard-won civil-service reforms of the Pendleton Act, Cleveland was forced by rapacious Democratic politicians to make wholesale replacements throughout the government, to the disgust of many of those who had voted for him.

Cleveland signed a landmark bill, the Interstate Commerce Act, on February 4, 1887. In the Midwest, Grange organizations of farmers had years before begun agitating against discriminatory rates and other railroad abuses. Elsewhere there had also been resentment against rebates, unfair variations in rates, and a host of monopolistic practices by the lines. From time to time Congress had held hearings that aired the public dissatisfaction, and various members of both houses had introduced regulatory bills. The railroad lobby, distributing bribes, passes, and other favors, had been too strong, however, and none of the measures had passed. By the mid-1880's many industrialists had joined those complaining about the railroads' monopolistic practices, and in 1885 a Senate committee headed by Republican Shelby M. Cullom of Illinois recommended the federal regulation of interstate commerce. A bill he introduced finally gathered support when, in 1886, the Supreme Court ruled that states could not regulate railroads that crossed state lines. Despite the vigorous opposition of Senator Aldrich—which established him as Congress' leading representative of finance capitalism—majorities in both parties worked out and passed a measure based on Cullom's bill. The act prohibited most of the objectionable railroad practices and created the Interstate Commerce Commission to oversee the enforcement of the provisions of the act. For years the railroads' many devices to circumvent the provisions, together with Supreme Court decisions that favored the railroads, rendered the commission all but powerless. In the wave of reforms during the twentieth century, however, other congressional acts strengthened the commission's authority over all carriers of interstate commerce, and as the federal government's first regulatory body for a particular segment of American industry—able to act independently of the three branches of the government but combining the functions of all of them—it served as a model for such future administrative agencies as the Federal Power Commission, the Federal Trade Commission, and the Federal Communications Commission.

Another measure passed early in 1887 attempted to write finish to the persistent Indian problem. Relations with the Indians, who everywhere had gradually been dispossessed of most of their lands, pacified by military force and treaties, and herded onto reservations, were still based on the premise that some of them would be assimilated and the rest would disappear. In 1871 the spoilsmen in Congress, responding to the pressure of the railroads and other interests that wanted the Indians' remaining lands and resources, ended treaty making and the recognition of tribes as independent political entities. Thereafter aggrandizers, encouraged by such congressional leaders as Conkling, Blaine, and Garfield and supported by troops and corrupt government agents, seized what they wanted, their aggressions leading to such desperate last stands of Indian resistance as the dramatic battle of the Little Bighorn in 1876. By 1887 most hostility had ended, and under the influence of reformers who hoped to save the Indian survivors by speeding their assimilation into white society, Congress passed the Dawes Severalty Act (named for its chief manager, Senator Henry L. Dawes of Massachusetts), providing for the division of the reservations into small private tracts that would be distributed to Indian families to farm like their white neighbors. The scheme, which proved impractical, was supported by the land-grabbers, for it provided that all reservation land left over after the distribution to the Indians could be sold to whites. By 1934, when the act was ended as a failure, some ninety million additional acres of Indian land had passed into white ownership. Far from assimilating the Indians, whose population began to increase, the measure made poverty a fixture on the reservations, robbing the tribes of water rights, timber, and much of the land needed for viable economies.

The Fiftieth Congress, convening in December, 1887, and lasting till March, 1889, climaxed all previous sessions as the most "do-nothing" Congress in American history. With a steadily mounting Treasury surplus becoming a menace, Cleveland devoted his entire annual message to a plea for a reduced tariff. Alarmed protectionists immediately attacked him. "The Democratic party in power is a standing menace to the industrial prosperity of the country," announced Blaine, who though out of Congress was still influential as an elder statesman of the Republicans. Nevertheless, hard times had returned, and much of the country supported Cleveland. In July, 1888, a new reduced tariff bill named for Roger Q. Mills of Texas, the short-tempered Democratic chairman of the Ways and Means Committee, passed the House, despite opposition led by Thomas B. Reed and William McKinley. In the Senate the Republicans decided to write their own version. Drawn up principally by Allison of Iowa and Aldrich of Rhode Island, the Republicans' protectionist measure reached the Senate floor in October. By the time the first session ended, no decision had been made on either the House or the Senate version, and the tariff quarrel, which the whole country had been watching, became the principal issue of the 1888 presidential campaign, then nearing its conclusion. Other than the tariff, the chief interests of the session were various subsidy and pork-barrel bills, many of which drew the scorn of a fiery thirty-three-year-old Wisconsin Representative, Robert M. La Follette. A Republican reformer, La Follette was serving his second term in the House, having been elected both times over the opposition of the powerful Wisconsin Republican machine headed by Senators Philetus Sawyer and John Coit Spooner. In the House La Follette flailed away at appropriations desired by the machine, and on one occasion Senator Sawyer

—a millionaire who had risen from lumberjacking and was believed to be so illiterate that he could not spell his first name, signing himself simply as "P. Sawyer"—came charging apoplectically onto the House floor, storming at La Follette as a "bolter." La Follette held his ground, replying that the Senator could not tell him how to vote, and Sawyer, realizing that he was violating congressional etiquette and rules, vanished as abruptly as he had appeared.

Though Cleveland's popular vote in the November election in 1888 was some 96,000 above that of his Republican opponent, Benjamin Harrison, a former Indiana Senator and grandson of William Henry Harrison's, the Republicans carried the key states of New York and Indiana, won the electoral vote 233 to 168, and regained control of both houses.

The "lame-duck" session of the Fiftieth Congress, held after the elections, was as barren of legislation as the first session. North Dakota, South Dakota, Montana, and Washington were admitted as states in February, 1889 (which, after the census of 1890, would increase House membership to 357), and the Department of Agriculture was raised to Cabinet status. Aside from that, the two parties in the House brought to a climax a decade of dilatory tactics that frustrated business with endless roll calls and filibusters and dismayed the more responsible legislators, including Reed and Henry Cabot Lodge, the latter a scholarly and patrician first-termer from Massachusetts. Lodge, a thirty-nine-year-old graduate of Harvard, a lawyer, lecturer, author of works on history, biography, and politics, and a reformer like his friend Theodore Roosevelt, could scarcely contain himself over the lowly state to which the House of Representatives had fallen. It had become, he wrote in the *North American Review*, "a complete travesty upon representative government, upon popular government, and upon government by the majority." Drastic revisions of the rules were needed, he said, to "change the condition of the House from dead rot to vitality." The people, he declared, were "thoroughly tired of the stagnation of business and the general inaction of Congress. They are disgusted to see year after year go by and great measures affecting the business and political interests of the country accumulate at the doors of Congress and never reach the stage of action." In his impatience with the House rules that permitted the continuance of obstructionist tactics, Lodge was not alone. Many newspapers in the country were urging reform. The year before, in January, 1888, an editorial in the Washington *Post*, titled "Slowly Doing Nothing," observed that the "system of rules is the prime cause of the wonderful inertia of this unwieldy and self-shackled body. . . . In stalling legislation and keeping everybody else from doing anything a few members are all powerful. . . ."

Such calls for action were echoed by the huge, portly Reed, who had been the minority leader of the House and was now chief candidate for the new Republican Speaker in the Fifty-first Congress. In contrast to the Democratic Speakers, he held that "the rules of this House are not for the purpose of protecting the rights of the minority, but to promote the orderly conduct of the business of the House," and in an article in *Century* magazine in 1889 he hinted that a revolution was coming by demanding a check on dilatory motions and the establishment of majority rule. Mentally as well as physically Reed was one of the biggest men ever to sit in Congress. "Big head, big brain," another Speaker, Sam Rayburn, said about him years later. He was also one of the most engaging figures in congressional lore—charming, genial, a master of epigrams and bon mots, the very soul of intellectual honesty. He was a radiant conversationalist and had a sharp, rapierlike wit. His impalements of colleagues were legion. Of two Representatives, he commented, "They never open up their mouths without subtracting from the sum of human knowledge." When a New York Democrat remarked, "The Republican party drinks a good deal of whiskey clandestinely that we do not know anything about," Reed shot back, "When my friend from New York takes it, it does not remain clandestine very long." One member, having learned that Reed had helped kill his bill, demanded to know why. "To get rid of you," Reed replied. Asked to comment on a certain member's chances of re-election, he observed, "Oh, the gentleman from Texas is safe. His district is Democratic naturally. The common school system does not prevail there." And to one Republican who had muffed in guiding a bill through the House, he remarked in his Down East drawl, "You are too big a fool to lead and you haven't got sense enough to follow."

When Congress convened on December 2, 1889, Reed had numerous competitors for the speakership, and his Republican colleagues, meeting in caucus, hesitated at first to choose him because they thought that the Speaker should come from a state more populous, more central, and more politically important than Maine and because they were afraid that too many members would resent his sharp tongue. With the help of Lodge and other New Englanders, however, he was selected, and in the contest in the House—where the Republicans held only a slim majority—he defeated Carlisle by 12 votes and became Speaker. He immediately named McKinley chairman of the Ways and Means Committee and Joseph G. Cannon of Illinois chairman of Appropriations. Cannon, a testy, profane, and somewhat uncouth man of fifty-three, had been in the House since 1873 and in his earlier years in Congress had been known as the "Hayseed Member from Illinois" because of his crude manners. Now he was known as "Foul-mouthed Joe." The three men constituted a majority of the Rules Committee, which on December 3 began to draft rules for the new session. Reed's principal goal, however, was to end the precedent—observed since the First Congress—of establishing quorums by a count of those who voted, rather than those who were actually present, and he would have to do it before presenting the new rules. With the House so evenly divided and the Democrats remaining silent for any roll call on a subject of which they disapproved, the Republicans would be hard put to get a quorum at any time during the session when the Democrats wished to block them. On January 29, 1890, the House began to consider contested elections. When the first one—a West Virginia case—was reported by the Committee on Elections, awarding the disputed seat to a Republican, Democrat Charles F. Crisp of Georgia moved for consideration —the tactic of obstruction. When the roll was called no Democrat answered to his name, and the vote—with all 163 Republicans present voting—was short of a quorum. But Reed was ready, having assured himself of the constitutionality of what he was about to do and hoping that every Republican would support him. If they did not, he intended to resign.

Calmly he said, "The Chair directs the clerk to record the names of the following members present and refusing to vote." He then began to call out the names of Democrats who were sitting in the House. Immediately the hall exploded in an uproar. Democrats leaped to their feet, shouting that the Speaker could not count them present and rushing up to try to stop Reed. The pandemonium increased, with Democrats "yelling and shrieking and pounding their desks," demanding the right to appeal, and—while Reed continued calling their names, and Republicans applauded, whistled, and cheered—calling the Speaker's action revolutionary and dictatorial. The disorder continued as Reed finished his counting. "I deny your right, Mr. Speaker, to count me as present!" shouted a Democratic Representative from Kentucky. Unperturbed, Reed answered him: "The Chair is making a statement of fact that the gentleman from Kentucky is present. Does he deny it?" Then, as the House fell silent, Reed announced the basis for what he had done. Under the Constitution, he said, the House could compel the attendance of members. If attendance were not to be the basis of a quorum, the provision was meaningless. For a quorum, "attendance is enough. If more was needed the Constitution would have provided for more." He then ruled that within the meaning of the Constitution, a quorum was present.

The ruling produced another tumult and a great battle that lasted for three days amid the most disorderly scenes the House had ever witnessed. Again and again the furious Democrats, led by Carlisle and Crisp, demanded roll calls, and each time Reed read off the names of those present, but not voting, and declared a quorum. He was called tyrant, despot, and czar (the last name sticking to him, so that he became known as "Czar" Reed), but outwardly he remained cool and undisturbed and at last he had his way. After one climactic scene in which he ordered the doors of the hall locked to prevent Democrats from leaving and creating a genuine lack of a quorum (the enraged Democrats then hid under their desks, behind screens, and anywhere they could find to keep from being counted), enough Republicans showed up to constitute a quorum on their own—two were brought in on sickbeds—Reed's ruling was approved, and the battle was over. On February 6 the Rules Committee reported the new rules, written largely by Reed and known thereafter as the Reed Rules, and after four days of debate the House, with quorums now based on those present, approved them, 161 to 144, with 23 abstaining. The rules, which revolutionized House procedure and gave the Speaker immense new powers, provided among other things that every member must vote; that all present would be counted for a quorum; that one hundred would constitute a quorum in Committee of the Whole; that motions which the Speaker considered dilatory would not be entertained; and that the Committee of the Whole could close debate on any paragraph or section of a bill under consideration. "Disappearing quorums" and other obstructionist tactics would now be a thing of the past, and Congress, thanks to Reed, could conduct its business efficiently and with dispatch. In the next Congress, which the Democrats overwhelmingly controlled, Reed's changes were abandoned, but in the Congress after that the Democrats, with a slimmer majority, saw the wisdom of Reed's rulings, readopted them, and they became permanent. As Reed pointed out, the new rules meant that party responsibility in the House had begun, "and with it also the responsibility of the people, for they can no longer elect a Democratic House and hope the minority will neutralize their action or a Republican House without being sure that it will keep its pledges." The majority party, led by its Speaker, would now be able to rule the House.

To a large extent, Reed's revolution in 1890 was motivated by the Republicans' determination in that session—now that they occupied the White House and possessed majorities in both houses—to push through legislation, particularly a higher tariff. In his first message to Congress Harrison, a dour little man with a big body and short legs, took up the issue that had dominated much of the campaign, urging a reversal of Cleveland's tariff policy. McKinley handled the measure in the House and Aldrich in the Senate, and the new bill, known as the McKinley Tariff and raising the average level to 49.5 percent, passed on October 1, 1890, though not without bitter debate and compromises that affected the passage of another measure in the same session, the Sherman Silver Purchase Act. A renewed economic depression and a steady drop in the price of silver had strengthened the agitation of the inflationists, and a proposed program for the government's increased purchase of silver had been sent to the House by the secretary of the treasury. The House passed a bill moderately increasing the government's monthly purchase of silver, but the Senate, with a stronger silver bloc, added an amendment for the free and unlimited coinage of silver. When the House refused to accept the change as too inflationary, western silver Republicans in the Senate threatened to vote against the McKinley Tariff. The silver bill finally went to a conference, where the veteran currency expert "Uncle John" Sherman, now sixty-eight years old, worked out a satisfactory compromise, requiring the Treasury to buy 4.5 million ounces of silver each month—the estimated total United States production at the time—and issue legal tender notes, redeemable in gold or silver at the government's option. The silver-purchase bill then passed both houses, became law, and the westerners voted for the McKinley Tariff.

The tariff debate became entwined, also, with another Republican measure, the new Federal Election Bill, reflecting a growing Republican anger over the disenfranchisement of the blacks in the South and providing for renewed federal supervision of elections in states whose laws discriminated against black voters. Vigorously supported by Lodge and McKinley, who hoped to turn the South Republican again, the bill passed the House but stalled in the Senate. Not wishing to lose votes for the tariff, Republican Senators let the election bill lie dormant during that session, retaining the tariff votes of several southern protectionist Democrats headed by Arthur P. Gorman, a tough politician who ran a notoriously corrupt machine in Maryland. In the next session, when the election bill was revived, Gorman led a long filibuster against it, finally killing the measure.

The most historic legislation of the Fifty-first Congress, the Sherman Antitrust Act, was drafted by the Senate Judiciary Committee, principally by two of the Senate's most venerable and distinguished members, sixty-four-year-old George Frisbie Hoar of Massachusetts, the grandson of Roger Sherman and chairman of the committee, and George F. Edmunds of Vermont, who was sixty-two and had been in the Senate since 1866. Throughout the country public indignation had been growing against the monopolistic power and practices of industry, stemming from the development, under finance capitalist direction, of pools, holding companies, and trusts that controlled various commodities. Many states had tried to cope with the trusts, but their laws were generally powerless since they could not deal with combinations engaged in interstate commerce. Recognizing the threat to free enterprise and healthy competition, the Judiciary Committee's bill—again bearing the name of John Sherman, the committee member who reported it on the Senate floor—prohibited "conspiracies in restraint of trade" and gave somewhat ambiguously written powers of enforcement to the federal government. The law was enacted on July 2, 1890, but its obscure wording impaired its effectiveness. For years it was used more often against labor unions than industry. In its infrequent employment against trusts, its powers were limited by the courts, and eventually Congress had to supersede it with new legislation.

The Fifty-first Congress was also the first "Billion-Dollar Congress," slightly more than that sum having been appropriated for pensions, subsidies, and new naval construction as well as for the usual expenses of government. Reed dismissed the criticism of appalled citizens with the explanation that "this is a billion-dollar country," but that fall the Republicans—despite their productive record—suffered a stunning defeat in the congressional elections. The McKinley Tariff, the heavy spending, and the agitation for the Federal Election Bill were all blamed; even McKinley, his district gerrymandered to his disadvantage by the Ohio legislature, was beaten, and the new House, with 231 Democrats, only 88 Republicans, and 14 Populists, was returned to Democratic control. Crisp of Georgia was chosen Speaker (Carlisle had been elected to the Senate), and the division between the two houses in the Fifty-second Congress during Harrison's last two years in office resulted in the passage of little significant legislation. In the summer of 1892 a violence-ridden strike against the Carnegie Steel Company's Homestead, Pennsylvania, works focused the nation's attention on the growing helplessness of labor under the big corporations. Committees in both houses held hearings on the causes of the industrial unrest, but although they heard industry denounced for such practices as the hiring of private police forces to break strikes, they took no legislative action. During the year, however, Congress did decree an eight-hour working day for government employees.

The labor problems were symptomatic of renewed economic distress among many elements of the population. A farm depression had intensified, and organizations of agrarians, debtors, and the laboring poor were proliferating in the Midwest, West, and South. In 1892 they organized the People's Party of the USA, better known as the Populists, and nominated the 1880 Greenback presidential candidate, James B. Weaver of Iowa, for President on a platform that included the free and unlimited coinage of silver at a ratio of 16 to 1 to gold; government ownership of all transportation and communication facilities; a graduated income tax; the direct election of Senators; adoption of the secret ballot, the initiative, and referendum; a shorter working day for industrial workers; and restrictions on immigration. The new party represented a large coalition of homespun reformers and radicals and numbered among its leaders several highly vocal members of Congress, including Senators James H. Kyle of South Dakota, a former Congregationalist pastor, and William A. Peffer of Kansas, editor of *The Kansas Farmer*, and Representatives Thomas E. Watson of Georgia and Jeremiah Simpson of Medicine Lodge, Kansas, who was known as "Sockless Jerry" because he had once campaigned among the dirt farmers of his district without wearing socks. A big sunburned man with a gnarled face, gold-rimmed eyeglasses, and huge hands, Simpson, like Davy Crockett, affected an earthy quality and relished his nickname, for it got him votes at home. Nevertheless, he was a genuine battler for the small farmer hard pressed by eastern capitalists. "Man must have access to land or be a slave," he proclaimed, and he summed up the national issue, in the Populists' view, as "a struggle between the robbers and the robbed."

The Republicans in 1892 renominated Harrison, and the Democrats renominated Cleveland. In the campaign the Democrats made capital of the labor disturbances and the McKinley Tariff, which not only was keeping prices high for consumers in the hard times but was causing a decline in federal revenues from imports. At the same time Cleveland, a strong advocate of the gold standard, gained support from eastern bankers and industrialists by campaigning against the Sherman Silver Purchase Act, which was increasing the circulation of redeemable paper currency and causing a dangerous drain on the federal reserve of gold being used to redeem the paper. On Election Day the Democrats came back into power, even winning the Senate. For the first time since 1859 they controlled the White House and both branches of Congress. The Populists also did well, receiving more than a million votes.

Cleveland had hardly been inaugurated in March, 1893, when adverse fiscal developments, including a drop of the gold reserve below $100 million, caused the Panic of 1893 on Wall Street. The depression sharpened quickly as banks failed, factories closed, unemployment rose, and farm prices declined further. To halt the drain on the gold supply, Cleveland called the Fifty-third Congress into an extra session on August 7, 1893, and, flying in the face of the free-silver and southern and midwestern agrarians and inflationists in his own party, demanded the repeal of the Sherman Silver Purchase Act, causing a sensation by announcing that he would keep Congress in session in Washington through the torturous "dog days" of summer until it complied. The conflict in both houses was intensely bitter, opening wounds in the Democratic party and making free silver a national issue that dominated the next presidential campaign. In the House of Representatives Democrat William Jennings Bryan of Nebraska, thirty-three years old, a second-termer known as "the Boy Orator of the Platte," won national prominence by thundering against the President and denouncing repeal as benefiting only Wall Street. In the Senate Daniel Voorhees of Indiana, chairman of the Finance Committee and a former criminal lawyer termed by newspapermen "the Tall Sycamore of the Wabash," reported the bill for the administration and ran into immediate opposition. For forty-six days free-silver men, most of them Democrats, tied up the Senate in a filibuster, one Senator, Nebraska Populist William V. Allen, holding the floor for fourteen hours. The perspiring and angry Republicans, most of whom, including Sherman himself, agreeing to give repeal all the votes it needed for passage, were furious with the Democrats, urging their leaders to hold a party caucus, make what compromises were necessary to end the split in their ranks, and stop the filibuster. But Cleveland was adamant against compromise, and no caucus was held. When repeated moves for cloture failed, some Senators talked openly of forcing Vice President Adlai Stevenson to halt the filibuster arbitrarily and put the question for repeal. Finally the opposition was worn down, and repeal, approved by the House on August 28, passed the Senate on October 30. Cleveland had his way, and the session ended on November 3.

The split in the Democratic party, which would harm it for many years to come, was further widened during the first regular session of the Fifty-third Congress, which began in December, 1893. With Cleveland's approval, House Democrats began carrying out their campaign pledge to reduce the tariff, and early in 1894 they passed a bill, introduced by William L. Wilson of West Virginia, chairman of the Ways and Means Committee, that repealed the high McKinley Tariff, put sugar, iron ore, and wool on the free list, drastically reduced the general level of duties, and included an amendment providing for a tax on incomes over $4,000. The Senate Finance Committee reported the bill with amendments; but lobbyists then went to work, and protectionist Senators, including a group of Democrats led by Gorman of Maryland, riddled the House's handiwork with amendments that shot the duties up again. The Senate amendments went back to the House, where

Wilson and others fought against them, making public a letter from Cleveland in which the President accused the Gorman Democratic group in the Senate of "party perfidy and party dishonor." The letter so stiffened the backs of the infuriated Democratic protectionist Senators that they dominated the conference committee and forced the House to accept a tariff that fell far short of Democratic campaign promises. Cleveland was in a dilemma. The Wilson-Gorman Tariff, passed on August 28, 1894, was a slight improvement over the McKinley Tariff, but it lowered rates only to an average of forty percent. Disapproving of the measure, Cleveland let it become a law without his signature. The income-tax provision, largely the work of reformers in both parties, was included, but the next year the Supreme Court ruled it unconstitutional as a direct tax.

Throughout 1894 the economic situation remained serious. The nation's distress was highlighted by a march on Washington of Jacob S. Coxey's ragtag "army" of unemployed and by bitter strikes of coal miners and Pullman employees, the latter led by Eugene V. Debs and broken by Cleveland's use of federal troops. During the same period Congress, reflecting a growing national support for the more prudent disposal and conservation of the country's remaining natural resources, passed on August 18, 1894, the Carey Act, named for a huge, doltish Senator from Wyoming, Joseph M. Carey, which authorized the President to grant to each public-land state up to one million acres of federal land within its boundaries to use for irrigation and reclamation projects. The repeal of the Sherman Silver Purchase Act did not halt the drain of the Treasury's gold reserve, and by early 1895 the government was in more serious difficulties than before, unable to place loans with New York banks. In response to a desperate appeal by Cleveland, the New York financial giant J. P. Morgan visited the White House, and he and August Belmont finally helped to stem the crisis, putting together a syndicate that lent the Treasury money to purchase more gold, but at a large profit for themselves. In time the gold drain slowed, finally ending after the decisive election of 1896 assured the future of the gold standard. But in the meantime the Silver Democrats, led by "Silver Dick" Bland and Bryan, increased their agitation in and out of Congress for the restoration of the free and unlimited coinage of silver at the ratio of 16 to 1.

When the Fifty-fourth Congress met in December, 1895, the Republicans took over the House and Reed was again elected Speaker. Because of Maine's long record of Republicanism, seniority boosted each of that state's three other Representatives into an important committee chairmanship— Nelson Dingley, a mournful-looking sixty-three-year-old former governor of Maine, became head of Ways and Means as well as Republican floor leader; Charles Boutelle chaired Naval Affairs; and Seth Milliken Public Buildings —and Reed and his three Maine colleagues exercised a large measure of authority over House business. Because Cleveland was still in the White House, however, legislation on controversial domestic issues was avoided, and the attention of both the executive and Congress was directed to foreign affairs, particularly to Cuba, where revolutionary activities against Spain— exacerbated by the Wilson-Gorman Tariff's high duty on sugar—had drawn the interest and sympathies of Americans. Within the United States, at the same time, restlessness among labor, the southern and midwestern agrarians, the western silverites, and reformer critics of the monopolies and eastern financiers continued to intensify, and with the holding of the presidential nominating conventions in the summer of 1896 the country's sharpening internal differences burst to the surface. Backed by Mark Hanna, the Ohio industrialist and Republican organizer, McKinley, who after his congressional defeat in 1890 had become governor of that state, won the Republican nomination, embittering Tom Reed, whose supporters gave way to Hanna. The Republican platform endorsed a high protective tariff and the gold standard. At the Democratic convention in Chicago, the silverites, agrarians, and enemies of Cleveland's conservatism seized control of the Democratic party from its eastern, Wall Street-backed wing and turned in wrath against the President. Focusing on the silver issue, Bryan threw the convention into hysteria with a ringing speech challenging the gold-standard advocates. "You shall not press down upon the brow of labor this crown of thorns, you shall not crucify mankind upon a cross of gold," he roared. The delegates thundered their approval and nominated Bryan. The platform called for the free and unlimited coinage of silver at a 16-to-1 ratio and condemned trusts and monopolies, the high protective tariff, injunctions against labor, and the Supreme Court decision on the income tax. When they met at St. Louis, the Populists happily endorsed Bryan.

McKinley was a moderate conservative, who as Ohio governor had shown a paternalistic interest in the workingman, and he had considerable labor support. But to most Republicans, as well as to Cleveland and conservative Democrats, Bryan and his backers represented a coalition of devils threatening the future of America. Raising alarm among business and industry, Mark Hanna, who took command of the campaign for the Republicans, dragooned banks, insurance companies, railroads, and large and small businesses into raising a war chest for McKinley estimated as high as $16.5 million. While Bryan, hailed by his followers as "the Great Commoner," tirelessly stumped the country, making six hundred speeches in twenty-nine states during fourteen weeks, McKinley ran a publicized "front-porch" campaign from his Canton, Ohio, home, addressing hundreds of delegations that, accompanied by the press, were shepherded to him by Hanna with all their expenses paid by the Republicans. Hanna, meanwhile, stepped up the field campaign against Bryan, getting him labeled a communist, anarchist, and lunatic and encouraging businesses to threaten their employees with factory closings and the loss of their jobs if Bryan won. The combination of money and scare tactics succeeded, and McKinley triumphed, beginning his term of office with a Republican majority in the House and a plurality in the

Senate (where a group of Populists and Independents held the balance of power) and with conservative, business-oriented, gold-standard supporters firmly in control of the nation's affairs.

The new President made John Sherman his secretary of state, and Hanna took Sherman's seat in the Senate, adding the voice of another multimillionaire to that body (between 1869 and 1901, forty-two percent of the Senate's members were among the nation's wealthiest men, eighteen percent being considered extremely wealthy). Re-elected Speaker, Reed again maintained a strong party hand over the House, naming for the first time a Republican whip, Representative James A. Tawney of Minnesota, to keep party members on the floor and voting with the leadership. A new development that finally brought party control to the Senate as well greatly strengthened the prestige and authority of that body's leadership of the legislative branch. To succeed Sherman as chairman of their Senate caucus, the Republicans chose sixty-eight-year-old William B. Allison, who had been in the Senate for twenty-five years, longer than any other Republican. For some years Allison had been perhaps the most influential member of a close group of Republican Senators who met frequently at the Washington home of Michigan's Senator James McMillan, a shipping and manufacturing magnate, to play poker and discuss legislation and strategy. Calling themselves the Philosophers' Club, they numbered some of the most powerful men in the Senate, principally Nelson Aldrich, Eugene Hale of Maine, Orville H. Platt and Joseph R. Hawley of Connecticut, and John C. Spooner of Wisconsin. All of them had come to wish for tighter party control over legislation, but the leadership of Sherman and his predecessor, Senator George Edmunds of Vermont, had been weak. Nevertheless, since the 1880's the Republican *ad hoc* groups that worked out legislative schedules for the party had been strengthened into a formal Committee on the Order of Business, or Steering Committee, whose chairman and ten other members were named by the caucus chairman. Allison, who also headed the Appropriations Committee, now took over the chairmanship of the Steering Committee himself and began the practice of naming his poker-playing colleagues and men who shared his views to other seats in that body, which increasingly managed every detail of the order of business as well as the proceedings on the Senate floor. At the same time Allison dominated the Committee on Committees, naming McMillan as its chairman and seeing that its other positions were also filled by men on whom he could rely. Since the Committee on Committees named the chairmen and members of all the other Senate committees, the little group of the Philosophers' Club, sometimes called the Allison-Aldrich circle for its two most powerful members, came quickly to exercise strict party control throughout the Senate.

Though seniority dictated the committee chairmanships, they were usually filled by members of the Allison group or Senators who would follow its wishes. But seniority did not necessarily rule the appointments to other seats on the committee, and, giving some due to geographic representation, the Committee on Committees meted out assignments generally to reward the party faithful and punish those who were independent-minded. The effect was to offer opportunity for advancement and authority to those who followed the leadership of the Allison-Aldrich circle and deny influence to dissidents, even though they might make national reputations through their speeches and maverick activities. At the same time, since appointments to positions of influence depended on the support and favor of Allison and the party leaders, power became centralized. "I feel that the greatest single point is gained in the possession of your friendship. I will labor very hard, strive very earnestly to deserve your consideration," said an ambitious newcomer, Senator Albert Beveridge of Indiana, to Allison in 1899. Even Tom Platt, the New York Republican boss and former Conkling henchman, who returned to the Senate in 1897, told Allison, "What you say goes. Kindly keep me posted as to what you do, so that I may not go astray."

The Democrats kept pace with the Republicans, though with somewhat less effectiveness because they were in the minority and did not possess the full measure of power at the disposal of the Allison-Aldrich group. As chairman of the Democratic caucus, Arthur Gorman of Maryland headed both the Democratic Steering Committee and the Committee on Committees and asserted control over committee assignments. Nevertheless, the Democrats split so often that the lack of unity led them, in 1903, to adopt a rule binding all members to decisions made by a two-thirds vote in the caucus. Such a rule was unnecessary among the Republicans under the Allison-Aldrich leadership; the Republican caucus had little difficulty in compromising differences among its members and seeing to it that the party spoke with a single voice on the floor. The working out of party decisions in councils, in fact, so cut down on the need for speeches on the Senate floor that for some Senators sessions became a tedious bore. "It would be a delightful thing to be a United States Senator if you did not have to attend the sessions of the Senate," complained George Hoar of Massachusetts. Increasingly, men wandered off the floor and found other things to do, save when there were roll calls or other business to which they were summoned. In time the American people showed concern at the growth of behind-the-scenes party control, but the development endured, less pronounced from time to time when the party leaders were weaker men.

The effectiveness of the new Republican control was apparent in the ease and speed with which the party passed another protective tariff in a special session of the Fifty-fifth Congress, which McKinley called for that purpose as soon as he was inaugurated. The new measure, with greatly increased rates, was quickly reported to the House in March, 1897, by Nelson Dingley, the chairman of the Ways and Means Committee, and with Reed controlling debate it was passed by the Republican majority in less than two weeks, after the members had discussed only fifteen percent of its provisions. In the Senate Aldrich labored over the bill only with the Republicans on his Finance Committee, who were a majority of that body, then presented the completed measure to the committee Democrats, who lacked the votes to amend it. When the committee sent the bill to the floor, the Republican caucus, under Allison and Aldrich, won approval for it from all but three Republicans; and on the floor the Republicans stood by the caucus decision, passing the measure, with only a few changes to satisfy independents, over the solid opposition of the Democrats. In the conference the Senate Republicans had their way, and the bill, known as the Dingley Tariff and raising rates to an unprecedented average of fifty-seven percent, became law on July 7, 1897. In somewhat similar fashion, the Republicans three years later settled the currency question, pushing through Congress a Gold Standard Act that firmly established gold as the basis of the nation's currency.

McKinley's message to the first regular session of the Fifty-fifth Congress in December, 1897, dealt largely with Cuba, a subject which climaxed a variety of overseas interests—mostly in the Western Hemisphere and the Pacific—that had drawn the attention of the American people and Congress from time to time since the Civil War. In 1867 the expansionist urge that resulted in Seward's purchase of Alaska from Russia had extended the country beyond its west-coast boundary, and despite opposition by many members of Congress who mocked the acquisition of the little-known and frigid region as "Seward's Folly," Sumner and others, glad to help another colonial power leave the continent, had got the Senate to ratify the agreement and the House to appropriate the $7.2 million purchase price. In the same year an American naval officer discovered and claimed the Midway Islands, some eleven hundred miles west of Hawaii in the Pacific. By the end of the century naval outposts had also been established on American Samoa and the mid-Pacific island of Wake.

The activity in the Pacific was part of a growing American imperialism, this phase eyeing the markets of the Far East and China. In 1882, after landings of Marines in Korea, the United States signed a treaty of commerce and amity with that country. Relations with China, however, were complicated by an intense feeling against the Chinese in the United States stemming from their importation as laborers by western railroad builders. By 1882 anti-Chinese sentiment, spreading eastward from the Pacific Coast, induced Congress to pass an exclusion act that restricted Chinese immigration for ten years. Still agitation continued, and six years later Congress passed a much more drastic exclusion act. Though American trade with China remained small, the United States resisted attempts by foreign powers to secure rights in China that would discriminate against other countries and in 1900 announced an "Open Door" policy asserting the right of all countries, including the United States, to trade equally with China. That same year United States troops, with congressional assent, joined those of other nations in putting down an uprising in China of an antiforeign group known as Boxers, and thereafter an American military presence protected the interests of American businessmen in that country.

270

In the meantime, the largest chain of islands in the mid-Pacific, the Hawaiian Islands, became American. Long under the influence of American missionaries, the native rulers in 1875 agreed to a treaty of commercial reciprocity and in 1887 gave the United States the exclusive right to establish a naval base at Pearl Harbor. Six years later conflict broke out between the native royal government and American planters, and the American minister to the islands, on his own, proclaimed Hawaii an American protectorate. Cleveland told Congress that he would not support annexation. Under the influence of the sugar planters and their Washington lobby, however, the Republicans took an opposite position, and in 1897 McKinley negotiated an annexation treaty. It met considerable opposition from Democrats and anti-imperialist Republicans, including Speaker Reed, but the Spanish-American War demonstrated the islands' strategic value to the United States, and in 1898, substituting a joint congressional resolution, which required only a majority vote, for Senate ratification, which needed a two-thirds vote in that body, the two houses approved annexation.

Of even greater importance to the United States were its relations with Latin America. The longest-standing interest was the building of an interoceanic canal across Central America, the subject of the Clayton-Bulwer Treaty of 1850 with Great Britain, in which each country agreed not to exercise exclusive control of such a project. In 1880, when interest in the undertaking reawakened, Hayes told Congress that since the canal would be "virtually a part of the coast line of the United States," the Americans would have to control it. Congress responded with a resolution authorizing the President to abrogate the Clayton-Bulwer Treaty. When the Arthur administration signed a canal treaty with Nicaragua in 1884, however, the British protested the violation of the Clayton-Bulwer agreement, and the Senate failed to ratify the Nicaraguan accord. American dreams did not die, and in 1901, by the Hay-Pauncefote Treaty, Great Britain at last renounced joint rights to a canal. Interest shifted to a Panama route, but a treaty for the lease of a right-of-way was rejected by the senate of Colombia, which owned Panama. In November, 1903, Panama (with the questionable connivance of the impatient Theodore Roosevelt) declared its independence of Colombia and concluded the Hay-Bunau-Varilla Treaty with the United States, granting the United States sovereignty over a canal zone ten miles wide across the Isthmus of Panama for $10 million and an annual fee of $250,000. The Senate ratified the treaty on February 23, 1904, and construction began on the canal, which opened to traffic on August 15, 1914.

The United States also extended its growing interest and power elsewhere in Latin America. As secretary of state, Blaine had vigorously advocated contesting British and European political and commercial inroads in Latin America by an aggressive expansion of American influence and trade. In a highhanded, imperialistic way he bumbled attempts to settle disputes between Chile and Peru and Bolivia, Costa Rica and Colombia, and Mexico and Guatemala, but in 1888 Congress authorized Cleveland to call a peace conference in Washington. The meeting, in 1889, failed to achieve its principal goals, the establishment of arbitration machinery and a customs union, but it set up the International Bureau of American Republics (which in time became the Pan-American Union) and focused attention on the use of reciprocal tariffs made by executive agreement, which the McKinley Tariff adopted as policy and authorized in 1890. During the next decade American aggressiveness became increasingly pronounced. In 1891 an attack on American sailors in Valparaiso nearly brought on a shooting war with Chile, and two years later another petty crisis, this one involving a United States attempt to arbitrate a border quarrel between Venezuela and British Guiana, set off a fever of anti-British sentiment. Congress responded as if the country's honor were at stake and as if war were just around the corner, but finally the border question was settled peaceably.

The conflict with Spain over Cuba saw the full flowering of America's imperialism and its self-confidence as a principal world power. Tension over Cuba began to build in 1895, when the latest in a series of rebellions against Spanish rule broke out on the island. Traditionally sympathetic to the independence struggles of the Latin peoples, Americans were aroused by a stream of stories in the yellow press about Spanish atrocities in Cuba. Although Cleveland opposed American involvement and issued a proclamation of neutrality, various Senators and Representatives introduced resolutions recognizing Cuban independence. After many jingoistic speeches, the resolutions were combined into a concurrent resolution, which passed both houses in 1896, urging recognition of the belligerent rights of the Cubans and offering the services of the United States to Spain for the recognition of Cuban independence. Without consulting Congress, Cleveland had already offered America's services to Spain to help find a formula that would grant the Cubans local autonomy but retain Spanish sovereignty. Spain turned down his offer, and Cleveland did nothing about Congress' resolution.

The yellow press, with William Randolph Hearst's New York *Journal* in the lead, increased its outpourings of emotional stories on the Cubans' plight. By and large, both McKinley and the leaders of American business opposed the raising of a crisis and the prospect of a war, viewing them as unsettling to the American economy. But various militant and expansionist Republicans, including Henry Cabot Lodge, now a leading member of the Senate Foreign Relations Committee, put McKinley in an awkward position. Most of the angriest voices for war were those of southern and western Bryan Democrats, some of whom thought that a conflict would help the adoption of free silver but the majority of whom endorsed the righteous cause of freeing Cuba from Spanish bondage and considered Republican objections a conspiracy that placed big business ahead of human liberty. Lodge and other Republicans feared that, unless their party led the way against Spain, the Democrats would have an enormously emotional issue to use against them in the 1898 and 1900 campaigns, and they argued this point with the President. Nevertheless, McKinley's message to Congress in December, 1897, was basically a peaceful one, holding out hope that the new Spanish policy would make American action unnecessary but leaving the door open "if it shall hereafter appear to be a duty imposed by our obligations to ourselves, to civilization, and humanity, to intervene with force. . . ."

The situation did not improve, and numerous members of both houses again introduced resolutions supporting the Cubans' belligerency and independence. After pro-Spanish riots occurred in Havana in January, 1898, pressure from Congress and the public induced McKinley to dispatch the battleship *Maine* to Havana Harbor, where on the evening of February 15, 1898, it was mysteriously blown up with the loss of 260 men. In the public hysteria—aroused again by the yellow press, which was quick to attribute the tragedy to Spanish agents—both houses without dissent passed an emergency bill appropriating $50 million for national defense. Though McKinley strove to maintain an antiwar policy, Congress rang with Democratic resolutions demanding war and the recognition of Cuban independence, and Reed, who was personally against a war, and other members of the Republican leadership in both houses had a difficult time restraining the belligerency of their own party members. On March 17 the militants received strong support from Republican Senator Redfield Proctor of Vermont, who had visited Cuba to make his own investigation of conditions on the island and who now confirmed the charges of those who had been attacking Spain. The speech by Proctor, who was greatly respected by his colleagues and was not regarded as a jingoist, was restrained yet full of facts and was a great influence on many of those who had not yet made up their minds. Under the increasing pressure, the administration on March 27 finally delivered an ultimatum to Spain, demanding an armistice in Cuba and the revocation of Spain's policy of forcing rural people into "reconcentration" camps to prevent their supplying the rebels. The next day McKinley released the report of a naval court of inquiry, which implied that Spain was responsible for the *Maine* disaster, and on March 30 the impatient Democratic floor leader in the House, Joseph Bailey of Texas, threw the hall into a scene of wild approval with a resolution recognizing Cuba's independence. Barely held in line by their leaders, the Republicans agreed to mark time while a committee visited the President and served notice that the House would not wait for a reply from Spain, or for decisive presidential action, beyond April 4.

Swayed by opinion in and out of Congress, McKinley finally planned to deliver a war message on April 4 but delayed it when he learned from Madrid that Spain was preparing a satisfactory reply to the ultimatum. It reached Washington on April 10, conveying Spain's submission to both American demands. By then, however, McKinley had lost his willingness to resist the war fever. With the concurrence of Senators Aldrich and Lodge, who agreed with him that the Spanish assurances could not be trusted,

McKinley sent his message to Congress on April 11, recommending "forcible intervention" in Cuba. The two houses took up the message, the House of Representatives erupting in melees over how far to go toward actual war and the Senate, with more restraint, considering whether Cuba, once free, should be truly independent or should be taken under American control. A conference committee ironed out the wording of a joint resolution, and on the night of April 18, while it was carried back and forth between the two chambers and the committee room, members of the House and spectators in the galleries sang patriotic songs. At three o'clock in the morning of April 19 the two houses adopted the resolution, recognizing Cuban independence, demanding Spain's withdrawal from the island, and empowering the President to use the army, navy, and militia units to enforce these objectives. A fourth point, included as an amendment by Senator Henry M. Teller of Colorado, disclaimed American intentions to assert sovereignty or control over Cuba, stating that the future government and control of the island would be left to its people. McKinley signed the resolution on April 20. The next day Spain broke relations with the United States and on April 24 declared war; on April 25 Congress responded with its own formal war declaration, making it retroactive to April 21.

Despite the fact that the army was woefully unprepared and suffered greatly through poor management and supply, a string of swift and decisive American naval and land victories in the Philippines and Cuba forced Spain to sue for peace by the last week in July. On December 10, 1898, a peace commission, meeting in Paris, concluded a treaty by which Spain relinquished Cuba, though assuming liability for some $400 million in Cuban debts, and ceded to the United States Puerto Rico, Guam, and, for $20 million, the Philippines. The cession of the Philippines, lying some seven thousand miles west of the United States, divided the nation in a new controversy over imperialism and moral right and wrong. The American seizure of the islands had been greatly aided by a strong insurrectionary group led by Emilio Aguinaldo, who believed that the United States had intended to help the Philippines attain freedom and independence. The four Republican members of the five-member American peace commission in Paris thought the United States should retain the islands, but the fifth member, Democratic Senator George Gray of Delaware, protested. The war, he maintained, had been to assist oppressed subjects of Spain to achieve their freedom. When it came time to submit the treaty to the Senate, McKinley himself, at first, did not know what to do. "I walked the floor of the White House night after night until midnight," he later told some visitors. "I went down on my knees and prayed Almighty God for light and guidance. . . . And one night late it came to me . . . we could not leave them to themselves—they were unfit for self-government . . . there was nothing left for us to do but to take them all, and to educate the Filipinos, and uplift them and civilize and Christianize them, and by God's grace do the very best we could by them as our fellow men for whom Christ also died. And then I went to bed and went to sleep and slept soundly."

When the President submitted the peace treaty to the Fifty-fifth Congress, the Philippine question caused a sharp debate between Senate imperialists and anti-imperialists, the latter composed mainly of Democrats, Populists, and a few New England Republicans. With the help of Bryan, who urged his followers to approve the treaty and end the war (and make Philippine independence a 1900 campaign issue), the treaty was ratified on February 6, 1899, by only two votes more than the required two-thirds margin. At the same time the disillusioned Filipinos under Aguinaldo rose in revolt for independence from the United States, leading to a new, controversial war in the Philippines, the ruthless suppression of Aguinaldo's forces by American troops, and the crushing of the independence movement by mid-1902. In the United States the conflict intensified congressional soul-searching over the latest stage of America's expansionism and treatment of weaker peoples, the brutality of the racially tinged aggression against the Filipinos being likened by some critics to the wars waged against the American Indians. Defenders of American policy, such as Indiana's new Republican Senator, Albert J. Beveridge—who with a maiden speech on the Philippine question leaped to national fame—echoed McKinley's theme of America's civilizing mission but intermixed in their ringing oratory practical reminders of the economic and strategic advantages of the Philippines to the United States. "The Philippines are ours forever," declaimed the thirty-seven-year-old Beveridge. "And just beyond the Philippines are China's illimitable markets. We will not retreat from either. We will not repudiate our duty in the archipelago. We will not abandon our opportunity in the Orient. We will not renounce our part in the mission of our race, trustees under God, of the civilization of the world. . . . God . . . has marked us as His chosen people, henceforth to lead in the regeneration of the world. . . . He has made us the master organizers of the world to establish system where chaos reigns. . . . He has made us adept in government that we may administer government among savages and senile peoples. . . ."

Thunderous applause on the Senate floor and in the galleries greeted such oratory, but other Senators, including the scholarly and elderly George Hoar of Massachusetts, questioned not only the wisdom of acquiring far-distant lands of people of different backgrounds and cultures, but the more fundamental issue of violating American values and principles. And while Hoar observed tartly that from the speeches of such men as Beveridge, "the words Right, Duty, Freedom, were absent," the great Speaker, Thomas B. Reed, true to the Shakespearean injunction "To thine own self be true," on September 4, 1899, resigned the speakership, as well as his seat in Congress, no longer able to associate himself with his party's foreign policy. He had gone along with the Spanish-American War, though he deplored the wild jingoism that launched the country into it. But regarding self-government he had said, "The best government of which a people is capable is a government which they establish for themselves. With all its imperfections, with all its shortcomings, it is always better adapted to them than any other government, even though invented by wiser men." He meant it, for on that ground he had opposed the annexation of Hawaii and delayed House consideration of the Hawaiian annexation resolution in 1898 until his friend Nelson Dingley convinced him that the overwhelming sentiment of the House and the nation was against him. But he could not accept the assertion of American control over the people of the Philippines. "I have tried, perhaps not always successfully, to make the acts of my public life accord with my conscience, and I cannot now do this thing," he said. Retiring from public life, he joined a New York law firm and died on December 7, 1902, having been, after Clay, the greatest Speaker the Congress had known.

Meanwhile, in the Fifty-sixth Congress—where a fifty-nine-year-old one-legged Civil War veteran, Iowa Republican David B. Henderson, succeeded Reed as Speaker—the debate on imperialism continued. Maintaining that "the Constitution follows the flag," anti-imperialist Democratic Senators argued that the new territorial acquisitions were an organic part of the United States and were entitled to all constitutional guarantees, including the right of free trade with the rest of the nation. Republicans replied, however, that the new possessions were dependencies and that Congress could make rules for them in any way it chose. Puerto Rico was made an unorganized territory, with a governor general and upper house appointed by the President and a lower house elected by the people, and the Dingley Tariff was extended to the island, with a provision limiting duties to fifteen percent of the authorized rates for Puerto Rican exports to the United States. Soon afterward, in several rulings, the Supreme Court decreed that the Constitution did not automatically apply to the people of an annexed territory but that Congress could extend constitutional provisions as it wished.

In April, 1900, McKinley appointed a Philippine Commission under William Howard Taft, a federal circuit court judge, to establish a civil government for the Philippines, and on July 1, 1902, Congress passed the Philippine Government Act, making the islands an unorganized territory and the commission its governing body. In Cuba, though the Teller Amendment had disclaimed American intentions of asserting control over that country once Spain was ousted, difficulties arose when the newly liberated Cubans wrote a constitution declaring themselves a sovereign and independent nation. Congress now balked at a total American withdrawal, fearing the Cubans' inability to govern themselves and determined also to protect United States strategic and business interests in the island. In the last session of the Fifty-sixth Congress, Republican Senator Orville H. Platt of Connecticut introduced an amendment to the army's appropriation bill, encompassing a group of additions to the Cuban constitution. Among them were a prohibition against Cuba's entering into a treaty with any foreign power that would impair Cuba's independence; a limitation on the Cuban public debt; the right of the United States to intervene in Cuba at any time to safeguard "life, property, and individual liberty"; and an agreement to sell or lease areas for American naval or coaling stations. The Platt Amendment was passed on March 2, 1901, and under American pressure Cuba added the measure's provisions to its constitution, becoming, in effect, a quasi protectorate of the United States.

In June, 1900, the Republicans renominated McKinley for President, naming as his running mate—despite Mark Hanna's objection—the forty-two-year-old governor of New York, Theodore Roosevelt, who had become a popular hero as leader of the Rough Riders in Cuba during the war. Dynamic, hard-driving, and progressive, Roosevelt was a thorn in the side of the New York boss, Tom Platt, who told the other Republican leaders, "I want to get rid of the bastard" and engineered a draft movement to help him eliminate Roosevelt from the New York gubernatorial contest by tucking him safely away in the harmless obscurity of the vice presidency. The Democrats nominated Bryan, who ran on a platform of anti-imperialism, free silver, and hostility to trusts. As a result of the war the country was prosperous again; McKinley and Roosevelt, in a campaign directed by Hanna and based on the gold standard, the administration's successful expansive foreign policy, and the "Full Dinner Pail" as a symbol of the good times, had no difficulty raising contributions from big industry, and in November they defeated the Democrats. The Republicans retained control of both houses.

On September 6, 1901, before the Fifty-seventh Congress met, McKinley was shot by an anarchist at the Pan-American Exposition at Buffalo and died on September 14. Despite his immediate announcement that he would "continue, absolutely unbroken, the policy of President McKinley," Roosevelt's unexpected accession to power raised fear and apprehension among many of the stunned Republican conservatives in Congress. "Now look," exclaimed Hanna, "that damned cowboy is President of the United States!" They had reason to be concerned, for the progressive movement for political, economic, and social reform and change was growing stronger and more insistent in the United States, and Roosevelt, a brash, energetic, and outspoken activist, had a record of independence and impulsiveness. Roosevelt, indeed, could not be pigeonholed—or controlled. Aggressive and determined to have his own way, he sometimes sounded and acted like an arch-conservative and sometimes like a flaming radical. As a masterful politician who won the enthusiastic support of the majority of the American people by championing their anger against the excesses of powerful forces within the country and their feeling of national superiority in the world, he possessed a strength that helped him dominate and frustrate opponents in and out of Congress. Yet he had a middle-of-the-roader's sense of responsibility and expediency, which until his last year in office restrained him from moving too far too fast and kept him, in sum, from being anything more than a moderate reformer, despite the images he created by his loud threats and gnashing of teeth. To the public, for instance, he became "the trust buster."

But Finley Peter Dunne's contemporary newspaper-column observer, Mr. Dooley, came closer to characterizing Roosevelt's real attitude toward trusts: "On wan hand I wud stamp them undher fut; on th' other hand, not so fast."

Even Roosevelt's moderate stance, however, was to the left of the Senate's "Big Four," Aldrich, Allison, Spooner, and Orville Platt, and such other Republican "standpat" conservatives in that body as Hanna, Tom Platt, Eugene Hale of Maine, Matthew Quay and Boies Penrose, the Pennsylvania bosses, Joseph B. Foraker of Ohio, and (to a lesser extent, since he was more independent, as well as a close friend of Roosevelt's) Henry Cabot Lodge. He was, as well, to the left of the autocratic Representative Joseph G. Cannon, who would be elected Speaker in 1903 and, employing the Reed Rules with greater ruthlessness even than "Czar" Reed, become the most powerful individual ever to sit in Congress. Cannon—sixty-seven years old in 1903, already in the House for twenty-eight years, gregarious, lovable, cigar-chewing, unabashedly tyrannical—despised reformers of both parties, saw no need to change the status quo, and would regard Roosevelt's policies as Republican party heresies. "That fellow at the other end of the Avenue wants everything from the birth of Christ to the death of the devil," he said.

Nevertheless, with tact and deference during his first term in office, Roosevelt, whose principal goal was to be nominated and elected in 1904, achieved generally good initial relations with Cannon and the arrogant strong men of the Senate, often sparing them involvement in controversial issues by using his executive powers rather than asking them for new legislation. When he did need a law that might be distasteful to them, he would discuss it with them in the White House, sometimes with a chummy exuberance that they found embarrassing, persuading them that he was only trying to save the free-enterprise system and protect capitalism from its own errors and from socialism or worse, and frequently agreeing to follow their advice on how to handle it in Congress. The result during Roosevelt's first years was substantial agreement between a reluctant congressional leadership and the strongest, zestiest chief executive since the Civil War. After Roosevelt was returned to the White House in 1905, the relationship—which the President had accepted only as a matter of convenience and had limited to legislative and not executive matters—changed, and Roosevelt gave increasingly stronger, and more independent, leadership to the progressives in Congress, alienating the conservatives and contributing influentially to a division in the Republican party.

Before delivering his first message to Congress in 1901, the new President consulted with the Senate Big Four and showed the message to Hanna. It supported large corporations as a "natural" development but recommended "practical efforts" to correct their "real and grave evils" and asked for the creation of a Department of Commerce, with a Bureau of Corporations to gather and issue information on interstate industry. Save for reservations about the intent of those items, the conservatives found the message relatively "safe." Roosevelt's program also included an act to strengthen the Sherman Antitrust law and one to bar railroad rebates; the reorganization and strengthening of the armed forces; a national conservation and reclamation program; the construction of an isthmian canal; and a bill, supported by Aldrich, to permit the contraction and expansion of currency. That congressional session saw only the ratification of the Hay-Pauncefote Treaty, opening the way for the building of a canal, and the passage of the Newlands Act, based on a plan drawn up by Nevada Representative Francis G. Newlands to use part of the receipts from public-land sales in the sixteen western states for the construction of irrigation projects in the semiarid West. The bill established a Reclamation Service and inaugurated a vast conservation program, pushed by Roosevelt during his years in office, that set aside almost 150 million acres for public use and extended to forests, coal, mineral- and oil-bearing lands, wildfowl and game preserves, national parks and monuments, and power sites.

Meanwhile, with considerable disapproval—but glad that they were not involved—the conservatives in Congress watched during 1902 as the President, on his own and without previous consultation with congressional leaders, exercised his executive powers, first to file suit under the Sherman Act to dissolve the Northern Securities Company, a giant holding company formed by James J. Hill, E. H. Harriman, and the Morgan and Rockefeller interests to create a transportation monopoly in the Northwest, and second to intervene in a huge anthracite coal strike in Pennsylvania. The Northern Securities suit rocked Wall Street but gained Roosevelt support from large numbers of the American people. The government won the case in the Supreme Court in 1904, and in the face of Congress' reluctance to pass tight laws prohibiting such monopolistic combinations as holding companies and trusts, the Roosevelt administration continued—though only sporadically—to take the court route against them. In the case of the coal strike, management's highhanded refusal to negotiate aroused public sympathy for the strikers and so infuriated Roosevelt that he threatened to seize the coal fields and have the government operate them. With the help of Elihu Root, his secretary of war, several Senators, and J. P. Morgan, he finally put pressure on the coal operators and achieved a settlement. Roosevelt's intervention in a labor dispute—calling management and labor to meet with him in the White House, appointing an arbitration board, threatening to use troops to take over and run an industry—set precedents for future Presidents.

In the second session of the Fifty-seventh Congress, beginning on December 1, 1902, Roosevelt got some of the legislation he had requested in his first message. On February 11, 1903, an act was passed expediting the trying of antitrust suits. Three days later the President signed an army reform bill based on a comprehensive plan that Root had submitted to Congress the year before. On the same day, February 14, Congress established the Department of Commerce and Labor, which included a Bureau of Corporations with the power to subpoena and compel testimony. Aldrich's support for the bill was won in a "stand-up fight" with the President, ending with Roosevelt's agreement to have his attorney general issue a public statement that, on the question of trusts, "Congress has now enacted all that is practicable and all that is desirable to do." Senator Quay and Pennsylvania Representatives had opposed the bill so strongly that Roosevelt threatened to call a special session unless the measure was passed. Finally the President charged that John D. Rockefeller was back of the opposition. The public reaction alarmed Congress, and both houses quickly passed the measure. Another bill, the Elkins Act, outlawing railroad rebates and introduced by Senator Stephen B. Elkins of West Virginia, was signed by the President on February 19. Since court decisions continued to favor the railroads, the act proved largely ineffective, and at a later date Roosevelt had to ask for still stricter legislation on the subject. The session finally ended in confusion over an amendment offered by South Carolina's Senator Ben Tillman for the payment by the federal government of a $47,000 claim to his state. When Cannon in the House refused to accept the amendment, claiming that the proper sum should be thirty-four cents, Tillman filibustered. At three in the morning on the last day of the session, with the members of both houses waiting wearily to pass the bill containing some $20 million of urgent government appropriations, Cannon finally gave in to Tillman but charged him with "legislative blackmail" and attacked the procedures of the Senate. The House members cheered, but when the new session convened the next day, Allison and other Senators blazed away at Cannon for his intemperate language and his breaking of the House rules to criticize the other branch of Congress. Cannon easily shrugged it off.

For a time conservative Republican support seemed to be mobilizing to replace Roosevelt with Hanna as the party's 1904 candidate. But the Ohio Senator died on February 15, 1904, and Roosevelt then had clear sailing, winning renomination by acclamation and defeating the lackluster Democratic candidate, Alton B. Parker, in November. Although Roosevelt had alienated many big businessmen, they accepted him as a safety valve for something worse, preferring, as the New York *Sun* said, "the impulsive candidate of the party of conservatism to the conservative candidate of the party which the business interests regard as permanently and dangerously impulsive." Even J. P. Morgan contributed $150,000 to the Republicans. On the night of his election, Roosevelt announced that he would not run for another term, suggesting that he might now be more independent of Congress but permitting the conservative leadership in Congress, also, to plan to be more independent of him.

Roosevelt's message to the last session of the Fifty-eighth Congress, which assembled in December after the election, reflected his increased determination to deal with festering social and economic problems. He proposed a long list of measures that included protective laws for railroad workers; the licensing of all interstate business by the Bureau of Corporations and the empowering of the bureau to investigate the insurance business; child labor, slum clearance, factory inspection, juvenile court, and compulsory school attendance laws for the District of Columbia to make it a model for states to copy; and the strengthening of the Interstate Commerce Commission. To implement Roosevelt's proposals, several bills were introduced in the House. One of them, offered by Representative William P. Hepburn of Iowa, a great-grandson of the fiery Matthew Lyon, gave the ICC broad authority to fix railroad rates. It passed the House by an overwhelming bipartisan vote, but the conservatives' opposition and the delaying testimony of railroad executives held it up in the Senate Interstate Commerce Committee and the lame-duck session ended with none of Roosevelt's programs achieved.

The conservatives' obstruction angered Roosevelt, who called such Senators as Foraker, Spooner, and Hale a curse and in his message to the new Fifty-ninth Congress, in December, 1905, attacked the power that the big corporations had over the government and termed their supervision by the national government a necessity. Again the public supported him and the House quickly repassed the Hepburn rate-fixing bill, 346 to 7. Despite the lower house's lopsided vote, the Senate conservative majority dug in, reflecting big industry's rock-ribbed position, and a long and divisive controversy wracked the upper chamber over the bill. With Roosevelt's support, Senator Jonathan P. Dolliver of Iowa handled the measure and became increasingly more progressive as he clashed with Aldrich, the Republican leader. In a complex maneuver, Aldrich managed to have the bill transferred from Dolliver's sponsorship to that of Senator Tillman, a Democrat who supported the measure, with permission given to committee members to offer amendments from the floor, an almost unprecedented move and one designed to wreck the bill by amending it. The transfer of the bill to Tillman was also a problem for Roosevelt, since the two men were not talking to each other. Earlier, truculent "Pitchfork Ben" had had a fist fight on the Senate floor with Senator John L. McLaurin, also of South Carolina, and after the Senate censured both men Roosevelt had not included Tillman in an invitation to a White House affair. But Roosevelt now made peace and supported Tillman's efforts to get the Hepburn Bill passed.

As the debate continued, discipline among both parties in the Senate almost collapsed. Robert M. La Follette, who was now in the upper house after having made a national reputation as a progressive reform governor of Wisconsin, attacked the bill as too lenient toward the railroads, and though many conservatives walked out of the chamber when he spoke, he won the support of Dolliver and several other Republicans. On an unsuccessful conservative motion to reject the bill, Beveridge also broke decisively with the Republican leadership. "We'll get you for this," Aldrich snapped at the influential young Indiana Senator. With confusion mounting, Roosevelt, who had been intervening first with the conservatives, then with the progressives, finally prevailed on Allison to save the measure with a compromise amendment. Still attacked by both the extreme conservatives and progressives, the bill at last passed the Senate and became law on June 29, 1906. It empowered the ICC, on the complaint of a shipper, to fix reasonable rates, subject to court review. Though the progressives had failed to achieve some of their goals, the measure was a large step in the direction of government regulation of industry. Of equal significance—as a result of the intransigence of the old guard Republicans—was a lowering of the Senate's prestige in the eyes of the general public, which, viewing Senators as defenders of the rich corporations and not accountable to the people because the politicians (often venal machine politicians) of the state legislatures elected them, gave increasing support to agitation for their popular election.

During the same session Congress reluctantly considered a Meat Inspection Act, introduced by Senator Beveridge and requiring sanitary conditions in packing houses and the inspection of companies selling meat in interstate commerce. For a time the meat-packing industry and its allies, bankers and western cattle raisers, induced Representative James Wadsworth of New York, the conservative chairman of the House Committee on Agriculture, to sit on the legislation. But the publication of *The Jungle*, an exposé of filthy conditions in the Chicago packing houses, by Upton Sinclair, one of the leading reformer-writers whom Roosevelt called muckrakers, angered the country, and the President, sickened by the revelations of his own investigation of the industry, pressured Wadsworth into freeing the legislation. It became law on June 30, 1906, along with a Pure Food and Drug Act, for which large segments of the public, the medical profession, and the press had long been clamoring, forbidding the adulteration or misbranding of foods and drugs sold in interstate commerce.

In December, 1906, when the second session of the Fifty-ninth Congress met, the President renewed his attack on the abuses of big corporations and the unequal distribution of wealth in the country. Roosevelt, it was clear, was gradually adopting, as his own, proposals that Republicans had regarded as extremely radical when the Populists and Bryan had supported them late in the nineteenth century. Yet Roosevelt was only keeping up with the nation as a whole, for in many states reformers and progressives were now moving into power and pushing through their state legislatures political, social, and economic laws that often went beyond Roosevelt's requests. At the same time the wave of reform stiffened the backs of the conservatives. The courts ruled much of the state legislation unconstitutional, and in Congress the Republican old guard in the Senate and in the House agreed between the two sessions of 1906 to bottle up progressive legislation in committees and try to deny the floor to, or call out of order whenever possible, the proponents of "obnoxious" legislation. The result was practical dictation in the House, where Cannon's tyrannical use of his powers infuriated—but quashed—the Democrats and Republican reformers. In the Senate Beveridge, Dolliver, and La Follette gave valiant leadership to a small band of Republican progressives, but they and the Democrats were beaten repeatedly. Only two of Roosevelt's requests were passed in the session—a limit of seventeen consecutive work-hours for railroad employees, and a prohibition on corporation contributions to federal campaigns. Roosevelt himself did little to further any of his proposals and refused to support a campaign that Beveridge waged with a moving, heavily documented four-day speech for a law prohibiting child labor in industries in interstate commerce. Spooner and others attacked such a law as unconstitutional and the President hung back as if believing that he had already done enough to antagonize big business.

It was the President's method, as some historians have termed it, of playing both sides of the street. He gave vocal leadership to the progressives, then emasculated their programs by compromising with the conservatives or failing to stay with them when they needed him most. At the same time, the conservatives saw him as the Pied Piper of their enemies. In January, 1907, John D. Rockefeller warned that Roosevelt's attacks on business and finance would bring a depression. When a financial panic and depression did occur later that year, many conservatives blamed Roosevelt, though the true causes lay in an inelasticity of the currency and an overextension of credit. Roosevelt used Treasury resources to stabilize the financial situation and even won kind words from industrialists and bankers by letting the giant United States Steel Corporation acquire the Tennessee Coal and Iron Company and promising not to institute antitrust action. At the same time, he stepped up his attacks on "certain malefactors of great wealth" and promised to continue his crusade for government control of big industry. When the Sixtieth Congress convened in December, 1907, he stuck to his word, asking again for an inheritance and income tax, the national incorporation and regulation of companies engaged in interstate business, and a limitation on court injunctions in labor disputes; and he broadened his program to include the regulation of railroad securities, compulsory investigation of large-scale labor conflicts, and the extension of workmen's compensation and the eight-hour day. His program stood no chance. Again, Cannon in the House and the conservatives in the Senate blocked all attempts by progressives and Democrats to win victories.

Roosevelt had meanwhile been busy in the field of foreign affairs, winning the country's plaudits for accomplishments that included the mediating of the Russo-Japanese conflict; the conclusion of a "Gentlemen's Agreement" with Japan regarding Japanese immigration; the adoption at a Hague Peace Conference of agreement by European powers not to employ force to collect debts owed by nations in the Americas; and the holding of a Central American Peace Conference in Washington in 1907. In his handling of foreign relations he consulted Congress only rarely, carrying out most of his actions by executive order. "I should not dream of asking the permission of Congress . . . ," he once told William Howard Taft. "You know as well as I do that it is for the enormous interest of this government to strengthen and give independence to the executive in dealing with foreign powers. . . . Therefore the important thing to do is for a President who is willing to accept reponsibility to establish precedents which successors may follow. . . ." Nevertheless, by 1908 the conservative leadership in Congress felt so independent of Roosevelt that it refused at first to vote his requested appropriation for four new battleships, and after pressure from the President's followers it finally approved only two.

As early as 1906 Roosevelt had chosen Taft as his successor. In the months before the Republican convention, Roosevelt had wished wistfully that he could run for his own second term, and he knew that the nomination was his if he wanted it. There was even talk of drafting him. But he had given his word that he would not run again, and to forestall a draft he saw to it that Taft was named on the first ballot. With everything else at the convention the old guard had its way, writing a conservative platform that promised a revision of the tariff (Taft had wanted it to read "downward," but it merely said "a revision," without indicating which direction) and nominating for Vice President one of Cannon's henchmen in the House, Representative James S. "Sunny Jim" Sherman of New York. The Populists nominated Tom Watson; the Socialists, Eugene V. Debs, the militant labor leader; and the Democrats again named Bryan. With Roosevelt campaigning for Taft, the Ohioan had no trouble winning the election on November 3, and the Republicans retained control of both houses.

On March 4, 1909, there was a snowstorm, and the huge, genial Taft took his oath of office in the Senate chamber. Soon afterward Roosevelt departed on an African big-game hunt. He had been a strong President, who boasted that he had used "every ounce of power there was in the office" to establish precedents for future chief executives in a world in which the American government was assuming vast new responsibilities. For better or worse, he had started the United States in new directions both at home and abroad. He also left behind him an unfulfilled blueprint for domestic reform, a widening cleavage in the Republican party, and a Congress whose Democratic and progressive Republican members seethed with revolt against Cannon in the House and the Republican old guard in the Senate.

8. Seesaw of Power

In his campaign and after his election, Taft assured the country that he would carry on the philosophy and substance of Roosevelt's reform policies, and the progressive Republicans in both houses of Congress looked forward to White House support against the standpat obstructionism of Cannon and Aldrich. But Roosevelt himself was less sure. "He means well, and he'll do his best," he told newspaperman Mark Sullivan. "But he's weak. They'll get around him." Taft, indeed, soon proved an infuriating disappointment to the hard-fighting liberals in the legislature— as well as to the majority of the country's voters, who wanted Roosevelt's reforms to continue. Slow, 350 pounds in weight, seemingly more interested in golf and food than in the presidency, Taft had neither the energy nor the will his office required. While he did not abandon the cause of reform (and in some respects, particularly in antitrust actions, compiled an impressive record), he hated political maneuvering and infighting and repeatedly rationalized the need to accept the verdicts of the conservatives in Congress rather than to stand by, much less lead, the progressives. The conservatives still controlled Congress, and Taft, something of a latter-day Buchanan, was afraid—and too lazy— to risk having them turn against him. In addition, he was an extremely conservative man himself, who felt comfortable with respectable men such as Aldrich and shared with them a measure of contempt for the firebrand reformers in his party. When such "radicals" as Senators La Follette, Dolliver, and Albert B. Cummins (who succeeded to Allison's seat after that venerable Iowan finally died in August, 1908) pressured him or complained of lack of support, he bridled as if they were of a distastefully fanatic ilk that was beneath him, labeling them "blatant demagogues" and "yellow dogs."

The progressives' disillusionment with Taft began soon after his inauguration. Overwhelmingly, the country was in a mood for a reduced tariff and a drastic modification of the protectionist principle that subsidized excessive big-business profits, aided monopolies, and kept prices high for the average American.

Taft had campaigned for a lowering of the high rates of the Dingley Tariff, now twelve years old and out of date, and deciding to live up to his campaign commitment at once, he summoned the Sixty-first Congress into extra session in March, 1909. The conservative chairman of the House Ways and Means Committee, New York Representative Sereno Payne, joined by Cannon, advised Taft that while he might confer with the leaders, he should not interfere with the legislative discussions of a bill until it reached conference stage—a suggestion that Taft accepted by reminding himself that the three branches of government should indeed be independent of each other. For the same reason he gave ground again when Cannon, Aldrich, and Payne told him of an expected attempt by a coalition of Democrats and insurgent Republicans to unseat Cannon by forcing a change in the House rules and warned him that the rebels had to be beaten if the tariff was to pass. Taft disliked the "dirty and vulgar" Cannon and believed that the Speaker's tyrannical rule of the House made him a millstone around his own neck as well as that of the Republican party. But once more he gave in and reassured the conservatives that he would support Cannon against the progressives.

When Congress convened, the Democrats, aided by a dozen Republican insurgents, did make a futile effort to supplant Cannon with the Democratic leader of the House, fifty-nine-year-old James Beauchamp "Champ" Clark of Missouri. Clark, an able parliamentarian and a forceful debater, then tried, unsuccessfully, to enlarge the Rules Committee. Supported by the Republican progressives, who were led by George W. Norris of Nebraska, forty-seven years old and a fearless and ruggedly honest former judge, Clark finally put through some minor rules changes, but Cannon, as usual, had the last licks. He waited for the disposition of the tariff bill to see what other members he might have to punish, then demoted insurgents from committee chairmanships or shifted them to the least desirable committees. "Adam and Eve were insurgents and ate of the forbidden fruit, expecting to become gods," he chided the rebels. "They only learned to see their own nakedness."

The tariff bill Payne's committee reported to the House distressed the low-tariff advocates, for while it reduced some rates, it raised others and represented scarcely any overall change from the Dingley Tariff. With Cannon restricting the offering of amendments and limiting floor debate, he and his hierarchy had no difficulty getting the measure passed, since a two-thirds vote in the Republican caucus bound all the House Republicans—save the insurgents, who boycotted the party caucus—to vote for the bill. The measure then went to Aldrich and the conservatives of the Senate Finance Committee. At that point La Follette called on Taft to tell him that the Payne bill was not a downward revision and therefore violated the Republicans' campaign pledge. Taft promised that if this was true of the final version he would veto it, but he would not interfere with the legislative process. For two days Aldrich's Finance Committee worked behind closed doors, consulting in secrecy with a stream of lobbyists for protected industries. Then Aldrich presented the bill to the Senate, shocking the nation with a measure that now included some six hundred increases in the tariff.

The debate that followed was as dramatic as any the Senate had ever seen, and it was followed closely by the press and the public. Many of Aldrich's old guard colleagues—Allison, Orville Platt, Spooner, Foraker, Matt Quay—were dead, defeated, or retired, but the aging Rhode Island Senator, aided by such conservatives as Lodge, Boies Penrose, Julius Burrows of Michigan, and Reed Smoot, a newcomer from Utah, still had the upper hand. Six Republican insurgents, however—La Follette, Beveridge, Dolliver, Cummins, Joseph L. Bristow of Kansas, and Moses E. Clapp of Minnesota—all of them among the Senate's ablest debaters, battled the conservatives day after day through the hot, humid weeks of June and July. Pressing for a vote and determined to deny his opponents a chance to study the bill, Aldrich secured a ruling that kept the Senate in session without recess or adjournment from ten in the morning until eleven at night. The six insurgents divided the bill among themselves, one taking the schedules on wool, another on iron and steel, and so on, and worked each night until the early morning hours to master the complexities of the three-hundred-page document. Though the sympathies of much of the nation were with them, the President gave them no help, and on one occasion he even intervened to assist Aldrich. This happened when Cummins and Democratic Senator Joseph W. Bailey of Texas introduced an amendment for an income tax on individuals and corporations. When it seemed certain that the Democrats and Republican insurgents had enough votes to pass it, Aldrich called on Taft for help. The President supported an income tax, but he felt that the Supreme Court would again find it unconstitutional. On June 16, without warning, the President startled the progressives by sending a message to Congress supporting a corporate tax in the tariff bill but recommending the adoption of an income-tax amendment to the Constitution before passing any legislation on that subject. It was something of a victory for Taft, who had persuaded Aldrich to accept a corporation tax for two years by satisfying him that the constitutional amendment would postpone an income tax. Though the progressives were now angry with the President, they offered a separate resolution for an income-tax amendment. It passed both houses in July and on February 25, 1913, was adopted as the Sixteenth Amendment.

The tariff debate, meanwhile, was becoming increasingly harmful to the Republican party, sowing the seeds of a nationwide revolt against its conservative leadership. The progressives, beaten down repeatedly on their amendments, called the conservatives reactionary tools of the corrupt trusts and eastern monopolists. On July 8, 1909, the Senate finally passed the bill, La Follette branding it "the consummation of privilege more reprehensible than had ever found a place in the statutes of the country." Aldrich read out of the party the ten insurgents who voted with the Democrats against the measure. La Follette again called on Taft to live up to his pledge and veto the bill when it reached him, but the President replied by saying that he would now take a hand and straighten things out in the Senate-House conference on the bill. But the conservatives neutralized him. Aldrich, when bearded, professed ignorance that the Republicans had pledged downward revision—the platform had said only "revision"—and he and Cannon stacked the conference committee with loyal protectionists. Taft not only failed to bring pressure on the committee members by such tactics as withholding patronage or going over their heads to the people as Roosevelt had done, but let it be known that he would not veto the measure because he did not want to lose the support of the congressional leadership.

On July 31 the House passed the bill, with twenty Republicans and all but two Democrats opposing it. "Not all the perfumes of Araby the Blest can sweeten the Payne-Aldrich Tariff Bill to please the nostrils of the American people," said Champ Clark. The Senate passed it, 47 to 31, on August 5, with the ten insurgent Republicans still voting against it. The next day Taft signed the measure and the special session ended. The Republican progressives were now determined that Taft would not be renominated in 1912, and the Democrats, not too long before described in the House as a "disorganized, undisciplined mob," gained new unity and the hope of a return to national power—a vision that became more real in the fall when the President raised a storm of disapproval across the country by terming the session's handiwork "the best tariff bill that the Republican party has ever passed."

Further conflict between the progressives and Taft arose over a new railroad rate bill. In an attempt to strengthen the Hepburn Act, passed under Roosevelt, George W. Wickersham, Taft's attorney general, prepared a bill embodying Taft's wishes and the President sent it to Congress. Although previous Presidents had used countless methods, in addition to their messages, to further their legislative wishes in Congress, this was the first time a chief executive had had one of his departments assume the legislature's function of drawing up a bill. House Democrats, in particular, registered their anger at what later Presidents would do as a matter of course. In the Senate Aldrich handled the bill, but the Democrats and progressive Republicans, led by La Follette and Cummins, offered so many amendments that Aldrich and the administration forces finally lost control, and to get the bill passed Aldrich had to make deals with the Democrats.

The progressives' setback to Aldrich's control in the Senate was matched by the sudden smashing of Cannon's authoritarian rule in the House. By 1910 the gleeful—but deadly serious—way in which the Speaker exercised his stifling control over the legislative process, frustrating all progressive measures and reducing to impotence the people's representatives (the House, after the 1910 census, would go to 435 members), had made "Cannonism" a national issue. The white-bearded seventy-three-year-old "Uncle Joe," seemingly impregnable, gloried in his notoriety. "Behold Mr. Cannon, the Beelzebub of Congress!" he chortled at one public meeting. "Gaze on this noble manly form—me, Beelzebub! Me, the Czar!" It was said that one Representative simply sent out Cannon's picture when constituents requested a copy of the House rules. But much of the nation's press was now paraphrasing what Norris had once written: "The House of Representatives bears about the same relation to the national government as the appendix does to the human body. It has no well-recognized function. For all practical purposes our national government, like Gaul of old, is divided into three parts: the Senate, the President, and the Speaker." In the face of that reality, Cannon's remark "Everything is all right out West and around Danville. The country don't need any legislation" was no longer amusing. To editors, the country at large, and a growing number of Congressmen, the nation's needs made intolerable such standpat tyranny, which throttled every new idea that came into the House.

For weeks Norris had been carrying around a resolution he and a number of other insurgent Republicans had prepared. The problem was to gain recognition to introduce it. On March 16, 1910, the break he had been waiting for suddenly came. Another Representative asked that a joint resolution regarding the 1910 census be taken up out of order, arguing that the Constitution called for a census and that a constitutional mandate overrode any rule of the House. Cannon ruled the argument valid, and Norris had his chance. The next day he rose and asked to offer a resolution he claimed was also privileged by the Constitution. "The gentleman will present it," Cannon said. The Constitution, Norris explained, provided that the House make its own rules. There was a hush as he began to read his resolution. It proposed the creation of a new fifteen-member Rules Committee, elected by the House, which "shall select its own chairman." Moreover, the Speaker "shall not be eligible to membership of said committee." The hall was suddenly charged with electricity. The resolution would mean the end of the five-member Rules Committee dominated by the all-powerful Speaker. Despite the precedent of Cannon's ruling on the census resolution, one of the Speaker's men immediately raised a point of order against the introduction of Norris's resolution. Since it was St. Patrick's Day, many of Cannon's supporters were out of town attending parades and banquets, and the Speaker postponed a ruling but kept the House in session. All that day, that night, and the next day, Cannon and the Republican leadership sent hurriedly for absent members and tried to plot strategy to head off the debacle. Champ Clark and his whips also sent for all Democrats to come in, and through the newspapers the whole country watched the drama of the sudden revolution against Cannonism. After Norris turned down Cannon's attempt to compromise, the Speaker on March 19 said to some of his friends, "Boys, it looks as though we're beaten, but we'll die game," and returned to the Speaker's chair to rule Norris's resolution not in order. Clark immediately appealed, and amid tremendous tension the House voted, 182 to 163, to overrule the Speaker. Norris's resolution, amended to create a ten-member Rules Committee, with six from the majority and four from the minority and with power to elect its own chairman, was then carried, 191 to 156, and the revolution had won.

In the 1912 Democratic landslide Cannon was defeated, but he returned to Congress two years later and remained there, good-natured, friendly, but politically reactionary, until 1923, when after forty-six years of service in the House he retired at eighty-seven. Three years later he died in Illinois, still remembered by some as the archenemy of the reformers. "Emma Goldman [an American anarchist leader] in her palmiest days," said William Allen White, the Kansas editor, "never made as many anarchists as Cannon."

Back from his African game hunt and angry and disgusted with Taft, who had struck off on his own with the conservatives, Theodore Roosevelt in August, 1910, re-entered the political scene with a fighting speech at Osawatomie, Kansas, attacking the "lawbreakers of great wealth" and proposing a broad program of social legislation that he termed the "New Nationalism." The speech did Taft no good, and in the elections that fall the Democrats won the House, and the Senate passed to the control of a Democratic-insurgent Republican coalition. (Aldrich himself did not run again, but finished out his service on the National Monetary Commission, retiring to Providence and dying in 1915.) When the new Sixty-second Congress met in special session in April, 1911, Champ Clark was elected Speaker.

Without an all-powerful Speaker, the Democratic caucus assumed the task of organizing the House, naming Oscar W. Underwood of Alabama, a tariff expert of strong Jeffersonian principles who had been in Congress since 1897, majority leader and chairman of Ways and Means. The Democratic members of that committee were designated the party's Committee on Committees to draw up assignments of all Democratic committee chairmen and members—the Republican leadership being permitted to compile its own committee lists—and both slates were then perfunctorily endorsed by the caucus. The principal power in the House passed from the Speaker to Underwood, who became the majority leader in fact as well as in name, dominating the Democratic committee-assignment process as head of Ways and Means and employing the caucus to mold the Democrats into a well-organized and disciplined body. A two-thirds vote in the caucus bound members to support party positions, save when individuals had made contrary pledges to their constituencies or differed with the caucus on constitutional grounds.

On December 4, 1911, the legislators reassembled for the first regular session, which saw the passage of a resolution for the adoption of the Seventeenth Amendment, for the popular election of Senators. The amendment, expected to democratize the Senate and end a system blamed for filling the upper chamber with men who represented political machines and corporate interests rather than the people, had long been a principal goal of reformers. Many states had employed such methods as direct primaries, the initiative and referendum, and calls for a national constitutional convention to adopt the amendment to force their legislatures to observe the popular will when they chose Senators. As an increasing number of men who had first been nominated in direct primaries entered the Senate, resistance to the amendment began to crumble. Starting in 1910 a fight in its behalf, led by Senator William E. Borah, a first-term Republican lawyer from Idaho, made headway, and both houses at last approved the amendment in 1912. It became part of the Constitution on May 31, 1913.

During the same first session of the Sixty-second Congress, the Democrats in the House satisfied another long-time goal, authorizing a subcommittee of the Committee on Banking and Currency under Representative Arsène Pujo of Louisiana to inquire into the so-called money trust, the most powerful trust of all, and to examine the interrelationships among the major financial interests of the nation, including the largest investment banking houses, commercial banks, insurance companies, railroads, and corporations. The star witness was J. P. Morgan, and he and other semi-legendary figures of finance provided dramatic headlines for the newspapers as they reluctantly revealed interlocking directorates, monopolistic practices, and other devices and activities that had concentrated the private money power of the nation in the hands of five banks in New York and Boston. With the White House and Congress split between the two parties, no immediate legislation resulted from the testimony, but under Woodrow Wilson and the Democrats the investigation would bear fruit.

In the Senate, as they had done in the House, the Democrats sought to achieve party unity, beginning in 1911 a custom of electing for each session a floor leader who was also chairman of the party caucus, and in 1913 adding party whips, or assistant floor leaders. The Republicans soon followed the Democrats' example. The majority and minority leaders, however, often had difficulty maintaining party unity, since the party caucuses, which were beginning to be called conferences, had lost their power to bind the votes of members, and the leaders had to fall back on the use of personal influence and pressure.

That first session of the Sixty-second Congress witnessed, meanwhile, the Senate's approval of a "corollary" to the Monroe Doctrine, which was introduced by Henry Cabot Lodge. Stemming from reports that a private Japanese syndicate was negotiating to purchase coastal land on Mexico's Lower California peninsula, it proclaimed American opposition to the acquisition of strategic areas in the Western Hemisphere by private companies that might give control of such sites to foreign powers. The Japanese negotiations fell through, but Lodge's Corollary, in effect, denied to other countries the right to do in the Americas what the United States itself was doing under an aggressive foreign policy enunciated by Taft and known as dollar diplomacy, which provided government support for strategic purposes to American bankers and businessmen abroad, particularly in Latin America and the Far East. Although that policy, which Taft characterized as "substituting dollars for bullets," fell into disrepute from time to time, it was still, in the 1970's, an inherent influence in the conduct of foreign relations. In a similar vein, Taft continued Roosevelt's policy of intervening in Latin American countries to further American interests, acting on his own and without Senate advice and consent and even without a war declaration when he sent Marines to put down an insurrection in Nicaragua in 1912. The Marines remained in Nicaragua, policing that country's affairs, until 1933, and Taft's action in sending them served as a precedent for armed and clandestine intrusions, without a war declaration, in the affairs of Haiti and other Latin American countries by Presidents who followed him. Whether such assertions of executive power were unconstitutional was a moot question; Congress and the American people acquiesced and seemingly thought as did future Supreme Court Justice Felix Frankfurter, who in regard to America's seizure of Veracruz in Mexico in 1914 said cynically, "It would be an act of war against a great nation; it isn't against a small nation."

By the time of the 1912 campaign, Roosevelt's break with Taft was complete, and he announced that he would oppose the President for the Republican nomination. Taft's tight control of the Republican convention at Chicago in June, however, rebuffed Roosevelt, and when the conservatives in the party renominated Taft, a new Progressive party (also called Bull Moose for Roosevelt's statement that he felt as strong as a bull moose) met in August and nominated Roosevelt for President on a platform that called for numerous reforms, including nationwide preferential primaries for presidential candidates, tariff revision, stricter regulation of industry, the recall of judicial decisions, the prohibition of child labor, woman suffrage, and the initiative, referendum, and recall. The Democrats met at Baltimore in June, and though Champ Clark began as the leading candidate, he was unable to secure the necessary two-thirds vote. Finally the still-influential William Jennings Bryan shifted his support to Woodrow Wilson, the liberal governor of New Jersey, and on the forty-sixth ballot the convention named Wilson and, as his running mate, Thomas R. Marshall, governor of Indiana (known for his wit, he would remark one day while presiding over the Senate and listening to a boring speech on the needs of the nation, "What this country needs is a really good five-cent cigar").

The campaign was fought principally between Roosevelt and Wilson, the two candidates' progressivism differing mainly in their philosophies of how best to cope with the powers and privileges of the monopolies. Roosevelt's New Nationalism envisioned a strong central government to control and regulate business and legislate social reform, while Wilson's creed of a New Freedom, developed with the help of Louis D. Brandeis, a brilliant progressive lawyer, proposed a restoration of competition and free private enterprise by destroying the special privileges that permitted monopolies to exist. In a sense Roosevelt's program, the forerunner of the planned economy and welfare state of the future, contained strong Hamiltonian elements, while Wilson's New Freedom—laissez faire, ideally shorn of its evils—was Jeffersonian. On November 5 Wilson defeated Roosevelt, who ran ahead of Taft. Reform and liberalism were in the air; even Eugene V. Debs, the Socialist candidate, received almost a million votes, and the Democrats won control of both houses of Congress. When on March 4, 1913, the long-faced

Wilson, idealistic, self-confident, and eloquent—but preachy, overbearing, and convinced of his own rightness ("Talking to Wilson is something like talking to Jesus Christ," the French statesman Georges Clemenceau would later say)—was inaugurated, the ground swell of reform finally came into power.

During the new President's first years in office, relations between the White House and Congress underwent a drastic change. Roosevelt had fought Congress and had often gone over its head to the people to get it to act, but he was never able to establish the primacy of his office over the conservative leadership in the legislature. Taft had shied away from even contesting for dominance. But it was now a different Congress. Wilson had no such opposition as Cannonism in the House or the powerful Aldrich hold on the Senate. His Democratic majorities were well organized and led by, and to a large extent composed of, men who shared the chief executive's goals, were as eager as he to compile a record of party achievement, and were willing to follow or cooperate with him. It was a situation made to order for a man of Wilson's commitment and temperament. "He had to hold the reins and do the driving alone," wrote historian Arthur S. Link in *Woodrow Wilson: The Road to the White House;* "it was the only kind of leadership he knew." Believing strongly in party government and in his responsibility to be the nation's political head, Wilson gave forceful leadership to his party in Congress from his first day in office, telling it what he wanted it to do, introducing and sponsoring legislation, working closely with the Democratic leaders, committee heads, and individual members to achieve his programs, and in the process strengthening and broadening the powers and prestige of the presidency.

Wilson's close association with his party in Congress went far to break down the invisible barrier between the two branches of government, and one of his first actions as President dramatized this. His program envisioned destroying monopolies by eliminating the economic foundations on which they rested, and his initial goal was to end one of those supports, the high protective tariff, which the Republicans had maintained since the Civil War. He called a special session of the new Sixty-third Congress to reform the tariff, and on April 8, 1913, the day after Congress assembled, he addressed the two houses in person—the first President to do so since Jefferson stopped the practice in 1801. He wanted the members of Congress to see that he was a real person and a partner in their work, he told them, not "a mere department of the Government hailing Congress from some isolated island of jealous power."

The tariff bill, introduced in the House by Underwood, chairman of the Ways and Means Committee, had been worked out with Wilson and was a sharp and historic reversal of all previous tariffs, lowering the average rates to about twenty-nine percent, putting scores of everyday items on the free list so their cost to consumers would come down, and all but ending the principle of protection. To make up for the expected drop in government revenues, the committee included a provision for a graduated income tax, drafted by Representative Cordell Hull, a forty-two-year-old former judge from Tennessee. The measure easily passed the House but ran into trouble in the Senate when the expected hordes of lobbyists—so numerous, said Wilson, that "a brick couldn't be thrown without hitting one of them"—went to work on the members of the upper house. Faced with a repetition of previous failures to reduce the tariff, Wilson issued a public statement denouncing the "insidious" lobby that was trying to defeat "the interests of the public for [its] private profit." The press backed the President, and his bold move also aided the insurgent Republicans Cummins and La Follette, who maneuvered the Senate Judiciary Committee into holding an investigation of the lobbyists' activities and forced every Senator to reveal publicly his investments and property holdings that might be affected by a tariff reduction. The exposure of the lobby and the Senators' private interests undermined the fight of the protectionists, and after long debates over individual items the Senate passed the bill, the two houses approved a conference report, and Wilson signed the measure on October 3, joyously calling attention to the achievement of the united Democrats in breaking the monopolists' hold on the government. Indeed, not only was it a historic reversal of tariff policy, withdrawing artificial supports that kept prices high, but, taking advantage of the newly ratified Sixteenth Amendment, it was a start in the democratization of the federal tax structure.

At the same time, Congress worked on a second administration bill designed to achieve another of Wilson's goals, the ending of the monopolists' control of money and its availability as revealed in the Pujo Committee's hearings. Recognizing the need for a reorganization of the banking and money system that would ensure a sounder, more flexible currency and make credit more readily available for the country's expanding requirements, most bankers and businessmen supported a change, though they differed over what should be done. The reform measure was handled by Representative Carter Glass of Virginia, a gentlemanly but irascible little man weighing about one hundred pounds, who chaired the House Banking and Currency Committee. Again and again Wilson, stemming party revolts in both houses, took the lead in effecting compromises that resulted finally in a bill for a banking and currency system with a mix of private and governmental control. After standing off attacks by bankers who wanted no government control and denunciations by La Follette and other progressives who wanted complete government control, Wilson helped the Democratic leaders guide the measure through both houses and signed it on December 23, 1913. The Federal Reserve Act established a system of twelve regional banks, each one owned and controlled by private member banks and empowered to issue a new flexible currency, Federal Reserve notes, to the member banks. The whole decentralized system would be supervised and partially controlled by a single Federal Reserve Board, whose seven long-term members would be appointed by the President with the consent of the

Senate. The measure was a significant reform of the heart of the American economy. It destroyed the control of money and credit by a few banks centered in Wall Street, created a new flexible and sound currency, and permitted a planned supervision of banking reserves to meet the country's needs.

Wilson's third goal, the enactment of laws that would cripple trusts and restore free competition, resulted in more reform measures. In January, 1914, Wilson for the fifth time addressed a joint congressional session, outlining his ideas for a new antitrust act that would outlaw certain specific unfair trade practices, ban interlocking directorates, and give private parties the benefit of decisions when the government brought suits. A bill introduced by Representative Henry D. Clayton of Alabama, chairman of the House Judiciary Committee, contained these proposals, while another one, presented by Representative James H. Covington of Maryland, proposed the establishment of an interstate trade commission that, supplanting the Bureau of Corporations, would gather information on businesses and assist the Justice Department in antitrust activities. The bills aroused a variety of opposition—from progressives who thought the Clayton bill a futile way of coping with the problem; from small businessmen who wanted a stronger trade commission; from southern Democrats, agrarians, and followers of Bryan, who wanted to destroy the trusts and big corporations instead of regulating their practices; and from labor unions that wanted the Clayton bill to exempt labor and farm organizations as combinations in restraint of trade and free them from all threats of prosecution for their activities.

Wilson and the Democratic leaders finally agreed to compromise wording on labor's demands, recognizing that farm and labor groups were not illegal combinations as viewed by the Sherman Act, and on June 5 the House passed the Clayton bill and Covington's interstate trade commission measure. Meanwhile, pressure on Wilson had begun to convince him that Covington's measure was not strong enough. Another bill, drafted by Brandeis and one of his associates and establishing a federal trade commission with authority to issue cease-and-desist orders to halt whatever practices it found to be unfair or in restraint of trade, was introduced in the House by Democratic Representative Raymond B. Stevens of New Hampshire. The measure was passed by both the Senate and House, and the Federal Trade Commission Act became law in September, 1914. The five-member bipartisan commission for many years disappointed its advocates. Wilson himself hoped the commission would be "a counselor and friend to the business world," not "a policeman to wield a club over the head of the business community." The commission did so little to carry out its mandate, however, that the progressives regarded it as a failure. From time to time in later years it became more conscientious, but critics in and out of Congress often wondered whether the regulators were not being regulated by those whom they were supposed to regulate.

The Clayton Antitrust Bill, meanwhile, had been seriously weakened in the Senate. When it finally passed both houses and in October, 1914, became law, Democratic Senator James A. Reed of Missouri termed it "a sort of legislative apology to the trusts, delivered hat in hand, and accompanied by assurances that no discourtesy is intended." Nevertheless, its prohibitions supplemented and strengthened the Sherman Act, and with its passage Wilson considered his program of economic reform complete. Few progressives agreed with him, and such groups as agrarians and organized labor still pressed for passage of a host of measures to commit the federal government to further social and economic reforms. Many of them had been part of Roosevelt's New Nationalism platform, and Wilson opposed them as violations of his own New Freedom concept because they conferred special privileges on individual groups. He managed to block the passage of a bill for long-term rural credits, refused to support woman suffrage—claiming that it should be left to the states—and gave no help to a child-labor bill, declaring that such interference in the affairs of industry was unconstitutional.

In foreign affairs Wilson and Bryan, whom the President made his secretary of state in payment for his support at the 1912 convention, began on a high note of idealism and anti-imperialism, which most Democrats and progressives in Congress—reflecting the nation's current mood of liberalism and desire for international justice and peace—applauded and conservatives eyed warily. Where Roosevelt and Taft had had difficulties winning Senate approval for treaties with foreign nations that agreed to the settlement of disputes by arbitration, Bryan dropped arbitration and negotiated conciliation treaties with thirty countries, providing for one-year "cooling-off" periods during which the parties to a dispute would submit their argument to an investigation commission whose findings they could either accept or reject; Bryan thought that their belligerency would evaporate during the breathing-spell period. Cynics' attacks on the realism of these treaties were underscored when they were submitted to the Senate for ratification in August, 1914, just as Europe exploded in war. "No one except Bryan," noted Democratic Senator Henry Ashurst of Arizona, "believes that his treaties will preserve the peace." Nevertheless, the Senate ratified most of them.

On other matters Wilson's idealism gradually acquired the character of a stern, crusading self-righteousness—resulting, paradoxically, in high-handed, imperialistic interferences in the affairs of other countries that, playing up to feelings of pride, honor, and the cultural pre-eminence of the United States, foreshadowed popular backing for similar unilateral overseas "police" activities on a much grander scale after World War II. Wilson took the lead in opposing Japanese moves that threatened the independence of China, finally—without popular or congressional opposition—reviving dollar diplomacy to assert American interests in China and block Japanese ambitions there during the First World War. Though the President avoided serious conflict with Japan, his actions in temporarily frustrating her militant expansionism began a period of increasing distrust and tension between the two nations that ended eventually in war in 1941. Similarly, Wilson's missionary-like interventions in Nicaragua, Santo Domingo, Haiti, and Mexico—announced as necessary to save those nations from themselves ("I am going to teach the South American republics to elect good men!" he once exclaimed)—increased anti-Americanism throughout Latin America. Even as Wilson and Bryan denounced financial imperialism, their announced altruistic motives to stabilize the governments and economies of foreign countries stemmed from military and financial pressures to expand or protect American business and political hegemony.

The start of the great war in Europe came as a sobering surprise to most Americans, but despite divided sympathies, Congress, like the President, viewed it as none of America's affair and supported strict neutrality. Gradually, however, commercial and financial ties, together with the natural bonds between America and England and an effective British propaganda campaign, began to edge the United States toward the side of the Allies. The Germans themselves accelerated this development when their use of submarines to blockade Britain resulted in the torpedoing of the *Lusitania* with the loss of 128 American lives on May 7, 1915. Though an anti-German shock wave ran through America, many people, including Senators and Congressmen, urged Wilson to continue to keep the nation out of the conflict. "There is such a thing as a man being too proud to fight," Wilson remarked, but in a series of stiff notes to Germany he won a German promise to halt unrestricted submarine warfare.

At the same time, a growing division within the United States between the peace forces and those who demanded defense of America's rights on the seas led to two conflicts in 1915 and 1916 between Wilson and the Democrats in Congress, whose leadership—reflecting the sentiments of Bryan and the progressives—was committed to staying out of the war and continuing domestic reforms. One of the clashes was triggered by a German announcement, during Wilson's complicated maneuvers to cope with submarine warfare, that her U-boats would sink armed merchantmen without warning. Determined to maintain American rights and hold Germany to strict account, Wilson precipitated a storm among his supporters in Congress by refusing to issue a warning to American citizens against traveling on such vessels. When Democratic leaders pleaded with the President not to risk a provocative situation and he continued to resist them, the Democratic majority on the House Foreign Affairs Committee threw its unanimous support behind a warning of its own to the American people in the form of a resolution against traveling on armed ships introduced by Texas's A. Jeff McLemore. Oklahoma's Thomas P. Gore presented a similar resolution in the Senate; Speaker Clark, House majority leader Claude Kitchin of North Carolina, and Democratic committee heads in both houses advised Wilson that the resolutions would pass; and the stage was set for the formulating of foreign policy by Congress rather than the President. Wilson countered vigorously, enlisting, according to Neil MacNeil in *Forge of Democracy*,

Texas Representative John Nance Garner of the Ways and Means Committee to serve "as a confidential liaison man inside the House" and twice a week visit the White House secretly to confer with the President. With the full use of presidential power and influence, as well as the help of Lodge and other Republicans and the support of much of the nation's press, the resolutions in both houses—backed mostly by midwesterners and southerners—were finally tabled, and the crisis was passed.

The second controversy arose when Wilson, moved by an awareness of America's military weakness, gave in to those pushing for preparedness and was again opposed by the peace elements in Congress, most notably a House bloc led by majority leader Kitchin that controlled the Military Affairs Committee. In December, 1915, Wilson laid before the first session of the Sixty-fourth Congress a comprehensive War Department program for preparedness, including a new national volunteer "Continental Army" of 400,000 men. When the House committee blocked the Continental Army plan, Wilson had to yield, and the final bill was a compromise, providing for the immediate expansion of the regular army and the enlargement of the National Guard and its integration into the federal military structure. Congress also passed a $315 million appropriation bill for a large navy construction and expansion program, an act establishing the Council of National Defense to prepare for the possible mobilization of industry and labor, and a Shipping Act to develop the American merchant marine. Southern and midwestern Democrats dominating the House Ways and Means Committee also revolted against the administration, rejecting its proposed plan for financing the preparedness measures by a tax that hit all levels of the population and substituting a "soak-the-rich" measure that hit hard at those with high incomes, doubling the income tax and adding levies on estates and the receipts of munitions makers. In the Senate such progressives as La Follette and Norris aimed it even more sharply against the wealthy, and the final bill was regarded as a victory by the liberals and followers of Bryan.

Meanwhile, the continuing pressure of progressives and social reformers, the congressional elections of 1914, which had cut into Democratic strength and started Wilson worrying about his re-election in 1916, and his own change of mind concerning the need for additional social and economic legislation moved the President to support a number of reform measures passed by the Democrats and progressive Republicans. In the summer of 1916 Wilson signed the Federal Farm Loan Act, establishing twelve regional Farm Loan Banks to provide long-term, low-interest credit to farmers, and the Warehouse Act to aid farmers in financing their crops. Continuing this about-face, in which he was now endorsing the federal government's assistance to individual groups, Wilson signed the Keating-Owen Child Labor Act, which barred from interstate commerce products made by the labor of children under sixteen (in 1918 the Supreme Court ruled it unconstitutional), and the Adamson Act, establishing an eight-hour day for railroad workers.

In June, 1916, the Republicans met at Chicago and nominated for President Supreme Court Justice Charles Evans Hughes, who had earlier been governor of New York. The Progressives, meeting at the same time in Chicago, nominated Theodore Roosevelt, who declined and gave his support to Hughes. When the Democrats met at St. Louis the following week and renominated Wilson and Marshall, many former supporters of Roosevelt, recognizing that the Democrats had enacted almost every plank in the Progressives' 1912 platform, backed Wilson, especially after his campaign got under way with the peace theme "He kept us out of war." Although Hughes ran an inept campaign, he came close to defeating Wilson, the final verdict becoming known only after late returns put California in Wilson's column, giving him an electoral-vote victory of 277 to 254. The Democrats maintained control of the Senate but divided the House seats almost evenly with the Republicans, so that a few Progressives and independents would hold the balance of power. Among the victorious Republicans was Jeannette Rankin, a thirty-six-year-old social worker and suffragette leader from Montana, who earlier in her life had written in her diary, "Go! Go! Go! It makes no difference where just so you go!" Winning one of Montana's two congressional seats, both representing the state at large, she became the first woman ever elected to Congress and received applause and cheers from her colleagues on the House floor and from suffragettes in the galleries when she was sworn in on the opening day of the new Sixty-fifth Congress, April 2, 1917.

After the election Wilson made fruitless efforts to find a way to end the war, asking both sides to state their war aims, and on January 22, 1917, going before the Senate to state his own formula—a "peace without victory" and without indemnities and annexations, and an international organization after the war to safeguard a lasting peace. Most Americans supported his idealism—La Follette called his address "the greatest message of a century"—but on January 31 Germany, having decided to try to win quickly even if it risked American entry in the conflict, stunned Wilson by announcing a resumption of unrestricted submarine warfare. On February 3 the Germans sank an American ship without warning, and the same day Wilson addressed Congress, breaking diplomatic relations with Germany, a decision the Senate endorsed on February 7. On February 26 Wilson asked Congress for authority to arm merchant ships and to use other "instrumentalities or methods" to protect American commerce on the high seas. Both houses indicated rapid support for the arming of ships, but when opposition was raised to the other part of the request, which might permit Wilson to wage an undeclared naval war, the President released the text of an intercepted dispatch from the German foreign secretary, Alfred Zimmermann, to the German minister in Mexico proposing the return of Texas, New Mexico, and Arizona to Mexico if she joined Germany in war against the United States. The note, rousing a wave of anti-German hysteria, changed peace advocates into supporters of war overnight, and on March 1 the House passed the Armed Ship Bill, 403 to 13, though still withholding from the President permission to use other methods against Germany. When the administration pressed for the Senate's approval of its full request, a group of a dozen adamant noninterventionists, led by La Follette and Norris, filibustered against giving the President what they considered would be the power to make war and blocked the bill until the session ended on March 3.

A patriotic intolerance that would take many forms for years to come now began to sweep the country, fed by an indignant attack by Wilson on La Follette and his colleagues. "A little group of willful men, representing no opinion but their own, have rendered the great Government of the United States helpless and contemptible," the President charged, and newspapers, large elements of the public, and members of both parties savagely denounced those who had filibustered as "descendants of Benedict Arnold" who would be rewarded with "an eternity of execration." Seventy-five Senators signed a manifesto recording their support of Wilson's bill and noting that "the Senate favors this legislation and would pass it if a vote could be had"; and when Wilson angrily called the new Senate into special session on March 5 and demanded it amend its rules so that it would be able to act and "save the country from disaster," that body, after only six hours of debate, passed its first cloture rule, 76 to 3, on March 8. The provision, known as Rule 22, permitted the limitation of debate by a two-thirds vote two days after sixteen Senators submitted a cloture motion. Thereafter, each Senator could speak for only one hour on the bill and all amendments and motions affecting it, and could introduce an amendment only by unanimous consent. At the same time, Secretary of State Robert Lansing (the neutralist Bryan had resigned in 1915) advised the President that he could arm the ships by an executive order, without congressional approval, and Wilson promptly took that step, also calling both houses of the Sixty-fifth Congress to meet in special session on April 16. On March 16 submarines sank three American ships with heavy loss of life; soon afterward Theodore Roosevelt raised the nation's patriotic fever by demanding war; and as the torpedoings continued, Wilson pushed up the convening of Congress to April 2.

On that day the Democrats, aided by the votes of the independents, again organized the House and re-elected Clark as Speaker. The Capitol was filled with excited crowds, some frantically urging continued neutrality, others arguing for war. In the crush a pacifist and his wife lunged angrily at Senator Lodge but were pulled away. At eight-thirty in the evening Wilson somberly addressed a joint session, asking for a war declaration against Germany to make the world "safe for democracy." Against the continued opposition of La Follette and Norris, the Senate on April 4 adopted the resolution, 82 to 6, and at a little after three in the morning of Good Friday, April 6, the House concurred, 373 to 50, one of the opponents being Jeannette Rankin, who first remained silent when her name was called and then, when it was repeated, partly rose and, violating a House rule that forbade comment during a roll call, stated, "I wish to stand by my country, but I cannot vote for war. I vote 'No.'" The night was filled with drama. Many Congressmen wept openly as American neutrality ended.

There followed the passage of a stream of war legislation, beginning with appropriations of $4 billion for the army and navy and authorization for a Liberty Loan of bonds to be sold to the public (four Liberty Loan drives during the war and a Victory Loan in 1919 raised a total of $20.5 billion). A Selective Service Bill providing for universal conscription caused bitter controversy in the House, where Speaker Clark left his chair to oppose the measure. Its constitutionality—sending drafted men outside the United States—seemed open to question, but it was enacted on May 18, 1917. Prohibitionists under the leadership of the Anti-Saloon League, which was working hard for a constitutional amendment to ban the use of alcoholic beverages, persuaded Congress to protect the morals of the draftees by prohibiting the sale of such beverages at or near army camps. The prohibitionists again employed the emergency to secure a ban on the use of foodstuffs necessary to the war effort in the manufacture of distilled liquors, and finally, on December 18, 1917—adding to their arguments a shrill condemnation of distillers and brewers of German descent—they prevailed on Congress to go all the way and adopt the Eighteenth Amendment, prohibiting the manufacture, transportation, or sale of alcoholic liquors in the United States. The amendment was ratified on January 29, 1919, and was placed in operation under the provisions of the Volstead Act (passed over Wilson's veto) on January 16, 1920. Bitterly resisted and flouted by racketeers, gangsters, and the general public for more than a decade, it was repealed by the Twenty-first Amendment in 1933.

Congress also passed the War Revenue Act, which increased income and corporation taxes, imposed an inheritance tax and a graduated excess-profits tax, and sharply increased excise taxes on amusements, tobacco, alcoholic beverages, transportation, and various luxuries. It empowered the federal government to take over the operation of the nation's railroads, authorized reorganizations of executive-branch agencies to prosecute the war more efficiently and economically, and enacted the Trading with the Enemy Act, which prohibited commerce with enemy nations and created an Office of Alien Property Custodian to take over and dispose of property in the United States owned by persons in enemy countries. In addition, the national legislators supported the establishment of the Committee on Public Information under the journalist George Creel to direct war information and propaganda; the War Industries Board under Wall Street speculator Bernard Baruch to increase production of war materials, purchase supplies, fix prices, and eliminate waste; the War Finance Corporation to help supply credit to war industries; and the National War Labor Board to serve as a final court to settle labor disputes.

While the expansion of government power to deal with economic and social problems during the prewar progressive period had established precedents for this burst of federal regulations and controls, the war measures—frequently opposed by some Democrats, but passed with the support of many Republicans who observed something of a wartime political truce—marked an accelerated development away from Wilson's New Freedom concept of laissez faire and toward Theodore Roosevelt's New Nationalism idea of governmental responsibility for social and economic planning and served as precedents themselves for even greater concentrations of federal power during the New Deal and World War II. In addition, the need for cooperative enterprise to win the war encouraged the growth of labor unions by forcing management to deal with the workers' organizations; stimulated such long-sought reforms as a child-labor ban, workmen's compensation, health insurance, and woman suffrage; and, bringing together businessmen and military purchasing officers, laid the foundation for a future "military-industrial complex."

At the same time several acts, urged by the administration and supported by the fervent patriotism and anti-German feeling of a great majority of the American people and their representatives in Congress, broke sharply with the relatively benign atmosphere of political tolerance and freedom of dissent of the progressive period. Paralleling the emergency controls on business, they seriously abridged civil liberties and traditional American rights. The first was the Espionage Act, passed by Congress on June 15, 1917. Designed to combat disloyal and treasonable activities, it provided heavy fines and prison sentences for actions ranging from refusal to serve in the army to aiding the enemy and authorized the postmaster general to exclude from the mails materials he deemed seditious. On May 16, 1918, the measure was amended by the harsher Sedition Act, covering a variety of loosely worded crimes, including using "disloyal, profane, scurrilous, or abusive language" about the American government, the Constitution, the flag, or the military forces. Under both acts numerous pacifists, conscientious objectors, and political dissidents of various shades of radical belief were arrested. Eugene V. Debs, three times Socialist candidate for President, was sentenced to prison for ten years for "propaganda which advanced and played upon the theme that this was a capitalists' war," and Victor L. Berger, a Socialist Representative from Wisconsin, whose jail sentence of twenty years was upset by the Supreme Court, was twice barred by House resolutions from taking his seat in Congress because he opposed the war.

Even with the end of the conflict, the hysteria continued. The new Bolshevik regime, which angered Americans by taking Russia out of the war seemingly in collusion with the Germans, who were thus enabled to move all their troops to the Western Front, and which, in addition, appeared to threaten an atheistic, anti-capitalist world revolution, raised a new international menace for patriotic Americans to fear and oppose. The domestic violence of postwar labor disputes and the militant political action of a small number of bomb-throwing anarchists and other extreme radicals, many of them immigrants, aroused alarm that the revolution was spreading to the United States, and in 1919 and 1920 Wilson's attorney general, A. Mitchell Palmer, a former progressive, exploiting nativist bigotry and patriotic sentiment, led in generating a "Red Scare." Palmer conducted a repressive campaign against thousands of suspects, employing the wartime sedition measures, outdoing all previous violations of civil liberties, and receiving widespread support. Most of the country's fears were finally proved groundless, public opinion turned against the excesses of the anti-radical crusade, and the turmoil quieted. But in world communism America had a new potential enemy that required, in the minds of many citizens, constant vigilance against left-wing agents "boring from within" under various dissident and nonconformist guises to threaten the nation.

In 1918, meanwhile, American military power moved to Europe, helping to stem the final German offensives and launch the fierce drives that at last brought victory to the Allies. From time to time French and British leaders came to Washington and visited Congress to reinforce the feeling of partnership. On May 1, 1917, Marshal Joffre, the hero of the Battle of the Marne, was escorted to the Vice President's rostrum in the Senate by the Republicans' chief spokesman on foreign relations, Senator Lodge. Wearing scarlet breeches, the French military leader acknowledged the Senators' cheers, shouted, "I do not speak English," and, waving his cap, cried, "Vivient les États Unis!" Soon afterward the British Foreign Secretary, Arthur Balfour, visited the Senate, delivering a twenty-minute address in a weary monotone.

As the conflict in Europe neared an end, Wilson's uncompromising determination to handle foreign affairs himself and impose on the world his idealistic vision of an enduring peace headed him on a collision course with the Senate. On January 8, 1918, he delivered a stirring address to the Sixty-fifth Congress, boldly outlining fourteen points as a basis for a moral peace. Among them were proposals for open diplomacy, freedom of the seas, the reduction of armaments, and "a general association of nations." Liberals in America and the Allied countries supported the Fourteen Points with enthusiasm, but many of the Republicans and militants in Congress were cynical, fearing that Wilson would not be stern enough with Germany and showing signs of resentment at his aggrandizement of the role of sole arbiter of postwar settlements. To Lodge, who with nationalistic loyalty had generally supported Wilson's war measures, most of the Fourteen Points sounded like "mere words and general bleat about virtue being better than vice." Democratic Senator Charles S. Thomas, an earthy sixty-eight-year-old pioneer from Colorado, commented that Wilson was being "bushwhacked." Nevertheless, the President hewed to his course, promising in another eloquent message to Congress on February 11 that the peace would include "no annexations, no contributions, no punitive damages."

Soon Lodge and other Republicans separated from Wilson, demanding

Germany's unconditional surrender. "The thing to do," Lodge insisted, "is to lick Germany and tell her what arrangements we are going to make." As the congressional elections approached, Wilson recognized the need to unite as much of the country as possible behind his policies. Seeing the danger to his authority if the Republicans took control of Congress, he appealed to the voters to return Democratic majorities to both houses. It was a mistake. Angry Republicans took it as an attack on their patriotism as well as a violation of the wartime truce on politics, and ex-Presidents Roosevelt and Taft issued a jointly signed statement denouncing Wilson. When, largely as a result of other forces including economic discontent, the Republicans won the House by fifty seats and the Senate by two seats, Wilson not only lost his hold over Congress and his goal of a strong national unity behind him, but because of his ill-advised appeal seemed even to have suffered a repudiation of his peace policies on the eve of the war's end.

Under attack after the armistice for not having demanded Germany's unconditional surrender, Wilson soon afterward aroused another storm of criticism by announcing that he would personally attend the peace conference at Paris (a questionable right, according to some Americans, since it would be the first time that a President had left the country while in office) and would take with him a peace commission that would include no Senators and only one Republican, Henry White, a former ambassador to Italy. With him, as his chief adviser, would go his little-known personal confidant and counselor Colonel Edward M. House, whose credentials for the assignment even Democratic Senators questioned. "Who is this Colonel House. . . ? Whence did he come, what has he accomplished, and whither is he headed?" asked Arizona's Senator Ashurst. Overnight Wilson's popularity in Congress plummeted, and it was said that he did not have twenty friends there. "Mr. President, the House of Representatives would impeach you and the Senate convict you if they had the courage. Their lack of nerve is all that saves your removal from office," one Senator told Wilson privately. "Congress has a brainstorm but as soon as I am on the high seas they will recover," the President replied. Nevertheless, he received a chilly greeting when he addressed the opening of the last session of the Sixty-fifth Congress on December 2, 1918. The principal sore point was his snub to the prestige and importance of the Senate by excluding its participation at the peace conference. Lodge, now sixty-eight years old, slim, natty, and cantankerous, with curly gray hair and a trim white mustache and beard, was slated to become Senate majority leader and the powerful chairman of the Foreign Relations Committee, but he said that he did not care about Wilson's slight to him because he would have refused to be a rubber stamp for the President at Paris. But most Senators worried about what Wilson would do when left on his own. The threat of subordinating America's sovereignty and independence to an international League of Nations particularly concerned them. It is "a spider's web into which the American fly is invited," said Missouri's Democratic Senator James A. Reed. Wilson made no explanation of his cold indifference to Congress, but his motive appeared to be his determination to have no opposition in the American delegation.

It was just as well. The European leaders made the peace conference at Versailles a trial for Wilson, ripping apart his Fourteen Points and agreeing to his idea of a League of Nations only after he had given in to innumerable compromises—including the fastening of sole war guilt and impossible reparations of $56 billion on Germany—that made a shambles of his hopes for a just and lasting peace. Nevertheless, he believed that the League would eventually rectify the treaty's wrongs, and while a draft covenant was worked out he returned briefly to the United States, inviting the members of the foreign affairs committees of both houses to dine with him on February 26, 1919, where amid coolness and skepticism on the part of most of them he explained the treaty provisions. Two days later Lodge—now seething with a mixture of hatred for Wilson, a principled belief that the idea of a League might be all right if only it were worked out with much more care and attention to America's interests, and a tawdry political perspective that looked to Republican advantage in the 1920 presidential election—attacked the League in the Senate, pointing out that its covenant did not recognize the Monroe Doctrine, did not protect the United States from League interference in such internal matters as tariff and immigration policies, and would make the nation responsible for helping to guarantee the territorial integrity and independence of every country in the world. In a follow-up, he read to the Senate at midnight on March 3, just prior to the adjournment of the Sixty-fifth Congress, a "Round Robin" that he had prepared with Republican Senators Philander Knox of Pennsylvania and Frank Brandegee of Connecticut and that thirty-nine Senators and Senators-elect had signed. It called the League "in the form now proposed" unacceptable to the United States and urged that it be separated from the peace treaty and carefully reconsidered after "negotiating peace terms with Germany. . . ."

Wilson, about to return to Paris, was defiant, announcing that the League's covenant would be so tightly interwoven in the treaty that the Senate would not be able to separate the two but would have to vote for them together. "The Senate," he said to France's ambassador, "must take its medicine." On his return to Paris, however, Wilson secured most of the changes in the covenant that Lodge had sought. The treaty was signed at Versailles on June 28, and Wilson presented the document to the Senate of the Sixty-sixth Congress on July 10. The battle lines in that body had already formed. Leading the opposition was a group of some twelve to fifteen extreme isolationist "irreconcilables," headed by Senators La Follette, Borah of Idaho, Hiram W. Johnson of California, Miles Poindexter of Washington, and Reed of Missouri, who had already embarked on a vociferous crusade to keep America free from European entanglements. The great majority of the Republicans favored ratification after making certain changes to protect American interests; several had only mild reservations, the rest had strong reservations. Save for a few who also had mild reservations, the Democrats supported Wilson.

With public sentiment in the United States seemingly strong for ratification, Lodge—determined to win the 1920 elections by holding together the Republican irreconcilables and those with reservations—played a devious game to beat Wilson, naming irreconcilables to six of the ten Republican positions on the Foreign Relations Committee, planning to cripple the treaty with so many strong reservations that Wilson would refuse to accept them, and bottling the treaty within the committee long enough to give League opponents a chance to change public opinion. For six weeks he held public hearings while Wilson's enemies flooded the nation with anti-League propaganda financed by Andrew Mellon, a multimillionaire Pittsburgh banker, and his colleague Henry C. Frick, the coal and steel baron. Finally the President, though in poor health, took his cause directly to the people, traveling ninety-five hundred miles through the country and making thirty-seven speeches during the first three weeks in September. Suffering a collapse after a speech in Pueblo, Colorado, Wilson was rushed back to Washington, where on October 2 he was felled by a stroke that paralyzed him and placed his life in danger for several weeks. Meanwhile, on September 10, Lodge reported the treaty to the Senate with four reservations to the League's covenant and forty-five amendments to the rest of the instrument. The Democrats, aided by twelve mild-reservation Republicans, defeated the amendments. On November 6 Lodge presented the treaty again, but with fourteen, instead of four, reservations. After a stormy battle the Senate approved twelve of the reservations and added two others. Friends of the League sent messages to the incapacitated President urging him to accept the reservations, but when the minority leader, Nebraska's Gilbert M. Hitchcock, saw Wilson the President told him that Lodge's reservations provided for nullification, rather than ratification, of the treaty, and he hoped that the Democrats would vote against Lodge's resolution to ratify the treaty with the reservations. On November 19 the dutiful Democrats, almost to a man, joined the irreconcilables to defeat Lodge's ratification resolution, 55 to 35. A Democratic motion to ratify the treaty without Lodge's reservations was then beaten, 53 to 38. That night Borah, Lodge, Brandegee, Reed, and other opponents of the League celebrated their victory at the home of Republican Representative Nicholas Longworth of Ohio, who was married to Theodore Roosevelt's daughter, Alice. The scrambled eggs were cooked by the wife of another Republican from Ohio, Senator Warren G. Harding, a Lodge supporter on the Foreign Relations Committee.

The battle was not over. When a public demand arose for Wilson and Lodge to compromise their differences and allow the United States to join the League, Wilson refused, releasing a letter from his sickroom suggesting that the voters decide the issue in the 1920 presidential election, which, he said, could be a "great and solemn referendum." A bipartisan move in the

Senate reopened the debate early in 1920, but it did little good. When the irreconcilables threatened to defect from the Republican party and produce an election-year split such as had occurred in 1912, Lodge gave in to their demand not to change his original reservations. Wilson, in turn, sent messages insisting on ratification of the treaty without the Lodge reservations. In the stalemate produced by the two unyielding enemies, the treaty went down to a second, and final, defeat on March 19. Wilson's hope that the people's verdict in the fall election would reopen the treaty question was dashed by the election of Harding, who announced in his inaugural, "We seek no part in directing the destinies of the world" and, turning his back on the League, retreated, in Wilson's embittered words, into "sullen and selfish isolation." On July 2, 1921, a congressional joint resolution finally officially ended the war with Germany and Austria-Hungary.

In the meantime the United States—lacking executive direction and without any guidance or planning by Congress—moved precipitously from war to peace. The armistice was followed by rapid demobilization and by the abrupt ending of most of the war agencies and their emergency measures. The War Industries Board, halting its numerous activities, "was dissipated in a day," wrote its chief historian. The public operation of the railroads in a single system had been so successful that the railroad unions and brotherhoods urged adoption of a plan to nationalize the lines and allow the workers to participate in their management and profit. Both Wilson and the Congress rejected the proposal, and when the President announced that he would return the railroads to their private owners on March 1, 1920, Senator Albert Cummins of Iowa and Representative John J. Esch of Wisconsin quickly introduced legislation to achieve the progressive movement's last unfulfilled goals for the control of the railroads. Enacted on February 28, 1920, their Transportation Act further strengthened the ICC, empowering it to regulate all traffic and service, set rates, supervise railroad financing, consolidate lines, and permit the pooling of freight. Other progressive-supported measures followed, including the establishment of the federally owned Merchant Fleet Corporation to operate vessels built during the war and still in government hands, and the Federal Power Commission to license the building, operation, and regulation of hydroelectric projects on waters in the public domain. Finally, with women already able to vote in twenty-three states, Congress, in June, 1919, approved the Nineteenth Amendment. Prohibiting the denial of the right to vote on account of sex, it became part of the Constitution on August 26, 1920, in time for women in every state to vote in that year's presidential election.

In June the Republicans met at Chicago with no outstanding presidential candidate (Roosevelt had died in January, 1919). The delegates finally settled on Ohio's "favorite son," Senator Warren G. Harding, a cheerful and gregarious man whose handsome chiseled features, silver hair, and dark eyebrows conveyed to many an image of what a President ought to look like, but whose genius, wrote historian John D. Hicks, "lay not so much in his ability to conceal his thought as in the absence of any serious thought to reveal." Babbitt-like, superficial, anxious to be in step with public opinion, Harding lacked strong convictions on most issues. For Vice President the delegates chose the cold and aloof governor of Massachusetts, Calvin Coolidge, who had become a hero to conservatives by helping to break a strike of Boston policemen. Coolidge appeared so austere and joyless that H. L. Mencken later characterized him as having been "weaned on a pickle." The Democrats, who met at San Francisco on June 28, also lacked a front-runner and were as confused as the Republicans. Finally the bosses of several of the largest states took over, and on the forty-fourth ballot the weary delegates accepted their choice, James M. Cox, the governor of Ohio. The delegates then named Cox's vice-presidential selection, Franklin D. Roosevelt of New York, Wilson's assistant secretary of the navy and a prominent supporter of the League.

The Republican platform rejected Wilson's League but approved an "agreement among nations to preserve the peace of the world"—a deliberately ambiguous statement written by Elihu Root to mean all things to all people. Implying, also, an end to social and economic progressivism and a return to pre-Theodore Roosevelt conservatism, the platform promised an increased tariff and tax reductions. Though Cox and Roosevelt labored to make the election the "great and solemn referendum" on the League that Wilson desired, the American people, tired of world problems and turning inward, were more captivated by Harding's "back to normalcy" and "America First" appeals, and on Election Day they gave the Republicans a landslide victory. Harding's electoral-vote margin, 404 to 127, was matched by sweeping congressional triumphs that gave the Republicans majorities of 167 in the next House of Representatives and 22 in the Senate. Even Champ Clark, the popular former Democratic Speaker, was beaten in Missouri.

The winter months of 1920–21 were bitter ones for Wilson, who had partly recovered from his stroke but whose feeble condition made him a recluse in the White House, guarded from the outside world by his wife and physician. On March 4, 1921, he rode to the Capitol in an open car with Harding, Senator Knox, and the aging "Uncle Joe" Cannon. At the Capitol steps the three Republicans left him, and Wilson was taken in a wheelchair through a side entrance to the President's Room, where he signed a few last bills. He did not wait to see Harding take the oath of office, but left for the Washington house he had bought for his retirement. There he lived in semi-seclusion, cast aside by Americans as thoroughly as his dream for the League, and on February 3, 1924, he died. Senator Lodge was named to a committee to represent Congress at his funeral, but at Mrs. Wilson's request the Massachusetts Senator was excluded from the service.

The return to "normalcy" proclaimed by Harding lasted for twelve years under three relatively passive Republican Presidents and was marked by an isolationist policy of withdrawal from overseas "entanglements"—an impossibility, since the United States was the capitalist world's chief creditor and economically the strongest and most influential nation on earth—and a domestic philosophy that frankly favored big business, abandoned social and economic reforms, and looked to free private enterprise rather than government to solve problems. In effect an irresponsible attempt to turn back the clock to a less complicated time, the period's failings, ending in catastrophe, stemmed in large measure from the shortsighted and selfish desires of an electorate grown cynical and materialistic in the aftermath of the war. Nor was all consensus. Conflicting economic and regional groups, as well as progressive and reform minorities, pulled and tugged on the unwilling Presidents and kept Congress, through most of the period, at odds with itself and with the chief executives.

In a reaction to its difficulties with Wilson, the Senate intended to reassert its authority over the White House. Even during the 1920 campaign, Lodge and other Republican Senators let their candidate know not too subtly that they expected him, when elected, to "sign whatever bill the Senate sent him and not send bills for the Senate to pass," and Harding demonstrated in his few ineffectual attempts to exert control that he had neither the will nor the capacity to dominate Congress. His successor, Calvin Coolidge, who presided over an unprecedented national prosperity and opposed any governmental action that might rock the boat, refrained almost entirely from pushing legislation and sat in the White House largely ignored by Congress. The last of the triumvirate, the rigid and petulant Herbert Hoover, was politically awkward, felt that the government should be no more than an umpire even when the boom collapsed, and got nowhere with a hostile Congress.

Despite the weakness of the executives, the Senate provided little leadership. In April, 1921, the Republican Committee on Committees, headed by Senator Brandegee, forced through a long-overdue consolidation of standing Senate committees, reducing them from seventy-four to thirty-four, abolishing some that were obsolete (including one on Revolutionary War Claims), and increasing the Republican membership on the various committees. When the Democrats complained Brandegee retorted, "The Republicans are responsible to the country for legislation and must have control of committees. That's not tyranny; that's . . . the rule of the majority." The next year, to mesh with the establishment of the executive branch's Bureau of the Budget and the initiation of a single overall annual budget, the Senate—following similar action by the House in 1920—reconcentrated authority over all spending in the Appropriations Committee. Despite such centralizing moves, however, the Republicans were rent by divisions that not only precluded the reinstatement of a tight party control such as Allison and Aldrich had once maintained, but put the actual power in the Senate in the hands of a large group of insurgent Republicans, mostly from the Midwest and Northwest, who, under the leadership of such men as William S. Kenyon of Iowa, Arthur Capper of Kansas, Charles L. McNary of Oregon, and Edwin F. Ladd of North Dakota, as well as La Follette and

Norris, stood together as a "farm bloc" and, opposing legislation favorable to big business, cooperated more with southern agrarian Democrats than with the old guard regulars of their own party. Brandegee, Philander Knox, and others called them traitors to the party, for although they did not consider themselves antiadministration, they—as well as other special-interest blocs—created chaos in the legislative process and frustrated the passage of party measures.

The situation became worse after the Republicans suffered disastrous losses in the 1922 congressional elections and had their Senate majority cut from twenty-two to six. As part of an insurgent attempt in the next Congress to gain control of the Senate from the regulars, La Follette, the second-ranking Republican on the Interstate Commerce Committee, attempted to win the chairmanship. The regulars resisted in a fight that disrupted the Senate for a month and finally helped to elect the committee's ranking Democrat, Senator Ellison D. "Cotton Ed" Smith, a large, lumbering demagogue from South Carolina, rather than give the post to La Follette. In 1924 the Wisconsin Senator split with the Republicans and ran for President as a Progressive against Coolidge and the Democratic candidate, John W. Davis. He won sixteen percent of the popular vote but carried only his own state, and the Republicans, picking up five more seats in the Senate, punished the insurgent Senators in the next Congress by barring them from Republican conferences and appointments to Republican vacancies on committees. La Follette died in June, 1925; his thirty-year-old son, Robert M. La Follette, Jr., also a progressive Republican, was elected to fill his vacancy; and he and other insurgent Republicans continued to frustrate the conservative party leadership, finally voting regularly with the Democratic liberals during Hoover's administration and being castigated by an angry Senator George H. Moses of New Hampshire as "sons of the wild jackass."

In the House the Republican leaders were able to maintain stronger party control, but even that accomplished little, for it enabled the House to challenge the Senate for mastery, leading to conflicts that further hobbled the party's legislative programs. In 1921 the Republicans re-elected as Speaker Frederick H. Gillett of Massachusetts, first named to the post in 1919, but they centered their leadership in an eight-member Steering Committee chaired by the majority leader, which, with the Speaker and the Rules Committee chairman, met almost every day. The arbitrary action of the leadership and of powerful committee chairmen in blocking consideration of bills they opposed often produced complaints by Representatives. "You can go to hell," the Rules Committee chairman once told his committee members whose resolutions he had pocketed. "It makes no difference what a majority of you decide. If it meets with my disapproval, it shall not be done; I am the committee; in me repose absolute obstructive powers." When the 1922 elections cut the Republican majority in the House, a controlling faction of progressives held up the re-election of Speaker Gillett for two days until Nicholas Longworth, the new majority leader, agreed to a full debate that produced a number of reforms, including one that made it easier to discharge a committee from further consideration of a bill and force its chairman to return it to the House. That reform was short-lived. After La Follette's defeat in 1924, the increased Republican majority in the House punished progressive members, who were ousted from important committees and dropped to the bottom of others. Longworth was elected Speaker and a new discharge rule was adopted, so strong that Democratic Representative Charles R. Crisp of Georgia (the son of the former Speaker) complained that it "hermetically seals the door against any bill ever coming out of a committee when the Steering Committee or the majority leaders desire to kill the bill without putting the members of this House on record on the measure." Thereafter, for the next six years of Republican control, Longworth—bald, businesslike, a stern practitioner of majority-party rule—ran the House on a tight rein.

Among the many measures that Republicans in the House and Senate bounced back and forth in disagreement with each other was a so-called Lame Duck Amendment, which Norris first introduced in 1923. Norris hoped to cut down on Senate filibusters by ending the short sessions of Congress after elections, when men who had been defeated still sat in Congress and so many of the filibusters occurred. The House leaders had a different idea; they liked the short sessions, whose definite termination date on March 3 helped them control legislation. Five times the Republicans in the Senate voted for Norris's resolution, and five times the House Republicans blocked it. Finally, on the sixth attempt, in 1932, the House, now controlled by Democrats, passed it, and on February 6, 1933, it was declared ratified as the Twentieth Amendment, providing that Congress should meet annually on January 3, that the terms of Senators and Representatives would begin on January 3 of the year following an election, and that the President and Vice President would take office on January 20. The amendment, however, did not end filibusters, and the principal weapon against them remained the cloture provision of Rule 22, which the Senate had passed in 1917 and which it modified on several occasions.

During the twelve years of Republican Presidents there were considerable stresses over America's foreign relations. Republican realists such as Elihu Root and Harding's secretary of state, Charles Evans Hughes—and even the three Presidents themselves—recognized that the United States, simply for the protection of its own interests, had to assume a responsible role in world affairs. But the League's opponents had done such a masterful propaganda job that few in politics would risk the wrath of public opinion, which had become overwhelmingly xenophobic and stayed so throughout the period. As a result, American foreign actions were either forthright assertions of national interests—for example, a 1921 treaty with Colombia, pushed behind the scenes in the Senate by the oil companies, that opened that country's oil fields to Americans—or compromising, self-defeating attempts by the realists to be responsible and yet not be attacked by Borah and other senatorial watchdogs alert for "foreign entanglements."

Borah, who after the war began to urge naval disarmament as one way to reduce sources of international friction, unwittingly provided the Harding administration with a chance to show responsible world leadership without getting involved in the League. After the Idaho Senator, a shaggy, publicity-conscious independent who pursued causes with the zeal of a holy crusader, continued during three sessions of Congress to offer a resolution calling on the United States to invite Great Britain and Japan to a conference to reduce naval expenditures, Harding finally accepted the proposal and expanded on it, hosting, with Senate assent, a huge Armament Conference of nine of the world's principal powers in Washington during the winter of 1921–22. Appointing both Lodge and the Democratic leader, Senator Underwood, to the American delegation, Harding ensured Senate ratification of the conference's results—nine separate treaties, ranging from one that provided for a ten-year naval construction holiday and set a ratio of capital ships among the five leading naval powers, to agreements over China, peace-keeping in the Pacific, the restricting of submarine warfare, and the outlawing of poison gas in war. The treaties eased tensions with Japan and seemed a step in the right direction, and in ratifying them the Senate underscored the public's feeling that while they would not interfere with the nation's freedom of independent action, they were still somehow an American triumph that would guarantee, better than the League, an enduring world peace.

Somewhat similarly, the United States participated in another naval conference in Geneva in 1927 (which failed in its attempt to curb the construction of smaller naval vessels), the Kellogg-Briand Pact signed in Paris in 1928 renouncing war and pledging to settle all future disputes by peaceful means (a moralistic promise so free of legal obligations that the Senate ratified it 85 to 1), and in additional disarmament conferences at London in 1930 and at Geneva from 1932 to 1934. The Republican administrations trod gingerly at home about such involvements, consulting dutifully with Borah and other isolationists and putting Senators of both parties on American delegations, but the bankruptcy of their policy of avoiding commitments to collective action became evident with Japan's 1931 aggression in Manchuria. Hoover's secretary of state, Henry L. Stimson, denounced the Japanese actions, but when the British refused to join in a joint declaration of nonrecognition of Japan's conquest of Manchuria, preferring to work through the League, and the League in turn threatened to impose sanctions on Japan, Hoover forced Stimson to announce that "we do not intend to get into war with Japan." The League backed down, Stimson had to be content with a hollow declaration that the United States would never recognize conquests made in violation of treaties to which she was a party, and Japan continued her aggressions in China unhindered.

312

Unrealism and lack of executive responsibility also helped pave the way for disaster in Europe. The impossible war reparations the Allies had fastened on Germany soon brought that nation to the point of collapse. When she was unable to continue paying the Allies, they found it difficult to repay their own war debts to the United States—a problem for which the American people and the Congress had little sympathy and which the Republicans compounded by raising high tariffs against the purchase of European products. The Republican administrations first demanded repayment of the war debts in full, but gradually parts of the debts were canceled and interest was lowered. The worldwide depression and the raising of American tariff barriers even higher continued to squeeze the European nations, and in 1931 Hoover had to declare a one-year moratorium on the payment of all inter-Allied debts and reparations. Two years later more than ninety percent of the Germans' reparations were canceled, but by then the damage had been done. Germany's humiliation and inability to recover economically helped the rise of Hitler, who renounced the Versailles Treaty, and, save for Finland, all the Allies, for their part, simply defaulted after 1933 on any further payments of their war debts to the United States.

Among domestic issues in the 1920's, the plight of the farmer, whose booming wartime economy had crashed and then—in contrast to the rising prosperity of the country as a whole—had stayed depressed, was a principal factor in the conflicts within Congress and between Congress and the Presidents. The farm bloc and its progressive allies not only pushed for specific legislation that the administration and the Republican leadership often opposed, but frustrated administration measures if they seemed to favor other interests at the expense of the farmers. Considerable time was given to agricultural measures during the twelve-year period, and a number of bills were enacted, though—because of the basic conservatism of the farm bloc leaders—they dealt mostly with the symptoms rather than the causes of the farmers' problems and were generally unsuccessful. In a special session of the Sixty-seventh Congress that Harding called soon after his inaugural to lower the wartime taxes and reinstitute the old-time Republican nostrum of higher tariffs for business, the farm-state members of Congress threw the leadership into confusion by insisting that consideration of an "emergency" tariff, with high protection for agricultural products, precede work on tax revision. The farm spokesmen won, and in 1921 Harding signed a tariff act, pushed through by Representative Joseph W. Fordney of Michigan, chairman of the House Ways and Means Committee, ignoring duties on most manufactured items but placing high rates on wheat, corn, meat, and other agricultural products. This did not satisfy the farm bloc, however, and the Sixty-seventh Congress produced a spate of farm legislation that included establishing controls on packers, stockyards, and grain exchanges; increasing credit and the availability of loans; permitting farmers' cooperatives to buy and sell in interstate commerce without fear of antitrust prosecution; and seeking to raise prices by disposing of surpluses. The farmers, however, continued to be confronted by glutted markets and low prices. In 1924 Oregon's Senator McNary and Representative Gilbert N. Haugen of Iowa began a five-year campaign for a relief bill that—by authorizing the government to purchase the annual surplus of various commodities and either hold them until prices rose or sell them overseas, recouping any losses by an "equalization fee" that the producers would pay—was designed to increase demand, remove surpluses, and make prices rise. Much modified, the plan was enacted in 1929 as the Agricultural Marketing Act, but because it had no provision for controlling production, farmers simply produced more and the government kept paying for their surpluses. Deemed a failure after the spending of $180 million, the program was ended in 1933.

As had happened after the Civil War, veterans too became a special-interest pressure group. The American Legion and other veterans' groups demanded a bonus to pay veterans the difference between their servicemen's compensation and the wages civilian war workers had received. The proposal became a sure vote-getting device for members of Congress (conversely, veterans' groups impugned their patriotism if they opposed it), and in 1921 Harding was able to stave off passage of a prohibitively expensive bonus only by making a special visit to the Senate and pleading with members to put aside a bonus bill until they revised taxes and balanced the budget. Several Senators denounced the President for interfering in the Senate's business, and the House complained that Harding should have talked to the Representatives, who had authority over money bills, but the bonus was temporarily shelved. The next year a bonus bill was passed but Harding vetoed it. The veterans did not give up their fight, and in 1924, a presidential election year, Congress again passed the bill and managed to override Coolidge's veto. The act provided veterans with twenty-year endowment policies of $1.25 a day for overseas service and $1 a day for service in the United States, on which they could borrow from the government up to about twenty-three percent of the policy's value. In 1931, when the Depression sharpened, a new bill was introduced to permit loans of fifty percent of the value of the policies. Hoover vetoed it but Congress overrode his veto, and the Democrats then proposed that the full bonus be paid immediately in cash. As distress mounted, veterans took up this demand, and to bring pressure on the government some seventeen thousand of them joined a "Bonus March" on Washington in the spring of 1932. On June 15, with the veterans living in makeshift camps around the Capitol, the House passed the Patman Bonus Bill, introduced by Wright Patman of Texas, to pay the bonus, but the Senate defeated the measure. The government then provided money to help the veterans return home, and all but about two thousand departed. On July 28 Hoover, overreacting to his fear of their continued presence in Washington, called out federal troops, who forcibly drove the rest of the marchers out of the city. Three years later a New Deal Congress passed the Patman bill again. This time President Roosevelt established a precedent by going before a joint session of Congress on May 22, 1935, to announce his veto, explaining that it was too inflationary. The Senate sustained the veto, but the next year, when both houses passed a somewhat modified version of the measure and then overrode another presidential veto, the government finally paid the bonus.

As early as the first year of Harding's administration, rumors of graft and corruption began to circulate in Washington, some of them implying collusion between the executive branch and oil interests. In 1921 Harding had signed an executive order transferring jurisdiction over two naval oil reserves from the Navy Department to the Interior Department, and both of them, Elk Hills in California and Teapot Dome in Wyoming, had then been leased to private oil operators. Though pressure mounted for a congressional investigation, the Republican leaders in the House refused to act. In April 1922, Senate Democrats and insurgent Republicans authorized such an investigation by the Senate Committee on Public Lands and Surveys, and for more than a year Democratic Senator Thomas J. Walsh of Montana headed a quiet but thorough inquiry. Harding died suddenly in San Francisco on August 2, 1923, and shortly afterward scandals in other parts of his administration began to come to light. A Senate investigation of the Veterans' Bureau resulted in the exposure of wholesale bribery and corruption on the part of its director, who was ultimately sent to jail. Walsh, a soft-spoken sixty-four-year-old lawyer with a clipped mustache, began his hearings on Teapot Dome and Elk Hills on October 25, soon revealing that Secretary of the Interior Albert B. Fall, a former Senator from New Mexico, had accepted bribes for the naval reserve leases from oilmen Edward L. Doheny and Harry F. Sinclair. The testimony created a sensation, and both Fall and the secretary of the navy resigned, Fall being sent to prison and fined $100,000.

Still the scandals went on. The Alien Property Custodian was investigated and sent to jail, and another Senate inquiry, more melodramatic than all the others, revealed favoritism, corruption, and various sordid activities in the Justice Department, centered on Attorney General Harry M. Daugherty, a ruthless and unsavory hack politician and lobbyist from Ohio who had managed Harding's presidential campaign. The inquiry, conducted in free-swinging style by Montana's other Senator, Burton K. Wheeler, a tough first-term progressive Democrat, provided headlines about an "Ohio gang" of Harding's cronies who had followed the President to Washington and set themselves up around Daugherty as influence peddlers. During Wheeler's hearings files were rifled, papers stolen, and threats and espionage engaged in, and the feisty Senator himself was subjected to a false charge of bribery—all of it traced to the Federal Bureau of Investigation, which was working for Daugherty. In the end Coolidge fired Daugherty and the head of the FBI, who was succeeded by his assistant, J. Edgar Hoover. Though Harding himself was not implicated in the scandals, he had undoubtedly helped to obstruct justice before his death by concealing knowledge or suspicion about some of them, and the Senate's revelations cast an enduring cloud over the reputation of his administration. Only the unquestionable moral character of the new President, Calvin Coolidge, permitted the Republicans to regain the nation's faith and retain the Presidency in 1924.

Standing above the scandals also was the unperturbed symbol of all that the business elements most trusted in the Republican administrations, Andrew Mellon, who served as secretary of the treasury from 1921 to 1932. As economic mentor of the three Presidents ("The business of the United States is business," agreed Coolidge, his chief admirer), Mellon encouraged government economy, balanced budgets, debt reduction, and low interest rates for business, worked for tax, tariff, and fiscal legislation that had the effect of concentrating wealth and purchasing power in the hands of the few, and even after the Depression closed in claimed that the only cure was to give business freedom and assistance to make money so it could provide jobs. Some called it the trickle-down theory—give to the top, and some will trickle down to everyone—a notion reversed by the New Deal, which made a better case for the opposite belief that money given to the top stays there, while money given to everyone moves upward. Mellon was bitterly opposed by the western and southern farm bloc and the progressives in Congress and often had to compromise with them, but he got much of what he wanted in the revenue acts of the twenties, which steadily reduced taxes on corporations and the wealthy. At the same time he supported increased tariffs. The Fordney-McCumber Tariff of 1922 started a reversion to the pre-Wilson principle of a high protective tariff climaxed by the Smoot-Hawley Tariff of 1931, which in the face of increasing international economic stress, raised outrageously high barriers against countries that could not pay their debts and thereafter had to devalue their currencies and erect retaliatory tariffs of their own.

The Wall Street crash of October and November, 1929, began the bankruptcy of the economic policies of Mellon and the administrations he served. As the Depression deepened he—as well as the conservative leadership of both parties in Congress—clung to belief in the automatic workings of the business cycle to effect a cure. "Let the slump liquidate itself," Mellon advised. "Liquidate labor, liquidate stocks, liquidate the farmers. . . . People will work harder, live a more moral life. Values will be adjusted, and enterprising people will pick up the wrecks from less competent people." Congressional leaders seemed to agree, for they too did nothing. The off-year elections of 1930, reflecting the nation's growing distress, finally brought a change. The Democrats won control of the House for the first time since 1919 and reduced the Republicans' control of the Senate to one. With a leadership that was still essentially conservative, the Democrats named as Speaker of the Seventy-second Congress white-haired, ruddy-faced John Nance "Cactus Jack" Garner of Texas, who was sixty-two years old and had been in the House for twenty-eight years. At the same time Hoover, under mounting pressure, at last began to try to stem the economy's deterioration.

Though Hoover differed with Mellon—who resigned in 1932—and now

316

accepted the need for governmental action, the measures he supported failed because of limitations he placed on their implementation. Many of them relied on voluntary action or on execution by states and localities rather than the federal government. Others were designed to help business in ways that had become impractical. None offered aid or relief directly to the people, since Hoover considered such use of federal funds unconstitutional. Nevertheless, the first session of the Seventy-second Congress, which met on December 7, 1931, passed a number of the administration's emergency bills, including one setting up the Reconstruction Finance Corporation (RFC) to make loans to hard-pressed banks, insurance companies, railroads, and farm mortgage associations; the Glass-Steagall Banking Act to counteract a run on bank gold reserves that had led to a contraction of credit; and the Federal Home Loan Bank Act, which set up regional banks to assist building-and-loan associations, savings banks, and insurance companies in providing long-term loans for mortgages and housing construction.

At the same time, an effort to raise new taxes to balance the federal budget resulted in a dramatic revolt in the House against a general sales tax, led by the diminutive but fiery Fiorello LaGuardia of New York, who through most of the 1920's—as a Republican, a Socialist, and a Progressive —had been an eastern ally of the insurgents, and North Carolina's Robert L. Doughton, a tall, dour Democratic member of the Ways and Means Committee. Heralding a new, temporary alliance between the northern labor and urban interests and those of the farmers, the two men succeeded in having the House kill the sales tax, which LaGuardia, in a ringing speech, characterized as a "soak-the-poor" measure. The volatile New Yorker, with Senator Norris, also achieved the passage of the Norris-LaGuardia Act, which outlawed "yellow dog" contracts (binding an employee to an agreement not to join a union) and limited the use of federal injunctions in labor disputes. Another measure, the Wagner-Garner Bill, worked out principally by Senator Robert F. Wagner of New York and passed in the House under Speaker Garner's direction, provided for a huge public-works program for the unemployed and added capital for the RFC to lend, but Hoover quickly vetoed it as a "pork-barrel" measure, and his veto was sustained.

At the Democratic convention in Chicago in June, 1932, Garner broke up a "stop Roosevelt" movement by throwing his support to New York Governor Franklin D. Roosevelt; former New York governor Alfred E. Smith, who had run unsuccessfully against Hoover in 1928, walked out in a huff; and the delegates nominated Roosevelt for President and Garner for Vice President. Roosevelt pledged to the delegates "a new deal for the American people." Renominated by the Republicans, Hoover went down to a crushing defeat in the November elections, which saw the Democrats win the House and Senate by large majorities. In the last of the lame-duck sessions, during the gloomy winter of 1932–33, Congress overcame a one-man filibuster by Senator Morris Sheppard of Texas, who in 1917 had introduced the resolution for the Eighteenth Amendment, to approve the Twenty-first

Amendment, repealing the much-hated prohibition law. Even President Harding and members of Congress had violated that measure, a scandal having occurred on one occasion when a bootlegger, known to Congressmen as the "Man in the Green Hat," was arrested while making deliveries in the House Office Building. The nation hailed repeal, which went into effect on December 5, 1933.

The economy, meanwhile, went into a climactic crisis as banks closed throughout the country, and members of Congress appeared on the House and Senate floors wearing money belts that contained all their cash. In the last days of the session, with fourteen million unemployed, industry coming to a halt, and the nation facing complete collapse, Congress became turbulent, arguing ineffectively but, like the outgoing President, taking no steps to cope with the emergency. The country was filled with angry talk of revolution and the need for a dictator when Congress, reflecting a sense of helplessness and approaching doom, finally adjourned on March 3, 1933. The next day Roosevelt, radiating the assurance and determination of a commander in chief, took over, inspiring sudden confidence with his dynamic assertions that "the only thing we have to fear is fear itself" and that "this nation asks for action, and action now. . . ." Declaring that, if necessary, he would ask Congress for "broad Executive power to wage a war against the emergency," he promptly set in motion a whirlwind program of action. He called Congress into special session on March 9 and, making use of an almost-forgotten authority contained in the Trading with the Enemy Act of 1917, declared a four-day national bank "holiday" (the connotation of the word even worked to reduce anxiety) and placed an embargo on the exportation of gold. When Congress met he was ready for it with the Emergency Banking Relief Act, outlawing the hoarding of gold, giving the President broad authority over the Federal Reserve system, and providing for the orderly reopening of the banks. The bill had not yet been printed: the only copy was read to the House while new members were still looking for their seats, and after thirty-eight minutes of supporting speeches the House with a unanimous shout passed the measure. The Senate approved the bill, 73 to 7, at seven-thirty that evening, and an hour later the President signed it. With confidence restored, the banks soon started to reopen.

Roosevelt had intended only to present the banking act in the special session, but the support of the nation and the receptive mood of Congress decided him to keep going. Aided by his Cabinet members, a "brain trust" of academic advisers headed by Raymond Moley, Rexford Guy Tugwell, and Adolf A. Berle, Jr., and numerous experts in each field, he sent a torrent of bills to Congress, and in a dramatic period of one hundred days the legislators enacted a major program of New Deal laws for relief and recovery.

Among the principal measures were the Economy Act, to balance normal expenditures by permitting the President to cut the salaries of government employees and veterans' pensions for nonservice-connected disabilities, enacted on March 20; the Beer-Wine Revenue Act, legalizing and taxing beer and light wines (March 22); an act establishing the Civilian Conservation Corps (CCC) to provide work in reforestation and on conservation projects for 250,000 jobless men (March 31); the Federal Emergency Relief Act (FERA), with $500 million to be granted to states and municipalities for relief through the Reconstruction Finance Corporation (May 12); the sweeping Agricultural Adjustment Act (AAA), to lift agricultural prices to "parity" with industrial prices, to grant subsidies to farmers who curtailed acreage or production to eliminate surpluses, to refinance farm mortgages, and to give the President authority to inflate the currency (May 12); the Tennessee Valley Authority (TVA), expanding on a measure twice introduced by the public power advocate, Senator Norris, and twice vetoed by Coolidge and Hoover, to set up an independent public corporation to construct dams and power plants, sell electric power and nitrogen fertilizer, and develop the economy and social welfare in the Tennessee River basin (May 18); the Federal Securities Act, to require full disclosure to investors of information regarding new securities (May 27); a joint resolution supporting the abandonment of the gold standard (June 5); the Banking Act of 1933, creating a Federal Bank Deposit Insurance Corporation to guarantee deposits up to $5,000 and make modifications in the banking system (June 16); the Emergency Railroad Transportation Act, to aid the financial reorganization of railroads and eliminate duplication of service (June 16); and, finally, the innovative National Industrial Recovery Act, developed from a bill introduced by Senator Hugo L. Black of Alabama, to revive business and reduce unemployment by creating the National Recovery Administration (NRA) to supervise the drawing up of industry-wide codes of fair practices by business in order to raise prices and limit production without fear of antitrust prosecution, the Public Works Administration (PWA) to spend $3.3 billion putting the unemployed to work on a vast construction program of roads, public buildings, and other projects, and the National Labor Board to enforce the rights of labor "to organize and bargain collectively through representatives of their own choosing" (June 16).

All these measures, passed hastily (eleven of the major bills received a total of only forty hours of debate in Congress) and setting up numerous new "alphabet agencies" (known popularly only by their initials), rebuilt the nation's self-assurance and reinvigorated the economy. As a whole, they reflected no overall plan but were amalgamations of old ideas, innovative concepts, and improvisations culled from hundreds of sources to cope with emergencies and try to bring about long-needed reforms. They were, said Roosevelt in his book *On Our Way*, published in 1934, "a satisfactory combination" of "the progressive ideas expounded by Theodore Roosevelt of a partnership between business and government and also of the determination of Woodrow Wilson that business should be subjected, through the power of government, to drastic legal limitations against abuses." Certain acts were contradictory (some economizing, others spending heavily), some had harmful side effects (the AAA, while helping most farmers, hurt sharecroppers and tenant farmers when owners took their lands out of production), and others failed to achieve their purpose. Frankly, explained Roosevelt, it was all experimentation; if one thing did not work, something else could be tried.

The members of Congress were bewildered. They sensed an inconsistency in the bills, and most of them had little idea what they were voting on or what the effects of individual bills would be. When one reporter surveyed Congressmen about where the New Deal was going, several replied, "That's what I want to ask you." Senator Ashurst wrote, "Under our new laws (some of them half-baked), many of our tested standards . . . may be jettisoned. . . . Social control over competitive and economic enterprise may be on the way. Who knows?" The fact was that in the Hundred Days a combination of circumstances—the crisis conditions, Roosevelt's immense popular support, the presence of large Democratic majorities in both houses (including 131 freshmen Democratic Representatives who were mostly willing to do what they were told), Republican memberships that were small, leaderless, and cowed, the eager loyalty on the part of the Democratic congressional leadership, and Roosevelt's own tactical genius—permitted the new President to dictate the course of legislation.

Both houses of Congress contained numerous potential dissidents but serious resistance was rare, and many Republicans supported the administration's bills rather than risk the lash of public opinion for obstructing recovery. In the Senate, where many southern Democrats, through long years of being re-elected, had forged by seniority to the chairmanship of committees, Roosevelt was his own legislative leader, being aided principally by Vice President Garner and a trio of southerners—the blunt and bulldog-like majority leader, Joseph T. Robinson of Arkansas, Finance Committee Chairman Byron "Pat" Harrison of Mississippi, and James F. Byrnes of South Carolina. Robinson revived the Democratic caucus, and, by a 50–3 vote, he won agreement from the Democratic Senators to make a majority vote in the caucus binding on them all, unless a Senator felt it violated his conscientious judgment or a pledge made to his constituents.

In the House (where a census-reapportionment bill had finally been passed in 1929 stabilizing membership at 435 and establishing a permanent system for reapportionment after each census) the big Democratic majority, led by a new Speaker, Henry T. Rainey of Illinois, and majority leader Joseph W. Byrns of Tennessee, set up a Steering Committee composed of Rainey, Byrns, the whip, the chairmen of Ways and Means, Rules, and the party caucus, and fifteen regional spokesmen. But the real power in the House lay with the Rules Committee, chaired by Edward W. Pou of North Carolina, which brought most of Roosevelt's measures to the House floor under special "closed" or "gag" rules that limited debate, waived points of order, and barred all but committee amendments. Little opposition was registered during the Hundred Days in 1933, but in January, 1934, the Rules Committee, wishing to smother developing opposition to the slashes in government salaries and veterans' pensions under the Economy Act of 1933, brought in a rule barring amendments during the new session to appropriation bills that would conflict with the Economy Act. Minority leader Bertrand H. Snell of New York objected, calling it "the most vicious, the most far-reaching special rule" ever proposed. The Rules Committee just managed to get the rule approved, 197 to 192, with many Democrats joining the Republicans to show their displeasure at being "hog-tied" through the whole session. The practical result of such tight control was that most work on bills was accomplished, as in the Senate, in committees, and both houses, particularly during the 1933 session, often had from ten to twenty committees busy in sessions day and night.

In foreign affairs Roosevelt also moved with drama, implementing a "Good Neighbor policy" toward Latin America (which Hoover had actually begun though with less fanfare) that agreed, to the satisfaction of the Latin nations, that "no state has the right to intervene in the internal or external affairs of another"; pulling out of—and wrecking—the London Economic Conference in July, 1933, because he would not cooperate in the stabilization of currencies until the United States dollar had become further depreciated; and on November 16, 1933, extending recognition to Soviet Russia after sixteen years of refusing to accredit its Communist government.

When the first New Deal Congress ended on June 15, 1933, not all Democratic members were happy with what had happened. Roosevelt had gone far beyond any other President in asserting executive authority, not only asking for legislation but sending over a brief message and a detailed draft of each bill he had wanted passed, and many Congressmen resented the feeling of being "lackeys" or "rubber stamps" of a chief executive who had taken over the legislative function. Others were contemptuous of the intellectual advisers, nonpoliticians, and New Deal bureaucrats who had framed the bills, pushed them through the legislature, and now held high positions in the executive branch. Not a few, moreover, were distrustful of what they had legislated and of where the New Deal was taking the country. They shared the fears of the conservative Republicans—the progressives, almost to a man, supported Roosevelt—worrying whether the President's advisers, many of whom were suspected of being ultra-radical, were insidiously steering the nation toward fascism or communism; a number of southerners, particularly, were concerned about the extension of federal power at the expense of the states.

Five conservative southern Democratic Senators, as historian James T. Patterson makes clear in *Congressional Conservatism and the New Deal,* "consistently opposed the President" and, with one exception, would continue to do so through World War II, providing a determined nucleus of opposition to Roosevelt. They were the peppery Carter Glass of Virginia, Wilson's secretary of the treasury, now seventy-five years old; Oklahoma's blind and angry Thomas P. Gore, sixty-three years old and so hostile to government paternalism, even when the Depression had rendered private enterprise helpless, that he would lose his Senate seat in 1936; Millard E. Tydings, forty-three years old, a slim Maryland lawyer with a handsome, impeccable appearance and top-drawer business and social connections; Josiah W. Bailey of North Carolina, sixty, solemn and moralistic; and Harry F. Byrd, Virginia's junior Senator, forty-six, former governor and head of the powerful Virginia Democratic political machine, a Shenandoah Valley apple-growing squire, and brother of the famous aviator-explorer Admiral Richard E. Byrd.

Despite such rumblings and elements of dissent, Roosevelt, by and large, continued to have his own way in the next session of Congress, which began in January, 1934, and dutifully passed a stream of relief and reform legislation to supplement and extend the laws enacted in 1933. Among the more significant new measures were the Gold Reserve Act, permitting the President to fix the price of gold; an act creating the Securities and Exchange Commission (SEC) to regulate the nation's securities markets; the Communications Act, setting up a Federal Communications Commission; the National Housing Act, creating a Federal Housing Administration (FHA); and various agricultural and urban relief measures. The executive's mastery over the legislature, still supported by public opinion, was never seriously in question.

Congress, meanwhile, gained attention for itself through two highly spectacular investigations. One of them, conducted by the Senate Banking and Currency Committee, with Ferdinand Pecora as its chief counsel, made sensational headlines during 1933 by studying the stock market collapse, the practices of the securities exchanges, and the financial dealings of major banking houses. The nation's leading bankers were subpoenaed by the committee and day after day were forced to reveal malpractices, dubious financial operations, and details of personal transactions that incensed most members of Congress. The evidence resulted in many of the regulations and reforms contained in New Deal measures. The second investigation, resulting from the long growth of revulsion against World War I and a belief that munitions makers, the "merchants of death," had played a sinister role in America's entry into that conflict, was authorized by the Senate in April, 1934. A special committee, with a majority of Democrats but chaired by Senator Gerald P. Nye, an eloquent Progressive Republican from North Dakota, set out to prove the guilt of the munitions industry. In public hearings that continued until 1936, businessmen, industrialists, and bankers revealed the international dealings of the arms makers and their large profits, but the committee failed to establish anything more than the need to control the munitions industry. Various revelations of bribery, conniving, and arms deals that involved foreign nationals and other nations, however, increased isolationist sentiment and strengthened national support for neutrality legislation as conflict erupted overseas.

In the 1934 fall congressional elections the Democrats won another enormous victory, increasing by nine their majorities in each house. Speaker

Rainey had died, and when the Seventy-fourth Congress met on January 3, 1935, the 319 Democratic Representatives, who almost engulfed the Republican membership on the floor, advanced Joseph W. Byrns to Speaker and William B. Bankhead of Alabama to majority leader. Sensing the formation already of special-interest blocs that might make the large party membership unmanageable, the Democratic leadership quickly put through a rules revision, returning to the former requirement of a majority (rather than a one-third) vote to force the discharge of a bill from committee. Despite the voters' mandate, Roosevelt had begun to come under pressure from both the left and the right in the country. The crisis had been halted but recovery had not been achieved, millions were still unemployed, and most people were still pressed down by hard times and uncertainty. Roosevelt himself was partly at fault, for many of his relief and recovery programs had been crippled by their halfheartedness, and the rich and powerful had tended to receive the most help from them. Intent on revitalizing the capitalist system so that it could save itself, the President had shied away from massive doses of medicine or drastic surgery; he had feared, for instance, to "prime the pump" with deficit spending that would unbalance the budget "too much," or to unsettle the country's financial leaders by anything that smacked of a redistribution of wealth. In the face of the continuing depression, his moderation opened him to attack by all manner of radicals, who felt that he was trying to save big business and the bankers. A few of them, such as the ranting and clowning Louisiana Senator Huey Long with his "Share-Our-Wealth" program, Dr. Francis E. Townsend, who proposed a fanciful $200-a-month old-age revolving pension plan, and Father Charles E. Coughlin, an unscrupulous demagogic priest in Detroit who filled the air with radio appeals for Nazi-tinged demands for "social justice," began to threaten the administration, turning their huge followings against Roosevelt. Conservative businessmen and bankers, who had benefited most from the New Deal measures and who felt that the emergency was over, also became increasingly hostile to the administration, demanding a return to the laissez-faire philosophy of government and, when the President ignored them, dubbing his program the Raw Deal.

During the first months of the new session, Roosevelt seemed less aggressive than before, and, left largely to itself, the Senate, under a flood of oratory by Hiram Johnson, Huey Long, and other isolationists, rejected Roosevelt's plea for American adherence to the World Court of International Justice. At the same time, the House wrestled with a $4.8 billion relief program. To get it passed the Rules Committee put through another gag rule, which after its approval caused Republican Representative Dewey Short of Missouri to rage at the House as a "supine, subservient, soporific, superfluous, supercilious, pusillanimous body of nitwits." The relief measure finally passed both houses on April 8, establishing the Works Progress Administration (WPA), which put millions of jobless employables to work on a large-scale public-works program.

Meanwhile, angered by a Supreme Court decision that ruled the NIRA unconstitutional and by the mounting hostility of businessmen, Roosevelt took the counsel of advisers who urged him to counter the left by moving in that direction himself, and beginning in June he gave aggressive support to a new mass of controversial legislation, which some historians call a second New Deal and which kept a harassed and rebellious Congress in session during the long hot summer in Washington. The first measures to pass were the least controversial. On July 5 Senator Wagner's labor bill was enacted, setting up a National Labor Relations Board (NLRB) with unprecedented powers to supervise union elections, enforce the rights of workers to join unions and bargain collectively, and halt unfair labor practices by management. Hailed as a Magna Charta for labor, the bill was furiously condemned by conservatives as unconstitutional, but in 1937 the Supreme Court upheld it and it opened the door for the rapid growth of union membership and power. On August 14 (after Representative Doughton held hearings of his Ways and Means Committee to convince Dr. Townsend's followers that his old-age pension plan was a pie-in-the-sky delusion) the Social Security Act established federal old-age insurance and a federal-state system of unemployment insurance, financed by taxes levied on employers and employees. Though conservatives denounced this measure too, it passed Congress with little trouble and was also sustained by the Supreme Court in 1937.

Three other measures, meanwhile, were wracking the two houses. To put an end to the pyramiding of public utilities by irresponsible holding companies, which established monopolies and kept rates high, the administration drew up a bill correcting the utilities' evils and containing a "death-sentence" clause that provided for the virtual dissolution of the holding companies. The measure was introduced by Montana's Senator Wheeler and Representative Sam Rayburn of Texas, the chairmen of their respective commerce committees, and was immediately assaulted in an enormous lobbying and propaganda campaign by power companies, led by Wendell L. Willkie, president of the Commonwealth and Southern Utility Company, and by holding-company executives and lawyers, including two prestigious Wall Street attorneys, John Foster Dulles and John W. Davis, the Democrats' 1924 presidential candidate. After stormy revolts against the measure by otherwise-loyal New Dealers who were threatened by the utility interests in their home states (freshman Senator Harry S. Truman of Missouri was one of those who stood up defiantly to this " 'wrecking crew' of Wall Street," as he called them), a series of sensational investigations of the utility lobby by Senator Hugo Black helped effect a compromise between the President, now fighting mad at the arrogant utility magnates, and Democratic opponents of the bill in the House, and the measure was enacted on August 28. Democrats raised an even greater tempest over the Wealth Tax Bill, which Roosevelt—taking the steam out of Huey Long's "Share-Our-Wealth" plan—demanded Congress pass as a means of breaking up large concentrations of capital and redistributing wealth in the United States. Moderate conservative Democrats, including Roosevelt's loyal Senate leaders Joseph Robinson and Pat Harrison, who had been raised in the Democratic tradition of taxation for revenue only, were appalled by the conviction that the bill was simply a vindictive weapon aimed at the President's enemies; but because of party loyalty, a desire to maintain the prestige and patronage of their positions, and the need to be re-elected in 1936, the leadership stayed with the President, overcoming the opposition in Congress and pushing the measure through with slight compromises. The bill levied steeply graduated taxes on large individual incomes, as well as estate taxes and excess-profits taxes on the bigger corporations.

Before the session ended it was marked by several antiadministration filibusters by Senator Long (one of them, lasting fifteen and a half hours, established a record) and by the defeat of a Food and Drug bill, which was torn to pieces by a drug company lobby with the help of New York's Democratic Senator Royal S. Copeland, something of a quack doctor who wrote a newspaper column of medical advice and kept his pockets full of nuts and raisins on which he munched "for his health" during Senate sessions. When Congress adjourned on August 26 Roosevelt had achieved another series of major victories, but at a cost. He had finally declared war on the wealthy and powerful whom he would call "economic royalists," and they would fight him tooth and nail. But he had weakened the support of his congressional leadership and driven into hostility and future unreliability a number of formerly loyal followers in the House and more than a dozen moderate conservative Democratic Senators, who were now courted by such men who consistently opposed him as Glass and Bailey.

None of this seemed important in the months ahead, as Roosevelt's position, explained to the people in his radio "fireside chats," became stronger than ever among the electorate. On September 8, 1935, his major threat from the left disappeared when Huey Long—now a strange mixture of benevolent populist and ruthless dictator in Louisiana, and to some in other parts of the country the menacing figure of a would-be American-style Mussolini—was assassinated in Baton Rouge. Roosevelt again dominated Congress during its 1936 session, forcing through the Soil Conservation Act and, after acrimonious debate and compromises, the Revenue Act, which levied a tax on the undistributed profits of corporations, further enraging businessmen, who claimed they were being penalized for setting aside funds for reserves and expansion. In the presidential election that fall, Roosevelt led a powerful coalition of urban dwellers, relief workers, union members, farmers, blacks, southern Democrats, and the underprivileged everywhere in a massive victory over his enemies. "I should like to have it said of my first administration," he declared, "that in it the forces of selfishness and lust for power met their match. I should like to have it said of my second administration that in it these forces met their master." The nation gave him 60.4 percent of the popular vote over his Republican rival, Governor Alf Landon of Kansas, who lost every state but Maine and Vermont. Republican membership in the Senate reached a low of sixteen and in the House it fell to eighty-nine.

Joseph Byrns had died in June, 1936, and Alabama's William B. Bankhead was now Speaker, with Texan Sam Rayburn, a quiet, persuasive team player, moving up to majority leader. The new session of Congress started off quietly on January 5, 1937, but exactly a month later it exploded suddenly over the most divisive issue that had yet struck the New Deal. Following its decision against the NIRA, the Supreme Court had invalidated the AAA, the Guffey-Snyder Coal Act (closely regulating the coal industry), and a New York State minimum-wage law. Angry with the "horse-and-buggy" mentality of the reactionary Court majority, which seemed to bar progressive social and economic legislation by states as well as the federal government, and fearing for the fate of the advanced measures passed in 1935, Roosevelt called the Democratic leaders of both houses to the White House on February 5 and told them abruptly of a message he was about to send to Congress asking for authorization to appoint a new federal judge whenever one who had already served ten years failed to retire six months after he became seventy. For the Supreme Court, which then had six justices over seventy, he would appoint a maximum of six additional judges.

The audacious plan shocked the congressional leaders. "Boys, here's where I cash in," said Representative Hatton W. Sumners of Texas, chairman of the House Judiciary Committee, as the Democrats rode back to the Capitol. Because of Sumners's opposition, the bill began in the Senate Judiciary Committee, headed by the usually compliant Senator Ashurst. But Ashurst held it up there until June, finally reporting it unfavorably. Meanwhile, vehement opposition to the plan had mounted throughout the country as well as in Congress. To many, the Supreme Court was sacred, the ultimate barrier against tyranny. Conservatives were horrified by Roosevelt's "immoral" attempt to assert executive control over the third branch of government. Even liberals, fearing the loss of protection against future assaults on civil rights, viewed the "court-packing" plan as dangerous. In Congress progressive Republicans such as Hiram Johnson, who had generally supported Roosevelt, drew away from him in anger and united with the conservatives in their party—though they remained silent, letting the Democratic opponents of the bill lead the attack. Among the latter were the conservatives who had already shown their opposition to the New Deal as well as a number of previously loyal moderates such as Montana's Burton Wheeler, Bennett "Champ" Clark of Missouri, the son of the former Speaker, and Thomas T. Connally of Texas, a large, florid man whose big black hat, shoestring tie, and long gray hair curling up at the back matched the cartoonists' symbol of a Senator. Within weeks the opponents in the two parties were working together, and by spring a powerful bipartisan coalition, led by Wheeler and with enough votes to block the measure on the Senate floor, had been formed.

326

Roosevelt's desperate supporters, fearful about the party's split, urged him to settle for a constitutional amendment, but he had already discarded that idea as requiring too long a process. For months he let the issue stew, still confident that in the end he would win. Gradually, however, circumstances gathered against him. A number of Supreme Court decisions, beginning even before he had announced his plan, upheld such measures as the National Labor Relations and Social Security acts, about which Roosevelt had been worried, and indicated that a majority of the Court had made a change on its own and would now support New Deal measures. Then one of the justices announced his retirement, and on July 14 Robinson, Roosevelt's strong right arm in the Senate, died. As a tense fight broke out among Senate Democrats over his successor, raising party tempers higher, Roosevelt asked Garner to settle the Supreme Court issue with Wheeler. A mild bill was finally passed, limited to minor reforms but barring changes in the membership of the courts. "Glory be to God!" exclaimed Hiram Johnson when the result was announced.

The Democratic majority in the Senate had suffered enormous damage, and more was on the way. The split, marked by the willingness of many of the Democrats to work in a loose coalition with Republicans, was already exacerbated by other serious intraparty differences. During the spring a rash of sitdown strikes had been supported by the Democratic liberals and had seemingly enjoyed the sympathy of Roosevelt, who resisted all efforts by conservatives to get him to intervene to protect private property. The strikes angered such southern Democratic leaders as Garner, Robinson, Harrison, and Byrnes, and by April they were in a quiet revolt of their own against the New Deal's decided tilt toward labor, northern urban interests, and blacks and against states' rights and moderate spending. Backed by a large number of southern Democrats in both houses and supported by most Republicans, they began to steer a course that frequently found them at odds with Roosevelt's legislative requests. On one measure—a $1.5 billion appropriation bill for the WPA—Roosevelt had to rely on Senator Alben W. Barkley of Kentucky for leadership. As a result, when Robinson died Roosevelt intervened pointedly in the Senate's affairs, sending his new lieutenant a "Dear Alben" letter that showed the loyal New Dealers for whom to vote and aided Barkley in beating Pat Harrison for the majority leader post. The episode widened the split over administration legislation, and Congress adjourned on August 21 with the Democrats in bad humor but with the legislative branch, oddly, having taken a long step toward reasserting its independence from the executive.

On November 15 Roosevelt called Congress back into special session to take up unfinished business, but resistance was again running high and nothing was accomplished. In the Senate the coalition between southern Democratic conservatives and the Republicans became a reality, and together they blocked Barkley and the liberal New Dealers. In the House the administration was hobbled by the Rules Committee, which was now controlled by a majority coalition of conservative southern Democrats, led by Edward E. Cox of Georgia and Howard W. Smith of Virginia, and Republicans and chaired by John J. O'Connor, a Tammany Democrat from New York who had little enthusiasm for the New Deal. In the regular session of 1938 Roosevelt continued to have trouble with these coalitions in both houses, being forced to accept (though he did not sign) a new Revenue Act that reduced some of the earlier taxes against the rich and the big corporations. By resorting to a discharge petition in a bold defiance of the Rules Committee, Congresswoman Mary T. Norton of New Jersey and other determined House liberals finally got a Fair Labor Standards Bill out onto the floor of the House. Abolishing child labor and setting national minimum wages and maximum hours of work, this landmark measure became law on June 25, 1938. Other administration bills enacted included a $3.75 billion relief-and-recovery program to reverse a new recession that had set in and new farm legislation to deal with surpluses and price declines.

As the fall elections approached, Roosevelt set out to "purge" some of his most obstructionist foes in both houses, supporting their primary opponents, but amid much criticism his efforts failed against Senator Tydings in Maryland, Walter F. George in Georgia, and "Cotton Ed" Smith in South Carolina, and he succeeded only in effecting the defeat of Representative O'Connor in New York. O'Connor's place as chairman of Rules was taken by a loyal but ineffectual liberal, Adolph J. Sabath of Illinois, and the crusty Howard Smith, who was noted for wearing wing collars and pince-nez, and his coalition of southern conservatives and Republicans retained their stranglehold over the committee, clearing bills that Roosevelt opposed and blocking, or forcing substantive changes in, bills he supported.

By the time the Seventy-sixth Congress met on January 3, 1939, Roosevelt's ability to achieve further New Deal domestic reform and recovery legislation had all but vanished, and Congress and the executive were close to an angry stalemate. Republican membership in the House had risen to 169, and, combining under the astute leadership of Massachusetts's Joseph W. Martin, Jr., with the Democratic conservatives, it, together with the anti-New Deal coalition in the Senate, hamstrung and cut administration requests for more relief appropriations; abolished the undistributed profits tax; killed a housing bill; passed the Hatch Act, which barred federal employees from political activity (the result of an investigation of WPA involvement in the 1938 elections); and authorized a committee under Howard Smith to investigate the National Labor Relations Board. But by the time Congress adjourned on August 5, 1939, forces were fast gathering elsewhere in the world that would shift Americans' attention from domestic to foreign affairs, finally end the Depression, and result in the President's acquiring greater powers than ever over the affairs of the nation. On September 1, Germany invaded Poland.

9. Congress in Crisis

In large measure, the predominant isolationist mood of the American people and of Congress that lasted until the late 1930's reflected not only disillusionment and cynicism about World War I, but also a sentiment—which Senator Nye's 1934–36 investigation of the munitions industry furthered—that conspiracies of arms makers and their bankers had pushed the United States into that war. Consequently, when international tensions erupted into new wars in the 1930's, American policy had a twofold aim: to remain diplomatically disentangled and to prevent American arms makers from involving the nation in the conflicts. While Hoover's secretary of state, Henry L. Stimson, and most internationalists did not support the conspiratorial theory of the role of the munitions makers, they did view America's ability to withhold arms from aggressors and make them available to victims of aggression as a potent deterrent to war. In 1931, when Japan invaded Manchuria, a resolution was introduced in Congress to ban the sale of arms to any country that violated the Kellogg-Briand Pact. Munitions lobbyists held up the bill, but Stimson supported its discretionary principle of halting arms only to aggressors, and so, on the eve of his inauguration, did President-elect Roosevelt. But the isolationists then amended the congressional resolution to bar shipments to *all* belligerents—removing the deterrent factor—and the resolution died, as did Roosevelt's interest in it.

The new Democratic administration sought to ease economic tensions by lowering the high Smoot-Hawley tariffs—while at the same time using them as economic weapons—and at Roosevelt's request Congress in mid-1934 went back to the old Blaine-McKinley idea of reciprocal tariffs, passing the Trade Agreements Act, which authorized the President to lower duties by up to fifty percent for "most-favored nations" that reciprocated with similar concessions. Though Secretary of State Cordell Hull made sixteen such treaties in the next four years, the policy had little effect other than to halt a further deterioration of international trade relations. When Mussolini threatened Ethiopia in 1935, Congress approved the Neutrality Act, introduced by Democratic Senator Key Pittman of Nevada, which forbade the export of munitions to all belligerents. Roosevelt opposed it as penalizing Ethiopia, but isolationist feeling was so strong that he succeeded only in winning agreement to limit it to six months. Not only did the Neutrality Act fail to deter Italy, but when Hull asked American business to place a "moral embargo" on other products that Italy needed, the oil industry ignored him and supplied Mussolini with petroleum, his most pressing requirement.

When the Pittman bill expired in February, 1936, Congress, led by the rigid isolationist Senators Borah, Johnson, and Nye, rejected Roosevelt's plea for discretionary authority to apply the embargo only against aggressors, extended the act to May 1, 1937, and added a prohibition against the granting of war loans and credits to belligerents. In the summer of 1936, Francisco Franco's fascists commenced a civil war against the Republican government of Spain, and Roosevelt, fearing involvement and the large American Catholic vote that favored Franco, joined England and France in a nonintervention policy. In April, 1937, with the Neutrality Act again expiring, Congress passed a permanent law. It empowered the President to determine when a war or civil war threatened international peace, at which time arms and credits would be embargoed against all belligerents, but it permitted him to authorize the belligerents to purchase nonmilitary commodities in the United States on a "cash-and-carry" basis, paying cash and transporting the goods in their own vessels. Roosevelt's support of this measure puzzled many of his liberal followers. They saw it as favoring Franco—whom both Mussolini and Hitler were openly assisting—and indicating that the isolationists in Congress were in control of an American foreign policy that would do nothing to halt the fascist menace.

Their concern was reinforced in July, when Japan again attacked China. This time Roosevelt declined to invoke the Neutrality Act and permitted the sale of arms to both sides. On October 5, however, he began to reveal his distress when, in a speech at Chicago, he suggested a "quarantine" of nations that created a state of international anarchy and instability. But he was ahead of American public opinion; the isolationists attacked him ruthlessly, and for the time being he dropped further thought of seeking collective security. Instead he focused the nation's attention on its own military unpreparedness, asking Congress for a $1 billion increase in appropriations for defense, including a huge naval construction program. Congress responded in May, 1938, with the Naval Expansion Act, largely authored by Representative Carl Vinson of Georgia, for the building of a two-ocean navy.

Congressional opinion on foreign affairs was beginning to polarize. Southern Democrats, who opposed Roosevelt on the New Deal and domestic matters, were growing more internationalist, while isolationism was hardening among many midwestern and western Democrats, conservative Republicans, and former Progressives. Hitler's Austrian "Anschluss" and demands on Czechoslovakia that culminated in his appeasement by Great

Britain and France at Munich in September, 1938, accelerated this polarization and finally persuaded Roosevelt of the urgent need to alter the nonintervention policy inherent in the neutrality laws and to concentrate on the rearmament of the United States. The Pacific threat was growing apace as Japan, in reply to American protests against aggression in China, announced that the Open Door Policy was "inapplicable" to conditions "of today and tomorrow." In January, 1939, Roosevelt asked Congress for another huge defense appropriation, a large part of it for military aircraft, and again Congress responded affirmatively, appropriating $2 billion, more than he had asked for, and authorizing him to begin stockpiling strategic war materials. At the same time the President appealed to Senator Pittman, chairman of the Foreign Relations Committee, to repeal the 1937 Neutrality Act and allow him to discriminate between aggressors and their victims in supplying arms. Pittman worked out a compromise, but the isolationists on his committee refused to report out a bill that made any changes in the 1937 act. When Hitler violated the Munich Pact and dismembered Czechoslovakia, the President, calling for methods "short of war" to resist aggression, encouraged Democratic Representative Sol Bloom of New York, chairman of the House Foreign Affairs Committee, to sponsor a bill for repeal of the arms embargo. Isolationists were still too strong, however, and they amended the Bloom measure to impotence. Roosevelt again turned to Pittman, but without success: the Senate committee, 12 to 11, would not endorse a repeal measure. Still Roosevelt tried, calling Senate leaders to the White House. When a poll of them showed that they were against repeal, Vice President Garner remarked to the President, "Well, Captain, we may as well face the facts. You haven't got the votes, and that's all there is to it."

In August Germany and Russia signed a nonaggression pact, and on September 1 the long-dreaded war in Europe began. Issuing a Proclamation of Neutrality, Roosevelt, now more determined than ever, summoned a special session of Congress on September 21, 1939, and once more asked for repeal of the arms embargo. Though he was angrily attacked by Borah and others, he finally had his way. Pittman drafted a bill that lifted the embargo, permitting the sale of munitions and other contraband on a cash-and-carry basis and allowing short-term loans to belligerents. Roosevelt echoed the belief of most Americans that, given access to arms, Britain and France could defeat Hitler while the United States remained neutral; despite vigorous opposition from isolationists the measure passed Congress, and Roosevelt signed it on November 4. In January, 1940, the President asked for almost $2 billion for defense, and in May, during the spectacular German blitzkrieg on the Western Front, he sought from a stunned and worried Congress another $2.5 billion for defense and called for the production of fifty thousand airplanes a year. Meanwhile, he had sold Britain and France surplus government arms without authority from Congress, and when Italy entered the war on June 10, he castigated Mussolini and dropped all pretense of neutrality in favor of a state of nonbelligerency.

American defense efforts now quickened. Congress authorized arms sales to Western Hemisphere nations and passed measures to finance military production. To emphasize nonpartisanship, Roosevelt—though intensely distrusted by such veteran Republican isolationists as Senators Nye, Johnson, and La Follette and by newcomers Arthur H.Vandenberg of Michigan and Robert A. Taft of Ohio (Borah died in January, 1940)—appointed two Republican internationalists to his Cabinet, Henry L. Stimson as secretary of war (a post he had held under Taft) and Frank Knox as secretary of the navy. He named a National Defense Advisory Board and a National Defense Research Committee (eventually supplanted by the Office of Scientific Research and Development), and as a result of information about a nuclear scientific breakthrough that Albert Einstein communicated to him in October, 1939, he directed the latter agency to begin work on developing an atomic bomb. Throughout the war expenditures for that secret undertaking, code-named the Manhattan Project, were slipped into military appropriation bills under engineering and other guises. At one point, when Democratic Representative Clarence Cannon of Missouri, chairman of the House Appropriations Committee, began to notice exorbitant requests for various projects in the budget, he called Army Chief of Staff George C. Marshall to a committee meeting for an explanation. Marshall would say only that the money was for something that could win the war for the United States—or for Germany, if Hitler solved the problem first. The committee agreed to go along, asking no more questions, but when the appropriations reached $2 billion with no apparent results, Cannon balked again, and Secretary Stimson had to arrange for Cannon and four members of the committee to visit the huge research installation at Oak Ridge, Tennessee, and learn the secret. The leaders of both parties were also let in on the project so that they could quiet any objections to the necessary appropriations, and all of them kept the secret until the bomb was dropped on Hiroshima in 1945.

Meanwhile, over England, the RAF during the summer of 1940 fought and won the Battle of Britain. But German submarines were imperiling the sea lanes between the United States and Great Britain, and to continue receiving arms Prime Minister Winston Churchill appealed to Roosevelt for fifty old World War I American destroyers to help combat the U-boats. A direct sale or loan of the vessels would have been illegal, and Roosevelt did not dare open a divisive debate on the subject in Congress. On September 3, instead, he traded the destroyers to Britain for leases on a number of naval bases in British Caribbean possessions and Newfoundland. Though the canniness of the destroyer deal incensed the isolationists, its strengthening of Western Hemisphere defenses neutralized them, and the transfer of the warships helped save Britain in its darkest hour. Against the mounting fears of isolationists, Congress federalized the National Guard, enacted the nation's first peacetime draft (the call-up was for one year of military duty), and placed the export of scrap iron and gasoline to Japan under license.

As division within the United States became sharper, a swelling coalition of isolationists—now known as noninterventionists—accelerated a national debate. Such organizations as the America First Committee attacked pro-British interventionists, who were rallied principally by the Committee to Defend America by Aiding the Allies, founded by Kansas newspaper editor William Allen White. Both sides were bipartisan and were helped by members of Congress, the most vehement being Senators Wheeler and Nye, who spoke throughout the country for the America First Committee. The noninterventionists merged their fight for neutrality with an assault on Roosevelt, and the President, now actively campaigning for re-election to a third term, responded with vigor. On November 5 Roosevelt was re-elected with a five-million-vote majority over the former utility magnate Wendell Willkie, and both houses remained Democratic.

That same month a new crisis arose when Churchill informed the President that Britain was exhausting its financial resources and would soon be unable to pay for additional arms and supplies. Unwilling to revive the memories of unpaid World War I debts by proposing a loan, Roosevelt came up with a daring plan to lease and lend material to England, first employing a fireside chat on December 29, 1940, to explain the idea to the American people and win their support, and then asking the new Seventy-seventh Congress, in January, 1941, for $7 billion for war materials to sell, lend, lease, exchange, or transfer to any country whose defense the President deemed vital to that of the United States. Proclaiming, in the same message, the Four Freedoms, he called on the United States to become the "arsenal of democracy." The noninterventionists viewed the issue as their last stand and waged a bitter two-month fight against the Lend-Lease Act, which became law on March 11. "I had the feeling . . . that I was witnessing the suicide of the Republic," wrote Vandenberg when the Senate approved the measure.

As America's own defense effort increased, the President set up an array of agencies to administer defense production, cope with labor disputes, and try to combat inflationary forces. At the same time the Senate, on March 1, 1941, created what became perhaps the most businesslike and effective investigating committee in congressional history, the Special Committee to Investigate the National Defense Program. Headed by Democratic Senator Harry S. Truman of Missouri and composed of a number of freshman Senators with adequate time to devote to the committee, it was given broad latitude to oversee the entire defense program. Truman himself had proposed the committee after fretting about the confusion in carrying out some programs and the awarding of defense contracts primarily to large companies. An avid student of American history, he was determined not to repeat the excesses of Congress' Civil War investigating committee and refused to probe into military policy or operations. Ranging over the entire area of defense—and then war—mobilization, working closely and quietly with the executive branch to uncover and end shortages, deficiencies in allocations and product quality, interagency conflicts, and frauds, the Truman Committee compiled a notable record of rapid corrective action.

After the passage of the Lend-Lease Act, America moved steadily toward war. German submarine warfare increased, and the President, declaring a state of unlimited national emergency on May 27, 1941, permitted the navy to convoy British supply vessels part way across the North Atlantic. On July 3, with the one-year draft period approaching an end, the administration asked Congress to extend the draft act for eighteen months and permit servicemen to be sent outside the Western Hemisphere. The request, seeming to imply that Roosevelt was now bent on entering the conflict, raised a new storm of opposition in Congress. After a reassuring explanation from General Marshall that the men were needed only for the nation's security, the Senate approved the request, but an angry fight in the House foretold a close vote. Sam Rayburn of Texas, fifty-nine years old, a short, kindly man who was immensely popular among his colleagues because of his integrity and consideration and because of his preference to persuade rather than command his fellow Democrats, had become Speaker when Alabama's William B. Bankhead died in September, 1940. Well known for his advice to freshman Representatives, "To get along, go along," he now appealed personally to every wavering Congressman to stand by the President, using any argument he could think of and falling back in some cases on the plea, "Do this for me. I won't forget it." On August 12, in a tensely dramatic roll call, the House approved the measure by only one vote, 203 to 202.

Thereafter the progression toward war accelerated. German submarines began to attack American destroyers, and after issuing orders to the navy to attack enemy craft on sight, the President requested permission from Congress to arm American merchant ships and allow them to carry cargoes to Allied ports. The appeal again stirred opposition in Congress, but it collapsed after a few weeks of sharp debate, and the requested authorization became law on November 17, 1941. Meanwhile, a quiet but uncompromising diplomatic effort by Secretary of State Hull, accompanied by an embargo on oil and other vital materials, to force the Japanese to withdraw from China caused a fateful conflict in Japan between peace elements and military expansionists. The latter won and on December 7 launched a huge offensive in the Pacific and Southeast Asia with a surprise attack on Pearl Harbor. The stunning blow united the American people, and Congress on December 8 declared war on Japan with only a single dissenting vote—that of Montana's Republican Representative Jeannette Rankin, who had also voted against war in 1917 and who, still an active pacifist, had been recently re-elected to Congress after an absence of twenty-two years. Her colleagues pleaded with her to change her vote, but she refused, went to a telephone in the cloakroom to call the Capitol police, and escorted by them made her way to her office in the Cannon House Office Building, where she remained behind her locked door for the rest of the day. Three days later, Germany and Italy declared war on the United States.

Although most members of Congress, including the former isolationist leaders, closed ranks immediately to confirm national unity and purpose, the public's trust in the President as the determined and reassuring commander in chief soared, while its regard for the legislature, stereotyped as a rancorous body of self-serving, shortsighted obstructionists, fell. Congressmen were criticized for demanding unlimited gasoline ration cards and for including themselves in a bill that provided retirement benefits for civil-service employees. When some Representatives complained that wooden decoy guns, rather than real antiaircraft artillery, had been placed atop the House Office Building, the newspapers derided them, especially when one Congressman angrily suggested that the decoys might be a plot to lure enemy bombers away from the White House. Nevertheless, making good its authorization to the President "to employ . . . the resources of the government to carry on war," Congress in short order broadened and extended the draft act, and passed two War Powers Acts, which gave the President enormous authority to create war agencies, reorganize the executive branch, and enforce regulations and controls.

As the initiative in the prosecution of the war was assumed by the executive, the unity achieved after Pearl Harbor gradually disintegrated. As in the early days of the New Deal, new agencies were created and new bureaucracies mushroomed, causing suspicion, fear, jealousy, and antagonism among former isolationists, conservative Democrats, and Roosevelt-hating Republicans in Congress. Both chambers rang daily with denunciations of "arrogant, war-shirking bureaucrats," of infiltrating radicals, and of agencies "misusing the power granted by Congress" to extend the New Deal or institute new social and economic reforms under the cloak of war measures. Some agencies existed and operated with little or no legal authority even under the War Powers Acts, and while Congress in general recognized them as necessary to the war effort, the two houses responded to the more persistent criticisms of particular agencies and their policies by authorizing more than one hundred investigations during the war. In addition to the ongoing Truman Committee of the Senate, the most notable special investigating committee was one authorized by the House Rules Committee early in 1943 and named for its chairman and sponsor, conservative Democrat Howard W. Smith of Virginia, "to investigate acts of executive agencies beyond the scope of their authority." The Smith Committee, reflecting a broad conservative distrust of the war agencies, received warm support from Representatives who denounced the "cancerous growth of bureaucracy . . . eating the heart of our American way of life."

Much of Congress' antagonism to the war agencies stemmed from a recognition that the gigantic executive establishment was making it increasingly difficult for the legislature to maintain its function as a coequal branch of government. As the war progressed, the problem became so disturbing to the responsible leaders of both parties that there was general agreement that something would have to be done about it when the war was over. Meanwhile, though Congress had plenty to do, its subsidiary war role was evidenced by the relative paucity of bills it was required to pass. Most of them sparked debates that showed a gradual regrouping of Republicans and conservative southern Democrats against measures, or provisions within them, that hinted of liberal New Deal philosophy or attitudes. In 1942 the principal legislation enacted included the Emergency Price Control Act, which established the Office of Price Administration (OPA) to set price ceilings, control rents in defense areas, and administer rationing; an act to create the Office of Economic Stabilization to stabilize prices, salaries, and wages; and the Revenue Act of 1942 (described by Roosevelt as "the greatest tax bill in American history"), which increased revenues by more than $7 billion a year through higher corporate and excess-profits taxes and a broadening of the income-tax base and the levying of almost confiscatory taxes on higher incomes. A request by the President for a third War Powers Act died in committee at the end of the year, reflecting the deterioration in relations between the administration and Congress.

In the 1942 elections the Democrats retained nominal leadership of both houses, but their majority in the House of Representatives was reduced to thirteen (at one time during the new Congress, because of deaths, it fell to two), and though Rayburn was re-elected Speaker (with slender, ashen-faced John W. McCormack of Massachusetts renamed majority leader), a coalition of Republicans and southern Democrats asserted control over legislation. A similar coalition dominated in the Senate. In this Seventy-eighth Congress sniping at the administration increased. "Government by bureaucrats must be broken, and broken now," insisted Georgia's pugnacious Democratic Representative Edward E. Cox of the Rules Committee. In the growing tensions and frustrations of the war economy, citizens registered complaints of every kind to their Congressmen—against administrative ineptitudes, against highhanded bureaucrats, controls, and rationing, against the forty-hour work week and strikes, and against real or assumed injustices to relatives in the armed forces. Many members of both houses were quick to champion such causes, waging something of a guerrilla war in the two chambers and through the newspapers and radio against war agencies and their administrators. Much of the drumfire was of more than momentary significance, for it reflected a growing offensive to try to dismantle Roosevelt's prewar domestic reforms and halt any moves that tended to impose new social ideas. Congress must "win the war from the New Deal," Republican Charles L. Gifford of Massachusetts told the House.

During the turbulent year of 1943 Congress abolished many New Deal agencies, including the WPA, the CCC, and the National Youth Agency; terminated one of its principal "hates," the National Resources Planning Board, which operated in the White House and kept devising New Dealish proposals for postwar social legislation; and waged running ideological and policy fights with the administration over such issues as farm price controls, organized labor, new taxes, and actions by the President's Fair Employment Practice Committee to end racial discrimination. The conflict over labor had long been brewing. From the beginning of the war, workers—who made more money than soldiers and could enjoy the benefits of civilian life—were popular targets of the more demagogic Congressmen, who equated them with draft dodgers. The hostility of Republicans and conservative Democrats toward organized labor increased as the unions' power expanded rapidly under prewar and wartime legislation that favored them. In 1943 congressional anger exploded when John L. Lewis, the formidable head of the United Mine Workers, called a strike of coal miners for higher wages in defiance of the government's "hold-the-line" policy on wages and prices. When the miners ignored a presidential plea and a War Labor Board order to return to work, a furious Congress passed the Smith-Connally Anti-Strike Act, which ordered thirty days advance notice by a union intending to strike a war industry, authorized the government to take over struck war plants, and banned contributions to political campaigns by labor organizations. Roosevelt vetoed the measure, but both houses easily overrode his veto, indicating a widespread antilabor resentment that smoldered in Congress for many more years.

Particularly disturbing to southern Democrats were war measures that tended to favor blacks and undermine the "Jim Crow" segregationist policy that had settled firmly over the South in the latter part of the nineteenth century. The migration of blacks to northern and western urban areas led to a demand for the end of racial discrimination in war industries and the armed forces. Through the Fair Employment Practice Committee, created by executive act in June, 1941, and the regulations of the military services and war agencies, discrimination in many spheres of war activity was gradually prohibited, and though most southern Democrats fretted and fumed over the eroding of racial barriers, they could do nothing about it, for on this issue they lost the support of most Republicans. Their one defense continued to be the weapon of the filibuster in the Senate, which they had used in the 1930's to halt anti-lynching legislation and which they now employed to block attempts to ban the poll tax, a favorite means of denying the vote to southern blacks. With the ending of the war they would turn the filibuster against peacetime legislative efforts to outlaw discrimination, holding up bills for a permanent national FEPC in 1946 and again in 1950. In the South segregation and discrimination would continue virtually free of interference until the civil-rights revolution of the 1950's and 1960's.

There was in the wartime Congresses a growing acceptance of the responsibility of the United States not to repeat the retreat into isolationism that had followed World War I but instead to participate as a leader in world affairs at the end of the current global conflict. This development began in March, 1943, with the introduction in the Senate of a bipartisan resolution by Republicans Joseph H. Ball of Minnesota and Harold H. Burton of Ohio and Democrats Lister Hill of Alabama and Carl A. Hatch of New Mexico, recommending that America take the lead in establishing a United Nations body. Soon afterward more specific resolutions were introduced by Tom Connally of Texas, chairman of the Senate Foreign Relations Committee, and J. William Fulbright of Arkansas, a cultured, soft-spoken thirty-eight-year-old Rhodes scholar, former president of the University of Arkansas, and first-term Democrat in the House. Despite alarmist opposition from such die-hard isolationists as Republican Representative Clare E. Hoffman of Michigan, who declared that the Fulbright Resolution would "repeal the Declaration of Independence," the House passed it readily on September 21, 1943, by a vote of 360 to 29. On November 5 Connally's resolution passed the Senate, 85 to 5, with opposition from Senators Johnson, Wheeler, Robert R. Reynolds of North Carolina, William Langer of North Dakota, and Henrik Shipstead of Minnesota, all prewar isolationists.

Both votes provided evidence of the war's effect in turning the American people away from isolationism. Since Pearl Harbor many former isolationists in both houses, most notably Senator Vandenberg, the Michigan Republican, had changed their position. Vandenberg had become a dedicated believer in the need for bipartisan support of efforts to secure the peace, and he gave enthusiastic assistance to the Connally Resolution. Unlike Wilson, who had snubbed Congress, Roosevelt's advisers and State Department officials worked closely with Connally, Vandenberg, and members of the two foreign affairs committees of Congress, and on April 25, 1945, when fifty nations met at San Francisco to sign the United Nations Charter, the eight-member American delegation included Connally, Vandenberg, and Sol Bloom of New York and Charles A. Eaton of New Jersey, the chairman and ranking Republican member respectively of the House Foreign Affairs Committee. The cooperation between the two branches of government and Vandenberg's bipartisan support proved their worth when the UN charter was presented to the Senate for ratification in July, 1945. The lessons of 1919 had been learned: all Senator Lodge's principal objections to the League covenant were absent from the UN charter, and the veto right clearly protected the United States from an obligation to enforce collective security without the approval of Congress. The Senate ratified the UN charter on July 28 by the overwhelming vote of 89 to 2, the negative votes being cast by Senators Langer and Shipstead. Hiram Johnson, who was ill and not present, announced his opposition, and nine days later, on August 6, at the age of seventy-nine, this last of the old original isolationists died.

The 1944 session of Congress, attuned to the presidential election of that year, was more partisan and quarrelsome than the one of the year before. Militarily the tide had turned and victory was in the air, but a sense of unity in the common effort against the foe scarcely existed in the Capitol. The year before Roosevelt had asked Congress for a $16 billion increase in taxes, not simply for revenue but to help control inflation and prevent war wealth from becoming concentrated in the hands of a few. Congress failed to act, despite a lowering of the request to $10.5 billion. In February, 1944, it finally passed a revenue act with an increased yield of only $2.2 billion. Roosevelt angrily vetoed the measure, returning it to his faithful Senate majority leader, Alben Barkley, with a rebuke so stinging that Barkley resigned his party leadership and denounced the veto. What might have been a serious party schism was healed quickly when Senate Democrats, with the encouragement of a contrite President, re-elected Barkley majority leader, and Congress then went on to override the veto. In addition, that year, Congress, looking toward the end of the war, passed in a burst of patriotism and gratitude (with only forty minutes of debate in the Senate) a "GI Bill of Rights," providing educational and other benefits to World War II veterans. With less unanimity, it began to prepare for the period of conversion to peace by creating the Office of War Mobilization and Reconversion, which was given authority over all phases of the transition from war to peace. Debate was contentious and highly partisan, largely because some members of Congress feared a postwar depression and others were determined to prevent the start of another round of New Deal-style measures.

In June the Republicans nominated Thomas E. Dewey of New York for President, providing him with a platform that was internationalist (confirming the end of Republican support for isolationism) and recognized the fact that many major reforms of the New Deal were permanent. In July the Democrats renominated Roosevelt for a fourth term and chose for Vice President the bespectacled and beaming little Senator from Missouri, Harry Truman, who was enormously respected both in Congress and in the administration for his fair and effective direction of his Senate investigating committee. On November 7 Roosevelt was handily re-elected, carrying along, once again, Democratic majorities in both houses. Roosevelt's victory did not quiet his enemies. During the campaign he had made it plain that after the war he intended to resume progressive economic and social policies at home while giving strong leadership in foreign affairs. When the Seventy-ninth Congress met on January 3, 1945, it was divided more sharply than ever between the liberal followers of the President and an adamant coalition of Republicans and conservative Democrats. After the Yalta Conference, Roosevelt reported to Congress on his meeting with Churchill and Stalin and then went to Warm Springs, Georgia, for a rest.

In the days of Longworth and Garner the Speaker of the House had maintained a hideaway room in the Capitol to which he could invite colleagues of both parties to have a drink in privacy, exchange gossip and stories, provide information about what was going on among the House members, and plan tactics and strategy. The room became known as the "Board of Education" because, as Garner explained, "you get a couple of drinks in a young Congressman and then you know what he knows and what he can do. We pay the tuition by supplying the liquor." Sam Rayburn kept up the tradition, although he changed the hideaway to a small room on the Capitol's first floor and called it simply "downstairs." On April 12, 1945, a little after five in the afternoon, when the Senate had adjourned, Rayburn asked Vice President Truman to join him "downstairs" to discuss, as Truman later wrote his mother, "policy and procedure and, as Alice in Wonderland would say, 'shoes and ships and sealing wax and things.'" By the time Truman reached the room, there was a message for him to call the White House. He did so, and Steve Early, Roosevelt's press secretary, told him in a strained voice to come right over. There Mrs. Roosevelt gave him the shocking news that the President had just died at Warm Springs.

Amid the overwhelming grief of the nation the government went on. On April 16 Truman delivered his first address as President to a joint session of Congress. He was so affected that he mounted the rostrum and immediately began to speak. "Just a minute, Harry," Rayburn, who was sitting behind him, interrupted, "let me introduce you." The Speaker faced the crowded chamber. "The President of the United States," he announced, and Truman began again. There was still a war to win and many grave decisions for the new President to make. In the beginning his popularity in Congress served him well, and the party leaders of both houses once again closed ranks to give him support and advice and make his huge task easier. The UN Conference at San Francisco, which he hosted, was followed by V-E Day, May 8, and the end of the war in Europe. On July 16 the Manhattan Project was crowned with success in a test at Alamogordo, New Mexico. At the time Truman was at the Potsdam Conference, but he had already issued orders for the use of the atomic bomb, and on August 6 the first one was dropped on Hiroshima. On August 15 Japan surrendered, ending the most terrible war in history.

Already Congress had taken the first steps to try to regain the capacity to function as a coequal of the executive branch. On the one hand, it plowed through the job of trying to bring the executive back to manageable size (some twenty-nine war agencies had sprung up under the Office of Emergency Management alone, which the President had created by an executive order). As quickly as it could, Congress reduced the massive wartime apparatus by repealing authorizations and grants of power, terminating agencies, abolishing administrative positions, and providing for the transfer of government undertakings to private business. On the other hand, recognizing that the vast new requirements of the atomic age and America's complex society would demand the continuation of a huge bureaucracy of specialized agencies, it tried, in effect, to lift itself by its own bootstraps to a coequal level, rectifying its deficiencies and attempting to give itself new vigor and strength. "Congress must modernize its machinery and methods to fit modern conditions," said a study of the American Political Science Association in 1945. "This is a better approach than that which seeks to meet the problem by reducing and hamstringing the Executive. A strong and more representative Legislature, in closer touch with and better informed about the administration, is the antidote to bureaucracy."

340

In line with such thinking, the two houses early in 1945 established a bipartisan Joint Committee on the Organization of Congress, headed by Senator La Follette, with Democratic Representative A. S. Mike Monroney of Oklahoma as vice chairman. The group conducted extensive hearings, listening to many members of Congress as well as outside experts, and in March, 1946, presented its recommendations. Because of disagreements within the committee, it failed to cope with major areas of complaint, including the concentration of power in the House Rules Committee, the selection of committee chairmen by seniority, and the inability to limit debate in the Senate. Nevertheless, it proposed numerous measures to modernize procedures and reduce congressional workloads. Most of these management-type proposals were adopted in the Legislative Reorganization Act of 1946. Among its principal effects was the reduction of the number of standing committees in the House from forty-eight to nineteen and in the Senate from thirty-three to fifteen. The committees, as well as both houses, were subjected to a variety of new rules and procedures to increase efficiency and effectiveness, a method was proposed to give Congress control over the budget, and staff and research assistance was increased. In addition, lobbyists were directed to register and report their expenditures to the clerk of the House.

On the whole, the act increased the housekeeping efficiency of some of the mechanisms of Congress and buttressed the institutionalizing of its own bureaucracy, but in significant ways it was ineffective. Its provisions for budget control soon broke down and were discarded. The executive branch habitually asked for more money than the House Appropriations Committee—trying to curb expenditures—wished to grant; the Senate tended to side with the executive and raise or add appropriations; and the House could not maintain its ceilings. The two houses engaged in an internal feud over the right of the Senate to increase appropriations, which finally surfaced in 1962. In an acrimonious flurry of charges and countercharges that year, the House declared that the Senate's repeated advocacy of larger appropriations and increased spending was "an infringement on the privileges" of the House, and the Senate retorted that it possessed "coequal power to originate any bill not expressly 'raising revenue.'" The arguments were finally abandoned without resolution, obscuring the real fact that, under Senate pressure, the appropriations committees of both houses throughout the postwar period acquiesced so regularly to executive spending requests that, far from increasing its control over the budget, Congress at best exercised only a limited authority over that aspect of its constitutional power of the purse.

At the same time, the attempt of the 1946 Reorganization Act to lighten the workload by reducing the number of committees came to nothing when both houses began to create numerous subcommittees and special committees. The goal of helping members of Congress in their work was corrupted by an unprecedented expansion of questionable emoluments and perquisites for Senators and Representatives—voted from time to time over the next thirty years by both houses—that ranged from a vast number of free and subsidized personal services, rapidly increased expense accounts and salaries (more than quadrupled, to $57,500, by the late 1970's), and wide-ranging, government-paid travel opportunities to the burgeoning of staffs and the construction of wasteful facilities (the Rayburn Office Building included an estimated 440 bathrooms to serve 169 Representatives, their staffs, and visitors). All this periodically angered taxpayers, further eroding the prestige of the legislature, and served, ironically, to stultify Congress by deadening its vitality and aggressiveness amid the enervating trappings of a privileged bureaucracy. The provisions regarding lobbyists also failed as ways were quickly found to get around them without penalty.

More importantly, the 1946 act failed to cope with the significant questions of the distribution of power within Congress and the equality of power between Congress and the executive branch—two problems that dominated congressional history after World War II. For a number of years the conflict over power in the House raged around the tight control exercised by the ultraconservative majority of the Rules Committee, dominated at first by the belligerent Edward Cox and then by the highhanded Howard Smith. Reduced from fourteen to twelve members in 1945, the Rules Committee, with Cox and Smith usually voting with four Republicans, managed repeatedly to frustrate administration and liberal-supported legislation. In 1945 it turned down requests from President Truman for rules that would permit the House to vote on a bill for a permanent Fair Employment Practice Committee and consider raising the minimum wage. The Rules Committee the next year refused to clear for House discussion an administration labor-relations bill and instead reported out a stern antilabor measure framed by Republican Representative Francis H. Case of South Dakota. When Congress, in a punitive postwar mood toward union labor, passed that bill, Truman vetoed it, but in 1947 the Eightieth Congress passed—and made stick over another Truman veto—the Taft-Hartley Act, which outlawed the closed shop.

For years the power of the Rules Committee could not be bridled. During the Eightieth Congress it made the House Banking and Currency Committee delete provisions for public housing and slum clearance from one of its bills and held up the consideration of administration measures for universal military training and the revival of the draft. In 1949 the liberal Democratic majority in the House, with Speaker Rayburn's support, approved in caucus a rule by which a committee chairman could force a measure to the floor if the Rules Committee failed to act on it in twenty-one calendar days. The twenty-one-day rule was used eight times during the Eighty-first Congress, but in 1951 the Democratic caucus repealed it, and for the next ten years the Rules Committee's coalition of Republicans and southern Democrats was able to exercise censorship over much of the legislation in the House. In 1955 Smith became chairman of the committee and ran it as he pleased, outraging his enemies by often disappearing and becoming unreachable so that rules he opposed could not be issued. (To prevent a committee meeting on a civil-rights bill, he once went home to Virginia "to check on a burned barn," moving Speaker Rayburn to declare that while he knew Judge Smith would do almost anything to defeat a civil-rights measure, he had not thought that he would commit arson.)

With the election of President Kennedy in 1960 the liberal members of the Democratic House caucus, organized in a Democratic Study Group under the leadership of Representative Chet Holifield of California, finally decided that they had to take drastic action against the Rules Committee if they expected to pass any measures for the new President. In one of his last major efforts in the House (he died of cancer on November 16, 1961), the persuasive Rayburn took on Smith, rounding up enough votes to increase the Rules Committee's membership to fifteen. The vote against Smith on January 31, 1961, was close, 217 to 212, but Rayburn's victory allowed him to "liberalize" the committee. Even so, the new anti-Smith majority was a slim one, and the liberals continued to have trouble with the Rules group. In 1961 it killed an administration school-aid bill and the next year temporarily quashed a move to create a Department of Urban Affairs after learning that Kennedy intended to appoint a black—the first one of Cabinet status—as its head. Then in 1966 Smith was beaten for re-election in Virginia, and by February, 1967, the committee was finally able to adopt a strict set of rules for itself that formalized its procedures and satisfied the liberals. When Representative Ray J. Madden, an Indiana liberal, became chairman in 1973 ground was at last established for Rules to become an arm of the House leaders rather than the independently acting and self-constituted censoring body it had been since the days of the New Deal.

During the same period, both houses were thrown on the defensive by widespread public criticism of the extreme and injudicious methods of some of their investigating committees and the antics of some of their members. In trying to assert equality with the executive branch, Congress increasingly relied on its function of legislative oversight of the executive through investigating committees. The number of such investigations swelled, and most of them attempted efficiently to keep tabs on the huge bureaucracy. But a few, exploiting the fears and tensions of the Cold War or other subjects that generated sensational news headlines, trod ruthlessly on the constitutional rights of individuals and blatantly overstepped legal and ethical bounds, outraging the sense of decency of large segments of the public and—as had happened after World War I—creating a genuine threat to basic American liberties. In the area of investigating loyalty to the United States, excesses on the part of committees became almost a hallmark. The postwar anxiety about world communism was accompanied by an intense fear of internal disloyalty and subversion, and some members of both houses discovered that they could gain celebrity overnight and advance their political fortunes by sitting on committees that exposed suspected spies, Communists, and Communist sympathizers. The development was not an entirely new one, for even before the war the House Un-American Activities Committee, under a bullying, xenophobic chairman, Martin Dies, Jr., of Texas, had acquired an unsavory reputation by grilling radicals and members of left-wing organizations in a sustained attempt to link them with the New Deal and discredit Roosevelt. The committee continued to function after the war under the chairmanship of J. Parnell Thomas, a New Jersey Republican, who eventually was himself jailed for ordering his staff to pay him kickbacks from their salaries.

Reacting to reports of spy plots and evidence that is still debatable, President Truman early in his administration unwittingly helped to aggravate the postwar concern about internal subversion by ordering the rooting out of "security risks" in the federal bureaucracy. The resulting loyalty checks trampled on the rights of employees and found few real subversives, but they aroused a national hysteria that the Un-American Activities Committee and others heightened with witch hunts of their own. After first conducting a well-publicized inquiry of Communists in the motion-picture industry, Thomas's committee in 1948 picked up some of the threads developed by Truman's loyalty checks of the bureaucracy and paraded in public hearings a host of bizarre witnesses whose charges implied that the government had been, and still was, riddled with spies. The most dramatic testimony was furnished by a drab, lumpish former Communist, Whittaker Chambers, who in a face-to-face confrontation before the committee in August, 1948, accused Alger Hiss, a former high State Department official, of having been a member of a Communist group. When Chambers repeated his accusation on a radio program, Hiss sued him, but he lost the suit and went to jail on a perjury charge. One member of the committee who leaped to fame as an ardent interrogator of Hiss was Richard M. Nixon, a Republican Representative from California, who was already known for his anti-Communist zeal. In 1946 Nixon had won his first election to the House by insinuating that the incumbent, Representative Jerry Voorhis, a loyal Roosevelt supporter with a national reputation, was pro-Communist. In 1950 Nixon, labeled "Tricky Dick" by Democrats, employed the same methods to defeat Democrat Helen Gahagan Douglas for the Senate, hinting to the voters that she, too, was a "pink."

Nixon's successful use of communism as an issue rubbed off on other members of Congress, including freshman Senator Joseph R. McCarthy, a Wisconsin Republican, who had served in the Pacific with the Marines and been elected to the Senate the year after the war. Generally unknown until 1950, McCarthy on February 9 of that year made a speech in Wheeling, West Virginia, claiming to hold in his hand a list of 205 persons "known to the Secretary of State as being members of the Communist party and who, nevertheless, are still working and shaping policy in the State Department." The sensational charge, which McCarthy on several occasions refused to substantiate, led to a stormy investigation by a subcommittee of the Senate

Foreign Relations Committee, chaired by Maryland's Millard E. Tydings, who had weathered Roosevelt's "purge" attempt in 1938. Tydings failed to weather McCarthy, who used the hearings to accuse a number of persons of Communist activity and to charge that Tydings was "soft" on communism. That fall McCarthy took credit for Tydings's defeat for re-election in Maryland and then tangled with Democratic Senator William Benton of Connecticut, who urged the ouster of McCarthy from the Senate for his role in the Maryland election. In 1952 Benton was beaten in Connecticut, and McCarthy took credit for his defeat as well.

McCarthy's principal weapon—a highly suggestive ability to persuade the public that anyone who opposed him was part of an international Communist conspiracy—began to seem not only invincible but perilous to the future of the country, for the fanaticism that he aroused and was able to direct against some of the most respectable figures in the nation was fast spreading fear and undermining nonconformity and freedom of dissent. And he had only begun. In the 1952 elections the Republicans won control of both houses, and McCarthy became chairman of the Senate Government Operations Committee and its Permanent Investigations Subcommittee. With carte blanche given him by his fearful Republican colleagues in the Senate, he launched a series of investigations—more accurately described as inquisitions and persecutions—that ranged in many directions, targeting the Voice of America, the State Department, the army, the United Nations, Harvard University, and elements of the press. In July, 1953, the three Democratic Senators on his committee, Henry M. Jackson of Washington, John L. McClellan of Arkansas, and Stuart Symington of Missouri, resigned in protest at his extremist behavior, but they rejoined the committee the following January when he reformed some of his procedures. By that time McCarthy had taken on high officials of the army and, indirectly, the whole Eisenhower administration. When the army filed charges with the Senate against McCarthy and his chief counsel, Roy M. Cohn, McCarthy filed countercharges against the secretary of the army and other defense officials, making them all appear to have been willing dupes of communism.

Beginning in April, 1954, McCarthy's committee, now chaired by Senator Karl E. Mundt of South Dakota (McCarthy temporarily stepped down for the hearings), in effect investigated itself, listening to the angry counteraccusations of McCarthy and the army officials. The hearings were televised and a huge audience watched the proceedings, for the first time getting a close look at the phenomenon of character assassination that American newspapers were calling "McCarthyism." Abrasive, aggressive, still casting suspicion on the loyalty of all opponents, McCarthy finally taxed credulity and was at last discredited by the soft, quiet questioning of the army's special counsel, Boston attorney Joseph N. Welch. When the hearings ended, McCarthy had lost millions of his former supporters. With the worst of his sting gone, resolutions introduced in the Senate by Republican Ralph E. Flanders of Vermont and others, charging McCarthy with "personal contempt" of the Senate, were referred to a Select Committee to Study Censure Charges, headed by conservative Republican Arthur V. Watkins of Utah. Despite a continued defense of the Wisconsin Senator by the Republican majority leader, William F. Knowland of California, the committee unanimously recommended censure, and on December 2 the Senate voted, 67 to 22, to condemn McCarthy for various abuses of Senators and Senate committees. When control of the Senate returned to the Democrats the following January, McCarthy lost his committee chairmanships. His investigations and charges were at an end, and by the time he died on May 2, 1957, he was no longer in the news.

In the meantime, many reputations had been sullied. Accusations by McCarthy and members of the House Un-American Activities Committee had aroused suspicions about a host of leading figures, ranging from General George C. Marshall to Albert Einstein. In the hysteria such persons as J. Robert Oppenheimer, who had been in overall charge of the development of the atomic bomb, were declared security risks. Other freewheeling congressional investigations, making full use of television to dramatize their charges to the public, also impaired the rights of witnesses. Even before McCarthy's investigations, a Senate Special Committee to Investigate Organized Crime, headed by Estes Kefauver, an awkward, gangly Tennessee Democrat with presidential ambitions, conducted a sensational televised inquiry of gangsters and racketeers, hauling a host of crime figures before the cameras. By 1954 there was a reaction to such investigations. While providing entertainment, they were now seen as dangerous assaults on fundamental American liberties. Rayburn himself, responding to attacks on the procedures of the Un-American Activities Committee, had angrily banned television, radio, and film coverage of all House committee hearings in 1952.

Principally as a result of McCarthy's conduct, the rules committees of both houses decided after McCarthy's censure to hold hearings on reform proposals. On March 23, 1955, the House adopted ten reform rules for committee conduct, providing long-overdue safeguards for witnesses and for persons accused in testimony. The Senate Rules Committee recommended similar standards, but that body voted to leave acceptance to its individual committees. As a matter of practice, the committees adopted the new safeguards. When John McClellan became chairman of the Senate Permanent Investigations Subcommittee, which McCarthy had headed, he approved rules similar to those accepted by the House and implemented them when he led the committee in a 1957 investigation of labor racketeering.

On occasion, the misconduct of individual members of Congress or persons associated with the leadership also brought public outcries and resulted in attempts at reform. Little could be done about most cases of personal eccentricities and antics. Since the days of John Randolph, the legislature had always had its share of alcoholics and mental cases, and their colleagues did their best to shelter them from publicity that would discredit Congress as a whole. At times they failed, and momentarily the nation would laugh cruelly at the pathetic and aberrant public conduct of a Marion Zioncheck (a Democratic Representative from Washington who became deranged in the 1930's) or a Wilbur Mills (a powerful Arkansas Democrat who lost his chairmanship of the House Ways and Means Committee in 1974 after eccentric public behavior resulting from a breakdown). More serious were criminal activities, and again the history of Congress is replete with instances of members who faced trial and went to jail for misdemeanors and felonies. Often they involved actions that had nothing to do with congressional business, but sometimes the misconduct struck close to home and, focusing national attention on conflicts of interest, influence peddling, nepotism, and the illegal use of public or campaign funds, raised questions of corruption and ethics that Congress could not ignore.

In the 1960's a sudden rash of such scandals, coming hard on the heels of Congress' long patience with McCarthy's disreputable conduct, disturbed the leadership of both houses. In 1963 Robert G. "Bobby" Baker, secretary of the Senate majority, was charged with having used his powerful position to accumulate a fortune through outside business activities. Though the Democrats were shaken and tried to mute an investigation, fearing that it might implicate Lyndon Johnson, for whom Baker had worked, a report by the Senate Rules Committee led ultimately to Baker's being tried and sentenced to prison for income-tax evasion, theft, and conspiracy to defraud the government. Largely because of the episode, the Senate in 1964 established a six-member bipartisan Select Committee on Standards and Conduct to investigate "allegations of improper conduct" by Senators and Senate employees and to prepare a code of ethical conduct. In its first investigation, in 1966, it looked into public disclosures charging Democratic Senator Thomas J. Dodd of Connecticut with misuse of political campaign contributions and double-billing for official and private travel; as a result of the inquiry the Senate censured Dodd on the first charge. The matter was then closed, and Dodd served in the Senate until his defeat for re-election in 1970. The select committee recommended, and the Senate adopted, a set of reform rules regulating the outside employment of Senate personnel, directing an accounting of Senators' campaign contributions and limiting their use, and requiring Senators and higher-paid employees to file copies of their tax returns and other financial data with the controller general; public disclosure of its members' finances, however, was rejected. This club-atmosphere protection of the membership was severely criticized in May, 1975, when the Senate, with almost no debate, directed the controller general to refuse a subpoena from a Florida prosecutor for the financial statement of former Florida Republican Senator Edward J. Gurney, who was then on trial for allegedly soliciting and accepting bribes for federal housing subsidies. "An arrangement by which Senators 'disclose' their finances secretly to a committee of their colleagues is obviously a sham," said the New York *Times*. The case awakened new interest in a bill previously introduced—but not acted upon—by Republican Senator Clifford Case of New Jersey, requiring full public disclosure of personal financial interests by the President, the Vice President, members of Congress, the judiciary, and all federal employees making more than $25,000 a year.

The House, meanwhile, became embroiled in a scandal of its own in 1967, when the Democratic caucus, reacting to a prolonged series of complaints of misconduct against Democrat Adam Clayton Powell, Jr., a black Representative from New York, removed him from the chairmanship of the Education and Labor Committee, which he had headed since 1961, and the House at the same time voted to deny him his seat pending an investigation by a special committee. One of the few black members of Congress at the time, Powell, a tall, ruggedly handsome man, had been in and out of the headlines with tax and personal problems, but the members charged him particularly with long absences, use of public funds for personal travel, and highhanded leadership of his committee. After an inquiry the House, on March 1, 1967, voted to declare Powell's seat vacant. Though his constituency immediately re-elected him, Powell made no effort to reclaim his seat but took his case to court. The next year he was again re-elected, and when the Ninety-first Congress met early in 1969 he was permitted to take his seat but was fined $25,000 and stripped of his seniority. In June of the same year the Supreme Court ruled that he had been improperly excluded from the House in 1967. Powell served the rest of his term but was defeated in a primary in 1970.

As a result of that case, and the action by the Senate, the House in 1967 established its own bipartisan Committee on Standards of Official Conduct, and the next year adopted a Code of Official Conduct somewhat stronger than the one approved by the Senate. The House also instituted a rule requiring the annual filing of certain financial interests of its members— which were to be open to public scrutiny—and a report on income from those interests, which could be disclosed according to the judgment of the Committee on Standards of Official Conduct. Neither of the rules passed by the House and Senate could, of themselves, end misconduct or quiet criticism of congressional ethics. Questions of conflict of interest and influence peddling would continue to arise. Opportunities for gifts and favors, inherent throughout Congress' history, became greater than ever in the years after World War II, and the most powerful and respected members of both houses, under the delusion that there was nothing wrong with accepting them, utilized them without inhibition, even standardizing the practice of encouraging executive agencies—particularly the military—to curry their favor by enriching their home districts or states with government installations. Senator Case's bill, meanwhile, provided a vague, continuing hope that full financial disclosure would ultimately end most complaints.

None of the postwar reforms significantly affected Congress' most discernible problem—its steadily deteriorating position as a coequal of the executive branch. Concerned legislators hoped that, by another attempt at internal modernization and the streamlining of procedures and organization, Congress could better meet its constitutional responsibilities and in that way pull itself up to the executive's level. The result was the Legislative Reorganization Act of 1970, which instituted a considerable number of new procedural and operational rules in both chambers, improved access to information, and met various demands to assist the legislative process. It fell far short of the reformers' objectives, however. It did not deal with the power of the House Rules Committee (which the House itself was then still trying to bring under control) or with the problem of Senate filibusters, which the Senate sought unsuccessfully to curb by making slight changes in the number of votes needed for cloture (in 1949 cloture required support by two thirds of the membership; in 1959 it required two thirds of those voting; in 1975 it required two thirds of those voting to end debate on a change of rules and three fifths of the membership on all other matters—hairline changes). More significantly, the Reorganization Act did nothing about the seniority system, which some members of both houses felt lay at the heart of Congress' weak posture in relation to the executive.

That assertion was debatable. Opponents of seniority argued that the continuation of aged men in positions of leadership—some lacking initiative, creative drive, combative determination, even the ability to stay awake—"delivered" the Congress in the tense crisis-ridden postwar years into the hands of an aggressive, power-usurping executive. It was charged that committee chairmen, secure as barons in their fiefdoms, throttled questioning or dissent in their committees, abandoned an adversary role for one of deference to what they accepted as the superior knowledge and expertise of the executive, and arranged mutually beneficial collusive working relations with the military and administrative agencies with which they dealt. There was considerable accuracy in such criticism, but it was also an exaggerated generalization that did not hold true for many committee chairmen (for example, during the 1960's Colorado's Democratic Representative Wayne Aspinall, in his seventies, presided autocratically over the House Committee on Interior and Insular Affairs, ferociously contesting executive departments at every turn). Moreover, it was a simplistic distortion of the complex day-to-day working relations between the committees and their staffs on one side and executive department personnel on the other and reflected a belief in a conspiratorial version of government that overlooked the pressures and influences of forces beyond the halls of Congress.

Throughout the thirty years after World War II, one overriding subject —the fear of expanding world communism—dominated American public affairs. On April 13, 1945, the day after he was sworn into office, President Truman was briefed on Stalin's refusal to allow American and British observers into Poland in violation of the Yalta agreements, and from that day on the country's executive leadership committed the United States to an international civil war, sometimes hot, sometimes cold, and with only weak dissent and occasional periods of mild questioning until 1968 the American people and Congress went along. Believing the issue to be survival against a monolithic tyranny expanding from the Soviet Union, Congress and the people looked to the central direction of the executive, as they had during World War II, to take the responsibility of leadership in halting and repulsing the enemy. Since unity was required in war, great deference was shown to the commander-in-chief–President, particularly in foreign affairs, where congressional legislation unquestionably increased his powers. But it went on from there, for intertwined with the struggle to secure the United States and as much of the world as possible from communism were a host of other subjects of legislation, ranging from military procurement, weapons development, mutual security, foreign aid, space flight, and intelligence to taxation, control of basic resources, availability of energy, immigration policy, international trade, and the production and use of foodstuffs. Nor were these all, for accompanying the long political crisis were an unprecedented technological explosion, a constant shifting among uncommitted nations, and the emergence of overwhelmingly complex international and domestic socioeconomic problems. Most of them called for ongoing expertise and decisive leadership that seemed beyond Congress' powers, and as the legislators' workload increased they tended to place more reliance on the executive and delegated responsibility to federal agencies and commissions, which they could monitor only sporadically and superficially through the General Accounting Office or by committee oversight.

The fountainhead of presidential primacy was foreign affairs. The Senate had the constitutional power to ratify treaties and the House to appropriate funds for their implementation, but commencing with the wartime summit meetings much of foreign affairs was determined by executive agreements with foreign leaders. Most of them were communicated to Congress (though not all: for example, President Nixon's private assurances to South Vietnam in 1973 that the United States would come to that country's aid again in the event of a serious North Vietnamese violation of the Paris peace accords of that year), but they did not require Senate approval as did treaties. Thus when Congress became involved with them—enacting such support measures as foreign aid—the legislators were in a subordinate position of following the leader. In a theoretical sense their power over foreign affairs actually grew, because the executive's periodic need for authorizations and appropriations for the burgeoning programs—military assistance, import quotas, trade bills, economic aid, and so forth—provided them with vastly increased roles to play, yet they could only question and exercise vetoes; the executive alone had set the policy without congressional participation. Sometimes the President did not even establish policy by an agreement but instead by the enunciation of a "doctrine," which spelled out no specific action but which Congress endorsed by a broad authorization that permitted implementation by whatever actions the executive deemed necessary. Either way, committee chairmen and the congressional leadership generally induced a majority of the membership of the two houses, year after year, to give patriotic support to the President's leadership in foreign affairs and defer to the executive branch's expertise in managing all aspects of the contest against communism.

In the thirty-year period the trend toward presidential aggrandizement of power in international relations was marked by a number of milestones. Russia's insistence on compliant governments in neighboring states and the resulting emergence of "satellite" countries committed the United States as early as 1945 to an adversary position that risked confrontation and recurrent diplomatic and military crises. The fear that the Soviets would eventually possess their own nuclear capability increased tensions, and Congressmen occasionally joined influential public leaders in calling for a preventative war before Russia acquired the bomb. While resisting such action, Truman and his secretary of state, James F. Byrnes, with the bipartisan support of Senator Vandenberg, decided that it was impossible to seek a policy of mutual trust and collaboration with Russia. The developing Cold War led early in 1947 to a fateful step. When Great Britain informed Truman that she would no longer be able to maintain protective forces in the eastern Mediterranean and the Mideast, the President went before a joint session of Congress on March 12 to enunciate what became known as the Truman Doctrine, proposing that the United States immediately fill the vacuum in the region and use military and economic resources to contain Soviet expansion in Greece, Turkey, and wherever else it threatened in Europe, whether openly or by subversion. By May 9 both houses had overwhelmingly endorsed the new doctrine.

This was the beginning of a congressional habit of placing broad, vaguely limited powers in the hands of the executive, who made the fullest use of the authority. There was little concern expressed in Congress that the President might imperil the nation with the containment policy. A few members agreed with Senator Taft that the United States was being maneuvered into "pulling Britain's chestnuts out of the fire," but most Senators and Representatives were willing to back forceful anti-Communist leadership. In the same year, to stave off the economic collapse of other European nations and set them on the road to reconstruction, the administration devised the Marshall Plan (first described by Secretary of State George C. Marshall in a commencement address at Harvard University). Offering aid to all European countries (the Communist states decided not to participate), the plan had no strings attached to it, though its supporters hoped that by reinvigorating European economies it would strengthen anticommunism. Truman did his homework well, gaining advance support from Vandenberg and Republican Representative Charles A. Eaton, the chairmen respectively of the Senate Foreign Relations and the House Foreign Affairs committees—the Republicans had won control of both houses in 1946—and from an eighteen-member bipartisan group of Representatives, led by Republican Christian A. Herter of Massachusetts, that had toured the devastated areas of Europe and seen the desperate need for aid. On November 17 Truman called a special session of Congress, presenting the Marshall Plan and asking for $17 billion for its long-term implementation. The proposal drew sharp criticism from various Republicans: Senator Homer Ferguson of Michigan dismissed it as "a global WPA," and the newly elected Senator McCarthy demanded that for every dollar given a European country the United States receive a dollar's worth of foreign bases or strategic supplies. But Russia, by staging a Communist coup in Czechoslovakia in February, 1948, and restricting access to West Berlin, roused Congress' anti-Soviet feelings, and the Marshall Plan was approved on April 2, 1948.

Even before the Marshall Plan went into effect, five western European countries joined in a fifty-year political and military alliance, aimed principally against Communist expansion. Truman believed that it should be enlarged and with American participation converted into a strong defensive bulwark against the Soviet Union. To prepare the Republican-controlled Congress for this new foreign venture (the idea of "no entangling alliances" was still strong among the legislature's many former isolationists), he prevailed on Vandenberg to assist him. The Michigan Senator, now an enthusiastic convert to collective security against Russia, needed no persuading. He offered a "sense of the Senate" resolution, declaring the right of members of the United Nations to join in regional arrangements for their collective defense and asserting the intention of the United States to join such arrangements "should any armed attack occur threatening its national security." The Senate Foreign Relations Committee endorsed it unanimously, and on June 11, 1948, the Senate approved it, 64 to 4.

The Vandenberg Resolution paved the way for Truman to negotiate with the European countries for an enlarged defense organization that would include the United States. On April 4, 1949, twelve nations signed the North Atlantic Treaty, agreeing that an attack against one would be considered an attack against all, and binding all of them to the defense of the one attacked. To implement the treaty Truman had to ask Congress for arms for the alliance members, but fearing defeat in the Senate if he made it sound too militaristic, he first submitted the treaty alone for ratification. The Foreign Relations Committee reported it unanimously, but the Senate witnessed a sharp debate over its implications. Like the rejected covenant of the League of Nations, the treaty would involve the nation in a "moral commitment" to fight other people's wars, charged Republican Forrest C. Donnell of Missouri. Others pointed out that it would take away from Congress and put in the hands of the executive the right to declare war. In his last major fight (he would soon be gone from Congress, incapacitated by illness), Vandenberg defended the treaty, blunting most of the opposition from members of his own party and maintaining for the President a bipartisan majority. After beating down crippling reservations by Republican Senators Taft, Watkins of Utah, and Kenneth S. Wherry of Nebraska, the Senate approved the treaty, 82 to 13, on July 21, 1949, with its opponents still charging that the action delivered Congress' war power to the President.

Two days later Truman requested $1.45 billion for military assistance for the other nations in the pact, as well as for Iran, the Philippines, and South Korea. Containment was now worldwide, with the United States giving it direction and footing the bill. The request shocked even Vandenberg, and a new debate broke out, this time in both houses. Many members thought the nation was going too far, too fast, overextending itself as a "policeman of the world"; even the House Armed Services Committee, whose leadership habitually came close to giving the Pentagon all it asked for, missed by one vote cutting the request in half. Again an overseas event decided the issue. In September, 1949, the United States learned with a shock that Russia had exploded an atomic bomb. The Mutual Defense Assistance Act promptly roared through both houses with big majorities, and by September, 1950, NATO—the North Atlantic Treaty Organization— was an established fact.

In 1949, meanwhile, the Chinese Communists had gained control of their country, sending the Nationalists in flight to Formosa, loosing a torrent of criticism of the Truman administration by the so-called "China lobby" and its vocal supporters in Congress—including California's Republican Senator William Knowland and Minnesota's Republican Representative Walter H. Judd—for having "given China away." The charge was illogical—the United States had withdrawn from China after having failed to work out a *modus vivendi* between the Communists and the Nationalists, whose corruption and ineffectiveness were the true causes of their defeat. Nevertheless, many Republicans, sensing a popular political issue, delivered blunderbuss attacks on the administration and the Democrats for not having stood up to Chinese communism. As if responding to this criticism— though obviously he was following his developing policy of containment— Truman took another fateful step in May, 1950, announcing, under the blanket authorization given him by the Truman Doctrine, that the United States would aid France's colonial administration in fighting the Communist-led Vietminh in Indochina. Viewing the Vietminh as an arm of monolithic Russian and Chinese communism bent on seizing Southeast Asia, the United States paid $4 billion—some eighty percent of the war's cost—before the French were defeated in 1954.

With the same reasoning, Truman, on June 27, 1950—without consulting Congress—ordered American forces to aid South Korea, which had been attacked by the Communist government of North Korea. The United Nations gave Truman justification for his action by calling on all UN members for help in defending South Korea. Though Truman did not ask Congress for a war declaration, insisting that he was using emergency powers authorized during World War II, there was little opposition to his intervention until the end of the year, after China had entered the war and inflicted serious reverses on the American forces. Various public figures questioned the nation's military commitments abroad, and when others defended NATO and the Korean action, a "great debate" began. In January, 1951,

Senators Wherry and Taft opened an attack on the President in Congress. Wherry introduced a resolution opposing the commitment of ground troops to duty in Europe without congressional authorization, which Taft supported with an impassioned assertion that the President "had no authority whatever to commit American troops to Korea without consulting Congress and without congressional approval," adding that he had no power, either, "to agree to send American troops to fight in Europe in a war between the members of the Atlantic Pact and Soviet Russia." In his State of the Union message to the Democratic-controlled Eighty-second Congress Truman attacked Wherry's resolution, as did NATO's supreme commander, General Dwight D. Eisenhower, in an address to a joint congressional session. The debate gradually focused on the commitment of troops to Europe rather than to Korea, and it ended on April 4 with a victory for the Democrats and the internationalist Republicans. Two resolutions, substituted for Wherry's, were passed, endorsing the dispatch of four American divisions to Europe but stating that it was the sense of the Senate that the President send no additional ground troops to Europe without congressional approval. Since neither resolution had the force of law, Truman hailed them, but he continued to disregard Congress in the matter of military commitments. The weak conclusion of the "great debate" confirmed Congress' continued abdication of power. It gave the coloration of endorsement of broad authorization and leadership to the President and to the military and administrative agencies that supported the overseas commitments.

In 1952 another attempt was made in the Senate to curb the President's foreign-policy powers. Senator John W. Bricker of Ohio, a Republican isolationist, and fifty-eight cosponsors proposed a constitutional amendment that reflected a growing concern over American adherence to UN conventions and agreements that had the effect of treaties and therefore under the Constitution had to be accepted as the "supreme law of the land." Appealing to the resentment of many conservative lawmakers at the President's increasing use of executive agreements that were not subject to their ratification, the Bricker Amendment, revised and reintroduced the next year with sixty-three cosponsors, would have limited the scope of treaties and imposed congressional controls on the making of international agreements. The proposal was the subject of heated debate in the Senate during 1953 and again in 1954, when on one occasion it came within one vote of receiving the two-thirds majority required for approval. Largely because it implied retreat from collective security and participation in the UN, it did not receive support from the Eisenhower administration, however, and after it was raised again briefly in 1956, the leadership of the Senate, again controlled by the Democrats, let it die without a vote. Once more Congress, fearful of hobbling executive leadership in the face of continuing confrontations with communism, rejected an opportunity to regain some of its authority.

For the last six of his eight years in office (1953–61), Eisenhower had the unique experience of facing a Senate and House ruled by the opposite party. He was favored, however, by the coalition of Republicans and conservative Democrats who on many issues exercised actual control over legislation and generally supported the President, and by a harmonious working relationship with Speaker Rayburn and Rayburn's Texas protégé, the influential Senate majority leader, Lyndon B. Johnson. Tall, gracious, and outgoing, Johnson cultivated superb personal relations with other members of Congress and built up a network of loyal followers in both parties whom he shrewdly manipulated by an intimate knowledge of their personalities, needs, and thinking. Johnson first entered the House in 1937 and idolized President Roosevelt, but though he supported a continuation and extension of Roosevelt's domestic and foreign policies, he, like Rayburn, practiced politics as "the art of the possible" and gained respect and prestige even among conservative Democrats and Republicans by catering and deferring to them. He was elected to the Senate in 1948 and by 1953 had become minority leader. By force of personality, cunning use of his power to make committee assignments, and what became known as the Johnson Treatment—the overwhelming and often theatrical employment of every facet of human emotion to win support from an individual—he dominated the Senate until his retirement to run for Vice President in 1960. In the cadre of his Senate supporters he counted a bizarre mixture of legislators of every persuasion, ranging from the conservative southern Democrats Harry F. Byrd of Virginia and Richard B. Russell of Georgia and the Senate's senior Republican, H. Styles Bridges of New Hampshire, to liberal Democrats Hubert Humphrey of Minnesota and Richard Neuberger of Oregon and liberal Republican Margaret Chase Smith of Maine. With such a backing, Johnson was essential to Eisenhower, and the two men frequently worked together as a team.

Though Johnson and Rayburn encouraged congressional deference to the executive in foreign and military affairs, Johnson as minority leader in 1954 managed to exercise a personal restraint on the President when the Vietminh surrounded French forces at Dienbienphu in Vietnam and threatened France's ability to contain communism in that country. Eisenhower and Secretary of State John Foster Dulles prepared to intervene with American air power, but in a rare show of congressional independence Johnson, supported by Senator Russell, the ranking Democrat on the Armed Services Committee, and other Senators, interposed an objection and persuaded the President to change his mind. The experience of Korea, from which the United States had extricated itself with great difficulty, was still fresh in mind, and the Democratic leaders convinced the administration that the American people would not support another military involvement in Southeast Asia. Nevertheless, when France did evacuate its troops from Vietnam after being overwhelmed at Dienbienphu, the critical need—as it was seen at the time—to continue containing communism in that part of the world induced the administration to take France's place as rapidly as possible in all Indochina. The first steps were diplomatic. The United States attended a conference at Geneva in April, 1954, where accords were framed that divided Vietnam into a Communist-controlled north and an anti-Communist south, but provided for a referendum on reunification. From that point on the administration worked actively and largely in secrecy—withholding information from Congress except for a few selected members of the leadership—to bolster the anti-Communist forces in Indochina and scuttle the referendum in South Vietnam. With the support of Congress, appropriations were made each year from 1955 to 1961 for military aid to South Vietnam, Cambodia, and Laos, and advisory functions and clandestine missions were assumed by an increasing number of American personnel, whose activities, without specific congressional authorization, steadily raised the level of American involvement in Southeast Asian affairs.

Early in 1955, when the Chinese Communists threatened to seize offshore islands as a prelude to an invasion of Formosa, Eisenhower asked Congress for authority to use American forces to protect Formosa and "related positions and territories," stating that he wanted Congress to make clear to the Communists the nation's intention "to fight if necessary." Though a number of Democrats balked at the ambiguity of the request, maintaining suspicions that it would involve the United States in an attempt by Nationalist China to regain the mainland, Johnson, Rayburn, and the Democratic leaders supported another broad conveyal of power to the executive. On January 25, by a vote of 410 to 3, the House approved a resolution authorizing the President to "employ the armed forces . . . as he deems necessary" in the defense of Formosa. The resolution met considerably stronger opposition in the Senate, where Estes Kefauver, Hubert Humphrey, Ralph Flanders, Wayne Morse of Oregon, Herbert H. Lehman of New York, and William Langer of North Dakota all attacked its ambiguity and tried to limit the President's authority. They were beaten down, and the resolution was passed by the Senate on January 28.

Communist China made no serious move toward Formosa, and as a weapon of containment the resolution was deemed successful. In 1957 the man who devised it, Secretary of State Dulles, believed that a similar expression of congressional support was required to meet a developing Russian threat to the Middle East. Eisenhower went before a joint session of Congress to ask for authorization to give military and economic aid to Middle Eastern nations and to use the armed forces to protect that area against "overt armed aggression from any nation controlled by international communism." Dubbed the Eisenhower Doctrine, the proposal was attacked at first by members of both parties as "vague" and a "blank check." When Lyndon Johnson complained of the generalities and lack of specific information in the administration's draft resolution, Dulles replied, "If we have to pinpoint everything we propose to do, this program will not serve its purpose. If Congress is not willing to trust the President to the extent he asks, we can't win this battle." Congress agreed to trust the President again and gave Eisenhower the authorization he requested. A year later, when internal disorder stirred fear of Russian intervention in Lebanon, Eisenhower used the blanket authorization to land American Marines in that country. Though the risk of war with Russia seemed great, he did not consult Congress. The Soviets did not intervene, however.

Even more completely beyond Congress' control than foreign and military affairs were clandestine operations carried out by the intelligence branches of the armed services and the Central Intelligence Agency. Deemed necessary weapons in the Cold War, the intelligence organizations had the potential of involving the United States in international complications that could, if serious enough, lead to war, yet because of the secrecy their operations required, Congress handled their appropriations and oversight in minimal fashion. CIA expenditures were disguised and rarely questioned, and even the committees of the two houses charged with overseeing the CIA abdicated their roles, neither asking for nor receiving detailed information on CIA activities. "I don't know anything about it, and I don't want to know anything about it," said one Representative when a newspaper once disclosed a questionable CIA activity.

Freed of meaningful accountability, the intelligence services fought totalitarianism with the methods of totalitarianism, abandoning the niceties —and the morals and values—of America's democratic traditions. Knowledge that the United States was countering Communist spies and subversion with a spy system of its own generated a sense of security, but the American people, and most members of Congress, were unprepared for an announcement by Russia in May, 1960, that she had brought down an American U-2 spy plane, one of a number that for four years had been making secret photographic reconnaissance flights over the U.S.S.R. At first the Eisenhower administration denied the Russian assertion categorically. Finally, however, Eisenhower revealed that the Russians were correct, and that he himself had authorized the espionage flights. The incident resulted in the Russians' cancellation of a forthcoming summit meeting; but the government's dissemblance was more of a shock to America than the U-2 flight or the canceled conference.

In the Cold War against communism, the executive branch's deception of Congress and the people became thereafter almost a matter of habit, spreading from the concealing of secret intelligence activities to the hiding of ineptitude, maladministration, and fraud in other phases of government operations, and during the Nixon administration to unprecedented lying by the President of the United States, the Vice President, and other high officials about political and domestic matters that had nothing to do with foreign relations. To the extent that "power corrupts and absolute power corrupts absolutely," the flow of broad authorizations from Congress to the executive, compounded by congressional deference, collusion, and weak leadership, contributed to an erosion of executive credibility that reached a climax in 1974. Although the CIA was a special case, it played a continuing rule in the deterioration of general accountability and trust. Within a year after the U-2 affair, President Kennedy was trapped in a skein of falsehoods woven around a CIA-directed attempt by Cuban exiles to retake their island from Fidel Castro, who had established a revolutionary pro-Communist Cuban government. Kennedy shouldered the blame for the botched invasion of Cuba that foundered in April, 1961, at the Bay of Pigs, but Congress permitted the CIA's role to remain so dark and mysterious that a welter of rumors in later years linked the event with the assassination of President Kennedy and with the Watergate burglary.

The CIA in time became associated in the public's mind with the growing American involvement in Southeast Asia; the overthrow of governments in Asia, Africa, and Central and South America; and with the assassination of heads of state and political leaders unfriendly to the United States. In no case did Congress conduct a meaningful inquiry, call the CIA to account, or lay down admissible guidelines for the agency. The CIA was the most notable example of an element of government that had slipped from the harness that the framers of the Constitution had fashioned to restrain tyranny. In the aftermath of the 1974 Watergate scandals, Congress was at last goaded into calling the CIA to account. Investigations by select committees in both houses, as well as a less demanding administration commission headed by Vice President Nelson A. Rockefeller, at last, in 1975, began to throw light on more than twenty-five years of the agency's operations. Even so, Congress' old, fixed habit of acquiescence to the CIA's need for secrecy was still so strong that in June, 1975, when it was revealed that the chairman of the lower chamber's investigating group had concealed for more than a year knowledge of CIA plans to assassinate foreign leaders, conflict raged in the House over whether Representatives had a right to make such information public.

Meanwhile, the building of the Berlin Wall between East and West Berlin and Soviet threats to Allied rights in Berlin led Kennedy to ask Congress in July, 1961, for authority to call certain reservists and extend the enlistment period of men on active duty. Congress readily granted his request in a joint resolution. A long-smoldering crisis followed, and a year later, in October, 1962, Congress on its own gave support to the President's determined stand on the Berlin question by passing a "sense of the Congress" resolution, designed, said its sponsor, Democratic Representative Clement J. Zablocki of Wisconsin, to let Russia "know that our nation stands united behind the Administration's firm policy on Berlin." It passed without a single vote of opposition in either house. At the same time a new crisis loomed in Cuba, when it was learned that Russia was shipping missiles to that island. On September 7, 1962, Senator Everett McKinley Dirksen of Illinois and Representative Charles A. Halleck of Indiana, the Republican minority leaders, urged Congress to authorize the President to use military force to "meet the Cuban problem." Such a resolution was premature, and Kennedy headed it off by seeking—and receiving—authorization merely to call up reservists, as he had done the year before. When some members of Congress persisted in seeking specific action against Cuba, the administration forces once more headed them off with a joint resolution, passed overwhelmingly by both houses, declaring a determination to use force if necessary to prevent Cuba from extending subversive activities elsewhere in the hemisphere or permitting itself to become a base for foreign military installations that endangered the United States. With this backing, Kennedy led the nation to a firm, but perilous, confrontation with Russia over the missile bases being built in Cuba, declaring a naval and air quarantine of that island and finally forcing Soviet Premier Nikita Khrushchev to halt construction of the bases and remove the rockets.

In the months that followed the missile crisis, relations between the United States and Russia gradually improved. Efforts were begun to reach agreement over the proliferation of nuclear weapons (a treaty was finally signed in 1968 and ratified by the Senate the next year). On May 27, 1963, Senators Humphrey of Minnesota and Dodd of Connecticut, proposing a new approach to ease international tensions, introduced a resolution urging the United States to seek agreement on a ban of nuclear tests in the atmosphere or underwater. Kennedy supported the proposal, and by July such an agreement had been concluded. The President sent the treaty to the Senate, and after bipartisan majorities rejected reservations by Republican Senators Barry Goldwater of Arizona and John G. Tower of Texas, the upper chamber ratified it, 80 to 19, on September 24, 1963. In a short time more than one hundred nations signed the test-ban treaty.

Under already existing authorizations Kennedy, meanwhile, had steadily escalated the effort to bolster the Southeast Asian nations' ability to withstand Communist pressure, before his death increasing the number of American military men in South Vietnam to sixteen thousand and sending troops also to Thailand. To those who objected, he explained that the American ground forces in Vietnam were "not combat troops in the generally understood sense of the word." Actually, they included military advisers for the South Vietnamese army and units trained in jungle fighting, and by June, 1962, they were beginning to suffer casualties. Congress had very little control over what was going on in Vietnam, but with a few exceptions the leadership and members of both houses ardently backed the administration, some legislators such as Senator Goldwater pushing for even more vigorous action.

Together with Kennedy and his successor, Lyndon Johnson, the overwhelming majority of the members of Congress dismissed the claim of the insurgent Vietcong in South Vietnam that, having been denied the promised referendum, they were fighting a civil war to reunify their country. Instead, most of the legislators insisted that international communism was still monolithic and that the Vietcong and North Vietnamese were one of its spearheads, directed by China, bent on extending communism throughout Southeast Asia. Unless the Communist aggression was halted, they believed, all the countries in the area would topple like dominoes. To some extent, administration hawkishness was heightened by a fear of even more extreme hawks in Congress, particularly Senator Goldwater, whose growing stature as the Republicans' presidential candidate in 1964 threatened the Democrats with defeat. In addition, McCarthyism in the country was not dead. It had been revived by the John Birch Society, whose attacks on the administration for "softness" toward communism inevitably stiffened the policy planners' backs and moved them to prove their anti-communism by the zeal of their hawkishness. Still other pressures working on the administration, as well as on Congress, were the lobbyists of the military-industrial complex, which had grown more powerful as a political-economic force since President Eisenhower warned the nation against it in his farewell address, and the Air Force leadership of the Joint Chiefs of Staff, which had hoped for a provocation by China that would permit it to eliminate the centers where the Chinese were developing an atomic bomb of their own.

By the time Lyndon Johnson became President, Congress was in a warlike mood toward North Vietnam. Overt and covert aid to South Vietnam and Laos was increasing, and while Johnson, facing election in 1964, held out hope that he would send no ground combat troops to Indochina, the assaults of Vietcong guerrillas that were causing American deaths raised the intensity of the attacks of his opponent, Senator Goldwater, who led a growing movement for an uninhibited air-and-sea offensive against North Vietnam. As congressional support for such action increased, the administration's policy leaders finally fell in line, drawing up a draft resolution for Congress to give the President a free hand in stepping up the military pressure. Their opportunity came early in August, 1964, when two American destroyers on intelligence patrol in the Gulf of Tonkin off North Vietnam were attacked by North Vietnamese torpedo boats. In retaliation, on August 4, President Johnson issued orders that inaugurated the bombing of North Vietnam and the next day presented his joint resolution to Congress, asking approval "to take all necessary measures to repel any armed attack against the forces of the United States and to prevent further aggression." Amid an atmosphere of grave crisis, Congress on August 7 agreed to what would become the most fateful and controversial of all its presidential authorizations, the House, by a vote of 414 to 0, and the Senate, 88 to 2, registering their approval of the Tonkin Gulf Resolution. Only Democratic Senators Ernest Gruening of Alaska and Wayne Morse of Oregon opposed the resolution, Morse warning angrily that America would one day regret the vote.

In the ensuing stepped-up American intervention in Southeast Asia, the Democratic leadership of the House, composed of Speaker McCormack, majority leader Carl Albert of Oklahoma, and majority whip Thomas Hale

Boggs, Sr., of Louisiana, together with the chairmen of the Armed Services Committee and its subcommittees, gave the executive branch enthusiastic support. In 1965 the venerable Carl Vinson of Georgia, who had been in the House for a record-making fifty years, retired, and his post as chairman of the House Armed Services Committee was taken by L. Mendel Rivers of South Carolina, a combative man with a heavy shock of white hair that fell to his collar in the back, who at times kept a loaded derringer on his desk. Supported by a battery of hawkish Democratic subcommittee chairmen, including F. Edward Hébert of Louisiana, Chet Holifield of California, and Melvin Price of Illinois, Rivers gave the Pentagon what it requested, frequently arguing over details but becoming so obliging that some Pentagon officials regarded members of his committee as "stooges." Rivers had a considerable hold over Speaker McCormack, and the two men worked together to keep the House militantly behind the presidential war policy and bury any dove-like sentiment under an avalanche of loyal votes. Year after year, as the war dragged on and disillusionment and opposition arose among the American people, McCormack and Rivers held the Democrats in line, joined by Republicans under minority leader Gerald R. Ford of Michigan and Melvin R. Laird of Wisconsin, who differed with the Democrats only in their impatience with the administration for not taking more aggressive actions against North Vietnam—even if such actions risked Chinese and Russian intervention—to win the war.

In 1965 the first sign of Democratic opposition to the war appeared in the House when twenty-eight Democratic liberals requested Thomas E. Morgan of Pennsylvania, chairman of the Foreign Affairs Committee, to hold hearings on Vietnam policy. Morgan rejected the suggestion, and the halfheartedness of the doves was reflected when the House the same year voted, 393 to 1, for an amendment to the Selective Service Act, introduced by Rivers, to punish draft-card burners with a $10,000 fine and up to five years in prison. The lone negative vote was cast by a New York Republican Representative, Henry P. Smith III, who thought that a five-year prison sentence was too severe. After Republican Strom Thurmond of South Carolina spoke for the measure in the Senate, it rolled through that body by a voice vote, the entire debate in both houses having required less than ten minutes. It was in the Senate, nevertheless, that the escalating war received its first serious questioning when Democratic Senator John C. Stennis of Mississippi in 1966 told Secretary of State Dean Rusk, "You stand on mighty thin ice if you rely on the Tonkin Gulf Resolution as a constitutional basis for this war." That theme was pursued the following year when Democratic Senator Albert Gore of Tennessee and Republican Senators Charles H. Percy of Illinois and Bourke B. Hickenlooper of Iowa took issue with Under Secretary of State Nicholas deB. Katzenbach's description of the Tonkin Gulf Resolution as the "functional equivalent" of a declaration of war. The Senate made no move, however, to restrict activities in

Vietnam, though in the House that year many leading Democrats, including Thomas P. "Tip" O'Neill, Jr., of Massachusetts, Morris Udall of Arizona, and Claude Pepper of Florida, began to turn against the war.

Though the Communists' powerful Tet Offensive in January, 1968, made little impact on McCormack and the House hawks, revolt was brewing among liberal Democrats in both chambers, particularly among members of the Senate Foreign Relations Committee, led by its chairman, J. W. Fulbright of Arkansas. Events outside the Capitol—Minnesota Senator Eugene McCarthy's Democratic presidential primary victory on a peace platform in New Hampshire; New York Senator Robert F. Kennedy's entry in the presidential race, also as a dove; and President Johnson's announcements that he would not seek re-election, had ordered a bombing halt over three quarters of North Vietnam, and would pursue a nonmilitary solution of the war—strengthened the end-the-war advocates in Congress. Although peace talks opened in Paris on May 10, and the bombing of all North Vietnam ended on October 31, 1968, the war nevertheless continued. When Richard Nixon became President in 1969 and announced a policy of "Vietnamization"—the withdrawal of American troops and the turning over of the conduct of the war to South Vietnam—both houses of Congress, though still controlled by the Democrats, agreed to give him time. When nothing happened, patience wore thin in the Senate, which on June 25, 1969, adopted the National Commitments Resolution, declaring it to be the sense of the Senate that no troops should be committed to hostilities abroad in the future without "affirmative action" by Congress. On October 28 Fulbright charged that the United States had been conducting a war in Laos without the knowledge or consent of Congress, and on December 15 the Senate in an unusual secret session added an amendment to the defense appropriations bill forbidding the introduction of American ground combat troops into Laos or Thailand. House conferees agreed to the amendment, and President Nixon signed it.

Debate on the National Commitments Resolution had revealed the scope of Congress' abdication of its constitutional right to declare war. As a result of treaties, agreements, policy statements, and the existence of bases abroad, the United States had become committed to the military defense of more than forty-two countries. This realization helped spur new attempts to quicken withdrawal from Indochina. During 1970 a number of Senators, including majority leader Mike Mansfield of Montana, Democrats Frank Church of Idaho and George McGovern of South Dakota, and Republicans Mark O. Hatfield of Oregon, John Sherman Cooper of Kentucky, and Edward W. Brooke of Massachusetts, sponsored antiwar measures. None of them was adopted, but President Nixon's sudden decision to extend the war by sending troops into Cambodia in April, 1970, caused an uproar among antiwar groups across the country and led to a six-week debate in the Senate on an amendment to the Military Sales Bill, introduced by Cooper and Church, to bar the use of funds for military operations in Cambodia. A diluted version—applying only to ground troops—passed Congress in January, 1971, long after Nixon had withdrawn the ground forces from Cambodia. Meanwhile, on July 10, 1970, the Senate voted, 57 to 5, to repeal the Tonkin Gulf Resolution.

In 1971, with American troops still in action in South Vietnam, the Senate attached Mansfield amendments to three different bills, calling for the withdrawal of all forces by a certain date. Though the peace forces had greatly increased in the House, Carl Albert, who had become Speaker after McCormack's retirement, and Hale Boggs, who had become majority leader ("Tip" O'Neill was the Democratic whip), continued to muster a majority to give Nixon more time, and the House killed the Mansfield amendments and rejected similar proposals by its own members. The doves made no further progress in 1972, a presidential election year marked by Nixon's initiation of detente with China and Russia and a sudden heavy bombing of North Vietnam to try to force her to make peace. The Paris peace accords were finally signed on January 27, 1973, and the last American troops left South Vietnam on March 29. Finally, in May, the House, in its first antiwar action, voted to stop the bombing of Cambodia. With American forces and prisoners out of Vietnam, the majority of the Representatives had at last decided to end America's military involvement in Southeast Asia, and Speaker Albert and the Democratic leadership went along with the House in its first foreign-affairs rebuff to a President in decades. When the Senate went further, also banning the bombing of Laos, and tacking the provision on every urgent appropriations bill, the administration faced an operating crisis. Nixon finally agreed to the bans if the cutoff date were delayed, and the House accepted the compromise; but it hardened the final version of the amendment to bar all combat activity in North and South Vietnam as well as Cambodia and Laos. Congress passed the measure, and Nixon had to sign it on July 1, 1973, at last bringing all American overt military action in Southeast Asia to an end on August 15.

During the course of the peace negotiations in January, 1973, Nixon had secretly assured the South Vietnamese President, Nguyen Van Thieu, that the United States would give him new support if the North Vietnamese seriously breached the peace terms. The existence of this assurance was revealed only in the spring of 1975, when the North Vietnamese launched their final victorious offensive against Thieu's government. Even if the new President, Gerald Ford, had wished to honor Nixon's promise, he could no longer do so, for the congressional ban of August 15, 1973, made it impossible. Still, Ford came close to risking violation of the prohibition at the time of South Vietnam's collapse, first in the confusion attending the use of troops to evacuate Americans and South Vietnamese before the advancing Communist forces, and second in a brief use of military force to free the crew of the American merchant ship *Mayagüez,* seized by Cambodians in May, 1975. In both instances, Congress backed him up.

In what appeared to be a grand climax to the reversal of almost thirty years of deferring to Presidents in foreign affairs, Congress followed its 1973 ban on military action in Southeast Asia by passing the War Powers Act, which set a sixty-day limit on any presidential commitment of American forces overseas without congressional authorization. Congress, moreover, could make the time limit shorter by passing a concurrent resolution, which did not need the President's approval. This landmark bill reflected Congress' first determined act to reassert its constitutional power to declare war. On October 24, 1973, Nixon vetoed the measure, calling it "both unconstitutional and dangerous." It was certain that the Senate would override the veto, but on five previous occasions during that session the House had failed to override Nixon vetoes. In a dramatic vote on November 7, the House turned against the President, 284 to 135, with many conservative southern Democrats, as well as Republicans, providing the two-thirds majority. A few hours later the Senate also overrode the veto, 75 to 18. It was a severe defeat for Nixon and also a historic move in re-establishing coequality between the legislative and executive branches. In the potential crises that still faced the nation in the Mideast, Korea, and elsewhere, the President might still take the initiative, but if Congress wished to check him it would have the power to do so and could, at least, participate in the making of fateful international decisions.

Events during the Nixon administration also climaxed postwar relations between the executive and Congress in domestic affairs. At the close of World War II, the honeymoon between Truman and the legislature ended quickly when the new President, faced with spiraling inflation, bitter labor disputes, and an acute housing shortage, called for a program of measures that smacked too much of New Deal-type social and economic reforms for the coalition of southern Democrats and Republicans in Congress to accept. Truman bungled and lost a fight with Congress over the extension of price controls, managed to win passage of a so-called "Full Employment Act" in February, 1946, to help stabilize the economy, and provoked a long running fight with southerners (who engaged in a number of Senate filibusters) over his championing of a permanent Fair Employment Practice Committee. In 1945 the conservative coalition—in something of a posthumous slap at Roosevelt—put through the Twenty-second Amendment, limiting a President to two terms won by his own election (it was ratified on February 26, 1951). For the first time in sixteen years the Republicans took control of both houses in the 1946 fall elections and the next year achieved their aim of restricting the actions of labor unions by the passage of the Taft-Hartley Act over Truman's veto. With Joseph W. Martin of Massachusetts as Speaker and Robert A. Taft, the former President's son and a man of great integrity but cold personality, chairing the Senate's Republican Policy Committee, Congress also passed a measure coordinating the armed services into a single Department of Defense; an act to permit the entry of immigrants displaced in the aftermath of the war; an anti-inflation law; and a new presidential succession act, making the Speaker first, and the President *pro tempore* of the Senate next, in line after the Vice President.

On the whole, during the first three postwar years the dominant conservative coalition in Congress blocked a revival of progressive reforms, but, save for its anti-labor action, it lacked the strength to dismantle or seriously reverse the basic economic and social measures of the New Deal, which now seemed a permanent part of American life. Truman's troubles with the Republican Congress galled him, however, and running as an underdog for re-election in 1948 against Dewey, he attacked what he called the "do-nothing" Eightieth Congress and scored a stunning upset victory, helping to return control of both houses to the Democrats. Flushed with his victory, he urged congressional acceptance of his Fair Deal program of progressive legislation. The conservative coalition was still powerful, however, and during the next four years Truman was only partly successful. The minimum wage level was raised to 75 cents an hour, the President was given power at the time of the Korean War to stabilize wages and prices, social security was extended, and aid was given to highways and housing. At the same time two internal security measures, authored primarily by Nevada's Democratic Senator Pat McCarran (whom Truman hated), were passed over his vetoes, and his request for congressional approval of his seizure of steel mills during a 1952 wage-price dispute was ignored (the Supreme Court later ruled his action unconstitutional).

In 1952 moderate Republicans frustrated Taft's followers at the GOP convention and nominated General Eisenhower as their presidential candidate. The Democrats selected Governor Adlai E. Stevenson of Illinois, the grandson of Grover Cleveland's Vice President, and in the ensuing campaign the Republicans, led by Eisenhower's vice-presidential running mate, Senator Nixon, attacked the Democrats for "crime, corruption, and communism." Eisenhower won and the Republicans regained control of both houses, but with so slim a majority that when Senator Taft died in July, 1953, Wayne Morse, then an independent, controlled the balance of voting power in the upper chamber. Enjoying great personal prestige, "Ike" Eisenhower pursued a generally centrist, "standpat" program, using Republican Representative Charles Halleck of Indiana, House majority leader, as his chief lieutenant on Capitol Hill. Speaker Martin also helped him, but conservative Senator Knowland of California, who succeeded Taft as Republican leader in the Senate, frequently split with the President over his moderate policies, and when the Democrats regained control of both houses in 1955, Eisenhower often received more assistance from the Democratic leaders, Rayburn and Johnson, than from Knowland.

During Eisenhower's first term, Congress—after a 22½-hour filibuster by Wayne Morse—passed a bill that Truman had successfully vetoed in the previous session, giving states title to tidelands oil. It also approved a multibillion-dollar federal interstate highway system; urged the termination of federal relations with Indian tribes and the end of the reservation system (a policy so harmful to Indians that the government halted its implementation in 1958); passed the Atomic Energy Act, providing for peaceful uses of atomic energy; established flexible farm-price supports and a soil bank; increased housing programs; and stepped up foreign aid. The House, on March 1, 1954, was subjected to a frightening experience when four Puerto Rican nationalists in the visitors' gallery suddenly opened fire with pistols, wounding five Representatives on the floor. Capitol police quickly overcame the Puerto Ricans, pages became stretcher bearers, and all the Representatives recovered.

In 1956 Eisenhower again defeated Stevenson, but both houses remained in Democratic hands. With Johnson and Rayburn often angering Democratic liberals by their cooperation with the administration (a teamwork that also played a role in undermining congressional independence), Congress during Eisenhower's second term created the National Aeronautics and Space Administration (NASA) to develop an American outer-space program, and, in response to a sudden congressional panic resulting from Soviet space activities that revealed the U.S.S.R.'s advanced technological abilities, passed a tentative and weak National Defense Education Act, providing a minimal program of loans to students.

At the start of the Eighty-sixth Congress in January, 1959, a revolt occurred among House Republicans, who boosted Halleck to the post of minority leader, ousting the seventy-four-year-old Martin, who many Republicans felt had become too subservient to Rayburn and Johnson. With appropriations for foreign aid and the military steadily increasing, a reaction against high spending affected domestic programs, and a coalition of Republicans and southern Democrats, numbering in the Senate John C. Stennis of Mississippi, Sam J. Ervin, Jr., of North Carolina, Allen J. Ellender of Louisiana, Strom Thurmond of South Carolina, Harry F. Byrd of Virginia, and John L. McClellan of Arkansas, forced Johnson and Rayburn to withdraw support of such measures as aid for depressed areas and broadened educational assistance. In addition, they blocked a minimum-wage increase and medical care for the aged, both supported by liberal Democrats and moderate Republicans. Civil-rights legislation, for which a demand was growing, was also shunted aside. In September, 1957, despite a record-breaking one-man filibuster of twenty-four hours, eighteen minutes, by Senator Thurmond, Congress had passed the first civil-rights act since 1875. It met symptoms rather than causes and was toothless. In February, 1960, eighteen southern Senators began another long filibuster against a new civil-rights bill providing limited voting protections for blacks in southern states. The filibuster finally ended in compromise, and on April 8 President Eisenhower signed the measure, which was so watered down that one of its sponsors, Democratic Senator Joseph S. Clark of Pennsylvania, called it "only a pale ghost of our hopes."

Following the 1960 presidential conventions, the Senate presented an unusual scene: Republican candidate Richard Nixon presided as Vice President, and on the floor, as Senators, were the Democratic presidential and vice-presidential candidates, John F. Kennedy and Lyndon Johnson. Kennedy's victory in the fall was the closest in history: he received 49.7 percent of the total vote to Nixon's 49.6 percent. During the "thousand days" of his aborted administration, Kennedy, with stylish sophistication and polished oratory, proclaimed an idealism to meet the challenges of what he called the New Frontier and espoused most of the program that the Democratic liberals, including himself, had pushed in Congress during the last years of the Eisenhower administration. But Lyndon Johnson was no longer majority leader in the Senate and the popular Rayburn, affectionately known as "Mr. Sam," died near the end of 1961, and their successors— Mike Mansfield of Montana as Senate majority leader, John McCormack of Massachusetts as Speaker, and Carl Albert of Oklahoma as Democratic leader in the House—were all weak and permissive and did not enjoy the influence of their predecessors. At the same time, Republican strength in the House had increased and the Republican leaders in both chambers, Halleck in the House and Dirksen in the Senate, suddenly flowered with the disappearance of the overpowering Johnson-Rayburn command. Dirksen, a theatrical orator with a heavy mane of curly hair and a deep-pitched oily voice that gained him the nickname the "Wizard of Ooze," was a likable man despite his propensity for hamminess, which he projected to the nation in the "Ev and Charlie Show," a periodic Republican television fireside-chat type of program that he and Halleck conducted. In the Capitol the two men were astute negotiators, and their bargaining cooperation with southern Democrats blocked much of the new President's domestic program.

The coalition's strength in committees and on the floor of both houses constantly frustrated Kennedy, even though he deferred to his southern opponents and often accepted compromises with them. Nevertheless, before his assassination, Congress passed a minimum wage increase (up to $1.25 an hour), a comprehensive housing act, enabling legislation for the Peace Corps, a manpower development and retraining program, an accelerated public works bill, a tax revision measure, a bill empowering the Food and Drug Administration to evaluate the claims and safety of drugs, and measures for compulsory arbitration in rail disputes, aid for medical education and mental health and retardation, and equal pay for equal work regardless of sex. In addition, funds for the space program were increased, the Twenty-fourth Amendment, abolishing the poll tax, was approved (it was ratified on January 23, 1964), and Kennedy was given authority to cut tariffs under the Trade Expansion Act. Two milestones were reached in 1962: eighty-four-year-old Carl Hayden of Arizona, the Democratic President *pro tempore* of the Senate, marked his fiftieth anniversary as a member of Congress, and eighty-three-year-old Democratic Representative Clarence Cannon of Missouri, chairman of the Appropriations Committee, reported the first $100 billion peacetime budget in American history. The long service and advanced age of both men exemplified what an increasing number of critics felt was one of Congress' weaknesses.

Since the days of Roosevelt, who had concentrated the executive's ability to plan policy, manage the budget, and initiate legislative programs by creating the Executive Office of the President—which in time encompassed such agencies as the Bureau of the Budget, the Council of Economic Advisers, and the National Security Council—Congress had grown used to expecting the President to take the lead in proposing most legislation. This, too, had weakened Congress as a coequal branch, though the legislature believed that it fulfilled its constitutional role adequately by disposing what the President proposed. Kennedy, at any rate, bombarded Congress with legislative requests and got somewhat less than half of what he asked for, some of it in compromised and distorted form. In reaction to the shock of his murder in November, 1963, and in response to the legislative wisdom, astute tactics, and commanding personality of his artful successor, the congressional floodgates suddenly opened—especially after Johnson's landslide victory over Goldwater in 1964, which greatly increased Democratic strength in Congress—and in its most productive sessions since the first Congresses of Wilson and Roosevelt the legislature poured out a stream of bills, some of them measures that had been denied to Kennedy, some of them Johnson's. As a whole, they represented a new surge of liberalism.

Soon after Kennedy's death Congress enacted an aid-to-education bill, including loans for students, that it had long delayed. In the following four years, in general support of Johnson's promulgation of a "Great Society" aimed at encouraging the nation's increasing affluence and spreading it to all elements of the population, Congress, among landmark legislation, passed the Economic Opportunity Act (to wage "a war" on poverty); Medicare (medical aid for the elderly under social security); increased school and college aid; expanded housing acts, including one that set up the Cabinet-level Department of Housing and Urban Development; assistance for mass transit and a bill creating the Department of Transportation, also of Cabinet level; and measures for health research, the National Council on the Arts and the National Foundation on the Arts and Humanities, rent subsidies, auto and road safety, highway beautification, consumer protection, help for educational television and radio, broadened and increased social security, higher minimum wages, and a model cities program to help eliminate urban slums. Responding to a growing concern over the deterioration of the environment, Congress also approved administration bills to create a wilderness system and a Land and Water Conservation Fund, to combat air and water pollution, and to set standards for automobile exhaust emissions. The Twenty-fifth Amendment, clarifying procedure in the case of a disabled President, the death or removal of a President, and a vacancy of the vice presidency, was approved. It was declared ratified on February 10, 1967.

On August 14, 1962, during Kennedy's administration, the first successful cloture vote since 1927 halted a Senate filibuster and permitted passage of the Comsat Act, which created a semipublic corporation to control communications by satellites. Under Johnson's skillful guidance the Senate on June 10, 1964, for the first time in its history voted cloture on a civil-rights filibuster, 71 to 29, clearing the way for passage of the Civil Rights Act of 1964, which enforced the voting rights of blacks and their equal enjoyment of goods, services, and facilities in places of public accommodation. On March 15, 1965, amid tense conflict in the South over the blacks' civil-rights struggle, led by Martin Luther King, Jr., Johnson addressed a night session of Congress to request stronger voting rights legislation. A cloture vote again broke a Senate filibuster on May 25, and Congress passed the Voting Rights Act of 1965, providing for federal registrars to secure fair voting. In 1968 a third cloture vote halted another filibuster, and a new civil-rights measure, the Open Housing Act, went through, adding the capstone to a program that finally made good the promises of the civil-rights acts that Congress had passed and the Supreme Court had nullified a hundred years before.

In the fall of 1968 former Vice President Nixon defeated Johnson's Vice President, Hubert Humphrey, for the presidency, becoming the first chief executive since Zachary Taylor to have both houses of Congress in the hands of the opposing party at the start of his administration. Mansfield and McCormack still led the Democrats, but dissatisfaction surfaced at the start of the Ninety-first Congress in January, 1969, when Edward M. Kennedy of Massachusetts defeated Russell B. Long (the son of Huey Long) for majority whip in the Senate, and fifty-eight Democrats supported Representative Morris Udall of Arizona for the speakership, bringing an announcement from the victorious McCormack that this would be his last term in Congress. On the Republican side, Dirksen died in 1969 and was succeeded as Senate minority leader by Hugh Scott, a Pennsylvania moderate, who found it increasingly hard to represent the erratic, often-changing positions of the new President and his coterie of White House advisers. In the House Halleck had been replaced in 1965, his position as minority leader given to Gerald Ford of Michigan by the Republican conference after a revolt of younger Republican Representatives who wanted a more forceful leader.

Because of the administration's newness, Dirksen's death, and the Democratic congressional majorities, Nixon's legislative program got off to a slow start, and he had few serious confrontations with Congress. He appealed for a "New Federalism" of revenue sharing (the return of certain federal tax monies to the states), the reform of the welfare system and a minimum guaranteed family income, and law and order. Eventually the Democratic liberals began to clash with the President over Pentagon spending (the military budget was cut by $5 billion), the size of foreign aid (it, too, was cut), the building of an antiballistic missile system (Nixon won the necessary funding for it by the margin of one vote in the House), and the construction of a prototype supersonic transport plane (the Senate finally killed it in 1971). A Nixon choice for the Supreme Court was rejected by the Senate (which also rejected a second nominee in 1970).

As inflation began to threaten the economy, conflict arose between the Congress and the administration in 1970 over how to cope with it. Against Nixon's wishes, legislation was passed authorizing the use of a wage-price freeze if it became necessary. Congress also passed the landmark National Environmental Protection Act, setting up an independent agency with broad authority to protect the environment; the Clean Air Act; an anti-crime bill; a measure converting the Post Office Department into a government-owned corporation; and in 1971 the Twenty-sixth Amendment, lowering the voting age to eighteen, which was quickly ratified and became part of the Constitution on June 30 of that year. Nixon's own program of revenue sharing, welfare reform, health insurance, guaranteed family income, and full employment bogged down in 1970 and 1971, partly because of the ailing economy, which caused uncertainty in the administration and clashes with Congress over the best measures for its cure.

The economic situation eased somewhat in the presidential election year of 1972. Nixon's differences with Congress increased during the second session of the Ninety-second Congress (he vetoed sixteen bills), but he was finally given a revenue-sharing measure that authorized $30.2 billion in federal tax money to be distributed among states and local governments over a five-year period. Congress also enacted the Federal Election Campaign Practices Act, limiting campaign expenditures and requiring reports on contributions, and approved the proposed Twenty-seventh (Equal Rights) Amendment, barring discrimination for reasons of sex, and overrode a Nixon veto of a water pollution control act, authorizing some $24.7 billion over three years to fund state and municipal sewage plants and projects to clean up the nation's waters.

In the presidential election Nixon easily defeated Senator George McGovern of South Dakota, who ran a hapless campaign largely mismanaged for him by self-serving amateurs. In their eagerness to win, however, Nixon and his aides, including Cabinet officers, administration heads, and members of the White House staff, conducted the most foul and corrupt campaign in presidential history, indulging in a series of unethical and illegal actions that became known collectively as the Watergate scandals for the Watergate Apartments in the capital, where a foiled burglary led to disclosures of even greater evils in the Nixon administration. Because of the persistence of federal judge John J. Sirica and the Washington *Post* and other elements of the media, evidence was developed that in February, 1973, induced the Senate to create the bipartisan Select Committee on Presidential Campaign Activities under Democratic Senator Sam J. Ervin, Jr., of North Carolina to investigate the campaign. In hearings conducted in front of television cameras during the summer, the committee laid bare an assortment of executive-branch "horrors," centered on President Nixon and his closest aides and encompassing the illegal use and corruption of such agencies as the CIA, the FBI, and the Internal Revenue Service; the employment of government departments to reward administration friends and punish its enemies; the violation of the constitutional liberties of individuals by order of presidential aides; the breaking of election laws by administration members and corporation heads; and the use of the office of the presidency to create the potential for the tyranny of a small group of presidential assistants whom the people did not elect and who were not accountable to Congress.

As the charges broadened and became more grave the President tried to dismiss them, and Vice President Spiro Agnew conducted an abusive offensive against those making the disclosures of misconduct. In October, 1973, Agnew himself was caught in a scandal and forced to resign in disgrace. In his place the President appointed Representative Ford. Relations between Nixon and the Congress deteriorated. The President opened himself to additional charges of usurping Congress' constitutional power of the purse by impounding huge sums that Congress had appropriated for educational, water pollution control, and other programs (a series of court decisions forced Nixon to free the funds). In addition, Nixon flouted Congress by refusing to allow members of the administration to testify before congressional committees, invoked the questionable doctrine of executive privilege to withhold documents and other information that might have cast light on alleged Watergate-related crimes, and stubbornly insisted that he had been ignorant of illegalities for which many of his associates were indicted. His erratic attacks on investigating officials and special prosecutors, together with the release of damaging portions of tape recordings made of his conversations in the White House and the revelation of other charges, including possible income-tax fraud, led to a growing demand for his impeachment.

After deliberations, the House Judiciary Committee, chaired by Democrat Peter W. Rodino, Jr., of New Jersey, at the end of July, 1974, voted three articles of impeachment against Nixon. At the same time the Supreme Court directed the President to release certain tapes that he had continued to withhold. For Nixon this was the last straw; concluding that the House would inevitably impeach him and the Senate convict him, he made public a portion of the withheld tapes which disclosed that he had been engaged in the obstruction of justice and had been lying to Congress and the people for more than a year. To the end a small number of Republican and conservative Democratic members of both houses continued to defend the President. The final revelation shocked them, but also disclosed the extent to which thirty years of presidential primacy had undermined the coequal independence of the national legislature. Seeing it as his role to be the President's defender, Republican Representative David Dennis of Indiana, a member of the House Judiciary Committee who consistently voted against impeachment, remarked that this was not the first time a "client had lied to me." On August 9, 1974, Nixon became the first President to resign.

For a moment, Congress and the nation felt relief. The Constitution and the federal government had safely weathered the unprecedented crisis, and Nixon's personable successor, Gerald R. Ford, radiated integrity and a determination to restore the country's confidence in the Presidency. Popular with many members of both parties in Congress, Ford—the first person to become chief executive of the nation by appointment rather than election —promised the legislature a policy of "communication, conciliation, compromise and cooperation," and Congress, though filled with members anxious to assert Congressional dominance over the White House, responded with assurances of goodwill. In a month, however, the honeymoon ended when Ford angered a large part of the country and most of Congress by pardoning Nixon for all offenses which he committed "or may have committed" while he was President, thus ending the possibility of further action against the former President. Thereafter, the Democratic majorities in both houses showed little inclination to go along with Ford, even subjecting his vice presidential nominee, Nelson A. Rockefeller, to weeks of intensive inquiry and only confirming him one day before the Ninety-third Congress adjourned on December 20.

During its first session in 1973, that Congress, occupied largely with Watergate, passed a $20 billion highway and mass-transit bill that for the first time recognized the growing need to assist urban-area mass-transit facilities. Bucking the strong highway lobbies, the measure authorized the partial use of highway trust funds for such aid. Two other important pieces of legislation that year were an agriculture act that reformed the twenty-year-old method of paying subsidies to farmers and a bill, passed on November 13, 1973, authorizing the immediate construction of an Alaska pipeline to bring oil to a southern port in that state from newly opened fields on the Arctic coast. The latter measure, finally enacted after several years of opposition by conservationists who wished to protect the Alaskan wilderness against development, reflected sudden national impatience occasioned by a new crisis: on October 18, the Arab oil-producing nations of the Middle East, reacting to U.S. support of Israel in its war that month with Arab countries, imposed an oil embargo that struck America with alarming severity. The embargo, which lasted until March 18, 1974, served notice that the nation faced a new and long-range, multifaceted problem that, unless solved, posed grave danger to the country's economy and political stability. The guaranteeing of adequate energy resources, independent of uncertain foreign sources, was only part of the problem; the Arab embargo, which ultimately raised the cost of foreign oil more than 400 percent, gave a critical new impetus to the continuing inflation, which affected international trade, balances of payment, the soundness of the dollar, and the health of the economies of many countries, including the United States.

Although Congress and the Nixon and Ford administrations recognized the seriousness of the energy crisis and its impacts, there was little agreement about what should be done. Late in 1973, while the embargo was still in effect, the first session of the Ninety-third Congress authorized a fuel-allocation and price-control system to administer the distribution of petroleum supplies and avoid abuses resulting from shortages, as well as approving the Alaska pipeline in order to increase domestic oil supplies. The next year the second session approved the creation of a makeshift Federal Energy Administration to coordinate the government's energy-related activities and an Energy Research and Development Administration to try to stimulate the use of alternative energy sources. These, however, were only tentative first steps that fell far short of developing and implementing a necessary policy and program for the nation. Furthermore, when the Arab embargo ended and the immediate supply crisis disappeared, complacency set in. Wrangling over components of a comprehensive energy policy among regional and political interests within Congress, and between Congress and the Administration, frustrated all attempts by the Ninety-third and Ninety-fourth Congresses to pass a meaningful measure that would cut energy consumption, increase U.S. production, and develop new fuel sources within the country. By 1976, when the Ninety-fourth Congress and the Ford Administration were both nearing their end, Congress—which had refused to accept the President's energy program, but had failed to agree on one of its own—shouldered much of the blame, even from some of its own leaders, for the continuance of the interrelated energy-economic crisis. "Since the Arab oil embargo three years ago," complained Representative James C. Wright, Jr., of Texas, who had headed a task force to fashion an energy measure for the House Democratic leadership, "we have tried to do a few timid things . . . we have dabbled . . . But as far as doing anything practical to increase the supply of energy and reduce our dependence upon foreign sources in the foreseeable future, we have done nothing."

Part of the difficulty stemmed from intransigent conflicts between members of Congress who represented producing and consuming interests and different regions of the country, as well as interests of competing energy producers, and who argued for months over tax incentives, price and production controls, deregulation of sources of energy, and other proposals for increasing production and conserving supplies. Part also resulted from inhibited and weak Democratic leadership, which was not only split by the individual members' need to protect their respective constituencies (Speaker Carl Albert of Oklahoma came from an energy-producing state, House majority leader "Tip" O'Neill of Massachusetts represented northeastern fuel consumers), but lost overall control of the legislation by separating it into different elements and sending them to different committees whose bills often bogged down in contention or faced defeat when they were sent to the floor. But a portion of the problem reflected a new stand-off between Congress and the President. Despite its intent to dominate the White House, the Democratic-controlled Congress, largely through continued weakness in leadership, was unable to do so, while in the wake of Watergate Ford could not firmly establish the primacy of the executive.

The President's inability to persuade Congress to accept his energy program (to stimulate production and cut consumption by letting costs and prices rise, which, in the face of the recession, Congress felt would hurt consumers) was only one of many disagreements, often lengthy and rancorous, between the two branches of government. In 1974 the Ninety-third Congress quarreled with Ford for months over his foreign-aid program, forcing him to accept a ban on military aid and arms shipments to Turkey, which had used U.S.-supplied weapons during an invasion of Cyprus, but which was also the site of important American intelligence-gathering bases. It refused to act on an anti-inflation tax proposal that Ford considered essential for the economy, and it overrode the President's veto of a veterans' education bill by large margins in both houses. Ford, in turn, vetoed fourteen bills (one of them, regulating coal strip-mining, was pocket vetoed after Congress adjourned and could not override) and had four of his vetoes overridden, the largest number of such defeats for a President since Truman's difficulties with the Republican-controlled Eightieth Congress in 1948.

At the same time, during 1974, effective Congressional action produced a number of measures which the White House signed. Among them were a major housing act; bills that raised the minimum wage and extended school aid; a landmark act that established standards for private pension plans; a six-year, $11.9 billion mass-transit aid program; a trade-reform measure; and a package of bills creating emergency public jobs and broadening Unemployment Compensation provisions to offset the impacts of the economic recession.

Congress, in the meanwhile, had begun to take important new reform steps. In March, 1973, in the atmosphere of conflict with Nixon and increasing abuse of presidential power, the House voted to open to the public, subject to certain restrictions, all its committee meetings, including bill-drafting sessions. At the same time, the House Democratic caucus—whose use liberal and moderate Democrats had been working to revive as a vehicle to bring about reforms—voted to democratize somewhat the rule against permitting the offering of amendments to important bills on the floor of the House and formed a new House Steering and Policy Committee, headed by Speaker Albert. Albert, in turn, appointed a bipartisan select committee in 1973 to study the House committee system. Headed by Democratic Representative Richard Bolling of Missouri, it recommended changes that committee chairmen and senior members refused to approve. In 1974, however, the House accepted some mild alterations in the committee structure as well as procedural reforms, including one that allowed the organization of new Congresses before they convened. In November, after Nixon's resignation, the Democrats swept the 1974 elections, sending seventy-five new Democratic members to the House of Representatives. Meeting at the Capitol in December under the new rules, the Democratic caucus, charged with the vitality of the many newcomers, made dramatic changes in the House power structure, strengthening the Democratic leadership at the expense of the committee chairmen.

Having already begun the weakening of the seniority system by subjecting committee chairmen to biennial re-election by the Democratic caucus, the members capitalized on personal problems that had undermined the prestige and effectiveness of Wilbur D. Mills of Arkansas, the chairman of the House Ways and Means Committee, and stripped that committee of its power to make other committee assignments for Democrats, while transferring the power to the new Steering and Policy Committee, headed by the Speaker. In addition, the caucus increased the membership of Ways and Means, enlarged the Democratic majorities of all committees, ruled that the caucus must approve the nominations of all subcommittee chairmen of the Appropriations Committee, and further strengthened the Speaker by giving him the power to nominate all Democratic members of the Rules Committee, subject to caucus ratification. Finally, when the Ninety-fourth Congress convened in January, 1975, Representative Albert C. Ullman of Oregon replaced Mills as chairman of Ways and Means and the Democrats continued their attack on the House seniority system, deposing the chairmen of the Agriculture, Armed Services, and Banking and Currency committees. Among the victims was eighty-two-year-old Wright Patman of Texas, the Banking and Currency chairman, in support of whose bonus bill the veterans of World War I had made their ill-fated march on Washington in 1932.

On the Senate side, similar reforms were adopted beginning in 1975. In January of that year, the Democratic caucus struck hard at the Senate's seniority system, ruling that henceforth committee chairmen would be named by secret ballot whenever one-fifth of the members of the caucus requested it. Soon afterward, the Senate passed legislation providing additional staff to assist junior members with their committee work, and on November 5 it followed the example of the House and opened all Senate committee meetings to the public, subject to a number of restrictions. At the same time, it fell in line with another House action, taken earlier in 1975, and agreed to open conference committee sessions unless a majority of the conferees of either house voted to close them. Two years later, in 1977, the Senate drastically reorganized its committee system, cutting down once again the swollen number of its committees, revising their jurisdictions, and ruling that a Senator could serve on no more than three committees and eight subcommittees and, after the Ninety-fifth Congress, chair no more than three committees and subcommittees. In addition, it gave larger staffs to minority members of committees and ordered the computerization of committee meeting schedules to minimize conflicting obligations of the Senators.

The reforms did not stop there. In 1972, to assist the legislators with research and information that would permit them to cope with the executive agencies on measures involving complicated technical and scientific matters, Congress created the Office of Technology Assessment. Beginning its operations in January, 1974, it grew rapidly, meeting the increasing needs of Congress for expertise in energy, transportation, health, and other fields, and by 1979 had a staff of 140 full-time and 500 part-time employees. In 1974 the two houses, frequently overwhelmed in fiscal and budgetary matters by the executive's Office of Management and Budget and Council of Economic Advisers, set up their own budget committees as well as the Congressional Budget Office with a professional staff to establish annual overall spending and deficit ceilings and end the practice of appropriating money in a haphazard fashion without close regard to total revenue and expenditures. The measure also restricted the presidential impoundment of funds that Congress appropriated, one of the sources of conflict between Congress and Nixon. In the same year, finally, the Campaign Finance Act set limits on campaign contributions and expenditures and for the first time established the partial public financing of presidential campaign costs.

Ford's stalemate with Congress continued until the end of his administration. The Democrats' hopes of a veto-proof Ninety-fourth Congress, following their widespread victories in the 1974 post-Watergate elections, were dashed by a combination of ineffective leadership and independence and division among the Democrats in both houses. In the House of Representatives, where the members' average age was below fifty for the first time since World War II, the Democrats had a two-to-one majority, the biggest in ten years. In the Senate, where the youngest member, thirty-four-year-old Patrick J. Leahy, had succeeded eighty-two-year-old George D. Aiken to become Vermont's first Democratic Senator since the Civil War, the Democratic majority was almost as great. But throughout the two years of its existence, in 1975 and 1976, the Ninety-fourth Congress had no easier time with Ford than had the preceding Congress. The executive and the Democratic leadership argued and sparred over almost everything, frustrating each other on many issues, including inflation, the recession, energy, and foreign affairs, and usually achieving agreements only by reluctant compromises that satisfied neither side. Ford's major weapon was the veto power, which he used thirty-seven times and which Congress was able to override only eight times.

Again, much of the Democrats' difficulties resulted from weak leadership. Despite the rules changes that had strengthened the Speaker at the expense of committee chairmen, Albert, a short, amiable man, lacked the will and ability to be a strong disciplinarian. In the Senate, the reserved Democratic majority leader, Mike Mansfield of Montana, who tended to use such polite and restrained expressions as "I deplore" when he was good and mad, was also passive and permissive. In time, many Democratic liberals became upset because of their leadership's inability to muster enough votes to override Ford's vetoes. But other forces, which would become more pronounced and noticeable in the next Congress, were also at work, handicapping the leadership.

In the country at large cynicism and a declining public confidence in government, stemming largely from such demoralizing events of the 1960's and early 1970's as the assassinations of John and Robert Kennedy and Martin Luther King, Jr., the unpopular Vietnam war, and the Watergate scandals, were reflected by increasing public apathy and a weakening of the two-party system, based on party loyalty among the voters. Many members of the new Congress felt little or no obligation to their party; they had formed their own local organizations to win their elections and were less susceptible to helping the party leadership create a national consensus in Congress than to responding to their own constituencies or to one or another special-interest group that could threaten them with defeat back home. At the same time, the fragmentation was furthered by the new democratizing rules, which loosened discipline; by the rise of special-interest Congressional blocs or caucuses among the members that cut across party lines (there was a black caucus, a group of environmentally oriented Congressmen, a New England bloc, and so forth); and by the opening of committee sessions, which encouraged the growth of single- and special-interest lobbyists and the independence of individual Congressmen who felt their increased influence.

After much squabbling and compromise, the first session managed to pass—and the President unhappily signed—another limited-goal energy bill that phased out, rather than ended, the control of oil prices, set up a national oil reserve, and gave the President some emergency powers; two tax-reduction bills to combat the recession (mindful, also, of the simultaneous inflation, Ford had wanted no tax cut without an equal cut in federal spending, but the Democrats refused to go along with him); and an emergency employment bill, a housing subsidy act, a measure to aid New York City (which was facing bankruptcy), and a bill (which Ford had initially opposed) continuing the Food Stamp program in its existing form.

In the second session, the Democrats put through a major tax revision bill. Passed with an eye on the 1976 presidential elections, it raised taxes on the very rich, curbed some loopholes and tax shelters, and revised gift and estate taxation. Over two Ford vetoes, the same session also passed a large public-works-jobs program to cope with the rising unemployment (in 1975 it reached 8.5 percent, the highest rate since the Depression of the 1930's). In addition, over the objection of environmentalists, it approved landings in the United States by the European Concorde, a supersonic jet airplane; voted—after much contention between opposing interests—to ban the use of federal funds for abortions; and, insisting on voting more funds for social programs than Ford wished, overrode his veto of an appropriations bill that increased health, education, and welfare programs. At the same time, the Ninety-fourth Congress failed by three votes to override a second Ford veto of a coal strip-mining bill, and it either got nowhere with, or—knowing of the President's opposition—failed to pursue, a full-employment bill introduced by Senator Hubert Humphrey and Democratic Representative Augustus F. Hawkins of California; a national health insurance scheme proposed in various forms by different Democratic Senators, including Edward M. Kennedy of Massachusetts and Abraham A. Ribicoff of Connecticut; a consumer protection agency bill, also pushed by Ribicoff; bitterly contested gun-control legislation; measures to reform the banking industry and force oil companies to divest themselves of certain of their operations; and environmental amendments to the Clean Air Act and the 1972 water pollution law.

In the field of foreign affairs, the Democrats were able to launch an aggressive initiative against the administration, gaining support from the nation's reaction to the long, unhappy involvement in Southeast Asia, as well as to the Watergate revelations of improper activities of the CIA and FBI. Putting the President's formidable Secretary of State, Henry A. Kissinger, frequently on the defensive before their committees, the Democrats mandated an end to further military aid to South Vietnam and Cambodia; forced an examination of the Administration's soaring program of arms sales and gifts to foreign countries; assured controls over the use of American civilians in Middle East peacekeeping arrangements in the Sinai peninsula; and blocked possible American involvement in a civil war in Angola on the African continent.

At the same time, both the Senate and House established select investigating committees which, bringing to an end an era of ineffective and irresponsible oversight of the activities of the intelligence community, revealed numerous past abuses and illegal actions, within the United States as well as overseas, by the CIA and other intelligence agencies. A fifteen-month probe by the Senate panel, headed by Idaho's Frank Church, led to the creation, on May 19, 1976, of a permanent fifteen-member bipartisan Senate Select Committee on Intelligence. Established to oversee the future affairs and authorize the budgets of the CIA and other intelligence agencies, it shared jurisdiction over the intelligence units of the Defense Department and the FBI with the Senate Armed Services and Judiciary committees respectively. A similar intelligence probe in the House was torn by dissension and controversial actions, including the temporary citing of Kissinger for contempt of Congress when he refused to produce subpoenaed documents and the leaking of the committee's final report after a vote to bar its release for fear of harm to national security. The House took no immediate action on its committee's proposals, but on July 14, 1977, during the next Congress, it approved a resolution drafted by the Rules Committee, establishing its own thirteen-member Permanent Select Committee on Intelligence.

During 1976, various members of each house were involved in scandals which, along with the legislature's inconclusive wrangling with the President and lack of decisive progress on such worrisome issues as energy, inflation, and the recession, as well as revelations of abuses of Congressional perquisites and knowledge that Congress was about to raise its own pay, caused the public's regard for Congress to plummet once again. The most lurid scandal involved the powerful and imperious Chairman of the House Administration Committee, Democrat Wayne L. Hays of Ohio, who was charged with keeping on his office payroll a woman whose only function for her $14,000 government salary was to provide him with sex. "I can't type, I can't file. I can't even answer the phone," she told amazed reporters. Three other Democratic Congressmen were also enmeshed in sex-related scandals that year, and a fourth, Representative Robert L. F. Sikes of Florida, was accused of financial misconduct. In addition, a Republican House member, Andrew J. Hinshaw of California, was convicted on bribery charges; influential members of both parties, including Hugh Scott, the Republicans' leader in the Senate, were charged with having accepted illegal campaign funds from Gulf Oil Corporation in the past; and seventeen members of Congress, including Speaker Albert and the chairmen of both the Senate and House Ethics committees, acknowledged that they had made unreported hunting trips as guests of defense contractors.

The House forced Hays to resign and reprimanded Sikes, but little or no action was taken on the other cases. Instead, explanations were offered that Congressional rules and Constitutional injunctions, as well as the members' own reluctance to sit in judgment on each other, prevented effective proceedings. However, it was a period of "post-Watergate morality"; the finger of scorn, once pointed at the White House, was now pointing at Congress, and largely in response to the discomfort caused by the unseemly Hays scandal, the House on July 1 set up a fifteen-member bipartisan Commission on Administrative Review, chaired by Democratic Representative David R. Obey of Wisconsin, and including seven members of the public, to draft a new code of ethics for the lower house. Before the Commission finished its work, the Ninety-fourth Congress ended. When the Ninety-fifth convened in January, 1977, Obey's report was submitted to the House. In the meantime, the question of Congressional ethics had merged with the pay-raise issue. Fearing the resentment of the voters, Congress, just prior to the 1976 elections, repealed an automatic cost-of-living pay hike which it was about to receive in accordance with action it had taken the year before. After the elections, however, a federal commission recommended a pay increase for top government officials, including members of Congress, but added pointedly that the raises should be tied to a new code of ethical conduct.

The recommended Congressional pay raise ($12,900 a year, to an annual salary of $57,500) was quickly accepted by the new Ninety-fifth Congress in early 1977, becoming effective on February 20. To muffle the public's objection to so large an increase, however, the new Speaker, "Tip" O'Neill, and the new Senate majority leader, Robert C. Byrd of West Virginia (both Carl Albert and Mike Mansfield had retired at the end of the Ninety-fourth Congress), also forced their respective bodies to hasten acceptance of tough new ethics codes. Among the provisions of the House code, presented by the Obey Commission and adopted by the House on March 2, were limits on the amount of money a member could earn from an outside job or from making speeches; the ending of unofficial office accounts by which members had been able to accept unreported contributions and spend them in any way they wished; the detailed public disclosure of the sources and amount of members' income; and stipulations rectifying abuses of travel expense accounts and other perquisites. On April 1 the Senate adopted an even more stringent code, drawn up by a Special Committee on Official Conduct, headed by Democrat Gaylord Nelson of Wisconsin. (On March 8, 1979, the Senate quietly lifted the restrictions on outside earnings of Senators for the next four years.)

In both houses, most Republicans and many Democrats raised objections to the various provisions and to the brief time for debate, but O'Neill and Byrd, attuned to the need to improve Congress's image, showed more determination and skill than their predecessors and rammed through the codes. The Senate put the implementation and enforcement of its code in the hands of its Ethics Committee, while the House, which had adopted the code as a series of amendments to House rules, established a Select Committee on Ethics to implement the provisions, but left enforcement to such House bodies as the Committee on Standards of Official Conduct. Though the reforms demanded observance of the strictest standards in Congress's history, enforcement continued to be still largely dependent on the members' willingness to judge each other.

The election of the smiling Georgia peanut farmer, Democrat Jimmy Carter, to the Presidency in November, 1976, ended eight years of split control of the White House and Congress by the two parties. Both houses were still heavily Democratic and looked forward to working with a more cooperative President than Ford. With the departure of Mike Mansfield, the "gentle persuader," whose sixteen-year tenure as Senate majority leader set a record for longevity, a contest to succeed him developed between West Virginia's Byrd, a skillful parliamentarian and moderate conservative, and the Democratic Party's veteran liberal leader, Hubert Humphrey. Many Democratic Senators, worried about Humphrey's health (he had had an operation for cancer), and sensing both in Carter and in the country's mood a trend to the right, away from traditional Democratic liberalism, felt that Byrd would be a more effective leader in behalf of the new President's programs. Humphrey withdrew from the race, giving the post to Byrd. In a demonstration of regard for their sick, but still spirited and optimistic, colleague, who during three decades had led, or been in the thick of, almost every fight for civil rights and liberal legislation in the Senate, the Democrats created for him the honorary position of Senate deputy president pro tem, with an increased salary, a car and chauffeur, and other perquisites. Humphrey's health continued to deteriorate, however, and he died at his home in Minnesota on January 13, 1978. Senate Republicans, meanwhile, had chosen as their leader Howard H. Baker, Jr., of Tennessee, the son-in-law of the former Republican minority leader, Everett McKinley Dirksen.

Benefiting from the campaign public financing law of 1974, Carter, a former governor of Georgia but a relatively unknown on the national scene, had captured the Democratic nomination in 1976 and gone on to win the national election with promises to end the impasse between Congress and the executive and restore public confidence in the government's ability to deal effectively with such problems as inflation and the energy crisis. But once in the White House, the new President, a Washington outsider untutored in the ways of the capital's politics and surrounded by young, inexperienced, and often incompetent aides, floundered in his relations with Congress. In a burst of enthusiasm to carry out his campaign promises, he barraged Congress with a stream of legislative proposals, more than it could handle or sort out for priority action. His liaison and communications with the two houses were poor; though the Democratic leaders were anxious to work with him, he offended and confused them; and he was accused, time and again, of failing to consult with key legislators, of providing weak and amateurish lobbying support in behalf of his measures, and of making compromises or sudden changes of position that undermined and embarrassed those who were fighting for him. For a year and a half, throughout the first session of the Ninety-fifth Congress and well into the second, until he gained enough seasoning and experience to begin to assert authority and acquire respect, he projected the image—reflected by his declining ratings in public polls—of an honest President, but a poor and inept leader.

At the very start of his Administration, he angered many Congressmen, including the delegations of most western states, by attempting to kill eighteen dam-building, irrigation, and other large water projects under construction in various parts of the country, claiming that they were economically or environmentally unsound. His threat to withdraw requests for their funding struck at one of Congress's most sensitive nerves—the pork-barrel tradition—and Congress, whom Carter had failed to consult prior to his announcement, fought back. The President was forced temporarily to reduce his "hit list" to nine of the projects, but the battle over all of them see-sawed for two years. In the last hours of the Ninety-fifth Congress in 1978, Carter, aided by the legislators' growing fears of tax-revolt sentiment by economy-minded forces, finally had his way and halted most of the projects.

Despite the Administration's shortcomings, Byrd and the newly installed Speaker, "Tip" O'Neill, a towering, heavyset, one-time Speaker of the Massachusetts House of Representatives, with a handsome head of white hair, a loud, commanding voice, and a warm, gladhanding manner, proved loyal and powerful allies of the President, shepherding through their houses many of the disparate pieces of legislation with which Carter bombarded them. Among those passed during the first session was a measure authorizing the President to merge, end, or reorganize agencies in the executive branch, subject to Congressional veto; a bill establishing a new Cabinet-level Department of Energy to consolidate energy-related agencies and powers scattered through the government; a measure raising the minimum wage; and a new coal strip-mining regulation act, which Carter finally signed into law after two vetoes by his predecessor.

At the same time, Congress, often confused or irritated by the White House, took its own tack with many of the Administration's proposals, ignoring, blocking, or reshaping them and inducing the President to go along. Environmentalists, who had supported Carter, were dismayed by his compromises on bills that extended and changed environmental-protection provisions of the 1970 Clean Air Act and the Federal Water Pollution Control Act of 1972. A bill to put the Social Security system on a sounder financial basis (Carter wished to transfer general Treasury funds to the system when unemployment was high) wound up—with Presidential approval—levying steep increases in payroll taxes. Similarly, one of Carter's most urgent proposals, an "economic stimulus" package of tax cuts and increased public jobs to cope with the continuing recession and unemployment, was broken into several bills, refashioned in various committees, and finally passed after a number of disagreements between Congress and the Administration and an abrupt about-face by Carter on one of his principal enthusiasms, a $50 tax rebate.

During the first session, Congress, in addition, enacted a new farm bill that restored price supports for hard-pressed agricultural interests; extended the Food Stamp program; passed a Housing and Community Development Act that aided urban areas; and began work on a measure to raise the mandatory retirement age for most Americans to seventy, which it passed the next year. But, reflecting the country's growing mood of conservatism, as well as the marked increase in the number and influence of special-interest lobbyists who worked determinedly on individual Congressmen, many Democratic goals, jointly shared by the Administration and liberal leaders in the legislature, including the establishment of a consumer protection agency, welfare reform, a hospital cost-control program, election law changes, and a bill to assist organized labor, were defeated or postponed.

Once again, the sharpest conflicts revolved around an attempt by the new administration to give the country a coherent and effective energy policy. Carter's program, an omnibus bill with 113 separate proposals which he presented as "the moral equivalent of war," was adroitly steered through the House almost intact by O'Neill and the Democratic leadership; but when it reached the Senate, special-interest lobbyists attacked and tied up its components. Under their barrage, and following the lead of the canny and powerful chairman of the Senate Finance Committee, Louisiana's Russell B. Long, who was frank in his advocacy of energy-producing interests, the Senate broke the legislation into six bills and proceeded to rewrite much of what the House passed. Bitter conflict over the deregulation of natural gas prices was highlighted by a dramatic nine-day filibuster by Democratic Senators James Abourezk of South Dakota and Howard M. Metzenbaum of Ohio, who were defending the Administration's position on gas pricing as passed by the House. Though the Senate voted for cloture, Abourezk and

Metzenbaum used a loophole in the cloture rule to offer an endless stream of amendments to the bill, each one requiring time-consuming quorum and roll calls. Even Long, who opposed the two men, offered grudging admiration for their perseverance, remarking about Metzenbaum, a freshman Senator, "I never saw a man come in here and become an ace filibusterer so fast." Finally, as the Senate's patience wore thin, Byrd and the presiding officer of the Senate, Vice President Walter F. Mondale, reflecting a switch in Administration tactics, pulled the rug out from under the two Senators by a maneuver in which Mondale called all further amendments dilatory and out of order and refused to recognize Abourezk when he tried to appeal the ruling. Though many Senators in the uproar that followed angrily assailed Mondale and Byrd for a dictatorial action, the ruling stuck, and Abourezk and Metzenbaum, charging the President with betraying his allies, dropped the filibuster.

Carter had decided to get the measure out of the Senate and into conference, where he felt the will of the House—and of himself—would prevail. When the Senate finally passed its version of the energy program and sent it to conference, however, it ran into an impasse among the conferees over natural-gas prices and energy taxes that stalled it throughout the rest of that session and until the closing hours of the next one. In the end, the Administration accepted provisions for the pricing and deregulation of gas that the White House had earlier characterized as "war profiteering," and following another unsuccessful filibuster by Abourezk and Metzenbaum, a five-part bill passed the two houses just before the adjournment of the Ninety-fifth Congress on Sunday night, October 15, 1978. Satisfactory to neither side, the measure contained provisions won by the energy producers and their lobbyists and opposed by the Administration, but also a tax on gas-guzzling autos and incentives for the production and conservation of energy which the White House desired. Though the bill would not solve the energy crisis, it was a first step toward helping the country cope with its threats. In a final note to the long and heated debate, Abourezk, whose earlier frustrations in the Senate had decided him not to run for re-election, announced impatiently, "I can't wait to get out of this chickenshit outfit."

A number of other issues during both sessions of the Ninety-fifth Congress aroused strong emotions and occupied much of the members' time. Buffeted by the intense lobbying of opposing forces, and with its own debate often angry and confused, Congress again voted to ban the use of Medicaid funds for abortions, save in certain emergency cases. Despite the vote, it was certain that the question of whether, and to what extent, the government should pay for abortions would surface again in future Congresses. Over the strong opposition of its detractors, Congress also gave supporters of the proposed Twenty-seventh (Equal Rights) Amendment thirty-nine more months to gain ratification by the necessary three-fourths of the states. In addition, it gave the President authority to halt U.S. imports of chrome from Rhodesia as a sign to the world that America supported black majority rule and equal rights in that country; curbed the participation by American firms in the Arab states' boycott of Israel; prohibited U.S. companies from continuing to make payments to foreign officials to obtain business from their governments; and with a wary eye cast toward the Soviets' growing military power, approved production of the "neutron bomb," a tactical nuclear warhead—though after long debate, it agreed with the Administration and blocked funds for the Air Force's expensive B-1 bomber, opting, instead, to support the development of Cruise missiles.

The settling of a highly divisive issue, the Senate's ratification of two Panama Canal treaties, which Carter signed on September 7, 1977, was regarded as a turning point in the President's relations with Congress. The treaties, which gave Panama control of the canal after the year 2000 but permitted the United States to help maintain its neutrality, were bitterly attacked in Congress and throughout the country by conservatives, who felt that the United States should give up neither control nor possession of the waterway. Even though Carter met a second time with Panama's chief of state to clarify U.S. rights after the year 2000, Byrd waited until the second session before risking a ratification vote. By that time, Carter had mobilized greater support for the treaties by appealing directly to the nation and providing persuasive explanations to wavering Senators and groups of leading, opinion-forming citizens. Though the treaties would be debated again by the next Congress, when the House of Representatives would have to initiate legislation implementing their provisions, the Senate's two-vote margin in favor of ratification was Carter's first notable victory in his dealings with Congress. It was followed soon afterward by others: Congress's agreement to lift the Turkish arms embargo, to pass his foreign-aid bill and to permit the sale of fighter aircraft to Saudi Arabia and Egypt, as well as to Israel. The last decision paved the way for Carter to invite President Anwar Sadat of Egypt and Prime Minister Menachem Begin of Israel to a peace-seeking summit meeting at the chief executive's Camp David, Maryland, retreat.

As public polls reflected a rising regard for Carter, his relations with Congress improved. Having learned from experience, he now worked closely with the Democratic leadership, dropping many of his legislative proposals in favor of the most important ones, improving communications with his supporters in the legislature, and providing more effective lobbying assistance. At the same time, he assumed with more firmness and authority the leadership role of the Presidency. During the first session, in 1977, he had been reluctant to exercise the veto power and had used it only twice—to deny authorization for a demonstration nuclear breeder-reactor and to kill a measure dealing with the inspection of rabbit meat. The following year, in August, 1978, he stunned Congress by vetoing a defense appropriation bill that contained funds for a fifth nuclear-powered Navy supercarrier that he felt was superfluous, and two months later by vetoing a giant public-works bill containing the pork-barrel water projects he opposed. Unable to override the vetoes, the awed Congress, with new respect for the President, rewrote the measures to satisfy him.

Meanwhile, despite the new ethics codes, Congress was experiencing more cases of misconduct by some of its members. In January, 1977, the House Committee on Standards of Official Conduct was authorized to investigate charges of payoffs and the buying of members' influence by agents of the South Korean government. When the committee's chairman was accused of dragging his feet, Speaker O'Neill, angry at allegations that he and other Congressional leaders might be implicated, got the committee to hire the former Watergate special prosecutor, Leon A. Jaworski, to conduct a ruthless investigation of what the press was calling "the Koreagate scandals." A Korean businessman, Tongsun Park, had been identified as the man who had paid various members of both houses for alleged support on matters affecting U.S.–South Korean relations, but Park had already fled to London, and then to Korea. For a while, the Korean government's refusal to send him back to Washington to testify imperiled House approval of military aid for South Korea. Eventually, Park returned and testified, naming many Congressional recipients of his largesse. Most of his contributions, it appeared, had been accepted innocently and had had no influence on the legislators; some had been returned to Park; and serious charges were leveled against only a few individuals. One of them, former Democratic Representative Richard T. Hanna of California, had not been a member of Congress since 1974 and had already been indicted before the investigation began. As Park's partner, he had the distinction of being the first Congressman accused of having been an agent of a foreign country while still in office. The House Committee on Standards of Official Conduct recommended that another California Congressman be censured and two others reprimanded for taking money from Park; the House settled for "slap-on-the-wrist" reprimands for all three, and the matter was closed. Once again, it had been difficult for members to accuse and judge each other.

Other legislators got into graver trouble. Pennsylvania Democratic Representatives Joshua Eilberg and Daniel J. Flood, a former actor with a waxed moustache and a flamboyant manner, were both indicted on charges of taking money for their influence (Eilberg was not re-elected in 1978, and Flood's sensational trial in early 1979 ended in a mistrial). Republican Representative J. Herbert Burke of Florida was accused of resisting arrest after a fight and then trying to influence a witness to lie for him. Another Democrat, Representative Charles C. Diggs, Jr., of Michigan, who had been in the House since 1955 and was its senior black member, was convicted of padding his office payroll and using the money for personal expenses. The respected Massachusetts Republican senator, Edward W. Brooke, ran afoul of the law and was beaten for re-election in 1978 after he admitted lying in his divorce case. And in 1979 the Senate Ethics Committee went after Georgia's powerful Democratic Senator, Herman E. Talmadge, chairman of the Senate Agriculture Committee (and the only Senator still using a spittoon), on charges that he had misused his office and campaign funds.

The Ninety-fifth Congress ended on October 15, 1978, after a tumultuous, thirty-four-hour, nonstop session that saw the passage of two dozen major bills and a long list of minor ones. While the Senate waited impatiently to break the last of the Abourezk-Metzenbaum filibusters on the energy bill, and conferees of Long's Senate Finance Committee and Ullman's House Ways and Means Committee wrestled with the final compromises of a $19 billion tax-cut bill, the two houses rushed through measures that had been stalled in debate for months. During one hour, the Senate approved more than forty-five bills. At times, few bleary-eyed Senators could keep up with what was happening. "I don't understand what we're going to do and what bill we're going to do it on," objected New York's Republican Senator Jacob Javits. The presiding officer on occasion was also baffled. "I can't hear the member, but the request is granted," he waved at one Senator. In the House, from which many members were retiring, there was an air of "auld lang syne" and frivolity. A Financial Institutions Regulatory Act to end banking abuses revealed during an investigation of Bert Lance, Carter's first director of the Office of Management and Budget, was passed to the saxophone strains of "I'll Be Down to Get You in a Taxi, Honey," played by a celebrant in the Republican cloakroom. Among the legislation enacted in the last hours of the Congress were a large new mass-transit bill ("That's $51 billion [voted] in twelve minutes," observed one Senator); a compromise version of the Humphrey-Hawkins full-employment bill; measures to deregulate the airline industry, extend more aid to education, give new housing assistance, increase veterans' pensions, and continue the Endangered Species Act; and the tax-cut bill that finally emerged from conference.

The last measure reflected an historic shift from the redistribution-of-wealth policy that had underlain most tax bills since the days of the New Deal. The tax cuts gave little or no relief to low- and middle-income groups, but in an effort to help the economy by stimulating investments gave relief in various forms to corporations and upper-income people. In a sense, the bill mirrored profound changes that had affected not only Congress, but the President and the country as a whole, and that would also have influence on the fall elections of 1978 and the relations between the President and the new Ninety-Sixth Congress in 1979. In retrospect, after its adjournment, the Ninety-fifth Congress was seen by many persons to have been more responsive than previous Democratic-controlled Congresses to business and conservative interests. Organized labor, the minorities, the underprivileged, and the other elements of the coalition that had given a liberal thrust to Democratic policies for more than forty years had scored few successes and had suffered some sharp defeats.

This trend worried the liberal leaders in Congress, some of whom were quick to blame the powerful influences of corporation and conservative special-interest contributions to individual members of Congress and the resultant success of their lobbying. "Representative government on Capitol Hill is in the worst shape I have seen in my sixteen years in the Senate," said Democratic Senator Edward M. Kennedy of Massachusetts. "The heart of the problem is that the Senate and the House are awash in a sea of special-interest lobbying and special-interest campaign contributions . . . We're elected to represent all the people of our states or districts, not just those rich or powerful enough to have lobbyists holding megaphones constantly at our ears."

It was true that the corridors of the Capitol swarmed with more special-interest lobbyists than ever before (their number had risen from 8,000 to 15,000 since 1974), and that many votes reflected the influence of their power and contributions. But overall, their proliferation had resulted from the federal government's increased involvement in, and regulation of, many different facets of the economic and social affairs of the country. While a large number of them represented conservative economic interests, the lobbyists by and large were comprised of a multitude of pro- and anti- groups, each one interested in only one aspect or phase of the domestic scene or foreign affairs. In the fragmenting of interests, generating intense lobbying pressure on such varied single issues as gas deregulation, tax deductions for entertainment expenses, abortion, air pollution, women's rights, and gun control, the general public interest was seen to have suffered. Congressmen, already tending more and more to serve and respond to their own districts rather than to Congressional party leadership, cultivated and, in turn, were cultivated by particular special-interest groups who could help them. This led some observers, echoing Senator Kennedy, to complain that Congress was "becoming paralyzed in its ability to make decisions on behalf of all citizens."

But of equal influence on the change within Congress was the country's growing economic conservatism. The increasing pressures of soaring taxes and unrelieved inflation, pinching everyone, had given rise to public demands for less government spending, balanced budgets, and lower taxes. Since June, 1978, when California voters had approved Proposition 13, a dramatic state measure to cut property taxes and slash the state budget, the threat of tax revolts had lain heavy on the minds of state and federal officials. Following the lead of President Carter, who gave early signs of responding to the tax-revolt sentiment by veering away from support of high-cost social programs and toward economy in government, many Democratic Congressmen abandoned traditional Democratic liberal-oriented programs and caused Republicans to claim that they were "out-Republican-ing Republicans."

The trend toward conservatism was borne out by the 1978 fall elections. The Democrats still retained large majorities in both houses, but many new, as well as returning, members of both parties arrived in Washington for the convening of the Ninety-sixth Congress in January, 1979, hostile to new social programs and intent on holding down spending. At the same time, when Carter presented his "austere" annual budget to the new Congress, which reflected severe cuts in various assistance programs and aroused the ire of big labor, women, blacks, urban leaders, and other elements that had traditionally formed the Democratic coalition, Democratic liberals in both houses announced their determination to resist the "betrayals" of long-established Democratic policies. Carter, however, remained firm; in the wings, threatening him as well as Congress, were new, more extreme manifestations of the tax revolt, including a proposed Constitutional amendment, a state-initiated drive for a new Constitutional convention, and economy-minded Congressional bills, each mandating decreased federal spending, slashed taxes, and a balanced budget.

Other concerns faced the new Congress, including the settling of the disposition of public lands in Alaska; the public financing of Congressional campaigns; the final approval of the Panama Canal treaties; a national health-insurance program; and ratification of international trade agreements and SALT II, the difficult and sensitive extension of the Strategic Arms Limitation Treaty worked out between the Administration and the Soviet Union. In addition, Carter had presented the nation and Congress with a dramatic and divisive new issue by announcing on December 15, 1978, that he intended to normalize diplomatic relations with the People's Republic of China and terminate the 1955 defense treaty with the Chinese Nationalist government on Taiwan. Conservatives were shocked, and Arizona's Senator Barry Goldwater, Jr., immediately instituted suit to determine whether a President could abrogate a treaty without assent of the Senate, a Constitutional question that had never been tested. Following a visit to Washington and other cities by the Peking government's Deputy Prime Minister, however, together with assurances of support by liberal Democratic Senators for the continued security of Taiwan, Carter's moves, opening the prospects of vast new trade and a possible new source of oil for the United States, gathered Congressional backing.

The interrelated crises of inflation and energy, accentuated during the early months of the new Congress by events in the Middle East, continued to overshadow most of the other issues. The ousting of the Shah of Iran, accompanied by an interruption of Iranian oil exports, created shock waves in the Arab oil-producing states that posed additional threats to America's energy supplies. The situation was helped none by the continued frustration of Carter's persistent efforts to settle relations between Israel on the one hand and Egypt, the other Arab nations, and the Palestinians on the other. The worsening oil crisis, in turn, helped to sharpen inflation within the United States, presenting the President and Congress with an even more urgent need than before to cope with internal inflationary pressures. Facing action by the Ninety-sixth Congress were measures to roll back the high Social Security taxes voted in 1977; provide a wage-insurance plan of tax credits to encourage workers to moderate demands for increased pay; and a program to contain rising hospital costs.

As the legislators took up these grave and complex issues in 1979, there were observers who thought that Congress itself was facing a crisis. Despite an enormous increase in the number of Congressional employees on personal and committee staffs (from a total of 4,489 in 1969 to more than 17,000 in 1979), the workload on the individual member of Congress had become so onerous that many of them no longer found the job desirable. Putting in an average eleven-hour workday, Congressmen still had to rely on their staff personnel to serve, and respond to daily bags full of mail from, home-state constituents, research and prepare legislation, work with the staffs of other legislators and with pro- and anti- special interest groups, provide briefings on bills, and even give advice on how to vote. Many persons, indeed, saw the growth of the numbers and powers of the Congressional staffs as a menace: committee staff directors and aides, they believed, were becoming more powerful than the committee members themselves; the swollen staffs were adding to the workload by generating more bills, more hearings, and more reports; and, most alarming to some critics, staffs were not only writing much of the legislation, but once the bills were passed, were preparing directives for the executive agencies, specifying exactly how the legislation was to be carried out. On occasion, the executive with good reason complained that such attempted management by Congressional staffs violated or blurred the Constitutional separation of the two branches of government.

To other observers who saw in the growth of staffs an attempt by the legislature to recapture and maintain co-equality with the executive branch, Congress had been in a chronic crisis since before World War II. Such a view, however, was shortsighted, for within that period Congress on numerous occasions had lived up to the legacy of its greatest architects— Madison, Fisher Ames, Clay, Calhoun, Webster, Benton, Thaddeus Stevens, Thomas B. Reed, Joseph G. Cannon, Robert La Follette, and others—who sometimes led the American people and sometimes disappointed them. Even the shadow of Aaron Burr, who in 1805 proclaimed his faith in the Senate's ability to save the Constitution in times of crisis, may have watched approvingly over the shoulders of the Senators who voted the War Powers Act and conducted the Watergate hearings in 1973. And when the Judiciary Committee gained new prestige for the House of Representatives during its impeachment hearings in 1974, Congress, as never before in its history, testified to the wisdom of the writers of the Constitution in planning for the orderly continuation of a government equipped to meet crises.

In some respects, Congress has never satisfied the American people and will never be able to do so, for Congress *is* the people. But precisely for that reason, the legislative branch, as it was in colonial and revolutionary days, is still the people's voice and the people's hope, destined to frustration and conflict in synthesizing all the people's needs and aspirations. "Congress," declared Republican Senator (then Representative) William Cohen of Maine in 1975, "is designed to be slow and inefficient because it represents the total diversity in this country. Yet people are accustomed to instant gratification, and when they don't get it, they have instant disappointment and instant cynicism. I don't know if we will ever be able to measure up to public expectations."

Bibliography

Alexander, De Alva S. *History and Procedure of the House of Representatives.* Burt Franklin, 1970.

Almanac, 1977. Congressional Quarterly, Inc., 1977.

Ames, Seth, ed. *Works of Fisher Ames.* Burt Franklin, 1971, 2 vols.

Ashurst, Henry Fountain. *A Many Colored Toga: The Diary of Henry Fountain Ashurst.* University of Arizona, 1962.

Bailyn, Bernard. *The Origins of American Politics.* Knopf, 1968.

Barry, David. *Forty Years in Washington.* Beekman, 1974.

Bates, Ernest Sutherland. *The Story of Congress, 1789–1935.* Harper, 1936.

Bell, Rudolph M. *Party and Faction in American Politics.* Greenwood, 1973.

Bemis, Samuel Flagg. *John Quincy Adams and the Union.* Knopf, 1956.

Benton, Thomas Hart. *Thirty Years' View.* Greenwood, 1968, 2 vols.

Binkley, Wilfred E., and Malcolm C. Moos. *A Grammar of American Politics.* Knopf, 1952.

Biographical Directory of the American Congress, 1774–1961. Government Printing Office, 1961.

Blanchard, Robert O., ed. *Congress and the News Media.* Hastings House, 1974.

Bolling, Richard. *House Out of Order.* Dutton, 1965.

————. *Power in the House.* Dutton, 1968.

Brant, Irving. *James Madison.* Bobbs-Merrill, 1941–61, 6 vols.

Burdette, Franklin L. *Filibustering in the Senate.* Princeton University, 1940.

Burnett, Edmund Cody. *The Continental Congress.* Norton, 1964.

Burns, James MacGregor. *Congress on Trial.* Harper, 1949.

Capers, Gerald M. *Stephen A. Douglas, Defender of the Union.* Little, Brown, 1959.

Carroll, Holbert N. *The House of Representatives and Foreign Affairs.* University of Pittsburgh, 1958.

Chidsey, D. B. *The Gentleman from New York: A Life of Roscoe Conkling.* Yale University, 1935.

Ch'iu, Ch'ang Wei. *The Speaker of the House of Representatives Since 1896.* Columbia University, 1928.

Clapp, Charles L. *The Congressman: His Work as He Sees It.* Brookings Institution, 1963.

Clark, Champ. *My Quarter Century of American Politics.* Harper, 1920.

Clark, Joseph S. *Congress: The Sapless Branch.* Harper, 1964.

Coit, Margaret L. *John C. Calhoun.* Houghton Mifflin, 1950.

Colbourn, H. Trevor. *The Lamp of Experience.* Norton, 1965.

Coletta, Paolo E. *The Presidency of William Howard Taft.* University of Kansas, 1973.

Congress and the Nation. Vol. 4, 1973–76. Congressional Quarterly, Inc., 1977.

Congressional Quarterly's Guide to the Congress of the United States. Congressional Quarterly Service, 1971, 1973; 2d ed. 1976.

Crawford, Theron Clark. *James G. Blaine.* Edgewood, 1893.

Cunningham, Noble E., Jr. *The Jeffersonian Republicans: The Formation of Party Organization, 1789–1801.* University of North Carolina, 1957.

Current, Richard N. *Daniel Webster and the Rise of National Conservatism.* Little, Brown, 1955.

_____ *John C. Calhoun.* Washington Square Press, 1966.

Dalzell, Robert F., Jr. *Daniel Webster and the Trial of American Nationalism, 1843–52.* Houghton Mifflin, 1973.

Dangerfield, George. *The Awakening of American Nationalism.* Harper, 1965.

_____ *The Era of Good Feelings.* Harcourt Brace, 1952.

Dimock, Marshall E. *Congressional Investigating Committees.* Johns Hopkins University, 1929.

Dobson, John M. *Politics in the Gilded Age.* Praeger, 1972.

Documentary History of the First Federal Congress: 1789–91, Vol. I, *Senate Legislative Journal.* Johns Hopkins University, 1972.

Eaton, Clement. *Henry Clay and the Art of Politics.* Little, Brown, 1957.

Farrand, Max. *The Framing of the Constitution of the United States.* Yale University, 1962.

Faulkner, Harold U. *Politics, Reform and Expansion, 1890–1900.* Harper, 1959.

Fenno, Richard F. *The Power of the Purse: Appropriations Politics in Congress.* Little, Brown, 1966.

Follett, Mary P. *The Speaker of the House of Representatives.* Longmans, Green, 1896.

Fribourg, Marjorie G. *The U.S. Congress: Men Who Steered Its Course, 1787–1867.* Macrae Smith, 1972.

Frye, Alton. *A Responsible Congress.* McGraw-Hill, 1975.

Galloway, George B. *History of the House of Representatives.* Crowell, 1969.

Garraty, John A. *Henry Cabot Lodge.* Knopf, 1953.

Gould, Louis L., ed. *The Progressive Era.* Syracuse University, 1974.

Green, Mark J., et al. *Who Runs Congress?* Bantam, 1972.

Hamilton, Alexander, et al. *The Federalist Papers.* New American Library, 1961.

Harlow, Ralph V. *The History of Legislative Methods in the Period Before 1825.* Yale University, 1917.

Hartmann, Susan M. *Truman and the 80th Congress.* University of Missouri, 1971.

Haynes, George H. *The Senate of the United States: Its History and Practice.* Russell and Russell, 1960, 2 vols.

Hicks, John D. *Republican Ascendancy, 1921–33.* Harper, 1960.

Hinds, Asher C., and Clarence Cannon. *Precedents of the House of Representatives of the United States.* Government Printing Office, 1907, 1936, 11 vols.

Hofstadter, Richard. *The Age of Reform.* Knopf, 1955.

Korngold, Ralph. *Thaddeus Stevens.* Harcourt, Brace, 1955.

James, Marquis. *The Life of Andrew Jackson.* Bobbs-Merrill, 1938.

_____ *The Raven.* Bobbs-Merrill, 1929.

Jensen, Merrill. *The New Nation.* Knopf, 1950.

Jones, Charles O. *The Minority Party in Congress.* Little, Brown, 1970.

Josephson, Matthew. *The Politicos.* Harcourt Brace, 1938.

Leuchtenburg, William E. *Franklin D. Roosevelt and the New Deal, 1932–40.* Harper, 1963.

Link, Arthur S. *American Epoch.* Knopf, 1955.

_____ *Woodrow Wilson and the Progressive Era, 1910-17.* Harper, 1954.

Luce, Robert. *Legislative Procedure.* Houghton Mifflin, 1922.

McCall, Samuel W. *The Life of Thomas Brackett Reed.* Houghton Mifflin, 1914.

McConachie, L. G. *Congressional Committees: A Study of the Origin and Development of Our National and Local Legislative Methods.* Crowell, 1898.

McDonald, Forrest. *The Presidency of George Washington.* University of Kansas, 1974.

McGeary, M. Nelson. *The Development of Congressional Investigative Power.* Octagon, 1973.

Maclay, William. *The Journal of William Maclay, United States Senator from Pennsylvania, 1789–91.* Frederick Ungar, 1965.

MacNeil, Neil. *Forge of Democracy: The House of Representatives.* David McKay, 1963.

392

Madison, James. *Notes of Debate in the Federal Convention of 1787,* ed. A. Koch. Ohio University, 1966.

Main, Jackson Turner. *The Sovereign States, 1775–83.* New Viewpoints, 1973.

Malone, Dumas. *Jefferson and His Time.* Little, Brown, 1948–74, 5 vols.

Mantell, Martin F. *Johnson, Grant, and the Politics of Reconstruction.* Columbia University, 1973.

Miller, John C. *The Federalist Era, 1789–1801.* Harper, 1960.

Mooney, Booth. *Mr. Speaker.* Follett, 1964.

Mowry, George E. *The Era of Theodore Roosevelt, 1900–1912.* Harper, 1958.

Murray, Robert K. *The Harding Era.* University of Minnesota, 1969.

Nichols, Roy F. *The Invention of the American Political Parties.* Macmillan, 1967.

Patterson, James T. *Congressional Conservatism and the New Deal.* University of Kentucky, 1967.

Peck, Harry Thurston. *Twenty Years of the Republic.* Dodd, Mead, 1906.

Phillips, Cabell. *The Truman Presidency.* Macmillan, 1966.

Plumer, William. *William Plumer's Memorandum of Proceedings in the United States Senate, 1803–7,* ed. Everett S. Brown. Da Capo, 1969.

Poore, Ben Perley. *Perley's Reminiscences of Sixty Years in the National Metropolis.* Hubbard Brothers, 1886, 2 vols.

Randall, James G. *Lincoln the President.* Dodd, Mead, 1945–55, 4 vols.

Rapoport, Daniel. *Inside the House.* Follett, 1975.

Riddle, Donald W. *Congressman Abraham Lincoln.* University of Illinois, 1957.

Ripley, Randall B. *Party Leaders in the House of Representatives.* Brookings Institution, 1967.

––––––. *Power in the Senate.* St. Martin's Press, 1969.

Robinson, James A. *The House Rules Committee.* Bobbs-Merrill, 1963.

Rodgers, Lindsay. *The American Senate.* Knopf, 1926.

Rossiter, Clinton. *1787: The Grand Convention.* Macmillan, 1966.

Rothman, David J. *Politics and Power: The United States Senate, 1869–1901.* Harvard University, 1966.

Schlesinger, Arthur M., Jr. *A Thousand Days.* Houghton Mifflin, 1965.

Sellers, Charles. *James K. Polk, Continentalist, 1843–46.* Princeton University, 1966.

Sherman, John. *Recollections of Forty Years in the House, Senate and Cabinet.* Werner, 1895, 2 vols.

Silbey, Joel H. *The Shrine of Party: Congressional Voting Behavior, 1841–52.* University of Pittsburgh, 1967.

Smelser, Marshall. *The Democratic Republic, 1801–15.* Harper, 1968

Stampp, Kenneth M. *The Era of Reconstruction, 1865–77.* Knopf, 1965.

Taussig, Frederick W. *The Tariff History of the U.S.* Putnam's, 1923.

Taylor, Telford. *Grand Inquest.* Simon & Schuster, 1955.

Van Deusen, Glyndon G. *The Jacksonian Era, 1828–48.* Harper, 1959.

Walters, Raymond, Jr. *Albert Gallatin.* Macmillan, 1957.

Weaver, Warren, Jr. *Both Your Houses.* Praeger, 1972.

White, Leonard D. *The Jeffersonians: A Study in Administrative History, 1801–29.* Macmillan, 1951.

White, William S. *Citadel: The Story of the U.S. Senate.* Harper, 1956, 1957.

Wicker, Tom. *JFK and LBJ.* William Morrow, 1968.

Wilson, Woodrow. *Congressional Government.* Peter Smith, 1973.

Wolfinger, Raymond E., ed. *Readings on Congress.* Prentice-Hall, 1971.

Young, Roland. *The American Congress.* Harper, 1958.

––––––. *Congressional Politics in the Second World War.* Columbia University, 1956.

Index

224, 256, 260, 268, 309, 332, 341, 367

Arkansas, 172

Armed Services Committee: House, 35, 353, 361, 370, 375; Senate, 356, 358

Armed Ship Bill, 299

Army: British, 41, 42, 101-2, 148-149; Confederate, 213-14, 216, 223; Continental, 10, 14, 19, 25-27, 47; U.S., 34, 64-68, 81-82, 96-98, 109-12, 120, 126, 136-37, 140, 143-50, 152-53, 170, 172, 190-91, 213, 216, 218, 227, 239, 244, 253, 256-58, 266, 270-77, 279, 297, 300-3, 314, 331-34, 337, 345, 353-57, 359-66

Army Appropriation Act, 228, 229

Army-McCarthy hearings, 345-46

Arthur, Chester A., 238, 248-51, 254, 256, 271

Articles of Association, 19

Articles of Confederation, 7, 17, 19, 25-27, 34, 37, 58, 65-66

Ashley, James M., 228

Ashurst, Henry F., 296, 304, 320, 326

Aspinall, Wayne N., 349

Astor, John Jacob, 43

Atchison, David R., 201-3

Atomic Energy Act, 366

B

Babcock, Orville E., 235, 236

Bache, Benjamin, 101

Bailey, Joseph W., 273, 287

Baker, Edward D., 216

Baker, Howard, Jr., 380

Baker, Robert G., 347

Balfour, Arthur, 303

Ball, Joseph H., 338

Baltimore, Md., 73, 125, 135, 148, 174, 176, 187, 210, 213, 238, 292

Bankhead, William B., 323, 326, 334

Banking and Currency Committee: House, 224, 290, 294, 342, 375; Senate, 321

Bank of the U.S., 75-77, 79, 89, 104, 141-42, 145, 149, 150, 161, 172-180, 185

Banks, Nathaniel P., 204

Barbary states, 128

Barbour, Philip P., 156

Barkley, Alben W., 327, 339

Barksdale, William, 209

Barron, James, 136

Baruch, Bernard, 302

Bassett, Richard, 79

Bayard, James A., 117, 148

Beckley, John, 14, 87-88, 137

Beer-Wine Revenue Act, 318

Begin, Menachem, 384

Bell, John, 210

Belmont, August, 252, 266

Bemis, Samuel Flagg, 183

Benson, Egbert, 72

Benton, Thomas Hart, 156, 160-61, 166, 168-70, 172-73, 175-78, 184, 184-86, 186-91, 197, 198, 207

Benton, William, 345

Berger, Victor L., 302

Berle, Adolph A., Jr., 318

Berlin, Germany, 352, 356

Beveridge, Albert J., 269, 275, 281-282, 287

Bibb, William W., 144

Biddle, Nicholas, 172, 174, 177

Bidwell, Barnabas, 122, 132

Bingham, John A., 224, 229-30

Birney, James G., 188

Black, Hugo L., 319, 324

Black Codes, 223

Blackfoot Indians, 129

Black Hawk, 172

Bladensburg, Md., 148, 182

Blaine, James G., 219, 232-33, 237, 239, 242-43, 247, 249-50, 256, 258, 271, 329

Blair, Francis P., 231

Blair, John, 30

Blañd, Richard P., 252, 267

Bland, Theodoric, 55, 63, 71

Bland-Allison Act, 253

Bloom, Sol, 331, 338

Boggs, Thomas Hale, Sr., 360-61, 369, 393

Bolivia, 271

Bolling, Richard W., 374

Boone, Daniel, 153

Borah, William E., 290, 305, 306, 312, 330, 332

Boston, Mass., 24, 42, 72, 87, 135, 145, 156, 158, 291, 308

Boudinot, Elias, 13-14, 18, 58, 63, 70, 72

Boundaries, 100, 105-6, 153-54, 186-87, 189-91

Boutelle, Charles, 266

Boutwell, George S., 230, 235, 239

Boxer Rebellion, 271

Brandegee, Frank, 305-6, 310

Brandeis, Louis D., 292, 295

Breckinridge, John C., 122-23, 210

Bricker, John W., 354

Bridges, H. Styles, 355

Bright, Jesse D., 203, 216-17

Bristow, Joseph L., 287

Brooke, Edward W., 362, 385

Brooks, James, 239

Hamlin, Hannibal, 210
Hampden, John, 15
Hampton, Wade, 246
Hancock, John, 24, 37
Hancock, Winfield S., 249
Hanna, Marcus A., 250, 267–68,
  277–80
Hanna, Richard T., 385
Harding, Warren G., 306–9, 311–15,
  338
Harmar, Josiah, 75, 80
Harper, John A., 143
Harper, Robert Goodloe, 107, 108,
  112, 115
Harriman, E. H., 279
Harrison, Benjamin, 259, 262–64
Harrison, Byron "Pat," 320, 325, 327
Harrison, William Henry, 144, 176,
  184, 194, 210, 259
Hartford Convention, 149–50, 168
Harvard, 10–12, 61, 180, 345
Hatch, Carl A., 338
Hatfield, Mark O., 362
Haugen, Gilbert N., 314
Hawaii, 270–71, 276
Hawkins, Augustus F., 378
Hawkins, Benjamin, 94
Hawley, Joseph R., 268
Hay-Bunau-Varilla Treaty, 21
Hayden, Carl, 367
Hayes, John L., 233
Hayes, Rutherford B., 230, 243–45,
  248–49, 252–54, 271
Hayne, Robert Y., 157, 167–68
Hay-Pauncefote Treaty, 271
Hays, Wayne L., 379
Hearst, George, 232, 248
Hearst, William Randolph, 272
Hébert, F. Edward, 361
Henderson, David B., 276
Henry, Patrick, 17, 24, 30, 37, 38, 40,
  57–61, 74, 114
Hepburn, William P., 281
Hepburn Act, 281, 288
Herbert, Philemon, 205
Herter, Christian A., 351
Hickenlooper, Bourke B., 361
Hickman, "Beau," 165
Hicks, John D., 307
Hill, James J., 279
Hill, Lister, 338
Hinshaw, Andrew J., 379
Hiroshima, Japan, 340
Hiss, Alger, 344
*History of the House of
  Representatives* (Galloway), 14, 51
Hitchcock, Gilbert M., 306
Hitler, Adolph, 313, 330–32
Hoar, George Frisbie, 262, 269, 275
Hoffman, Clare E., 338

Holifield, Chet, 343, 361
Holland, 11, 42, 67, 89, 90
Homestead acts, 208, 217, 226, 234,
  238
Hoover, Herbert, 309–10, 312, 314,
  316–17, 319, 329
Hoover, J. Edgar, 315
House, Edward M., 304
House of Representatives, 8, 10, 12
  12–19, 34–39, 41, 44–77, 79–85,
  87–90, 92–96, 99, 102–5, 107–11,
  113–17, 119–25, 127–38, 140,
  142–62, 165–67, 170, 172–76,
  178–95, 197–200, 203–44, 246–
  262, 265–70, 272–73, 276, 280–
  283, 286, 288–91, 293–301, 303–4,
  308–11, 314–17, 320, 322, 326–28,
  334–44, 346–56, 358, 360–64,
  366–69, 371–72, 374, 376, 378–80
Housing, 322, 365, 367–69, 374, 377,
  382
Houston, Sam, 58–59, 179, 191, 193,
  202–3
Howe, Timothy, 237
Huger, Daniel, 189
Hughes, Charles Evans, 299, 311
Hull, Cordell, 294, 329–30, 334
Humphrey, Hubert H., 356, 359, 369,
  377, 380
Huntington, Collis P., 233, 247
Hylton, David, 97

I Illinois, 153, 172, 192–93, 200, 208–
  209, 233, 237
Illinois Central Railroad, 201
Immigration, 112–13, 204, 264, 270,
  284, 303, 305, 350, 365, 395
Impeachment, 34, 64, 103, 107, 125–
  126, 131, 175–76, 228–31, 235,
  239–40, 245, 371, 389
Imperialism, 267, 270–77, 296–97
Implied powers, 103–4, 131, 151, 160
Impressment, 135, 140
Income tax, 215, 219, 253, 264–67,
  283, 287, 294, 302, 325, 336–7
Independent Treasury Act, 179, 185,
  189
Indian Affairs Bureau, 172
Indian Removal Bill, 171
Indiana, 81, 144, 153, 208, 233, 243,
  259
Indians, 9, 10, 25, 27, 35, 53, 76, 80–
  81, 83–84, 92, 96, 104, 130, 143,
  171–72, 225, 240, 256, 257–58,
  274–75, 366
Indochina, 360–63
Industry, 84–85, 157, 161, 214, 219,
  233–34, 237, 245–47, 250, 252–57,

403

M

48, 50–52, 56, 62, 64, 65, 69–72, 76, 77, 79, 206
McLemore, A. Jeff, 297
McMillan, James, 268
McNary, Charles L., 310, 314
MacNeil, Neil, 310, 314
Macomb, Alexander, 147
Macon, Nathaniel, 115, 121–22, 132, 136, 138, 140, 160, 167
Madden, Ray J., 343
Madison, Dolly Todd, 107, 139, 148
Madison, James, 12–13, 16, 19, 27, 29–30, 37, 38, 49–51, 75–77, 79–80, 81–89, 93, 95, 97, 99, 103–5, 107–8, 112–13, 121, 125, 128, 131–32, 135, 137–41, 142–52, 160, 165, 170, 243, 389
Magna Charta, 21
Maine, 149, 155, 260, 266, 326
Maine, ship, 273
Manchuria, 312, 329
Manhattan Project, 332, 340
Mansfield, Mike, 362–63, 367, 369, 376, 379, 380
Manufactures, 55, 57, 74, 84–85, 97, 147, 150–51, 157, 161, 174–75, 180, 206, 212, 219, 246, 254, 255
Marbury v. Madison, 63, 97, 125
Marcy, William L., 163–64
Marine Corps, 111, 128, 270, 292, 357
Marshall, George C., 332, 334, 346, 351–52
Marshall, Humphrey, 101
Marshall, John, 38, 63, 76, 98, 108, 115, 117, 118, 123, 124–26, 134, 141, 171
Marshall, Thomas R., 292, 299
Martin, Joseph W., Jr. 328, 364–66
Maryland, 22–25, 26, 28–29, 56, 71, 76–77, 98, 117–18, 125, 195, 263, 345
Mason, George, 30
Mason, James M., 196
Mason, Jeremiah, 148
Mason, Stevens T., 101
Massachusetts, 11, 16, 22–26, 29, 34, 37, 41–42, 55, 57, 60–61, 70–71, 86, 89, 93, 145, 149, 151, 156, 167, 176, 183, 196, 204–5, 213, 238
Mathers, James, 18
Maxwell, Cornelius, 19
Mayaguez, ship, 363
Maysville Road, 171, 173
Meat Inspection Act, 282
Medicaid, 383
Medicare, 368
Mediterranean Sea, 92, 128, 135, 136, 351
Mellon, Andrew, 306, 316

Mencken, H. L., 308
Merry, Anthony, 120
Metzenbaum, Howard, M., 382–83, 386
Mexican War, 188, 189, 190
Mexico, Gulf of, 9, 132, 216
Michigan, 233
Middle East, 351, 356, 363, 372, 378, 384, 388
Midway Islands, 270
Midwest, 241, 257, 282, 288, 297, 309, 330
Mifflin, Thomas, 77
Military Affairs Committee: House, 191, 298; Senate, 151, 191, 214
Military Reconstruction Act, 227–28
Militia Committee, Senate, 151
Miller, John C., 86
Milliken, Seth, 262
Mills, Roger Q., 258
Mills, Wilbur D., 347, 375
Mining, 233, 241–42, 246, 252, 265, 279, 337, 377, 382
Mississippi, 153, 162, 181, 193, 198, 211, 238, 253
Mississippi River, 9, 27, 106, 129–130, 133, 153, 165, 171, 173, 242
Missouri, 153–55, 156, 201, 204, 216, 238
Missouri Compromise, 155, 156, 158, 193, 196, 201–2, 207, 211
Mitchill, Samuel, 126
Moley, Raymond, 318
Mondale, Walter F., 383
Monopoly, 173, 177, 233, 248, 254, 257, 262–63, 267–68, 278–79, 285, 288, 291–95, 324
Monroe, James, 38, 79, 88, 92–93, 96, 101, 107, 129–30, 134–37, 141–44, 148, 151–53, 155, 156–58, 160, 168, 170
Monroe Doctrine, 156, 291, 305
Monroney, A. S. Mike, 340
Montana, 259, 299
Montesquieu, Baron de, 30, 33
Monticello, Va., 94–95, 139, 155
Moore, Andrew, 55
Morgan, J. P., 266, 279–80, 291
Morgan, Thomas E., 361
Morrill, Justin S., 209, 212, 217, 224
Morris, Gouveneur, 36, 97, 115, 119
Morris, Robert, 10, 52–54, 56, 59, 69–73, 75, 93–94
Morse, Wayne, 356, 360, 365
Morton, Levi P., 250
Morton, Oliver H. P. T., 231, 237, 243
Moses, George H., 310
Mount Vernon, Va., 28, 45, 47, 86
Muckrakers, 282

About the Author

Alvin M. Josephy, Jr., an historian and former editor of *American Heritage,* is a nationally known expert on American Indian affairs and author of such prize-winning books as *The Patriot Chiefs, Red Power,* and *The Indian Heritage of America* (a National Book Award Nominee for History). He is also a diligent student of politics who once campaigned for Congress from Connecticut and has served as a consultant to leaders in both the executive and legislative branches of the federal government.